The Final Colossus
With the Valor of Archangels
AD 2016-2018

by
William L. Roth
Timothy Parsons-Heather

My brother and I live under obedience to the Most Blessed Virgin Mary who has initiated, consecrated, guided, flourished, and propagated a mystical body of work received through Her precious Immaculate Heart. We are solemnly consecrated in faithfulness to Her and to all the principles delineated within these written texts in union with and interpreted through the spiritual catechesis of the Roman Catholic Church. It is our intention and mission to spread Her messages to the world in celebration of the Holy Gospel of Christianity for the sake of the Glory of our Lord Jesus Christ.

Copyright © 2022   William L. Roth
All rights reserved.   Timothy Parsons-Heather

Publish Date: May 13, 2022

ISBN: 978-0-9793334-6-0

Our Marian Consecration

We hold our Holy Mother's gracious favor as the most precious and sacred thing that we could have ever had deposited into our hands, noting that we receive the Eucharistic Body of Jesus upon our tongues. One of our strictest intentions is to never allow the thought to arise in the Most Blessed Virgin's mind that Her words and intercession are not the most welcome and appreciated gift that we could ever have received in our lives. We accept all that we have been given as mankind's treasure, as if we were all humanity receiving Her. She loves us. We want Her to feel loved in return. No sorrow will arise in Her thoughts from any lack of receptivity of Her mystical grace on our part. This is our commitment. This is how we want our lives to be recorded in the Book of Life.

When Our Lady gazes across the world looking for love, we want Her to immediately see us. We will venerate everything from Her, even if we are the last two standing. We will respond to Her with the fullest measure of our strength and devotion. Our faculties and lives are in Her service. We will obey Her every request and progress on every path She points out to us, even if it is to our own cross. The flesh may be weak at times, but we are determined that our spirit will always be strong. We will hold in infinite regard all that She dispenses and will protect it with our integrity and honesty until we meet Her in Heaven face-to-face. And there, we will thank Her again. And, all of this is because of Her Son whom we love in our unity.

Wisdom
7:22b–8:1

In Wisdom is a spirit
intelligent, holy, unique,
Manifold, subtle, agile,
clear, unstained, certain,
Not baneful, loving the good, keen,
unhampered, beneficent, kindly,
Firm, secure, tranquil,
all-powerful, all-seeing,
And pervading all spirits,
though they be intelligent, pure and very subtle.
For Wisdom is mobile beyond all motion,
and she penetrates and pervades all things by reason of her purity.
For she is an aura of the might of God
and a pure effusion of the glory of the Almighty;
therefore nought that is sullied enters into her.
For she is the refulgence of eternal light,
the spotless mirror of the power of God,
the image of his goodness.
And she, who is one, can do all things,
and renews everything while herself perduring;
And passing into holy souls from age to age,
she produces friends of God and prophets.
For there is nought God loves,
be it not one who dwells with Wisdom.
For she is fairer than the sun
and surpasses every constellation of the stars.
Compared to light, she takes precedence;
for that, indeed, night supplants,
but wickedness prevails not over Wisdom.

Indeed, she reaches from end to end mightily
and governs all things well.

The Final Colossus
With the Valor of Archangels
AD 2016-2018

Prologue

Part I - Our Recital of Divinity 1

Part II - Orientation, Transition, Conversion, Transfiguration 5

Part III - Admonish for Truth's Sake 11

Part IV - Sanctifying the Inner Sanctuary 17

Part V - Advocatus Mater Dei, The Promoters of Her Cause 33

Part VI - Casting Down the Mighty 47

Part VII - Sacralized Spiritual Deduction 53

Part VIII - Justice's Final Verdict 69

Part IX - Rejecting the Lie 77

Part X - Conjugating an Angel's Valor 81

Anthology of Messages

AD 2016
95

AD 2017
275

AD 2018
433

Sunday, April 2, 2000
2:58 p.m.

Yesterday, I was in the process of emptying my small garage so it could be demolished. I was removing truckloads of old materials that had been laid above the ceiling braces many decades ago. As I neared completion of the task, I lifted some old pieces of wood, and beneath them was a picture frame laying face-down on the rafters. It was covered with a thick layer of dust that had accumulated over the many years it had been there. I grabbed it as another item of junk and was ready to throw it into the bed of my truck, but as I turned it over, I saw that the frame contained one of the most beautiful images I had ever seen—Jesus elevating His Eucharistic Body as He did at the Last Supper. His countenance was majestically somber, yet emanated a peaceful power. The black-and-white picture was a framed First Communion gift that belonged to the previous resident of my home that dated back to June 1, 1919. I sat for a moment in wonderment about how something so beautiful came to be placed in the attic of a garage, and remained there unharmed for so many years, only to be discovered on this day. I considered it a great gift from God that had waited there for me to find it. During Her words, Our Lady referred to the picture.

"I am happy that you discovered the First Communion relic from 1919. Do you know what night the picture celebrates? Yes, the Last Supper. I ask you to keep this relic as a gift from the Saint who used to live in this house. My Special son, of all the depictions of the Face of Jesus which have been made in the world, this one is the most accurate. I thank you for cherishing it so well."

This is the picture that is presented on the front cover of this book.

The Final Colossus
With the Valor of Archangels
AD 2016-2018

"I have said that the Morning Star Over America is not only a work for the ages, but a transcendent blessing beyond those ages as well. It contains everything I would like to have said after the Resurrection of Jesus and the moment of My Assumption. All the sentiments, all the guidance and comfort, all the shared pity and wisdom—these are the things that a world of any millennium should have always known. I have come to you and your brother during the 20th and 21st centuries because these are the decades in which you have lived. The Providence of God is no more complex than this. What you have given to humanity in the form of your obedience to Me is as great as the fruitful outcome of any world war. Your own eloquence combined with Mine has crafted wisdom and created brilliance that will last into perpetuity. My Special son, can you not sense that this is true? We have more than developed a plan for the conversion of the lost. We have literally taken their hands and lifted them to the presence of God. We have strengthened their faith from whence they first had it. And, we have given them a new definition of piety and truth that they could never have gained on their own. When you think about it, My Special son, it may be even difficult for you to comprehend what this means for the Church. My messages and your deposit of works need not be feared by those who are loyal to Jesus. They should be looked upon as not only a sanctifying grace for those with open hearts, but a means to authenticate the sureness and goodness of those who have been true from the start."

- The Blessed Virgin Mary
Saturday, July 9, 2016

"When a man stumbles a single time, the world will define him as corrupt and he will live out the rest of his days bearing the ignominy of his weakness. But, if a man accepts His Savior, a single good act can esteem his soul in Heaven for Eternity."

- William Roth Jr.

Prologue

Part I
Our Recital of Divinity

> *There is an ethical problem at the root of our philosophical difficulties; for men are most anxious to find truth, but very reluctant to accept it. We do not like to be cornered by rational evidence, and even when truth is there, in its impersonal and commanding objectivity, our greatest difficulty still remains; it is for me to bow to it in spite of the fact that it is not exclusively mine, for you to accept it though it cannot be exclusively yours. In short, finding out truth is not so hard; what is hard is to not run away from the truth once we have found it. ...The greatest among philosophers are those who do not flinch in the presence of the truth, but welcome it with the simple words: yes, Amen.*
>
> - Etienne Gilson
> 'The Unity of Philosophical Experience,' p. 49

May the Glory of Jesus Christ come to this age of turmoil. May His Kingship be extolled throughout the nations, to man and beast alike, from the mountains to the seas; across meadows and deserts may Divine Light shine into the souls that the King of kings came to save. Petition the conversion of men and sing out Salvation in the Blood of the Lamb; He who has conquered the world; He who has brought the majestic Eternal Light into the darkness; He who has split open the tomb of man's perfection where laid in death and decay the children of His sacred image. Hail Thrice-Blessed Trinity of Deific Love! Announce Divine Redemption to the ages of Thy servants and call us into Thy presence in company with the Angels. Before Thee we kneel, to Thee we pray, for Thee we live, and by Thee we are saved. May the doors of the converting realms be opened and the waters of divine absolution inundate the arid chambers that thirst for your pardon and praise. Say the Word that shall force the vaults to defer to Thy Glorious Coming; part their curtained exile of men and happily splay them as bunting across the rafters of celebration where the children of Creation may revel once again in being united with you who conceived us good. Colossal and magnificent are your ways; purposeful and peaceful do your sentiments resound; permanent and perfect does your mighty wisdom dictate the beauty that flourishes from Thy creative thought. Intent and intense is the passion by which you reign sovereign in the Creation that proceeds from you. In flourishing magnanimity did you raise your image and likeness into being, into whose reflection you might see your own glorious face, knowing that your own praise would echo from your divine creation, your Word returning to its source fruitful. Singing thy praises and proclaiming thy plaudits is the order of the faithful heart. Honest and intrepid are the convictions that search for you in an exiled world. Sing on humanity of the great love your God has dispensed to you. Rally the ages and call forth the legacies of Patriarchs, Pontiffs, Prophets and Martyrs. But, woe to you who do not inhale the scent of their legacies where good men find deliverance. Woe to you who defy the Sacrifice of the Lord of Creation, He who came to save you into Glory while prideful men wallowed in agony, darkness and death. Out of the firmament has transcended the Father's Queen who brought forth His Son in inestimable light whose soul was the nature of the Infinite God, a perfect Lamb prepared to accept Passion and Death so that death itself would be vanquished by Eternal Life. Oh, what a story! What a sacrificial epic, the aria of God's Only Son, His memoir of human salvation!

How must this recital of Divinity be presented to humankind in order that all may listen and have their hearts touched and drawn into Heaven's Light? What is the wage that ears may be opened and eyes see? What price must be paid when words fail to matter and parables ricochet off steely spirits of pride, when sentiments bow only before matter, material, position and worldly power? When the miraculous testimony of God and the miracles of His Queen are rejected by presidents, prelates, emperors and kings; when the stewards, bellhops and doormen have commandeered the throne rooms and stationed rhetorical guards before their vestibules, whom can God send to reclaim His Dominion? When arrogance has grown to the towering heights of redwoods and hubris deploys its canopy of jurisdiction to darken the earthen floor, what then? When the wolves secure their fleece more tightly at their collars like alabaster tombs shrouding their haunting emptiness, what will remove their cerement to reveal the death within? How is one to approach a world that will not seize its moment of maternal grace before it cascades into the abyss? When Jesus' tears before Jerusalem echo in our time, what is the Father to do? [Luke 19:41-44] What words can be said to those who are too proud to hear? How does one dislodge human consciences which are imprisoned in Dante's ice and disposed therein to dominate and suppress the work of God's mighty Spirit? Do not such people conduct us to a fate that will horribly perfect us all? Will those ominous strains of Saint Luke's Gospel not play out upon us? Not one stone atop another.

How often is our demand that we be spoken to respectfully become nothing more than a justification to dismiss those whom we force to speak to us stridently because our pride refuses to listen? Whitewashed tombs and empty vessels, we cry! Calumny, they respond. Yet, admonish and rebuke says the works of mercy. In a world paled to the darkest ink of midnight, gentle words are disregarded to no effect before pride that rules by authoritarian whim, threat, decree, and intimidation. Passionate declarations are derided, as well, as extremist excesses beyond the boundaries of the dignified Spirit of the Prince of Peace. And ultimately, even ominous prophecies and harsh rebukes are mocked and disqualified as being no more than delusions from subjective unbalanced minds [Matthew 11:16-19]. What tenor, tone and volume must Heaven's messengers assume for their words to be heard? Speak up, I say! God wishes to know because He will call forth that soul so disposed by His Spirit and bring them to the fore. How loudly does Heaven allow its evangelizers to bellow if their mellow words are ignored? What has to be torn down before sinners recognize that the Almighty Father is serious and that we are being put on notice before the eternal ages? They taunted the Messiah, "What sign can You show us to prove Your authority to do these things?" He said, "Destroy this temple and I will rebuild it in three days." The King of kings prophesied what sinners would require before they would listen. He knew that a Crucifixion and Resurrection of a Perfect Lamb was the only thing that would matter. And, generations of humanity have proven Him right in the martyrdom of His Saints.

Pride is masterful at finding excuses to ignore spiritual correction, from meek encouragement to the harshest of admonishments. So, from which perspective is God to inject His wishes now in these latest of times? Through the gentlest Creature ever birthed in Creation or through the scorching of continents in the righteous fires of His final chastisement? Yes, it is through humanity's own suffering, if we will not listen to this Immaculate Creature. The Heavenly Father will unabashedly unite humanity with His Son on the Cross and defeat human pride through every age by a Sacrificial Hecatomb so mighty that it will force the bending of every knee and the attestation of every soul, even the damned. Human pride will ultimately be humiliated by the recognition that it killed its own salvation on a Cross and thereafter impeded the message of Salvation dispensed by the heavens all throughout history. This is how God brings ultimate defeat to those who will not listen. He removes the restraint and lets His enemies defeat themselves by tasting the bitter cup. He lets them consume the fruits of their own rebellion. Their own teeth they will gnash, and their own vomit they will eat. He conquers the sins of men with their own pride by revealing to them the beautiful mystery they rejected right in the midst of their very own lives. The God they rejected was with them all along. 'The stone the builders rejected has become the cornerstone,' indeed!

All of the obstacles strewn across the pathways of mystical grace, all the rejection of prophetic voices sent by the Father, all of the intellectual hubris claiming prestige and provenance, all the denigrating of miraculous intercession is turned back upon the pride from which such arrogance came, and the guilty realize then they need grace like one lost in a desert begging for a drop of water. The Woman clothed with the Sun beams down upon our existence in these times in very profound ways seeking our obedience. She quenches the spiritual thirst of humanity with the waters from Her Son's pierced side. She sweeps up the nectar from this Eternal Flower, adores it within Her immaculate maternal heart and pours it upon the Earth to those with the humility to listen. In Her Immaculate Heart is where Jesus finds us born again. She is without flaw, of a composure of pure truth, stature beyond history, and present now and throughout the expanse of Eternity at the side of the Lord of Creation as His Mother and as ours. Wisdom lies in heeding Her presence, profiting from Her Motherhood and sanctifying our faith in obedience to the call of the Church-Triumphant.

Part II
Orientation, Transition, Conversion, Transfiguration

"Moral principles do not depend on a majority vote. Wrong is wrong, even if everybody is wrong. Right is right, even if nobody is right."

- Archbishop Fulton J. Sheen

I believe it might be universally accepted by every person that we live amidst a whirlwind of beliefs, perspectives, ideologies, preferences and positions that are as individualistic, turbulent and conflicting as the people who possess them. What is not necessarily accepted in this churning sea of motion is that there is a peaceful truth that transcends and permeates it all. Commentators try to ascribe names to it, give descriptions for it, and attach generalizations to circumscribe it, such as "we need to come together; we must put our differences aside; our diversity is a strength." Yet, none of these describe the truth that must be known, nor are they anything more than meaningless stereotypical platitudes conjured by people who are at a loss as to what more to say. Should we not better discern the landscape of our lives through the lens of human excellence in order to make sense of what is happening to our humanity and why we are mercilessly treading such paths of contention and suffering? And, should we not define human excellence from a plateau of spiritual wisdom as opposed to the gutters of ideological self-contempt? Truth is objective, meaning that it is true in itself and is not subject to the manipulation or modification by any other beliefs or opinions about it, or actions against it. There is no such thing as "your" truth or "my" truth. Truth simply "is." All else is just transient opinion and perception which is stirred in the cauldron of our mutual divisions. The world is filled with truth, laws, and precepts that are immutable and permanent. Many of them bind us into the natural parameters of our mortal lives in exile, such as gravity holding our feet to the ground so we can walk or fire being able to injure and even kill us. We might call these empirical truths. Others are spiritual, such as love possessing unimaginable power to move the human heart or that there are underpinnings to human motivations and actions which flourish these movements, such as 'out of the mouth, the heart speaks,' as the Bible states. It is a part of truth itself that each of us is inspired and motivated by interior drives and instincts whose origins we do not necessarily grasp or even recognize. We do not consider that our emotions and habits come from somewhere. Most people simply see the resultant outcomes of these mysterious actions and concede to their choreography on the surface of their everyday lives, which are then mixed with impacts against the obvious truths of the material world such as a car cannot be driven through a concrete wall. The natural world is very good at holding human beings bound to its truths because they do not give way to what any creature might think about them. Men can jump off mountains all day long until the end of time, and they will always fall, most probably to their deaths, unless they have contravened the empirical truth of gravity by artificial means. The question is how many artificial means are we employing in order to circumvent the spiritual truths in our lives?

Spiritual truths, such as the presence of the Kingdom of Heaven residing in the spiritual heart, are what many people are reticent to consider. These truths defer to no one, not even to the heart that contains them. The spiritual heart accepts them or dies just as one might forfeit their life by piling into a concrete wall that will not give them way. In the material world, we inevitably learn to exist in communion with the truths of our environment, lest we become victims of all kinds of unpleasant physical circumstances and pain. But, oftentimes, it takes wars of unimaginable death and destruction before we get the message. Nearly everyone wishes to live in a semblance of peace, even if it is only a cold war detente among would-be combatants. Nevertheless, we see a world that is not at peace due to the rebellion of multitudes of people who have surrendered themselves to the artifices of deception. Why? Because there are so many who do not abide by the spiritual truths which stand aside for no man. We may refrain from running into every concrete wall in our lives to maintain our comfort, but we may still be defiantly impacting spiritual truths whereupon we experience the contentions of not being in communion with the Spirit of Peace that unites all humanity in the ultimate truth of existence. Natural truths of the material world reflect and preserve the intentions of the spiritual truths where both find synchronization with the beatitude of the Divine Kingdom that flourishes in and around us. I believe every reasonable person instinctively wants to be right; we all want coherence in our thoughts in order to avoid both interior dissonance and outward suffering; we want to live by what is true, as well as understand it at every moment so that our decisions would be good and that we would not stumble, skinning everything from our hearts to our knees. So, the search to reconcile ourselves with spiritual truth is imperative if we truly desire to be people of peace and live in a world where goodness and comfort reign instead of derangement, wickedness and suffering.

Many might ask how we descended into this vulnerable position of disorientation, or blindness as some may call it. Or, is it that we never learned these truths from the beginning? We were born as human creatures who are anything but immortal and omnipotent. God created us and then confined our souls in this material world in the flesh, exiled from the unobstructed vision of Himself, for the opportunity of preparing for Paradise or succumbing to damnation. Even if someone were not to believe this about our existence, simple logic should tell them that the world they live in is limited and limiting. Do not our hearts conceive far greater things than what we seem to be able to manifest? Yet, what we see with our eyes and what we contemplate in our hearts must be reconciled for there to be true peace. The world we live in must become the image that we see in our hearts. And, if we do not open our perceptions to see clearly with our hearts, the things we see with our eyes in the material world obscure the great spiritual truths of Creation from our understanding. No matter the state of our enlightenment, whether it be of dullness or wisdom, of curiosity or indifference, or of sanctity or wickedness, we progress through a cordoned arena of life that is structured to subject us to its truths through the process of our maturity or the experiences inflicted upon us by our violating them. So, in our engagement with life, even these words serve as an orienting grace for a person's perceptions toward truth. We must realize that knowledge is not truth, per se. People can have all kinds of seeming knowledge about things that have nothing to do with orienting them toward the truth. For example, a person may have the knowledge and skill to ride a skateboard in death-defying stunts, but that knowledge and those actions have almost no power to affect the orientation of the soul toward spiritual truth, unless maybe as a result of a person daring the empirical truth of the material world and ending up in a hospital bed searching for the wisdom as to why such suffering has come upon them. Here again, the truths of the physical world and our own ignorance can have an orienting effect toward the greater spiritual truths. Our Lady says that such reckless acts which risk our gifts of good health, life, and safety are not a search for truth, nor are they a prayer to God; they are examples of where truth could have been accepted and prayers said in order to decline these temptations to satisfy simple emotional gratification. People such as these are merely toying with the machinations of their own physicality.

So, we can see the disorientation which impedes us from uniting the truths of the material world with the spiritual truths that are communicated by God to the human heart. The Good News is that we can seek out and live in harmony with the highest truths where impenetrable walls, material or spiritual, become a companion to our joy, comfort, unity, and protection, instead of instruments of suffering which too often demarcate where we violated them. God created us and He desires to show our hearts how to live our potential if we will look for Him within the light of wisdom. Every person possesses the capacity to perceive and become aware of the truth. We simply must become curious enough to turn in our orientation and hungry enough to know as much of the simple truth, material and spiritual, that our heart and understanding can contain. This is why we both study in our schools to the depths of our minds, as well as pray to our God across the sanctuary of our hearts. If we admit that there is truly an orientation to be gained, then it implies there must be a direction to look; a place where truth can be located, understood and incorporated into our perceptions, thoughts, reasoning, and finally our actions. It implies a present location for our perspective to come alive, as well as a destination where truths can be more clearly recognized and readily accepted. Therefore, the orientation we should seek is in the direction of the destination.

Consider being told the direction to a city and turning to look out across the landscape toward that horizon and seeing nothing but plains and wilderness as far as the eye can see. Could someone not say, "I don't see any city that you claim is out there." Well, might our response to them be, "Look in every other direction. Do you see the city there either?" So, the ability to see the destination is not the most important bit of knowledge when trying to gain an orientation toward your destination. It is more one's willingness to believe the word of someone who knows where it is. Those who accept this witness can then turn themselves in the direction of the truth which bestows upon them the blessing of actually someday arriving at their destination. Those who refuse to be oriented in the right direction do not even have a chance. So, the orientation is just the beginning, and it originates in one's acceptance of the word of someone who knows where the destination is located. Furthermore, anyone seeking the truth must not only be willing to accept their reorientation toward their destination, but they must also be willing to step forward into the transitions that present themselves in their journey to that destination. And, what are these transitions that will be experienced? They are transitions in the traveler's beliefs, ideas, perspectives and understandings that compose who they believe themselves to be. These transitions can be as difficult to experience as someone engaging the impediments and trappings of the wild outdoors. Outdoor impediments are most often physical, where the transitions in the journey toward the truth are spiritual and entwined in the comforts that enslave us in our lost itineraries of interior thought. Imagine living in the wilderness and you begin a walk toward an unknown place called "civilization" which you have been told about. Consider all the terrains that you might be required to traverse and the transitions you would have to accept. But, do you notice that not all transitions are necessarily difficult? Do not the appointments of your surroundings present greater organization and ease as you approach the great cities? Do not overgrown paths in the forests become dirt roads carved out by bulldozers which give way to paved county roads, then to state highways, then on to interstates which pour into cloverleaf exchanges that serve all the people in orderly peace? And, what do these noticeable transitions in the landscape tell you as you transcend them? There truly must be a city in the distance, for why else would life become more refined. And, it is in this sense of inevitability that the destination exists where the consciousness gains the scent of conversion because the difficulties that are overcome and the perspective gained upon their passage become evidence for the intellect. A foundation of truth based in the spiritual senses comes alive. The truth starts to make sense to the heart, and the will begins to say yes to the reality of the destination which one may still not be able to see. This is conversion, and it becomes stronger and more multidimensional in the experience and acceptance of the transitions which produce the conversion.

So, we must set out in the right direction, make the choice to step forward, and be determined to overcome any obstacles in order to arrive at our destination in oneness with the truth. Then comes the reward, the gifts of transfiguration begin to resonate throughout our person, both body and soul, in a cohesive, impenetrable, sanctified identity of eternal genius which is the living embodiment of God's envisionment of our being when He created us. This state of being is an archetype of the Second Person of the Most Holy Trinity, who is Jesus Christ crucified and resurrected. And, in this state of sanctifying grace, we share in the life of the Holy Trinity forever. This is Truth. Vast majorities of humanity are presently lost in the worldly turbulence of ignorance and defiance that is obscuring their orientation and first steps toward this beatific destination. They are not ready to make the journey, disinterested in the treasure to be sought, too obstinate to endure the excursion, too weak to transcend their own obstacles, and just plain ignorant as to how lost they are in the worldly wilderness. They will never reach their eternal homeland. Yet, they will, each and all, find themselves staring at Truth across an unbreachable canyon upon their passing from this life; for the first and only time, they will see the Paradisial City that they never sought out, with no way to get there across such an inhospitable expanse of sin. In that moment of Truth, there will be no intimidation to employ, no opinion that will matter, no success to be purchased, no argument that can be won, no violence to perpetrate to any effect, no deception that can be hidden, no lie that will find legitimacy, no error that will not be vacated, and only a Crucifixion standing before them which they will be required to accept in every chamber of their heart and fiber of their soul. For some, they will wish that they had died in a flaming inferno with their flesh falling off their bones than to appear at the Throne of God after having rejected the orientation of the Holy Spirit. This is Truth. All the rest who surrendered their perceptions and tendered their will to be oriented in the truth and engaged in the pilgrimage of sanctification will rejoice with every fiber of their being on that day because they will find themselves walking on the streets of gold in that great City of Light. They will see themselves with Jesus on the Cross when that Crucifixion comes to light before them. They will know that every effort they made, every self-denying forfeiture they surrendered, every sacrifice they offered, every kindness they portrayed, and every holy sentiment they harbored in their transitions and conversions has reaped for them the ecstasy of transfiguration into endless bliss. Our Holy Mother is presenting us a vision between the Truth and the lie. If She has to plead with us to trust Her, She will. Her intercession and resultant messages and graces are like fireworks launched above the great destination so that everyone knows the direction to the city that they cannot yet see. Her presence is an act of great merciful assist. Can it be defined as part of the Divine Mercy before the final day? The answer is yes.

Part III
Admonish for Truth's Sake

"The proud look of man will be humbled,
and the loftiness of men brought low,
the Lord alone will be exalted in that day."

- Isaiah 2:11

What does it mean to admonish someone? First of all, it implies a recognition of some action in another person or group of people that has impacted our awareness which we compare with our moral sense of correct behavior and thinking. Secondly, our sense of correct deportment comes from our unity with righteousness and truth after the beam has been removed from our own eye through the graces of sanctification. Sanctification gives us the refinement to know the difference between instructing the ignorant, counseling the doubtful, and admonishing the sinner. Being ignorant or doubtful is not a sin, except when it is willful, we know better, and we have been given sufficient grace that manifests culpability. The question we should consider is that after 2,000 years of Christianity calling throughout the globe, may we perhaps be far more culpable than we would like to admit? Possibly the first true Christian admonishment ever heard is recorded for us in Mark 1:15 where Jesus proclaimed, "This is the time of fulfillment. The kingdom of God is at hand. Repent, and believe in the Gospel." Repent is a pretty aggressive word for a person's ego to hear through the lens of pluralism in our relativistic secular culture, but it is one of the first things Jesus uttered at the beginning of His public ministry. He did not consider winning anyone's affections first or creating some kind of diverse ecumenism where He might hoodwink others into loving Him as their peer. The house He was building would stand on solid foundations, not on placating any sinner or bowing before anyone's ego-stricken feelings. He was the respecter of no man at the expense of righteousness and truth. This is admonishment in its clearest form: Repent and believe.

What meaning lies within the word repent and what are we to believe as a basis for our thinking and conduct? It is first of all a recognition that a supreme objective realm of authority claims its reign over us and will ultimately decide who and what we have been according to some standard. Repent declares implicitly that a better state of being exists which one is evidently separated from, a higher order of dignity of the human person. Then, it inspires each of us to ask why that would matter to us. Why should it be anyone else's business how another person lives their life? The answer is in the Holy Gospel which we are asked to believe based upon the greatest supernatural testimony in human history, a Testament filled with miracles that still thrives after two millennia. In these Sacred Scriptures is revealed the knowledge which will bring us into alignment with the perfection encouraged unreservedly in every holy admonishment. It is this perfection which prepares us to be granted Eternal Life in the paradisial Kingdom which is at hand in the Messiah of the Cross, He who once appeared among us in the flesh and has promised to come again in Glory to judge the living and the dead. And, the time of fulfillment is 'now' through the eternal reality where Jesus descends and becomes substantially present on the Altar through the miracle of Transubstantiation in every Holy Mass of the Roman Catholic Church. The Most Blessed Sacrament is the Bread of Life which comes down from Heaven, and he who eats of it faithfully will live forever [John 6:51]. The Lamb of God offered His life to the Sacrifice of the Cross so that we might receive the fruit of repentance, which is His forgiveness of all of our imperfections. And, upon attaining this sanctified state, He has promised that we will be allowed entrance into His paradisial Kingdom upon our passing from this life, instead of languishing in horror forever in the fires of hell as the punishment for rejecting such an eternal gift. So, by what authority does one reprimand his brother or sister? It is through the Holy Spirit of this same King. The Gospel Testament imparts the responsibility of the Great Commission which calls us to make disciples of all nations and teach them to observe all that He commanded [Matthew 28:19-20]. The Gospel, the Beatitudes and the Works of Mercy authorize and instruct us to admonish from a position of unity with the righteousness and truth of Jesus' Life, Death and Resurrection. All of this comes because we are asked to love one another as He has loved us, and to assist those we love with the truth that they may be saved. Helping our brothers and sisters to gain Heaven by our sharing what it means to live the Gospel is a great act of love, and often one of laying down our reputations and lives before the derision of many who will never believe.

Now, when pondering human idiosyncrasy, it is interesting to watch the choreography of people's responses when reproached about their less than dignified beliefs, conduct or speech. Our Holy Mother characterized it to me as them saying, "How dare anyone talk to little ol' me like that," as they stampede through Creation like a million buffalo across a flower garden. There are so many parables, analogies, and even cinematic depictions that portray the concept of our spiritual soul rotating or turning into the path of great power and becoming synchronized with it in order to participate in a synergy of historical or galactic providence. We have artistic works galore which attempt to communicate the spiritual themes of great heroism, virtue, honor, and glory which summon almost superhuman conviction from normal, nondescript participants. We see the best of humanity portrayed with devotion, principle, righteousness, courage, suffering, sacrifice, and yes, noble conduct brought to the surface of life and thrown into the crucible fires of great tribulation from which they rise triumphant. And yet, there are also depictions of the simple turning of the focus on an old spyglass from distortion to clarity by an early century ship captain so that he might see what approaches from the horizon. Where does man get the ideas to create these artistic scenes? Where do these themes arise? They come from the Holy Spirit of the Father of Lights who impresses "scents" of His Son's Sacrifice into the human spirit that we may see the ultimate triumph in Him and be saved. They are a form of evangelization of the higher orders of dignity of the human person which every heart can sense, even the atheist. And, if we rotate our identity, motivations and intentions into the path of Jesus' Life, Death and Resurrection, our colonial spyglass becomes a state-of-the-art Webb telescope that can see across the universe and the eons of time. Admonishment is simply a means of gaining humanity's attention, one person at a time, to look up and beyond who they presently are and see the child of God they inhibit themselves from becoming. It is a display of hope for them when they do not even know how to contemplate that such spiritual stature might exist within them.

Admonishment is why Our Lady has appeared in the world. She has come to call mankind to Glory, to encourage us to transcend the obscene decadence that we have been lured into making the definition of our contemporary lives. We are a super-race of sentient creatures. We may not be invulnerable or immortal, but look at what has been accomplished through the works of our own hands coupled with our highest aspirations and dreams. Look at what has been propagated from one generation to the next across millennia. Expand your vision across the epochs of history and witness the spiritual genius that has flowed from the hearts of humankind at its best. And, in all of this, it is only the Son of God on Mount Calvary who implanted perfection on the mountaintop of human experience and testified across the limits of history to the Divine Love which was crucified there. The Love of Jesus Christ is the eternal power that will reign over Eternity. Almost no one on the face of the Earth is speaking of the preservation of human hearts in this Love before they can be deformed, poisoned, and deranged by the forces and fanaticism of the secular void which wallows in darkness and corruption. And, it is getting worse as the darkness descends. Each human heart which comes into the world as a beautiful baby is a precious perfection of existence and awareness. It comes into the world for a lifetime of engagement, growth, expansion of awareness, development of perception, discovery of identity, destined to consolidate beliefs, organize knowledge, deal with its temperament, overcome its trials, secure its happiness, evolve its wisdom and ultimately come to the eternal enlightenment that a Creator conceived them beautiful from the beginning. Why do we not take seriously this magnificent process called life and do everything in our power to conform and protect our civilization by nurturing this light within every human consciousness and bringing it to perfection in its awareness? Why do we allow the most despicable and deranged human beings; the devil's minions; they who will never embrace their true identity, to corrupt the landscape that each beautiful child will greet when they enter this world? It is not simply the atheist that our Heavenly Mother hopes to bring to this Light through Her miraculous intercession, but also the common man, the esteemed, the publicans, the scholarly, the religious, the clerics, as well as those of every other religious sect and secular denomination which has tried to seat themselves on the Throne of the Son of God Most Holy.

    Our Lady's presence is a gift to humanity. She wishes every child born into this world to be birthed into Her hands, to have and hold, to caress and protect, and to guide and teach. She wishes those who believe themselves to be wise to consider Her Immaculate Power. Can we imagine what it was like for Jesus to be born to a Mother so beautiful? He grew into His stature as the Angelic King because He came to adulthood having the visage of Heaven's Queen blessing His attention every day of His Life. Our Lady is offering that royal visage to us at this moment if we will open the eyes of our awareness. She asks us to take a simple moment to consider how much She loves us, and with what power, and what She wishes to help us overcome; all our pain, all of our mistakes, every sickness and depression, all the indignity, the stress, and anything that would diminish our royal nature as children of the God of Heaven. She asks us not to be people who would deflect our own eternal glory for a passing world of material artifacts which will be consumed by the final fires. She says, 'Love wins. Nothing can stop Him. His Church will receive its crown of victory. It will be judged worthy as having fulfilled Her commission. The Church Militant of every generation declared faithfully the Eternal Light to a darkened world.' And, each of us who believed will be recognized in that Mystical Body. We will be found standing in the brilliant rays of that Light because we came of age in the torments of this world. We overcame the deceptions and lies to stand with conviction in the Crucifixion of a Man who came forth from a Tomb to declare the Redemption of all those who would believe in Him. And, to this day, millions atop of tens of millions have invoked the courage to believe this. Our Lady asks the rest to believe Her now, and for those who think they can impede Her to stand down and step aside.

Part IV
Sanctifying the Inner Sanctuary

Love justice, you who judge the earth;
think of the Lord in goodness,
and seek him in integrity of heart;
Because he is found by those who test him not,
and he manifests himself to those who do not disbelieve him.

Wisdom 1:1-7

Discernment of mystical revelations, and the recognition of the presence of the Holy Spirit as their Author, is a topic that has been debated, analyzed, researched, pondered, and documented since the early days of the Church. Most every faithful Christian acknowledges, although some begrudgingly these days, that the Third Person of the Most Blessed Trinity continues to work in human history to assist us in the cause of conversion and sanctification, even to the level of extraordinary manifestations such as the Miracle of the Sun at Fatima in 1917, the miraculous tilma of Juan Diego in Guadalupe, Mexico, and our Holy Mother's appearances in Lourdes and Medjugorje. The list of these spiritual manifestations goes on and on throughout the globe. Moreover, both history and the Church well recognize that the devil has been allowed a reign of influence in the fallen domain to strike at our lives and incite turbulence in our hearts by creating deception and cultivating error through the leveraging of our vulnerabilities as sinners. In addition, great Saints have given their opinions and perspectives describing certain dimensions of mystical phenomena based on the particulars of what some of them experienced. Yet, none of them experienced it all. God is simply too creative and each person too unique. There have also been people who have been well-meaning, curious, opportunistic, fearful, scrupulous, etc., who have attempted to decipher what these Saints wrote, hoping to apply their metaphysical insights in their own lives and to assist them in discerning the truth when others present such manifestations to them as evidence of God's prophetic intentions. Then, there are still others who dismiss it all and generate worldly agendas as a worthless substitute for what the Holy Spirit would have them do instead.

We must remember and always hold dear the perception of how beautiful it is for God to extend His recognizable presence into any soul or throughout our environment. Indeed, He does this for any soul who allows His Holy Spirit to reign within them. We should welcome Him within and not reject Him through a false humility or inordinate fear that something difficult might be asked of us. We should believe that He pines to be recognized as present in our soul, especially in His Coming through our reception of the Holy Sacrament of Confirmation whereafter His graces and gifts flourish in each faithful heart throughout their life of sacrifice. Make no mistake, no sinner has ever been owed or earned any spiritual gift from the Heavenly Father. We live in an inherited state of exile due to the disobedience of Adam and Eve who fettered human spiritual evolution in darkness. But, know true that God yet loves everything He has created. Everything that exists, indeed Creation itself, has an intimate connection with Him by its very existence. His image resides in us and behind everything through which He wishes to reveal His divine attributes, most supremely in His very likeness impressed in the creation of man. Nonetheless, there are an extraordinary number of supernatural revelations from God that do occur, each in their precious uniqueness, in each human soul as part of His love for what He has created. This is the way of grace and of oneness with His Kingdom. Each moment of grace has distinctive characteristics based upon the intimacy that God shares with each of His children. Signs appear throughout the landscape and skies. Events astonish us with revelation and spiritual elevation. Signal graces abound. Actual graces are overwhelming and present. Sanctifying grace is sacred and abundant. The questions which we might ponder are: Is our heart tender, disposed, and sanctified to recognize and accept the presence of the Holy Spirit around us, within us and in others? Who is the Holy Spirit? Do we realize that He is a Person who is alive within us, closer to us than our own thoughts? How can our will become synchronized and remain in union with His will as opposed to living an existence which denies Him? Can and do we live in perpetual communion with His distinguishable presence within us? God resides in the soul of every person where He attempts to communicate with us, if we will listen. He reveals Himself to us, if we will open the door. He will not break it down but rather calls through it with the beckoning of Divine Love and righteous truth. When a person answers with an open heart, the extraordinary commences, the mundane is eclipsed, and the mystical senses become operative as if a blind man were given sight. This is what Saint Paul was saying in his letter to the Ephesians.

Ephesians 3:14-21
Brothers and sisters: I kneel before the Father,
from whom every family in heaven and on earth is named,
that he may grant you in accord with the riches of his glory
to be strengthened with power through his Spirit in the inner self,

and that Christ may dwell in your hearts through faith;
that you, rooted and grounded in love,
may have strength to comprehend with all the holy ones
what is the breadth and length and height and depth,
and to know the love of Christ that surpasses knowledge,
so that you may be filled with all the fullness of God.
Now to him who is able to accomplish far more than all we ask or imagine,
by the power at work within us,
to him be glory in the Church and in Christ Jesus
to all generations, forever and ever. Amen.

    In the midst of all this mystical "normalcy" which defines the authentic Christian life, there are also souls of conspicuous Providence to whom God invokes His calling in special ways. The Almighty Father can, and often does, manifest extraordinary prerogatives of sacrificial conscription upon souls whose hearts may or may not be tender, disposed, or sanctified at all, all for His purposes of His Glory and the drawing of human hearts to Himself. Saint Paul would admit this, and the miracle on the road to Damascus confirms it. Not only saints, but many a rogue has received miracles, premonitions, signs, and deliverance through the power of God's Right Hand. Notwithstanding these extraordinary movements of the Holy Spirit, we should see the mystical normalcy of the Holy Spirit in each of our lives no matter who we are, and thereafter consider how we might refrain from becoming distracted from the operations of His divine grace. We are like divine fish who are supposed to swim in mystical grace and commune with our God through the Spirit of His Son Jesus Christ. Being a fish who jumps out of the water onto the bank is no way to be a fish. The Bible states, "Blessed are the pure of heart for they shall see God." How many only wish to admit this to be true after we pass from this life? The Kingdom of Heaven is at hand now. We are supposed to recognize His mystical presence within our soul. And, we should not be reticent to acknowledge His work out of fear that these mystical graces are always deceptive aberrations. How can we be thankful for something we are determined to deny? Our Heavenly Father loves us. The question is how do we get from blindness to sight, from darkness to Light, and from lost to found? It is directly related to humility and the purity of a heart which can see Him and hear His voice.

    If someone were to ask how a person can move into the perception of these truths, I would begin by asking, "Are you prepared to surrender what you presently believe? Will you allow your perceptions to be remolded, replaced, and rearranged? Will you allow your vision to come into focus?" If the answer is no, there is not much that can be done further. But, all is not lost because suffering is very effective in teaching the lessons of spiritual truth; and no one escapes suffering. It is simply more beneficial to embrace suffering with clear vision as opposed to being ignorant as to why it has come upon us. Imagine a person who realizes they have the ability to nail wooden studs together as a carpenter would do. They have a hammer and a bag of nails and a stack of two by fours; and they just start nailing together a structure as they see fit. Now, after completing the ground level according to their measure of expertise, which is often none, an engineer happens by and tells them that they will never be able to safely construct the second story because their ground level construction could never sustain the load. This is how it is with most human beings at some time in their life. They already have their ground floor frame of reference erected and nailed together. So, what are they tempted to think when the engineer tells them that they cannot go higher because what they have built is inadequate? Are they not usually inclined to dismiss the instruction and attempt to build upon their previous work, no matter the consequences? Should they not consider the questions originally asked? "Are you prepared to surrender what you presently believe? Will you allow your perceptions to be remolded, replaced, and rearranged? Will you allow your vision to come into focus?" There are multitudes, perhaps most, who have built scholarly rat traps as their ground floor that are as woven together and cemented into place as nuclear blast bunkers. Pride is the concrete. This is why our Heavenly Mother asks us to begin to pray willingly from the heart and season our lives with the self-denial that allows Her to clear our original job site of anything that is detrimental to the construction of our spiritual mansion. She also wishes us to know that She will preserve every wooden beam and vertical wall stud that was placed in the proper alignment when She arrives. She cares about how we desire to sacrifice for Jesus. She appreciates the things we have laid in place in our good efforts to be virtuous people. Nothing of goodness will ever be lost, but instead, will be magnified and incorporated into the construction of our interior dwelling. She will convert hemlock two by fours into polished stainless steel beams and wooden posts into massive marble columns directly from the mystical quarries of God's divinity.

I believe many people learn by comparison. For example, a writer often becomes excellent in his field by having been a voracious reader of the compositions of other great writers. Great orators study the valedictory homilies and triumphant addresses of history's ceremonial voices. They consume the excellence of others and incorporate these artifacts of elevation, technique and style into their composure for magnification in their own works. This can be seen everywhere throughout the advancement of human civilization. People can also learn what not to do by comparing themselves with those who have miserably failed or by what they have suffered themselves. This is why we look to the life of Jesus Christ and all the exultant wisdom and sacrificial suffering that is preserved in the New Testament, as well as seek to imitate His voice in every realm of virtue and knowledge that came from His Word. Each soul is a unique presence and reflector of God's divinity in Creation. Each person is of breathtaking value. And, each of us profits by comparison with those who embrace the Christian life. This is why the Catholic Church elevates Saints for veneration. We become light to others in our presence, attitudes, actions and decisions. Grace comes from somewhere and leads ever onward to the heights of perfection through our conversion and proclamation of the Christian Gospel. Even Saint Paul stated somewhat emphatically, "Be imitators of me, as I am of Christ" [1 Corinthians 11:1].

Imagine being told that you were going to enter into a room where someone of great stature was ready to greet you. You are not told what they look like, but simply that they are ready to meet you beyond the next door. Anxiously, you open the door and enter, but are stymied when you come face-to-face with a roomful of people. Imagine scanning the room looking for evidence of which person that you are expected to meet. We may look at the body language of others in attempt to recognize to whom they are deferring. Where are people congregated, and around whom? We look for a head table, a podium, and who has the microphone. We look for the best dressed, the person with the most dignified bearing. The person is in the room, but you experience the dilemma of not knowing who it is, while discerning the people, stature, and appointments of the room to fortify your perceptive deduction. This is how the presence of the Truth often exists in the human person. He is there, but oftentimes we do not know who He is amidst the crowd. Nor do any others in the crowd give us clues as to who He is within us. Within the Saints, when their perception walks into the room, everything and everyone is kneeling and worshiping the King of kings. Everyone who enters the room sees through every sentiment, posture, poise, presence and appointment who the Truth of Creation is. My point here is that your interior perceptions are your friends if they assist you in recognizing your Redeemer when you enter the room. If they are your enemy, they will push the Truth into an obscure corner of the room, not to be seen, and create all kinds of distracting pandemonium to draw your attention elsewhere. We benefit by our comparison of posture to all those looking in the direction of the Truth. This is not only an interior phenomenon, but also a social one. Christians who lead lives oriented toward Jesus Christ are examples and motivators to all those looking for Truth in the room.

So, in light of this benefit by comparison, people may wish to purify their perceptions by comparing their own with the interior landscape by which Our Lady has directed my brother and me. We are looking in the direction of Christ Crucified and His Mother Crowned. And, if one would wish to benefit by comparison with facets of our perception, the following list may provide some substance for this comparative exercise. These sentiments are simply a salting of mental impressions that may provide some identification and direction to one's orientation.

1. Ignore the deceptions that the secular world is peddling. Ignore its tenets, rules and demands. Disregard where it is pointing. There is no spiritual truth in it and no wisdom guiding it. It is a spiritual wasteland. It is being influenced and directed by those who are blind and lost. Allow it to bring you no spiritual disturbance. Observe it only to make note of that for which you must pray and who you must engage with the truth.

2. Begin to pray the Most Holy Rosary every day. This is obedience because this is what Our Lady has asked us to do. It is a reciprocal signal to Heaven that you are prepared to give God reign over your own will. It is not just a random devotion. It is a sign of obedience to your Heavenly Mother and will be rewarded with Her immaculate grace upon your soul. She denies no one. It prepares the contemplative arena of the heart. It clears the job site for building.

3. When you pray, manifest your affirmation of the presence of the Heavenly Hosts with you through your demeanor, composure, respect, deference, humility, and faith. Act like Jesus and His Mother are there because they truly are. It is an affirmation of spiritual reality. It is deception to believe they are not, simply because you may not physically see them. Remember that blind people cannot see who is in the room with them either. If you have knelt to pray with Jesus and Our Lady, recognize their presence like you believe it because in doing so you confirm the truth within yourself. 'Where two or more are gathered, there am I in their presence.' Our Lady says that She is always one of the two that are gathered in Her Son's presence when you kneel alone in prayer. Allow your heart to become immersed in their Love through your

interior vision being attentive to Jesus' Life, Suffering, Death and Resurrection. How did their Hearts embrace the Sacrifice on Mount Calvary? Why did they sacrifice? Unite with them in the Calvarian Sacrifice. Go to Mount Calvary. Bring your sufferings into that sacred union with them. Make your suffering the point of connection with Jesus on the Cross. If you can find no suffering to bring to them, perform some penance, some act of self-denial and bring it to them as a flower.

4. Do not suffer Our Lord to hear your babbling. No hysteria, no hand-wringing, no drama, no fear, no wild-running mind. No pleading, no begging that life be otherwise. Manifest simple acceptance, sincerity and honesty from a humble heart. Do not fear holy emotions or tears of awe and gratitude. Show Jesus that you have confidence in Him and His will for your life. Be respectful to receive His attention. Be peaceful and of few words, but meaningful. Leave disturbance behind, show Him your strong, long-suffering, well-intentioned adoration of His Sacred Heart which is the Source of all the Beauty you are looking for.

5. Never require or demand that Jesus or the Heavenly Hosts talk back to you in any extraordinary ways, as you understand extraordinary. Accept that a mere sinner simply having the grace to acknowledge the presence of God as being the extraordinary event in itself, because without that grace you would not be able to lift a prayer. Be comfortable and at peace in your submission to the Heavenly Hosts and expect nothing, but ask for great things for the world. Be grateful to be in their presence. Ask for love and light to flood all souls, not just your own. Desire Jesus' Will by diminishing your own will to extinction, if possible. Never doubt that they are with you and hear your every sentiment, even those unspoken. Know that they are united with your soul from the inside. They know you and are present. They have seen your entire life and have been with you through it all. They have suffered your life with you. Suffer theirs with them through your compassion.

6. Do not act as if anything wildly extraordinary has happened if you believe they have spoken to you by apparition, locution, holy sentiment, vision, or if you feel they have choreographed your intellectual meditation. Note the moment as you would reflect on a sunset, and go on. Do not believe it is a sign to willfully do something more. In the beginning, you should not even express thanksgiving for anything you believe may be

extraordinarily occurring in your soul so as not to make the mistake of affirming your own willful mental conjuring. Personal desires related to the world can create extraordinary deceptions. Jesus' desires are the only thing that matters. Patience should become your virtue. When the desires of Jesus become your own, then light comes. Otherwise, all kinds of thoughts swirl for attention which the human will attempts to grab onto instead. If you extend thanksgiving for your own conjuring, it is your will that has decided to do so. Your perceptions must become purified by self-denial until the denial is fluently welcomed. Then, God can build His Kingdom in you. Your sentiments must become measured and balanced so that you are at peace throughout the entire spectrum of human thought and engagement. They must be disciplined to endure the buffeting of the devil; fortified by lashes and wounds accepted with grace, and undisturbed by any personal sentiments in order to achieve the level of discernment where you recognize that your spiritual impulses are of the Holy Spirit and not of your own imagination or worldly desires. This is not so hard because it is an action of addition, not subtraction, although it is a purification. Add the vision of Love to the measure of being overflowing in your interior prayers. Then, all that I have referred to will occur mystically by the grace of God.

7. Do not allow yourself to construct any path as if you are willing a goal into being in your prayers. Do not dig for graces as if none have been given to you. Those who dig for graces are admitting that they don't have any which they recognize. Simply ask the Holy Spirit to help you adore Jesus' Sacred Heart and His Mother's Immaculate Heart at the Crucifixion. Allow your heart to extend compassion and yearn for graces for the world, but never anything extraordinary for yourself, only what you need to remain in sanctifying grace. Your goal is to show Jesus and Our Lady that you love them no matter what, and from beginning to all ends. You have one life of sacrifice to give to them, a few short smattering of years in exchange for an Eternity of glory. Will you be faithful even if they never speak audibly to you in your life? Remember that union with Christ and any manifestation of mystical gifts comes through the diminishment of the flesh, through sacrifice, suffering and pain. Beware what you ask, but pray for the gifts of the Holy Spirit. In my case, it never entered my imagination that I would be the recipient of Our Lady's miraculous intercession, even though I have loved Her as my Heavenly Mother since I was old enough to remember.

8. Ask Jesus and Our Lady to teach you to become holy and to bring sanctifying grace to your soul. Then, believe they have begun the moment the words formed in your mind. Patience is the first lesson. Be patient. Life itself is the arena in which they will teach you virtue, and the lessons will come; accept them all.

9. Practice quieting your will throughout your life, and contradict your pleasures and contentment with the fluency of peace. Never rebel from the sacrifice. Practice doing what you do not want to do. Give effort that surpasses where you wish to quit in your sacrifices. Go with God the two miles if He asks for one. Rouse your spirit to sacrifice in simple things. Be willing to contradict your will at any moment, but never obey someone who asks you to violate the truth out of a false command of obedience. Invoke your will with power and refuse to accept anything that is not the truth. This is the will of the Holy Spirit.

10. Remember this principle. Do not assume you do not have something you may indeed already have. Our Lady asked, "How do you get someone to accept the blessings they have been given but refuse to recognize? Rescind the blessings and let them ponder what they previously had." Notwithstanding, presume nothing outlandish, either of benefit or detriment. Do not tell God you are poor when He is trying to tell you that He has given you great riches. Do not tell Him it is dark when He is shining light right into your eyes. Do not tell Him you are heavy when He is trying to lift you up. He already knows. All of this banter is prattle; it is all self-will. It is a false attempt at self-justification, false littleness. Confirm your belief by repeating 'yes' to Him. In other words, accept His disciplines upon you as quickly as you might accept His compliments.

11. Do not embrace the habit of criticizing yourself. God created a magnificent creature when He formed you. It is false humility to heap negative self-criticism upon yourself in order to somehow confirm your nothingness to yourself. Tell Jesus that you realize that you could do nothing without Him, and mean it, then thank Him for all that He helps you do. Our Lady once asked me to write a meditation for Her. I sat down to try, but could generate nothing in my mind to write, which left me terribly distressed because I believed She expected me to have something for Her when She came again. I would have to go to Her with

nothing. When She came again, She said, "Now do you see what you can do without Me?" Give thanks to Jesus for the little things. It is easy to fall onto one's knees for the great things. Simply be honest, be penitent, be humble, and go on with confidence in Him to accomplish the things that He asks of you.

12. Do not wallow in self-pity if you fall to a mistake. The world's condemnation, whether it be from enemy or family, is meaningless. Ignore it. God does not care one whit about the torches and pitchforks of those who refuse to show mercy. Any presumptuous sinner who wishes to pile on a penitent person who has fallen will hear the Mother of God rise up against them saying, "Weep for your own sins." But, condemnation by the Spirit of God is ominous. So, do not remain in sin. Simply tell Jesus that you want to do better, and ask Him to help you. Remember that it is only the past that has been soiled. The future lies before you with its unstained thoroughfare. Step into that future with the intention not to soil it but to magnify it with the grace in your heart. Allow God to cleanse the past of anything you might have done to it. The Universal Church prays in its penitential liturgies for the purification of the world. We forgive you. Accept our prayers as help in purifying your past. Confess serious sins to a priest in the confessional with trust that Jesus is filled with joy that you have approached Him with such faith and openness. He loves to forgive and make right. Pray away the memory of your sins with charitable penance as did the woman who bathed Jesus' feet with her tears. Also, remember what Archbishop Fulton Sheen said about confession, "Hearing nuns' confessions is like being stoned to death with popcorn." Do not rattle on about trifles in confession. Simply be honest about your weaknesses and failures with a firm purpose of amendment; meditate on the occasion of sin that you encountered so as to repair your perception and avoid the sin, and concentrate on the Love that Jesus shares with you. Do not repeat your sins in your thoughts like a metronome. Fill your thoughts with the Love of Jesus in the Crucifixion, then temptations have no room for influence.

13. Union with God is in the astounding revelation of Infinite Love to the soul. Seek to see and experience the love in the Holy Sacrifice of Jesus. Then, if a specific interior revelation were to manifest itself, you will recognize and understand it through Infinite Love in the pains of His Sacrifice and embrace it with the innocence of a child.

14. Make the decision, however radical it may seem, to become completely open and receptive to the magisterial teachings of the Roman Catholic Church; not the musings of clerics or religious who have surrendered to the secular world, not religious politicians and pundits, but the true teachings manifested in the history of Pontificates. Be determined to get the big moral questions right, such as abortion, divorce and the teachings of purity. Make sure your spiritual pilings are anchored in the dogmatic bedrock of Catholic truth. Read the Roman Catholic Catechism. It is a repository of the Truth.

The barometer for measuring the spiritual state of your soul is the constant state of quiet even in the midst of worldly activity. Our Lady asked me to recognize "motion" in my soul from the earliest days of Her intercession to my brother and me. She defines "motion" as being that which creates disturbance and dissonance within us. She asked me to not allow myself to get into motion caused by the world or anyone in it, although I still have to invoke my reminding efforts to this day because my exile is not completed. Our Lady once admonished certain members of our prayer group when they were belaboring the failures of others by saying, "You say that others are blind. Sometimes Satan makes you see so much that you become blind." What disturbs or overcomes the peace within our soul? What makes our mind fly and causes our emotions to become riled? Do our intentions, decisions and actions arise from serenity, or do they originate in the turbulence? Rebellion against sacrifice and suffering generates turbulence in the quiet. Fluently accepting sacrifice and suffering defends the quiet from being disturbed. Yet, this perception of peace is not as simple as many people try to make it. Many think that anything which contradicts their own will and disturbs them is a violation of their peace, and thus, not of the Holy Spirit. For example, many are summarily afraid of miraculous intercession, so they reject these holy occurrences out of hand because they disturb what they believe. This leaves them often in contradiction to the truth. The position of peace from which they are judging is not the peace founded on the Holy Spirit. For example, the perception of the heart can also be afflicted by the acknowledgment of sin and injustice in the world, but the peace of God can remain intact even so in a steady heart. Suffering in the soul caused by the recognition of sin in the world is part of holy vision. Our actions in response to our recognition of this suffering must always arise from the quiet, not from a reaction to the suffering as if in rebellion to it. In addition, do not be deceived when the Holy Spirit tests you. The Holy Spirit can disturb our interior state when we are rooted in the hollow solitude of darkness, mediocrity, or lukewarmness. The voice of conscience can cut against the grain of our temporal composure. This is when the disturbance of our "peace" is often mistaken as a sign that something is not of the Holy Spirit. Our Lady said that it is oftentimes God simply disturbing people in the silence of their dead souls. The human ego will create a fortress within us where it implements its own terms of peace to the exclusion of God. This is not true peace at all. Then, when God comes to enter this kingdom, the ego screams how disruptive to peace that God is because He is knocking so loudly. This is what the Saints convoked writ large within societies by their presence. We may be thrown into many fires of discernment by the Holy Spirit to sanctify our perceptions of true peace. And, you only know if you can maintain your peace through faith if you are thrown into these fires where it is tested. God can level us any time He chooses in His efforts to reveal how faithful we really are to Him. These are grace-filled moments. These fires are realms where our intellectual sense of logic is upended by His Almighty Power, and everything that previously supported our composure is removed. It is then we find out what our faith truly rests upon. The arrogant and prideful have no idea how fragile their mental composure actually is. They have houses built on shifting sand and do not realize it. Theologians beware! It is in the unfolding of human life in our sufferings and sacrifices where sanctification plays-out and reveals this mystery. Faith moves mountains, while the reasoning of men often stumbles around trying to decide how many dump trucks it would take. Oftentimes, dump trucks have absolutely nothing to do with it.

Our Heavenly Mother has been my spiritual director in these themes since February of 1991, and probably in more inconspicuous ways before that time in preparation for my serving Her. I have had access to Her wisdom and comfort every day for over thirty years last count. This does not mean that I have availed myself of this grace extraordinarily, as She has asked me to live a normal life as would any other person. Her spiritual direction of my brother and me disturbs some people, thinking that we should have been accompanied in Her intercession by theologians who could critique Her along the way, which they most assuredly would have done, just as they do now. Imagine that. They have never heard of a spiritual gift where the Queen of Heaven would become so present to two of Her children for this purpose. She said that She has been with my brother and me in a special way since before we were born from our mothers' wombs to assist us in the lives Jesus would ask us to live in witness to Him. There is Providence in our lives, that sacrificial conscription previously mentioned, which was part of our calling from conception to serve Her as the Morning Star Over America. It has been a unique experience to watch how She has guided my heart and understanding through the years. I would call it "fluent" with my life in exile. It has been unique to my spiritual composure, just as She used a particular approach to my brother. I think Her overtures are an example that all spiritual directors should follow, although Her direction has singularly unique qualities. For instance, She knows everything. There is nothing that I can hide from Her, even if I wanted to. Our relationship is one of complete honesty with no subjective interpretation on Her part. This is not the case with any other spiritual director. In addition, and this is important, there is no impediment to my surrendering of my perception to Her because She does not possess the exilic limitations of any mortal spiritual director. I never have to test Her Spirit. There is never a moment when I hear, wonder, perceive or experience dissonance from the truth when She speaks. It is a reciprocal spiritual union to the deepest essence of the heart. For example, you may ask a group of one hundred theological experts about a facet of the truth, and you would get one hundred perspectives, each posited from the perspective of a sinner who is locked in exile. Some would be irreconcilable, and many speculative. Uncertainty exists in this human dynamic and causes one to pause in one's conviction and unity with the other person. Sometimes this pause lasts centuries before the uncertainty is reconciled. Spiritual directors are most often not united at all in this deep way with those whom they direct. They are merely observers who pray as any person for unity with the Holy Spirit. There is often no true sacrificial oneness with the one being directed, but merely a sense of authority, responsibility, or lordly affection. Many would never think of dying out of love for the person sitting in front of them. And, rare few are prepared to sacrifice their own perceptions. In contrast to the theologians mentioned, Our Lady is able to tell us which of the one hundred are absolutely accurate, and where each of the others diverge from Her beatific vision. She has the authority to focus our perceptions of the truth with complete certainty. Why? Because Her perception comes from a state of eternal perfection in the Beatific Vision. Her wisdom is completely divested from any uncertainty. As I have said before, speculation is not part of Her immaculate composure. She does not guess about my spiritual disposition, or any other person's for that matter, as an earthbound spiritual director might. She comes from a position of pure unadulterated vision. This is rarely, if ever, the case with any earthly spiritual director, although many of them with humble heart do possess the faculties to accompany a wandering soul and sharpen their vision to a more refined state, much in the same way that my perceptions might serve a person seeking a deeper relationship with Jesus and our Heavenly Mother. Our beautiful Immaculate Mother has been my maternal Advocate and has made every effort to form my spiritual composure in complete union with Hers, which is none other than a reflection of Her Son's image. I am somewhere on that path of sanctification. I hope I have been successful to this point, according to Her intentions. It has never been Her intention to teach me the most refined nuances of theological thought that human beings have conjured. She has not attempted to break or subdue me. She has not made any explicit efforts to violate my will, intrude upon my decisions or force me to succumb to Her sentiments. It has simply happened by Her mere presence. She has magnified Her Love to such heights that it has transformed my will, decisions and perceptions into being closer to what She wishes them to be. I so much wish that I could generate the presence of the Love that She possesses. I simply have not suffered enough. Her grace and beauty are infinite in what She has suffered. My, oh my! Considerable violence is often done to souls by spiritual directors, and even ecclesial authorities, who are seduced by their self-perceived stature where they either presume greater vision than they actually possess or surrender to no vision at all where nothing but their egocentric whims can reign. There has been much violence done to the souls of messengers and visionaries in history, indeed the faithful, who have been granted mystical relationships with the Heavenly Hosts. Mystical gifts are often seen as requiring imposed affliction and the denigrating of dignity where the recipient must be subdued by spiritual violence and ignobleness in order to convince doubters that a seer's will is not involved. Our Lady does not direct our hearts this way. She lifts up and nurtures our hearts. We must remember that God does not expect no will from His children, He asks for a holy will in union with His own. Any spiritual or physical indignity endured by His messengers and visionaries is a sacrifice that Jesus has asked them to bear as part of the opportunity for the world to receive His graces. But, said spiritual persecutors will meet judgment for what they do just as assuredly as those who placed Jesus on the Cross.

All discernment by spiritual directors must be focused on the desire for the presence of Infinite Love in the soul they are directing. They should be sacrificial companions in the elevation of a soul to perfection, not its critics or scourgers. Often it is the soul of the spiritual director that is being challenged to greater perfection in their interaction with a gifted soul. Their role is not to make sure their brother or sister is broken in submission to authority to convince themselves and their frail faith that a soul is actually guided by the Holy Spirit, nor is it to implement their will in the soul of another. Where is faith or love anywhere in such oppressive and manipulative conduct? They are not to take Christ to Crucifixion in a blessed soul to prove it is His work in that soul. Their intention should be, 'How do I help make this soul as strong as Christ Himself? How do I administer the grace of Jesus' Mother upon this soul? How do I help them do the Father's will? How do I affirm all the good in a way that is more beautiful than the enticements of the lesser?' The answer is to heap the Love of Our Lady upon them, just as She did to Her Son. Spiritual directors are to protect, share and magnify the grace they see growing in a soul. They must help them complete their sacrifice. I do not believe it has anything to do with blind obedience to any doubter or skeptic just because they supposedly hold a title of authority. Tyrants hurl demands of obedience. And, dictators with tin-pot crowns are the first to bellow for silence from their ragged thrones. Christ did not surrender His soul to the Sanhedrin. He stood resolute to the completion of His Sacrifice. He did not allow two minds nor two loyalties to be created within Himself. If the sentiment of Infinite Love is present and a spiritual director denies it as being from God, their perceptions of discernment are flawed, and their willfulness can bring great sacrificial suffering to a soul that resides beneath their direction. Spiritual directors are not God, nor are they chosen by God. They are companions in the unity of love and sacrifice in the Mystical Body of Christ, if they accept the nature of their affirming role. Great suffering can be inflicted on holy souls by those who have not remained in the presence of Infinite Love through their own humility, prayers and sacrifices. Signs of a strong will are not necessarily signs of human wilfulness that are detrimental to the spiritual life. Do we actually believe that Jesus did not have a strong will? He still has a strong will, but a holy will united with His Father, as have His Saints. Were not many Saints described as having wills of steel? We could go on and on naming them. I relate these perspectives so that everyone can sense the nature of Our Lady's relationship with my brother and me as our spiritual director. Her presence allows us to bypass many impediments that are oftentimes present in earthly spiritual direction. This has allowed us to progress through Her spiritual teaching with great acceleration and clarity. Now, just because we have been taught does not mean that we are dispensed from the sacrifice of implementing each day what we have learned. Uniting ourselves with Jesus' Sacrifice is the same for every Christian every day of their lives. We must do it in unity with one another. And, this is the essence of the Church's call to unite at the Altar as one Body in the Sacrifice of Jesus on the Cross which is made present in each Holy Mass. If spiritual directors are to "direct" a soul in a particular direction, the Catholic Altar is the destination for that direction. It is the Source of All Infinite Love that we wish to flourish within us, in every perception, thought, action and intention.

As a final thought, exaggeration in the mystical life is often seen by many as a flaw which brings on the tension between opinions about objectivity and subjectivity. The Kingdom of Heaven is filled with mystical realities that theology cannot grab hold of with its intellectualism. But, stubborn men only wish to accept what can be circumscribed by the protractor of their limited intellectual vernacular, then they label anything they cannot grasp as hyperbole or overstatement, relegating it into being a subject of a sinner's imagination. I would say that the presence of seeming exaggeration may be a soul trying to push the human language to describe heavenly things, which human words and expressions are too anemic to describe. There can also be multiple unique descriptions of the same mystical truth. There is no true language that has the semantics to describe the beauties of Heaven and its Savior and Queen, or His Wisdom in governing all Creation. It is like asking someone to describe love to you in detail. Poets have been trying to capture that description for centuries. God captures the zenith of love on Earth with one Calvarian Cross. Indeed, how might we describe it? Saints have been trying to describe it with their lives for two millennia. One could push human words to the celestial edges of mortal linguistics and still not grasp all the dimensions of Jesus' Crucifixion and Resurrection, or the yet veiled mysteries of the Kingdom of Heaven. The only exaggerations that I feel are non-productive when speaking of God are exaggerations of oneself by oneself. We must remember that when all is said and done, we are nothing more than servants to the Glory of God who is the Author and Sustainer of our lives. One does well if they are very cautious, even indifferent, to accolades from others, except those received from the Heavenly Hosts. And, the reason? The judgment of the Heavenly Hosts is real and true. One should never generate even the slightest intention to refute a sentiment or declaration from the Holy Spirit. In those cases, one must assent to the perceptions of God, even about oneself, and give glory to the Son for the reflection of grace that is recognized because it all comes from Him. Our Holy Mother has heaped copious thanksgiving and accolades upon my brother and me, as well as certain people whom She tells us She is proud of. She does not allow me to deflect or minimize Her words, but asks me to be humble and have the faith to accept the love and truth which She dispenses. She is serious about the command to love our neighbor as ourselves. She has never let my brother or me become lost in the idea that we are irrelevant to God. It has been quite the opposite. She tells us how special each of us is. And, that is part of our message to the world. Humanity is special in the universe, right down to the most despicable person to have ever been given the breath of life. It is better that we see ourselves this way, and be thankful that we are loved so dearly.

Part V
Advocatus Mater Dei
The Promoters of Her Cause

You have been told, O man, what is good,
and what the LORD requires of you:
Only to do the right and to love goodness,
and to walk humbly with your God.

- Micah 6:8

The Holy Gospel embodies both a sweet and a bitter message. The "taste" of the Gospel message is sweet to the penitent palate, but bitter in the belly of our worldly appetites. A phenomenon presently exists where many supposedly religious people, many who sit in pews every Sunday or preside before altars, recoil at any hint of righteous truth or calls to repentance in a Christian's voice because they wish to hear only pleasing rhymes of leniency behind which their lukewarm indifference and secular agendas can hide. They embrace the delusion of chasing a false peace whose terms are dictated by compromisers and cultural activists who will walk away from fraternity if the smallest correction were directed their way. It is their tendency to overlook the mediocrities of sin and defend those who commit them because they personally refuse to embrace the heights of sanctification which are necessary for spiritual holiness. They excuse wickedness without requiring amendment because they cannot accept the self-denial to overcome sin themselves. And, standing for the Gospel with an angelic conviction that would take them to the Cross is light-years beyond the excuses they generate to avoid its sacrificial burden. Then, they confuse mercy with permissiveness, and Christian truth with relativism. They caricature the King of kings as a grand liberal parent who gives them license to do whatever they wish without consequences, somehow believing it is honoring human dignity and a sign of great mercy. The Spiritual Works of Mercy declare something quite different. Perfection knows not this kind of leniency, but it is adorned with patience and forbearance. Sanctity cannot be tolerant of evil and sin, but it can forgive, mitigate, and heal. This is when the taste of the Gospel takes on its flavor in and out of season, and when salt should not lose its taste. Ironically, it is usually these same people who are on alert with worry about whether everyone else maintains an outward facade of humility and self-abasing submission, the people who assail confidence anytime they see it in another person. Their predictability would be humorous if it were not so tragic. Humility does not mean standing around with our heads down demeaning ourselves so that we become convinced that we are worthless with no redeeming contribution to the Great Commission. Genuine humility extinguishes the self which cowers from the sacrificial acts of authentic faithfulness. Authentic humility is having the power to believe when Our Lady mystically presents Herself before us. Humility is when one realizes that worldly stature and titles are straw in the fires of the Crucifixion. True humility comes with being in awe of how much we are loved, and knowing what power sustains our existence at every moment of life. Then comes thanksgiving for every gift, peace in the midst of any storm, joy in every breath of life, sacrifice for God's glory, and the audacity to ploughshare the New Covenant Gospel of Jesus Christ into every ear.

Problems arise when evil must be confronted and exposed in defense of the truth and human dignity. It is an act of love for all humankind, as well as the Earth and Nature, when these moments arrive. The two Spiritual Works of Mercy, instructing the ignorant and admonishing the sinner, are usually very difficult to do in a world that holds sacred its supposedly charitable relativism. Hence, deep reticence normally exists toward speaking the truth of Christian conversion and sanctification because the truth we impart is regurgitated back into our faces because it tastes so bad to those lost in defilement. Then, as a compromise, the mantra peals that Jesus 'accepts us exactly the way we are' because He is so loving. Yes, His Divine Mercy has the infinite breadth which provides Him the power to unilaterally execute that gift of acceptance, should He so desire. He proved that power on the Holy Cross. But, we must realize that His Divine Mercy is not the entire story. He declared that we have a part to play in obtaining the rewards of His Paradisial Kingdom through our conversion and acceptance of all that He commands. The measure of our sacrifices in union with His Crucifixion effects the integrity of our sanctification. Will we judge ourselves mercifully when we come face-to-Face with His Glory and realize then what we should have accepted and how we should have conducted ourselves in full view of what we did instead? Will we consider ourselves acceptable to be anywhere near Him? Do we realize that we will see a lifetime of Truth's admonitions shining upon us in scrutiny in that moment? If we detest these Truths now, are we going to accept them then in the finality of that last hour?

The Gospel proclaims many a parable about the requirements thrust upon souls who were waiting for the Bridegroom to arrive with their lamps lit and oil abundant; about those wishing to enter the wedding feast; and those who were removed because they were not well dressed. There will be no stolen entry into Heaven [Matthew 22:11-13]. The best preparation for our greeting Jesus Christ is to conform ourselves to the truths He reveals, imitate the perfection which He embodies, embrace the Holy Spirit to recognize the Father, and make the sacrifices that will identify us as having been obedient to His Word. These are all interior acts originating in the beatific aura of sanctifying grace. Scripture states, "*If anyone is ashamed of Me and My words in this adulterous and sinful generation, the Son of Man will also be ashamed of him when He comes in His Father's glory with the holy angels*" [Mark 8:38]. How should this Gospel truth affect our perceptions of our own lukewarmness, mediocrity, inattention, and distraction, indeed our sin; all those things that steal away our reverence for He who gave us life? This dichotomy of conflict between the light and darkness is why humanity's spiritual perception remains entangled in the deceptive errors of this militantly secular age and its chimera of salvation. It is also why strong declarations of the truth, the outward defense of human dignity, and allegiance to the unity embodied in the Original Apostolic Church are so necessary. The secular roar must be penetrated with the truth as a claim of dominion for Christ.

The American culture is lost in a glaring anomaly that seems much like rank hypocrisy when the Truth begins its winnowing of human intentions. To wit, not every partisan claim is based on wisdom and truth; nor is any absurdity, no matter how nobly adorned, worthy of being fostered or equally treated, and this seems hypocritical to secular relativists. Evil does not deserve due deference alongside the majesty of goodness, truth, and faith. Being charitable toward the goals of the devil's minions is no way to progress toward the beatitude of Paradise. Choices can lead to the damnation of souls and the destruction of nations. Purity, virtue, and honor are not accidents. Multitudes of people seek power, wealth, and fame by creating artifices of stature, constructing flourishings of grandiose and sympathetic rhetoric, contriving claims rooted in seduction, and setting out the trappings of false virtue in order to seduce others into surrendering the noble orders of the world and populations of the planet to their demonic patronage and menacing misguidance. Nearly all cultural image-makers in our contemporary era are malignant producers of shimmering deceptions of no less demonic origin than Satan slithering with appeal in the Tree of the Garden. The messengers of the secular world are masterful at creating themes and strains that waft base enticements before the senses of the masses for their own profit and megalomania. It is a self-celebrating concoction of lies being marketed as a more sophisticated reality. It is no more than propaganda from the father of lies and those who serve him.

One of the most confining states to exist is worldly prosperity, esteem and comfort while in spiritual darkness. Why would anyone wish to consider turning their perceptions away from material advantage, the adulation of other people, and their own physical comforts? The entire focus and perception of life becomes centered upon that which provides them this estate. The contemporary world has been filled with the secular canon of financial and material success with the Internet bringing the illusion of esteem to the children of darkness in the counting of mouse clicks which glorify sinful flesh, heathen relativism and Marxist demonism. In these times, the ideology of "diversity for its own sake" has proven itself to be a transgressor of prudent wisdom, unhinged from the anchoring of truth, and empowered to distract, distort and destroy the only true vision humanity could ever gain. The good news is that the God of Heaven loves us too much to sit back on the laurels of His Crucified Son and not reach out with His almighty divinity to open our blinded eyes; and so comes the Immaculate Virgin Mary in Her miraculous intercessions. Yet, what do we see as humanity's response? The teeming multitudes of the planet, including millions of professing Christians and their leaders, are found to be unable to transcend their realms of worldly comfort and social esteem to accept Her presence when She appears within their midst. The sacrifice to believe is too much for them, the rewards too immaterial, and eternal judgment too delayed. It makes one ponder the contrasting perspectives between those who do believe and those who do not. In a world blinkered by exilic perception, secular darkness and diabolical deception, the manifestation of this chasm of division seems all too human, predictable, and impenetrable. It is an utterly amazing phenomenon to witness in the presence of so much grace. Every person of sound faith should concede that if God has sent His Immaculate Virgin Mother to deliver a message to the Earth, it is humanity's opportunity, in fact its veritable duty, to respond and obey with swift dispatch, even as quickly as She responded to the Archangel Gabriel at the Annunciation as our example. Yet, what has been humanity's proven response across salvation history instead? Excuses abound because people love the darkness more than the Light, just as the Gospel writers bore witness [John 3:19]. And, oftentimes that darkness reveals itself as being most prevalent in the authoritarian obduracy of those who esteem themselves as Christianity's stewards. Autistic theological intellectuals caution people into the confines of their own personal doubts, and obedience to the Queen of Heaven dies away. The wholesale conversion of humankind in one generation after another is impeded from coming to pass because people refuse to answer the call of Heaven of their own free will, and those with the responsibility to encourage the faithful to respond to these grace-filled manifestations slink off into wilful rejection, hoping not to offend the protesting ecumenism they maintain with unbelievers in a washed-out compromise of the Gospel truth. Some might lament, 'if only God would reveal Himself more apparently.' Well, His spiritual gifts are dispensed through the conduit of humanity's faith. Those who believe, receive. Faith is the enlightening power that brings vision to those who make the sacrifice to believe. And, the fruits of that faith, namely the vision to recognize God's mystical beckoning, flourish in those who have invoked the courage to believe in the Man of all men and His Immaculate Virgin Mother. Those who do not believe ultimately receive nothing but the rebuke of their own consciences in the end. God provides the graces, but it is for human beings to invoke the faith that makes them fruitful for the transformation of the collective human spirit. Humanity will revere the Cross or rue it by being placed upon it. We will touch the Wounds of Jesus with our faithful hearts or with our obstinate flesh. We are headed for the mountaintop of Calvary where we will together see the Truth, some to great joy, while others to absolute horror and humiliation at the sight of what they could have accomplished, had they believed.

When people are presented with the "moment of faith" upon being asked to respond to our Immaculate Mother's miraculous intercession, they often surrender themselves into a suspended animation of mentalism which sometimes lasts for the rest of their lives because they can never escape their doubts about what they are being asked to believe. A rattling metronome of apprehension begins sounding its toll, which they often conclude is the voice of the Holy Spirit cautioning them, when it is actually quite the opposite. The truth is a burr that will never go away. It is the same with atheists and agnostics who are presented with the truth of the Gospel itself. Some spend their entire worldly lives in efforts intended to discredit Christianity, yet they never ask themselves why it sticks in their craw. Again, the Gospel lies bitter in the belly of their worldliness. Their composure of reason, more or less darkened by a prevailing secular world, inflames across the expanse of their minds. For those with little faith, this exilic reasoning, such as it is, runs like a wild stallion across the acreages of their intellect, never stopping until it is exhausted, whereafter they find themselves confronted with the same simple dilemma of believing or not believing standing right in front of them, still bearing its challenge of faith. Then, they either renew their faithlessness and continue running, or in a moment of self-effacing submission, reevaluate their lives that have thus far left them so vacant of meaning. It is almost like breaking a wild horse in a circular pen. The horse turns one direction, then the other, over and back again until it realizes that it is futile to attempt to evade the influence that is being imposed upon it by the trainer, and it comes to a stop. God is like that trainer. Our Holy Mother's miraculous intercession is not going away until She has completed every intention for which She has been sent by the Almighty Father. The good news is that She told me that She has come because She knew there would be multitudes who would listen with open hearts. There are children who will welcome Her as their Mother, and She knows who they are. The rest will keep running and someday wish they would have listened. If there were none to embrace Her, She would have never come, and Jesus would have already allowed "the end" to commence. He would never countenance His Immaculate Mother to be treated so disrespectfully by the sinners who deny Her mystical gifts.

Two facets of believing any truth are believing in that truth and thereafter accepting the myriad of implications of that truth. Truth cascades from truth as does Light from Light, true God from true God. For example, it is a great thing to accept the Marian Dogmas of our Blessed Virgin Mother enshrined by the Roman Catholic Church because they are definitively true. But, it is difficult to accept the consequent implications of these dogmatic truths with a completely open heart, most particularly all the facets of Her intercession that flow from the truth in these Dogmas. If one rejects the implications of a truth, have they really accepted that original truth? No, they have not, and conviction becomes no more than vacuous words. They have severed themselves from mystical reasoning. Dissonance is created in the Church when the truth and it cascading implications are not united in oneness. This is why a better case needs to be made for our obedience to our Heavenly Mother through Her miraculous intercession. The origin of this dissonance is in those of weak faith whose hearts do not recognize the Spirit of their Divine Shepherd at work within the Church. They are deaf to His beckoning call, oftentimes believing that the sound of their own ego is the Voice of God. The divine light reconciles this dissonance and confirms the Mind of God in the body of the faithful. Consider the certitude that comes from the divine light shining on the mind of one who has directly experienced extraordinary supernatural revelation from the Holy Spirit compared to the perceptions of those who yet disbelieve all the cascading implications of the truths they rhetorically profess. It is a fascinating contrast on the spectrum of perception related to humanity's sanctification. What is the difference between these two minds? What does the "certainty" bring? It brings unity and magnification to the spirit of the person in communion with the Holy Spirit. It brings a hallowedness of perspective that is a gift that must not be squandered or squelched. It brings a spiritual resonance to our interior vision much like harmonic physics as an analogy. Sacred Scripture recalls:

"(Jesus) answered, 'Because you have so little faith. In truth I tell you, if your faith is the size of a mustard seed you will say to this mountain, "Move from here to there," and it will move; nothing will be impossible for you." [Matthew 17:20]

The Catechism states, *"Faith is certain. It is more certain than all human knowledge because it is founded on the very word of God who cannot lie. To be sure, revealed truths can seem obscure to human reason and experience, but "the certainty that the divine light gives is greater than that which the light of natural reason gives." "Ten thousand difficulties do not make one doubt."* [Catechism 157].

"What moves us to believe is not the fact that revealed truths appear as true and intelligible in the light of our natural reason: we believe "because of the authority of God himself who reveals them, who can neither deceive nor be deceived" [Catechism 156].

These teachings from the Catechism reflect why messengers of Our Lady do not necessarily petition natural reasoning to defend their claims, nor might they be able to. It is God Himself who trumps the intellect and confirms their witness with divine light that often surpasses human reason. This is why what moves us to stand firm in witness is not the fact that it is reasonable to any human rationale, but rather because God said it. We believe in obedience to the authority of God Himself who reveals Himself to us, He who can neither deceive nor be deceived. Pope Benedict XIV compiled a great work of perceptions and pastoral advice on private revelation in his treatise on Heroic Virtue in the 18th century. In it, he recorded the following:

"Are they to whom a revelation is made, and who are certain it comes from God, bound to give a firm assent thereto? The answer is in the affirmative…"

Heroic Virtue, Vol. III, p. 390

"He to whom that private revelation is proposed and announced, ought to believe and obey the command or message of God, if it be proposed to him on sufficient evidence; …For God speaks to him, at least by means of another, and therefore requires him to believe; hence it is, that he is bound to believe God, Who requires him to do so."

Ibid, p. 394

As the first statement reasonably alludes, every soul who has been given the grace to know that God is the initiator of a revelation to them must never deny Him, even at the tip of a sword. Has every soul been able to generate this kind of conviction in the testing moment? No. Some have forsaken the graces they have received. Others have been deceived into rejecting such graces through the intimidation of others, even by some possessing authority in the Church. For those spoken about in the second statement to whom these private revelations are proposed, the question should arise as to how much faith does God wish us to have? When attempting to satisfy the necessary discernment to fulfill one's spiritual responsibility when God is calling, what is "sufficient evidence?" Should we not ponder what God believes sufficient evidence to be? If an intercession is authentic, surely He has dispensed the evidence. Is not the more difficult part our recognizing what that evidence is and having the courage to accept it as such? We are not going to escape our judgment; and we are going to admit in truth whether or not we extended our faith in response to the evidence He did dispense to us. God very rarely in history performs miracles that doubters demand, but He does dispense sufficient evidence of His work right in front of their eyes on His own terms. He does not necessarily perform miracles to force people to believe, but He often grants them as a reward for the faith of the people who do. I say this: Everyone who receives authentic miraculous revelation from God knows it, and they are bound by this knowledge because they know it is God who has imparted it. And, expectations are in effect. It becomes part of the composure of their responsibilities for which they will one day answer, as God has stated to whom much is given, much is expected. It becomes a dimension of a seer's self-judgment before the Throne of God. For me, I know Our Lady's presence in my life with divine Catholic faith which I cannot deny without the risk of losing my soul. If I deny Her, it is a sin against the Holy Spirit for which I will have to atone deeply in the agonies of Purgatory, if I attain that position at all. Simply said, I know better, and God knows that I know better because He knows the graces that He has given me through no merit of my own. I have no excuse. For those to whom we propose and announce Our Lady's miraculous intercession as the Morning Star Over America, what is the sufficient evidence that God has given on His terms which bear expectations upon us to respond to Her wishes? For those who would wait for a personal supernatural miracle of confirmation, are not the works and the great messages in them the miracle? I submit that there is no person alive who could have, or would have, possessed the spiritual faculties and invested the time, effort, sacrifice, suffering, and devotion in order to compose the messages in relative anonymity without interruption over the span of more than thirty years, while attending to normal daily obligations in a secular world to survive and prosper. Those who doubt do not seem to ask themselves, where then did all this come from? Do they actually believe that my brother and I made them up? We might appreciate the accolades for our spiritual genius from these people, but we do not deserve it because we are not the origin of them. A mighty rock of mystical revelation has been laid on the tabletop of Creation by the Queen of Heaven. It is yet for Heaven to watch whether humanity embraces it for the conversion of millions, or attempts to kick it away as an unwelcome distraction.

Notwithstanding these previous sentiments, most everyone who is asked to believe a revelation of the Holy Spirit such as Our Lady's miraculous intercession engages human reasoning before extending spiritual faith in the process of searching for sufficient evidence to extinguish their doubts. The most faithful of the children of Mary extend faith first because they trust Jesus, His Mother, and their brothers and sisters to greater degrees at the outset than most. This trust, which is a grace, informs and encourages their immediate acceptance of the sufficient evidence that always surrounds Our Lady's intercessions. They don't need as much evidence to quell the turbulence of human reason as do the doubting intellectuals because their faith is greater and humility more profound. For some, great supernatural miracles are required as sufficient evidence, which really means the abdication of their faith altogether. It all resides on a great spectrum of discernment where God is asking, "Just how much is it going to require before you will believe?" Sometimes exalted members of the Church hierarchy who should be of the greatest faith are the very ones who require the most evidence. And, what a shame this is. They believe they are protecting the Church when in actuality they are rejecting the very graces they are seeking to protect the Church and advance its mission of converting a lost humanity. They claim they must test the spirit, but fail to test their own. And, therein is the devil's surreptitious victory. Our Lord wishes us instead to be Advocatus Mater Dei, the Promoters of Her Cause, for the sake of the conversion of millions. The magnitude of our trust and faith influences the measure of sufficient evidence that we will require to convince our human reasoning to stand aside, believe, conform, and begin the march of faithful obedience toward the Cross. Nonetheless, those who engage human reasoning at the outset do not do so in vain if they are humble because their reasoning when perfected and sanctified will take them to the door where only their faith can walk through.

The point to be pondered is that the intellectual mechanics of the mind can injure and overshadow the responsive invocation of belief that our God desires. He wants us to trust Him, and He usually asks us to do so through other people whom He sends. Faithful Catholic parishioners extend this trust every day of their lives as a matter of course in the respect and deference they show to their priests and Prelates. Our Lady asks when are Prelates going to reciprocate that trust to the faithful in true regard, especially to Her messengers whom She sends to them. Do we not more often make the choice to engage a wandering excursion of skepticism through a forest of supposedly expert excuses, none of which help us generate the intention of arriving at the door where faith would matter? We must see the exception displayed to us by little children who possess humble souls. This is why Jesus pointed them out as being so precious. They do not market in the apprehensions of scholarly mentalists, nor do they have any stature to risk or pride to stand upon. They step up with faithful enthusiasm because they love Jesus and trust that He will always care for them. They step right up to the door wanting to see the other side because they love the One whose voice is sweetly calling from the other side. They are the little lambs who know their Shepherd, and recognize His voice [John 10:27].

What is it that children and humble souls possess that shames the proud? Humble innocence, faithful deference, fearless trust, and the desire to be united with great love. They do not count the cost to themselves. They are not afraid of being wrong because they have nothing to lose. They are vacant of worldly artifices that would impede their spiritual gravitation toward the revelation of love. Conversely, how often have sterile intellectualism and clerical hubris revealed themselves to be combatants of mystical grace throughout history? The examples of yore are legion. Satan anchors haughty skepticism in the orders of discernment, an elitism that flies in the face of God, whether it be through imperious theological traditions, obtuse religious hubris, ad hominem suspicion of messengers, the convenient abuse of the wisdom of the great mystics of the Church, the barricaded doors of clericalism, the trite dimensions of our faith, or through the outright demonic frame of reference of the lost who arbitrarily deny God's gifts ex post facto to the moment of the Annunciation of the Archangel Gabriel. The presence of unsanctified thinking, analyzing, comparing, debating, deciphering, deciding and marginalizing serves as a blatant obstacle to anyone fluently accepting the mystical graces that God offers in His relationship with us. Our Lady's Fiat at the Annunciation testifies to something far different, something that is perfect. Most critics are vacant of the holy fear that might otherwise caution them to avoid becoming obstinate adversaries of the Holy Spirit. Their mansion (claim) of holy prudence is often the shanty of faithlessness which doubters such as themselves believe to be a hallmark of integrity in the Holy Spirit. While in its exalted confines, the graces of God are summarily rejected by these false discerners who consign messengers to being merely sinners afflicted with delusions while they simultaneously make the fatal mistake of presuming upon their personal infallibility, which is often based on nothing more than a common ideology of disbelief shared with the rest of their cynical brethren [John 7:47-49]. Rationalism that is conscripted by fears rooted in pride and lack of trust in God inevitably relegate these doubting Thomas's to perpetually debating "whether" to believe any supernatural private revelation at all. And, they continue running like wild stallions through the thicket of their own excuses. The worst of their lot are also the ones who are tempted to rationalize away every miracle ever performed as recorded in the New Testament. It is discernment that has lost the fear of God which should be the admonishing impetus for wisely embracing all that He does instead. Rationalists rarely engage in honest self-reflection, self-criticism, or consider the measure of their own perfect unity with the Holy Spirit. They live in the echoing chamber of their doubting clan who fortify the faithlessness that defines them all. And, they are the first to administer their own uniformed scrutinies upon messengers as if the light of God emanates from their towering intellects alone. Our Lady says that they are mere spectators and speculators who hold nothing but irrelevant opinions, who risk their opportunities to display their loyalty to God and convert thousands and millions in the process with the assistance of the Heavenly Hosts. They act as if they are already at the pinnacle of sanctified intelligence, having nothing more to offer their God by way of their sacrifices. They have irrelevant worldly agendas, while God possesses the plan which unfolds His Salvation as He intends. Simple innocence of the heart which would recognize His provident action and comply with joy for the sake of the magnification of Christ and His Mother is lost to them. "Blessed are the pure of heart, for they shall see God." Yet, this is what children mirror instinctively, at least until they grow old enough to be scandalized by the doubters, skeptics and worldlings that I speak of. Intellectualism should not be a white-knuckled grip on theoretical structures of mentalism, intoxicated with the prospect of superior enlightenment, and haunted that its entire cerebral superstructure will become unbalanced and begin crashing to the ground if they happen to get out of the boat and face the storm. To them, water can never be walked upon, and no mountain could ever be moved. They fear God's spontaneity like an autistic paranoiac finding an odd number of socks in the drawer of an anonymous one-legged man. Any psychologist would tell us that developing a psyche which tries to meticulously control every minute aspect of its existence is a pathological state of engagement with one's life. Yet, that is exactly what some of these people spend their lives doing when trying to define the human person and its relationship with our omnipotent unseen God. Beatific grace is far more fluent and beautiful in every person than they will concede it to be. We must remember that there are many extremely astute intellectuals whose hearts are as cold and dark as a tomb. For all their genius, they are destined for the revelation of their failure. What a place for so many thinkers to have congregated — All sitting in a cavern, debating a light they have never truly seen.

The exiled intellect conjures distraction by generating mental turbulence based in uncertainty and the defense of self-autonomy, instead of falling into the unity of contemplative obedience to the ways that our God speaks to us and forms us. Obedience to Divine Love does not require any intellectualism at all. It comes from a sacrificial heart that knows of its nothingness, and thus its God, without reservation. This is the heart of Saint John who stood beneath the Cross while all the others fled. He was in contemplation of the One he loved at the expense of everything he possessed, everything he knew, and everything he thought might happen to him. Our Lady has stated that She wishes us to get past "whether" it is Her appearing, and move into contemplative obedience to what She has to say as our Heavenly Mother, and then, tell the world! There are over 7 billion people on a planet of nearly 8 billion who either reject or do not know Jesus Christ. What a shame after 2,000 years. She is trying to amplify the story of human Salvation to them with miracles, and restore the simple vision and unity of hearts in the Sacred Heart of Her Son. Think about it! The Mother of God has appeared with great revelation and dispensed thousands of pages of wisdom and encouragement across the globe to numerous messengers as fruits of the Holy Gospel. Thus far, however, fainthearted discernment is stumbling and bumbling, confirming itself as being faithlessness looking for a reason not to believe. This ideological vacuum has nothing to do with the advancement of any soul in the grace of God's revelation of Himself through His Immaculate Mother. Of course He expects theologians to ponder the Morning Star Over America, indeed, until the end of the world. But, woe to those who reject it before having spent a lifetime meditating upon what has been delivered in it. Jesus has not asked for heady criticisms of His Immaculate Mother or the children who suffer to receive Her, but only for humanity's faithful openness to receive everything She has to say and put it into practice.

Souls made in the image and likeness of God know when He touches them. They also know when the Heavenly Hosts stand before them. And, the great revelations and intercessions of Our Lady leave no defensible alternative than for us to cooperate with them as swiftly as Her Fiat was given to the Archangel Gabriel. Belief opens the door to our fluent relationship with supernatural grace that can be believed through the prescriptions of divine faith. Sufficient grace becomes efficacious through the invocation of faith. Nowhere in the Dogma and Teachings of the Divine Faith does it say that one should reject supernatural gifts and revelations given throughout the Body of Christ because they are inconvenient to us. But, that is what many evangelize as their creed because they fear to have faith. The Holy Scriptures state, "Strive eagerly for the greatest spiritual gifts" [1 Corinthians 12:31]. Saint Paul also speaks clearly in those same First Corinthian verses about the spiritual gifts bestowed upon Christ's Mystical Body by the Holy Spirit, and how each performs its service unto the Lord for the edification and building up of the Church. If the Church en masse were to have been stripped of its mystical sensibilities over the course of a darkened century, do we think that God would not now send the heavenly luminaries to encourage and admonish everyone in sight to return to the true path? Would the Dominion Angels not make their presence felt and perform their duties of justice? Verily, they are doing it now. The contemporary mountain of exilic irrationalism that defines our age of scientific skepticism must be leveled and made straight in the same way that mental analysis evaporates on the mountaintops of mystical contemplation. Saint John of the Cross would say as much. There is no theological intellectualism on the mountaintop of supernatural revelation. Man is left speechless and the intellect dumbfounded in the sight of God just as Peter, James and John on Mount Tabor could find nothing meaningful to put into words before the Transfigured Christ. It is the experience of oneness with the Creator of the universe and the origin of our being that surpasses all human understanding which a thousand skeptics could neither disturb nor overrule.

Part VI
Casting Down the Mighty

*"One person practicing holiness is better
than a thousand people theologizing over it."*

We live in an age immersed in secularized hype that is nothing more than mindless propaganda twittered by those with the audacity to cultivate lies about their stature or boast about a tomorrow which they have forgotten they will only see by the grace of their God. Deception advances itself with zealotry, sophistry, fury, contrivances, ostentation, seduction, manipulation, elitist intellectualism, intimidation, threats, fear, and paranoia. Disorientation dons the majestic pageantry of rhetorical compassion and anchors itself in sanctimonious conviction like the General Sherman sequoia piling its taproot into the northwestern forest floor. Nonetheless, we must see instead that the truth needs no hype, and it will always reign supreme. It stands in peace as an impenetrable icon of certainty that will outlast the ages and all the derangements of deceivers, demagogues and despots, long after the last redwood has been toppled to the ground. The truth does not need to march in mindless mobs, chant divisive hatred, launch its salvos of revolution, burn its cities or scorch its continents. It does not need to intimidate and persecute its detractors, screech its worldly entitlements, or wail its victimhood. The truth is peaceable and kind, slow to anger, rich in kindness and mercy, but mighty in righteousness and wisdom, decisive with flashing sword in the face of monstrous evil, while being inclusive of anyone who wishes to contribute themselves to the Sacrifice in order to become a good and noble member of the human family. It thinks well of its brothers and sisters, even in the midst of their unintentional struggles and failures, and admonishes with compassion and asks for a common sacrifice that all may live with dignity. But, woe to the riotous and the renegade. Woe to the atheists and anarchists. Woe to the taunters and tyrants. Woe to the marauders and Marxists. Woe to the tongues dripping with nihilism and vanity. Woe to the dividers and the dregs. The judgment of Truth is near! And on that day, these purveyors of ungodly darkness will wish they had never been born. These are the rebellious lot who will be searching for a mountain to crawl under to escape the righteous judgment of Almighty God [Revelation 6:16]. This is a truth that needs no hype; it needs no cadenced slogans nor any chants short of the Gregorian psalms. It requires no acknowledgment before it will command its own entrance. It dares to step forward, despite the scorn of all its enemies. It will come like a thief in the night when irreligious defiance is all the rage. And, it is then that the fires of God will rage instead, consuming the elements where they stand. These two companions, Wisdom and Truth, will brand all Creation and the entire expanse of human history with the heat of their own Glorious Song. The meek and humble will be vested with authority, while the arrogant and proud will look back across the chasm of their audacity, hoping a moist finger would reach out to soothe their arid tongues.

While resting beneath this foreboding shadow of judgment, what are we to think when peering across the sorrowful landscapes of human life and seeing the ominous scriptural prophecies of Revelation playing-out their mystical choreography in our presence? First of all, we must recognize that delusions brought upon us by the conscripting remnants of original sin are all too present to distract us from the eternal realities in our lives. Thunderheads of hysteria sweep their shadows of division across otherwise sunlit plains of peaceful unity. Modes of communication and their limitations across generations, nationalities, dialects and pedagogies of knowledge are belaboring the flourish of divine revelation which is instead washed away without compunction in the riptides of autocratic opprobrium. Lost majorities are oblivious and unconscious to the restorative graces of Christian faith that are heralded in the Sacred Scriptures and manifested by Saints and Martyrs throughout the ages. Minuscule numbers and barely a remnant concede attention to the procession of God's convalescent miracles, let alone lay down their lives in cooperation with His Spirit that He may be glorified instead of themselves. Prophetic voices are then silenced; messengers go unheeded, visionaries are derided as dreamers, mystics are mocked as eccentrics, heroic priests are ostracized and punished, great mystical works are delegitimized by theologically autistic experts, spiritual martyrs are forced to the Cross in reparation, and the Queen of Heaven is treated like Lazarus lying beside the rich man's door. How is it possible that so many mystical graces and miracles from the vaults of God's Kingdom process before the awareness of humanity but thereafter find themselves relegated to dustbins of private irrelevance by the religious 'haut monde'? In favor of what are they being displaced? Where is the voice of Truth that would stand as herald to God's mystical interventions? Who is responsible for the sacrilege and dishonor that assails the abounding graces of the Father's Queen? Who is it that considers themselves to be of such great stature as to fly in the face of Heaven's Matriarch? Who is it that offends my Heavenly Mother? Why are Her immaculate intercessions not at least respected, if not honorably enshrined atop the summit of mystical credibility of the Roman Catholic

Church as part of our motiva credibilitatis? Those who believe they can defer ecclesial approbation for Heaven's work for centuries are not only deluding themselves while cheating the present age, but they are also failing to realize that they may, in fact and truth, be running out of years to portray such calculated indifference. There will come a time for all justice! Furthermore, do we not see the injustice in being routinely forced to accept ecclesial silence as the only alternative, lest one finds oneself accused before humanity of the remnant of Adam's sin of disobedience? This is nothing more than a convenient abuse of authority, reminiscent of the most rogue inquisitors of Church history, all in a nation of liberty where godless secularists better secure the great right of free speech for atheism than do the religious for their God. Luke 16:8 says, "For the children of this world are more prudent in dealing with their own generation than are the children of light." I say again, we watch the Gospel prophecies play out right before our eyes, and many are the doubting Thomas's wrapped in the hubris of their provenance and superficial discernment; they who will certify to the ages that they were indifferent, at best, to the Providential Will of the Almighty Father and the gifts He granted into their stewardship for dispensation to a lost world for its own conversion. Shame upon them at the Judgment of the Ages!

Our beautiful Virgin Mother has encouraged me not to be silent no matter anyone's scorn, but to proclaim all that She has taught me, admonish where necessary, confront the arrogant, forgive at every opportunity, caress every open heart, charge the gates of mentalism, thunder against sin, and pray as if there may be no tomorrow. She has told me to waste no time responding with confrontational recriminations against Her adversaries because She said their day will come and their excuses, edicts, and opprobrium against Her work will die with them. In obedience to the Beauty that has succored the pantheon of Saints, my brother and I have compiled page after page, perspective atop of parable, with metaphor, example and analogy, year after year, decade upon decade, tapping out words, sentences and phrases from the Spirit of God while saturating our laps with tears, attempting with single-hearted consecration to give a viable reason for humanity to believe our Queen's intercession against every skeptic's doubt. Alas, even this will fail to be 'sufficient evidence' for the most hard hearted who sit atop the laurels of their pride. But, they will fall in the end, nonetheless. Our Lady will be triumphant despite them! Here again is the sweet and bitter message of the Gospel. Christian duty calls us to share both the spiritual gifts and the ethereal resplendence of human deliverance celebrated in the Sacred Scriptures, calling everyone to obediently surrender to the Maternal guidance of the Most Immaculate Virgin Mary in preparation for the Return of Jesus Christ in Glory. The Virgin Mary is not a figurehead Mother, nor is She the static object of dogma. Indeed, She is the Mediatrix of All Divine Graces from Heaven through the perfect Son of Her Immaculate Womb. The Woman clothed with the Sun is standing in human history and hovering near the consciences of Her faithful children in testament to the unfolding Revelation of Her Son.

The call of the ages is resounding throughout the architectures of Creation and the hallowed halls of Paradise. The Heavenly Hosts are trembling with the pent-up anticipation storehoused in the millennia during which they have prayed. Humanity is presently receiving a final call to trust our Heavenly Mother and to respond as one body of faithful believers, each in our own way for the conversion of those who will hold out until the last mortal moment. Just as a single drop of rain turns into a monsoon, She comes asking for our obedience for our own sake, hoping the individual voices of Her children will become a hurricane roar of acclamation for the King of kings. We must remember that trust cannot exist if one waits until all human reasoning satisfies its gluttony for indifference before accepting Jesus through the power of faith. Human reasoning is like an inspector examining a diving tower at an Olympic swimming pool to determine its structural integrity in order to accomplish its purpose. Faith is diving off its ten-meter tower. Our Lady's miraculous intercession is on an entirely different level. It testifies to Her children diving from mountainous cliffs, while the inspectors are grousing about the safety of a diminutive diving tower. They are retorting to the crowds, "Are you going to believe us or your lying eyes?," while Christ says, "Behold!" as His children dive from the immaculate granite towers He erected in the opening days of Creation. We tempt Him when we demand our own confirming supernatural miracles before we tender allegiance to Heaven's appellate remonstrations of our conduct. Where is faith in that, Our Lady asks. There is no virtue to be gained in waiting for a supernatural sign to crush our stubbornness before we invoke our trust and believe. The miracles and wonders already stare us in the face, ominously and unapologetically. God can convince humanity with overwhelming beatific riches any time He chooses; He can turn up the lights in the house at any next moment. However, He gauges these graces during this Advent in order to maintain faith intact so that great gifts of forgiveness and mercy may be granted, should we invoke the virtue to respond. After the Day of Mercy, the flames of Judgment will come!

Our Blessed Mother says that moral intellectuals who consider themselves gatekeepers should revisit what it means to trust. God uses the weak and insignificant to shame the proud, and He will continue to do so until the last day of the mortal world. He can do anything He pleases, and mankind is left with no option but to say 'thank you, I accept and concur.' His little ones are His weapons of mass destruction of human pride. They believe when the esteemed and scholarly do not. And, why do they not? Because the learned have too much intellectual reasoning to satisfy before they believe. They have too many intellectuals to battle in their vaunted halls to make the effort. They never get around to believing with conviction because their sacrificial hearts are never in it. The first shall be last [Matthew 19:30]. It is a commendable grace and a sign of humility for one to consider God's perfect impartiality when one is challenged by mystical gifts presented into our midst by the Holy Spirit. There are always reasons why He does. He gives no person a dispensation from the requirement of invoking their faith when He calls in these extraordinary ways, notwithstanding that perfection can still be gained through suffering, even if one disbelieves. It is good to remember that the Holy Sacraments inflame triumphant graces within the soul of any person who partakes of them with faith in their efficacy. They are not static dogma either. The law becomes written upon the heart in full view of our awareness, which gives volume to the holy conscience and direction to all didactic acts of Christian evangelization. God shows no favoritism nor discrimination when dispensing His grace where He wills. Yet, history is flush with the witness of grace rejected because it did not originate in those who believed they were the sole proprietors of God's sacred vineyard instead of the humble servants within it. It testifies to rearing faith locked in the stalls of other men's doubts. It glares of admonishment to cowards who skulk in the shadows, watching greater men stand in the breach against the horrors of the ages. Valor out-thunders tepid rhetoric, especially when the darkness of uncertainty looms. Those with faith know that stepping from the boat does not mean falling to the bottom of the ocean's fathoms when responding to the Lord calling, "Come!"

Sacred Scripture implores within the strains of its mighty Testament that we recognize the seasons of our times and the immaculate grace that He has been pleased to present in His Mother whom He is glorifying. It is about a love and unity in the Holy Spirit who reigns without end and across every micron of Creation; Wisdom that is above and beyond anything humanity has been able to generate in the eons of stale intellectualism. We are brothers and sisters in the God who comes to us and reigns without fail in every human heart which is open to receive His grace. "All who are guided by the Spirit of God are sons of God. The Spirit himself joins with our spirit to bear witness that we are children of God" [Romans 8:14,16]. Trust implies that we do not yet know all the answers, for what human mind can circumscribe the breathtaking motivations of an infinite God in one Sacred Heart. But, when the fruits are present and integrity stands atop its pedestal unshaded, our confidence must rise to kiss the challenge of the unseen with the same allegiance as Abraham giving his fealty to the Almighty Father in the offering of Isaac, his son. We must acknowledge our responsibility to accompany and nurture the veritable grace of God, and to comply with as much faith as Our Lady when She said "Be it done unto Me" to an Archangelic Saint. We trust that our God will never lead us astray, and He will respond by making every word we utter bound in Heaven as it is proclaimed on Earth. It is Satan's worst nightmare that we might invoke this kind of loyalty toward one another and the Most Holy Trinity in every way that God speaks, especially through His Immaculate Mother. It all boils down to each person deciding to respond through an act of faith in defiance of every disbeliever and allow the grace of God to reconfigure our frame of reference, no matter what; to concede to the therapeutic piety that heals the disfigurement of our mystical intellect and transfigures our entire identity through the Holy Sacrifice consummated on one Calvarian Cross. Our confirmation in faith thereafter bestows upon us the right to convoke all the graces and powers of Heaven, and move into the freedom of the Sacred Heart of Jesus as newly christened children of the Almighty Father.

Part VII
Sacralized Spiritual Deduction

1 Corinthians 2:12-16
We have not received the spirit of the world but the Spirit who is from God, so that we may understand the things freely given us by God. And we speak about them not with words taught by human wisdom, but with words taught by the Spirit, describing spiritual realities in spiritual terms. Now the natural man does not accept what pertains to the Spirit of God, for to him it is foolishness, and he cannot understand it, because it is judged spiritually. The one who is spiritual, however, can judge everything but is not subject to judgment by anyone. For "who has known the mind of the Lord, so as to counsel him?" But we have the mind of Christ.

Fallen humanity is battling a consistent deficiency across human evolution whereby we too often succumb to the intellectual composure of Saint Thomas the Apostle who asserted that he would not believe until he had touched the Wounds of the Resurrected Messiah. Scripture does not say whether Saint Thomas rose to the challenge when Christ appeared to him. Can you imagine the moment? Everyone startled at the appearance of Our Lord in the room. The lightning of material apparition striking throughout Thomas' soul when his eyes fell upon the Risen Christ. And then the Lord staring directly into his eyes and voicing the words, "(Thomas) Put your finger here, and look at My hands. Reach out your hand and put it into My side. Stop doubting, and believe" [John 20:27]. Oh, what a moment in human history as the walls fell! The power of God obliterating the mental constitution and regenerating it in the Truth of His Glory. The human tendency to be closed-hearted is a symptomatic state of stubbornness in doubt, deceived by the material world, fearful of being wrong, replete with questioning, defensive in pride, worried about personal stature, and brazen in debate until one has their mental reasoning demolished and reconstituted by the breathtaking beauty of the miraculous. It is mechanistic cynicism ignited outside abandonment to God, unable to hear His Voice, vacant of love, severed from holy conviction, while wandering around in exilic mentalism that respects only what can be interrogated, weighed, measured, and dissected. Doubt, suspicion, and apprehension become the squatters of the mind when faith falters and leaves the heart untethered from trust in God who cares for us beyond the lilies of the meadows. It is a precarious mental state absent the enlightening, focusing, purifying freedom conceived beneath the rays of a bright and shining faith. It is raw earthly intellect, indentured by questions demanding answers like a slaver holding keys with a money bag open for tithes. It possesses not the power to loose itself from the conscripting definitions demanded by human reason, locked in the depleted perspectives of exile.

The human intellect from birth is subject to mature within this conscription if it is not fed the warmth of God's mystical graces, beginning with those manifested through the Holy Sacraments of Roman Catholic Christendom. Deception reigns without the waters of the Spirit of Christ Crucified. It is life without the practicability of the supernatural, locked in mental conjuring, mulling worldly possibilities but never accepting mystical facts, meandering in cowardly equivocation at the expense of human suffering, skulking in conjecture but never taking a stand, observing the procession of the miraculous but never joining the Passion, and resigning itself regrettably to being unable to manifest the grace that leads the rescue of humanity from suffering, captivity, sin and death. This conscripted vision requires that the eyes of men should see before they are allowed to believe, while the heavens declare that everyone must believe or they will never flourish in the freedom of divine vision. Those who prostrate their reasoned deduction beneath only what they can see, touch, and what the secular world approves, inevitably diminish themselves and everyone else as being separated from God simply because He has not revealed Himself before their doubting eyes. The worldly intellect says, "No, I will not believe unless I see, and I will not trust anyone unless I see for myself. If I cannot intellectually comprehend and judge it, then lord over it, it could not possibly be true." The Heavenly Father will not succumb to the extortion of sinners who say, "I'll only believe in the mystical things you do if you do them through me first." People who think this are utterly oblivious to the limits of their power to command anything from God at all. He has set the terms for human redemption — we offended His Glory. But, He established each person as a sovereign creature with a heart which could know Him, which will leave no excuse found exonerating in the end. Wickedness harbored in the hearts of men is an enigma of self-possessed iniquity. There is really no logical or moral sense to it, and a heart filled with holiness knows it. Stubbornness in pride without self-reflection is the empty keep of the penitentiary of everlasting doom. Our Lady said that people will continue in Eternity the composure of wickedness in which they confirmed themselves in a life without repentance. These deranged minds find no ability to reason in the ways of divine light because their mental frames of reference have been enslaved by seemingly rational prerequisites which demand that nothing be accepted as reasonable unless it complies with the doubting standards of their bounded worldly criticisms. They are doubters in life; they will be doubters of their own salvation in death because they require God to compete with their mentalism when He is only trying to save them from their own pontificating hubris. Imagine that! The mystical beauty of Heaven's Sacred Heart never has a chance in these lost souls because Jesus Christ does not dance to the fifing dictates of acceptability that they impose upon themselves and everyone around them. But, look at humble Catholic priests who obey Jesus and their Heavenly Mother; those who are ostracized for speaking unvarnished truth; those who believe in miraculous intercession, the gifts of the Holy Spirit, the power of Sacramental Confirmation, and give their entire lives in testament to the greater vision of Truth about the relationship of God with His children. Scorned by the world, but resoundingly exalted in Heaven!

The morning of the Easter Resurrection of the King of kings reveals quite a lot about the human intellectual constitution. The Tomb lay empty, and the stone rolled away when the holy women of the Lord arrived that morn. Mary Magdalene saw the empty Tomb and ran to Jesus' disciples saying, "They have taken the Lord out of the tomb, and we do not know where they have put Him!" What was the state of Mary Magdalene's intellectual composure where her reasoning could deduce no more than that Jesus' Body had been taken from the Tomb by others? Simon Peter then made haste to the burial site and went in, followed by John whom Scripture states "saw and believed." What compelled John to believe with seemingly nothing more than an empty Sepulcher? Then, Jesus began His appearances among them to resurrect their faith from the horrors of Mount Calvary. There was an entire spectrum of intellectual composure among the disciples which would require differing measures of "sufficient evidence" before their mental deductions could be penetrated by the truth of His Paschal Resurrection from among the dead. It ranged from Mary Magdalene to Peter, to John, the holy women, the remaining apostles and disciples, and yes, Thomas. But, John's faith reigned supreme, even though he '...did not yet understand from Scripture that Jesus had to rise from the dead' as his Gospel states [John 20:9]. Not from intellectualism, but from the heart did John come to know. What a magnificent spiritual deduction from his heart of the wisdom of God! This is true reasoning of the Holy Spirit. He saw nothing supernatural before he believed, just the relics of the greatest miracle the world will ever know lying folded on the Sepulcher stone. Maybe the perceptions of his conscience were tweaked by that morning's aftershock of Good Friday's earthquake which removed the stone from the entrance to the Tomb. Then, the breathless arrival of Mary Magdalene and her frantic announcement to them. So spontaneous and unexpected. How the small hint of a smile must have come across the immaculate visage of the Blessed Virgin Mother, She who knew the Resurrection was imminent, She who knew what the earthquake of that morning signified. Then, Peter rising at Mary Magdalene's word to go see for himself, searching for evidence to rationalize the truth that was pouring-forth upon him. Did he more move because he too believed that Jesus' Body had been taken, or did he have a sense of faith, hoping that it all may be true? When running to the Tomb and seeing the stone rolled back, did John immediately recall Jesus petitioning for the stone to be removed to bring forth Lazarus's rising from the dead? Did the words "Destroy this temple and I will rebuild it in three days," ring anew in his thoughts? Did he conclude, "Oh, could it be so? Surely, this is His ultimate triumph. Did He not show us His power by raising Lazarus? Did He not tell us what He was going to accomplish?" It all added up for Saint John, just as it had added up for Simon Peter when he exclaimed, "Thou art the Christ, the Son of the Living God" upon being asked by Jesus, "Whom do you say that I am?" [Matthew 16:15]. This is sacralized spiritual deduction straight from the Heart of the Father.

The flood of perceptions that was inundating consciences on the Resurrection morning was splendorous and magnificent; yes, Veritatis Splendor! The boulders of stagnancy in the solemnity of death were being shaken loose and displaced as the moments unfolded through the Providence of Life bursting forth from its interment. Yet, it was John whose heart put it all together first, who manifested the greatest spiritual deduction of Christianity that the Christ had indeed vanquished mortality by being raised from the dead! His spiritual deduction supported by great trust in the goodness, words, example, and actions of His Savior created a platform for his faith where his heart began screaming "Yes" to him. But, what of the others? What about Thomas? For over a week, the simple loving witness and joy of his apostolic brothers was not enough to support him in transcending his doubt about his Lord's conquering of death. His worldly hopes had been dashed, and he dared not lift new ones because the Crucifixion had been too painful and permanent for his reasoning mind to witness. To him, the declarations of resurrection bordered on mere hysterical fanaticism. What else could they have been? How do we respond to ecstatic witnesses whom we do not believe? How do we respond to Marian messengers bringing great news into our midst of Our Lady's appearances? The unity he experienced throughout three years in his Savior's presence should have been enough to encourage his intellect to believe the factual witness of his fellow disciples to the Messiah's Glorious

Resurrection, even though from the frame of reference of worldlings, his response of doubt was completely reasonable through any measure of human deduction in his time, and probably ours. His mind represented the world that was passing away through Christ's Death and Resurrection. There is something eschatological about these moments of revelation to Saint Thomas that can teach us about what is old and what is of the coming new world. For him, the mustard plant had yet to break the soil. His intellect cultivated in the old world could not transcend its own exilic reasoning, notwithstanding all the miracles that he had witnessed. He was bound by worldly reasonableness which told him Christ's Resurrection was unreasonable. Not even the raising of Lazarus from the dead after four days in a tomb was revelation enough to support the words of Peter and John petitioning him to believe the Lord had risen. Saint Thomas was afflicted by the residue of original sin matured in the intellect. This intellectual phenomenon is afflicting humanity even now across vast swathes of the Earth, and even in the bosom of the hierarchical Church of Rome by many of its most esteemed. And, it is one of the primary reasons that Christ's Salvation is not being thundered from one end of the Earth to the other with the power of Pentecost.

One can be inspired to believe through scents of spiritual faith before intellectual deduction can organize into a reasoned understanding, and Saint John proved it. This is why the mystical always triumphs over the theological, which is always attempting to catch up. There is great sorrow to be felt for hardened intellectuals and so-called theological experts who live as a self-referential group of doubters in personal mental frameworks of nuance, analysis, speculation and postulating, not to mention bureaucracy and politics, which they feel must be satisfied to the very last jot and tittle before any evidence of the miraculous would inspire them into reverent obedience. The miraculous never has a chance in the mortal combat with their intellectualism. They would never run to an empty tomb at the testimony of someone's voice. They will look for any reason other than the miraculous to rest their convictions upon. They will not believe in Emmanuel, God with us, until they are forced to touch His open Wounds, and touch His Wounds they eventually will. They will reject all witnesses to the divine action of God, assailing them all as lacking in scholarly competence to proclaim anything as fact in their religious vineyard. They will refuse to accept or respond to anything mystical that does not come to them personally or to one of their lettered clan who is of like mind. They are the contemporary Thomas the Doubter. It is a state of trusting no one, lording over everyone, and rejecting out of hand every individual in the communion of witnesses, including messengers sent to them by the God they autopsy. Their brothers and sisters so blessed have nothing of value to contribute to their inordinate estimation of themselves and the compartmentalization they believe they have achieved of the infinite God whom they personally do not know all that well. They have lost the wisdom that would inform them that all the erudite thinking pondered by exiled intellectuals across the ages is but a brief flicker of the genius of the Almighty Father, and that the unilateral freedom of His divine will possesses a spontaneity that will not, and cannot, be mocked. They simply demand compliance with their interpretations of theologized intellectual rhetoric which in effect dismisses as extraneous any mystical action of the Holy Spirit that has not come to them first. Their hearts have gone dark beneath bushel baskets placed upon them by the sinners to whom they have entrusted the formation of their intellectual and spiritual composure. It is so sorrowful when doubters have formed their acolytes as images of themselves. Would that Love would make them famished and thirsting for their own sanctification instead, to be immersed in the Calvarian Sacrifice of the Lord Jesus Christ; lost in the Sacred Mystery whose rays of divinity have no need to be interrogated or debated. Our Lady told me, "*Hair-splitting theology is no match for the universal goodness that no man has the power to dissect. That goodness is the singular Love of God for His people, present as the Messiah, the Holy Spirit, and the Most Blessed Sacrament. Jesus is truly alive and dwelling in and among you only because I have borne Him to humanity, a solemn rite that I still confer upon My children, especially those who pray. This is not My will, but the Divine Will of the Creator of the Universe who has told Me in undeniable terms that I am the Mediatrix of all Graces, the New Eve, and the Queen of Heaven and Earth. Anyone who would approach the King of all Creation should bear this in mind, lest He sends them away with shame written across their faces.*" [Morning Star Over America-Twentieth Century Anthology 1997-1999, December 5, 1999]

Notwithstanding this frank perspective of circumspection, in no way should one impugn benign intellectual pursuits or those who humbly seek deeper knowledge of their God so as to imitate His Son. Respect must be given to the value of reasoned hierarchies in one's engagement with the life that God has given to each of us. But, none of this should impede our love for our brothers and sisters when asked to believe them, should they present themselves and declare that God has done something magnificent with their lives. Thirty-five years ago, I believed six children in Medjugorje from the first moment I heard of them because I had every reason to trust them and God Himself. It added up instantly in my spiritual deduction. Every soul knows when God has truly touched them, and they rarely if ever lie after He has done so. And, if the circumstances should require a pause for discernment, we must do so in imitation, urgency and disposition of Our Lady when She asked the Archangel about the course She was to take, "How can this be...?" But, should it really take forty years to believe that the Queen of Heaven visits Medjugorje in a special way to this day? We must give honesty and sincerity a fighting chance and accompany our brothers and sisters in our prayers, if our faith cannot generate more, to the destination to which God is calling. Simply said, we must love them and not become their stumbling block. They are on a mission from which no man of any stripe of authority can deter them. God endows great prodigies within spiritual communities of childlike faith. Jesus' Life, Death and Resurrection in communion with the unfolding of conversion and redemption throughout history is a beautiful tapestry of revelation in each human heart. Our Lady said to me, *"God wishes to listen to His children speaking the strains, '...I am doing this because Jesus asked me to.' These, My Special son, are the most beautiful words that God could ever hear. They represent the obedience to Him that Jesus asked them to convey to the world and to Creation itself. ...There are no words to even broach the glory that those who believe in Jesus' Blood on the Cross will receive when He finally calls them home. It is simply that you believe, My Special son, and that the Church believes. It is that children believe without seeing, without knowing the reasons why, that they take things based on trust alone, and that they walk with the innocence that Jesus brought into the world from My Womb. I knew that it would happen, the Great Archangel Gabriel knew that it was true, and the waiting world knew, even in all its emptiness, that God would eventually fill its void, its lacking, its future, and its posterity with the Salvation that it deserves. This is what Our Loving God does best, My Special son. He loves us. He takes care of those who have lived with faith and who have died in Him. He cherishes His people from long ago, even to this day, with Him and inside His Holy Kingdom. It is only a matter of time, My Special son, and the lost would do better to believe it."* [The Final Colossus, August 22, 2020]

We must share an honest and meaningful recognition of the limits and liabilities associated with the machinations of our mortal brains which are only relevant to the worldly side of the veil. Every honest person must admit that all of our detailed interior intellectualism is subject to dissipation into a fog of generalizations over time, and usurpation and extinction upon our deaths, leaving our mortal body of deductive construction to be a very fragile and opaque thing in the moment. The human mind strains to remember complex intricate details over long periods of time. Likewise, the mind is incapable of maintaining the infinite associative comparisons required to balance its judgments with the infinite thoughts of God. This is why we call them Sacred Mysteries. We believe because God says it, not because we comprehend it. We should also believe God's miraculous intercession because He does it, not because we fully grasp it. Life lived in union with the Sacred Heart of Jesus is God's explanation of Himself to us. The expertise one is hailed to possess in the past, such as it is, often eludes us in the present, yet we ride the accolades of prior academic achievement to our graves like conquering heroes with faces upturned for the showering of rose petals thrown by our partisans. For example, very few have ever truly maintained a conversational command of all that Saint Thomas Aquinas postulated in his gigantic framework of philosophical reasoning about God, and the rest are not the lesser because they might rather focus on being simple faithful children who trust His Immaculate Mother. Many of them live everything Saint Thomas spoke about without ever reading a word he wrote. In addition, sanctity is not measured by the comprehensive mastery of all the facets, events and commentary that the historical Church has experienced, suffered, contained and grown to be in two thousand years. The composition of the Holy Gospel is not growing by the day according to the velocity of the churning brains of theologians and historians and their high-brow speculations. The professor is no more than the child. People with the best memories and mental mechanics are not by default the holiest. We are vulnerable creatures that do not possess intellectual invulnerability in our reasoning because we are subject to reasoning from the dark caverns of the perspective of our exile as sinners. And, no one is immune to this liability. Yet, Our Lady encourages us to recognize that we possess heart-imbued souls that are immortal, and have the potential to magnify eternal genius through the simplicity of divine love and obedience to Her. We have allowed a detrimental imbalance, inversion or eclipse to occur where the mental intellectualism of exiled sinners is being worshiped as god, absent the heartrending sacrifices of true faith that bring the supremacy of their own reason. Has God not said that His ways are not our ways, and His thoughts higher than our thoughts [Isaiah 55:8-9]? Did not Saint Paul write to the Corinthians, "For it is written: 'I will destroy the wisdom of the wise, and the learning of the learned I will set aside,' and 'For the foolishness of God is wiser than human wisdom, and the weakness of God is stronger than human strength?'" Why do these words not manifest a far greater humility amongst those who consider themselves learned, especially in the hierarchy of the Church when Our Lady comes to bless Her children and convert the rest? Instead, She is kicked to the curb, alongside the testimony of the children who believe Her.

Mental reasoning which is dismissive of divine revelations manifested in the Body of Christ is merely hubris locked in its own exile, a sad attempt to build a tower of elitist mentalism, hoping to reach the pinnacles of God's intellect; a fortress defined by the pride of intellectual gluttony, unable to open its gates to accompany the chasteness required to unite itself completely with the loving genius of the Sacred Heart of the King of kings, just like Saint John the Apostle. How many will profess their love for "the Church" but never manifest their love or respect for any living soul in it when they come bearing their gifts, unless of course, it is that of financial resources? Oh, it is then we snap to attention and roll out the red carpet of our respect and gratitude. Do I go too far to say that the rich have bought themselves into all kinds of influence within the Church? Yet, let a messenger deliver them the gifts of Our Lady's Queenship, and their passionate defense of truth and propriety then comes back from the dead. It is then that they will strain integrity of any gnats, force scrupulous discernment to dive to the depths of theology's trenches, and inflict letters of moratoria silence to complement history's inquisitors. Am I speaking falsehood here? Our Lady would tell them that this is no way to confirm their imitation of their Lord and Savior, or any of the original Apostles who surrounded Her and listened to the Holy Spirit like angelic infants suckling at the breast of their mothers.

To manifest the grace and purity of little children is Jesus' call. Mental reasoning will never join Our Lord on the Cross because the calculating mind never finds the "reason" to embrace that Sacrifice, for it is only found in the vulnerable faith, heartfelt trust, and sacrificial allegiance displayed by the Church's greatest Saints, beginning with the Most Blessed Virgin Mary at the Annunciation. "No greater love hath man than to lay down his life for those he loves." This is the pinnacle which the intellectuals risk never embracing because they are too enamored with whom they believe themselves to be and the intellectual superiority they believe they have achieved. The pride of their personal identities is staked in their intellectualism, whereafter they shy away from allegiance with Love's Great Sacrifice by saying, 'Let's be more reasonable. Let's find a balance. Let's not cause a disturbance. We need to analyze this further. This is just your subjective imagination. You're not a lettered theological authority. You presume to own a competence that you do not have.' They retort a torrent of a thousand excuses culled from their like-minded peers to justify their calculated indifference toward our Holy Mother's presence and works. Our Lady says instead, *"Give me one good man who will trust My Son!"* She informs the world that the balance between Heaven and Earth is when the Earth becomes the image of Heaven by being united with the

Crucifixion of the Lamb of God in complete abandonment to the Holy Spirit. There is no balancing the intellect of the world with the supreme genius of the Most Blessed Trinity, God On High, Most Holy. The human creature is not capable of this total knowledge possessing infinite perspectives and such stratospheric dimensions of Divine Love. Therefore, faith and obedience are imperative. There is no balance on Earth without faith in the King of kings so that His mighty Will may be done instead of our own. The fulcrum of this perfect balance is at the veil of our faith in our inner sanctum. The worldly intellect loathes sacrificing itself to realms that are reached only through the mystery of divine faith, flourishing in the courage of a soul who will bear the Calvarian derision for proclaiming the Mystical Truth that thrives within the redeemed human identity. He is looking for companions who will remain loyal to His Word in the dark night of the soul, who will walk amidst the horror with the courage of Martyrs, those who will remain firm in their conviction that the third day's first light is imminent.

Deficiency, distortion, and disorientation have crept into the frame of reference of too many men of title and esteem; they who reject the mystical works of the Holy Spirit because the orbits of their intellectualism revolve only around their vaunted estimation of themselves. Beatific unity for them means a compacted authoritarian uniformity of no more expanse than their own subjective fears. How many observe both the fruits and facts of miraculous graces such as Our Lady's gracious intercession, but thereafter commence their teeming trifles and tittles, hoping to outrun any responsibility to contribute to Her wishes? They force their Virgin Mother to the margins. They throw up defenses, then marginalize, manipulate and remonstrate, claiming that heavenly wisdom only rests in them. Their agendas are not a reflection of those of the Immaculate Mother of God, so they reject Her in everything but lip service. People such as these who hold sways of power are merely gatekeepers who flaunt their authority and retreat into the caverns of their theologically-interpreted doubts, there to begin their pseudo-orthodox equivocation when obedience to the Church's Queen is the more valorous path. The gifts of the Church Triumphant are then squandered and desecrated in the consciousness of the Church Militant who were hoping that, this time, it may have all been true. There exists an elitist diminishment of the faithful which never acknowledges the graces of anyone's Sacramental Confirmation, the same Spirit that generates the wonder and awe of our Immaculate Mother that Her humble children offer to Her with pious abandonment every day of the world. Read the Catholic Catechism about the graces petitioned from God by the successors of the Apostles in this beautiful Sacrament. Are they not granted?

All-powerful God, Father of our Lord Jesus Christ,
by water and the Holy Spirit
you freed your sons and daughters from sin
and gave them new life.
Send your Holy Spirit upon them
to be their helper and guide.
Give them the spirit of wisdom and understanding,
the spirit of right judgment and courage,
the spirit of knowledge and reverence.
Fill them with the spirit of wonder and awe in your presence.
We ask this through Christ our Lord, Amen.

- Catholic Catechism, 1299

"Recall then that you have received the spiritual seal, the spirit of wisdom and understanding, the spirit of right judgment and courage, the spirit of knowledge and reverence, the spirit of holy fear in God's presence. Guard what you have received. God the Father has marked you with his sign; Christ the Lord has confirmed you and has placed his pledge, the Spirit, in your hearts."

- Saint Ambrose

Do the gifts of the Spirit; wisdom, understanding, right judgment, courage, knowledge, reverence and holy fear, only stretch as far as the doubts of the most feckless theologian? Every one of them seems to think so. Guard what you have received, indeed! Let no one disqualify you. Do not seek unity in the world, but unity with Heaven. We have received the Holy Spirit that allows us to know our God. There are some who seem to harbor and nurture the belief that the graces of Confirmation are only of effect upon those with ecclesial stature, and they prove it with the arrogance by which they reject the children, recipients and faithful believers alike, who come to them bearing witness to the miraculous intercession of their Heavenly Mother. All these graces come through Her familial Motherhood and mediating stature, and in Her presence we have the opportunity to embrace the power of the Resurrection right before our eyes. While the Matriarch of Heaven is trying to kiss the holdouts, deniers and doubters, they are instead lost in mind-streams of fearful calculation of their provenance, authority, public stature, and doubts about the veracity of everyone else's faith except theirs, while being flooded with deductive ambivalence as to whether it is even Her at all. Then, they hurl indicting insults against messengers like "lacking in competence" and "subjective inner experience" to diminish their culpability for rejecting the works of God outright. Mystics, messengers and visionaries are judged unworthy of belief with an effortless nod of the zucchetto, and they are stigmatized as being afflicted with delusional subjective mental deceptions. Our Lady told me to fear them not because they did as much to Jesus, and Her Immaculate Triumph will come nonetheless, to the shame and chagrin of them all.

We are workers in the earthly vineyard, and we must not grumble due to how generous the Lord may be with His grace to the workers He calls forth at the close of the day. God spoke to Ananias thus when he did not want to accept Paul's witness as an apostle, *"Go!" said the Lord. "This man is My chosen instrument to carry My name before the Gentiles and their kings, and before the people of Israel. I will show him how much he must suffer for My name"* [Acts 9:15-16]. It can be a very difficult test of humility for a person who has faithfully given his entire life to Jesus and the Church for 40 or 50 years or more, who has sacrificed deeply, having to face a person with no recognizable credentials who has received the great mystical gift of Our Lady' appearance to them, while they may have never received or recognized a mystical revelation in their lives. But, we must consider that we do not know the private suffering and sacrifices that God is requiring from each of His workers that appear before us. Beware what they suffer to bring you such gifts! Their cross as well may stare you in the eyes at your judgment alongside that of the King of kings. Rare few discerners pause to consider that the test of faith that they are facing may be the door to their being granted mystical revelations as servants of the Gospel. It may be the moment when God is asking that He be allowed to flood their life with visionary wisdom. When God comes asking for conversion into a deeper relationship with His Kingdom, one should not be too tightfisted about how they believe the vineyard ought to be overseen, particularly when it already lies so obviously smoldering in the rubble of humanity's decadence, destruction and diabolism. They should be far more worried about the state into which it has descended under their stewardship and the accounting they are going to have to make to the Owner. We must make room for the Master's wishes who has sent His workers bearing their spiritual tools of labor for His purposes of cultivation and fertilization. He is trying to bring the ultimate Resurrection of His vineyard from the ravages of faithless death. Rebellion, fear, and discomfort inflamed by these challenges of faith cause many to self-manipulate their own powers of discernment into a lockdown of ego-stricken scrupulosity which suits their purposes for oppressive control. They really do not trust their Savior. Many an authoritarian believes their ego to be the will of God speaking to them, and woe to you if you do not bow before that ego. These are the blind ones who lead by no example of the Crucified Lamb, but often claim to be fearless defenders of orthodoxy. They are doing no more than catering to their own fears while feting their own self-importance. In this dynamic, God's great gifts fail to fruitfully impact their judgment unless He invokes thundering supersessions of the laws of physics and phenomena where their skeptical minds become afraid not to believe, and even then it is often decades before they offer their reciprocal trust and thanksgiving to Heaven in any evangelizing way. We must do better by Jesus and His Mother during these days of tremendous revelation, here at the cusp of the end of times.

When a person witnesses to a supernatural event manifested to them by God in this secular age, it places them immediately upon the pathway to Calvary because these events generate the "moment of faith." They manifest the mystical Rock of Truth from the objective source of God that intellectuals cannot physically touch with their human reasoning in order to confirm their superiority over it. We must become aware of this "moment of faith" and what impedes its flourishing because, I believe, it is the key to the doorway to the finishing of our faith and the end of the ages. It is the moment of Abraham's faith. It is the moment of the Annunciation. It is the mystical moment which allows our entrance into the vestibule of God's sacrificial power. Our Lady is offering the Moment of Faith to the entire world through Her miraculous intercession. True faith comes with the plunge off the cliff where human deduction skids to a stop. It is conviction that stares into the storm without fear, and steps into the miraculous at the beckoning of the Lord, out upon perilous waves with the peaceful confidence of a prince standing beside his King. Faith is not to be misconstrued as being merely a body of intellectual knowledge by which one is measured acceptable or found wanting like a yardstick telling a toddler that he is not tall enough to sit at the adults' dinner table. Little children mirror what Our Lady desires better than any adult I have ever seen. It is based in a humility and innocence that allows the power of the Holy Spirit to prosper creative life to our person and flourishing to its example. It fosters a welling-up of mystical confidence, a joy, and an impregnable conviction that stands on the Truth of the Crucifixion and Resurrection of Jesus Christ, knowing through great trust that our souls have been redeemed if we but follow Him throughout the remaining moments of our lives, come what may. Woe to those who damage the innocent faith of children with the doubts that terrorize their own personal intellectualism. Vision comes through the painful process of sanctification and the sacrificial crucifixion of our worldly perspectives, but it is only painful to those who have not maintained their childlike spiritual disposition. For the childlike, it is always a beautiful expansion; it is always a release, like watering flowers and watching them grow. But, for those who have already had their garden overgrown with weeds, much disruption, tilling, and planting must occur before they will ever see flowers. If Our Lady's messengers are required to lower the cultivator into the soil to prepare for planting, then so shall it be. But, as I have said before, the dirt clods don't like it much.

Our Lady's children, along with Her priests and Prelates who have maintained their humble innocence, are rejoicing in Her miraculous presence, while the rest of the religious intelligentsia are disconcerted over why everyone is not paying attention to their cerebral calisthenics instead. Our Virgin Mother's intentions are to admonish with prodding, perspective, and parable hoping that all who impede the path of Her immaculate grace would stand down their opposition to Her intercession. They need to invoke their belief or step aside and dismiss themselves from any influence into penance and prayer because finding oneself in the end as having been a roadblock against the Queen of Heaven is no way to complete a life. The moment of acceptance of divine grace is presented to us every day of our lives in all the different experiences we have, sacrifices we are asked to accept, beauties that we witness, and the testimony of the faithful throughout the world who have gathered beneath Our Lady's Mantle. Scripture states that we should not be forgetful to entertain those we do not know because some have entertained angels unaware [Hebrews 13:2]. Others have been merely sinners who were entrusted to bear messages from the Heavenly Hosts who are doing so to the best of their obedience, while facing a hailstorm of derision from those who should have believed from the first sound of their voice, just like Saint Elizabeth greeting Our Lady. I asked our Holy Mother one time what Saint Elizabeth did after she became aware that She bore the Savior when She visited her. She said, *"Saint Elizabeth told everyone in sight. She told everyone within the sound of her voice. Nothing could keep her silent about her Savior."* So, this should give a wider perspective to those who casually dismiss recipients of miraculous intercession who do not run away and hide these graces until future times which may never come. In many cases, this was done as a gift of the Holy Spirit upon the blessed soul where God knew that public disclosure of the grace would bring them unimaginable suffering, and even death. In His kindness, their deferential silence was His gift of protection to them. But, there comes a time.

Moments abound where the transcending light of God is present, giving us every reason; intellectual, spiritual and experiential, to decide to believe, to make way and embrace the revelations of His grace so that a world of sinners may spiritually profit from them. He does so as verifiable confirmations of His relationship and care for our souls. 'The Lord be with you' is invoked upon us at every Holy Mass. I would ask whether we believe it? Have we considered what this means? Does our faith meet the invocation to allow His omnipotent presence to become manifest? It begins with a simple 'yes.' Amen! Our Lord asked us, for our own sake, to not persist in our unbelief, but to believe. Now is the moment that He was speaking about even then. It is what He speaks to us when we encounter the miraculous intercession of His Immaculate Mother. With all due respect, Our Lady is sinless and immaculate, while the rest of us are not. Do we think we have the authority to dismiss Her? Her reasoning has never been compromised by the obscuring veil of original sin. It is labored by nothing, and it is not qualified by anything. It is beautifully simple so a child could understand it. How Christ tried to give the human intellect the flavor of mystical reasoning over the course of His ministry, to accept the reality that the God of Creation has indeed appeared amongst men. He struggles still to give us this perception today through His Immaculate Mother and a Great Eucharistic Sacrament so sublime. The intercession of the Saints is a Sacred Truth of the Roman Catholic Church. Do we embrace the implications of this truth? Do we not risk rendering our dogmas to be hollow by rejecting the manifestations that flourish from them? So, how might we better discern the workings of our reasoning, and thereafter sacralize our spiritual deduction, when asked to accept these manifestation of God's loving engagement with His children? Rejoice, I say! Rejoice and tell everyone within earshot! Indeed, tell the world!

Part VIII
Justice's Final Verdict

*"Learning comes from books;
penetration of a mystery from suffering."*

- Archbishop Fulton J. Sheen
Life of Christ

Any effort to forthrightly address humanity's reticence to accept Our Lord's blessings of intercession is 'salt.' But, we must apply salt as seasoning, not in such measures as to lay waste to fields as the ancient Romans did to those they conquered. Faith is like a ballerina balancing on her tiptoes, not a goliath in work boots stomping out a forced march. Humility allows belief; ego allows nothing that is not centered in itself. The key is to center our humility in our trust in the Holy Spirit. God intends for us to know Him in very discernible ways from the plateau of the heart. Many seem to believe, at least in practice, that their trust will grow commensurate with the growth of the compendium of knowledge they keep warm in their memory for recall at any defensive moment of apologetics. I find the exact opposite to be more often true. More intellectual thought does not equate to levels of trust; and laying the trajectory of our soul in the hands of those who do not trust is like placing our journey in the hands of a blind man. Jesus said both will fall into the pit [Matthew 15:14]. When our humility is centered in our trust in God, our soul and its vision becomes moldable and accepting instead of combative and deliberative. Then, comes the opportunity to pass the tests of faith like Abraham because the test is always presented from the midst of darkness where the intellect is challenged as to its spiritual identity, and whether it is supple and ready to assent to the will of God without question. Trust comes to the fore in the testing moment, which means its integrity is assessed while in the veiled thicket of the unknown and uncertain.

There are a good many people of acclaimed stature who do an awful lot of circumscribing of God who is omnipotent, infinite and indescribable, He than which nothing greater could be conceived, as the ontological argument posits. Human pride is a seductive and voracious beast that prowls around looking for every opportunity to esteem itself instead of its servitude to the Lord. It will fight against anything it feels is diminishing or obscuring it. Ego loves to stand atop the achievements of cognitive discipline in a world of elitist aggrandizement. Pride loves educational titles and inflates itself when it is conferred authority. It has ears that only listen to itself. Archbishop Fulton Sheen once said, "Pride is an admission of weakness; it secretly fears all competition and dreads all rivals." The simplicity of Our Lady is the ultimate competition, for you see, having a great memory and being intellectually adroit oftentimes has nothing to do with the sacrifices of Divine Love, the humility to obey the calling of the Holy Spirit, or the courage to embrace the Cross in order to convince a world of sinners of an unseen Kingdom. Contemporary mores mistakenly predicate that attempting to penetrate the sacred mysteries of the Most Holy Trinity is more an intellectual exercise of inebriating oneself with mental frameworks of scholarly argument, encyclical quote mining, and dogmatic fact-checking than pining for the light dispensed amidst suffering and sacrifice out of redemptive love. Unfortunately, unity with God is purported to be achieved by filling oneself with the orthodox strictures of intellectual theory than emptying oneself to embrace the transcending gifts of the Cross. Did not the Scribes and Pharisees do as much? All their parsing, pondering and pontificating, and they killed the Chosen One they were intellectually mincing.

    Our Heavenly Mother is facing a wall of human obstinance masquerading as prudent discernment created and sustained by the fearful intellectualism of hypercritical men. She says that She is not trying to encroach upon what anyone believes to be their authoritative domain, but is trying to make clear where She stands as Queen in an Eternity they hope to one day enter. We are living amidst a theological vernacular whose personification has strayed from communion with history's greatest Christian witnesses, many of whom were not educational achievers at all. What did the Cure of Ars teach us? He was nearly incapable of satisfying his theological studies, but ranks in holiness as one of the greatest and most extraordinary Saints whom the devil simply despised. This is why our humble priests so admire him as their patron. We risk equating holiness with complex theological intellectualism, and superordinate moral enlightenment with mere mental aptitude. If I may be so bold as to quote-mine myself, Saint John Paul the Great said in Fides et Ratio (Faith and Reason, 14 September 1998), "*It has happened therefore that reason, rather than voicing the human orientation towards truth, has wilted under the weight of so much knowledge that little by little it has lost the capacity to lift its gaze to the heights, not daring to rise to the truth of being.*" Gatekeepers and their roadblocks obstruct the corridors of Christian evangelization in our time. I suppose they have always been there to certain degrees, for most of the world still stands as a spiritual wasteland after 2,000 years as proof. There is an artifice of callous detachment rooted in the illusion of moral superiority in those who feel they are not required to listen to anyone unless God's graces come directly through the thoroughfares of their own will. The worshipers of theological intellectualism dissect every nuance of the definition of grace, but often reject its extraordinary presence most everywhere it beckons them to comply. Ah, it is then that faith divulges its sacrificial requisitions. The example shown to us in Christ and His Mother is not to live in the mode of uncertain conjecture and compromise, for it suffers us incapable of generating any supernatural conviction, evangelic eloquence, or even simple obedience when He calls.

What should be our perfect response when faced with the miraculous intercession of our Heavenly Queen? How do we prevent scandalizing ourselves with analytical evaluation of distracting trifles? A perfect fiat is difficult to invoke, if not impossible, for those who see Jesus' Resurrection as confined by an historical age. Their approach to the Faith proves their orientation has not embraced a resurrected Savior in our time in imitation of the faith that Saint Peter raised from his benevolent heart. Christ's Proto-Vicar did something more than just believe something had occurred. He was martyred after walking into the pagan unknown advancing the Gospel of the One whom he knew was alive and preparing to one day come again. He just did not know how soon, but evangelized that it might be before the close of day. He was familiar with the mystical graces of the Holy Spirit, and was surely humbled before the power of Jesus' miracles. He commenced his great commission with the absolute conviction of making disciples of all nations through the powerful grace of the Holy Spirit that instructed him from within. How much closer is the return of Jesus than when Saint Peter proclaimed it on the pagan streets of the Eternal City? A healthy dose of wisdom rooted in fear of God should warn us that theological intellectualism is the dead tree that Jesus cursed if that tree will not return Him the fruit of sacrificial concession when He calls. And, without the abandonment of the heart and an authentic humility robed in sacrifice, every moral subject studied becomes a blunt instrument of elitist authoritarianism, seeking only the dictatorial mediation of mental facts to the exclusion of any dialect it does not recognize as its own. We study to maintain the strictures of academic language while God is speaking sentiments of ethereal beauty in the sanctity of the spiritual heart. This is why so many do not acknowledge the voice of their Immaculate Mother calling to them throughout the world in our time. There is nothing that they recognize in the academic trenches of the theological deep that would require them to respond; and trust in God is a faithful leap just a bit too far to maintain the comforts of their authoritative self-autonomy. It is because they conjure in their brains instead of surrendering through the love in their hearts. Why? Because their love has grown cold, and they do not fear offending God or facing the reality of their own judgment. Our Lady's presence is foreign and insignificant to those who presume that they have sufficiently deciphered the mind of God to the exclusion of everyone else. She speaks in the language of the Sacred Heart of Her Son, while they are lost in the forest of their mentalism and calling it "The Church;" again, to the exclusion of everyone else's sense of the faith imparted at their Sacramental Confirmation. They force the Queen of Heaven to run their gauntlet by dismissing with prejudice the faithful children that She molds and sends before them to deliver Her intentions. It is God's test of faith brought to their exalted doorstep, and they trample on it like a doormat for wiping their feet. It has been the same with almost every messenger in history, those who have felt the inquisitorial wrought and wrath of thinkers, thugs and theocrats.

What depth of attention do we suppose contemporary theologians would give to any of the Original Apostles if they walked again in the world today with no ability to prove who they were? Each of them would be disqualified forthwith as lacking competence to contribute anything to the evangelization of the Gospel because they would be seen as ignorant of 2,000 years of Church history and theology. They could claim direct conversations with Jesus and His Mother, and it would all be for naught. No one is trusted to proclaim Christ if they, firstly, have not been fully vetted and immersed in deep theological inquiry with a diploma hanging prominently behind their desk on the wall, or secondly, crushed with unimaginable suffering that shames people into believing that only God could actually be generating the power they are witnessing. Is respect for honesty and integrity so rare that we do not even recognize them when we see them anymore? Has brother actually become so skeptical of brother? As I said, Peter, James and John would not be seen as competent to speak of the Gospel. The lost world will be converted by touching the heart, not the mind. For all the reasoned intelligence in Saint Thomas Aquinas's great works and others of his theological caliber, I doubt their exchanges have actually converted many, and surely not capable in themselves of impacting the bewildered masses wandering the world looking for a Shepherd. If you took Saint Aquinas's great works to an inner-city and placed them before lost souls, none would pay any attention to you because they are not works of the heart, but of the mind. They do not scream of the beauty of Creation and the love of human hearts, but only instruct in their dissection.

It is like presenting a group of people from a desolate land a stack of books describing all the botanical, biological, chemical and molecular facets of flowers, and another person laying the beauty of a dozen bouquets before them. Upon which do you think these people are going to turn their eyes? This is why testimony to Our Lady's miraculous intercession is so powerful. They are the bouquets. She has come out of their Book. She is the beauty that cannot be described with formulas. She is transcendent of mental dissection, and supersedes those who scandalize themselves and everyone around them with their mentalism. She speaks of Her beatific love to Her children in ways where they recognize Her. And, these hearers take notice because they want to be loved. Ah, it is here that lost souls are confronted by something from beyond the firmament, only to find it has always resided within them. It is then that the first scent of conversion wafts through the lost soul. 'Maybe there is something more to this world. Maybe this time it's true. Maybe the world is more beautiful than it seems. Maybe there is a Heaven. Maybe somebody does love me.' This is why there has been so little success in evangelizing a world of seven and a half billion people, approaching eight. We are getting it wrong, and are too stubborn to admit it. We have made it a function of the brain and not the heart. When I see Our Lady, I do not see theology, although it is there muttering, trying to describe Her so inadequately. I see immediate Truth. I see Light blinding to the intellect. I see astounding Love. I see majestic authority anchored in that Truth. I see unending Beauty reflected from the Sacrifice of the Beautiful One! I see the Crucifixion in Her eyes and every Mass that has ever been said gazing at me! "Beauty itself doth of itself persuade the eyes of men without orator," said William Shakespeare.

It would seem that I have spent exceeding amounts of time admonishing those who will not listen, and describing why I believe they will not. And, they will not like it much. They will gather in their comradery of critics to soothe the pangs of their faithlessness. They will critique, criticize and condemn me based upon their aversion to my tone being anything but what they would see as charitably deferential to them. Our Lady says that there is no tone to which it seems they will bow, so we should concentrate instead on taking the truth to the rest who will listen. She told me that it has nothing to do with my tone; it is with what is being said. For them, the Gospel is bitter tasting. And, beyond their present understanding, our Holy Mother's insistence that we engage humanity's thinking with this tenor has nonetheless been a grace for them that She wishes to be fruitful to Her cause, should they ever reevaluate their recalcitrance. She knows that pride-filled people always have swift retorts and refutations about anything that challenges what they believe about themselves and the world they have subordinated beneath their autocratic feet. Believe it or not, the "cancel culture" did not start in our contemporary social era. It began at the Birth of the Son of God in a manger, and faithful Christians have been subject to its societal sentence since the moment Jesus said, "If they persecuted Me, they will also persecute you" [John 15:17-20]. And, this persecution comes from those whose frames of reference are soiled with the self-referential claptrap of the world and thereafter refuse to consider that they may in fact be the very ones who need to reevaluate the depths of their faith or whether they even believe at all. Rare few of them who engage life with their worldly minds accept that Our Lady is actually alive and appearing to Her children with any authority that might convoke a responsibility upon them. Someday, we will see if they are right. Those who know the truth have the faith, patience, and forbearance to wait. At present, the supposed freedom not to believe is defended as the highest dictum, instead of realizing that their Immaculate Mother wishes they would. It is indistinguishable from a secularist cursing the most profane utterances in public to validate their Constitutional right to speak freely. Does uttering such horrible vitriol in the public square actually display proof of the right to speak? Or, women who vindicate their right to choose by militantly defending the slaughter of infants in their wombs. Is committing outright murder actually the validation of a person's right to choose? Similarly, does it really confirm our faith when we claim the authority that we are not required to believe anything extraordinary that Our Lady does? Is stretching God's Mercy all the way to the horrific depths of the Crucifixion the only way that humanity will become convinced that He is merciful? Is requiring Our Lady to miraculously conquer all Her detractors with apocalyptic miraculous signs the only way to prove these graces come from Her? Only people filled with pride and completely vacant of faith would further demands like these against so much evidence. Many speak of faith, but require God to oblige them with earthshaking supernatural omens before they will tender theirs. Thomas the Doubter did as much. Our Lady says this is no faith at all.

    It is both sorrowful and ironic to watch those who are instructing others in the truth stumbling over the mystical realities of what they teach. It is analogous to a professor instructing others in the technique of opening doors by grasping doorknobs and turning them, whereafter we find him standing in front of a double-swing door stupefied as to what to do next because he cannot locate a doorknob. Then, a toddler scurries past him, pushes the door wide open and runs through, trailed by the family pet, and the professor feels his jurisdiction as an intellectual authority has been offended because his ideology requires that all doors must have doorknobs. And, before the door swings back and strikes him in the forehead, he begins speculating that what he is confronted with may not be a real door and warning everyone away before he has looked at what may be in the next room. These confounded people sift human life with the colander of their theological hair-splitting, and presume to declare anyone not of their rigid and autistic schooled dialect as bereft of competence. They even do it amongst themselves. Look at the religious wars and ideological skirmishes that have gone on amongst supposedly righteous thinkers and speculators for 2,000 years. We must remember that the origin of the word "scrupulous" is not in 'an attention to detail,' but in one who is 'troubled with doubts,' doubts that can be conquered with faith as personified by Catholic Saints, Martyrs and Mystics for two millennia.

Imagine this irony! As we revere great theological scholarship to every end with accolades, deference and reverence, lamentations are lifted throughout their lot that the Great Commission has come to near extinction, leaving modern Christian civilization all but collapsed on every continent. And, the intellectual titans simply wash their hands as they look on in silence. On their watch, this has happened. And, of all the audacity, the laity are left to bear their public accusations that we have surrendered our responsibilities by not doing our part of evangelizing the atheistic secular void. They pontificate to the choir while we face down wolves every single day of our lives without so much as a syllable of affirmation to encourage us. The voice of the Great Commission has been ridiculed into silence by cowardly men who lack trust in the Holy Spirit, who possess no defensible loyalty to Jesus and His Virgin Mother, and then fail to support the children of the Church in their mission of evangelic witness. Is there any other explanation for the stiff arm that is applied to any parishioner who wishes to speak at large about how their hearts have been touched by Our Lady's miraculous intercession? It is hard being hated for defending the truth we know that so many yet refuse to accept. It is a cross to weather the aggressive storm of secularized liberal parishioners who have surrendered their faith to the ideologies of leftist indoctrination, but dominate and intimidate every holy priest into veiling the truth, lest they throw a fit and storm the Chanceries to force punishment upon these servants of God. Instead of the faithful finding encouragement to be of good strength and embrace the Cross, scrutinies and criticisms are heaped upon their backs by their own. The doors of mystical grace that are opened through their faith are slammed in their faces in order to maintain a false sense of peace, anchored in the compromises of a phoney pluralistic secular ecumenism. Withholding affirmation to the faithful in the midst of their sacrificial evangelism is a horrible act of provocation for a child to wonder whether the Holy Spirit within them even matters at all. And, we wonder why Christian civilization has collapsed? By contrast and example, Our Lady offered complete and total affirmation to Her Son throughout His Life, and especially as She stood beneath the Cross and helped Him complete His Holy Sacrifice.

Our Holy Mother does not make the mistake of denying Her avowal of approbation to Her children. Her love is so great as to make Her children wish to die in Her service because She validates our innocent beauty and encourages from us all the sacrificial gifts that we could possibly extract from our lives. She loves us. She supports us. She teaches us by Her very presence. She knows that each child of God possesses a measurable contribution to human conversion. Her encouragement is tantamount to the creation of saints through the testament She composes with our lives. She never found it a priority to train my brother and me in the scrupulous nuances of accepted theological dialects before She told us to share Her presence and messages with anyone who will listen. In fact, She has never come into the world by miraculous intercession to teach theology to anyone that I am aware of, but I am willing to be apprised about this point. Might we ponder what She has done instead? She has shared the unvarnished responsibilities of the Gospel truth with all the beautiful love She can muster as Jesus' Immaculate Mother. She is trying to touch the hearts of little children who will listen, not add to the mountain of intellectual theory that Her children are required to climb before they are deemed "informed" by others. We are acceptable to Her no matter how small or insignificant we seem; and She says that we have something to offer our brothers and sisters. While teaching us to pray the Most Holy Rosary has been Her preeminent call, history records and we testify that Her mystical appearances most often bear warnings, admonishments, prophecies and instructions as part of Her matriarchal role as our Heavenly Mother. It has been no different here with my brother and me. She encourages us to pray from our hearts so we can better come to know God. She is trying to teach us to see unseen wonders that are believable through faith and Her word. And in the process, She performs supernatural works of mercy, and encourages us to make the sacrifices to do the same. This has become my perspective after basking in Her purity and eloquence for over thirty years. I grieve that She is being rejected by the supposedly brightest and most admired among us. Hate my brother and me, if you must. Throw us into the dustbin of human contempt. Tell the world that we bear neither competence nor consequence. Profess to everyone who will hear that we are below their dignity and beneath their respect. It simply does not matter to us. But listen and take heed now; beware discarding Our Lady's blessings into the darkness of the night, for the Truth shall have its day, and the voice of Justice is about to issue its final verdict.

Part IX
Rejecting the Lie

Therefore, God is sending them a deceiving power so that they may believe the lie, that all who have not believed the truth but have approved wrongdoing may be condemned.

2 Thessalonians 2:11-12

"Politics is the framework in which lying takes its most essential form."

Timothy Parsons-Heather
January 12, 2022

Any ideology or agenda that does not hold itself accountable to the staple requirements of human excellence, virtue, wisdom and self-sacrifice is surely a deadbeat deception, if not an outright lie. Demagogues leverage unstable minds with the stirring frenzy of their vacuous partisan rhetoric. It has always been thus amongst the dregs of civilizations' despots. For all the talk about a mandate of "equality of outcomes," none are achieved but through tyranny, the unjust manipulation and scandalizing of the gifts of human freedom, and the violation of the 7th and 10th Commandments of God. It is the "equality of honor" that we should be fighting for; a harbor of equity that is conferred as a fruit upon those who embrace the sacrifices that prove themselves to be good and decent members of humanity en masse. The sacrifices of human love are the ultimate equalizer. They espouse no partiality. They have no axe to grind or politics to please. They hail those who advance the profiles of greatness. The communion of love is the only true "privilege" that mankind will ever know; and it comforts and sustains only a humble and sacrificial people. It is the sweetness of sacred dewdrops raining down upon us from our grateful Father in Heaven. Yes, peaceable and true, slow to anger and rich in kindness, but just and righteous in all human affairs. God invokes privilege with the grace of His own being upon those who love Him and follow His ways. His faithful people are the embodiment of everything that is noble and resilient about our far-flung American nation and its vast multitudes of lives and families, in their shared good will, their lineage and heritage, in their daily duties where they have labored long and served well, and in their repentance and promises to do better by their countrymen whom the Holy Spirit has inspired them to love.

Our country has risen as the world's only safe harbor for a sacrificial people who wished to seek out that elusive union with perfection in a republic of citizens culled from a planet of sinners. From the shores where the Statue of Liberty has welcomed the lost to the footstool of the Pacific Northwest where the towering sequoias grow; from the lone tip of Texas to the northern slopes of Alaska's mighty tundra; from the purple mountaintops to the meadows of our sprawling smokey valleys, our country is beloved by the heavens because of the generations of wheat that have flourished amidst the tares. Good men reverence those who had the wisdom to conceive her. Families imitate the selflessness of those who have sacrificed to make her shine. Veneration flows in the pageantry of America's heart upon those who have had the courage to fight for her. Awe is deserved upon those who have had the endurance to sustain her. Hallowed are the souls who possessed the compassion to heal her. The faithful flocks humble themselves before those who had the mystical grace to bring her spirit to perfection in the great Sacrament of the Altar. We hail those brave enough to stand to defend her. And, we celebrate everyone who has made the effort, even while struggling and stumbling, to make themselves a triumphant part of her historical testament by their selfless acts of service. If there be any excellence among us, let it be our sacrifices that foster peace, good will, virtue and truth; knowing that these sacrifices for humanity are the ultimate victory, for no one is ever promised a kingdom without a cross before it.

Yet, must we not also be chastened by the vision of absolute horror that will greet the unrepentant enemies of our Lord Jesus Christ, the King of kings, on the day of His Great Return, upon the rising of those with the seal of His love within them to everlasting life, and the unbelieving loathers to their perpetual demise? Let us pronounce to all the people who spend their lives sowing hatred and division against their fellow human beings that their judgment day will come, and our vindication will be the last shovel full of truth piled atop their graves. Lost are those who lead lives filled with arrogance, self-absorption, worshiping their celebrity, feeling that they have the right to hurl slanderous epithets against virtuous and honorable people; they who persecute and 'cancel' those who challenge their unprincipled rampages; they who think they have the authority to kill infants in the womb with impunity, they who nullify the words of those who would speak to them the valor of truth, silence those who proclaim the virtues of Christ, they who sow animosity and elitism against their neighbors, snuff-out the worthy legacies of our nation, and dismiss the magnitude of its righteous sacrifices. Yes, let all these reprobates know that the total summation of their pride, arrogance, high-minded authoritarianism, worldly esteem, and political successes will be stripped away from them. In the cauldron of naked terror before the judgment of the ages, they shall stand. Their minds have not yet conceived such eternal desolation. It will matter not whether one was a master legislating Speaker of the House, a ranking congressman for half a century or a charismatic president hailing radical social justice; nor will it be of any repute whether one was a university chancellor, a wealthy entrepreneur or venture capitalist, a magnetic social influencer or ostentatious pop star, a garrulous populist hailed by the electorate, or an earthshaking activist revered by their partisans. When that great day arrives, evildoers will have no place to hide, not a syllable of rebuttal to speak, no defense to offer, no excuses to pitch, no podium to stand on, no microphones to crackle their quips, no cameras recording their every move, no media to publish their lies, no doctoral hoods to vaunt their stature, no advocates to plead their cause, no experts to validate their delusions; their worldly dominion evaporated, esteem blasted away, frozen in a furnace of molten truth with nothing to save them from the eternal grief they deserve. They will lie face down in the steaming excrement of their own making, fuming in the noxious sewage that they spewed forth like poison and worshiped without shame. Imagine this moment because it is a reality that is coming to those who reject wisdom and truth; and it does not matter whether they believe it or not. It will come with the justice of angelic ferocity, and they will wish they had never been born. They will plead to the deaf ears of the righteous that it surely cannot be so, and they will display their rage at God with their final 'I hate you.' Ponder the moment upon their realizing that their ultimate miscalculation has been their undoing, wrought by their own arrogance, with no appeal to any court or power. No turning back; everything lost. Dreams evaporated in the wake of their personal and social corruption. No friends, no compatriots, no adorers, no hearers; no one to share a kind word or mitigating sentiment. No families to hold, no refuges to be found, nary a hope to glimmer anew, no food to savor on their lips, eyes to never imagine a hint of beauty, deprived of every fulfillment and satisfaction, a mind rendered incapable of conjuring a soothing thought, living in a moment of inconsolable rage that becomes eternal itself; worse than looking at your child's broken body lying limp beneath your car wheel and just wishing for those ten seconds back; worse than seeing your home burning to the ground with your family still inside it, more excruciating than a final agony without respite, more desolate than the moment of dread when the tether from a rescue ship slips from your grasp, never to return, leaving you marooned in the dark expanse of intergalactic space to die, worse than breaking your neck and knowing at that moment that you'll never walk again, more bloodcurdling than standing in a shower stall with Zyklon-B gas pouring from the vents, worse than a nuclear explosion above your house and the fire charring the skin off your bones. This is the moment of horror that will come upon the unrepentant, the instant when they will be forced to realize that their damnation is complete without annulment, with no reprieve and no relenting. The Gates of Paradise closed forever to the sound of wailing cries and the gritty grind of their own gnashing teeth. Endless punishment for their inexplicable wickedness. "It will be finished" because there is no life within them; the human soul forever extinguished into the hellish darkness, with nothing there to reignite its flame. Sheer hopelessness and abject horror. Eternally punished for the suffering they inflicted on their fellow man and rejecting a beautiful Savior who only asked them to love. What they did to the 'least of these' will torment them with self-loathing forever beyond their deaths.

So, never doubt that victory and the everlasting hills belong to those who love Jesus Christ, and follow in His ways. Follow His ways indeed, not with scholastic dissertations or dogmatic droning, but with sacrifice, prayer, unity, virtue, deed, and truth. Those who refuse to do so will wish they had walked in this truth. Across the great chasm with the rich man, they will watch Lazarus and all they assailed standing in triumph in the glories of God's Kingdom from which they have been banned by the Three Archangels. They are the reason why Scriptures say that the mountains will be sought out to cover them upon the last judgment of the Son of Man. So, this is their hour. Now is the time for them to convert their hearts and accept the only redemption they will ever know. None has been so detestable that God cannot make them new, but they must put forth their confession that they have finally repented, recognize Jesus as their Savior, and walk in His ways of virtue and light. We must realize that the Heavens do not grieve that evildoers have been thrown into Hell to agonize with the Beast they have served. The Heavens rejoice at the judgment of the Thrice-Blessed Trinity! No devil or condemned sinner has ever held a place in Heaven. There are no empty seats at the Feast Table of the Lamb of God that would inspire regret that someone is missing. The celebration is in the Victory of Christ and His people, and that every evil will be vanquished for life, cast into the hottest flames of Gehenna's fires.

Part X
Conjugating an Angel's Valor

"And he who is not sufficiently courageous to even defend his soul – don't let him be proud of his "progressive" views, and don't let him boast that he is an academician or a people's artist, a distinguished figure or a general. Let him say to himself: I am a part of the herd, and a coward. It's all the same to me as long as I'm fed and kept."

Alexander Solzhenitsyn, *"Live Not By Lies"*

From the beginning of Our Lady's gracious intercession, I was compelled to offer Her a blank slate of cooperative faith, trust, and absolute obedience because I knew She definitively transcended the intellectual composure of the world and that we were no more than tiny children before Her. Everything I had previously learned about my faith and spirituality was an earthly rendition that gave way to its heavenly purpose in Her presence. I did not believe that fostering opinions contrary to Her facts served to maintain my unity with Her Queenship. Why would one fracture their union with Her by becoming one of Her critics? What opinions of a sinner would ever matter before Her unstained perfection? Debating faculties, argumentative analysis, and even so-called prudent indifference have no standing and cease to exist in Her presence. The unity my brother and I have shared with our Blessed Virgin Mother has been maintained by remaining in communion with the perspective She has nurtured in us, and obeying Her every sentiment. We remain in Her Immaculate Heart in the very center of the Original Apostolic Church. We are not worshipers of human beings, nor do we expect anyone to worship us, but we venerate and affirm great holiness when we see it. Positions of authority are not de facto indicators of honor or plateaus of sanctity, and oftentimes privileged regalia does nothing more than conceal the corruption of dead souls. Yes, our Virgin Mother told us to be as wise as serpents, but gentle as doves. She cares about our thoughts and often asks us to share them with Her, but I believe it is only to confirm that we reflect back to Her the nature of our unity. She is brought great joy when She sees Her words alive in any of Her children. It is not the best use of our faith to entertain any inclinations to doubt Her or move away from Her perspective, no matter the cost. She exudes no rigidity or closed-mindedness. We are simply not to be of two minds if we expect to receive anything from the Lord Jesus [James 1:4-8]. It is not the best use of our faculties to generate a mind different from Hers at the behest of anyone, not even one possessing a title of Bishop. We should invest and partake in what builds up, and dismiss what is stagnant and tears down. All in all, it is edifying to read the lives of the great Saints and Mystics. It is fruitful to imbibe in the perspectives of the great orthodox theologians and Church Fathers. It is constructive to unity to be in union with the best intentions of one's Bishop, for it is an object of the faith to be in communion as the Mystical Body of Christ. And, it is also wise to be attentive and intuitive to the sensus fidelium, the "sense of the faithful," that echoes its consistent historical fidelity which testifies to a beautiful collage of mystical multiplicity in those who invoke their faith at the calling of the Lord.

Our allegiance to our Heavenly Mother must be in imitation of the devotion to Her by the Communion of Saints, to the best of our ability. Can we imagine how much the Church Triumphant loves Her? Out of the mouth, the heart speaks, which means any discussions we engage would be well-placed if they come from Her perspective, which we must not knowingly contradict. Our intentions should be that our words reflect that commitment and consecration, while seasoned with edifying instruction and admonishment as the Holy Spirit prompts. We should not bounce around seeking palatable perspectives that satisfy nothing but our druthers or anyone else's. Her perspective is one of pure beauty and intent, a spiraling outward manifestation of love, which is receptive to the creative mystical genius of the Holy Spirit. My brother and I testify to our Holy Mother's presence, and we obey Her, while many of the supposedly learned among us rarely seem to arrive at any hard conclusion about whether She matters to them much at all, except as a rhetorical device to chatter the orthodox axioms of their faith. The graces of divine light that we have been given in no way inflate our esteem beyond what God would have it be as His children and messengers of His Sacred New Covenant. Any vagrant on the street given the same graces may prove to be a far greater saint than I might ever hope to become. Yet, Scripture states that to whom much is given, much is expected; and woe to they who do not proclaim the Gospel upon seeing the seed of faith firsthand. My brother and I live within the realms of that expectation, and it is because we have received the mystical grace to "know" the truth in our Heavenly Mother's intercession, a divine light 'where ten-thousand difficulties will not make one doubt,' and before no threats or punishment will we ever cower. Our Lady told us that, "Faith becomes knowledge to those who serve." 'Non serviam' when our Lord calls is the testament of no knowledge of the faith at all. We serve Our Lady as the Queen of Heaven and Matriarch of the whole of Creation.

If asked to elaborate on this divine light, I might describe it as a mystical grace in the form of a "conjugation" of my frame of reference manifested by the revelation of Her miraculous presence. Many people who have visited our Holy Mother's shrines have felt varying degrees of this conjugation. Consider the conjugation of a verb into past, present and future derivatives of the same action, such as rose, rise, and will rise. A person could say, "I rose yesterday," or "I rise," and finally, "I will rise tomorrow." While trying to be very simple with this metaphor, the reference to time as past, present and future is not the main point. Rather, it is the sense of vision in the transformation of perception through the conjugating process and the differing states and inflections manifested of the same principal verb. Properties are shifted or added to the perception through the mechanism of conjugation. It is a spectrum that someone can traverse. A new vision is created, much like a new person is created from two spouses in the Sacrament of Marriage, or someone intellectually learning about the grace of Our Lady, and then having everything they ever learned, and more, confirmed upon seeing the Lady of Grace Herself. Something is added; something new is created or revealed; something becomes. A transversion occurs through the spectrum of conjugation. Intellectual titans are often tempted to believe that their vision is the only true vision, and they act as such to everyone, even as Scripture states, 'At present we see indistinctly, as in a mirror, but then face to face. At present I know partially; then I shall know fully, as I am fully known' [1 Corinthians 13:12]. In the conjugation, the intellectual vision is revealed as being the indistinct vision which the heavenly vision supersedes as the only true reality. Many intellectuals refuse the realization that they may only be seeing indistinctly while sequestered in exile; and trained theologians are often the worst.

To continue the discussion of this conjugation, before Our Lady revealed Herself to my brother and me, my perceptions were bounded by the parabolic past and present tenses, which spoke in their individual ways to the reality of what we know by faith and sacrificially experience in exile. Her presence revealed a mystical tense, or dimension, to my frame of reference in many of its facets of vision, perception and judgment, much like a heavenly body coming very close, and the gravity of wisdom becoming noticeably more affective. Or, like metal filings snapping into uniform alignment when a powerful magnet is placed beside them. They align according to the invisible field that surrounds them. Before the magnetic effect comes near, no one recognizes the magnet's lines of force, and the filings have no set pattern. In the normal course of life, we do not recognize these lines of unseen grace unless we have visionary faith, but they are there nonetheless, and we see them when the "filings" of our life are sprinkled in the presence of the great Heavenly Bodies. This is why so many in the Church do not see, and thereafter decline to accept, the power in Our Lady's miraculous intercession. They refuse to sacrificially sprinkle the "filings" of their life before Her presence with any conviction that would matter. The ultimate unseen power is manifested at the Moment of Consecration during the celebration of the Holy Sacrifice of the Mass. Everything that is of eternal consequence in this world becomes aligned. Our God of Creation becomes present in the realms of exile on the Sacred Altar as the authentic Bread of Life. And, this is why the Catholic world kneels at attention as one body; hundreds of millions of filings, all in the alignment of beatific grace. This is also why Satan has expended so much effort attacking the structural environments of Catholic churches over the past 75 years, while creating all kinds of abominations and calling it sacred architecture. He is trying to bring aberrations to distort the historical alignments of beatific grace and our communion with the Church Triumphant.

To further this description of tenses, consider what perceptive facets are added to a person's understanding of an action upon its conjugation into the future tense that are not part of the original perspective of the past and present. Consider if you never knew anything about future tense verbs, and no one used the future tense to interact. Imagine if no one knew tomorrow existed. Would we then immediately recognize something strange about a person's speech when talking to us using the future tense? What if a person's sense of orthodoxy only spans the breadth of the past and present tenses? Might they refuse to accept the future tense as orthodox, even though the same verb is in action? An identical action of the verb is present in all tenses at the same time, but there are different perspectives between the three frames of reference as similarly as God exists in Three Divine Persons of the Most Holy Trinity; One God in three frames of reference; Almighty Father, the Son who became Man, and the Holy Spirit who descended upon the Church at Pentecost to permeate Creation. Knowing this fact is the conjugated future tense of believing in our Salvation, which is revealed by God through His mystical grace, given by Jesus on the Cross to the penitent soul. God still reveals Himself to us, and as He does, our entire being snaps into alignment with the Divine Light of His beatific Kingdom. And, it is the reward of faith that allows a person to 'know in fact' the things they earlier only believed. It is the difference between blandly acknowledging the theological framework of the Gospel as many intellectuals do, or spiritually living it in one's heart because the Christ of the Gospel has revealed Himself to us, as He said He would do for those having true faith. Just because one may have a verb conjugated to its future tense by mystical grace does not mean that the past and present tenses have been violated or are irrelevant to the framework of salvation. It is a communing, connecting, and completing movement in unity with the Church Triumphant. We must remember that theologians are simply 'learners' like the rest of us. And, a life of sacrifice is the sacred institution of learning into which many of them never enroll. They are on the path to sanctification just as surely as everyone else, and so are their fragile theologies. But, there remains a spiritual certainty that is often conveniently dismissed and overshadowed by arrogance. No one can teach what they themselves have yet to learn. Until then, it is detrimental to embed one's perspectives only in the past and present derivatives of one's perspective because it diminishes all other tenses of mystical grace that would nourish a person in the presence of great sacrifice. Mystical grace is a living component of Divine Faith.

Another example is the idea of depth perception. A person with one eye closed cannot easily see dimensions of depth. A one-eyed person may not know that a circle is actually a sphere. If we see life, or faith, as a circle, what is it really? Here, if the person opens the other eye and sees with a conjugated vision, they see facets that were previously unknown to them. While remaining with one eye closed, they risk denying the spherical surface of a mystical faith because they only see a circle laying flat on the tabletop of exile. For many who have appointed themselves as 'deciders' for everyone else, they oftentimes do not see the depth of the truth because they are only looking through the bias of one eye without knowing it. The revealing grace has simply yet to reach them. But, once it does, it completes and re-balances their entire perspective of a faithful life and gives dimension and depth which reveals greater facets and realms of wisdom. This, I believe, is the meaning behind Saint Thomas Aquinas' heavenly vision that he experienced three months before his death, whereafter he said that he would not finish his great Summa Theologiae work, believing it to be so much straw. He saw his work anew as the 'indistinct vision' in a way he had never seen before. The Holy Spirit conjugated his vision with the parabolic future tense of mystical grace, and it re-calibrated and completed his perspective of the thrice-holy domain that had prospered his life as a gift to humanity and the Church. Can we imagine if he would have been given ten more years to live, and what his gigantic new heart would have wrought thereafter? Nonetheless, he served his Savior well in what he chose to accomplish during his life of sacrifice. And, we are the better for his contribution before the majesty of God.

There are two principal qualities that I feel are added when one receives a facet of this conjugated vision. First, tremendous conviction wells up in the soul, a passion to be completely united with Divine Love in the Sacrifice of Jesus. And second, directly alongside this conviction is a deep humility before God that slams the human ego to the floor and razes the intellectual constitution to dust, initiating its reconstruction. Although the Church is filled with the mystical witness of its Saints in the future tense, it is a perspective that many contemporary intellectuals gloss over as part of their 'knowing.' They believe they know, but they actually do not. They see themselves as participants when they remain as only speculators. Then, Our Lady comes speaking the strains of future times, and they marginalize Her by maintaining that Her presence is a subjective and private matter, perhaps even unorthodox, and then relegate Her to irrelevance because they have one eye closed, not recognizing the depths of the future being prophesied by the Holy Spirit. They reject Her beatific gifts before the masses outright by donning their intellectual mortarboards and hoods, and intimidating everyone into complying with their monocle vision.

The Seven Great Sacraments of Roman Catholicism are seven great "verbs" instituted by Jesus Christ to initiate, consecrate, and nourish each soul's mystical communion with the Almighty Father in Heaven. In addition, there are unlimited propagating "verbs," or actions, of the Holy Spirit that flourish from the Great Seven, each having their tenses which awaken man to the reality of Jesus' Life, Death and Resurrection, and His Coming again in Glory. People have a tendency to study things to their last whit of reality. They do this for self-fulfillment, to possess the lordship of command over bodies of knowledge, to then be seen as an authority, and to advance their own wilful perspectives and interests just as the great psychologist Abraham Maslow postulated. Many do this with the Faith itself, not knowing that God reigns supreme and will not be circumscribed by any sinner. One can never claim a supremacy of knowledge about God as if to control Him because it would be the same as placing a quantity on the infinite in order to hold command and authority over its breadth. God will not subject Himself to the authority of a sinner's intellect before they have been perfected in the Holy Spirit to the degree of Jesus' Crucifixion. He expects great faith from everyone because it is the only way to transcend the frailties of exile and death. Consecrated religious leaders have not been made oracles of the truth of God and human affairs in order to protract their own will. They have not been made the deciders possessing a miraculous knowledge from which all others are deprived by a lower station. Indeed, they have instead been conferred a responsibility to believe, to obey and to do the Divine Will of Jesus Christ until their last breath. It is like a little boy walking across the sand to the ocean's edge, and with his tiny pail in hand tells his mother that he has come to empty the ocean. He bails and bails, and bails some more, dumping a puddle at his feet, but never making a dent in the ocean. Then, he looks at his puddle and beams with self-assurance that he now controls the ocean. And the mother, even while knowing that her little boy's perspective is a bit lacking, affirms him by saying, "Yes, you do have the ocean, my courageous little one." This is the sum total of our intellectual knowledge about God. She knows as he plays in his puddle that he can say with confidence that he knows "of" the waters that the ocean is composed. He gets just as wet, even while what immerses him has come from an infinitude of conjugated oceanic verbs which he will never completely comprehend in his time. Does his puddle give him the tenses of an endless horizon or the silence of the ocean's uninhabitable trenches? Does it tell him of its teeming creatures, its thermal flows, or its terrifying tsunamis? Does it show him colossal waves that heave warships and tankers on their crests? Does it divulge the sea creatures that awe ocean-goers or the schools of fishes that fill the cargo-holds of trawlers on their way to feed humanity? Our Holy Mother's miraculous intercession is as if Heaven opens up and douses a person to the soul as an action verb in that vast ocean of the Holy Spirit. We know we are soaked with waters from those seas of beatitude and, by comparison, we can imitate the grace of that Infinitude of Deific Love. We must never act to impede this inundation of grace upon humanity, even if it were possible, so that we may not find ourselves in the end as having attempted to build a seawall to hold back the Living Waters. We could erect mountain ranges of Everest's height at our shores to hold back the breaching waters, but those jutting towers of rock would only be destroyed and washed away like diminutive sand castles by the colossal tsunami of Glory that is bearing down upon this world. The Triumph of the Immaculate Heart of Mary is coming. Imagine what happens immediately before a tsunami crashes into a coastline. The tidal waves retreat far into the ocean, leaving huge expanses of coastline exposed. Then comes the wall of returning water magnified by the earthquake or impact that created it. The receding of faith across the world is the harbinger of Our Lady's Triumph.

    The Queen of Heaven can never be accused of deception when She offers Her heavenly insights and asks us to make way for what She teaches. It is we who are sinners who stumble over events and interpretations, where we scandalize and scatter each other through our personal fears, and then disparage the event as being unworthy of belief using our own faithless fruits as evidence. Indeed, we are all sinners, but Our Lady is not. Her truth is the Truth. She holds a special claim on the Truth of Her Son as His Mother, and as the

Suffering Matriarch of Mount Calvary. She is the Bearer of Truth himself. One thing that may be said is that the truth one experiences is often indescribable in human terms. This has the effect of causing difficulties at times when one translates it in order to make it describable to others; and it is often the discerners who fail in this translation, not the original orators or scribes. There is no spoken or written language to effectively describe heavenly beatitude. It is always an analogous effort. But, we must remember that all our parables and analogies go away upon our entrance into Heaven. Until then, we must do our best in hailing that Eternal Kingdom with the most heartfelt descriptions conceivable through the power of the Holy Spirit. This is the discerning realm where the Holy Spirit must not be squelched because He is boundless to the human intellectual constitution. But, if someone is determined nonetheless to live in that menial mental box, it is to their great misfortune in a world of such universal grandeur and eternal mystery. Great leeway must be given to the Holy Spirit to touch the manifest diversity of hearts with the scents of beatified vision. Our Lady speaking to a blank slate of humility is a far more constructive state for us to offer Her than being convinced of our own mental judgments, and then batting away Her tenses of divine grace like a prize-winning goalie deflecting a hockey puck.

When this humility is not extended by those who discern, the simple recognition that the recipients of divine intercession are exiled creatures inevitably becomes the small window of concession that radical skeptics hurl themselves into like high-divers into a teacup to manipulate, refute, slander and oppose the tender relationships that God allows His Mother to engage with Her children. Should not the celebrated discerners search themselves instead for the faith and wisdom that Eli summoned when Samuel came to him in the night at the beckoning of the Lord [1 Samuel 3:1-19]? Indeed, speak Lord for your servant is listening! Why can we not venerate and celebrate these occurrences instead for the building up of the body, and discern why such beauty has touched the Earth? In this age of such outrageous atheistic darkness, why do we employ an extremist scrupulosity of such magnitude that even Jesus Himself could not satisfy? Of all the atrocious conclusions that the modern world could draw in our time, there is no doubt that we would crucify Him again. Should we not instead see these mystical graces as beautiful gifts for the Church, and place their fruits on evangelic pedestals so that their aesthetic magnificence can touch the hearts of all who might be converted by their presence? Do we love the hearts of our brothers and sisters enough to believe them when they bring us their gifts? What kind of stone cold-hearted elitist trashes the couplets and quatrains of the innocent poems of a child that are brought forward for their family to see? Presently, the Queen of Heaven offers Her pure mystical poetry in Her messages, while the haughty among us slander them as though they have the authority to critique the Mother of God and Her triumphal Church. Our Holy Mother's presence, validated by the 'sufficient evidence' of Her messages, graces, and the spiritual example of Her messengers, emanates the ethereal resplendence of the Crucifixion and Resurrection of Jesus Christ. She proves that the Gospel still applies, and Her Son still lives and reigns as Lord, Savior, and King. She moves about the lives of Her children at will with the power of God. We must simply recognize it. Only the human will can push God away for Eternity. It is called Hell, and its anticipation begins here in how we act and the decisions we make. The Immaculate Virgin's assistance is not only in the messages that She offers, but through Her mystical Motherhood by which She nurtures us, should we make ourselves the conduit through which Her grace and blessings flow. This conduit is the faithful human heart, supported by the collective affirmation of the Church which is open to receive and respond to Her in obedient love.

I concede that it is technically true as Her detractors charge, that if She never said an audible word to any of Her children nor appeared in Her majesty to any of us, then for Her part, She would be just as present to each of us. But, I ask, what kind of person thinks like that? It is much like saying that God would be just as present to humanity if Jesus had never been born, and the Holy Spirit never sent. Jesus came so that we would know Him and the Father who sent Him, to have life and to have it more abundantly. Life is more abundant with Our Lady in it wielding all the powers of Her Motherhood. And, we would do well to recognize it. But, what do we see instead? The Heavenly Matriarch who possesses the Beatific Power of the Queenship of Paradise is, in effect, told to go back and sit on Her Throne and just look pretty. How did the world reject Jesus Christ? Well, the same way it is rejecting the miraculous intercession of His Queen Mother. And, it is that serious. The way to defeat this darkness is for everyone to consider what mental mechanics causes this horrible calculated indifference to happen. How often are the mystical gifts of God slandered and rebutted as if they are beneath the dignity and integrity of our faith traditions? They are our faith traditions, flourishing and flashing, marvelous and magnificent! How much damage is done to little souls in the infancy of their faith by people filled with pride who think they know more than anyone else about an ocean when they are only standing in a puddle of water.

The manifestations of Jesus' intentions are to be neither audited nor dismissed by any sinner. Religious intellectuals study about the pathway to

Heaven, but how often do they refuse to set out on the journey of sanctification, which begins in the denial of the self that would allow them to believe? The Dominion Angels told my brother and me, "*Most men desire to know God not out of love, but in the pursuit of authoritative legitimacy.*" Should we not contemplate the unity of all hearts within the communion manifested by the common sacrifice of the Church Triumphant? Oh, what love is present there! The Saints would die again in defense of one another. The Church Triumphant believes the Virgin Mother's intercession with a passion that leaves them trembling in tears of joy that God would be so merciful and gracious through the person of His Immaculate Mother. Should we not be united with them in this joy? Despite all the reasons to believe lying right before them, most gnat-straining authoritarians never do until they are forced by earthshaking supernatural miracles. They are the least of men. They have other worldly agendas and popular sentiments to satiate alongside their egos. They let the true work of faith be accomplished by better men and women who embrace the solitary sacrifice of believing unto knowing.

The impartial test of humility leveled by God through the stones the builders are rejecting is being failed by those who think they are learned. It is only from a pure childlike heart filled with the Spirit of sacrifice that we extend a faithful allegiance in the image of Abraham and Our Lady. Think about it! Yes, the Savior of the world established a Church that is comprised of a Mystical Body of believers who embrace the Cross in the image of our Redeemer. We know that our Redeemer lives! But, the test of our faith must be met by a reciprocal fiat at every moment of our lives, no matter what challenge God lays before us. Faith is a living state of sanctifying grace that professes and proceeds upon the path to knowing as God chooses to reveal Himself. It is fettered when pride and intellectual arrogance attempt to supersede it, and then quash revelation for the sake of authoritarian control. Faith is not a gigantic library of intellectual knowledge to be consumed by a mind that will ultimately be conjugated into Glory. It is a love in the heart so profound that it becomes heroically sacrificial, and will mount a cross in the image of Christ the King that humanity might be converted and saved. It is not defensive from a standpoint of weakness, but offensive in the beatitude of power wielded through prayer, piety, and a Divine Love that cannot be impeded, even by being sequestered in the inhospitable defiance of an old rugged tomb.

Can one humbly ask without being scorned how much theology is enough? Is more theology going to convert the world, or should we somehow renew our humility and concentrate on announcing the simple truth of Jesus'

Sacrifice on Calvary? Does greater intellectual knowledge equate to the greater sanctity of man? How many libraries of philosophical and theological analysis of our faith is enough before we testify to its implementation as Our Lady counsels? How many doctoral dissertations do we need, most of which will do no more than lie on dusty shelves for the remainder of human history, testifying that someone merely ran the gauntlet of scholarly intellectualism in order to be proven worthy in the halls of the hooded? Is holiness defined by study or practice? Do we ponder the parameters of intellectual gluttony? Do we realize that theology itself is in the process of pursuing its own legitimacy, purification and sanctification? Have we ever noticed how religious intellectuals talk? Oftentimes, it seems that they are from another planet. Anthropologically this, ontologically that, epistemological here, systematically there, patristically forward and aft. How about a simple 'I love you' and living in a unity at the Altar that testifies to it being true? How about teaching the world what it means to pray, how to pray, and what can be gained if we all turn our hearts toward the God of the Holy Cross?

    I can remember only two clerics tell me in 60 years that they loved me, and one was only because I said it first. Our Lady tells me that She loves me every day, and She proves it by lifting up my heart into Her immaculate grace where I feel I possess the pearl of great price, and I could conquer the world with Her single teardrop if I could find a way to capture it. She encourages my brother and me to tell as many people who will listen about everything that our hearts conceive and have learned from Her. Could it sometimes seem to be a wandering description of sentiments that risk being snubbed as useless by esteemed theological scholars? Perhaps, but I relate it more as a massaging of the perspectives of all who might listen where we touch places that need to be reoriented and healed in the most delicate ways possible, because there is often chaos and pain in the hearts of lost sinners. They have thousands of questions requiring answers before they will believe. It is not my intention to give them the answers to all their questions. Rather, I try to give them an understanding of their heart where their questions will no longer matter to them. Questions arise from the disorientation in dissonant perspectives. Once one understands that there is peaceful rest for the heart which is in perfect consonance with Divine Love, then there is no disturbance to be questioned. Are we to be faulted when trying to meet our lost brothers and sisters where they are, when we are required to cut across the grain of intellectual fashion and theological style, or ask them both to get out of the way altogether? Both the Holy Spirit and Our Lady trust us to have the words to say, whether it is when we are called to interact with our humble brothers and sisters or hauled before the courts of doubters and dissemblers. Does Scripture not say that we should be confident of this [Matthew 10:19] ?

Our Heavenly Mother cheers our resolute determination to see Her work through. She cares not who we challenge to do better. She has told us to be unafraid of anyone who presumes to disqualify or silence us. She says they did as much to Jesus, and He never relented, even unto His death on a Cross. She knows that we know what love is because we have seen Her, and She has helped us through the suffering that has confirmed it within us. No one needs a doctoral degree to speak of their allegiance to the Son of God, and why. We are measured by lashes and scars, not diplomas, degrees, or coats of arms. The wisdom of Heaven is written upon the heart that fears its God and worships His Son through the Holy Spirit. Beatific truth has been gifted to humanity in the Cross of Jesus Christ through the Holy Sacrifice of the Mass and all the graces and gifts flowing from that Sacrifice, including the miraculous intercession of our Heavenly Mother and every grace of our Sacramental Confirmation. It is not the possession of an elite faction who are authorized to erect barriers demanding they be feted before the gates of Heaven defer to the passing of humanity [Matthew 23]. It was all so simple in the beginning when the Holy Spirit came down upon the faithful at Pentecost. And, it is likewise as simple in the supernatural presence of the Queen of Heaven. Her Immaculate Heart possesses and contains the ultimate Pentecost of the Holy Spirit upon the Church. The sincerity is so palpable and deep. The unity is impregnable and indivisible. The love, so genuine and selfless. The allegiance in the face of miraculous events as instantaneous as Her Fiat. The wisdom in the fear of God, so spectacular, courageous and vibrant. We are being called out of a world that demands ten thousand reasons before believing in Our Lady's immaculate light that shines a security where ten thousand difficulties cannot make one doubt.

My heart can only imagine what it would be like for those possessing lecterns and podia to love Our Lady with the verbal tense of the Church Triumphant. It is an awesome envisioning that the pulpits of the Earth would proclaim Her beauty with full-throated thunder, with Prelates magnifying the Church's venues to speak of Her immaculate grace with the holy fear that their salvation depended upon it. When such a coming ensues, the Voice of the Original Apostolic Church filled with love for Jesus and Mary will convert billions. I can only imagine standing before the masses with tears flowing down my cheeks, speaking about the love I have for the Immaculate Virgin and Her Sacred Son. It is yet just a vision that I would see Christians being led by prelature saints to take command of Creation and fold it into the will of Jesus

Christ with determination like lightning striking before Satan's minions. Lit up, passionate, bold and rearing with conviction as on that first Pentecost of the Church. Saint Peter, you spoke well that day! Stopping for no sword, remaining silent before no threat, breaching every barrier, shearing every chain, advancing upon secular citadels, and commanding the attention of a world in disarray to come to believe that God would love them so much as to send His Immaculate Mother to convert them, lest they die in horror in the bowels of hell.

Dear God, give us hearts to rise in allegiance to the Most Holy Trinity and call the world to its eternal destination in an Immaculate and Sacred Heart in a Kingdom of Light over which you reign as Father. Let encouragement and accolades go forth to those who do believe. He says, you are the Light of the World! 'May your Light shine before men that they may see the good that you do and give Glory to God!' Toss the bushel baskets from atop your faith into the roaring fires of commitment along with every fear you may harbor in the silent recesses of your heart. You have the approbation of the Queen of Heaven to proclaim your King! The Savior of the World came into the darkness for you! He trusts you, He commissions you, He strengthens you, He elevates you, He speaks to you, and He accompanies you in every endeavor and act that you advance in His Holy Name. Your words and intentions are bound in Heaven as you bind them on Earth when done for His sake. It is confidence that He wishes you to have, just as toddlers giggle when their father tosses them into the air, knowing they will be caught in his embrace. He desires that you know that your sins are forgiven in the Blood of His Sacrifice on Calvary that gushes from the Catholic confessionals and down from its Altars. There is nothing that you have done that He cannot wipe away from the mind of Creation. Purify He must. Come and witness the Divinity and Power of the King of Heaven, He who fashioned the moon and the stars, the expanse of every universe, He who came to deliver His own from the darkness, to accompany humanity through this nighttime in the flesh, He who suffered everything that we have suffered, yet did so without forsaking His obedience to the Father — all in our name, that we could pass the threshold of Paradise and bask in our greatest dreams with Him in the Beatific Vision of the Most Blessed Trinity. Where is fear in this? Where can doubts survive? Who dares to stand in our way? The secular world can do no harm to your soul, so stare it in the eyes and spit so that its eyes may be opened by your healing balm, mixed with your sacrifices of the Earth. Admonish the perennial cowards like slayers wielding sabers of light. Make Saint Michael the Archangel smile that mere mortals could have such heart to fight with an angel's valor. Prostrate evildoers with truth so mighty that they cry for Divine Mercy. Call out the fakers and frauds, those who flirt with secular surrender. Polish the compromisers with abrasive truth, and call them to order. Speak in the face of tyrannical ideologues who demand your silence in rebuttal to your truth about their lukewarmness and mediocrity. Remember that not every one may go to Heaven. It is not only the great despots, tyrants and murderers of human history who will find themselves before the judgment of God for what they have done, but every person who has invoked a sinful intention against the God of Heaven and His people. Whatever you do to the least of these, you do to Him. Therefore, let all we do be for His Glory, Praise and Honor.

The Final Colossus
With the Valor of Archangels
AD 2016

Saturday, January 2, 2016
9:34 a.m.

"Ruing the past, milking the present, hedging the future – all change is based on blood, moved or shed; plied like water, rocket fuel or rosin; archived by pen and brush, and the sanctity of memory and life of the heart."

- The Dominion Angels

"My holy little sons, we have embarked on another year of prayer for lost humanity, and we will succeed in finding them. The Father desires you to know that all your works will bear the fruit that He has implanted and nourished in you. You have clearly known that the sound of God's voice emits tremendous light, and your pious works will last beyond the eras of the world. They have an eternal shelf life, and no one can enter Paradise until they have first read, heard and internalized what they say. Jesus has promised this as a gift to My own dignity. Therefore today, I have come to open this new month and year with you through My Maternal Queenship on your sacred journey to Heaven. My Special son, for a Woman who has said so many things to you and your brother over the decades, your writing for your next book (*The Final Colossus - In Battle Array*) has rendered Me searching for words. And, the title! It is truly the Holy Spirit who has seeded in you the wisdom and kindness to proceed in your labor of love. The Dominions Angels' passage to begin our message today is another gift to humanity who is struggling to understand their role in the world. You have said that it is likely the most visionary piece of genius you have read, and it has the capacity to prove to any Bishop that your Marian apostolate is a work of the Holy Spirit. You have written so many things in your new book in the past forty eight hours alone that I would not know where to begin to commend you. I wish to express My gratitude for opening your heart to the message of love that the Father is dispensing through you. I also ask that you know that your writing is not too admonishing. It is benign compared to the reproval that God would otherwise inflict on the world. Why does He not? Because He is reminded of the Divine Mercy of His Crucified Son. If it is a reckoning that the Lord should seek, it will surely be done by the Messiah on the Cross. If peace and mercy will prevail at the end of time, Jesus will choose when and where they will be applied. It is depending on the response of humanity during these crucial times. I always add that My prayers are in favor of those who are consecrated to My Most

Immaculate Heart, and for the many who have yet to come to the Sacrifice of My Son for the meaning of life. I know that the sound of the Light of Christ is awakening millions of sinners from their sleep and allowing them to see their way through the darkness that has overcome the nations. If we persist in our prayers and take to heart the meaning of solemn redemption, we will live knowing that the work of the Saints will claim their final relevance.

Therefore, I share your concerns for the modern world, just as I have done for 2,000 years. There have never been more distractions from the Faith during these centuries, but there have also never been as many venues to share the Gospel. In earlier times when Christians would sit on their porches and in their parlors in prayer, they connected with humanity through the Heart of the Father. While this remains true today, there is much more emphasis on communicating by way of electronic conveyance and other messaging. As you and your brother have said, the world is not as large as it used to be. I ask you to remember that the graces and blessings of your lives with Me keep pouring-down from beyond the heavenly vaults into the exiled realms of men. Over and over, new gifts are generated by your prayers. The Father is stirred, awed and amazed by what you have done for Him. He stands erect and claps His palms together in thanksgiving and applause that you, in this new year of the 21st century, are still fighting the good fight for your faith. I have often asked you to consider how the earthly domain appears from the other side of time. God has the ability to see all the historical phases of human existence simultaneously. He has seen the radicalism as well as the monotony as they have been combined and divided, come and gone. He is aware of the motivations of men before they are transformed into discernible thoughts. He knows what actions will surface that will serve Him, and those that cause tremendous upheaval where His Spirit is not welcome. My Special son, the Father would rather watch this fight ensue than see indifference in a world without Him. We have the ability to stir Him to action to manipulate the events and endeavors of modern men, and our prayers are doing precisely this. I told you last week that humanity bears the responsibility for effecting the changes that must come. Every time an exiled person dies without doing so, another opportunity is lost. My Special and Chosen ones, we are active people; we know the power that remains in our hands to transfer the lost sinners of the Earth into the recognizable apostles with whom Jesus has been trying to interact. Even if it takes until the end of time, we will reach them. I declare, your works are miraculous gifts to the Earth; they have an eternal shelf life. When the epochs and eras are finally drawn to a close, your works bearing My messages and your renditions will always remain.

My Special son, while the relationship between God and His people is one that must be nourished, it should include the unification of men with the identity of Jesus. 'It is not I who live, but Christ who lives in me.' When exiled men understand what this means, they will learn the questions that the Father will ask at the end of time. They will prepare their response before the interrogatories are put before them. They will become maestros of their own fate because they will know what Jesus expects of them based on their wisdom and faith. They will be able to transfer their perception of life the same way that I looked down upon you and your brother at the Saint Augustine Cemetery on Palm Sunday 1991. They will see the purpose of their lives through My eyes. Thereafter, instead of wandering from place to place as though guessing what they must do, they will be self-apprised that they must 'go here, and go there' because these are the steps that Jesus would have taken. They will stop twisting their heads like puppies trying to decide what they are seeing, and they will look peacefully and confidently knowing that their vision has been clarified by the Church. This way, when the completeness of the Christian experience becomes full in their hearts, they will know why people live and die, why the sun rises in the east, and why suffering is a far greater gift for the conversion of the world than comfort. All humanity belongs not only to Jesus as His brothers and sisters, not only to God as His faithful flock, but to a guild of enlightened believers beneath the guiding light of the Cross. Focusing on the Cross of Mount Calvary is the origin of human genius. It encapsulates all the sunrises and sunsets that have ever dawned in the annals of the world. The Cross bears the signature of the entire New Covenant Gospel of the Man-God who was crucified there. It is the lighthouse that glows beside the dark crests of the seas, and it will remain there as a buoy when the Earth is flooded in suffering – not by water this time, but an overwhelming fiery catastrophe of dire mourning and grief. The Holy Cross will shield those who are given to Jesus from the agonies that will accompany these events. All change is based on blood – moved or shed. There is no question about what this means.

My Special son, it is fitting upon the opening of this new year to say that the ages are passing; humanity is growing older, and the traits of the created world are maturing. However, I have said that everything is unfolding backward. The souls of men are returning to their youth by the hour and day. The so-called 'fountain' of this youth resides in the human heart; it has always been stationed there. You and your brother, as My children, are beneficiaries of this fountain because you have refused to be distracted from your mission, and you have declined to see yourselves as old. It may have seemed strange through the ages that a young maiden such as Myself who was crowned Queen of Heaven and Earth has, throughout the centuries, referred to various Popes, Cardinals, Bishops and elder lay persons alike as My children. I have done this because they have become united in the Sacred Heart of Jesus; they have been unified in the Divine Love by which He has sanctioned their redemption. So, when the Angels speak about such things as mansions and sacrifices, they are referring to the destiny of men in their identity in Jesus. What has been archived by pen and brush can be read and viewed in this same identity. It is nurtured, shared and safeguarded inside the sanctity of the human memory that is always guided by the life of the heart. My Heart, My Most Immaculate Heart, is beating with love for you and your brother because you are one with Me. I have said that the years have not only borne this out, they have ratified that you have been situated alongside the Father's greatest blessings to the Church. Your lives and legacies rest between the front and back covers of the Sacred Scriptures and the teachings of the Roman Catholic Catechism. You have consecrated yourselves sacrificially and benevolently to the magnification of the Messianic message that will ultimately apprise the world about the shape and scope of its final destiny. It is more than an appearance about which I am speaking, it is the deliverance of Creation back to its origin in God. We must say 'Thank God!' and hallelujah that these things are true. You are willing to fight for the truth and the mission of the Church. God is indeed merciful. Bishop Daniel Ryan is in Heaven with Me. *"I'm so happy about the Divine Mercy granted him. Let him know how much he is loved, and thank him for his episcopal blessing on our home."* The good Saint just heard what you said, and My little boy began crying with his face in his hands. My Special and Chosen ones, God is good. You will someday hear what He will say to you. 'My little sons – you bow to no one!' *"It is indeed an amazing adventure."* Yes, My Special one, it will assist you in describing how difficult it is to bear the exile in which humanity is stationed."

Saturday, January 9, 2016
9:11 a.m.

"We have inherited at our disposal and brandished to our advantage our own enigmatic and oracular weapons, reams, tongues and verses – even as we are imbedded to the depths of struggle these days, we ride in triumph over the hordes that despise us. Such is the battle of blind-faith believers. This is the cause of our victory over the Church's tormentors, over pain that cannot stop us, over the bloodstains discoloring our faces, over the tortured perceptions to which atheists subscribe about the true meaning of life. Trusting the faith in one's own heart does not require mastering mainstream social etiquette or having a keen cultural intellect. It is a product of the simple acknowledgment that everything humanity will ever need to know or believe to be successful in this life is based on the eternal promises of the next."

- William Roth Jr.

"My dear little children, you are worthy and wise. You do not yield to the unruly mob. You keep your faith pulled tightly. And, you realize that there is no neutral side to the Cross on which Jesus was crucified. This is not only your record, it is your sacred identity. It is to these things that your purpose is given, addressing the casualties that inevitably come, reminding the world that it is truly broken. Today, we pray that those who are far from the Church will open their hearts and believe; not that they will see as you, My little sons, have seen, but that they will grow their faith in the image of giants. I hold in My Immaculate Heart the key that opens the door on which Jesus knocks. My Special son, the writing that you have composed to open our message today comes from deep within your heart and the depths of your faith where Jesus lives in you and touches you. The writing that you are composing for your next book, the strains of beauty and glory that you just imbedded into our message today, is of this same origin of divine perfection. Here, we are seeing what happens when holy men hand their goodness to Jesus in the form of faith and righteous works. You have completed the passage for our message in the same spirit in which you spoke and wept a few days ago when referring to General and President George Washington riding as a leader into battle. My Special son, there are hundreds of poems and sonnets that will be written about what you and your brother have done. You will be uplifted as examples of what God expects from His people. It is done by working together with Jesus through the Church. Yes, the Holy Trinity is the tripod on which human Salvation is stationed. And, it sings the songs of absolution to the world – God the bass, Jesus the baritone, and the Holy Spirit the tenor. Anyone has the capacity to hear it, but this is dependent on whether they are inclined to listen.

I come again this morning to make your day an auspicious occasion for the Church and humanity around the globe. It is not so much that they will know anytime soon what I have said today, but that our assembling here with your brother is seen as a prayer to Jesus and the Father who have dispatched Me to celebrate the Good News in yet another form. What we have done through the decades is ask God to touch the world the same way that I have been your mediator between the Lord and from the Lord back to you. This is not only My spiritual right as your Mother, it is My honor as your Lady in the presence of the Church. When we pray for the Father to bring pardon and peace to the world, we have seen in our hearts what form it will take when He does. Humanity needs to defer and allow Jesus and the Holy Spirit to do Heaven's work. Pride, gluttony, envy, sloth – all these things are manifestations of the devil. They hail from a world of infamy; they have no place in the halls of sanctified humanity. I have always spoken My Heart when it comes to such matters as these, but it seems that I am forced to beg My children to change, lest I lose the gentle sense for which I have been centuries known. I stood beneath the Cross on Good Friday without anger, but with sorrow and hope overcoming My thoughts. You might imagine what a bittersweet tragedy this was for Me. It was the day that My Immaculate Heart was devastated by the knowledge that My Son had died. Yet, it was simultaneously the same hour that I knew He would rise again on the Third Day; and centuries later, I would be dictating this message to you and your brother here. The Crucifixion and Resurrection of Jesus are timeless events that happened within the setting of humanity's exiled years. The world is blessed not just because Jesus was willing to die, and God was willing to surrender Him to death, but that humanity would be the beneficiaries of these redemptive events. The Sorrowful Passion and Crucifixion of Jesus Christ are the most monumental tragedies in the history of the Earth and the universes surrounding it. And, even with all the sin and malevolence of the earthly domain, the exiled people who live here are heirs to the divine gifts that the Father has deigned. I have spoken to you on many occasions about little people and spiritual giants. These are not dimensions that would describe someone's physical stature, but the inner-being of who they are. Jesus does not care about anything else but this.

Hence, you and your brother have inherited a portion of what the world will come to know. You have been recipients of the interaction from Heaven to Earth in your home and elsewhere. I am not saying that this has not solicited your faith; you have trusted God perhaps more than anyone else through time. How could you have anticipated that He would come to you and your brother with everything we have done? After all, you are both more humble than anyone in the world. There was a vast fortune of time given you when you were young because you are still living today. You could not have known that this would occur. You embrace the words coming to you now and say, '...yes, this is the Mother of God.' And, you do not surrender your faith in any way to generate this belief. It is given to you by the same spirit of wisdom that comes to all men. I refer to you as being Special and Chosen not just because you have aided the transfer of My messages into the physical realms, but because you have been distinguished as special and chosen based on your trust in what Jesus will allow. If God allows suffering and mourning to prevail worldwide, He will permit His miracles to unfold as well. Many of these miracles reveal that God is both active and proactive. Other miracles include gifts of omission because God could have blown the world to pieces by now and never batted an eye. Through Jesus, the Father is merciful; through His justice, He is sometimes vengeful. Humanity decides which of these approaches will define the conclusion of the ages. I have given you reasons aplenty to know that Jesus has His moments too. There are times when He is reminded of His own Crucifixion and everything He promised the Father He would do. Jesus always wished to be the benevolent teacher who was born in Bethlehem to usher in a new age of peace. Indeed, He was born the Prince of Peace. However, He also came as the divider and conqueror. He is the Man-God who would separate the sheep from the goats and the wheat from the chaff, not because this is what He willed from the beginning, but because humanity would reject who He is and what He desires for His Kingdom. Human beings are the dividers. They have become the adversaries of the same peace they claim to be denied.

During this second message of 2016, I have come to bless you and your brother for your dedication to your mission and devotion to Me. It will forever be this way. I honor, admire and cherish who you are, what you mean to the Father, and how you have chosen to live. Please remember how you are loved! My Special one, will you promise to never forget? *"I won't forget. Thank you."* Bless you for your lovely prayers. I always tell Jesus that you are asking for His blessing not just because this is what you have learned to do, but because you mean it from the depths of your heart. *"Yes, thank you."* I will keep My holy embrace around you and your brother for the entirety of your lives – and we will someday hold one another in Heaven with a sense of victory that cannot be annulled. Please pray for your Bishop because he is postponing what we have asked of him. I will not wait to proceed toward My Immaculate Triumph. I will accomplish what I set out to do with or without him."

Saturday, January 16, 2016
9:33 a.m.

"The human soul is eternal – mortality cannot claim it; suffering cannot conquer it, malice cannot offend it, darkness cannot conceal it, sorrow cannot subdue it, and death will never write its epitaph."

- Jesus of Nazareth

"Good morning, My dear little sons! I have come bearing the Good News that humanity is indeed amending their ways because of our daily prayers. My Special son, you received from behind the veil an unknown quotation of Jesus at the beginning of our message today. It is one that must always be remembered by those who wish to strengthen their relationship with God. My little son, you do not 'have' a soul, you 'are' a soul. Your soul is your essential 'being' in this world and the next. This is why I told humanity through My Magnificat that My Soul magnifies the Lord in the same way that My children become Jesus' Mystical Body through their unity in Him. And, unless someone trips over their own mind trying to understand this, it is as simple as anything a human being will ever know. Every person on Earth must magnify the Lord in His sacred love and perfection. This is what Jesus has called the Church to teach. Men may not yet be able to detect what perfection in God means because so many of them, your brothers and sisters, have never tried the way you and your brother have given yourselves, your souls, to Jesus on the Cross. I have come today, therefore, to remind you that this is the glory that has overwhelmed you and brought you to have the faith to which you are so dedicated. Faith is factually a gift from the Father, and humanity must accept this gift in the same way that you have opened your heart to receive Him. My dear Special son, I wish that I could spend the next hours telling you how much I love you, but I cannot put it into words. There are no symbols or images that could possibly capture what you mean to Me. Your honesty and trustworthiness are beyond compare. Your desire to see the demise of the enemies of the Church is unmatched. The amount of effort and immense resources that you have devoted to your Marian apostolate are becoming of the greatest Saints who ever lived. I pray that, someday, I will be able to impress upon you in a discernible way what you mean to God. It is true that you are yet behind the veil that impedes your vision of Heaven, but you have already permeated that veil through the faith and love in your heart. You have more than value and worth. There are no instruments with which to measure the intensity of your perfection within the Glorious Kingdom. I am telling you that I am trying through My messages in the world to persuade My children, all of them, to become like you. It is your image that reflects the identity of Jesus, and makes My efforts here with you so worthwhile. "*Thank you, Mama. It is because of you.*" I wish for you every good fortune in this life, that you will be happy knowing the immensity of your sainthood, that you will forever feel the sensation of Jesus' arms wrapped around your soul, and that you will never forget what He has promised you because of your eminent love. There are no words to describe it.

I also wish that I could touch the rest of the world because they have their own potential to be more holy in their own way that approaches and manifests their identities in Jesus as prescribed in the Scriptures. "*It is going to take miracles to ignite them, and not just simple miracles.*" My little son, you have already seen that miracles are not enough. It is going to require a level of colossal devastation and suffering so intense that the lost will have no choice but to seek their God. "*Then, let it be.*" Yes, and in their pursuit of consolation in God, they will seek-out every fiber of human existence where He has given Himself to the world. It will be through My intercession, in My messages, and with the aid of the Holy Spirit that they will seek The Divine, the supernatural wisdom that will teach them where they have failed and how they can succeed. You have echoed a poster that once adorned a closet door in your brother's second floor bedroom in Ashland — 'Let it be.' This does not mean that you and I do not hope for something more benign to shock and awaken the hearts of men from their slumber in indifference. We still hope for that 'manifest abruption' that will bring all who yet do not know the truth to discover themselves immersed in it. We remain united, you and I, and we pray and live out our dreams because we realize that Jesus can do anything. He has already proven Himself to be the worker of miracles. This is what His Sorrowful Passion and Crucifixion have given to those who believe. The miracles about which you speak were patently ineffective in His earthly days – they killed Him anyway. "*But, they ignited His Gospel throughout the ages.*" Yes, and there is only one Gospel. There will never be another. We are praying that humanity will turn to the Gospel in the same way that Jesus turned to His betrayers and said that it is they who must change. As I say, many of them have been trying, but they often stumble over their own thoughts while treading the foothills of the Earth, trying to reach the summit of the heart. It is all too much a distraction that keeps them from becoming bare in front of Him and confessing their sins, faults and failings.

And, My Special one, this is the reason why I consistently focus on the joys of life, knowing that Jesus has already laid out the roadmap to Himself. He is both the Journey and the Destiny. I have said this before. And as such, He must also be the nourishment for all who are still trying to find their way. The Way, the Truth and the Life they seek, not yet knowing what it may look like when they arrive. The sacred beauty and holy power that I have been telling you about for the past several years is the beneficial divinity that will always and everywhere be the guidance of the lost into the Eternal Kingdom. Beauty is derived from humanity's concession to the Lord that they can neither exist nor survive without Him. This is a divine profession for lost sinners to eventually make. And, once it is done, then power, limitless power, is given to those who believe. My Special son, this is why I have said that humanity's perception of beauty, what people believe beauty to be, has always been flawed. It has nothing to do with visual fairness or something that is alluring to the mind or flesh. It is all about the future; this beauty about which I speak assists humanity to their future in Jesus on the Cross. Beauty is the Bloodbath on Mount Calvary that has preserved humanity from spending eternity in Hell. Beauty consists of the sound of the lashes that struck Jesus of Nazareth on His final mortal day. This is the irony of what the Father believes beauty to be. There can be no eternal power without His redemptive and sacrificial beauty. And, this is why the world is called there. Suffering is the balm for the agony of lost souls. If Jesus has not proved this to the nations by now, they will truly never know. The power that comes from beauty, therefore, has nothing to do with boasting of something that no one else has. It is not founded in priceless jewelry or fine fashions. It cannot be seeded in square-jawed men with tan complexions. It is about connecting the souls of men with their deliverance to the realms beyond the constraints of time. Now, this is power! Hence, when you are speaking to others in the years to come about what the Mother of God has said about the finer things of life, tell them they live in the tragedies that they need to overcome. Remind them that they are inherent in the plight of the poor, and those who are exploited for money, influence and fame. You have seen in your own life how worldly beauty tends to manipulate the innocent. It has caused pain, regret and sorrow that can linger for decades, and often lifetimes. This is why worldly beauty is not beautiful at all. It is something that just happens to contrast with the more unsightly visions of life, but it is not as pretty to the druthers of the soul.

Yes, I have told you about beauty and power to emphasize the magnitude of one more thing – innocence. Without the restoration of innocence, nobody could survive. Why? Because guilt is always damning. Guilt fosters darkness and destruction. It manifests condemning conditions over which no faithless man can prevail. It is not that Jesus proved humanity to be innocent when He died on the Cross, but that their innocence was restored in their acceptance of His Sacrifice. This is why I have said to you on many occasions, '...what sins?' I have no knowledge of anything evil that Jesus has reconciled to the Father. And, please allow Me to tell you another point that humanity has never known. Jesus the Messiah has the ability to erase the memory of God, Himself. The cleansing of the world on Good Friday also began the moment when God the Father ceded His capacity to hold vengeance over Adam and Eve and all who would follow them. Is this difficult to believe? For those without faith, it is. God can do anything He pleases. He can dispatch His Messianic Son anyplace in Creation to bless and absolve. He has vested Christ Jesus with the authority to call anything He chooses either bound or loosed. Why? Because Jesus suffered and died to change the veritable framework of human life and the previously held standards by which it will finally be judged. Jesus surrendered His life on behalf of an entire guilty race of human sinners so they could find themselves innocent once again. This is more than the world upside down, it is humanity turned inside out. It is bypassing the logical in favor of the Mystical. Jesus on Good Friday did more to sustain the dignity of the human race than the Father did when He first created it. So, when was the world really created? On the first day? In the first six days? Does not the rise of the redeemed Earth seem much more appealing than the downfall of the exiled one? Is not the New World to come more filled with light than the older order of halls? My Special son, these are among the many revelations that will come when the Book of Revelation itself is finally unfurled. I hope you have enjoyed My message today. *"Yes, I really did. Thank you so much."* Do you have any issues to discuss with Me this morning? *"Where are we in the unfurling of the Book of Revelation?"* Please make your question more specific. *"Where are we as far as the events that are prophesied to unfold?"* It is clear that you are asking for a theological explication of the End Times that will preclude your overwhelming sense of joy, should I tell you now. I say this not to be evasive, but because you and your brother are participants in the Divine Revelation due to your identities in the Morning Star. Also, the End Times are being prescribed as we speak by the prayers of the faithful on Earth and the Saints in

Heaven. *"I understand, and I trust you."* Please realize that you will at the last discover the fruits of your life with your brother included in this sacred domain. Yes, what we have done here together is this sacredly manifest. *"Thank you, Mama. I understand."* My Special son, your brother keeps telling Me that he knows who you are. He understands what your companionship with him means. It has been the difference between the world embracing the light rather than the darkness. All things will be made clear as the years unfold."

Saturday, January 23, 2016
9:48 a.m.

"An affirmation conducive to theological absolution –
Discovering the trousseau within the heart."

"My dear little sons, all the paraphernalia that a bride requires for her wedding day – all the collectibles, the gown, jewels, the collateral needs and all the rest – this is her trousseau. The trousseau is generally collected inside a hope chest for safekeeping in advance of the auspicious event to come. Yes, the dowry is deposited there as well. You already know where this is leading. The human heart is the environment in which all the needs of the spiritual person are generated in expectation of your final reward. Your faith is your affirmation that is conducive to your theological, mystical, Messianic redemption. I wish to not make My analogy between the contents of the heart and the wedding trousseau any more complex than this. My Special son, this affirmation, this environment about which I speak includes your own confident assurance that everything you are giving to Jesus through your faith is worthy of His Sacrifice. I have come today, My little sons, not only to reinforce your knowledge that you are blessed in these ways, but to promise you that you are held in the highest esteem in the Kingdom where you are bound. You have swept through the world like a force of Nature. You have refused to be held back, collared, encumbered or leashed by the hatred of your enemies. You are victorious over those who oppose you because you do not cower from what they say. It is true that Jesus was offended by His betrayers during His earthly years as well, but He did not focus on the offenses in any way that would distract Him from His mission. My Special son, you will discover only very little content in the Gospels indicating what Jesus was thinking during His mortal years. Plenty is recounted about what He said, what He taught and commanded, but rarely can you cite the context of those teachings and commandments that would lend you to understand the interior personality of the Savior of the world. Do you believe that most theologians would agree with Me? *"No, because they like to define Jesus, and then build from there."* What definition do you believe they have assigned to Him? *"That He was effeminate."* Yes, and why do they believe this? *"Because they don't recognize the power that this King is going to someday wield."* Yes, you are precisely correct. It is as true as anything else comprehensible by man. It is the principle of peace through strength. This is what the theologians are missing. You have seen what I am going to illustrate now, but think about it for a moment. What are some alphabetical letters that can be written on a page without lifting the pen? Let us use upper case letters. C...L...O...S...Z...U...V. Depending on who is doing the writing, there may be others, but you get the point of what I am saying. And, the thesis of this is that theologians refuse to believe that there has been a constant imprint of the hand of the Father in this world to create anything communicable to any host of believers. They maintain that miracles and blessings have come on intermittently, not with a constant outpouring of divine revelation. In other words, they believe that the language of Creation and the mandates of the Holy Word were handed down as though the Lord was speaking between breaths rather than one unending oration. They are wrong. You can write anything you desire without lifting your pen if you compose it in cursive longhand.

Here, I have given you another metaphor that reveals the placement of Jesus' hand on the pulse of His own Mystical Body. It is true that Jesus never said to the Church, '...Come to Me, or I will come get you.' He said instead, '...Come to Me, all who are tired and weary, the lonely, lost and brokenhearted.' Do you understand the simplicity of the difference? *"Yes."* The point of this issue is that Jesus stands as the lighthouse on the shore, but He also is willing to enter the water to rescue those who believe in Him, not to drag them back, but to prove that He is deeply imbedded in their suffering and strife. Every human creature on Earth needs to know that they can swim. This was the purpose of the Apostle who was urged to walk on water. It was not inability that caused the Apostle to fail, but a lack of trust. This is the fear that has beset most people in this century and beforehand from accepting that they can be perfected in Jesus. I am not suggesting that this perfection includes reading the future before it happens or healing one's neighbor from some crippling disease. It is more a matter of rational enlightenment from a seeming irrational origin. Here, I am using the term 'irrational' in the form of supernatural, not in the sense of being unable to apply logical reason. So, turning again to the passage that began our message today, the affirmation of men is one of self-induced agreement with the mystical elements of human life with the revelatory miraculous components of the sanctified human condition. Humanity needs to be able to write their future with God on a day-to-day basis without lifting the pen. This is the constant affirmation of men's faith to the gift of Salvation that they have found in Jesus on the Cross. Jesus remained on the Cross during the entire time span of the Crucifixion without suspending His constant pain. My Special son, if this can be equated to the worldly human experience, then all who believe in Jesus must find their comfort in Him with the sense that He never departs from their side. Does this seem simple enough? *"Yes."* I agree, but many theologians throughout the ages have said that Jesus could never apply that type of touch to His earthly domain because He went routinely alone and entered silent prayer. They have written that He took brief sabbaticals because He could not maintain the peace and patience to endure the secular void. They have written these things because they have neither identified nor understood the personality of Jesus to which I referred moments ago.

So, what can be said about Jesus' personality? First, He went to pray on His own to be one with the Father, and for no other reason. It was not that He was trying to avoid anyone. The best example of this type of prayer was last seen in Pope John Paul II. While the Pope may not have always worn sandals, his tennis shoes worked just fine. Jesus did not so much have disdain for the 'identity' of humanity as He was concerned whether He could change their identity into who He is. This had to be done by example, and this is where so many theologians believe that He was meek and weak-spirited in matters of justice and defending the faith. If anyone wishes to speak in metaphorical terms, Jesus has more destructive power in one fingertip than all the nuclear arsenals on Earth combined. So, it was not about His ability to destroy – it was about His capacity to restore. He wanted to saturate the world with His peace and grace to such a degree that exiled humanity would unilaterally disarm themselves. The reason I have made this point so clearly is because Jesus, and therefore God Himself, has not changed. I told you recently that Jesus sustains the Father's relenting in exacting justice where it should be rightly applied. This is the origin of the Father's Will that sent the Messiah into the exiled realms in the first place. Thus, the Church and humanity at large have learned that they can in fact write their future, but it must be done by taking up their own crosses as their pen and pouring out their lifeblood in the likeness of their Savior. This is not always done by physical means, but by being spiritually martyred for the good of The Faith. My Special and Chosen ones, nobody does this by lifting their pen and wondering what to write next.

It consists of the constant touching of the Lord's face and hands with faith inside the heart. This is the inception and completion of the affirmation that was broached at the beginning of our message today.

My Special son, I have said enough about theological designs for today. I wanted to relate to you that Jesus' personality is deeply rooted in a theology that cannot omit the immensity of His commitment to remain in uninterrupted contact with His exiled disciples. If ever there were a fitting definition of loyalty, piety, power and innocence, it can be found in the premise that Jesus has never surrendered His love for humanity. He has never ceded an inch to mortal men that rightly belongs to God. And, He has never lost sight of manifesting in the earthly domain a vision to which all good men must aspire for leading life the way it was exemplified through Him. You, My Special son, are the modern day example of what Jesus intended because you have believed what He comes to say through Me. It is sometimes maintained that sightless people can see better than sighted ones because they are not as prone to visual distractions. And, what this means is that those who have sight must do better at discerning what is truly worth focusing on, and what things should be ignored. It is this process that is occurring with men of spiritual faith. If something regales the legacies of the Saints, if its touch is reminiscent of Jesus on the Cross, if it has the fragrance of humility and sacrifice, you can be certain that all men's eyes should fall upon it. The constant touch of Jesus' Most Sacred Heart on His brothers and sisters on Earth is like God staring at His Church without so much as blinking an eye. It is always the matter of living in hopeful expectation – the Church celebrates this during every Holy Mass. Waiting in joyful hope means that humanity is forever aware of the touch of God on the cheek of the Church with compassion and tenderness. It is the focal point of the prayers of the Church, the celebration of the Lord's presence in the here and now, and the fostering of the kinship and friendship between this world and the next. My Special son, I again remind you that I rarely have other seers and locutionists who will listen to everything I say like you and your brother. It is not that they do not care, but that their patience wears thin. They cannot see the light because they are too worried about the darkness. They decline to feel the joy because they seem too traumatized by the sorrow. *"I'm so happy to be here with Timmy and with you, and have the opportunity to communicate everything you have ever said, and who you are, into a witness that will last throughout time."* You are so kind and gracious. You have made My eyes teary with thanksgiving that you are so special, so endlessly faithful to Me and Jesus. Your brother has issued his profound thankfulness that he is here with you as well. When asked by the Angels what he wanted for his birthday, he said thirty more years here with you. We all know that this will not be possible, but we will move forward one day at a time – these are indeed great and blessed days that you are living. Thank you, and bless you for praying for all My intentions every day. We have built a firestorm against the evils of this world that will turn them into ashes in their path. The winter will soon pass on, and you will be driving around the countryside with the warm breezes blowing across your faces."

Saturday, January 30, 2016
9:32 a.m.

*"Life to the fullest, finding one's voice –
and the liberation of talents."*

"My dear little children, so much love do I have for you, so much admiration and appreciation, so much desire that you always remember what you mean to Me. We have together made faith the reality for the generations that have preceded you. Yes, My little children, all who have come to Heaven have read your massive works, and Jesus has assigned everyone in Purgatory to read, hear and internalize not only My messages to you here, but everything you have written on your own. Every syllable of your devotionals, all your prologues and prefaces, the content of your prayers, and the ideals that you still pursue have already been shared with the tens of billions of people who have heretofore lived and died in this world. The first Saints in Heaven centuries ago saw your writings when they got here. The Poor Souls in Purgatory are hearing them now – not as a form of punishment, but a means to help them realize everything that should have been from the moment they were conceived. I am telling you here today that what we have done for the past quarter-century and more is this important to the conversion and redemption of the exiled human race. We have aided lost sinners to come to Jesus on the Cross for the fullness of life, to find their own voice amid the clamoring of the world, and to liberate from among their own sins the holy talents that the Father has given to them. My little sons, there is much to be said about the aspirations in all this. There has never been a soul born on Earth who did not at one time or another aspire to become something greater than merely human. This means that there is a seed of eternity implanted in everyone, but oftentimes the seed is left unnourished and trampled upon by a world that exploits and neglects them. Too many times, it is self-inflicted harm that comes upon them because they refuse to accept the fruits of true virtue that are begging to be savored at the depths of the human heart. Hence, living life to the fullest means that the exiled soul must break past the sights and sounds of the secular void to come to a fuller understanding of what Jesus desires from them. The entire identity of the human person must be shaped by everything taught in the Holy Gospel, and this same Gospel must be permitted conveyance from each person to whole societies at a time. This is how the individual and the world grow simultaneously to visibly meld the Earth with Heaven in every concurrent moment. And, one's own words must echo the voice of God, the sound of Truth ringing out not only around the globe, but throughout the epochs of time. Finding one's voice means that holiness and righteousness reign inside the heart, so that when a word is uttered, it resounds the Gospel about which I speak. None of this can be accomplished by men alone. It must be received by the world from the mouth of God. It is from His sacred lips that the future of humanity is pronounced.

And, this is likewise the way the talents of humanity are set free. The exercise of one's individuality must be to the advancement of the whole. Once properly practiced, once understood in the context of Jesus' Mystical Body, these talents are liberated – set free into the universe and beyond for the mission of the Church. My Special son, we know that the energy for everything I have thus far said is prayer. It is the making and remaking of the created realms into the identity of Jesus, now seated at the right hand of the Father. There are multiple forms of prayer. We are praying now. Tending to little children and lifting them up to their dignity is also prayer. Admonishing lost sinners is even a much more tremendous prayer. Feeding and housing the poor are viable prayers to eradicate poverty and disease. Jesus hears them; He confers them unto the Father, and the Holy Spirit provides the background melodies that sing God's responses back to the Earth. You and I can hear them now because we are attuned to His Will. And, this is why all our hopes are being realized both spontaneously and in rhythm with Jesus' words from the Cross. These professions were not only prophetic for the future, but ratifying for the virtuous acts that everyone who would ever live would commit in His name. I know that there are many invisible miracles happening every day because you see them when they finally occur. They are forthcoming now; they are unfolding at the behest of the Messiah who would never turn away from the calling of His Church. I would like to tell you today some news about My messages here in this place, and about your deposit of works and manuscripts, but you would be prompted to run outside into the street in front of this home, shout aloud and throw your fists into the air. I am unable to tell you about the magnitude of this mammoth miracle because the time has not yet come. All I can say is that you and your brother will drop to your knees in thankful adoration of the Son of Man once you hear news of the miracle about to be bestowed upon you. As I have said, however, you must wait in faith and joyful hope that what I am telling you is true. It is like the end of a football game when the winner has been determined, but the clock is still running, and the players are walking off the field. This is how I ask you and your brother to live, even if it requires another twenty-five years. There is no reason to believe that it will take near that long.

I have used the word 'ratify' in My message today with reference to the loosening and binding often related to the reign of Pope Peter. You and the Church have asked for certain occurrences to precede the Second Coming of Jesus, and He will indeed bind your wishes into being. The world believes that Jesus is much too silent, but it is because He wishes the Church to 'live out the message' that is worthy of a gallant warrior. To hear something in advance that could take another twenty-five years might seem anticlimactic, would it not? *"Yes."* Therefore, I beseech your patience and solicit your sentiments in realizing that God is the Master of timing. Present before you now in material form through your books, writings and apostolate stands the foundation upon which Jesus will place your miracle. It will coincide with the permanent miracle in Medjugorje as well, and the entire world will understand that the Queen of Peace and the Morning Star Over America are one and the same Mother of God. You have within you the youth to keep this hope alive, even as you are almost half-way through your sixth decade of life. Imagine how it must feel for Me to have such joyful pronouncements poised on My lips, but I am not yet able to utter the words. Have you seen the sight of a young girl sitting in class waving her hand with the correct answer, but the teacher will not call on her? *"Yes."* This is the way I am feeling right now. The key point I am making is that nothing can impede the victory you are about to see – nothing can stop it from happening. There are no manifest abruptions that can amend the course of events that will reveal the triumph in the offing. This is because you and your brothers and sisters have asked God for help. Yes, He knows about the agonies and ironies that you witness every day. He is aware that the individuals who are trying to stop the scourge of abortion by filming the murderers are themselves being charged with a crime. How backward can something be?

All of this tends toward something. It is the fact that those who are trying to reach for Heaven are having to battle the sinners already on their way to Hell. This is the ascension of the down staircase that Jesus wrote about when He was a child. It was a concept that was never revealed in the verses of the

Bible. He did not wish anyone to believe that they are irrevocably on the road to perdition before they have the opportunity to reverse their momentum. Does this make sense? "*Yes.*" Ascending the down staircase means that the pathway toward Hell is crowded with those who are attempting to hold everyone else back. This includes the persuasions and perversions that affect impressionable people who are distracted from discovering the truth for themselves. We have seen them in many places and times, and we know how fruitless the other paths have been. Yes, Jesus desires that His disciples have the fullness of life in Him. He prays that all who live will ultimately claim their own voice in speaking what He would have them say. He deigns the liberation of their talents so they can come of age in the teachings of the Church, and not something else that is generated from the secular void. If anything of innocence will ever bear fruit, it will begin in this. I have tremendous expectations that My children will heed the call of the Gospel to pursue the goodness that is plenteous for all, to open their hearts and believe, and work tirelessly for the protection of the nations against the evils of the devil. I pray every day for this – every morning where you live, and when the sun falls silently below the horizon at night. I have said in My Medjugorje messages that I am the Queen of Peace because of the obedience of humanity to the Cross, not despite the crosses that souls are asked to bear. Suffering and redemption are inseparable. It is much the same way that 'blace' is the union between 'blessing' and 'grace.' There is always ultimately a marriage of two forms that garners a greater Creation in the end. It is indeed the Cross and Salvation, beauty and the unsightly, the benefits of sorrow and laughter, and the way the children of God pray on their knees to remain upright in their faith. These are the words that I have come to share with you today. My Special son, thank you and your brother for allowing Me to offer them to you."

Saturday, February 6, 2016
9:36 a.m.

"I have come to the conclusion that exiled human existence, the whole expanse of it, is measurably estranged from remedial tenderness. With all its uncertainties, bloody turpitude, brash insults, cold incivility and reprehensible error, our lives on Earth will eventually boil down to one dynamic moment of cataclysmic revelation. Yes, the twisted wreckage of this world will someday come to rest, and only then will it claim its final victim. That is the hour when the ages themselves will testify that we made them the scapegoat for our own defiance against the exhortations of the Cross. The years and millennia bear no responsibility for what we have done, but we have too long brought them to mourning by our reluctance to heed their castigating knell."

- William Roth Jr.

"Touching the core of the human super-soul."

"Hear now, My little sons – this is My untold joy. I have come again to speak to you while we pray together for the conversion of lost sinners. You must realize that the Earth has been settling since it was first positioned in space. It is not that one would notice it, due to the ravages of humankind's corruption, but the Earth is settling-in as it was in the beginning. Since that time, God has come to recognize what has become the dregs on the surface of the Earth's foundation. It is not something that He dwells upon, but it has certainly become noticeable since human beings have lived. Yes, the word is dregs, or perhaps lees, and even the term 'sediment' applies. Whatever description one chooses to apply, there has long been the separation that is not unlike that of the sheep and the goats, the wheat and the chaff, spoken about in the Sacred Scriptures. When these layers of dregs finally form one atop another, there is a 'concretion' that forms consisting of their multiple layers. My point in telling you this is that there is no such thing as the perpetual state of the earthly realm – at least not in the sense that one might expect from such a sprawling domain. All around you, My dear sons, you are seeing which people and from what quarters those exist who are consecrated to Me and Jesus' Most Sacred Heart. I have come today, therefore, to dwell upon the uppermost strata of the world in which My pious children live. My Special son, I wish to commend you for your wonderful writing not only for your next book, but also your thoughts and observations that have begun our message this morning. I would like to tender your thoughts to the prospect that touching the core of the 'super-soul' is something that will alleviate all the evils that you have mentioned. The clarity of the meaning of the creation of man and the reason for human existence itself is found in the Holy Gospel, just as you have said, and most specifically in Jesus' Crucifixion on the Cross. Certain people might inquire about the reason for life being the suffering of humanity, and the answer is that this is the way the world is perfectly united with its eternal redemption.

First, therefore, it must be determined what a super-soul is. This is not someone who sails across the oceans at the behest of the most prolific trade winds. Neither is it a person who can fly without having wings. It is not even someone who can see a speck on a wall fifteen miles away. The concept of the super-soul is vested in those who can cast off not only their own failures when trying their best to succeed, but who come back with even more intensity and try again. And, this must be placed in the setting of Jesus' purpose for humanity, the mission of the Church, the ways of goodness and righteousness, and the founding of new avenues to propagate His Kingdom in the world. A super-soul is something that Jesus has named for you and your brother. It is not a term that has been used in this world or in Heaven. My Special one, you and your brother are each a super-soul because you have elevated the meaning of being souls. Remember that I recently told you that you do not have a soul; you 'are' souls. And in this, you have the most perfect identity in Jesus because He comes to gratefully consume you for the Father's appetite, reserving your place in Heaven. Human beings are not conscripted into Heaven because this would imply that they are taken against their will. You and your brother have given the Earth new reason to have hope that ordinary people will become super-souls through the teachings that Jesus professes. This is not a complicated prospect. So, what happens around the globe when this finally becomes the norm? The sediment is shaken up again. The lees and legions of dregs are allowed to see once more what their lives are for. They begin to recalculate what it means to be a human being. It gives them venue to ponder what else might be 'super' in their midst. Could it be true that there are such things as super Saints? The answer is yes, of course. Is there such thing as super grace? Super love? Super forgiveness? The responses are affirmative in all these cases. And, this is not meant to elevate everything to a 'super' status and devalue the meaning of the term the same way that the world is beginning to call everyone heroes. The reason why is because becoming 'super' involves the excavation of the sediment again. This is a spiritual manifestation, not a figurative one.

Touching the heart of the super-soul means living the spiritual dynamics that connect the actions of mortal men with their immortal station in Heaven. It is prayer with purpose, speech with relevance, engagement with integrity, and interaction with kindness. Indeed, you spoke in your opening writing today about people who defy the call of the Gospel for peace and good will. This, after all, is partly what caused the wreck that has yet to come to rest. If it can be made analogous to an automobile, it is still tossing through the air after becoming upended by the devil, and not yet landed solidly in place. No one knows better than you how this feels – it is simultaneously quick, but the rolling motion seems to take forever to end. (*Our Holy Mother refers to the seeming slowing-down of time during an accident. I was a passenger in a car during my youth which left the road and experienced a multiple roll-over crash on a trip returning from Canada. By the grace of God, neither my friend nor I was seriously hurt in the accident. In preparation for our travels, I had taken along a heavy metal toolbox filled with tools in case we experienced mechanical trouble along the way. On the night we left Canada to return home, while sitting in the driveway with the car running, my friend got out of the car to check the cabin door one last time. I was in the back seat ready to take a nap when I was inspired to say a prayer to my guardian angel to see us home safely. At that moment, I had a very powerful sense to move the heavy metal toolbox from the backseat floorboard to the trunk of the vehicle. If that toolbox had not been relocated from the backseat, I would have been seriously injured or killed in the accident as it would have flown around inside the vehicle as it rolled.*) There is a sense of disorientation and the feeling of helplessness as well. The purpose of My using this metaphor is to relate the fact that most people on Earth do not even realize that a wreck has happened. They seem unaware that their fate rests in the clutches of whatever external forces choose to affect their condition of unknown danger. It is somewhat like having to tell someone that they are standing in the very spot where a ten ton boulder is about to fall. How can humanity be this blind? This is the question that God has asked for centuries. What other signs are needed? What else must He do to awaken the paralyzed consciences of the lost? Well, My Special son, He found the answer in you and the Church. Yes, once the wreck of this world comes to rest, everyone alive will know that they have impacted the surface of the other side of time. Hence, your writing today is well taken and utterly visionary. And, I know that you do not dwell on all the negative and counterproductive aspects of human life that you have cited in your writing this morning. However, it would be imprudent and even erroneous to pretend that they are not even there. In all our messages and your personal writings throughout the years, we have cited the shortcomings and wrongdoings of exiled mortal men not simply to manifest more shame, but to guide them away from the actions and habits that keep their callousness going. Yes, it is true that the ages have the capacity to speak. Once the final life is claimed by the wreck about which you have written, the decades and epochs will have plenty to say, testifying at the inquest of humanity's death about the wasted opportunities and unused time frames during which the world of men could have made peace instead of war. If the world believes that time is not their friend, they have not seen anything yet.

My Special son, Jesus can mute the ages in the same way that He once calmed the seas. He can judge for Himself that those who have accepted His Holy Sacrifice need not stand trial for what they have done. This is the testimony that will be most beneficial to Christians. The generations will come forward and attest that they saw absolutely nothing that would infer any wrongdoing by those who have been bathed in the Blood of the Lamb. They will be unable to say anything indicting because they will not even know it. Yes, Jesus' Blood on the Cross not only saves souls, it expunges any record of the sins of those who believe. It eliminates any ability of life or Nature to know that humanity once had a corruptible frame. The Moon and stars, when prompted by the Messiah to speak, will testify that they did not see anything either. My Special son, this is the true meaning of the Heavenly Court that the world must come to know. It is more than the Angels and Communion of Saints. It is about the judgment of exiled men once they have passed into the presence of God. This is the venue that suffices your statement that there will someday be a dynamic moment of cataclysmic revelation. This is where the Gavel of Truth will impact the very essence of the human identity, and the remainder of time will take care of itself. What is this time? It is when each person decides for themselves whether they are worthy of the Divine Mercy of the King. All of our conversation here together, My Special son, is contingent on the prayers of good men from now until the end of the world. The Judgment will still arrive – there will never be any question about that. What humanity's prayers will do will have a bearing on what the proceedings look like when this cataclysm unfolds. So, you see that there is a building up of the Church and the Mystical Body of Christ since Jesus first put this holy framework into place. There are comers and goers, believers and naysayers, those who will ultimately embrace the Cross, and those who will reject it. There are high-flying intentions and bottom-feeding devilish works. And yes, there is sediment, lees and dregs that must be upended to decide for themselves where they wish to spend the eternity of the soul. This is My message today, My Special son. I pray that you have enjoyed it. *"Yes, thank you."* Please remember that you and your brother are so highly beloved and admired by Jesus that you have no way to comprehend it. Someday, you will."

Saturday, February 13, 2016
8:54 a.m.

"The Lord's compassion theory, worthy of hope – the stately, salutatory, unique, sublime, majestic utterances of exalted eloquence. This is construing the correct meaning from the appropriate symbols."

- The Dominion Angels

"My dear little sons, in the recipe to extinguish the movement against My role in the redemption of humanity, God plans to insert a full measure of saber steel into the gut of the perpetrators. And, this is all I need to say about that. Good morning! I come with the fullest joy today because we are praying for the conversion of lost sinners, and the Father and Lord Jesus will respond. Yes, the Dominion Angels have an enviable purview from which to witness not only the orations of Jesus, but to hear them even as they are being pondered in His mind. The worthiness of hope means that there is a future in something, an auspicious future, one that prescribes for the nations what courses to follow. If there is any accompaniment to beauty, power and innocence, it must surely consist of all things pure, majestic, stately, salutatory and eloquent. I have arrived here to tell you today that one's innocence speaks volumes about these strains – so much so that a new identity comes to those who accept these gifts from the Holy Spirit. The Angels hear this sublimeness and uniqueness because they are wholly united with God in Heaven and on Earth. This, My Special child, is the reason I have come into the world to strike a new accord between humanity and the blessings of redemptive suffering. This is not about suffering solely for the sake of pain, but suffering that brings enlightenment and expels poison from the veins of the human soul. The Angels have also said that there must be present the appropriate symbols that yield the correct meaning. I once invited them to show you something like this – 'Watt due ewe sea?' This is a phenomenon where you can deduce the correct meaning from inappropriate symbols. One would think that this would suffice for God, that it would be acceptable to procure the meaning of human sacrifice as long as the context is there. What is your opinion about this? *"It's still not a unified, pure vision."* Yes, and this is a premier example of why the Protestant Church is not in communion with the fullest truth of Christianity. They might pronounce the words, 'Watt due ewe sea' all day long, but they are only mouthing the strains without the underlying legitimacy in 'What do you see?' Do you understand how this is true? *"Yes."* I will stop short of saying that Protestant sects teach heresy, but they are telling humankind to shinny up a rope to reach the halls of Heaven, while the Catholic Church is saying that humanity should use the grand staircase. Here, I have not come to criticize the people who are living holy lives outside the Sacraments of the Catholic Church. This is not My purpose at all. But, any faith that summons the elimination of the Mother of God from the Salvation story is bidding for the devil.

I am humanity's strongest advocate in defeating the forces of evil. This is what the Catholic Church has always taught because it is the majestic truth. The Angels will collect themselves at the feet of no other woman. I am not saying that I have power that is not of God, but rather, I have influence with Jesus that belongs to no one else. I beseech you to believe, My Special son, that I am not boasting this morning. *"I understand."* This, therefore, lends to the discussion about what the Angels have identified as Jesus' compassion theory. It is cited already in the field of psychological medicine as a means of healing others by eradicating their feelings of self-deficiency. It is a process of building one's self-esteem by valuing the attributes of someone's individuality. In the case of Jesus Christ, however, it is to highlight and celebrate the approach that God has taken toward those who believe in Him for eternity's sake. This does not imply that Christ Jesus does not have compassion for the wicked, but that His compassion is tempered by the Father's desire for justice. Jesus has little tolerance for those who know who He is, but who conduct themselves in ways contrary to this knowledge. Millions upon millions of wicked people throughout the ages have been converted into worthy Christian Saints. I have made clear, and you have understood, that there is a difference between these two poles. The key element to this discussion is that all beauty, power, innocence, majesty, eloquence and so forth depend on someone's connection to and unity within the righteousness of God. The fullness of Heaven can be deposited within the parameters of the human heart in the same way that the whole universe could be placed on the head of a pin. It is a matter of dimension. After all, what does size matter to the spiritual dynamics of Heaven? What spacial elements could possibly be relevant to the limitless origins of Salvation? My Special son, I have broached this topic this morning with reference to the Dominion Angels' quotation as a means of explaining how you and your brother have found yourselves uniquely imbedded in the

Sacred Heart of Jesus. It is as though you are a butterfly in a cocoon that will take flight among the flowerbeds of Paradise sooner than you know. Images such as the one I just used come easily to those who are open to the prophesies, products and vestiges of the meaning and purpose of Jesus' Birth, Life, Death and Resurrection in the exiled world.

I pray that My children will all come to the same conclusion as the one I just made in My previous statement. If someone wants healing, they need to understand the reason they have fallen ill. If it is too dark inside someone's mind, they should begin to think about what conclusions they will draw once their thoughts are filled with light. In other words, being healed and enlightened are not ends in themselves, but the means to advancing to their destiny in God who first gave them the ability to envision and imagine. Hence, back to the first part of My message this morning, all symbolism and compassion, every form of salutatory eloquence, the smallest inklings of stateliness and exaltation must arise from one's understanding of the Glory of God. It is from this Glory that all goodness grows. If someone speaks in passing about the Crucifixion of Jesus without himself being willing to suffer in Jesus' likeness, then this is a simple remark from a man using hollow speech. Does this make sense? "*Yes.*" This is why someone can plagiarize the suffering of other people without having true empathy for what they have endured. It is not possible for a person to say that they have participated in the struggles of humanity unless they have undergone suffering too. The whole Body of Christ Jesus was crucified on Good Friday. If someone wants to speak with truth and eloquence, they will have learned these things through their own suffering the same way that you and your brother have learned. They will have spoken the truth about the Kingdom of God from having experienced the suffering that brings His Kingdom into being here in the exiled realms. I can attest that you and your brother have more than suffered for the good of this cause! "*Thank you, Mamma, and especially Timmy.*" This is an assertion that cannot be reversed. You have gained your honors, stripes, medals and badges from the City of Light to which you have given your lives. Even more than this, you have become the statesmen for the everlasting ages in the themes and rituals of Messianic Truth. You have esteemed yourselves in ways that only few men have been able to achieve. And, if there is any eloquence to be found in this world; if there is any stature, poise or stateliness; if there is any unification with the compassion theory that Jesus has professed, then they have found their home in you. This is as it should be.

My Special son, all holy principles can be deduced from the lives of people like you and your brother. Looking at who you are, seeing the fruits of love that you have espoused for the Church, giving your assets of faith and obedience to Jesus on the Cross – these are the evidence that provide for the world a renewed comprehension about whom they must become. Art and poetry are fine, as far as they may go, but your sacred personhood inside the Sacred Heart of Jesus is the final potential for which the entire world of men should aspire. I find eloquence sometimes by just looking at a flower. I have never once been stung by a bee! I oftentimes weep tears of joy when I see someone speaking in casual terms to strangers on the street – telling an elderly woman that she looks pretty today, or thanking a grandfather for giving his life to his family. There is more to be grateful for in the lives of men than there are reasons to regret. This is because of the beauty and innocence to which most people subscribe in their daily affairs, not centering their thoughts on what they can progressively steal or who they perceive the next victim of secular insolence might be. We have in our hands the key to the success of the completed human life. It is the Cross of Jesus Christ that opens His Most Sacred Heart to all who wish to come in. Let us look at the Dominion Angels' passage one more time today. Of all the words you just heard again, the most appropriate is 'hope.' Hope for the lost, hope for the Church, hope for peace, and hope for the destiny of the human spirit. All prayer is based on hope! I concede that I am not the most eloquent speaker that you will ever hear, My Special son, but I am a good listener to those who are. When I was assumed into Heaven, I was lacking in many of these themes until I reached the Father's side. It was there, My Special son, that I was gifted with the knowledge that you would someday be there with Me, that you would follow centuries later with your goodness and fineness in hand. I was overjoyed that I was reunited with Jesus in the High Kingdom of Supernal Love, but I was even more grateful that My having departed the exiled realms left so many Christians to act in My stead. I hope you have enjoyed My message today. *"Yes, very much, thank you."*

Saturday, February 20, 2016
9:03 a.m.

"Faith is about spark, energy, spiritual confluence, the spice of time and resilient trust, livelihood and flourishing wonder, melodrama, and the parting of the night at dawn. Beyond all these things – outside the bounds of human foresight, all guidance is indeed internal."

- The Dominion Angels

"Beauty springs forth from your lovely souls, My dear little sons, and the mission of the Church is strengthened by your prayers. I nurture you within My Immaculate Heart, and invite you into the Sacred Heart of Jesus who is likewise embraced there. The commonness of your relationship with Him is not very common at all – it is your extraordinary gift to which you have lent yourselves through the faith that the Dominion Angels celebrate in their opening remarks today. One would not think that livelihood and melodrama would be portions of the blessings of faith in the heart of the human person. The Angels are not speaking about livelihood in the sense of making money or spending it, but about the sustenance that you find through your faith, the nourishment that you receive through the Holy Spirit, and the Sacraments that prevail against the pressures of mortal life. And, the Dominions are not speaking about melodrama in counterintuitive emotional terms, but in a way that allows the world to see the deep spiritual romance that is imbedded in, and that flows from, the center of Jesus' Most Sacred Heart. It is the same as saying that something is 'awash' in something else. This has always had a negative secular connotation, but to be awash in grace and peace bears no adverse consequences. My message here this morning is not only to reecho the sentiments of the Angels, but to make clear that the manifestation of faith in human terms must move beyond the trials and tribulations of the physical realms, and be internalized from within. Yes, much the same way that the guidance of the spacecraft that you so admired became internal. It is the Father's way of saying that He has taught humanity through His Only Begotten Son what must be known in order to find one's way back to Him, and He thereafter says, '...Now, it is your turn. Walk to Me. Come to Me. Find your way through the darkness by the Divine Light that I have deposited in your hearts.' The guidance of the Holy Spirit is internal because everything else is external. And, while I will not attempt to replicate the pretty strains of the Dominion Angels, this is the reason you find such spark, energy and resilient trust in your faith. It is all spiritually bankrolled by God in Heaven. Jesus paid the price not only that you would be saved, but that in this Salvation, you would have the gift of faith to make your way to the fullness of belief. My Special son, we have spoken about the distractions that impede the journey of My children to the Cross, and this is why God chooses to bring the Cross to them. This is why there is suffering among you. There would be no suffering on Earth if the people were already aglow in the righteousness that Jesus was born to teach, and that He died to defend.

Jesus looks upon His Mystical Body the same way that mere mortals might observe an awe-striking vision. It could be a sight of tremendous glory that humanity may not see that way at all. For example, when you are writing your memoirs and receiving the Wisdom that He brings, it is as though God is nourishing the valor of the great Secretariat before his next run. And, He then watches you live here in this world with the same constructive emotion that you so profoundly experienced on June 9, 1973. Yes, this is what Jesus feels every time someone performs good deeds of faith and promise in His sacred name. There was only one Secretariat in the animal kingdom, but there have been millions of them in the human domain. Each of these souls touches Jesus differently. Just as no two people look alike or carry the same DNA, every Christian touches Jesus' Sacred Heart in a different way. Some seem larger than life to Him, while others somehow touch Him as the simplest little children. All are equally worthy in His sight. This is the way you and your brother have touched Him – and in both senses. You have attained for yourselves already in advance the title of Doctors of the Church, but you have also remained like little children playing with your dump trucks in a sandbox behind your house. The point I am making this morning is that you have found your dignity in Jesus from your identities as the great Secretariat to the likeness of Jesus in the manger of Bethlehem. And, this brings Me to the matter of spiritual confluence that the Angels mentioned today. It is the flowing together of all spirits into the bay of everlasting life. I spoke about this in one of your first thirty messages in 1991. This again refers to the way that Jesus views converted humanity as His Mystical Body. It is all one spiritual bloodline and bloodstream of holiness in Him, made manifest by His Sacrifice on the Cross. The Cross absolves all humanity of sin, and His Easter Resurrection has re-instituted humanity's right to live. This is the restoration that will never again give way to time or the elements of the material world. No friction can ever wear it down, and no motion can push it aside. Spiritual confluence. Just as human beings have arms and legs that look almost the same, they also have the capacity and opportunity to join in the one glorious spirit of humanity-redeemed in the heights of Paradise. There are no exceptions – even those born in exile without limbs and mobility have the same fullness and completeness of spiritual freedom as all the rest.

So, what does Jesus envision and actually see when He looks upon His faithful Church? It is an adoration to mirror that of the Church that looks so reverently back at Him. He turns to His faith-disciples for comfort when it is so obvious that His sacredness is being impugned by the world. He looks into the eyes of people like you and your brother, His friends and comforters, who pray for peace and healing in lands afar and near. Jesus has wept more tears for His Creation in the past 2,000 years than all the earthly oceans could possibly hold. These are tears not just of sorrow, but of gladness as well – just as I said about yourself seeing the great Secretariat running like a tremendous machine. I once told you and your brother that you have the right to decide how this story will end. Do you remember? *"Yes."* This is the reason that Jesus has hope. He does not yet know the hour upon which He will return, and it is in this same vein that He anticipates the heroism of those in whose faith He has deposited His Spirit. What I am saying is that the Church has the power to help in shaping the designs of the final ages of the Earth. It would not be living otherwise. It would be only a museum containing the vestiges and relics of the way things used to be. This living Spirit of God is not only ordaining and absolving, but delegating in the movement of His Will through the nations. He commissions to His apostles and disciples certain tasks that keep flourishing the wonders about which the Angels have spoken. This is also the reason why the Church, in all its statesmanship, will always be you. It has the sleekness of the sky-born mountains and the depth of the deepest seas. By all means, when you consider the ages of the Earth and the millennia that have passed, a 2,000 year old Church is young by contrast. This is the youth in which you find yourselves, My Special son. It is yours to take with you, even should you live another forty years. This breath of livelihood is for the inhaling by all who believe that there is more rejuvenation in being born again in Jesus than beginning one's life all over again. This is the spiritual essence of the meaning of being renewed. It will eventually come to everyone whose soul is allowed to fly freely in the Kingdom of Heaven once their earthly journey is done. It is the greatest 'welcome home' that could ever be imagined, and I will someday say it directly to you.

The whole idea of mankind looking up to Heaven and Jesus looking down on the world is rightly poised, but it is not completely accurate. Christ Jesus is here and united with you now, and you find Him by reaching your own inner-self. Heaven is not a spatial distance from you, as I have always said.

I am in Heaven and on Earth right now. All the souls who have entered Heaven are with us too. You just cannot see them. You are as close to them now as if you were launched aloft in any spaceship or atop any rocket. Why? Because when it comes to reaching for the domain of Glorious Love here in your time and in this place, the guidance you need is indeed internal. You are going there now. The prospect of Heaven being somewhere beyond the vaults of the skies is indeed accurate because the Father wants the world to imagine where Jesus was ascended, and where I was assumed. It is a metaphysical concept that keeps humanity's focus on the upward path of the heart to the divine, and away from the flaming dungeon of Hell. While being in Purgatory is more a condition than a place, living in Heaven is more of an infinite liberation than a measurable one. There is no need for a prescription if someone is not in need of medicine. This is the way of looking at it. I am not prescribing anything that humanity might require to remain alive here in this world, I am sharing with you the reason why staying alive in the material realms bears less consequence than what happens to the soul after someone passes away. The only medicine that humanity needs is Jesus' Blood on the Cross, the only antidote to the sentence of death. With great love does the Father make this known! My Special son, I pray as you pray. I see that your earthly father is advanced in years. He will soon realize that he became the biological father of one of the greatest Saints of the Church. It is not the Lord's intent that your father should suffer greatly before he shall inherit his heavenly reward, but I must tell you now that he has asked to join Jesus on the Cross through as much as he can possibly bear. This too is the signature of the greatest Saints. I am asked to bring the good wishes and intercessory prayers of your grandfather to remind you that your life here with your brother is rightly on track, and all the Saints are praying for your success."

Saturday, February 27, 2016
9:26 a.m.

"The United States of America has always been the brightest star, the best hope, and the most prolific symphony the nations have ever heard. This is what the world should never forget. Its ideals are not something to be taken for granted or shuffled behind a cloud. America should never be ashamed of its panoramic shores or refrain from revealing its own emotions. No country should shy away from its capability for filling the voids and cavities left when other societies, regions and republics refuse to hold fast to love. The United States of America should never be

reluctant to boast of its vast humanitarian gifts or hide from history, posterity or eternity its colossal strides toward the advancement of good will and world peace. Neither should it cringe from the extraordinary challenges still to come. As My children, I have asked you to be people; be holy people, good people. Therefore, do not fear to take your case for freedom into the world. Do not be too modest to expound upon your eternal inheritance in Jesus on the Cross. Indeed – be vigilant people. Be true and honest creatures. Never hide your smile from the glistening seas or shed your tears beneath a waterfall, hoping no one will notice. Your nation is about all things proficient, unique and consequential – the most vibrant the Earth has ever known. And it is I, your Patroness Saint and Queen Mother, who has ensured that the United States, the undaunted states of America, has been duly blessed by God. The Father in Heaven admires your courage. He loves your sprawling lands. He sees in living color your long held hopes and dreams. It is imbedded in the bravery of your heroes and the music of your prayers."

        Mary of Bethlehem, Mother of Jesus Christ
        25th Anniversary - The Morning Star Over America
        February 22, 2016

"My dear little children, there has never been a moment when pronouncing your names did not make Me smile. The Lord not only hears your prayers, He gratefully receives them as though He requires them for survival. We know that this is not so, but it is what God wants you to believe – just as believing in Jesus on the Cross has wrapped your souls in eternal redemption. I have come today to pray with you because you have invited Me here; you have asked this of Me. I have called you angels and darlings because you have acquired the dignity of the Saints already here in this world. My Special son, the greatest use of dynamic power is to set conditions so that it may never have to be exerted. This is the peace through strength premise that so many benevolent leaders have espoused. This is what the United States of America has always practiced. I am the Queen of Peace and Queen of Love, and this means that I hold reign over your country in the themes of holiness. As you know, I have come speaking to you and your brother to reshape the hearts and thoughts of your American brothers and sisters to be worthy of My blessing. It is in asking Jesus to wholly embrace the human person that My mission is made complete.

Today, I wish to tell you that even as Jesus the Messiah is the Man-God on the Cross, He is also your friend on the playgrounds of the world. He is the Child in My arms and the adolescent boy with whom you can chum from street corner to neighborhood. The Child Prodigy is the Savior of the World. It is in this youthful tenderness that Jesus comes calling upon those who require their own return to tenderness, their reunion with the innocence of Heaven that is trying to come in. This is the fullness of the heart that the Bible teaches, and it is in this fullness that humanity is again made whole. It is, therefore, possible that a man of 70 or 80 years can come calling on this young Messiah for wisdom that he could never have learned on his own. Genius and mobility in the tenets of God's righteousness come not from a stale or stagnant perception of the Holy Scriptures, as though they are somehow locked in time, but to see them as a rolling revelation of Divine Truth. Just as Jesus was raised from the dead on Easter morning, the consciences of men can be likewise resurrected from their death in the wreck of this world. I have told you on many occasions that the innocence of Jesus while hanging on the Cross was the most stark contradiction that the Earth will ever know. The most innocent Man alive was put to the most grotesque suffering and death that was meted out in His time. There have been countless people who have asked why it occurred twenty centuries ago. Why did the Father choose that particular century in linear time to effect this mode of human Salvation as opposed to another? The answer is not complicated. It was to ensure that exiled humanity could never misconstrue what really happened. It was because those who followed Him could be solely focused on His life and teachings. The redemption of humanity was manifested in a land of aridity and sand so the contrast of life and fruitfulness could be more clearly made. Indeed, what would be the need for faith if someone could capture on film the very absolution of a world in which films are routinely employed for so many illicit purposes? By all means, the Sacrifice of Jesus on the Cross has become an image on which only the human heart can focus. And, My Special son, it is this same impression that strengthens humanity's faith to believe in the deific miracle of the Cross. Within the spiritual heart, the Crucifixion is exempted from human manipulation, and protected from scandal. All of this must be remembered by those who refuse to believe. It is the same principle by which Pope Francis took the name he did. If you look at your electronic internet, there are people around the globe who have added names to would-be future papacies, and attributed to them scandalous events to mar and impugn the Roman Catholic Church. This is outright, unmitigated evil.

My Special son, this is another reason why I have caressed you and your brother within My Most Immaculate Heart. I desire to protect you from the battles that would have ensued. Life in exile is difficult enough without your having to thus far endure the ravages of slander and abuse. You have for the most part been spared these things because you have been harbored within My Immaculate Heart and here inside your home. It is in this same vein that Christ Jesus offers you the tenderness that I mentioned moments ago. All the power available in the universe has come consoling you. All the witness that the Father has to offer is present in this humble Man on the Cross. It is in Jesus that you have become conquerors; it is in the vastness of His glory that you have seated your souls. Imagine, My Special one, how it makes Me feel every time another child comes calling on Me. It is like a new candle being lit in the darkness of the world. And, this is important because Christians such as you and your brother provide the light by which others can find their way to Me. You are aglow with the love and truth that Jesus has deposited within you. This is not something that you can readily see with your eyes, but it is happening nonetheless. If you were to imagine the purpose of night-vision goggles, you would see what I am trying to say. Instead of heat being the reason others can see, it is the unbridled intensity of your love and devotion to God. It is your determination to succeed in Him, to be unified through Him, and to move along with the ever-extolling revelations of peace and virtue that are quietly reshaping the consciousness of men. It is the feeling of soft massage as well as the coarser facts of faith. So, when you feel a sense of peace coming over you when you pray, or when you stop and take a breath, or when you suddenly sense a flash of light, this is Jesus touching you where you live, as you live, with His kind and supple piety. He says through the touch of your heart from the eternal flame of His love that you belong to Him, that you are fighting the good fight to which Saint Paul rightly referred. This is the sensation of power from On High, telling you here in this life that you are worthy of everything promised by Jesus on the Cross.

When we speak about the Holy of Holies, the Great High Priest, and all the implications that this means for the exiled world, everyone should remember the simplicities too. Jesus was born a Child in My arms, and He was every ounce the Perfect King at that moment as He was on the Cross, and on the day He was ascended into Heaven. There was no such time of revelation to Him that comes to those who eventually believe in Him. He was aware from the moment He was conceived in My Womb that He was the Savior of condemned humanity. My Special son, I am telling you today that Christ Jesus knew that He was alive in My Womb. This is not something that could be easily grasped by theologians or philosophers who study the inflections of the human body. But, it is just as natural as the child you spoke about last night causing the mother's milk to be transformed to more fully ensure the health of the child. Do you understand the metaphor I just spoke? *"Yes. Does this mean that we didn't have that awareness in our mothers' wombs? Or, we just don't remember it?"* The answer rests in the state of the human soul at conception. What was the difference between Jesus and everyone else? *"We were born in sin."* Yes, this is your answer. *"So, Jesus didn't have the veil when He was conceived in your womb."* You are correct; there was never a moment when Jesus did not have access to the veil, and there were times when He chose not to look through it. *"I understand."* My Special son, I have told you things today that theologians could have only hoped to know. It has been pondered down through the centuries, but those who thought about it could not come to a conclusion. *"And, also Adam and Eve could see through the veil before they sinned?"* There was no veil when Adam and Eve were conceived. I ask you to remember that Jesus willingly shed His supernatural form to become as human as any other man, except sin. He had complete control of His faculties to do anything He wished, including striking down in death anyone who ever taunted, mocked, persecuted or lashed out at Him. This is the same power about which I spoke at the beginning of My message today. It is a sacred power that spawns from piety and innocence, and this power is transferred to any person on Earth who attains the likeness of Jesus in this life. There are souls who hold Heaven within them now; this is the reason you are capable of praying with such authenticity as Jesus. It is the reason you can write with the proficiency of the Saints. This is your share of glory that you are offering your brothers and sisters every day. You are asked to bear the same humanness that Jesus endured. I am so pleased that you enjoyed My message about the United States of America for your 25th anniversary year. It is something that you can publish in your next book, if you wish. I will love you always; it will never have an ending."

Saturday, March 5, 2016
9:26 a.m.

"Humanity's love response – Yes Lord, I too am music. To sing sweetly is to race toward the Crucifixion in melodious swarms, smiling smartly to the gusty winds, ringing in faith's luxurious poverty, marching down the world's sacrificial swaths, drowning in Heaven's pluvial truth, chanting the recessionals of the quieted Earth. The heart is the composer's finest piece! And, love is his crowning rendition. Men must disavow their insolent gall. So, swing wide open the windows of song, and never mind the shattered glass!"

- The Dominion Angels

"My dearly beloved children, today is the 25th anniversary of your kind and wonderful presence in Ashland where I gifted you with another miracle of faith. I mention this today because it also was a time when My Chosen one began weeping, saying that no one would believe what he was seeing. You, My Special one, are the Saint who believed! It is from that moment that the days, months and years have ensued, and you both now know the reason for all the highlights and low times that would follow. I come to you in tremendous joy again this morning, and I offer you the words of the Dominion Angels as My poem for the day. It is reminiscent of many earlier times when the Angels have brought to you visions and signs of the remaking of the Earth. As I told you on another occasion, humanity needs to convert so the Earth can be cleansed. Indeed, never mind the shattered glass. This does not mean that one should stomp with heavy feet around the globe, and slash and burn whatever stands in his path. It means that there is such resonate melodious righteousness that the glass shatters as if from a high-pitch note. There are many extremes that we have addressed during our time together; we have contrasted the light and the darkness, the good and the evil, and the ample and the scarce. We have spoken about the proverbial lackings and excesses because humanity rests between the two on any given day. I desire My children to learn that human life begins when they reach the end of their natural comfortableness. It is not that My children must always suffer; that pain, torment and agony are endemic to your lives in the Holy Cross. What I am saying is that you must be gathered in the potential of suffering; you must be willing to act when the Father prompts you to respond. Just as the Angels have said, you must voice your compliance to His call, and give of yourselves in ways that eradicate the pain of the innocent. Notice that I have not said that you must ease the pain of the guilty because they will soon know why it came. When Jesus said that His disciples should take up their crosses and follow Him, He did not mean that they were to be taken someplace else and laid down. My Special son, the record of your days has proved that Jesus' call was more than metaphorical. The whole world should know this by now, at least those who believe.

On the other hand, I have told you that Jesus is humanity's most unique and powerful comforter in union with Myself. We lovingly care for the souls of humanity and the hearts and spirits to which they belong. I ask all My children to believe in this consolation because they will not seek it if they do not. The whole idea revolves around the matter of consent and refusal. This is another moral contrast that I am drawing today to accompany the binaries of light and darkness, the good and bad, and all the rest. Remember the parable about the vineyard worker who arrived near the end of the day. It was not that he wanted to make himself present at all, but that he overcame his own opposition to finally do what he was asked. This is the way of many Christians today. Even if they do not know why they are asked to behave or perform a certain way, they will discover in doing so their identity in God. They will find the same purpose that Jesus knew He would find in bearing and dying on the Cross. It is not the same joy as having a picnic or winning a valuable prize, but that proves that one has the capacity to eradicate evil from the world or restore the newness that was lost. I must make clear today that Jesus did not have to overcome any of His own opposition to dying on the Cross. But, humanity does, and this is what it means to become perfected in Jesus here in this life. The choices of consent and refusal are inherent in the lives of humanity because of the forces of the human will. Jesus' Will was perfectly aligned with the Father who lived within Him. In other words, there was no such thing as spiritual dissonance in Jesus as He prepared for His Passion and Crucifixion. Jesus hung on the Cross for three hours, and honored the Father that He had been asked to bear it. His whole 'experience' at the hands of His persecutors, prosecutors and executioners was deemed a gift directly from the Heart of God, even by Jesus on the Cross. Why? Because the fate of the world rested in His love. If not for His love, if not for Christ Jesus' overwhelming love for lost sinners and the redemption of souls, there would be no merit in My speaking to you now.

My Special son, I am the Co-Redemptrix of humanity, and I wish for you to remember this. It is something that I have said before. As Co-Redemptrix, I have done many things for which there is no other origin. I can urge you and your brother to move to a choir loft so a priest can prepare for one of his final

Masses. I can cause runners to pass in front of the house to eliminate barking from dogs who would try to interrupt My words (*During Our Lady's opening strains today, my neighbor took her dogs inside her house because they were hysterically barking at passing marathoners.*) I have made plans for the future that will strike this world into shudders, wondering the origin of such miracles and blessings. There is no question that we have for many years done this together; Me as your Mother, and you as My children. It all blossoms from Mary and Jesus the Comforters. I have many titles. I have even been referred to as Our Lady Undoer of Knots. I have told you these things today because I wish to reinforce your strength and hope that we will prevail in our plans – perhaps the grandest and best will be when you and I and your brother have been united in the brilliance of Heaven. The point I am making is that it will happen, and the timing is truly irrelevant in the end. Having said this, My prayer is that it will not take too long. It will occur while you and your brother are here in exile, and the whole world responds with swift feet. This is also the plea of the Dominion Angels who have extolled so profoundly the passage to begin our message today. How could I be Mary the Comforter and not give you hope? Therefore, I have decided to bypass those who refuse to respond, and begin another movement to celebrate My Morning Star messages to the world. It is not that your previous encouragements did not take effect. Your prophetic direction has been subdued by those in the Catholic Church who have long been opposed to My appearances. You know the rest. Your evangelization of My love has done precisely what you have said – each word was a seed that has been planted in your nation. Each is being nourished beneath the spiritual soil, just beyond the sight of the secular void. They will have many more times the effect of the mustard seed mentioned in the Bible. The term 'exponential' is not sufficient to describe their efficacy.

This is a sign of great hope! This means that those in the Church will have to justify casting aside the words of their Immaculate Mother. You know that I would never be resentful, but I am capable of waking someone from their sleep. My Special son, all this is consistent with the Church's treatment of Saint Bernadette of Lourdes, Sister Faustina of the Divine Mercy, Saint Joan of Arc, and the others. You are in pious company here! As has been said, the universe is unfolding as it should. There has always been tremendous vindication of My messengers' lives and actions, and it commonly succeeds previous doubt. Here again, it is about contrasting human emotions – consent and refusal. I ask you to think back to the time of the Annunciation, and the events celebrated in the Joyful Mysteries. I have said that the devil has force, but no power. Did any of the scenes of the Joyful Mysteries undergo the influence of the devil when they occurred? Let us list them here. The Archangel Gabriel called on Me. I visited Saint Elizabeth who was with child. Jesus was born of My Womb. Jesus was presented at the temple. Jesus was found in the temple. There is no evidence that Satan had any influence over these gifts. This can be said of the Glorious Mysteries as well. Hence, you are seeing that Jesus faced the devil alone during the Sorrowful Mysteries. I am saying that humanity should remember that more joy can be found in the events of the Angelic Annunciation to My Crowning as Queen of Heaven and Earth than one might find sadness. Do you agree? *"Yes."* But, without the Passion of it, without the Agony in the Garden, Scourging at the Pillar, Crowning with Thorns, the Carrying of the Cross, and the Crucifixion of Jesus, there would be no joy. Therefore, the Church went from joy to sorrow, and back to joy again. This is the mystery of the Church. And, it is the same for all My messengers. I have come to bring you true joy. The world through the darkness of Satan makes you sad, but the fact that My messages are from God resurrects your happiness.

My Special son, I do not want you and your brother to wait until the whole assembly of humanity embraces My messages for you to be happy. *"I understand. I am happy now. I am happy to play this part and see the things from the perspective that you give me."* Yes, and do you remember saying that it would seem that you and your brother are living in an almost different world from everyone else? *"Yes."* This is the way Jesus lived. It does not mean that you cannot be happy during your preparation for the return of Jesus. I am telling you that you have every reason to believe that joy is yours here and now, with the fullest preservation of your dignity. Jesus is no less the Messianic Savior and King just because He was crucified. His death did not lessen His beatific identity. It did not ratify it either – it is innate to Him as the Second Person of the Trinity. I am saying that you and your brother, and all who believe in Jesus, will discover yourselves inside His Most Sacred Heart, Heaven itself, once the process of human redemption has been extracted from time. Truly, you are leading the life of Jesus, treading the same paths that He sanctioned through His teachings and blessings. His Blood has cleansed humanity of sin. Do you understand? *"Yes. Just as everything that those who diminish us do to us, cleanses them."* Yes, you have precisely repeated what I have said."

Saturday, March 12, 2016
9:28 a.m.

"Love has descended, grace is bestowed, redemption is complete – taut, pliable and decisive to the point of no return. Time will defer to glory once the last day finally dawns. No greater truth will ever be told. The faithless on Earth are fostering their own demise; the Crucifixion of Jesus Christ will never be waived, misspent, revoked, exceeded or undone."

- The Dominion Angels

"My dear little sons, you are overwhelmingly charitable to receive Me here in your home to pray with you and recount the blessings that humanity has received through the Most Sacred Heart of Jesus. You are giving Him a worthy Lent. You are making the most and the best of your lives in Him because His Spirit is living within you. I only ask that My other children imitate what you have done. There are more signs and blessings awaiting them than the airwaves could possibly tell. The Dominion Angels have again spoken to you about the necessity of lost sinners to come to the Cross. Speaking about the Crucifixion in such terms is not a matter that the world should take lightly because it speaks not only of a destination for believers, but a sorrowful fate for those who refuse to have faith. Yes, the Cross is irrevocable; the Crucifixion cannot be undone. God's love for His people is as paramount as Jesus' Sacred Body nailed to the Cross. My children, there is no symbolism in the Sacrifice of Jesus on the Cross. It was not about someone dying because He was branded a blasphemer. No, the death of this Man was the washing away of the sins of even those who killed Him. There are certain things that are absolute on Earth. The most absolute of all things is that Jesus was not taken down from the Cross until after He died. It is by delivering His Spirit to the Father that humanity was saved – and not just spared, but remade in the likeness of the Christ who redeemed them. My Special son, I am not telling you this today because you are unaware. I am telling you as a prayer to the nations, that God the Father will share My words to you and your brother in time and space in transcending ways. This is how prayer works, as you know. It is the same reason I wrapped My arms around humanity from the moment I was declared the Mother of all men on Good Friday. You must realize that Jesus handed Me a world of sinners who were as broken as His body taken down from the Cross. I remain devoted to the healing of My children. I pray that Jesus' Sacrifice will instill in all peoples the desire to build up instead of tear down. If there were ever more than one eternity, the hopes of a million lifetimes would be caught up in them. This is the reason the Angels' words this morning are so poignant.

Grace bestowed and redemption completed are more than implications to those who accept Jesus' Sacrifice on the Cross. These are eternal blessings that cannot pale like the skies or wither like flowers. They are the permanent signs of the eternal redemption of the converted human soul. This Man of God, this Man-God, is the finisher of all faith and the maker of every miracle. He does these things at My behest because, as I said, I recognized the broken nature of humanity from beneath the Cross on which He died. My Special son, I wish to issue a clarification. I have said that even in all its grotesqueness, the Crucifixion of Jesus was the most beautiful sight that any creature could behold. The same is not true of humanity I witnessed on Good Friday. In all their grotesqueness, men in the world were nothing less than ugly. Their souls and lives were ugly – their intentions were ugly as well. Faithless men had more persecuting to do; they had more killing to do, denying the witness of the Apostles, mocking the Gospel for which Jesus died, and dividing men along the lines of profit and death. I know that you have learned about these things during your years on Earth, and it is playing itself out around the world. This, My Special and Chosen ones, is the reason I have asked you to live in the comfort of My Immaculate Heart. If it were possible for Heaven to have measurable bounds, they would be within the succor of My Immaculate Heart. This is where Jesus has taken solace. And, My children, this is where the boundless expanse lives within each of you. It is the spiritual heart that breaks through the bonds of life to prove that the love of the Father is true. Another example is this – the entire Salvation of humanity is inscribed in the pages of the Bible. Eternity is captured between the covers of this Book. This is where prayer and promise intersect. It is the place in Creation where healing and deliverance hold hands. When a man takes up the Sacred Scriptures and promises Jesus that he will live out its meaning, this begins the resurrection of his soul. My Special son, it is all about Jesus' Blood on the Cross. This is the source of wisdom for all Christians. And in this, the pages of the Bible are like rungs on a ladder. They provide an ascension for the human heart to remain on an upward path to Salvation. Accordingly, they are far more than symbolic. The Holy Word is living in Heaven and in the hearts of humanity below, and the Bible is a fount from which thirsty souls find relief from the parching of the world. This is the clarity that must come when people think of one another. Each person who believes in God and lives for Him is a vessel containing His Holy Spirit. I am not saying that Christians should be worshiped themselves, but that the love and faith in their hearts must be treated like fine jewels because Jesus lives there. This is the reason that the hearts of the faithful should never be trod upon or spoken about irreverently. It is to this that My Motherly intercession was given to humanity on Good Friday. Even in all humanity's ugliness, I knew that Jesus would make them new – He would render humanity whole. If there were ever someone who could sense the content of the hearts of exiled men, it is Me. I have the ability to examine the intentions of the people of the world before they ever cast their thoughts into action. I have this ability because I am the Advocate for My children before Jesus in the same way that the Holy Spirit is your Advocate to the Father. There are unique ways that this can be manifested on Earth, and the best is when My children understand that they are not the nucleus of all universal action. I hold My children at the center of My Immaculate Heart who wish to be there. The ones who defy the teachings of the Church, who say that I gave birth to Jesus and have never been heard from since, the ones who spread body waste on My statues and painted relics, are holding themselves out. They refuse to come to the cradling peace of My Most Immaculate Love. I pity them when they do not allow Me to wrap My arms around their souls, but I do not embrace those who blaspheme the Sacrifice of Jesus on the Cross.

My Special son, I became the Mother of all the redeemed on Good Friday. Those who deny the life and Sacrifice of Jesus, the ones who refuse to believe in God, the people whose evil has already consumed them, will be orphans for the remainder of their days. I am saying that I am like the father waiting for his prodigal son. I have children who have yet to come home, the ones given to Me by Jesus on the Cross. Those who never arrive in the gentleness of My Motherly caress are failing to do so because they turned away from Me on the day Jesus died. And, they would be born centuries hence from Jesus' Holy Sacrifice. This is what I have told you about the peril of the human will. Jesus is the best friend of the faithful, but His Holy Sacrifice is the quandary for those who refuse to believe. And, this solicits a question from the beginning. Why would God give life to those whom He knew would enter Hell? The answer is that He never gave up on their ability to prove Him wrong. This is the reason we are believers in a living, sanctifying, viable, mind-changing God of the Old Testament and the New. Even in all His Divine Providence and Wisdom, God concealed from His own prescience the identities of those whom Jesus would save. Yes – the Father set in motion a surprise to Himself. There is nothing that the Father does not know – except those things that He chooses not to know. My Special son, you can wonder what a gift God has given Himself. The element of surprise; and this is the trust, power and providence that He has commissioned in Jesus. He vested His

Son with the ability to return to Him, to sit at His Right Hand, and never reveal whom His Blood has cleansed. This is the framing of two secrets. The Father has not yet revealed to Jesus when He will be sent back to Earth, and Jesus has not told the Father who will be coming home. I assure you, My Special son, that they will both be tenderly pleased. As for the timing of this? A great deal is depending on the Divine Mercy of Jesus. The Father has not yet sensed futility in allowing time to go on. There are conversions and life-altering events that Jesus wishes to fill the void between the life and death of exiled men. I have completed My message today. I am thankful to you and your brother for remaining steadfast in your prayers for the conversion of the lost. And, bless you for hearing of the infinite wisdom of God. I will speak to you again under the intercession of the great Saint Joseph."

Saturday, March 19, 2016
Feast of Saint Joseph, Husband of Mary
9:37 a.m.

"It is a question of reciprocal faith – should God believe in man? Yes, Jesus is the judge, but not the radical kind, not an outlier from the common good, not some unyielding avenger unequivocally bent on deathly justice, and certainly not a liquidator or wholesaler of discarded human souls. Jesus Christ is a Man of peace; there is really no need for arsenals, warships or time bombs anymore, no marketplace for flames, whipping posts and arrows, no venue for scathing vitriol or unchecked malice."

- The Dominion Angels

"The vernal and autumnal elements of redemptive prayer."

"My precious little children, I have come on this day to pray with you again – for this is what we do together to bring humanity to the foot of the Cross. I am pleased that the Dominion Angels, My Angels for sure, have brought you such profound words about Jesus' absolving Sacrifice. I will tell you today about the vernal elements of redemptive prayer because, just before midnight this evening, the season of spring will come. I will further speak about the autumnal elements of redemptive prayer because, as I have said, the world is in its autumn of life. I am saying that the spring of humanity's days have come in the promises that Jesus has made, and the autumn of life is here because the world is being folded in. My Special son, there is a difference between 'being' and 'doing,' but it need not be this way. A telegraph is an instrument, and a biograph is a document. There is rarely a time when the term biograph is used because it is usually supplanted by the term 'biography.' There is no such thing as telegraphy in the sense that one can hold it in his hand. There must be 'doing' in order for telegraphy to exist. This, therefore, forces the question that one must be living in order to bring being to his biograph. Do you understand? *"Yes."* If someone could measure his life using certain tools, he would likely use a biograph to do it. My point is to suggest that men can live without really having life. We know that the former is a manner of existence, and the latter is a person's unity with spiritual truth. Hence, in order for someone to accumulate a discernible record that can be transferred to Jesus, it must come from the life of spirituality based on its legitimacy in Him. There is nothing about the human person that matters if not vested in what their life means to Jesus. I told you in 1991 that Jesus is all the seasons of the climate of God. My message today expands this premise, as spring has arrived twenty-five years later.

I would be remiss in beginning if I did not relate to you the kind wishes and blessings of Saint Joseph, the Great Saint and stepfather of Jesus the Martyr. *"Thank you."* It is through his intercession that so many of your blessings have come – his name above the doorway of this prayer room is one of your greatest petitions to him. I speak about the vernal and autumnal elements of redemptive prayer in the sense that the world is changing; it was always meant to change. Therefore, the Father through Jesus and Myself summons prayers from the Church and all its lay people to seek from Him the intercessory graces that will make humanity more holy, and to end famine and wars. As I have said, spiritual springtime prayers requisition the recognition by the world that the Afterlife is coming to those who believe in Jesus' Crucifixion and accept His Blood on the Cross. These include the prayers for the Poor Souls in Purgatory. It is all about the imminent spring, the new growth and enlightenment, the invigoration of the Afterlife that appears once the dark, cold burdens of worldliness have been shed and gone. It is a time for seeding in one another a hope that flows from eternity itself, that becomes united with the Final Enlightenment that comes upon one's passage into Heaven. It is good and right that one should enlist the assistance of Jesus through these kinds of prayers. However, the world inside of time as you know it, as all humanity has known it, is nearing its final years. This means that the judgment of the Man-God is nearer than ever before. It is different from the Final Enlightenment because there are consequences and results that must still be faced. I can see by your thoughts that you know what I am saying. There is obedience required during one's earthly life that affects their judgment during the autumnal event. There are no such consequences in Heaven because judgment has been sufficed. I have broached this subject because vernal prayer involves someone's hopefulness beyond time, and autumnal prayers are related to the world as it must change. Do you understand? *"Yes, I understand."* While I do not wish My children to stop hoping, I have always desired that humanity take up prayerful lives so the autumn of the Earth is beautiful, precisely the way you see the autumn here in Illinois. I am saying that My messages to the world through the centuries have been reparative and converting, focused on the cleansing of the Earth before the end of time. I am not saying that I have never focused on the springtime or the Afterlife, but there are issues that must be addressed in the immediacy of the exiled human state.

When you look at My messages, and the Gospel, through the prism of this truth, you will see that Jesus' teachings are related to the sequence of human events first, and judgment second. This stands to reason. The constructional, redemptive elements of human prayer must always intertwine with the perfecting of the heart and soul, which in itself is a springtime prayer of final resurrection. You and your brother have struck a balance that is lent in favor of autumnal reparative prayer from which Jesus has sought from His disciples for 2,000 years. The world and the Earth have been in their fall season since Jesus was ascended into Heaven. I am praying that My children will recognize this passing of time, that the days and years are expiring not to never be renewed again, but to be superseded by the eternity of Salvation that will render time extinct. Why would someone have to get out of bed tomorrow if there is no need for him to retire for the night? And, to capitalize My discussion today, everything beautiful in life must be internalized by the converted heart because this beauty is inherent in the Promised Land. It is like imagining what something you have never seen might look like, and then having your imagination ratified once it is seen. I have said that Heaven cannot be described in words, but the image of Heaven, the blessings and sacred effects of Salvation, can be imagined in the heart from where prayer is derived. This is where the tether is attached, where the soul is infused with new life by Jesus' Blood on the Cross. My Special son, there are many dimensions and implications to this gift, and I could continue for hours. I know that you will ponder what I have said this morning, and reflect upon how to share My words with others. Someday you will, though not verbatim, through your own interpretation and spontaneous speech.

Yes, your Morning Star press release that you have sent to the newspapers of numerous cities has been received with as much shock as the mushroom cloud that you playfully sent your brother yesterday. It had this effect because it landed directly in the electronic mailboxes of those in charge. It is a matter of faith for them now, and some of them are Catholics who are searching for the signs that you mentioned. Jesus will induce them to act on their faith if they are not distracted by their secular colleagues. The pressure for them to act is often offset by their peers reminding them that there are some things that are too abstract to touch. My Morning Star Over America messages are one of them. Most newspaper editors are just looking for filler on their religious pages, where they may mention My messages. I am praying that humanity will realize what you and your brother already know – that I am the world's greatest advocate for the Crucifixion and Resurrection of Jesus. I will speak effectively to humanity if only they will recognize that I have come. My Special and Chosen ones, you must remember that the success of My messages and the impact of your works are not conditioned by those who choose not to believe. It is a matter of enduring the brashness of human affairs, and placing your gifts and lives before the Holy Cross and in the protection of Jesus' Easter Resurrection. We have never done things believing that humanity should just have greater hope, but that they will respond and change. It is not only that they will wait for spring to arrive, but that they will participate in the labors that will force the harvest and station the fruits of their lives in the Most Sacred Heart of Jesus. If humanity ever wanted to feed Heaven a spiritual feast of reconciliation from here in this world, they will do what I have commended today. My Special son, thank you and bless you for attending the wake of the father of your friends last evening. It was a gift of comfort and friendship for the family members who were there."

Saturday, March 26, 2016
Holy Saturday
9:31 a.m.

"It is not about the survival or maturation of truth – for truth has been clearly preserved; it has already conquered a billion heretics, given to the world the genius of God intact, with waves crashing against the wicked, hailing down tranquility upon the good and the wayward alike. The truth shines with grace, excellence, preeminence and revelations yet untold. This is the convergence and preservation of youth and the wisdom of the ages."

- The Dominion Angels

"My dear little children, the Dominion Angels have again given you strains of eternal delight. They are the leaders of Angels, and the ones with tremendous eloquence in holiness. They speak to you because Jesus sends them here. And, I come speaking to you and praying with you because Jesus believes that we can make a difference in these present days. We can claim for God more souls to open their hearts to His heavenly Kingdom. My Special son, your press releases are having a remarkable impact on those who receive them. You are accurate in that the hundreds of pamphlets you sent prepared their recipients for what My intercession means. Bless you for investing your time, resources and efforts in continuing your dedication to My mission in humanity's exile. If one would search for words to describe your standing before Jesus, he would be looking an extremely long time. News of your press release has landed on the desktops of several American Bishops. Bishop Thomas John Paprocki now knows that I imparted a response. It is a blessing for all the world!

The Dominion Angels spoke today about truth reconciling the Earth and Heaven through the preservation of God's Word carried out through the ages. They referred to the ability of the truth to hand defeat to heretics in the millions. This means that the same message of redemption has prevailed for 2,000 years, and it is the one that you are prospering in your day. It is not like democracy or philosophies that each new generation feels the need to modify because it is founded on the Cross that never yields to change. Democracies are constantly being amended by bodies of law and cultural preference, but the truth in the way the Angels have described it is immutable. It is the one principle from which all others follow. I am not saying that Christianity is rigid, but that the truth of the spoken word must be founded upon the Will of God. This is the 'fatherhood' of the truth that is forever stationed in the Godhead on His Throne in Heaven. Let us take another look at what the Angels have said. You see the reference to the preservation of youth and the wisdom of the ages. Does this mean that God can have it both ways? Yes, He certainly can. Humanity is called to maintain the innocence of their youth in its approach to Christian fealty, and this is best done by nurturing in the heart the seed of innocence, Jesus Christ. Here, I am alluding to the fact that human hearts are often crucified in a spiritual way the same way Jesus died on the Cross, and for the same reason. The heart is the seat of truth for those in exile the same way that the Crucifixion of Jesus is the seed of Salvation for those who believe in Him. I have told you that the heart cannot lie. It is the mind and thoughts that lie. I am not saying that the heart cannot be corrupted or filled with evil works. I am saying that people whose hearts are this way have thoughts that are filled with error. Their hearts cannot lie to them. This is why I have said that the heart must be changed; it must be transformed into the capacity for engaging the truth in order for the soul to submit to being cleansed by Jesus' Blood on the Cross. The heart is both the consciousness and subconsciousness of the individual, and it is upon these pillars that one erects his conscience. *"It is where the hierarchy of influence rests."* Yes, you are correct. When we pray for the conversion of lost sinners, we implore the Holy Spirit to infiltrate these realms of human 'being-ness' and foster the changes that will bring them to profess their belief in the Church.

My Special son, I have spent a great deal of time during My 2015 and 2016 messages speaking about the piety and power that resides in these things. I have spoken about them because they have the ability to remake the spiritual identity of the person on the inside the same way that external beauty affects one's capacity for preference and emotion. New energy, expectation and anticipation are generated on the inside that some type of movement will happen – the status at hand will give way to a new way of thinking. The Father has made Himself so appealing by His revelations to humanity that men desire to seek Him. It is not a prize that men have sought, but the seed of their destiny to a new home they have never seen. It is like the sweet fragrance of something that someone has never enjoyed. They are prompted to say, 'what is this?' And, they confess that whatever it is, they are drawn to it; they wish to partake of it. This is the instinct that becomes seeded in the newly converted Christian heart. It is not as much a blind curiosity as the desire for the satisfaction of a need. It is not like needing air to breathe because someone knows what oxygen is for. It is more like ingesting a drug on which someone becomes dependent the very first time. Becoming loyal to the Holy Spirit is not an addiction by the person with faith, but a recognition that faith can keep an entire Kingdom alive in their hearts. The newly formed Christian says, 'oh, this is where I am needed. This is where I am supposed to be.' It is the coupling of their youth with the wisdom of the ages within the framework of the heart. You know that men for centuries have desired to discover the secret to maintaining their youth, and they find it in the prescription I have just given. I ask you to notice that the Dominion Angels did not capitalize the word 'truth' in their passage today because they want you and your brother to know that truth and humanity are bound as one in Jesus' Holy Sacrifice. Jesus came down from Heaven. He came to the Earth and raised the world of men to Himself. Of course, men are supposed to surrender themselves to Jesus – it is for Jesus to live in them. The Spirit of Jesus supplants the spirit of men. The Will of God and the will of men must be one in yet another way. You cannot move your spirit aside, but God can. It is for men, therefore, to hand their will over to Him. This must happen before the transformation of the heart can generate the new light of truth within the identity of the soul bound for Salvation.

Christians know in advance that they have been saved. It is not something they will learn after they close their eyes in death. Christians know that only time separates them from seeing the Face of God and being seated at His eternal banquet table in Heaven. This is the way Saint Paul spoke. It is this confidence that brings the Christian to welcome one's judgment rather than fearing it. The people whose faith was doubtful are surprised by the prayers and gifts in their favor, and they enter Heaven knowing that they owe their redemption not only to the Blood of the Lamb, but to those who oathed themselves to Him as His disciples and apostles, the suffering and persecution they endured on His behalf. It is not that those who complement the works of the Cross know it beforehand. Tens of millions of souls will be given Salvation at the Final Judgment because they will see what you and your brother saw during dinner last evening. The girl who appeared to be paralyzed is clearly a Saint of the 21st century in whom Jesus has vested His Divine Mercy for those who can walk, who choose paths they should never have traveled. This is not about injustice or unfairness toward the person you saw at dinnertime. Since the world will end with this person having been stricken this way, she would have preferred to die a thousand deaths by fire than to have been healed. Do you understand? *"Yes."* In other words, Jesus would have healed her, just as you said you wished to heal her. But, her eternal station in Heaven after the brevity of one 80-year lifetime would not have been the same. It is not that she would not have been saved, but she would have been like the fastest runner who was not allowed to win. This is the way of all good Christians. It is the same as you and your brother choosing the sacrificial life for Jesus through Me that has brought your country and the unwitting world to the threshold of knowing the Morning Star Over America. You could have been living more comfortable lives, but in the end, would you have been happy for the fullness of eternity? We know the answer. I must tell you that the pity you took on the girl was worthy of Jesus in your compassionate heart. There are times when Jesus would do as you said – heal her in an instant. This would have been the crashing down of every hint of opposition to My messages, but what would it have done for faith? If you had healed her before My messages were recorded, would anyone leave you and your brother to your work for your manuscripts to be produced? Do you remember when Jesus told many of those He healed not to tell anyone? *"Yes."* He did so for the same reason. It is all a matter of timing and the Father's divine intent. *"I understand."* You are capturing the attention of media and religious organizations, and the curiosity of the masses will begin. I have warned what this would bring. Becoming known to the nations for what we have done is a heavy burden to bear. It is not without mocking, ridicule and rejection. You may say that you are prepared, but you and your brother are not. These are times when you will have to employ discretion about whom you speak with and the words you choose. Your brother has had it correct all along – just read the books. Thank you for your prayers, warm wishes and good will that you have accorded Me when I appear to you. My Special son, you are far too modest for Me to describe what you mean to Jesus. *"Thank you, Mama."*

Saturday, April 2, 2016
9:29 a.m.

The seen and unseen world –
the column upon the plinth,
the tree atop its roots,
a word defined, a phrase explained,
blood spent and souls redeemed,
the final command, an obedient response,
the war is done, peace now at hand,
a Kingdom is captured, an eternity won.

- The Dominion Angels

"The fire blazes rapidly, and the skies burn aloft –
Oh my goodness, the flames put the water out!"

"Hear Judas, Jesus was just resurrected –
and He's on His way over here now!"

"My dearly beloved little children, it is through your prayers that I am helping Jesus change the world and sanctify what must be cleansed. I am the Handmaid of the Lord who humbly serves as Queen of Heaven and Earth. Let us remember today those who do not know God, the ones who have shut His Kingdom out of their lives because they have become embittered against His ways. I have said today in Medjugorje that pain elevates. This can be seen not only throughout the lives of the Saints and in the mission of the Church, but inside each and every one of My children currently praying for peace where they live. I have not said that pain is purposeful just because it elevates, I have said that it elevates because it draws the world to prayer. Turning to Jesus and to God in order to alleviate human pain is elevating in ways that cannot be told in secular terms. Easing someone's pain is a means of emulating the life of Jesus; it is your way of joining Him with compassion here in your exile. So, even as I speak of pain as being the greatest prayer, I refer to the faith of the Christian as well. I speak about the ways My children are mocked and ridiculed, and yet they cling to their faith! My Special son, I have often said that it would be better to fight your enemies with cannon balls than soap bubbles – both are circular in shape. It is the premise of how much power one must use to defeat those forces and actions that oppose the teachings of the Church. This power is wrought from the prayer that I have mentioned, and it is a manifestation of the pain that often comes to those who believe. One does not know where to scratch until he knows the location of the itch. Grease cannot be applied to the proper wheel unless the wheel sounds loudly enough to be heard. These are the metaphoric ways that humanity knows what to say and where to focus their daily offices of compassion and Christian empathy.

My Special son, you and your brother have always been profoundly good. You have been scrupulous in your lives in Jesus. You have used discretion in your decisions and genuineness in your reverence. I was deeply pleased by your presentation to the Jacksonville newspaper reporter who himself is reviewing the intensity of his own Christian faith. One cannot encounter what we have done together without becoming a different person. Your answers to his questions were deeply spiritual and dynamic. They yielded for him a means by which he can explain what we have done through the perspectives of his own heart. He was nearly brought to tears upon asking your brother what made your brother so moved by the first Mass he ever attended – the Consecration of the bread and wine into the Body and Blood of Jesus. This man had never heard anyone say this before. Imagine undergoing the scrutiny you have had with regard to his own scrutiny of the issues that we have laid before him. I will tell you another matter that seemed interesting to the reporter. He is aware of all your books, of the intense amounts of time, effort and materials invested to produce them. He was impressed by the efficiency of what we have done together. There are no stockpiles of drafts or discarded pages. There is no inventory of antiquated machines. There are no wastebaskets brimming with trash. How can someone produce so prolifically such tremendous works, and yet their home looks like a maiden's den? This was for some reason extremely striking to him. And, this is something that you and your brother have taken for granted – but not in a negative way. One might have thought that after twenty-five years, your home would have taken on an academic author's setting, that it would be overrun by outdated books, remnants of papers and excised chapters. But, you have instead maintained the efficiency that I mentioned moments ago. This speaks volumes about your courtly state of mind, and your ability to sojourn through this world with little more than a tunic and sandals. I wish for you to realize that I have assisted you in this matter because I know where your focus has been. It is on the issues at hand. This, therefore, is the reason that the Dominion Angels have given you such pretty and energetic words this morning.

The second of their phrases today speaks about what some would believe to be nonsensical ideas. How could a fire put the water out? This is part of the counterintuitive mantra that the Angels have always told humanity through you. It does not seem natural to the thoughts of ordinary men that some of these things could be true. The skies are on fire? What does this mean? Surely in the backdrop of your faith and the viability of your spiritual insight, you have come to know that it streams from the Glory of God. The skies aloft cannot burn if there is nothing there to ignite. This makes perfect sense until someone says that God created man out of nothing. 'Hmm. Let us think about this some more.' This is what all men will eventually say. Third, if Judas had not taken his own life prior to the Paschal Resurrection, it should be considered that Jesus would have wished to speak to him on Easter morning to see what he would say. This is not solely about the hypothetical utterance spoken to Judas that the Angels provided in our message today. Imagine this sentence on a billboard along an interstate highway somewhere. This is all anyone would need to know about the Resurrection of Jesus Christ. The entire Kingdom of God is summed in this sequence of words. How many men are Judases driving down the street these days? It is somewhat of a miracle, if you think about it. When the Dominion Angels speak of the seen and unseen world, they are referring to what happens inside the human heart once the realization of the Cross becomes clear. Those who hear about such gifts as My apparitions around the globe, and how the New Covenant Gospel is being fulfilled in their day, are set to wondering what part they are playing in the here and now. They want to know if they are part of the problem or the solution. Are they like Judas Iscariot, or are they like Saint John the Beloved Apostle? My Special son, we are helping them answer this question. We are awakening those who work in the secular mainstream to see that miracles can be found in their midst for a quarter century, and they are only now learning about it. They are able to compare the visible distractions of their lives with the truth of

God in which you, your brother, and I are living. I am not suggesting that they are going to come knocking down the door of your home. And, they have not been ringing the telephone off the tabletop. However, I am saying that they have come to a sudden stop inside their collective consciousness. They saw your pamphlet as a holy devotional, but they also saw that your works are under the episcopal discernment of your diocesan Bishop. It is not that they care about My mission as your Mother, but from which of these prospects they can yield the greatest profits.

Therefore, a column upon a plinth suggests that one can see what upholds a passion or idea. The roots of a tree are assumed to be there because mankind has forever known that every tree has roots. Our purpose for many years has been to place a seed in their minds that everything about human life must have something beneath it that they cannot see that sustains and upholds it. When they realize that this is God, and Me as your Mother, they will understand their existence in human exile as being supported by the Providence of God, just as they know that trees have roots. It is not an indoctrination about the spiritual life, but an awakening from their sleep where they have lacked connection to the Kingdom of the Divine Spirit. My Special son, does My explanation make sense to you? "*Yes.*" You and your brother have been laborers in the Lord's vineyard who have transmitted from the unseen realms the truth of the Gospel. You have proved that the skies can be set aflame through the power of the Holy Spirit. You have laid the foundation and built the framework that will allow all sinners yet walking the globe to draw telling conclusions about whether they are Jesus' friends or His enemies. One cannot stand in the middle. You are either in the boat or standing on the dock. The departing of a ship cannot be expected to pull someone into halves. I wish you and your brother to remember that there are certain individuals who will only approach you as 'non-sanctioned' examiners, who wish to bring scandal upon your work. The person who recently contacted you is one of these men. He has put himself up as the judge of what God will and will not do. The best way to deal with him is to send him to the Bishop for everything he wishes to know. 'Read the books. Read the books. Then, there will be an interview with the visionaries who published them.' My Special son, if he were not the person I just described, he would have already celebrated My messages to you. I wish to repeat that we have prayed into being this morning the touching, healing and conversion of multitudes of hurting souls. You and your brother are blessed!"

Saturday, April 9, 2016
9:31 a.m.

*"It is drawn from the heart and written across the skies –
O' God, you collected us in your Son, and made us your victims.
Simply rendered – rocks fall and people die."*

- Saint Simon Peter

*A thunderstorm is God thinking out loud.
A rainbow is God dreaming with His eyes open.*

- The Dominion Angels

"My sweet, delightful, brilliant little children. It is on days like these that you capture in your hearts all the graces that any human beings could possibly imagine. You are free! It is, as Saint Simon Peter said, written across the skies that you have been rescued from the night. I come to you this morning to pray with you for lost sinners, as we always do. I come to offer My thoughts and reflections about your lives and the modern world, that we might help mend and reshape it by what we ask of the Father. It is not that we seek His commitment for the remaking of the Earth, for He has already done so – but we invoke His guiding assistance in brokering the manifest conversion of humanity to the Holy Cross with mercy and peace. My Special son, no one yet living in the world has heard the quotation of Saint Peter. It is not that God wants it that way, but only few have been given reason to know it. Why? Because it has an almost morbid view of human death, and Jesus wishes the Church to focus on life, new life and the Afterlife. I have given you Saint Peter's sentiments for your own spiritual consumption, but you have the latitude to share it with the rest of the world. I am not saying that Saint Peter was speaking ill of the burdens of Christianity, but he recognized that holy people find themselves caught up in the battles against evil, and they often become casualties of the fight. I tell you with affection that Saint Peter was not known for his eloquence. He was a resilient Apostle and practitioner of the Church. Hence, his quotation about rocks falling and people dying is evidence of his speaking to the core of the matter. The other two verses from the Dominion Angels are thoughtful and sightly; they were pleased by the opportunity today to share them with you. I know that there are times when you can detect their affable identities.

You see that Saint Peter spoke about the entire collective of the human family being reborn through the Crucifixion of Jesus. And, as this is true, does it not seem correct that humanity is the victim of its own sinfulness? You may respond. *"Yes, there is no doubt. And, good people are victims of other people's sinfulness."* This is the point Saint Peter was making. The whole issue rests on the prospect that to be saved, someone must walk the path of Jesus in all ways practical and beatific, in the likeness of Saint Simon Peter. This is what suffering is. It is the physical and mental anguish that accompanied Jesus' Agony in the Garden and as He carried the Cross on His journey to Mount Calvary. It would seem that these events encapsulate what human exile is like, but it need not be this way. I have told you and your brother that we speak about a Church that is already connected to its own resurrection, and within Jesus' Resurrection. You and your brother, and all believers, are united with the Living Christ here in this world not just through your faith, but in the Father's response to your faith. It is as though there is an invisible reciprocation that goes on between Heaven and Earth where this exchange is made – humanity's holiness for God's forgiveness. The fulcrum of this fusion is the Sacrifice of Jesus on the Cross. I am giving you common theological knowledge, and it can be revealed and energized by those who come to Me for divine intercession. This is the premise that you have imparted in your prologues and meditations since you began writing them. Another aspect of this reciprocity is that changes come in due season of their own accord because of the commitment that individuals give to the mystery of human redemption. You and your brother made your commitment long before I began speaking to you. I have never appeared to anyone who did not already believe in God. I bring with Me the benedictions of the Triune Deity, not to prove its existence to those who refuse to believe. Revealing this, it is within the power of the Church and Christians around the globe to provide the witnessing that I have just mentioned. You have the commission given by the Holy Spirit to do so; you are sanctioned by God through Jesus to assemble lost sinners beneath the Cross of their own volition. Someone cannot come to the Cross without desiring to do so, no more than they can accept the Blood of Jesus that was shed there, or accept their own entrance into Heaven unless it is in accordance with their will. This is another facet of the quotation from Saint Simon Peter. Everything that I have told you about the battles against evil are initiated in the darkness because this is where evil hides. If you could imagine what it would be like to stand in a valley in the pitch of night and hear a rockslide coming from atop a mountain, you can garner a sense for being deeply immersed in these battles. Truly, you already have; this is what Saint Peter was saying.

Rocks fall, and people die. It is not complicated to understand because history has borne it out. I am saying that blessed are they who endure the fight; who cope, engage and withstand the threat.

It is with tremendous gratitude that I remind you and your brother that, whether you believe it or not, you are champions in the yielding of truthful light from the dark corners of these battles; these enlightenments are in fact inscribed across the skies, visible to the human soul both day and night. It is not just that you will be crowned as Saints upon the culmination of your years, you will take with you the converted souls of nearly the entire western hemisphere. You are yet unaware because you still live in the flesh in the temporal realms, and you are subject to the same constraints that befall everyone else. However, you and your brother have overcome your susceptibility to being overwhelmed or controlled by these radical forces. You are already given to God and the Afterlife in ways that others will not know until they pass into His hands. I cannot overstate that you have done this by reason of your faith in connection with God's blessing for your having magnified the Crucifixion. This is part of the reciprocation that I spoke about moments ago. The changes are revealed over time. I ask you and your brother to continue to commit to the duties to which you have been given, and be peaceful in your ways. Please join Me in being patient as hearts and lives are changing; many are doing what Jesus is asking of them."

Saturday, April 16, 2016
Birthday of Pope Benedict XVI
Birthday of Alta M. Parsons Heather

The Morning Star Over America
Episcopal Commission

"The divinity of the Holy Spirit rests peacefully in your hearts, and gives you strength through your days. My little sons, it is to this divinity that humanity is called, to which I am dedicated, and from which the entire world is drawing inspiration. I have highlighted this morning the birthdays of two marvelous Christians – Pope Benedict XVI who is 89 mortal years old today, and Saint Alta M. Parsons Heather who would be 95 earthly years old today. It is through the prayers of Pope Benedict XVI and the intercession of Saint Alta that your work has been so fruitful. And, it is through the brilliance of your lives in Jesus that the world will never forget the title of My message today. 'The Morning Star Over America Episcopal Commission' will someday be the seminal invitation of humanity to the Cross in honor of the New Messianic Gospel. When the world reviews the magnitude of its gifts from God throughout the ages, 'The Morning Star Over America Episcopal Commission' will stand among the most profound. It will be viewed by the faithful and the unchurched alike as the greatest event in the history of the western hemisphere, even more than the founding of the American nations. My Special and Chosen sons, I am not exaggerating about what we have accomplished. If you were to become hermits on Earth, and no one heard from you again, everything you should have done has already been accomplished. I have told you this many times. You are living the extraordinary years that have been tendered to you from Heaven. And, if it were not for Jesus' desire that you join Him on the Cross, that you witness for the Gospel here in your time, you would have already been called to your heavenly rest. I am asking all My seers and messengers during My recent appearances to remember what it means to fashion for God an instrument with which the Angels can play the melodies of conversion and redemption to His people on Earth. You are their composers, My little sons! It is through your wisdom and within your holiness that humanity will be summoned to recognize their responsibilities to the Father. God does not ask all that much. If He did, He would have heretofore extracted all the measures from humanity that they should have scored – the melodies and harmonies that glorify Him alone. But, we have a merciful God. He wants His people to share in His glory and be unified through it by their faith in His Son. This is not the Will of a vindictive God, but God who believes that the peace of His Kingdom should inundate the souls of suffering men. This is the awakening that Jesus was trying to bring to His Apostles during His Sorrowful Agony in the Garden.

So today, My little sons, I make it My purpose to tell you that 'The Morning Star Over America Episcopal Commission' is not separate from the Church, but in harmony and communion with the Church. It is My Maternal signature on the conversion of humanity in the created realms. I ask that you remember what has been given to you, and what you have given to humanity. My Special son, you and your brother have the same beauty and dignity of everyone of piety who has lived in the exiled world or basked in the mansions of Heaven. I know that you will be humble in your awareness of this gift, of this tremendous energy by which Heaven continues to preside over the far-flung continents below. You are one with the Father through Jesus in precisely the way that the Holy Scriptures have taught. And, what has this brought you thus far? To no surprise, the world is shunning you. You are being cast aside as people who belong to a cult that has nothing to do with common human life. And as I have noted, you are being marginalized by the leaders and parishes of the Roman Catholic Church because your works are in addition to the Original Deposit of Faith. So, welcome to My Most Immaculate Heart! I am seemingly not needed in the equation of human redemption either. How many of the twenty-two million pilgrims to My shrine in Medjugorje have invested their faith and lives in relating what I have told them there, or have witnessed to what I am doing in their favor? My Special son, most of them have made pilgrimages to Medjugorje not to honor their Holy Mother or strengthen the faith they have been given, but to find out whether God exists at all. Once they believe they have the answer, they go back to their homes and turn their faith from lukewarmness to slightly moderate because they have found at least something to hold onto. They find out what they wish to know and congratulate themselves for not wasting their time on faith during the previous years. Can you imagine how this makes your Mother feel? "Yes." As I have said, welcome to My Immaculate Heart. "*Thank you. I love you so much, and I believe when most will not.*"

    My Special son, I am not telling you these things so you will have pity on Me, but to know that I identify with what you and your brother are experiencing. It is one of the reasons I have not prospered My Morning Star messages to the nations, even yours. I recently asked if you remember Jesus performing certain miracles and commending the recipients not to tell anyone. He did this for the same reason that you and your brother are not on national platforms. His time had not yet come, and your time is only now beginning. God has requested that I remind you that you could live 80 years' longevity and this new blessing would still be unfolding. Jesus depends on the faith of the Church to do His bidding. The messages of Medjugorje should have been published in every newspaper and broadcast on all television networks and radio airwaves combined, saturating the culture by now. This is not the case because sinners and secular deniers will not make it so. Even in light of these things, this does not stop us from trying. You must recall that Jesus' Crucifixion is not just about prospering the Gospel, He paid ransom for humanity's captivity to sin. Can you identify which passages from the Gospel that Jesus foretold from the Cross? It was not only that the Gospel was voiced from the Cross, but that the redemption of the world was manifested there too. The Gospel would come by the power of the Holy Spirit; it would be a miraculous account of what Jesus said and did during His ministry. I have through the Holy Spirit dictated to you 'The Morning Star Over America' messages, and you and your brother are living out what they say. This is the reason why these are such glorious days that you are living in the land where the Angels come to pray. Your faith and loyalties to God are not unlike the remark made about the slain President whom I have referenced through the years – 'He still lingers where his children used to play.' As for you and your brother, you remain very much alive, and the Angels pray in your company where you are of such comfort to Jesus, so holy and purposeful in righteousness, so capable of seeing the way God desires to sanctify the exiled human race.

My Special son, this is the reason I have said that your faith is the essence of your piety, power and capacity for persuading the nations that the Blood of Jesus is the antidote for death. Yes, this is as much a Sacred Mystery as was the Crucifixion of the Son of Man, but it is true nonetheless. What God will give the whole of the world if they will only turn to Jesus is permission to be who they wish to become in Him. It is only through this gift that the accounting of whom humanity should be will be realized. Anything less is to tell a man with two good legs that he will never walk again. Denying the prayers of the faithful would be like the Father complimenting His people on the beautiful color of their eyes, but withholding from them the ability to see. God knows that the function of faith is as important as its existence. It must have meaning if it is to dignify its conception. It is the same as thoughts of the mind being evolving and relevant. A mind with flourishing ideas is not the same as a barrel of basketballs. Innovative thinking is not remanded to the dimensions of shape and size. And, transcendental faith, the faith that everyone is given, cannot be constrained by human psychology The knowledge of the Gospel and living what the Gospel says cannot be separated one from the other. And, this is the same as the gift of 'The Morning Star Over America' being accepted for the miracle that it is, not rationalized as a questionable event for those who choose not to believe. My Special son, I have given you and your brother a great deal to think about today. *"Thank you so much. I understand."* I do not wish for you to dwell on the outcome of what I have said, but focus on the prayers that will render the outcome. You have always lived this way in the most blessed means possible, and I commend you for understanding why Jesus has such patience, even in the face of so many atrocities. These times are a turning point in the battle between His Church and nonbelievers. We shall see what the Father allows. *"I understand; it is a battle that has been ongoing since the day of Pentecost."* This is the trust that Jesus has implored from everyone whom the Holy Spirit has touched. *"I understand. I do trust you."* This will bear the marking of the tremendous learning of the nations because of your trust; this trust is a product of your faith. You will be repaid a hundredfold for serving Him. Yes, you are correct, the battle is underway."

Saturday, April 23, 2016
9:33 a.m.

"The United States must reclaim its ancient piety – sometimes there is a nation! This is the true freedom of a civilized world. But, if America rejects the Victim on the Cross, there can be no fixing its soul, nothing palatable to quench its thirst – no song, no medicine, no hope; only intense suffering to incalculable degrees, the loss of its spiritual heart, and the veritable absence of redeeming grace. For a nation to deny itself the lovely privilege of reaching its saturation point in holiness is to destroy it from the inside out."

- William Roth Jr.

"My dear-hearted little sons, it is My joy to come speaking to you as you pray for all the things that have been delineated in your hopes and writings. We are part of the cadence of Creation that leads good men to the Providence of God and teaches the lost the way to be found. 'In the beginning, God created...' 'The Angel said to Mary...' 'Jesus handed over His Spirit...' These are the five-word phrases that encapsulate the reunion of the Father and His lost creatures. And now six – 'Jesus was raised from the tomb.' Now, you see the addition of the one grand miracle by which humanity has been delivered into the presence of God, gift-wrapped in the Most Sacred Heart of His Son. My dear children, there are many five and six-word phrases such as these that contain the entire history of the Sacred Mysteries and the response of humanity in exile. There can be no question that what makes good men different from malevolent men is that they have recognized that they are not God, but that they belong to God in their acceptance of His Son's Holy Sacrifice. My Special one, I continue to be amazed by your capacity for being strong in the face of so much adversity in the world between societies, during the fires of public debate, and in the circumstances at your workplace. By handling the conflicting situation the way you chose to approach it, you have given a tremendous gift to yourself and your brother. I will allow you to live out your lives to see what it is, then I will tell you why it was connected to your recent good offices. Of the billions of ways that English syllables can be connected to communicate messages and transfer meaning, the writing that you have composed in your quotation this morning captures the essence of the godly manner. It is the Father who has spoken through the Holy Spirit within you. I assure you that you should not be concerned about when someone might hear

My messages or see them published. We have for the past twenty-five years been working to get them through the veil. This has been the focus of your writings as well. Getting them into Creation is the most difficult task because it requires tremendous time and effort. It has kept you and your brother sequestered from many settings and societies while we have done our work. And, as you have seen, you have not missed much.

Doing the important work of 'the Jesus mission' during your mortal years is the greatest investment of your time. You and your brother have superseded the element of time in favor of developing a 'mass' or 'cluster' of supernatural phenomena that will bring to the Earth the awakening that I have spoken about in recent weeks. This is the essence of your deposit of works. While the events of the world are saddening to humanity, your gifts to the Church and your lost brothers and sisters are bringing great joy and hope that the Kingdom of Heaven is near. This is the effecting of the Father's words 'I promise...' through the lives of you and your brother. Your work, faithfulness and trust have helped God not only keep His promise to those who love Him, but help shape the outcome of that promise as shared through the Life, Death and Resurrection of Jesus from the Sepulcher. You might consider it this way – you and your brother became incarnate through the same Will of God that brought Him to fashion Creation according to the first five words of Genesis. This is the same reason Jesus was Begotten, not made, of My Womb 2,000 years ago. You and your brother and Jesus have shared the same purpose for strengthening man's desire to seek the Kingdom of God and eradicating humanity's desire to pursue something else. And, we realize that the energy behind this grace is sacrifice. I have told you on many occasions that sacrifice is the basis for spiritual renewal; and in Jesus' life, the reason for the redemption of every soul who chooses to accept Him. The many theologians throughout the centuries have attempted to discern which is more important – the Cross or the Body of Jesus on the Cross. You can surely understand why some of them are confused. I know what you are thinking – the two of them cannot be separated, just as faith is founded and has life. *"The Cross was more inside Jesus than Him hanging on it."* Yes, and the sight of Jesus on the Cross is mankind's way of knowing that God loves them, even in their sin, to the point of the Passion and Crucifixion of His Son.

Men have said that dying is not the difficult part, but getting to the moment of death is. This is what happened to Jesus in His final hours. His suffering on behalf of lost sinners occurred as internally as the pain and agony that Christians around the globe endure today, but it need not be transformed into bodily harm to happen. *"It's the same as non-Catholic Christians having crosses that do not have Jesus' Body affixed to them. They don't recognize the inseparability of the two. And, they don't understand human suffering."* Everything you have said is true. Indeed, this speaks volumes in reflection of what you have written to begin our message today about the state of your country. It proves the relevance of Jesus' Holy Sacrifice here in the year AD 2016 because the same power that emboldened the Apostles is sufficing your strength in your time. Jesus' Body was taken down from the Cross, as you know, but the unseeable suffering about which you are speaking has continued by, and inside, good Christians through the ages. This makes you one with the Blessed Trinity in ways that many people do not know because they do not understand the Crucifixion through the imparting of Jesus' Holy Spirit in human hearts still in exile. You could say that apostles like you and your brother are ambassadors from Heaven. You have been vested and commissioned with the purpose of doing the Lord's work around the globe where Jesus laid the foundation of the Church. Jesus was the Church walking the Earth during His ministry, and all who believe in Him now bear the Church within them as they travel the world. You carry Jesus to humanity in the same way that Jesus carried you on His shoulders while teaching and preaching 2,000 years ago. There have been volumes published about this through the centuries, but most of them have made it more complicated. As I said at the beginning of My message today, one can outlay an entire redemptive framework in five or six words. I have always believed that as massive as your writings with your brother have been, they have this same simplicity about which I am speaking. This approach is also prevalent throughout the accountings of the Gospel. Some theologians have wished to know why there are four Gospelers in the New Testament instead of one. What is your opinion? *"I think multiple witnesses are the seed for even more."* Yes, and there are true and symphonic purposes for these witnesses – faith, hope, charity and love; north, south, east and west. It is a grand and miraculous design that speaks not only to what humanity must know, but what they can imagine hundreds of years from now.

Nowhere has this been made more clear than the Old and New Covenants of the Bible. There has always been a number of signs and seals, apostles, years and generations. There is even a Book of Numbers to emphasize it. There are given numbers of feasts and celebrations, and so on. These are the numerical facets of the Biblical Scriptures. On the other hand, it is the facets of piety that Jesus focused on through His parables, lessons and teachings. He spoke about opinions and preferences, ranges of conduct, the basis for the holiness of the human heart, and what hope inspires someone's actions that place them in accord with what God would have them do. My messages to you and your brother have been about the catechetical aspects of life, what behaviors place people in communion with what I have asked you to reveal. I am saying that the reams and volumes written by theologians about the mission of the Church have always been about interpretation. The facts surrounding Jesus' Life, Death and Resurrection are a coordination of qualitative and numerical events. This is the reason there are Five Mysteries in the Holy Rosary instead of six; there are ten Hail Mary's rather than eleven. These things have been prescribed according to the way the Father wishes the conversion of His people to happen. This is also the reason why the world keeps track of the days and the number of a particular year. There must be a universal reference point in time. As for the eternal part of humanity's life, the events of Jesus' life and Crucifixion are reference points beyond the ages. My Special son, I hope you enjoyed what I came to say today. *"Yes, thank you."*

Saturday, April 30, 2016
9:37 a.m.

"Everything we experience in life must ultimately be laid alongside our relationship with God, especially the motivations He instills in us to cultivate His Kingdom on Earth. Convincing a lost sinner to accept the Cross of Jesus Christ should not be difficult, but it is sometimes like pulling a bale of straw from the bottom of the seas, and trying to set it on fire. Nonetheless, this is the way we should live, breaking nonbelievers' defiance against the Rock of Ages and rolling them, upended if necessary, toward the summit of the sanctifying hills. Christian evangelization is our mission, the way we welcome the Holy Spirit into our lives, impart the Father's wisdom to the masses so our collective actions square with the truth, and keep afloat in our lifelong struggle against the cruelties of the night. This is the eminent triumph of our purpose, and the strategic character of our time."

- William Roth Jr.

"My Special son, you write and write, and write some more, and the world will be forever holier for your love. The Church is being inspired because you and your brother have dedicated yourselves to My Queenship, consecrated your lives to My Most Immaculate Heart, and devoted your souls to Jesus on the Cross. I wish to tell you this morning that everything you have written for God will be seen by all souls given the breath of life. All holy things will be known. Nothing will remain hidden. Whatever you desire humanity on Earth to see, it shall be done. Never mind the obstinance of time. You and your brother's work is playing out its purpose during these times, and you are now serving the Lord in the eternal realms. I ask that you forever remember that you have shaped the Earth into the likeness of the Cross because you have been given to Jesus from deep inside. You are not casual Christians. You do not perceive your religious faith as being just another facet of life. You are aware of the way time deceives sinners into believing that its expiration will amend the results of life without other agents of change. Hence, what you have written to begin our message today reflects the apostolic mission of the Christian person, even as the person is one and united with the community of the Church. And, My Special son, you and your brother have lived these benevolent ways not solely because the Bible commands it. You have given the decades of your lives to the conversion of lost sinners not just because Jesus has charged His disciples to reach out this way. No, you have worked tirelessly in the Lord's vineyard because you are one with, in, and through Him as believers in His Kingdom. You have accomplished your mission because you wish to be like Jesus, and you have become so. You have celebrated the righteousness of God the same way that Jesus teaches holiness through His Divine Spirit.

My little ones, there is so much distracting America and the rest of the nations during these days that it would seem that Jesus has to raise His hand, asking permission to be heard. We know that the world is upside down, and those responsible are only deceiving themselves. You, My Special son, have acquired a vision of life that transcends these distractions, even as you are required to engage the secular labor force to remain self-sufficient. The point I am making is that everyone has a private way of thinking about random social events. This is the everyday encounter that Christians face on Earth, the same way that Jesus lived among those whom He was trying to convert. It needs to be said that Jesus was asking humanity to be drawn to the Cross as much as to Himself. The fact that this path leads believers to the Crucifixion is because this is where Jesus eventually died. However, Jesus did not say that the Cross is the Way, the Truth and the Life, but He Himself. This means that those who follow Him must be willing to take up their own crosses. Theirs are converting crosses, borne from the perils, pressures and persecutions of the secular void. Therefore, Jesus on the Cross and Resurrected from the Tomb is the Way, the Truth and the Life. This is attuned to the Holy Sacrifice of the Mass being the Last Supper and the Crucifixion in one thanksgiving celebration. And, this is how someone can take tremendous joy in being persecuted for their Christian faith – their pain is the alleviation of evil from the earthly realms. This is your perfect union with Jesus that is ratified when you receive the Most Blessed Sacrament during the Mass. We know that these things are true; they are made manifest to humanity, especially to the nonbelievers that you have said must be touched, in such a way that guides them to the Cross of Mount Calvary. In other words, anyone who has yet to accept Jesus' Blood as expiation for their sins is directed there by your suffering. Your spiritual bloodshed, and sometimes bodily, is their recognition that something redemptive and restorative exists in someone dying for another. You said not long ago that it was to Jesus' life that men must be drawn, and I have said today that Jesus' Sacrifice proves your words correct.

Therefore, the true meaning of faith and power must be aligned in the conscience of men that allows for the possibility that suffering is good. If you asked a hundred people what beauty looks like, ninety-nine of them would never say the Crucifixion of Jesus Christ. This is the ninety-nine whom we are trying to reach. Moreover, your definition of evangelization is so truly accurate in your quotation this morning that it permits the human heart to see its purpose in life. It is to magnify the world's perception of success that fosters the reception of the Spirit of God, in all His sacrificial beauty, into places that were not previously known. This is done through prayer and the Word, and you and your brother are facilitating it. Many people at the end of time might have said that they not only did not read the signs, but they did not even see the signs. However, your welcoming Me as The Morning Star Over America has given them signs. The signs are here – and your definition of evangelization is that they must read them for themselves. This is one of those ironies where they can only see by closing their eyes and opening their hearts. Here, I would like for you and your brother to listen closely to what I am saying to you now. You have helped Me erect the signs of grace and love to which they will be drawn. You have already proven your allegiance to the Kingdom of the Father. I am not saying that you cannot evangelize all you wish. I am saying that others are responsible for spreading the message – the Church of Bishops, those who have a devotion to Me, the media, and all whose hearts are given to the transformation of the Earth to the likeness of Heaven. You and your brother should not feel as though you must rise from your beds and wonder how to propagate My messages to the world. This is not a burden that Jesus has laid upon you. There is nothing wrong with continuing to foster the relationship between My other children and Me, but you should know that you have attained emeritus status as My seers and messengers. This means that you are ranking dignitaries in Jesus' Church and the Kingdom of God on Earth and in Heaven. You are My little children at the same time you are fellows in the cause of human conversion.

I wish for you to read your final sentences this morning of your passage so you will recognize that your character as apostles in the Church has raised you to the level of princes alongside the Prince of Peace and the King of Heaven and Earth. These are among the sentiments that I ask you and your brother to never forget. It is imperative that you understand your stature in Jesus on the Cross and His Easter Resurrection. You have standing beside Jesus that you will find nowhere else. Hence, I wish to repeat that you possess the piety and power that Jesus holds before God and man. You are creatures in His likeness. My Special son, I have been watching what you have been writing for your next book, and it is as stunning as everything you have written heretofore. It is clear that the Holy Spirit cherishes permeating your heart and mind. It is as though seeds are being planted in you whose flowers will adorn the sacred corridors of Heaven in eternity. Do you have any observations to make today? *"I just pray for all those who are suffering, that need you to touch them as The Morning Star Over America. Please ask Jesus to allow you to be given venue in an astounding way in the United States."* Yes, thank you for your wonderful prayers and kind sentiments. I wish for you and your brother to remember that there will someday be another permanent sign given to the world that The Morning Star Over America is a true, real and valid manifestation of Myself and the identity of Christ Jesus in the final decade of the 20th century and several years into the 21st. *"Thank you so much."* No matter what happens in the future, or even what seems to not be occurring during some framework of time, I have not given you decades of messages for no reason. *"I understand."* You must remember that the Crucifixion of Jesus has transcended twenty centuries of ordinary time, even extraordinary and catastrophic times, and remains the only means of Salvation that humanity will ever know. When your spiritual eyes rest on the beauty of My presence in Heaven, you will remember that Jesus' Crucifixion is as beautiful as Me. This is of the redemptive mystery to which humankind is drawn within the sanctity of the Church. I ask you to never forget that you and your brother are loved in ways that cannot be told in human terms. It is not a gift that can be grasped with the mind."

Sunday, May 8, 2016
Mother's Day
9:27 a.m.

"Every launched vessel raises the waterline of the sea."

- The Dominion Angels

"My dear little children, you grant the earthly realms access to the profound healing graces that the Lord desires to give His people. It is My hope that the dire circumstances in which humanity has found itself can be supplanted by a new peace and wholesomeness as the future unfolds. Today, it is My sacred honor to speak with you about the love to which you have been given, the love that you hold for Jesus, the love about which I have been speaking to the world since before and after Jesus' Ascension into Heaven. You must know that I am the Mother of humanity because I hold the same timeless perfection that Jesus holds through the Providence of the Father. When Jesus arrived at the Father's side upon the Ascension, He told God that, '...we left our Queen Mother down there.' The Father replied that He wished Me to reign in Heaven and on Earth beyond the fullness of time, and so it has come to be. My Glorious Coronation was the celebration of My Queenship that began at My Immaculate Conception. The phrase that the sublime Dominion Angels have given you to ponder today expresses the requirement for all souls to join the cause of human conversion, purification and redemption. It would seem impossible to measure the waterline of the seas, but it is indeed changing with every new vessel that sails on its crests. It is one of those forces like the ticking away of the minutes and hours of the day. If humanity had some internal means of discerning how time expires, there would be no need for clocks. It is not 'natural' for the eternal soul to endure the ravages of time, even those who are still living on the exiled Earth. Time is often an encumbrance to one's perception of what the Lord wishes the Church to foresee. However, we have discussed that time itself is a friend of the Church because it allows Jesus to share His message and protract His absolution to those who are growing in years. It is always the same analogy; the proverbial drop of water in the ocean. A grain of sand on the beach. A new ship that takes sail on the splendorous high seas. Everything makes a difference, no matter how small. And this, My Special and Chosen ones, is the focus of My Medjugorje messages. It has been the thesis of My messages to you here in this place. Every thought, even the smallest intent that elevates the Cross in the world, matters in readying humanity for the Second Coming of Christ the King. Some people have said that Jesus will not return until He is welcomed with palm branches strewn in the streets. This is surely not true. He will return like the owner of the house who is unexpected. He has no issue about walking in on a world that is only halfway upright. He will find humanity at its best and its worst when He finally comes again. There will be new Saints prepared for admittance into Heaven, and there will be those who lay inebriated in street gutters who will wonder what has come upon them. There will be the good and the bad, the rich and the poor – all on the same unwary globe.

My Special son, it is clear that you and your brother are prepared for the return of the Messiah, but others, billions of them, are not yet there. I hope that you take intense comfort in knowing that this is your station before the Father. You have observed and measured the earthly realms according to the statutes laid out in the Holy Gospel and handed down through the ages by the Advocate from God. Everything we have done together through the years has been the fruit of the Holy Spirit in the same way that Salvation history was written by the Will of God. Jesus' sacred words, all of them spoken in the exiled world, were the dictation of the Holy Spirit through Him. This is what Jesus calls all those who believe in Him to reflect. Jesus is the Incarnation of the Love, Will and Spirit of the Father to those like you and your brother who not only believed what you heard from the beginning, but who made it the premise of your lives. You have taken upon yourselves the yoke of Christianity by reconciling the world to that which makes you holy in the Gospel of the Lord. It is not just that Jesus makes you righteous by what He has taught, but that He ratifies the holiness already in you. My Special son, I am telling you today that just as I was born without sin, you and your brother were born with the ability to know God from the moment you were conceived. You might respond that all men are born this way, but you and your brother were predisposed to live out the Will of God in ways that others did not acquire. This means that you and your brother have not only acknowledged the yoke that Jesus offers, but that of your own volition, you have vowed to carry it. This is a gift to God that many have declined to bestow. At the first hint of suffering, loss or deprivation, millions of lost sinners have proved that they wish to have nothing to do with His love. You and your brother, conversely, feed on the nourishment of suffering for the sake of the conversion of the lost. You anticipate what comes to you in the form of being shunned and ostracized by the secular void, just to make sure that everything they need to know when we gain their full attention is in place for them to hear. My little sons, they will learn what you have long understood.

Those vessels about which the Dominion Angels spoke to begin our message today are being commissioned through the power of the Holy Spirit and the decades-long effort we have invested in touching them. This is where the metaphor of flooding evolved in the setting of the spiritual conversion of the wicked. 'How high is the water today?' is more than an idea about protecting one's valuables from being submerged. Everything that matters in the Kingdom of God will be kept afloat by the Blood of Jesus on the Cross, while the rest of Creation succumbs to the depths of its own corruption. The watermark that is established is near its greatest height because Jesus is near to coming again. And, it is not 'when' He is returning that matters, but 'that' He is going to return. The entire encompassing purpose of the Church and those who espouse Christianity is based on the Second Coming of Jesus Christ. In this tremendous event rests the whole story of the Redemptive Covenant that fulfills the one it succeeds. The return of the Savior will outlast any imaginable eternity. It is the focus of the vision of the Genesis world. I cannot overstate, therefore, that what we have accomplished is wholly preparatory for those who do not know God. It would be irrational for someone to wait for an elevator if they did not know there is one nearby. It would be even less rational for someone to wait on an elevator if they did not even know what an elevator is. Imagine two 18th century Native Americans seated on horses taking a drink from a canteen, and near the stream next to them an elevator appears, the door opens, and a bell rings. My Special son, it is not an exaggeration to say that this kind of cultural shock will happen to many sinners, but the skyscraper in which the elevator is running will take shape as well. Is this the substance of awakening? Yes, as much as a 777 jetliner landing a mile from these same two Native Americans. It is a matter of knowing the environment. Jesus is transferring the wisdom of His Kingdom through the teachings of the Church, and the Holy Spirit is permeating the hearts that receive Him. We are giving this movement meaning by describing what must happen, and when. The purpose of My messages and apparitions for centuries has been to magnify God's wisdom for the generations to come.

My Special son, My role in converting humanity has been one of Mother and intercessor, of teacher and protector. I am like you and your brother. I have not known when Jesus will return. It is as though the Father turned to Me upon My Glorious Coronation and asked Me to weave a blanket in preparation for the closing of the ages and the celebration of Jesus' Mystical Body in Heaven. Now, one's first instinct would be to ask, 'How large should I make this blanket?' This question does not apply because of the ages that have already passed – there are too many questions about humanity's response, such as what would motivate the Father to call an end to the Old World; when will the final photograph of exiled men be sightly enough to take before the New World begins? In the meantime, I just keep weaving. I continue making the blanket requested by the Father with painstaking joy, not knowing when or if I will succeed in due time. And, it does not matter anyway. As I have said, it is not 'when' I complete the blanket, but 'that' I am weaving the blanket. This is the way good men should live. It is the purpose of setting one's sight on the Glory of the Church that already exists in Heaven. This is not so much a concession, but the honoring of God's Will. My Special son, I am like you and your brother in more ways than you know. Not only do I defer to the Father, I do so adoringly well. I cherish His every thought and reflection. I admire His determination to prevail. I am like you in that I question humanity's propensity to respond, but I do not doubt their ability. All of this is too precious to deny. It is more mystical than many people realize. It is the leading of humanity to their triumphal rest in Paradise, despite their best efforts to bide. God is a supernal genius. Hence, I have concluded My message for this morning. O' I hope you have enjoyed it. *"Yes, very much so. Thank you."* I wish to bless you and your brother for everything you have done for the Lord, for your devotion in handing over your lives to the Cross, and for receiving Me here in your home. What is it that the aria says about no one sleeping? 'In the morning, we shall win!' Please know that you and your brother are esteemed, treasured and adored by Jesus for everything you have done for Him."

Saturday, May 14, 2016
9:32 a.m.

"When counting backward from infinity, where do you begin?"

"All the glory you could imagine is saturating your hearts, My children. The heavens are rapt by your holiness because you have dedicated your lives and years to the conversion of humanity. My Special son, you have led a life worthy of the Saints. Since you were old enough to speak and walk, you have done everything right. You have never in your mortal years done anything wrong. You have always been a friend of Jesus. You have always been an enemy of the devil. Your thoughts and actions have been pure, prudent and righteous. It is My purpose here this morning to convince you that your goodness as an exiled human being is unprecedented in the history of man. I tell you these things not to stoke your self-impression, but to remind you that all that comprises you, everything that makes you who you are – the very essence of your conceptual and spiritual nature reflects your unity with God through Jesus. My little son, if there were a means by which I could prove that there is a gold-glowing halo over your head, I would do it now. You emit a unique countenance that has not been matched by any other mortal man in the annals of the Earth. I can only say that I love and bless you because there are no other words. To thank you and your brother for responding to My call would be insufficient to express the gratefulness of Jesus. How do I know these things? It is because I am Jesus' Mother. I am the Mother of God. I am the Queen of Heaven and Earth. And, when thinking about counting down from infinity to the beginning of all beginnings, it places the human mind at odds with everything logically known. God is eternal, and His sacred love is forever infinite. The question about where to begin counting down from infinity cannot be answered because there is no answer. What? Is there such thing as a question that has no answer? Yes. So, how can it be a question? This is the paradox that stands with all the mysteries surrounding the Messianic redemption of humankind. I ask that you believe to a permanent degree that you have been as singly enlightened by Me as any person could become. I am telling you who the Father sees when He looks at you. To say that the past twenty-five years have been a miraculous gift to the world would be stating it mildly, and you and your brother have been the agents who made it possible. When someone enlists a courier to deliver a letter or parcel for them, they place a tremendous amount of trust in them. This is the way God sees you. He knows your heart from the inside out. He is aware of the dignified way that you have endured the days, months and years. The Father is wholly apprised of the blessing you have been to your brothers and sisters, to the Church, and to the globe on which you live. I would like to continue describing what I am saying to you here, but I know that your Christian modesty would rather Me not. *"Thank you, Mama. I appreciate your kindness."*

Your brother will soon hear from the officials about the position at their workplace. The leader whom your brother assisted with such goodness and intelligence will be giving your brother a betrayer's kiss. They cannot overcome their opposition to My dictating to you and your brother My messages over the past twenty-five years. This is the way it was written, you know. The Gospel is being fulfilled. Your brother has been turned away 89 times for positions of employment for which he was more suited and qualified than anyone else. This is the way of people who assume positions of power, hold the reigns of choice, focus their attention on themselves, and turn away those who made it possible for them to lead. It was your brother, and solely your brother, who convinced the local newspaper to endorse the candidacy of this man. This is too ironic for most people to understand, but not for you and your brother. Please do not be dismayed. It further justifies the fact that the greatest prophets of God have for centuries been ridiculed and ostracized. Some things never change. Your brother could have not been better prepared for the position he was seeking. He builds strong relationships with others. In the end, however, he will be told that someone else has been hired. Your brother has been battered by this type of rejection so many times during the past twenty-five years that this will have no effect on him. He will take it in stride. He is not the type of person to become embittered or look for retribution. He is more mild-mannered than that. If it is a badge of honor for one of My messengers to be rejected by the secular void, then your brother will wear it proudly. I wish for you to know that I have deep compassion for him, and that the Will of God for the remaking of the Earth into the likeness of Heaven must be done in your day. Sadness has its way of seeping into situations like these, but we have set our sights on the ultimate victory of a world renewed in the Most Sacred Heart of My Son.

Today, therefore, I come speaking about that victory, about the Triumph of My Immaculate Heart, about the struggles that Christians everywhere endure for their religious faith. There seems to be pressure from all sides and seams to force the Holy Gospel from the debate in the public domain. Here again, the prophecies of Jesus are being fulfilled. I am not speaking from a platform of defeat. I am talking about realigning the priorities of human life according to the glories of the Cross. We have our mission, and the Lord has His ways. Keeping your faith strong means that you must focus on the everyday tasks of being a Christian, trying to be self-sufficient in the secular world. When speaking of miracles, imagine what it looks like in the Light of Heaven for two people on Earth to have amassed almost endless strains from the voice of the Mother of God without themselves being cloistered somewhere. This is a miracle in itself. And, this miracle has been manifested because you and your brother have continued to believe. All the messages that I have given you will be vindicated before the world. Every day that passes, something more from your books and anthologies will prove that I have been speaking to you. And, as backward as it sounds, even science itself will evidence to humanity what I have said here in this home. As I have told you, this may not unfold within your immediate sight at every new dawn. It is a daily process that brings legitimacy to those who are wise enough to see. Many works of the Saints in Heaven are only now being revealed through the actions and conditions in the world below. The whole life of most ordinary people is their gift to humanity. You and your brother are in good company when it comes to being recognized as premier blessings from the Father to His Kingdom on Earth.

My Special son, there are individuals who represent the holy attributes of Christ Jesus more than others. Not only are the acts of Jesus embodied by His disciples, but the veritable genius of His personality as well. It is not recorded in the Sacred Scriptures that Jesus was playful as a child, that His sense of humor was unsurpassed, and His compassion for His friends was as far-flung as the rainbows. Those who lived around Him, His playground friends and fellow mates, those from whom He gathered hope for Himself – all these relationships have not been written in the Book of Ages. The conversion and sanctification of the exiled human soul is far too serious to have included these events in the Bible. But, they happened. Jesus was and remains today fully human and divine in the image of God, in whose image humanity has been fashioned. I am telling you that the world of men does not have that far to travel to be standing on the same plateau of excellence as Jesus. It is not so much a distance to travel from the womb or across the universe, but in the commitment to be as loving as God and as pure as the divinity of His Son. It is about all the gifts of love and the Holy Spirit being welcomed into the human heart. And, billions who have lived have done so. They have fought the good fight, and finished the race. They have escaped from the darkness and embraced the light. My Special and Chosen sons, this is the purpose and mission of writing the esteem of humanity in the Blood of the Cross, and making permanent the residence of the world within the House of the Father beyond all time. I have said that prayer is the begetting of these miracles, and equally important is the obedience of humanity to the glory by which the Church is being redeemed. There will be mistakes and mistake-makers until the end of time. This has never been questioned. What seems to be in dispute right now is who will follow the Cross as their way of life, which people and societies will reach a sufficient mass to make Christian apostleship the mainstay of human affairs. With these prayers and faithful obedience, the whole Earth will get there. This is what Jesus believes, or I would not be here speaking to you now. My Special son, please never forget that nothing we have done to advance the message of the Gospel and the mission of the Church will be in vain. I pray deeply that those who are taking care of the sick and dying will be blessed by God in ways that allow their hearts to see the Cross."

Saturday, May 21, 2016
9:33 a.m.

When you can no longer run, you walk.
When you can no longer walk, you crawl.
When you can no longer crawl, you scoot.
When you can no longer scoot, what to do?
You conquer the world from where you sit.

- William Roth Jr.

"There are people who believe that the Earth is another planet's hell."

"A man is more than a sentient biped with distinguishing features, but how many people, if they could choose their own body, would pick a different one? How many people, if they could choose their own soul, would wish to be someone else?"

- The Dominion Angels

"My dear Special son, I thank you and the Dominion Angels for giving more food for thought for humanity to consume. I wish you all the blessings accorded from Heaven for being so enlightened. While I will not be expounding on the quotations beginning our message today, I know that you will think more about them at your leisure. I am here to bless you and your brother for your wonderful contributions to My intercession on behalf of those who refuse to see, those with the capacity to envision what the Father desires of their lives, but who are reticent to follow Him because of their fears. My little ones, I wish not to refer to your lost brothers and sisters as recalcitrant because they often do not realize that they are fighting against the very framework that makes them one with God. Yes, they are sentient, but they seem otherwise unaware of their part in promoting the constancy and consistency of holiness in the exiled realms. It has often been said that they are more ignorant than malevolent. This is something that can be addressed if those who need to learn will focus their eyes on the teachings of Jesus during His earthly ministry and His dire warnings from the hillsides and on the Cross. In this sense, everyone must remember that the fullness of wisdom cannot be imagined until after the human will permits the heart to be exposed to the truth begging to be known. There has never been a question about the accessibility of the Lord's wisdom, but there is some doubt as to whether every soul within the parameters of time will avail themselves to learn. I am saying that our prayers and your dedicated mission have become the mechanism for this transfer of knowledge.

My little sons, humanity will often not be interested in anything beyond their mortal constraints unless there is something paranormal about it. In other words, they decide that they will believe in God only after He sufficiently reveals Himself to them. This curiosity is thereafter substantiated only when someone believes that they have garnered sufficient proof that God and the Afterlife truly exist. We know that this type of thinking is contradictory to faith. It makes faith something only palatable to those who have already seen what they are required to invest their faith in. God will not have it this way. The Father hands down the gift of faith to those who seek it, but not to satisfy a premise that a person's human will never defers to faith without first seeing. Even in all I have given the nations throughout the centuries, I have never said that the world will need less faith because I have come. In fact, it must be said that humanity should invoke even more faith to comply with the love and sacrifices that the Father asks of His people. It requires little faith to accept what someone from Heaven is saying. But, it requires tremendous faith when one is fighting in the earthly trenches to endure, uphold, sustain and withstand the heated battles of true belief under intense scrutiny, rejection, pain and unrest. My Special son, I believe that this is often the basis for your wonderful writings, and rightly so, toward the end that Christians everywhere remember that the outcome is worth the investment, and that the new life is worth losing the old one. This is the underlayment of the exposure that I mentioned moments ago – that there must be a welcoming spirit in the human heart that prepares the warrior for anything that comes. Surprise is always the key element of conquest. We have, therefore, laid the foundation upon which this entire model of human achievement is built, and we have done so in the likeness of Jesus' teachings in the Gospel. You may have never heard before now that I am not only the Mother of God, I am also one of His most prolific disciples and apostles. This is the reason that I have recently told humanity in Medjugorje that they are apostles of Jesus' current-century Church. I am inviting the faithful to be like Me. There is nothing either secret or more specific to be known about what I just said – I am asking all My children to identify with what it means to believe in and make sacrifices on behalf of the Church in ways that convert lost sinners and clarifies what is expected of those who believe in God.

My Special son, it is always with tremendous joy that I come speaking to you and your brother, and all My visionaries and messengers around the globe, because it provides more time to reveal the intensity and dimensions of what Jesus would have you do as 21st century Christians. I spoke earlier about humanity focusing on God only when there seems to be something paranormal to be gleaned. Hence, I have given many secrets to My messengers to induce the response of the world. This often keeps them listening to everything else I have said about what they should learn from Me. The secrets are modes for enlisting their interest as they battle the worldly distractions that impact them from everywhere else. Do you understand? *"Yes."* And, it is not that these secrets will not have any lasting effect on the outcome of the world, but their content is subject to change based upon humanity's prayers. If humanity prays from the heart in the way of Jesus in the mountains and elsewhere, the fate of the Earth will change. No inconsistencies can be attributed to God because the world did not know the content of the secrets anyway. This is a method by which the Father enlists the prayers of the faithful for the mitigation of some secrets that have been incorporated into My apparitions. As for the secrets given to you and your brother, they will be utilized along with everything else that I have told you in providing a capstone to the Morning Star Over America supernatural blessing. They are connected with the reason I appeared to the first Marian seer centuries ago. The Morning Star Over America is a portion of that mission. It is a way for God to reveal that He perfectly understands what it means to have been cast from the Garden of Eden, and it provides the groundwork for what the future will bring based on the prayers of men. Why would it not be prudent to believe that one Son of Man who descended to the dead is now fixing humanity's gaze on one Morning Star? It is a matter of revealing to the world what the heavens already know. It is the exposure of the truth, come full circle, to humanity writhing in pain that their relief and release is Jesus on the Cross. Look up, and it shall be given to you. This is the message of the Crucifixion.

    Also today, My Special and Chosen ones, I wish you to remember that the sensation that the Church feels in believing that it is being spiritually crucified is well founded. Humanity has never been taught that Jesus was eager to die because of the barbaric nature of the way He was put to death. The Sacred Scriptures tell of the pain and agony that Jesus knew He was about to suffer, and which He ultimately did suffer. This is the key message that each Christian must remember because, for many, this is the same kind of torment, agony and pain that they endure. This does not mean, however, that Christians should refrain from joy in knowing that they are perfectly united with Jesus on the Cross. This is the source of the anticipation of the Church to know that it is being spiritually crucified. I realize that these two things seem contradictory. It almost makes no sense. It was as painful for the Father to see the Sorrowful Passion and Sacrifice of His Only Begotten Son as it was for Jesus to endure it. But, God has always said that the redemption of humanity was never about Himself. Of course, it was to make Him happy that His people would be coming to Heaven to live forever in His presence; this has never been in question. But, the idea that humanity would be eternally damned was not an option for God who embodies the epitome of divine love. Hence, the Salvation of the human race had to be done; the creatures whom the Father deigns to live in joy had to be delivered from the banishment that they had inherited. My Special son, this is what Jesus wants all who believe in Him, and especially those who do not believe, to accept. It was all about forgiveness from the beginning. I have spoken for generations and centuries about God's love for His people, and that it has been proven in the earthly domain by the Incarnation of Jesus. His donning of the flesh was the Father's way of declaring that He had sent His Son to represent Him in a world that was about to be condemned. Jesus was then, and remains still, the Father's Messianic Redeemer. And, Jesus delivered a Gospel that was soundly rejected. As a result, the Redeemer was not shot, but nailed to a tree to die as a heretic, when He was instead the Savior of the damned. Lineages of Saints from that moment forward have suffered in His name. It is true in the world today. We are helping, My Special one, to reveal to humanity the reason why this message must be accepted, that Jesus is the Way, the Truth and the Life."

Saturday, May 28, 2016
9:28 a.m.

"Blind faith and sheer good will, the Most Sacred Mysteries of human redemption, the sanctity of the Roman Catholic Church, triumph over evil, the acquittal of innocents, the birth of children, the sophistication of holiness, the esteem of the ready spirit, the Crown of the Blessed Virgin Mary, the Morning Star Over America, and the imminent return of Jesus Christ the King – these are the pillars that foretell the inheritance of man."

Humanity says – be the brick and not the window.
Christ the King says – be the door and not the wall.

- The Dominion Angels

"My lovely little children, how can I thank you for everything you have done for Me? How much more can you give – there is scarcely any more that God would expect. You are now in the process of adding to what you have accomplished to defeat the devil. My Special and Chosen ones, you must be particularly more wary in the future because of the exposure that My messages are going to receive in the media. And, My Special one, I wish to tell you that you must not be frustrated about what things will come. Now, the Angels have given you a list of exemplars that rightly speak about the Kingdom of God in this world and in Heaven. Notice that the Morning Star Over America has been included because My work with you is so important. You must remember that people can fall into complacency when thinking in terms of the crucial elements of the sanctification of men. I know that you and your brother are not prone to do so, but there are times when such lapses can seep into anyone's life. It is something that comes from being distracted by all the issues one faces in the secular void during the exhausting efforts of everyday life. We have entered a phase where you must remain on guard against anything that might bring you harm or attempt, successfully or otherwise, to impugn your name and tarnish the integrity of My messages. I wish to repeat this morning that I am not asking you to live in fear. I am advising you that we have arrived at a juncture where I am walking you around a corner in your corridors of life, and you must be adaptable when these things come. It is all the same grace and peace that accompanies you along the way. I would also like to say that you and your brother are committing to eternity the best of yourselves. You are withstanding the muster that has grown around you which seeks to batter the influence that I wish to have on the world and the Church. And, as you know, I come speaking to you with love and affection, and I will do so for as long as the Lord allows. I ask that you maintain your inner-peace, that you do not worry, and that you always remember that Jesus is with you, and in you, for your strength, vision and guidance. My Special son, do you have any issues to discuss with Me today? *"No, just that I'm proud of our Bishop for being so kind in his response to the newspaper regarding our work."* Yes, '...they seem sincere in their assertions' – this is something that could have never been written in a script. This is a paraphrase of what he is prone to believe, that what you are claiming is true. This is the way the world will view it. It is time for us to consider the consequences of the grand proceeding that we have placed before lost human exiles and Creation. It is all a stunning exercise in conversion. It is the celebration of the Great Revelation! Thank you, My sons, for being part of the finishing of the Earth within the Most Sacred Heart of Jesus, completing the destiny of humanity in Jesus on the Cross, and capitalizing on the wishes of the Father to have His people living with Him in Paradise once again."

Saturday, June 4, 2016
9:29 a.m.

"Jesus Christ – Holy Human and Wholly Divine."

"My dear little sons, every day, we are building up to something greater; we are stirring the environment in which mortal beings live, and we are creating an atmosphere where the Christian conscience can survive. It is in this that the Church has grown, and I wish for you to remember that you have been nourishing its seeds. What makes you beautiful beyond the beauty given you by the Father upon your conception is that you reflect this genesis of holy life back to Him. I come today to speak to you at the opening of the Month of the Sacred Heart, and I will do so by telling you what I know about the Child Jesus, Holy Human and Wholly Divine – and I will give you My impression of what this Child did upon entering the Temple, later preaching to the masses over the hills, mountains and valleys of the region, and consummating the Salvation of the world on the Cross in the presence of humanity and God the Father. My Special one, I wish to focus My message today particularly on Jesus' attributes because you embody them well. There are people around the globe who say that Jesus' healing of the sick and infirm stands as among His holiest acts. There is no such thing as Jesus' holiest acts. To suggest otherwise would be to say that there were times when the intensity of Jesus' holiness was stronger or brighter than others. There can be no such differentiation when speaking about the Son of Man. Jesus was on Earth and to this day in Heaven the infinite personification of the perfection of the Father. This, as I have said, is uniquely reflected by you in the exiled world. Another comparison that theologians and others attempt to strike is that there were discernible differences between Jesus' Humanity and His Divinity. Again, no such dichotomy exists. Third, there are many people who hear that Jesus was the Incarnation of the Love of God, but some say, 'compared to what?' The point I am making is that sinful mortals, especially those who lack faith to believe, insist on imposing qualifiers on their recognition and comprehension of Jesus in terms of who He is and what He represents. They need to know that Jesus represents them – in their most perfect form. Since it has been stated that God created man in the image of Himself, does it not stand to reason that this 'self' must be made perfect to complete humanity's essence? This is the cleansing, purification and cultivation about which the Sacred Scriptures speak. There are no degrees of holiness any more than there are degrees of life and death. One is either living or dead, and holy or unholy. A person is either perfect or flawed. Jesus made clear in His sermons and impressions that humanity can become perfect, just as the Father is perfect. It is therefore possible for a person to be holy in the likeness of Jesus to the extent that their humanity and piety cannot be separated. Do you understand what I am saying? *"Yes."* It is a matter of arriving at one's destination, and not turning back. If someone does not believe that they will complete a journey, they are not likely to undertake it.

As a Child in the manger, I recognized that the Son of My Womb was the exactness of God and the Holy Spirit who conceived Him. There were no such thoughts as an 'appreciative' likeness of the holiness of God, but the perfect likeness of God in the Flesh. Yes, Jesus was born the Son of God, and God Incarnate. This is the reason, clearly, that I am hailed as the Mother of God. It was not so much burdensome upon Me, but My joyful service to the redemption of the world to live out My role as the Mother of this Infinite Child, now come into the finite confines of the temporal Earth. I never surrendered that role, and I continue to fulfill it to this day. I realized even before Jesus' pronouncement from the Cross that I was the Mother of exiled humanity because I birthed the first perfect human being. Those whom I have adopted will ultimately become loving in His likeness because of His imprint on those who believe. Hence, Jesus is My Perfect Son, and all who accept His Crucifixion and Myself as their Immaculate Mother will be sinless in Heaven. My Special son, I lead My children to Jesus through His Holy Crucifixion. It is to convert lost sinners that I have come, to usher them to Jesus who died to redeem them."

Saturday, June 11, 2016
9:30 a.m.

"Truth is made manifest, Salvation remains a mystery."

"My dear little sons, it gives Me a feeling of tremendous honor to come to your home, into our home, where I can listen to the strains of genius, holiness, truth and righteousness that humanity needs to hear. My Special one, I recently told you that you are My esteemed son and the consummate Christian, and your writings prove what I have said. It is not just that you are writing these magnificent things, but that they will reach their intended audience, and have the intended effect. You are revealing to the world the 'Truth Made Manifest' about the Sacred Mysteries of human redemption in Jesus on the Cross. My little ones, the Mysteries are Sacred in so many ways that the Earth could not bear the full weight of their revelations. I must make clear to you today that the greatest sorrow known to man is to lose a child to death. This is the revelation of the Great Mystery that the Father was willing to undergo this grief to bring His lost children back to Him. And, for earthbound sinners in exile, Jesus' message was not only that they be saved in Him, but that there is no greater gift than to lay down one's life for his friends. There is tremendous humanity in this, My Special son, and there is even more humanity in how the Father protracted the Salvation of lost souls by sending His Son into the world to die. We know that Jesus shared a message from the Father's lips that was so profound to hear that it brought forth killing the Messenger. The fact that Jesus was begotten from the bounty of the Father's blessings and providentially born of My Sacred Womb is another Mystery that humanity does not wholly understand. There can be no question that I am the example of Motherhood for all Creation. I am lowly, but not in an impoverished way. I am capable of tremendous compassion, succor, and counsel to those willing to hear. And, I trust My Son, knowing that He was sent directly from the Heart of the Father to teach humanity everything large and small that must be known. These seem like simple prospects when viewed in the setting of communicating with children. But, trying to permeate the minds and obstinance of the world's rulers and gatekeepers is quite another thing. My Special son, I have just told you why the passage you shared with your brother this morning is so evocative. It solicits the human conscience to embrace the Truth that has been made manifest, and it instills in the hearer the Wisdom of Salvation to which everyone is being drawn. In other words, the Truth describes the problem, and the Sacred Mysteries of Salvation prescribe the solution. Your writing, My Special son, carries a miraculous tenor of healing and unification, even as you make clear that Jesus will separate the sheep from the goats. Your work is prescient in that you explain what the difference means in being a sheep or a goat. You talk about the path that each takes into the Eternal Dawn that finds its place in the Salvation that the Earth has been accorded.

So today, I come to pray with you and embrace you, to tell you again that you are beautiful, to offer My Motherly friendship, love and guidance, to remind you that My thoughts have gone where your meditations are now being derived. What you are writing cannot be contained inside the boundaries of time – it is as perpetual as the Gospel itself, and as revelatory as any word the Holy Spirit has ever shared. The tone of your vocabulary and phrases is exactly what the sinful world needs to hear. I have said to you and your brother that it would be different if the Earth were yet only 100 years beyond Jesus'

Ascension. But, you have now come twenty times that far in time. Indeed, the Return of Jesus in Glory is nigh, and surely the exhaustion of 2,000 years has brought the existence and anticipation of man immensely more close to receiving their Messiah once again. I have said that God has revealed the miracle of the Sacred Mysteries of human redemption. I have also told you that Jesus has leaned toward the Father in Heaven to receive His holy benison. He has risen to His feet and is adjusting His vestments in advance of coming again and judging the world, examining the conscience of every person who ever lived, hearing the confessions of those who repent, and destroying everything that the Catholic Church has proclaimed to be wrong. I am saying that these are timeless gifts, just as your lives in Jesus and on His behalf are timeless in themselves. My Special son, you are always so kind when anyone asks you to tell them that I am supportive of you, that I love you and the whole world more than they could possibly know. I wish today to tell you how grateful I am that you have shared this knowledge with your friends and neighbors. I believe, on the other hand, that you and your brother have the right to suggest to any interrogators that they should read the Morning Star Over America books before demanding a private audience. However, it would not be improper to share further details with those whom you know will not scandalize your work. Be as shrewd as serpents, and gentle as doves. Always summon the Wisdom of Jesus. My Special one, I have said what I came to share with you this morning. You are the sole person in the history of Creation to whom I have given messages of this magnitude. I have elevated you to be the image of Jesus in the exiled realms. *"I love you, Mama!"* And, I love you too. The month of the Sacred Heart of Jesus is particularly blessed this year because of the visionary intensity of your writing."

Saturday, June 18, 2016
9:29 a.m.

"Life is a song – music requires the passing of time to survive."

- The Dominion Angels

"What does a touched heart look like?
Do we dare believe that we will eventually get there?"

"This gracious and wonderful morning of holy joy is yours, My Special and Chosen sons, because the Lord has given it to you. I have come again to pray with you for the conversion of lost sinners. We ask Jesus to change a world that declines the grace that would foster this change. I also have come with blessings and promises that you have long awaited, that everything you have done, even the small things, are being accounted for in the Father's divine plan. It is as though you have the Providence of His Will within you when you ask Jesus to collect the whole of humanity inside His Most Sacred Heart, even if at the expense of the tremendous suffering of yourself and others. My Special son, when your brother on Wednesday described My first intonations to him in 1991 as having been awakened by an 'impulse,' this was the begetting of the modern world's understanding of what My intercession means. When your brother said that Mine was the voice of a young girl, but a voice with authority, he opened the door for everyone who reads your coverage in the newspaper to know that Divine Love is manifested by My Holy Innocence. It must be clear to you by now, My Special son, that you have made possible that there would be a venue in the created realms for God to teach His people about the sovereignty of His Kingdom and the Grace of His Mother. The Dominion Angels have given you a pretty point to ponder about life and song. There can be no music here in the exiled realms without the element of time because it is in sequence and succession that the notes are sounded. This is an appropriate metaphor for the life of a man. The song that we have often mentioned that lives in him requires the passing of time to be played out. It is obvious and logical that this be true – but this same song is heard beyond the element of time once a man's life has been fully heard. This is one of the beauties of life on Earth, and this leads to the second vignette for our message today.

What does a touched heart look like, and does the world dare believe that humanity will eventually arrive at the doorstep of redemptive forgiveness before the Father in Heaven? These questions are answered not only in the faith that the Church teaches, but by the hope in the hearts of those who believe. The answer to the second of these things is that, of course, humanity will ultimately rest in the Arms of Holy Grace. This is what Salvation and the promise of Heaven are about. Hence, this leads to the concept that a touched heart must surely appear differently before it is touched by the sublimeness of eternal joy than it looks once that joy has taken hold. There is something in this 'touch' that changes not only the perception of the receiver, but the very identity of the one who has opened himself to change. A touched heart takes on the impression and appearance of the Father, Himself. A touched heart reflects as if in a mirror the newfound dignity that God gives those who believe in Him and fight for His Truth. Some touched hearts emit the brilliance of a thousand suns; others take-on the humility of saints inhaling their next breath, and many humbly take to their knees in tears with gratitude for the gift of absolution. It is often the case that people do all three. My Special son, you likely saw something different recently. You noticed something more transcendental in your conversation with the newspaper reporter who visited you here on Wednesday a second time. He was sensing, feeling and exhibiting the attributes of having a touched heart while you were speaking to him. Of all the words any living being has ever uttered, your assurance to him that he is trusted by Me, that I would pronounce his name, that I would acknowledge that he exists, was as great an event as the Transfiguration. You did this with your charitable assurance that he too is a child of God. My Special son, this man has waited a half-century for his dignity to be confirmed by the Father in Heaven. This gift was bestowed by you. This is the fruit of your faith that I have been speaking to you for over twenty-five years. You were seated next to a man who is now someone different than he was a few weeks ago. He was transformed from observer to participant. I tell you this because, before we are through, the whole of humanity will undergo the same transition. My Special son, it is your faith, your dynamic and awesome belief, that has summoned Me to keep trying, keep striving and keep praying that we will make way for the Second Coming of Jesus with wholesale dispatch. We are not only soliciting the Return of the King, we are facilitating it. Jesus is pressing the urgency of the conversion of the world and the transformation of humanity. If it be by pain, let the hurting begin. If it be through simple piety, then let the buckets be filled to overflowing with the plenteous holiness of God. Yes, if it be through miracle, then let the miracles be too many to number. Let those who believe be rewarded for their faith in ways that not only suffice and ratify their faith, but that increase the gifts and blessings from Heaven for everyone else.

My Special son, your work on your next book is on course. The writings that you have recorded for the opening and imbedded texts are profound. I am pleased that it is not only Me who recognizes this, but you know it as well. There is nothing haughty in a writer looking at a finished work and saying that they are gratified by its final product. So, I wish for you to know that you have touched the Holy Heart of God the way I have described a touched heart in My message here today – not that He fell to His knees and wept, not that He needed Messianic absolution, but that He recognizes His own work in yours. He is able to comfort, console, teach and bless humanity through you, through your life and prayers, through everything you believe that His earthly Kingdom should become. I thank you immensely on His behalf."

Saturday, June 25, 2016
9:30 a.m.

"Our dear Lord Jesus has inherited the ages; and those of us who know Him have been privileged with a stream-side seat to a life of impeccable grace, wonder and imagining; of unblemished love, truth and compassion; of peace, wisdom, freedom and absolution."

- Simon Peter on Good Friday

"My dear little sons, on this anniversary of My messages in the holy place of Medjugorje, I come speaking to you not only as a fruit of that sacred shrine, but to fulfill its purpose. You have become privy to one of the most profound statements made by those Jesus left behind when He was put to death on the Cross, but the acclamations that came upon His Resurrection were even more inspiring. I will tell you what some of them are in the near future. I come praying today with you for the air to be cleared about what the Catholic Church teaches about the effects of human behavior, and how they create the pathway to Salvation for millions, indeed billions, of people around the globe. My Special son, I have told you that there is a pendulum effect that occurs through the waves of time when it would appear that evil works will always prevail against the righteousness of the Church. I ask you and your brother to always remember that the Catholic Church wins at the last! It is not that this journey of life and conversion was meant to be easy, that it would be a stroll through a mild greeny field. Not at all – it is a constant battle against the evils of the devil and against the plots and ruses of those who claim an allegiance to him. One would think after the passing of 2,000 years that humanity would recognize the futility in pursuing a life of evil instead of the righteousness of God. And, many who are committing evil acts do in fact know the difference, but they refuse to renounce their lives of luxury and lust. They are utterly against making the sacrifices that will heal the sick and tend to those who are living in poverty and neglect. It is impossible to exploit something or someone unless the perpetrator knows what they are doing – this is part of the definition of exploitation. Those who bring harm to others while not knowing what 'harm' is represent another breed of wrongdoers. We pray for them as well, and we know that most of them will amend their lives once learning about the mandates of the Gospel and the promises of Heaven. These are the ones most likely to walk the long journey toward reconciliation with the Father through their own repentance. As I say, however, those who do wrong and commit acts against the Will of God with malice and intention are at this moment on the road to eternal perdition. To choose to commit evil works rather than committing evil by accident are two distinctly separate matters.

My Special one, I have told you a seeming countless number of times that I come to you in joy. Very rare are the moments when I have come speaking to you and your brother that I have been in sorrow or with a feeling that I desired the world to be put down. And, it is not because I do not wish the world to be different, but that I know that it is on the pathway toward being so right now. All I can do is wait for My children to come to their senses and act based upon this new viewpoint of life. It is a prayer to wait patiently for the coming of the Lord, but it is also an even greater prayer to prompt your brothers and sisters to amend their ways and seek to live holy lives. This takes time because, as was stated last week, human life is a song that requires the passing of time to survive. A conductor of an orchestra playing a symphony would not need a wand if there were only one note. It would be like slapping one's palm down on a tabletop a single time and saying, 'There it is.' Here, we realize that the methodical reorientation of lost sinners to their newfound identity in Jesus on the Cross is a process, and not an event. One must remember that Jesus' life on the Earth was likewise a timely process that culminated in His redemptive Crucifixion and Resurrection from the Tomb. My little sons, I wish to make clear that this process need not be an agonizing one – it is the reluctance of humanity to accept the gift of faith that causes the evil that so much ignites the flames of hatred around the world. And, it is oftentimes that this seeming 'burden' of faith is too much to bear to those I have spoken about today. There is a means, a perfect means, by which the faithful can come to acknowledge that the burden of Christianity can be borne with joy and hopefulness. This means the realization that Jesus has done so before you. It is not only to Jesus that lost sinners are called, but also to emulate and imitate what Jesus has bequeathed to the Church. He has given Himself as the Hopeful Victim of the Salvation of lost souls worldwide. He asks not only the lost to come to Him, but those who already practice their faith so that He can teach them what happens next in a world of ensuing days. It is not so much a repetition, but a challenging exposure to the Revelation of the Will of the Father for the way the Earth ought to conclude. It is not that this should be an ending in the way of pricking a balloon, but being renewed and enlivened under the Scepter of Jesus and inside the Cross on which He died. He is asking humanity to find themselves within the very Cross on which He was crucified so they will simultaneously be safeguarded inside His Most Sacred Heart.

My Special son, so many people down through the centuries have spoken about the plight of Christians. This might have a meaning of being well-defined in some settings, but the modern world must come to understand that Christianity is a means of the liberation of the heart and soul, and freeing the human spirit to dream in the way of the Angels and the Doctors of the Church. I am not speaking about inordinate dreams like someone might have in the pitch of night, but the dreams that good people envision within their thoughts while they are fully awake and their eyes wide open to the gifts of the Truth. These are the dreams that foster hope and anticipation, that feed the joy that spreads good will around the globe. I have told you that if men have dreams, they should dream them. God reads the hearts of men through Jesus the Interpreter. So, what we are doing here this morning with your brother, what we have always done through our vast, magnificent 'relationship' that you have spoken about, is to ask Jesus to tender to the Father a testimony that humanity is changing for the better. Jesus can sing and play the songs of joy better than anyone else you will ever know. It just seems as though He is often required to stop and rebuke those who reject Him for reasons He often knows have nothing to do with the devil and everything to do with the fear and reticence of God's people in exile. 'Do not be afraid!' This was the proclamation of Pope John Paul II upon his 1978 election at the Vatican. He was not afraid because He knew that pain and suffering could not stop or impede his love for Jesus. He was not afraid because I came to him, just as I have come to you and your brother, and asked him to be courageous in the face of Satan's evil works. He never tired in his mission of holding close to his life with His Mother from Heaven who lives and reigns as the Queen of Heaven and Earth. So, My Special son, I ask you and your brother to remember this joy in whatever the future may hold – the good and the bad, please remain strong in your unity with Me. Thank you for your holiness and goodness, the light you bring into the world, and for the mitigation of many ills and wrongdoings by your lovely prayers to God. This has been a fruitful month dedicated to the Sacred Heart of Jesus. He has been consoled and stirred by the invocations of The Divine Mercy prayer that so many Roman Catholics around the world have yielded."

Monday, July 4, 2016
9:49 a.m.

"Not acquittal, but ordained clemency."

"My dear little children, it is with tremendous joy and sanctioning that I pray with you on this day of freedom. My Immaculate Heart is filled with the joy of Heaven to speak the strains of Salvation in the Sacred Heart of Jesus. My dear children, Jesus does not come to pronounce humanity innocent of the stain of sin, but absolved of sin by His Blood shed on the Cross. In the Crucifixion, you have been granted eternal clemency. Today, I ask you to pray for all who are held against their will. Pray for those in prisons and in captivity in foreign nations where hideous hatred and vile ugliness stand in such contradiction to the peace and grace of God. As you hold in your hands and hearts the ones you love, please pray with Me for those who have no one to pray for them. My Special son, you have known for many years last passed that the eternal light from Heaven shines truth over all lands. The divineness of the Father exposes the impurities and inequities of exiled men everywhere. We are called by Jesus to remember those who are far from God, that they will find their way through our works and requisitions to come home to the Cross. My Special one, we are under no illusion that this can be done before nightfall today. This is why I have returned time and again to beseech My children to pray for the conversion of lost souls. We hold in our hands that burden and gift of delivering them to Jesus for pardon and absolution. It is the conquest against indifference for which we have come. It is for the destruction of evil that Jesus died. It is for the renewal of Creation that Jesus was resurrected. I must make clear, My Special one, that the clemency about which I speak is not a conditional pardon, but a full and complete gift of redemption for those who believe. Now and forever, humanity will be pure and holy inside the Most Sacred Heart of Jesus through the Divine Will of the Father from whom all good things come. So this day of freedom in America must not just be about flags, symbols and patriotism, but about the remembrance that God has ordained through this nation that all men would choose in their freedom to accept His Son. I have overwhelming sympathy for those whose lives have been lost, and their families who grieve them. War is always unsightly. It is always toilsome and intolerable. This is why peace is the only perfect alternative for those who understand the Gospel of the Lord. It is here in this place during your time that the Morning Star Over America will bring the realization to the people of the United States and the world-over that the Queen of Peace is your Intercessor before Jesus.

My Special and Chosen sons, I always remind you that I come in joy and gratitude because Jesus is your eternal Joy and Peace. While you were viewing the motion picture "Risen," you were seeing not only an adequate rendition from a third-person view, you were seeing the Life, Death and Resurrection of My Son through fitting eyes. This true and real series of events can scarcely be captured in pictures and movie reels, but for the parameters of time, you are blessed for having seen the production. It is a prayer for those who believe, a blessing to the First Apostles, and a wish for holy things to come in a world that rejects righteousness outright. Please know that the story of the Resurrection that you have witnessed has within it the Providence of God and the power of the Papacy to be bound on Earth as it is bound in Heaven. My special children, I once told you that anyone who speaks benevolently of God speaks for God. Is this not the essence of prayer? Therefore, it is ordained that whatever you can imagine that can properly transfer the wisdom of the Father to His people on Earth has been dictated from the Father, Himself. This is part of the power that God dispenses to humanity through Jesus' Resurrection, Ascension and the Descent of the Holy Spirit. Therefore, if someone wants power, let him imagine for what this power will be used. Let him spread his intentions and lay out his designs before the Throne of God. Let him make his vision of goodness in the world replicate and imitate the goodness of Jesus Himself. I have said that we are under no illusions because we have the truth on our side. And, when we walk to those metaphorical ledges and raise our hands before the masses below, we are saying to them that they are the presence of God inspirited in a world destined for Glory. They shine and share; they believe and transpire, they hold fast to everything for which God would have them reach. Yes, My dear sons, we bless them because they are willing to receive, because they have within them the ability to build up the Church that has lasted through the ages. My hope on this day is that Americans everywhere will see freedom as a responsibility, and not just a blessing. Why would the Father ordain that a man, woman, or child be born in the western hemisphere or the east, or the north or south? It is because He understands the spiritual configuration of His earthly Kingdom more than any exiled mortal presently knows. This prize, this American nation, has within it a seed of righteousness so profound that no enemy, no contrarian, and no evil can stop it. I am at this very moment being handed a bouquet of loyalty from the hands of the American people that has bloomed from the center of your hearts themselves. I dispense My blessing over the United States with compassion, pity, and affection for all who are keeping God's work alive. I beg and beseech you to never surrender the fight to those who would accuse you of not loving them. Lessons and teachings are about more than the growth of the intellect. They are about an ultimate change of heart. So here, My Special one, you have seen the contrast of a world with such commotion and the one you have inherited in Me. Remember always that God's grace is upon you; Jesus' love is with you, and I am praying for you and your brother always."

Saturday, July 9, 2016
9:42 a.m.

"When prayer becomes sustenance."

"My dear little children, I come today soliciting and joining your prayers for the conversion of lost sinners. Humanity would be less human and less divine without our prayers. We must remember that we do these things at the behest of Jesus to satisfy the Father's desire for the hearts of His people. When we pray, we are giving God His grace-filled sustenance with which He energizes the Creation that He has fashioned. Today, I remind you that the worldwide turmoil about which you are aware is a result of the lack of prayer about which I am speaking. The Father desires most specifically the praying of the Holy Rosary because the decades contain the Sacred Mysteries of the life and love of Jesus. I have always said that Christians must be of simple mind and heart, altogether different from the complexities of the exiled domain. Even as I am in Eternity and reign as Queen of Heaven and Earth, I also reside with you here in this world. I ask you to gather at My feet during the days and months, and yes, even years of your lifetime on Earth so that I may share with you the imperatives of the mission of the Church and the grace of the Sacraments. Whenever the Holy Gospel speaks about the enlightenment of the world, when it refers to the purification of humanity, it is directing exiled men through the Wisdom of God to the blessings that usher His Kingdom into your presence. My messages to you have always been about the transformation of humanity into an even greater humanity that will hold Jesus' hand rather than batting it away. You know of His suffering; you know of His desire to bring everyone beneath the guidance of His ministry through His Sacrifice on the Cross.

My Special and Chosen sons, I shall never stop speaking to My children about the grace, peace, and blessings of the Roman Catholic Church. I will forever extol the holiness of My children and your ability to become the likeness of Jesus. With all My Heart, with all My strength, with the power of the Holy Spirit as My Wisdom, I bring the Good News and good tidings of Jesus of Nazareth to those still desiring to know the meaning of life. My Special son, I repeat to you and your brother here today that our every purpose is to satisfy the Father's Will for His Creation. He wants His people back. He aches through Jesus' Most Sacred Heart to feel the tenderness of His children once again. He yearns for new apostles and disciples with whom He has always desired to share the sovereign peace of His holy love. God the Father does not know what it means to abandon His flock. In all His genius and omnipotence, of everything He understands about the deep secrets of human life and longevity, He is absolutely unable to conjure a thought of what it would mean to turn His back on Creation. My Special one, this is a tremendous blessing for the people of the Earth, but it is also the source of great responsibility for those who would see Him again in Heaven. You and I, My Special one, are aware more than any two individuals have been able to know. We have that 'special relationship' that has been ordained by God the Father from the foundation of the world. When I see you walk, when I hear you speak, when I partake of the expressions on your face, I see inherent in the human realms the sanctity of the Son of My womb. It is not that other men are incapable of knowing this grace, but that they turn away in light of the sacrifices that arise from complying with My requests. They should all remember that I witnessed firsthand the life of Christ Jesus whose exemplary strength has laid the foundation upon which all weak men can walk. This again is the Will of the Father. This is the way humanity's prayers become the sustenance of their own presence before the Throne of God. While Jesus in the Eucharist is most assuredly the Bread of Life, humanity's commitment to be worthy of Him is His mandate to appear. Never has there been a Roman Catholic priest in communion with the Pope in Rome who has pronounced the Consecration of the Host that Jesus did not appear. He came even absent of the faith of many who were there. He does so still to this day. Jesus comes in the Sacred Host upon the Consecration, even in the absence of the faith of the priest. Just as God the Father imparts life through the means of procreation, He imparts spiritual life to humanity through the Body and Blood of His Crucified Son. If the hearts of humanity were to become as authentic as these gifts, if the faith of those who refuse to believe ever became as intense as the determination of God to bless them, there would be no more battles on Earth. The struggles and strains of rich and poor would vanish. The hatred between colors, races, creeds, and regions would be no more. All it would require is the affirmation by a world rife with lost sinners that they will give the Father a chance. No solution can be possible for a world that wishes to unite with its God without this mutual affirmation. My Special son, never let it be said that the Mother of God did not provide humanity the means to be exhumed from under the burden of their sins. Myself, this Mother of Sacred Love, and those who hold devotion to Me, are the conveyors of the light of the world with the Spirit of Jesus as our guide.

Now, the United States and those around the globe are dealing with the horrendous crimes of both secular legions and followers of radical beliefs. What does this mean for the future? It implies the same as it always has throughout history and its own culmination. It means that righteousness as prescribed by the God of Abraham, Isaac, Moses, and Jesus must prevail at all costs. While we know that this price has been paid by Jesus on the Cross, it must be received in the heart of every earthly man if this gift is to be wholly shared. God says to the world that He has laid before you a feast fit for kings, but He cannot force anyone to partake of this blessing against their will. There must be a hunger for truth that grows inside the spirit of men. There must be a search for light that casts away the darkness. There must be a struggle against everything that denies not only the existence of God, but His power to shape, remake, and reorient the veritable meaning of life. We have seen the workings of great men and women who have advanced this struggle. The Saints have left in their wake the models, templates, and frameworks to which all others must subscribe. They are with Me now. They hold these truths, as do I. While their fight in the exiled world has been concluded, their prayers still go on. And, My Special son, you and I realize that these are the reasons that hope in the redefinition of man will never die. There will be no broken chains here. The links between the past and its own subsequent eternity will last forever beyond the ages. The hallmark of the holiness of man can be found not only in his acts and legacies, but in the transformation of himself into the identity of the Church Triumphant. This, My Special son, is the reason I continue to come to you in joy and thanksgiving. Your work here with your brother is of this eternal firmament. It is a gift as profound as the Sacraments themselves. When your Bishop's commission moves to review My messages contained in your Morning Star body of work, they will be absorbed by the grace of My Immaculate Heart in ways they could have never foretold. The love of My Son will induce them to hunger even more for the reciprocal love that they hold for Me. You must also remember that it is difficult for the leaders of the Church to witness the presentation that I have dictated to you and your brother. Why? Because no man of any century has ever seen the likes of what we have laid before them.

I have said that the Morning Star Over America is not only a work for the ages, but a transcendent blessing beyond those ages as well. It contains everything I would like to have said after the Resurrection of Jesus and the moment of My Assumption. All the sentiments, all the guidance and comfort, all the shared pity and wisdom—these are the things that a world of any millennium should have always known. I have come to you and your brother during the 20th and 21st centuries because these are the decades in which you have lived. The Providence of God is no more complex than this. What you have given to humanity in the form of your obedience to Me is as great as the fruitful outcome of any world war. Your own eloquence combined with Mine has crafted wisdom and created brilliance that will last into perpetuity. My Special son, can you not sense that this is true? *"Yes. I wish everyone would begin their journey into your embrace."* We have more than developed a plan for the conversion of the lost. We have literally taken their hands and lifted them to the presence of God. We have strengthened their faith from whence they first had it. And, we have given them a new definition of piety and truth that they could never have gained on their own. When you think about it, My Special son, it may be even difficult for you to comprehend what this means for the Church. My messages and your deposit of works need not be feared by those who are loyal to Jesus. They should be looked upon as not only a sanctifying grace for those with open hearts, but a means to authenticate the sureness and goodness of those who have been true from the start. So, when you arise in the morning and feel My presence every day, you are understanding the plan of God unfolding in realtime. Your life on Earth with your brothers and sisters is indeed a subpart of the eternity of God. You are near and beside Him. All the days allotted to you are written in His Book. However, if God had preordained the destiny of men without the mission of the Church, without Jesus' Crucifixion on the Cross, I would not be here speaking to you now. There would be nothing to enliven the spirit of man from his sweltering indifference on the temporal plains. We have said that God is good. All men with true vision understand that redemption cannot come without sacrifice. Suffering is an innate portion of the purification of the world. And, even as there are sorrowed times and dark corners, we always turn ourselves to the Light of the Father for peace and comfort. You must remember that I was required to live on Earth through faith such as yours. This makes us unique and united with all who believe. My Special son, this is what I have come to share with you today. Thank you from the center of My Most Immaculate Heart for allowing Me to do so. And, bless you for committing yourself to resting over the past week. It is something that holy men do. I will remember your petitions as I refer My sacred prayers to Jesus."

Sunday, July 17, 2016
9:30 a.m.

"What exactly is the purpose of love?"

"My dear little children, it is with deep joy and reflection that I have come speaking to you today – on this auspicious occasion when Jesus has so blessed your lives. You cannot yet understand how overwhelming is His love for you because you are situated within the bounds of time. All of your emotions, your thoughts, sentiments and impressions having to do with God come through His Sacred Will, and this must be your reason for living. My Special son, this has certainly been the reason for your life here in this world with your brother, your friends, all believers and the destiny that is yours in the Cross. I have come today to speak to you with words of encouragement that I pray will enlighten you about the opportunities that have come into being. First, I wish to tell you that your father is with Me in Heaven, and with Jesus and all the Angels and Saints. There has never been any question about it, and I ask that you live your life with the joy of knowing that the entire Faith Church on Earth will someday join all the Saints in Heaven around the feet of God. Today's message begins with the question about what exactly is the purpose of love. This may seem like an elementary question, but it surely has an answer that seems to escape billions of people in exile around the globe. The purpose of love in love's essential form is to preserve the dignity of the human person. Love is the origin of life and happiness. Love is the sharing of peace, sacrifice and absolution. Love more than exists, it perpetuates the Will of God throughout Creation in such a way that makes His Divine Kingdom readily known.

And, My Special son, I will speak about the derision and ostracizing your brother endured yesterday before the funeral Mass in the Church this way – no greater happening could have occurred in the history of the world. The contrast between love and the lack of love was never more poignant. The distinction between the darkness and the light has never been so apparent. What I am saying is that the events at the Saint Augustine Catholic Church yesterday made Jesus so happy that He began to weep with joy. Please believe Me when I say this to you because it is true. Why was Jesus so filled with joy? Because He was given the gift of seeing His mark on this world with the distinction that I just spoke about. My Special one, think about this for a moment. How could something have been so dramatic? In what other way could a picture or a thousand natural sights have created a vision for what it means to love in the absence of love itself. Yes, My little son, you must realize how the truth was made clear. I know that you wish for the just to prevail over the unjust. There is no question that goodness and righteousness should sustain the dignity of the whole world. And, with the occurrence of yesterday in the Church, Jesus is even more heartened to exact His justice not only in the aftermath of that event, but throughout the nations and continents of the Earth. My Special son, I am in no way attempting to diminish the gravity of what you saw and heard. This is not the point of what I am trying to do. In fact, it is only through this gravity that the distinction I am making can be known. It is as though lightning hit the same place with successive strikes. Your brother reacted as a Saint – he was not hurt or insulted in any way. Why? Because he was able to see the joy within Jesus' Most Sacred Heart that such an event transpired. I am saying that your brother magnified His Savior. Anyone else might have been crushed or broken, but your brother was not. This is what made the miracle such a blessing.

All throughout the Earth and the history of man, Jesus has waited for moments like these. There is clarity and dimension to answer the question what love is for whenever things like this unfold. Just as you hear the thunder outside this prayer room right now, Jesus was touched and brought to elation by virtue of His own Sacrifice about to take place. The entire day was a perfect picture of what He asks His disciples to envision. Now that I have told you this, I remind you that I will never ask you to go anyplace or speak to anyone whom you believe to be an assault against your dignity. This will never change. I wish your heart to always be protected against the insults of the devil and those whom he assigns to act out his vitriol. You will see with the lives of all My messengers that I will protect them fully and wholeheartedly. You can have all the righteous indignation that you please toward such people as these and their corrupt regimes, but you are too much one with Jesus to give-in to hatred. I am like you in so many ways that it would defy your imagination to know. I have thought all the same thoughts that you have both manifested and inherited from others in this world. I have processed what I have heard and learned through My knowledge of Jesus, Himself. Jesus is your model for life; His Gospel is your mode, and He will mete out a response to what happens to good people every day by those who offend and exploit them. My little son, do you understand everything I have told you this morning? *"Yes."* Do you have any questions about anything I have said? (*I told our Heavenly Mother that*

I had never witnessed something so wicked in my life, firsthand. It was a vile instance of hatred in the center of a Roman Catholic church by a professing Catholic, right in front of the mortal remains of a saint and the Most Blessed Sacrament himself. If anything ever cried out for the justice of Almighty God, I stand as witness against what I saw. My heart was pierced at seeing the innocence of my brother attacked, his gentleness assailed, his compassion rejected, his blessing thrown back in his face.) I ask you to remember that justice will come to those involved in the incident yesterday at the Church. It may even be more stark than anything you could possibly imagine. And, My Special son, it will not be long in coming. You have seen the justice of God throughout the lives of those who assailed you and your brother for your witness to My intercession in 1991. This justice will come again. My dear little son, take joy in what has happened. The definition of right and wrong has been more clearly explained. Jesus hears your prayers from the moment they leave your lips. It is through this knowledge that I ask you to live in the confidence that all things will be made right. I can make it no more clear than this. God knows, and Jesus understands. They also know that to live in Jesus is to suffer the sacrifices that accompany The Faith.

So, our joy and hope continue to inspire what you know about the conversion of humanity and the work that we have laid out. My Special son, it is only through your faith that this has been done. You and your brother have been willing to receive Me here for so many years, and sustain the forces that try to impede you. You have given Me the same faith that you have offered Jesus to manifest the Will of God in the last century and this one. When searching for words, My Special son, how can I explain what this means to Me? With what sentiments can I describe how God is consoled by your lives? How could the miracle of Medjugorje be more clarified than the messages from the Morning Star Over America? This is what the Bishops will come to learn, whether they believe it now or not; and it is what the Angels know and what Creation reflects. It is all because you and your brother have given your lives to Me. You and your brother and I will go onward into the future the same way we have been praying for the conversion of the lost and the purification of the world. Please be joyful and filled with hope!"

On this day, Our Lady placed Her miraculous intercession on the front page of the west central Illinois newspaper, the Jacksonville Journal-Courier, with a Sunday circulation of almost 12,000 households. It was a great gift for our diocese, yet our Bishop told everyone in the article that they should ignore it.

Visions of Mary
Greg Olson
July 17, 2016
Jacksonville Journal Courier

Timothy Parsons-Heather was sound asleep early on Feb. 22, 1991, when he had the experience he said changed his life.

"I was awakened — not as if you would hear a sound, but as if an impulse came from inside you," he recalled. "After I awoke, I could hear a voice coming from outside me. It was a pleading voice from a very young girl. There was authority in her voice, even though it was very mild."

A Catholic Church commission is reviewing the communications Parsons-Heather believes are from the Virgin Mary, the mother of Jesus Christ.

Within a half hour of that first event, Parsons-Heather called his good friend, William Roth Jr., to explain what had occurred.

"As soon as Tim said what had happened, my mind raced, trying to grab an anchor to explain what he had just said," Roth said. "And at that moment, the Holy Mother spoke to me and said, 'You have always trusted him. He has never failed you. Believe him now.' As soon as I heard that, I felt a supernatural ecstasy, during which I have never doubted in 25 years it was the Virgin Mary."

Since going to Medjugorje, a town in what is now Bosnia-Herzegovina, in 1991, Parsons-Heather and William Roth Jr., former Ashland residents who now live in Springfield, said they have been receiving visions of and messages from Mary — communications they recently turned over to Bishop Thomas J. Paprocki of the Springfield Diocese for a commission to review.

Medjugorje has become a popular site of Catholic pilgrimage since 1981 because of reports of appearances by Mary.

Parsons-Heather and Roth said they have experienced visions, miraculous phenomenon, apparitions, prophetic knowledge and daily conversations with the Virgin Mary since February 1991.

"After the initial shock, she began teaching us about moral truth and what kind of people Jesus wishes us to become," Roth said. "I don't see mystical phenomena or miracles, per se, as something extraordinary or rare anymore. They accompany our faith. Many beautiful spiritual gifts become part of anyone's life when we are consecrated in obedience to Jesus through his mother's guidance."

A few weeks after first speaking to Parsons-Heather and Roth, they said the Virgin Mary appeared to them at St. Augustine's Catholic Church in Ashland.

"We were kneeling in prayer of the rosary at the back of the church," Roth recalled. "She appeared in the sanctuary in front of the tabernacle, which could be seen through her chest as if it were inside her. During the apparition, the parish priest, Father Murray, entered and proceeded to the sacristy to begin his preparation of the altar for the next morning's Mass. He did not see her, but she gazed at him intently while he was going about his pastoral duties. As he left the church, she returned her gaze upon us as we prayed."

From the very first message, Roth said he was inspired to begin an official record of the events and messages, which have been compiled into 12 volumes under the title "Morning Star Over America."

"That's the title that the Virgin Mary told us to use," Parsons-Heather said. "Over the course of the last 25 years, the Virgin Mary has appeared and spoken to us to help complete the contents of the religious works. She continues to appear and speak to us privately for the completion of the subsequent works. We have remained cloistered since 1991 because we were instructed by the Virgin Mary to do so and not become distracted by secular interests."

Paprocki has established a commission to study the messages from the Virgin Mary.

"The purpose of the commission is to study the body of literature concerning what is referred to as the 'Morning Star Over America' in accord with the 'Norms Regarding the Manner of Proceeding in the Discernment of Presumed Apparitions or Revelations,' in order to express a judgment regarding the authenticity and supernatural character if the case so merits," Paprocki said. "I would advise people to do nothing with the published 'Morning Star Over America' works until the commission yields a response.

"This is the only such request for the establishment of a commission to examine private revelations that I have had during my tenure as bishop of the Diocese of Springfield in Illinois, which began in June 2010. I do not have data on the frequency of the establishment of such requests in other dioceses," the bishop said. "I formed the commission in response to the request of Timothy Parsons-Heather and William L. Roth Jr., who seemed sincere in their assertions."

Parsons-Heather and Roth said there was nothing in their childhood or religious background that prepared them for what they have experienced in the past 25 years.

"I lived directly across the street from St. Augustine's Catholic Church in Ashland," Roth recalled. "My dad was instrumental in raising us in the Catholic faith, and he studied for the priesthood before marrying my mom. As I was growing up in the Catholic church, I was an instructor for the Christian Youth Organization for the high-school-age parishioners. I was just a normal person going about normal things in everyday life."

Roth's friend, Timothy Parsons-Heather, attended Ashland United Methodist Church before converting to Catholicism in 1979 at age 25.

"The first Mass I ever attended, I was asked to play 'Taps' for Bill Roth's grandfather, John J. Roth, in June 1977," Parsons-Heather recalled. "What happened was the miracle of the Mass. The most intriguing part of the Mass was the consecration of the body and blood of Jesus Christ. I knew I had found the physical presence of God at that Mass."

Despite Parsons-Heather being seven years older than Roth, the two became friends in the early 1970s through a common group of friends.

In 1989, Roth, while a Christian Youth Organization instructor, received a book about Medjugorje, Yugoslavia, and that inspired him to visit the holy site.

"It was probably the most profound experience of my life up to that time," Roth said. "I had grown up being taught about our Holy Mother's appearances at Fatima and Lourdes, and it struck me that it was happening right now, and I thought that we were very, very blessed to have an event like that happening."

"What I saw was the truth through the faith of the visionaries at Medjugorje. I became convinced that the power to change the world was through the Virgin Mary's miraculous intercession. I knew it was the gift that the world had been waiting for."

After Roth returned and shared his spiritual experiences with his family and Parsons-Heather, Parsons-Heather planned his own pilgrimage to the holy site.

"I invited Bill's father to join me on the trip to Medjugorje in November 1989," Parsons-Heather said. "I had a different experience than Bill. I saw many miraculous events that countless other pilgrims had seen at Medjugorje, including the miracle of the sun, where the sun begins spinning in the sky and pulsating like a heartbeat."

Then, in December 1989, Roth and Parsons-Heather returned to Medjugorje together, where they received a blessing of the laying on of the hands from one of the Medjugorje visionaries.

"We were pulled out of a crowd of hundreds of people to enter the private residence of the visionary to receive her blessing," Roth said. "We were the only ones selected. We didn't really know why we were selected. We went as we were asked. It was a transcendent moment to walk out of the house and have several hundred people look at you, wondering what had just happened. At Medjugorje, the Virgin Mary asks everyone, through the visionaries, to live her messages and pray the rosary."

Roth said that between December 1989 and February 1991, he and Parsons-Heather began to take their faith more seriously by doing what the Virgin Mary asked them to do.

"Our holy mother has appeared and spoken hundreds, if not thousands, of times in our home in Springfield while unfolding our work," Parsons-Heather said. "She has been unrestrained and prolific in her relationship with us. She has used the trust we have placed in Jesus and her, hoping to reach the hearts of the American people."

Saturday, July 23, 2016
9:24 a.m.

"The elements, dimensions and dynamics of eternal love."

"Hear now today, My little children, I have come to ask the Lord in your presence to bless you and all humanity, to strengthen your faith in ratification of what you already believe. My Special and Chosen ones, I wish for you to tell the world of My gentleness whenever you can because My poise and demeanor reflect the compassion of God. The elements, dimensions and dynamics of eternal love are endless. I cannot list them in My message today because I would be speaking for every minute of the remainder of your lives. The elements of love consist not only of the Providence of God in all His Glory, but of the essence of the Church and all the implications inherent in the Salvation of man. The dimensions are as innumerable as the stars. And, the dynamics of eternal love are said by those who believe that Jesus is the Savior of the world – all the individual and collective chants and songs of praise, the sacred utterances that laud His sinless person, and everything else that draws the human heart to the Cross and the soul to the boundless joy of Heaven. Today, I also come praying that all who have been awaiting the arrival of The Morning Star Over America will know that I have already come – I have been in the presence of this nation from a time long before it was scribed into sovereign states. Yes, the Mother of Jesus is gentle and composed, and My impressions of My children are given not only in My messages around the globe, but in every intent that I have held dear since I was conceived in My own mother's womb. I pray moreover that the Cross will be the standard by which all men on Earth begin to realize the purpose of life. I tell you that this is innate and inherent to the conscience and consciousness of Christians because each and every person of faith will ultimately taste the sting of the Cross before they enter Heaven. It is bitter only to those who have not understood the authenticity of the Christian life. Yes, it is the Cross that you have inherited from the Father in the aftermath of Jesus' Holy Sacrifice. His Son has died, and has risen again. Hence, your inheritance is also the joy and gladness of the fullness of pardon; it is filled with everything good that any man could conceive. In everything there is to know about the comparison between pain and glory, pain lasts only a while, but glory is eternal. This is part of the essence that I spoke about a few moments ago. This is the ceaseless dynamic to which all good men are drawn in the image of Jesus. And, it is an understanding by humanity in exile that Jesus was born full-fledged in the

Glory of God as the Son of Man. Here, I am saying that you have the capacity to share with your brothers and sisters what I have said because you have seen it personified by Me. There is no reason that My children should fear the days and years to come. Why? Because you presently and forever live beneath the guiding hand of Jesus, and you shall eternally bask in His Light by which you are led out of the dungeons of exile into the brilliance of eternal day.

Today, My Special son, I continue to bless you and your brother as your deposit of works becomes more widely known. You probably already know that the door has been opened that will allow hundreds-of-thousands to be exposed to My messages to you and your brother. You also are becoming aware that this comes at great stress to many who have lived their years against the Will of God as stated in My messages. And, My Special son, it would seem clear that you are seeing how blessed you and your brother have been to have lived anonymously. It is not too late for you to embrace this kind of life because the expanding release of My messages takes a great deal of time. You have seen that there are unstable people who are drawn to the miraculous manifestations of God, not because they either believe or disbelieve, but because they are not spiritually well-formed. There are people who have done nothing but remain absorbed and consumed by secularism and indifference over the past twenty-five years who will come to you and dictate what you should do and say now – even after you and your brother have devoted your lives to creating your holy deposit of works. There are others who will utterly lay claim to you, and they will demand what you should do in obedience to their demands. They do this because they are marking their territory in their previously-held perceptions of God. And, My Special son, there are untold others who will be curious and critical. They will tell you that you have been deluded for a quarter-century by the devil to believe that the Mother of Jesus Christ would stoop to communicating with nondescript Christians like you and your brother. They might even attempt to inflict physical harm. My Special one, none of this is new. Those who reject the Gospel of the Lord have slain good and holy men for centuries. And, even those who claim to have a grasp on the dynamics of the Church have burned its own Saints at the stake. This is the battle that has come to those who have been accorded the responsibility of sharing private revelations with the Universal Church. Yes, it is a gift, but it is a commission and a burden that no one should ever pray to receive. You and your brother have lived in the sheltered care of My Most Immaculate Heart for decades, and I will proceed in My protection as long as you, yourselves, remember to live prayerfully.

My little sons, I will tell you today that everything you will ever say and do on behalf of your Mother and Jesus will always be acceptable to us. It is for the reason that you and your brother have lived that the potential of the Church is being sustained. You have blessed the Church – you have reciprocally blessed Jesus at the same time that He has blessed the two of you. I cannot overstate the joy and sense of peace that you and your brother have given Me as you have lived, as you have accepted your burdens and responsibilities here in your age. There is a timeliness and timelessness about your lives that cannot be measured with the constructs of the Earth – this is too a gift to God who has pronounced you blessed before the world of nations. I am certain that few of My children truly understand what it means for God to be happy. Does this not imply that He can also be displeased? The answer is prescribed by the Old Testament and the New. The Lord is slow to anger, but He is swift to forgive. My Special son, the world that you have seen with your eyes has never deceived you because you have observed it through the vision of Jesus on the Cross. Never once have you yielded to evil spirits or given way to anything that would diminish your expectations of the Church. You have within you the same boundless designs that the Father flourishes in Heaven. Yours are the dimensions and dynamics that have taken this world from the threshold of condemnation to the gates of Paradise. You are wiser than even you are aware. There will come a time when you will see precisely what I am saying today from a fresh vantage point because you will see the good people who will react with joy to the messages that I have given to you and your brother. They will open their hearts in the millions – they will not be like those whom I previously described this morning. And, you will see that everything we have done here together will be worth the time, effort, resources and challenges that have become part of the process. All the prayers that you and your brother have said are written in gold lettering in the corridors of Heaven. Everything that you would have wished for humanity and the world will eventually come to pass. The history of the ages will be supplanted by the way Creation ought to have unfolded. The landmarks and milestones that have drawn mourners to mortal places will be replaced by flowerbeds and Marian shrines. My Special son, I beg you to believe that what I am saying is true. I also beg you to believe that, even in your own humility, you and your brother are giants among men upon whose shoulders the conversion of millions has been laid. God has staked in you the future of those who would not have known Jesus or the Cross through any other venue than the miraculous Morning Star Over America. *"I believe everything you are saying from the bottom of my heart."* Thank you for vesting Me with your trust in the same way that

God has vested Me in His Grace. These are joyful years and meaningful seasons to be touching humanity with the Glory of the Father. And, I wish for you to take seriously what I am going to tell you now. Thank you for everything you have done for your brother. It is utterly too much to put into words. I will forever be with you and your brother, at your side and in your hearts; and I will ask Jesus to bless you in every way known to God and to mortals on the Earth. Please remember to pray for travelers, for the safety of people in public and private places, and for the soliciting of prayers for the unborn whose lives are precious to God."

Saturday, July 30, 2016
Saint Bobby Dean Heather, 1945-2014*
9:46 a.m.

"Shed are our fears, gone are our doubts."

"It is because you love Me, My little children, that I keep coming back to you. Jesus has made you the prodigies of the Mother of God, and in this, you have reached far into the heights of Heaven for every intercession that the Father could possibly dispense. My little ones, it is also because you trust Him. You could have at the first dismissed My initial appearance more than twenty-five years ago as just an unknown happenstance, but you believed instead. You knew that Jesus would not lead you astray or allow you to travel errant paths. Look at this gift to humanity that your faith has wrought! I have come on the anniversary of the birth of Saint Bobby Dean Heather who would have been 71 years old today. He intercedes for you along with all the Saints in your families and those who have become your family members by virtue of your unity in Jesus on the Cross. Salvation has made you Saints in the spiritual bloodline that Jesus poured out on Good Friday. My Special one, you have said that your fears and doubts are gone because you have seen firsthand what can come from true belief. It is all about the Mercy of the Lord to those who yet walk the Earth and for the Poor Souls in Purgatory. It is also about the joy that comes from all this that transcends all worldly sorrows and disappointments. You and your brother have seen The Light in ways that many others have yet to see. Why? Because you have chosen to look directly into the origin of The Light. You permitted yourselves to refrain from becoming embedded in all the dimensions of the secular void that would have taken your time away from the Church. When I speak about the dimensions of the secular void, I am not speaking in spacial terms, but only in terms that are flat on the single dimension of the Earth. As you know, the Kingdom of God incorporates all dimensions, and yet it cannot be perceived in the context of dimensions. Limitless, boundless and infinite are better ways to refer to the Glory of God. And, to say that His Kingdom is great is to suggest that it could never be compared to anything else. The point I am making is that this is the source of your joy that has defined and encapsulated your days and years as Christians in the world. You have all the power and faith required to exemplify what the Holy Scriptures say about your entrance into Heaven. I will always be with you in this world and the perpetuity of the next because I am your Mother. Christ Jesus would have it no other way, and neither would I. He asks that you remember how cherished you are to God, for this will keep you mindful of why He remains so close to you.

My message today reflects your contention to humanity that fears and doubts have no place in human life. It must surely look easy for the Mother of God to say that Her children should have no fear, given everything evil that is happening in the world. It might likewise appear just as easy for Me to ask you to have no doubts in the face of what God has allowed to happen in the expanse of thousands of years. Perhaps I can cite a metaphor that will help. It has to do with the baseball sport that you and your brother watch in the summer and fall. When a pitcher gets himself into trouble, the first instinct of the manager is to remove him from the field. However, you have often stated that it is better to leave the player in the game to clean up the mess he has made. 'It is yours to win or lose.' This is the essence of what you have said. My Special son, this is the same reason why the Father does not dip His hand into the material realms and impose His manipulation on the actions of men. It is not because He does not love and trust humanity, but He is trying to bolster the confidence of men and the Church to know that they have the power to succeed. Evil can be eradicated by the holiness of mortal men. I beg you to not see My metaphor as too simplistic because it is rightly poised as exemplary of what God wills. And, when you put yourself in the vantage point of the Father, you would likely do the same. One does not tell a horseback rider who has fallen off his mount that he will never be allowed to ride again. You do not tell someone who has fallen into sin that he will never be pure again. The daylight that concedes to the darkness of night does not say that the sun will never shine again. This is the renewal that has made such strength of Christians prevail over the fears and doubts that you have rightly said to be shed and gone. My gracious – imagine a Church that does not realize what renewal and regeneration means! There would be no such Church at all. And, My Special son, I speak about the Church within the human heart because this is where it all begins. You already know that the Crucifixion of Jesus on the Cross was clearly a visual illustration of the Lord's love for His people, and it was also a means to intensify in the hearts of men what it means to love even unto death. No one's death but Jesus' Sacrifice on the Cross will ever lend to the expiation of human sinfulness, and this is what the heart gleans from the events of Good Friday. Everything begins and ends within the limitless expanse of the converted human heart. It is the heart that gives the soul to God, and it is this same heart that accompanies the soul freed from the bonds of the flesh into the House of the Father. We have known this forever, you and I.

Hence, I have come speaking to you and your brother to commend you for everything you are doing to substantiate your actions in alignment with the Will of God, and to bless you for the furtherance of your work with Me. You have been reading My messages from two and three years ago with joy that you have patiently listened. You have recorded what I have come to say because you do, in the fullness of every possibility, love Me just as I have said. The passing days and the components of time are proving that you have become part of the Providential Truth of God that lives and reigns in the Kingdom of Heaven. You and your brother have made yourselves particular to the conversion of exiled sinners in such a way that has established yourselves as Doctors of the Church. I know that you believe what I have told you here today, but you are having difficulty internalizing the immensity of what this means. It has everything to do with the fact that you could have already lived in a previous century, come to Heaven, and then asked God to go back to the Earth again in the 20th and 21st centuries of time. This is not what you have done, but it has the same effect. Do you understand how this could be true? "*Yes.*" In other words, I have given you this vision of the essence of Heaven within your hearts that will seem familiar to you once you get there. I cannot describe the power of all the glory or the magnitude of your joy while you are still in this life, but you have a concept of what it means to anticipate the infinity of that gift. We know that you and your brother must live in joyful hope for the Coming of the Lord along with everyone who believes in Jesus. Thank you for praying for everyone who lives in nursing homes and other institutions. It is clear that all these souls are sufficing the call of the spiritual domain."

Saturday, August 6, 2016
Feast of the Transfiguration
9:31 a.m.

"The Holy Paraclete and the Lord's subliminal message."

"My little sons, you are darlings and warriors in the same sublime identities. It is with intense joy that I have come speaking to you today because I know that our prayers make a difference in where peace lights in Creation, and in the ways that humanity responds to the overtures from God. I wish to make a distinction about these overtures that must be internalized by humanity. It is not possible to have a subliminal message if the hearer or seer knows in advance that a message might be imbedded. In other words, part of the intent of subliminal messaging is to catch someone unaware of a particular venue through which a parcel of knowledge might transmit. Those with faith know that God speaks to them in ways that they may not readily see, but they are aware that He reserves the right to do so. With this said, it is true that the Holy Spirit enlightens the world subliminally through many signs and wonders that are from the Heart of God. Christians should expect this to occur – they should not deny that they are knowing of the vast ways that the Father intervenes and enlightens them through every article He pleases. My Special little son, does this make sense to you? *"Yes. People shouldn't expect God to say 'ta da,' here I am."* Yes, this is precisely what I am conveying. It is that you have always known about the Father's capacity and willingness to make Himself present in your life. This has been imbedded in your heart and soul since you were a child. And, it has been reflected in your behavior for just as long. This is why you and your brother have been called to deliver My Morning Star messages to the world. My Special son, I have been vested to clarify another point. Along with your brother, you too have always been My 'Chosen one.' You have always been both My Chosen one and My Special one. I have for all these years referred to you as only My Special one because it has been a way for Me to refer to either you or your brother without ambiguity. You have been chosen to pursue the completion of My Morning Star Over America gift to humanity, and you have been special in your ability to complete many of the facets of your work that you alone were capable of achieving. So, you are also My Special one in the same way that Saint John was the disciple whom Jesus loved. This is in no way a diminishment of your brother who is a messenger for the Mother of God. It will complete his eternal joy to know that you hold the distinction of both designations. This is how profoundly he loves and admires what you mean to him and to the Church. He knows what I know about your dignity in Jesus and your stature before the Father in Heaven. Yes, this is another good day! I am pleased that you are seeing prayerful people around the world begin to take interest in acquiring your books and anthologies. It is in things like these, such flickers of holy light, that huge flames of goodness and mercy are ignited. My Special son, I am tremendously pleased that humanity in the world is becoming more open to hearing what I have said to you and your brother for the past twenty-five years. You are aware that the longevity that you and I have shared is one of the most authenticating aspects of My messages. How could someone keep hold of something for so long? Because it is true. And, when you and your brother take another look at your books after not having read their content for a long period of time, you are gladly taken aback by how beautiful they are. Imagine what those who have never seen them are feeling upon reading them the first time. It is a welcome tremoring of the soul, and an eternal uplifting of the heart. This is what miracles do.

I wish for you to bask in the knowledge that men and women far and wide are becoming aware of what we have been doing here together. You have said more than once that it would have been impossible for you and your brother to have compiled such a massive body of work unless you were 'sequestered' in your home with some assurance of privacy. It is because you have prayed for success that this has been done. I also would like to refer to the condition of the Roman Catholic Church in My message today. The Church is as strong as ever before. The Mass will always be the closest that any person will get to Salvation before their soul arrives in Heaven. Jesus remains in control of the Church Hierarchy the best He can through the hands of exiled sinners. There is no reason to believe that the power of the Cross will ever be diluted as times goes by. In fact, its impressions and power over the material world is becoming even more prominent. My Special son, the United States of America is headed toward a reckoning with itself, with its own identity, in advance of an uncertain future. My response is that if your home country can endure the tenure of its current president, then it can survive anything. You have nothing to worry about. And, it is not that your prayers are not having their intended effect. It was not a lack of prayer that caused the Planned Parenthood group to begin abortions in your hometown. It is because Satan has been so angered that you are praying for the cause of all life throughout the world that he has placed his evil works right in your own back yard. He will not do so for long. It is as though he has brought a kite to a warplane battle in the skies. So, My Special son, I ask for you and your brother to remain assured that there may someday be a movement to flush your privacy out into the public domain, in that you would not have time for the way you have currently lived. You have seen that your lives have been a blessing from God, and a gift to each other. I am telling you that our work would not have been accomplished if it had not been this way for the past twenty-five years. Your own goodness, your love for Jesus, your undying devotion to Me, your allegiance to the Roman Catholic Church, your determination to move forward, and your patience during the process have brought your successes into being. You are to be congratulated and vested in the dignity you deserve for giving your life to the Father in your every act of faith, in every hour, day and new year that you have fought for His Kingdom. I ask that you and your brother remember how much you are loved – as though this love could be measured – and that your lives in Christ Jesus have manifested untold mercy for those who repent. It is a bright and wondrous new world that has come to America and the nations of the globe because of your faith and good works. "*Thank you, Mama.*" I will pray for you and your brother endlessly until all the Earth knows of the Morning Star Over America."

Saturday, August 13, 2016
9:29 a.m.

"*Most of us can remember the day when American life seemed much more benign, when it was easier on the eyes and more comfortable to the ear, when it was like spontaneous music that we tossed into the air, and it fell back to the Earth again in meaningful song.*"

- William Roth Jr.

"The much heralded Glory of the Father is with you, My children, as you unfurl your seemly lives in His Grace. I am not capable of anything that even slightly resembles envy, but I know what it means to be in good stead before our Divine Creator – I am pleased that you have placed yourselves there with Me. My Special son, your quotation beginning our message today is indeed about the simple and the benign, and this is not lost to those who have accepted Jesus. You witness every day the scams and drudgery of the secular void, and you are forced to engage it for your self-sufficiency. But, this does not mean that it has a hold on you, or that it is imbedded in who you are. You have the melodies of purity and simplicity given you by the voice of the Holy Spirit, and this is what you lift to the heavens in prayer. What comes back to you is not the echo of your own sentiments, but the intonation of the Lord's response in love and affirmation. My Special one, you witnessed yesterday your brother's dealings with the business company and his frank conversations with the people of the city government. He endured both circumstances with confidence – he knew that he was dealing with people who have no idea what it means to be good and noble souls. He even felt sorry for them because of what they will eventually see. They laid My Morning Star Over America books aside for another time. They placed the newspaper coverage of you and your brother on a shelf with dozens of others. They will ultimately come to know the error of their ways and what they tossed aside. As your brother said, it is not that they are wicked; they are ignorant of what they need to do to fulfill their oaths to God.

Today, I have come praying with you for all the reasons that the world itself ought to be praying. We know the designs of God through His Church and in eternity where the Saints are piously gathered. This is the focus of truly good lives – you and your brother who have in mind the priorities of Jesus in a world still filled with sin. The recklessness and indifference that has saturated America and the other world nations seems to be natural themes these days. It is as though humanity has been accustomed to being 'mean' and callous in the place of the good will and compassion that Jesus teaches in the Gospel. I wish to repeat My promise that I am communicating with the world through the Wisdom of the Holy Spirit in every way that I properly can. I am trying to establish that 'relationship' with all My children that we have often mentioned in our shared conversations in this home. Humanity must come to realize that Jesus Christ is not just another idol. He is more than the Prophet that He was known to be in His day. And, I am not just the 'person' who gave birth to Jesus in Bethlehem. I am the Mother of God Himself, and the Queen of the Kingdom to which all men are being drawn. My little sons, it is the same in Heaven as it is on Earth. When the Queen speaks, everyone listens. And, this is what the Lord deigns for His exiled creatures here in this world. When His Mother says something, all humanity should stop and listen. I do not wish to give you the impression that I am the Truth and the Life, but that I have birthed unto mortal sinners the Truth and the Life, and this is the way that revelation and redemption have come into your midst. It is also the means through which the conversion of wicked men must be accomplished. All those who claim to be a child of God must also accept their new identity in My Grace and Virtue as their Mother. Imagine what it is like when those who do not understand this, the billions who have lived another way, finally hand their souls over to God and discover that they have been on the wrong side of His

Will their entire lives. It is nothing less than the shock of one's impact against a stone wall. And, it is only upon seeing the Roman Catholic Church, as we have said for decades, that these dead souls are able to see the crucified Christ and His crucified Mystical Body that have made such reparation for their sins. This is the only way they will agree to be saved. I wish that you remember this in your prayers because your petitions are the catalyst that makes their enlightenment possible.

It is to joy, My Special and Chosen ones, that I call you today and always! Perpetuating your obedience to Jesus mandates that you fully know what happiness He has given you during your lives. You have seen that your brothers and sisters have not yet completely recognized the difference between the darkness and the light. Their perceptions are skewed, and their confusion is aggravated. We are trying to seek in them the willingness to let go of their own control of worldly matters that mean nothing to God. They must lay down their toys and pick up their crosses that will make the Earth become the likeness of the Glory of Heaven. My dear children, there are so many components to what I have just spoken that you can barely take it in. Letting go means that you must learn to swim in the ocean of human thought and action. It would seem to the men of the world that God is asking them to let loose of their lifesaving devices and take hold of the burdens of life that would make them sink to the bottom of their own helplessness. This is where Jesus asks His disciples to walk on the crest of His Crucifixion in trust and dedication for the future He has planned. What pours forth from the Sacred Heart of Jesus creates life; it does not destroy it. He wishes to spread over the lands of the nations His intentions for the way His earthly Kingdom should eventually be. This is the manifesting of the Divine Love of the Father by exiled men who claim that they have no Father at all. When I speak about these things, My Special son, I am drawing humanity to abandon its own version of the future in favor of Jesus' vision for the future. This is precisely what we are doing here. You climb to the rooftops to see a community of nations that believes that these rooftops are as high as any man should climb. It is not standing there that matters, it is letting the soul fly freely in faith absent the encumbrance of temporal thought. Such perils as materialism, pride and envy are like snares that Satan has set for unsuspecting souls. Jesus has said that the way to avoid these traps is by seeing the truth more clearly, not by being able to maneuver more adeptly in their presence. Seeing the truth makes known to humanity that there are certain matters that have no place in the lives of good people or their future in the company of God. If the road seems too dark to travel; if there are obstacles and temptations that have nothing to do with one's life in Jesus, then take another way. Take Jesus, the Way! This is a simple message that I have given you today, My little sons, and I have not said anything that you do not already know. However, it speaks to the reasoning in your opening quotation that all things benign are found in Jesus.

My Special son, attention to your books will flourish like the mustard seed. We are having the impact that we desired because of the massive volume of your works and the content of My messages. A statement being made quite often is, 'Who in the world would keep this secret for twenty-five years? They would have done so only in obedience to the Mother of God.' Another contention is that this cannot be about fame or fortune because you would have tried to market your books long ago. I am saying this morning that these are the things that shape the music that you lift into the air. Your love and lives have been this music that is so joyful for the Father to hear. He will continue to send down the melodies that will draw all men to Him. It is clear, My Special and Chosen ones, that you have been patient in the echoing of all the years. You have lived as I have asked. You have kept your focus on your lives and prayers. You have held your oath perfectly and obediently to Jesus who is waiting for humanity to respond to His Ancient Sacrifice that has repatriated Heaven with all souls who have been lost. So, this is the joy to which I have called you. It is the reason that I am beaming with happiness. My Special son, I am desiring that you remember that you and your brother are leading the whole world to the golden streets of Heaven where the Saints will walk forever. It is a strange life that exiled men lead during the span of the years, but it is a miracle that they share the recognition of their new identity in the Cross. All who are given to Christ Jesus on the Cross see every potential realized that they could possibly imagine, even before they lay themselves down to die. Remember that the priest Father Leo Clifford once said that death is a person's loveliest moment. This is true beyond any words that language can describe."

Saturday, August 20, 2016
9:39 a.m.

"Not just commonness, but oneness –
here, now and forever renowned."

"My little sons, I wish for you to think of utterness, completeness, infinite profundity and genuine authenticity. This describes the joy with which I come speaking to you today. Take another look, My Special son, at the video that you have published of your speech to humanity about your Mother. No matter how many people see it for now, it is the beginning of the flourishing admiration that modern men will eventually hold for Me. I cannot thank you and your brother sufficiently for what you have done, what you are continuing to accomplish on Jesus' behalf, and what it all means to God. Giving one's life to the Church the way you have done portends greatness for the Salvation of the lost. It means that love and sacred obedience will never die. It is the precursor to the events that will finally change the world. When one speaks about being not just in common with love, but unified in love, this is what Jesus has asked. 'Not that I should live, but that Christ shall live in me.' This is the unity that supersedes commonality. It is taking on the identity of Jesus while in exile on the Earth. This is where the joy of humanity begins, so much so that men and women from all walks of life will lead their children to My feet here in the created realms. God will do the rest. I have come speaking to you with My Immaculate Heart overflowing with love for you. It is obvious that you and your brother have esteemed yourselves in being faithful Christians, and now you are pouring-out the wisdom that you have inherited into the far corners of the globe. And, My Special son, you are re-reading My messages from recent years that express My desire for humanity to learn about their own giantness in the Sacred Heart of Jesus. I have tried to lend further evidence, undeniable proof, that lost sinners and wicked men can shed their old selves and take on their new identity in Jesus on the Cross. This is the only way they will survive the Judgment of the Earth. My Special son, the quotations that you have included at the end of your video of My messages are being received so well that it is beyond description. You have chosen the most evocative passages that reflect your own words – that all the secular high-headers have lived during a time when the greatest miracles from God have passed before them on their watch, and they have ignored them. Your speech and the other elements of your presentation is a holy rebuke of those who deny Me as their Mother. I am saying that your video presentation harkens to the Sermon on the Mount and the mandates of Jesus from the Mount of Olives. This is the substance of the Father's feelings toward His people, and it reflects His Will for the conclusion of the ages. I tell you that you are blessed and adored.

Today, I have also come to share with you Jesus' commendation of you for the reasons I have said. It is never a waste of time when you think about it – you and your brother, My priests and religious, and all the pious lay people who are protracting their faith have become more than simple human beings. You are standing-in-wait for the Second Coming of Jesus while you proceed with your daily lives. This is a compatible complement to the Holy Spirit in your hearts. You have become components yourselves of the redemption of the world, even as you have been redeemed as well. Imagine, My Special son, what this means to the Father in Heaven. Think about what He sees as you live every day on Earth. With what righteous pride does He look upon you and all who serve Him, beaming with happiness that you are completing His work. And, ponder how Jesus receives your gifts to the Church on behalf of all who love Him. It can no more be placed into words than one might attempt to describe the beauty of Heaven, itself. I have said that your lives have purpose; there is no question about that. But, your lives have eclipsed the definition of purpose to include your heavenly function as an ally of God in the material world. You and your brother can always rest comfortably knowing that you have been the agents of change in a world that resists change for the good. There have been giants of history come and go, but none have had the impact that you and your brother have forged into being. I commend you and promise that you will be repaid a millionfold. It is a beatific certainty. Your prayers, compounded with Mine, are setting afire the deep oceans of indifference in which societies have been lost for centuries. 'We have something they all want; it will be their big surprise' (*Our Lady was apparently citing a popular music lyric here*). All the challenges and failures that mankind faces and undergoes are overcome by our prayers. We reverse the tides of history, and birth the legacy of humanity anew. This is what your lives in Christ Jesus and under My Holy Mantle have accomplished. I know that you will be relieved when I can one day tell you that the whole of the nations and all the centuries of time have finally focused on the Morning Star Over America as the capstone to My purpose in dispensing graces from Our God in Heaven. Everything we have done for Jesus will bear the sweet fruits that the Father has intended.

My Special son, I ask that you remember how good you are. I will keep repeating this until we see each other in Heaven. "*Thank you, Mama.*" We will speak to each other much the same way that we are at this very moment, and you will wonder where your mortal years went. I give you My earnest promise that I will stand with you and your brother against the world when the time comes to do so. Having said this, I wish to tell you that you already have attractors and admirers far and wide in the earthly domain. There are millions who will come to you as I have previously said, but you will not necessarily want them to. Sometimes they will approach you only in the spiritual realms, but they will know you nonetheless. Laid before humanity now is the Morning Star Over America iconography of the messages from the Mother of God. I could not have said this twenty-five years ago. You could not have imagined the lifetime of gifts that you would receive back then. You would never have guessed what you see when you look at the expanse of your work. *"I am so thankful. It has been worth every sacrifice."* And, I have told you that the joy in which I come reflects the gratitude that I have for you. It is a miracle beyond all other miracles because it has lasted long into this new millennium for the conversion of the lost. *"I hope my father can now see what his faith has produced."* Indeed, he knew it long before he came to Heaven a month ago. He knows it now before the backdrop of eternity. All your loved ones, all the good people of history, your family members and ordinary giants – everyone who has ever breathed-in the love of Jesus Christ knows what the faith of your father has manifested. It would seem that the most proud of all, however, is your grandfather John. And, yes, your grandmother Eula as well, and all whose generations have sustained your faith. It is a grand reunion that your father has joined with your family members who have come to Heaven, and your brother's loved ones, and all who have kept the faith during the most momentous times of the world. The word 'joy' has only three letters, and it is infinitely insufficient as a means of expressing the fulfillment that they know right now. Please remember everything I have told you about how you are loved and admired. I cannot tell you too often what you and your brother mean to Jesus. It is stunning to see His eyes glow with such love as He looks upon your lives."

Saturday, August 27, 2016
9:33 a.m.

"Faith and the virtuosity clause."

"Hear, My little children, of your truthful standing before Jesus and the Hosts of Heaven – you are Saints who have yet to pass through the veil to your eternal home with the Father. I have said in Medjugorje only two days ago that I bring the joy of Sacred Love to My visionaries, to be shared with all the world. This is the same joy that I celebrated with you a week ago, and it is the joy that you will bring with you when you join Me in Paradise. The beginning of My message today is about your talents and expertise in effecting the tenets of the Gospel in this world. To be a virtuoso means that you have virtuosity in a given discipline. It means that you are a master or prodigy. It means that you have overwhelmed humanity with your ability to know and relate your wisdom and capabilities to the exiled realms. My Special and Chosen sons, you have both achieved this status as those to whom Jesus turns for help in the conversion of lost sinners. It is not the same as virtue, although you also have plenty of that. But, it is about your stature and standing before God, even as you are yet living in His earthly Kingdom where the militance of your faith is played out. I do not declare these things lightly. As you have seen in My messages around the globe, it is necessary for Me to speak with disciplinary overtones, with rebuking and upbraiding words and phrases. But, not here. I feel at home here with you as though you were already with Me in the Light of the Eternal City. And, this is a standing that you shall never shed. I wish that you will somehow comprehend that I lack the words to describe the way Jesus sees you, the means by which He trusts and depends on you, the admiration with which He describes you to the Father and the Heavenly Hosts. Just as sure as your expert talents have given the world The Morning Star Over America, your prayers in reflection of your lives are mitigating the sins of the wrong and wicked. I will someday reveal to you an image of what this means, but it is hardly possible to place into human language. There are stark ways that others have approached their faith, some lukewarm, still more barely receptive, and many who see their relationship with God as though He is an inanimate object in a dark corner of a room. You have seen that the Lord requires them to come to Him through the gift of faith that He has accorded everyone who has asked. As backward as it sounds, God wants to take a picture of His children one at a time, but He wants them to first get out of the way. What? Yes, He wishes to take a photograph of someone who has to get out of the way of themselves to pose. I realize that this makes no sense, but it holds full logic in the spiritual realms. And, once the picture is processed, Heaven will see an image of Jesus. God asks that the burdensome nature of the individual will be put aside, that the Christian man will turn to the joy that I have described, and all who believe in Him shall expect and prepare for the miracles He has planned.

Today, therefore, I wish to re-emphasize that all glory and honor that is given to Jesus is reflected back to those who love Him. It is not just a novel notion that His disciples offer, but the intense dedication of their hearts and lives to the purification of the human family – one soul at a time. It would seem that there are many things in common with the people of the Earth, physically and ideologically. It is that living in the world brings problems to all, including the struggle for food, water and shelter; the hunger for love, peace and acceptance; a sense of purpose and the desire for self-fulfillment. My Special son, you have found that different societies suffice these needs in diverse ways. However, the difficulties arise when those who embrace contrasting ideologies attempt to force them onto people who do not share them. This is the cause of secular wars and sectarian battles. I have said many times that only the fight for the conversion of humanity to Jesus on the Cross is the battle worth waging. There will never be a time when this will not be true. This is the reason why I have such hope in My children on Earth. There is One Church located in one world to which all men should subscribe. This makes simple the pursuit of the Gospel, no matter what geographic location tends to see it. It is not as though Jesus came into the world and offered two, three or four different pathways to Salvation in Heaven. This would clearly have caused confusion and commotion on the Earth. Indeed, He offered Himself, the Person speaking, as the Way to redemption. Can you imagine how much turmoil there would be in the world if God had offered multiple avenues for the Salvation of the human soul? The point I am making is that there is only one pathway to Heaven; and even in this, many exiled human beings cannot decide what to do. They have delved into false choices and so-called alternative means. Yes, this is the error that is rampant in the world today. Not only is Jesus being rejected, which is bad enough, He is seen as just another messenger who might have an inward path to the portals of unseen dimensions. This diminishment does not bother Him. He is not insulted by those who reject Him as the Singular Truth. What does bother Him, however, is that sinners are condemning themselves. Once they reject and blaspheme His Crucifixion and Resurrection, He needs to do nothing more. Why? Because those who do these things have already chosen the eternal fires.

My Special son, this leads to the question of the efficacies of Divine Mercy. The answer is quite simple. Mercy is for the penitent. Anyone who rejects their previous identity, repents of their sins, claims their share of absolution in Jesus' Blood on the Cross, and who promises to amend their life is in good standing before the Father in Heaven. They will choose to accept the Divine Mercy of Jesus because they have become immersed in the infinite depths of His love for them. On the other hand, the billions who have not done this are sentenced to judge themselves and what must become of their unredeemed souls. This is the facility of human decision-making at its most crucial moment. There are those who decide for condemnation because they know they have not lived worthily in light of the Cross, and there are others who choose condemnation because they hate Jesus outright, even as they see Him upon their deaths. The first of these two groups is always embraced by suffering-humanity. This is what keeps them warm during their cold self-judgment before Jesus on the Cross. It is in finding themselves inside Jesus' Wounds that sinners who are truly sorry decide that they are worthy of His Holy Sacrifice. My Special son, the most crucial moment of advocacy, to every degree that advocacy is defined, is when the Saints in Heaven tell a penitent sinner that he is worthy too. Although humanity on the Earth does not see it, this is perhaps one of the most beautiful ethereal sights to behold. Imagine this. Someone who just could not get it right during their mortal years hands their spirit over to the Father in death, and the Father places them before the Son to be judged. They then see in full brilliance the magnified Glory of Truth that always glimmered inside their heart during their exiled years. And, through the intercession of the Angels and Saints, the sinner is reminded of the many times they raised their head even at the thought that God loved them. This was their connection with His Divine Will. And, this same Christ and these same Angels and Saints begin to recite the prayers that this sinner prayed during his mortal life on Earth. They are emblazoned in gold letters in the vaults of The Divine overhead. My Special son, this is where the sinner begins to recognize that he has returned to a home that he never knew he left. It is not like tempting somebody to take a leap across a chasm, it is the whole of Heaven reaching out to the sinner and asking him to join them because *they* need him. This is where the reunion is done, and the Communion of Saints becomes more whole. Another facet of Jesus' Mystical Body finds its rightful place in the presence of the Father. Another room in His House gains its proper tenant, reserved for him all along.

My Special and Chosen ones, I have described the collective virtuosity of the Angels and Saints to a holy degree, and I wish to tell you that this same power belongs to the Faith Church on Earth. In fact, when the Church Militant expedites its prayers on behalf of the faithful departed, the Church Triumphant stands aside and waits its turn. The door between Heaven and Earth is opened because the Faith Church decides to come in. When somebody says, 'Let us pray' in the earthly realms, it is as though Jesus Himself stands aside and tells His Divine Kingdom that it is His honor and privilege to introduce to them the presiders of His Gospel on Earth. This is the dignity and esteem that Christians have in the world. It is as though all eternity is called to stillness so those who yet live on Earth with the hope of the Cross can speak to those who have already seen. This is what that one sinner sees and hears that I spoke about moments ago. He once might have said, 'Dear God, I don't know if you are there, but if you are, please hear my prayers.' And, before he realizes it, he has come to a place where his simple prayer of faith is still echoing through the air. If he asks whose voice he hears, Jesus of Nazareth will say '…It is yours.' Yes, still fresh and viable, still resounding, still relevant and new, this found sinner's words are reflected back into the heart from whence they came. And, later when this new Saint writes his intercessory prayers to be dispensed to those he left behind, he will say, '...and I was saved. My life, heart and soul breached the veil, and I was saved.' This, My Special son, is the way the whole world should look with hope upon their destiny in the Lord."

Saturday, September 3, 2016
9:34 a.m.

"Benevolence yes, subservience no –
Sometimes you need a footstool to grab hold of a ladder.
It's like digging around the yard and unearthing another shovel."

"My little sons, My presence here today is all about My love for you, My intense desire to tell you that the world and all it contains belongs to you inside the Sacred Heart of Jesus. And, it is according to your discretion how you wish to deal with it – what you wish to keep and discard, what you cherish to achieve, whatever ideas and frameworks you wish to embrace for the glory of God. You are meant to be the same benevolent creatures as Jesus Himself, but you are not required to be subservient to anyone else in the world. Yes, you are co-creatures with Jesus; you are His likeness and advocates, and you have inherited in Him the dignity that the sinners of Earth would rather you not hold. It is for all these reasons that I come speaking to you, but mostly because I love you beyond all telling. My dear little sons, if I had never uttered a word to share with the rest of your brothers and sisters, I would have come anyway. I would have appeared to you and prayed beside you with no one else knowing because I love you so profoundly. It was you, My sons, who instilled in Me the desire to ask you to transmit My messages to the rest of the world. The inscriptions of faith and promise that are written in your hearts gave Me reason to believe that we could succeed. And, so it is – I am here again. I know that I am welcome here in your home bearing the Child Jesus in My Arms and the Holy Spirit in My Immaculate Heart. This is an auspicious time for all Christians, and it is an inauspicious time for those who decline the Truth of God. I realize that the actual deposit of news and information that you encounter every day would tell you otherwise. The content of the misinformation that comes from the media has an intentional bias against the Catholic Church. There is lacking in what they want holy people to know regarding the very facts that would destroy their own industry. We have spoken about this before. I have also said here and around the globe that the Holy Spirit of God is the arbiter of what must be judged by the converted human heart. It is not only clear, but wholly obvious that the truth belongs to Jesus; the truth is Jesus. And, this is where humanity must turn to discover its rightful place in space and time, in the annals of history, and what must become the future for those who have believed. Judge not lest you be judged does not imply that good people should turn their backs against those who suffer the perils of their own sins. It does not mean looking the other way when the secular void is painting such impure pictures for younger generations to see. One of the worst forms of child abuse is to tell them that evil acts are nothing more than acceptable alternative choices.

My Special son, you know in your heart the same as your brother what righteousness looks like when wholly revealed. I have told you in My 2015 and 2016 messages about the piety, power and innocence of the Sacred Divine when clothed in human flesh. It has nothing to do with skin and bones, but about holiness and goodness being able to be seen through eyes of prudence, wills of compassion, desires to be penitent in the face of the Lord's judgment, and the ability to reach beyond the center of the self to all the lives and peoples who must ultimately find themselves in God. My Special one, it is all about holding oneself accountable before the judgment of God prior to that judgment actually coming. This is the preparatory life that Christians must lead. And, as you have seen in the opening of My message today, it is about doubling back and rethinking what certain situations mean. Who would have guessed that someone might need a footstool to reach a ladder? This is how out of touch many people's thoughts have become. They believe that they will begin climbing out of their depraved lives once they see the ladder, not knowing that they are so muddled in sin that they will not be able to reach the first rung. Their own willing conversion and repentance is the footstool that will give them that first handhold. And, who on Earth ever found a shovel when they were digging a hole? It is such an awkward thought that things like this never come to mind. But, this is the uniqueness toward which Jesus leads the human mind. It is living within the world as self-sufficient people, and at the same time being individuals whose insights are far beyond ordinary life. My Special son, it is this approach that made Jesus seem like such an anomaly in His time. This is what caused His persecution, suffering and death. Imagine a man coming to the door and saying that He was a descendent of Saint John the Baptist. This would be very difficult for anyone to believe. But, if he threw water in your face, one could not be sure that it was not as holy as the River Jordan. I am saying all these things because this is the way My messages to you and your brother are being seen by many who have heard the news. This is not a poor prospect because they assume that they have heard all this before – except when they take another look at the divine messages that I have given you, and the accumulation of decades that you have responded. This says more about faith than miracles. And, this is another reason why you and your brother have been not only excellent in the eyes of the Father, but exceptional in the lineage of the Doctors of the Church.

I wish to impress upon you and your brother that Heaven has a 'presence,' even though it has not yet been seen by the eyes of mortal men. This presence is here within you, and you are aware of the glory that is being nurtured in your hearts. You are feeding the Kingdom of God here on Earth in the same way that the Holy Eucharist feeds you God's love. You have given Jesus 'the best of rooms' because you are aware of the ways He has touched you. Jesus is the consummate Man of instinct, maturity and stateliness, even as He is the Child in My Arms. He is the Incarnation of Wisdom and Truth in one Begotten Son. He was not 'made' like someone might construct an artifact, but begotten of the Father with whom He is eternally one. And in this, you and all believers are begotten into the perfection that God intends all creatures to become. It is all based on the stainless goodness that is the Lord. You might think about meeting Jesus in the Manger, and then seeing Him again when He was twelve, and then twenty, and finally at age 33. Your eyes would behold someone who certainly appeared different in accordance with the maturity of the body, but you would know deep within your heart that the Child of the Manger is present on the Cross, although years have passed. Perfect Love and Divine Innocence never change; they have no need to change. It is to the refinement of men in exile that this must be known. And, men on Earth can speak to Jesus not solely as the Savior of lost sinners, but as a friend and companion. Men can ask Jesus if He understands what happened in their families and on their jobs yesterday, and He would reply that He does. It is all about this 'presence' to which I am referring, the constancy of compassion and intervention that Jesus loves to give the world. There is no question that humankind on Earth should fear God; it says as much in the Sacred Scriptures. But, Jesus has the Father's ear. Jesus has made life for Christians bearable to undergo because He has lived here with you. My Special son, there is a fulcrum to the life of Jesus that no one ever talks about. Jesus was born into a world of men where everybody else born the day and even years before were older than Him. Now, you have moved into the 21st century, and everyone is centuries younger than Jesus was when He was crucified on the Cross. Mortal men tend to think in these terms. They admit that Jesus was born 2,000 years ago, but they refuse to heed His calling because He died when He was only 33. No person with true knowledge of God could have held the reigns for eternity, they say. But, these same men are themselves being called to accept the Child of Bethlehem.

Along with this paradox, these doubters are as wrong about Jesus' capacity for the fullness of wisdom as they are about their future without Him. They are not aware of the 'presence' that is calling them to know. It is like an invisible feather touching someone on the nose. They can feel it, and they might scratch it, but they do not know the origin of its touch. This is the same way that the Holy Spirit knocks on the door of the human heart. It is Jesus trying to enter. The 'presence' is imminently waiting to be admitted into the lives of those who do not know what they are missing. The void in their lives, hearts and souls is obvious, but they are ignorant as to the providence that will make them whole. My Special and Chosen ones, it is to this fact that I have spoken today when I have said that you are benevolent children, but not subservient ones. You need not bow down or pour yourselves out at the feet of other men to compel them to believe. Jesus does not kiss the feet of sinners, He washes them with love. Why? Because they are as unclean as the spirits inhabiting their flesh. This is the reason why we must pray for them, My children. Jesus will make them clean and kiss them with the affection of the truth that blooms from the love in His Sacred Heart. He will restore their innocence by making expiation for the errors of their past. Prayers not only invoke this 'presence' about which I speak, they manifest it in places where God has been unwelcome to go."

Saturday, September 10, 2016
9:28 a.m.

"The visceral intuition of the Christian heart –
robust proficiency in the spiritual vernacular."

"Never shall you surrender to the darkness of the world, My little children. You belong to the Divine Light that engulfs you, and this is where you will find your peace and comfort. I come speaking about the visceral intuition that keeps you positioned in the grace of God in the context of the dedication of your own will to Him. You have become robust in speaking the strains of spiritual Truth because you pray for the conversion of the lost and the Second Coming of the Son of Man. The term 'visceral' means that your faith is about immersion more than the intellect. It implies and outrightly signifies that you have internalized the teachings of the Gospel, that it has become your means of living and the purpose of your faith. My little sons, everything that is good begins from within. It is the seed and the thought, the instinct and the urgency. And, this is what the parable of the mustard seed means. There can be no true spiritual growth unless there is something to nurture the seed. This is the reason you must always turn to God in prayer. The Father nourishes your faith in the divinity of His Son. I ask that you take upon yourselves the initiatives that will keep you close to Him, for this is also according to the will of humanity. I see preciousness in everything you do for Jesus. You are creative and ingenious in these things because the newness of another day lives within you. No mind can possibly capture all the glory that you are manifesting this way. All goodness that you have ever thought about in your lifetimes has been archived in Heaven. It is not something that you need to dwell upon until you have reached that sacred shore. For now, here in this life, you are accustomed to accepting each new hour for the way you interact with it. There is no miracle in this, just that you remain keenly aware of where you are, and why you are living. With this in mind, humanity must always remember that the most important role of the inner-consciousness is to pursue the love of God. This, My Special and Chosen sons, is the visceral intuition about which I am speaking. It is not that a great skyscraper has been constructed, but that it has been built according to the plans that were laid out. These plans are always warehoused somewhere so everyone will know decades hence what is hidden behind its outer walls. This is the same as when a person professes Christian loyalty to the Savior on the Cross. There are no earthly skyscrapers in Heaven, but there are certainly reams of plans. It is what precedes the structures of life that matters most. It is what God instills in the human heart that determines what the rest of humanity will see. This is the visceral intuition and inclination by which Christians encounter the world and conduct the affairs of life.

My Special son, while this idea may seem a simple one, it is utterly foreign to those who live only by the intellect. All the public proceedings that you see and hear about every day are for the most part based on the exterior designs of life that have no inner core. They seem to be spontaneous outbursts of action and reaction that are not founded in this immersion. Yes, there are feelings and emotions for sure, but they are not righteous ones. Most emotions are based on someone wanting something that will only serve themselves. This is not the same as visceral intuition as practiced by the faithful Christian. For example, so-called eloquent speeches that stir listeners into emotion about the right to an abortion are not based on the faith of Christians. This is just secular blather that fights against the teachings of the Church. If there is feeling in these things, it is about desiring something so evil that one becomes hypnotized by its allure. There is no true eloquence in something that contradicts the mandates of the Gospel. I am calling all My children to recognize the difference, and not become entangled in the distracting webs of the devil. If someone discovers that they are heavy with child, God expects that child to be born into the world and pray for His Kingdom to prosper. This is the magnification of the infants who have been conceived in the wombs of mothers. My Special and Chosen sons, it is hardly possible to know what lies in the hearts of other people. They keep their spiritual identities concealed inside them like the blueprints of a skyscraper, but God knows what is there. His mystics and miracle workers know as well. Good faith loyalists like Saint Padre Pio were capable of reading the motivations inside someone's heart and soul. And, thanks to the power of the Holy Spirit, common Christians can acquire this knowledge by seeking the Wisdom of the Father in prayer. The Sacred Scriptures declare that you can judge a tree by its fruit. I am reconfirming here today that this is true, and I am adding that the presence of the Divine Paraclete in your heart can also make you aware. This is the 'reading of souls' about which I have spoken during the past 2,000 years. There is tremendous benefit in knowing this in advance, not only to recognize where there may be impending danger, but to understand where to orient one's prayers. I have said in Medjugorje that I cannot succeed with My plans in this world without My children's prayers. Why? Because it is through these prayers that I am capable of knowing where to devote My attention – yes, according to the calling of My little ones who are dependent upon My aid. I am saying that I see the motivations of My children based more upon their visceral intuition than the outward actions they take while exiled in the world.

My Special son, I have not told you anything here today that you did not already know. However, I am asking you to refer your prayers to magnifying the spiritual intuition of your Christian brethren in a way that I have never requested before. I ask you to remember that all action having to do with right and wrong is credentialed by this spiritual reality. I have said that spontaneous actions are not, but those that are pondered to any degree with a righteous outcome are formed by God's heavenly plan. I have always prayed that the intuitive nature of My children will find themselves aligned with the Will of the Father. In other words, I have prayed that the carrying out of the plans that will build a New Kingdom in the hearts of men will come with dispatch and without delay. The robust proficiency that I mentioned at the beginning of My message today is contingent on this. Having wisdom in the spiritual vernacular depends on the dedication of the heart that Jesus has sought to invoke from His brothers and sisters for twenty centuries. My dear little son, it all comes down to one tragic moment. As we speak right now, there are human souls entering Hell. This is what this implies. It is the worst outcome of any life that could possibly occur. It is the darkest dungeon of fiery torment that a person could endure. And yet, these sinners are doing it to themselves. They are coming to the awareness that there were no sacred plans within them. They are recognizing the void inside their heart and soul that could have been filled to overflowing with the Divine Mercy of Jesus – but they said 'no' to Him at their most critical hour. They were affluent at speaking about the spectacles of the Earth, but they had no eloquence that would have indicated their allegiance to God. They saw the skyscrapers towering above them, and ignored the titans that made them stand. I have asked you and your brother many times not to pity those who have done this because they did so out of their rebellious hatred toward the Cross. They chose the darkness so that no one could see that they were hollow inside. They thought about holiness with the intellect, but rejected it absent of spiritual goodness. I am telling you and your brother that this is a tragedy of the highest order of man. It is never God's fault when a soul enters the lightless Abyss.

My children, this is the reason why the disciples of Jesus stand tall before the world, and summon all lost sinners to listen. You are doing this in your prayers, poems and writings. You have scripted the lyrics and composed the songs of mercy through your dedication to the Cross and your consecration to Me. And, I ask you both to remember that the vast outcome of Heaven would not have been as inclusive of those who will ultimately occupy its sacred mansions if you had not lived the way you have. All the energies you have invested in the Kingdom of God have shepherded untold numbers of souls into the Light of Paradise. When the last trumpet in time reports about its legacies, this is what will be said about you and your brother. You have not only carried the Torch of Truth, you have resounded and magnified it. You have borne for Christ Jesus the burdens that He bequeathed to you from the Cross. You have inherited in Him the purpose of your years, here in this lovely place, so that all eternity can shine with the emeralds of converted men. This makes you giants among them, as humble as you are, and it causes all Creation to shine in the aftermath of your faith. My Special son, this is what the good life means. It is about changing the outcome of the Earth and all the universes in such a way that Heaven is different as well. It is the advancement of the visceral spirituality of intellectual men. It is the amassing of more sinners beneath the Cross by which their sins have been absolved – not vindicated, but forgiven. And, My little son, it is in gratitude for all this goodness that I continue to tell you not only that you are blessed, but that you have blessed Jesus and the

Church in return. You are the highlight of the grand production in which Creation and all its facets will conclude. It is the transformation of all that is corrupt into the incorruptible identity of the Church Triumphant. I ask that you and your brother realize that this is what you mean to Jesus; this is the esteem in which you pray beneath My Holy Mantle. And with this, I have concluded My message for today. I dearly hope that you have enjoyed it. "*Yes, very much. Thank you.*"

Saturday, September 17, 2016
9:37 a.m.

"The Love of One Man"

"It is crystal clear, little children, that you will allow nothing to impede our progress in effecting the conversion of your lost brothers and sisters, and it is for this reason that My messages of trust and faith continue to bless your lives. I have always asked My children to listen to the language of Creation and heed the call of the Holy Spirit to mend the wicked ways of the world. We have the designs of our prayers to seek the Father's intercession, to beseech Jesus to touch humanity with His sacred love, and instill in the Church the strength, hope and willingness to see beyond the trials it faces every day. There can be no question that this is the framework of our purpose. My Special son, I have always told you and your brother about the miraculous power of the Love of One Man. It is clear to you after twenty-five years of welcoming Me into this home that this power is not only about majesty and truth, but about simplicity and compassion. When the strongest among you is a benevolent being, then all should rejoice that communion will result. The Love of One Man. This speaks tremendous strains about the heights of the mountaintops and the depths of the seas within the human heart. The love of Jesus is the presence of God's gentlemanly Heart, given to men in exile so that everyone who embraces the Cross can know that it is not an abstract encounter with Heaven. We have spoken about ladders, sailing boats, and spacecraft in the context of tools and vessels to give peace to man. Climbing to the top of the clouds aboard your own humble prayers means that you have the capacity to reach toward God of your own accord. Sailing the seas of righteousness gives you the venue to travel beyond the horizon that holds you fast in a single day. Soaring into the heavens on your own spiritual triumphs allows you to touch the Face of the Father with your own holy peace.

Now, we have come, My Special son, toward a new week that will bring the anniversary of your birth. What a grand and precious gift this is for humanity! I beseech you to look at the record of your life. Hold your thoughts in the palms of your hands and see Jesus' Sacrifice there. See how you have harvested untold numbers of souls to fruitfully inhabit the Kingdom of Paradise. You and your brother have made possible that Jesus not only touches lost sinners with His Sacred Blood, but knows in advance who they are. These are but a few of the fruits that you have given the Church Triumphant through your obedience to Me. And, why did you do so? For the Love of One Man. These are not mere miracles that we have performed here together. This is the overarching purpose of human love and faith, combined to make way for the Return of the King. I speak about imminence because this is the promise that Jesus has made. There can be no true faith in an exiled man if he does not realize that this grand reunion between Savior and sinner will occur. You and your brother have explicitly expressed to lost humanity everywhere that this faith is nourished by human obedience. And, this obedience means accepting the trials, troubles and sacrifices that accompany your journey through life. However, it also means that you recognize God's hand in the triumph of the days, in the gift of newborn children, in the Sacraments that make humanity whole, in the Nature through which Creation is awed, and in the finality that will come when Jesus exchanges the old world for the new.

My dear little sons, I have tried to express My appreciation for what this means to the Father in Heaven. Unfortunately, the language that you speak allows Me only two words: Thank you. When all the precious pearls are counted after the last sunrise has come, the Father will look for the harvesters who laid them at His feet. And, He will see you there, My children. Indeed, it will be not just that you shall not bow to anyone, but that Heaven will bow to you. You have honed, polished, and wielded the saber of sacrifice in a wholly and profoundly beatific way. Hence, My Special son, I again ask you to look at the palms of your hands that have so shaped the goodness Jesus has taught into the likeness of the Cross. This is the freedom that every soul deserves. You have led humanity to the passageway of redemption, and this is your gift to them, not only on your birthday, but for eternity to come. So, let us imagine what the Love of One Man implies. Jesus has come knocking on the doorway of Creation on each single human heart, and on the collective conscience of the material world. Please think about His intentions before His first knock. You realize that He was not bearing confections and confetti. Truly, He still approaches all who will become His apostles just as He did in His earthly years. My Special son, Jesus knows in advance who will answer the door, and who will decline. As long as the tenant-heart knows who is knocking, this is their moment. This is the time when they must decide for God or turn way. Why? Because every sinner knows who is knocking on their heart when Jesus comes calling there. This is the first moment of the final judgment of men on Earth. Imagine what it is like to those who do not yet know Him. Does this fateful hour strike fear in them? Or, do they feel relieved, liberated and redeemed? These are the questions that must be answered in an instant, as soon as someone realizes that God is there. My children, I always watch in prayerful hope that My children on Earth will open the door. This has been My prayer since the Archangel's announcement. It is not whether someone is home, but will they reveal their intent from within? All the designs of God from Abraham and Isaac, to Moses and Jesus, and to all the prophets and messengers who have come down through the ages – the entirety of purposes encapsulated in all these identities are that God's Will shall be done. This, My dear children, is the essential nature of the touch of truth and loyalty. The world as you know it is not just withering away, it is deferring to a New Kingdom where there will be no sorrow, no tears or sadness, no darkness, no sickness or mourning. All of this is presently alive in the converted Christian heart. These things seem to accompany the hope that all joy and beatific love and truth manifest in good men and women reasons to go on. My Special son, I am asking My children to shape their hearts into the Triumph of My Most Immaculate Heart! In this way, when they hear Jesus knocking on the door, they will respond affirmatively and openly. They will anticipate what this means for them in the here and now. They will see that My Immaculate Heart receives them in prayer the same way Jesus asks them to open the door. Yes, Jesus comes with anticipation, with gifts of love and peace, with wisdom and comfort, and with the expectation that humanity will realize that His Crucifixion was not in vain. And, My Special son, it is true that this is a reciprocal gift. While Jesus comes calling on humanity, He implores lost sinners to search for Him. Yes, search for Him while He may be found. This is God's most meaningful wish. It is the direction in which the world is turning. It is the hunger of the elements of the Earth. There is no question that it is the Love of One Man.

My dear little sons, let us now imagine what happens when Jesus sees someone open the door. He not only brings a summons of faith and obedience, but gifts much too massive to measure. He says to those who greet Him that when you see Me again on the last day, you will remember what this means to your soul. Jesus comes to the heart with youthful energy, with promise and hope, purity and deliverance. And those who receive Him are the beneficiaries of these things. They see their own repentance as a receipt for His gifts. They urge the Father to accept their thankfulness that He has given them life anew. And, I dare speak today about the innocence that Jesus restores, the innocence that is reflective of Himself. He brings to the human heart an unassuming mandate to be quiet inside, to open wide and receive the pristine affection of the God of all the blessed. And, My Special son, while it would seem appropriate for Me to speak today about those who refuse to open the door, let us just pray that they eventually will. This message is about opportunity and gladness that was born in the Child of My Womb. We must dwell on this happiness, My Special son. We must make remarkable progress in ensuring that our prayers and the hopes of humanity in exile bear the most bountiful harvest they possibly can. God knows that we are trying. Jesus is aware that you are fighting for His Church. All the Angels and Saints join in your good intentions to uphold the promises made to God in your profession of faith. There is no such thing as not accomplishing the goals we have laid out. There is no such outcome as defeat. I have long spoken during centuries past about the Triumph of My Immaculate Heart. This is the Matriarchal Triumph celebrated in My messages around the globe. Everything that would seem to require being knitted together is being unified at this time. All that is untamed in the righteous sense; everything that is wonderful, holy, and awesome is happening now just beyond your level of comprehension. The darkness, confusion, and error that you see and hear about every day represent only the temporal acts of lost sinful men. Jesus handed the world a precious fabric of guidance and safekeeping, made from the garment of Good Friday. And, it is beneath My Mantle that you hold your greatest fortune for what you mean to God in Heaven. There are realities and symbols aplenty, wondrous signs, relics and manifestations, and truly remarkable events that are transpiring as we speak. Jesus desires all humanity to fashion for themselves an awareness that the whole of the Earth is preparing to receive Him. There is no question that Jesus knocking on the door of the human heart is paramount to His Resurrection from the Tomb. God said in the beginning that if you will receive Him here, He will welcome you there. All that is reciprocal between God and man is dependent upon the world's desire to be assembled in His presence once again. My dear little children, you surely must recognize how difficult it is for Me to choose appropriate language to describe such mystical events. During My time here with you, the Holy Spirit infuses in your hearts and thoughts the knowledge to understand. Hence, it is necessary for you again to turn to the love in your lives to comprehend what I am saying to you now. This is the way of all My messengers everywhere. While the veil is thin, it can be stubborn in permitting the fullness of wisdom to reach the hearts of the exiled. You, My Special and Chosen sons, have so lent yourselves, your holy lives, to Jesus and Me for so many years that your instincts are innate to the purposes of God. You are capable of seeing Creation in the way of the Father's Will, while others are only beginning to read it in braille. It would seem appropriate that I should say that these gifts come to you because of your faith and identities in Christ Jesus. Make no mistake about it here! It is you who have manifested this unity. Your worthy prayers and righteous lives have given meaning and piety to your brothers and sisters in this life. I invite you to look at any of the books in your deposit of works. You will notice that the hand of God is in everything you do. You will witness the providential touch of the Love of One Man. Time itself cannot nullify, negate, or reverse this spectacular miracle given to the Church. Yes, and when the door opens, Jesus walks in. He pronounces His purposes as if a tiny child. He waves His hands in blessing; touches the cheek of His receivers and proclaims, 'Welcome to the path of the Promised Land!' No greater fortune has ever come to someone in mortal flesh. There are no riches, no fame, no destiny, no charity of material that could possibly surpass the blessing of being known as a beneficiary of the Cross. All that is deposited in the heart of being human finds its meaning in this. Thank you, My Special and Chosen sons, for allowing Me to speak to you today."

Sunday, September 25, 2016
9:40 a.m.

"Penetrate and possess my whole being so utterly –
that all my life may be only a radiance of Thine."

- John Henry Cardinal Newman
1801-1890

"Vision imparts knowledge, knowledge conveys wisdom.
Wisdom sustains judgment, judgment compels reaction."

- The Dominion Angels

"Now, My beautiful children, the glories of Heaven are shining down upon you as always. Your Mother has come speaking with the ideals of God for His people on Earth. Today is a wonderful remembrance of the episcopal blessing of your home, and I have dictated a compassionate message at the holy shrine of Medjugorje. My dear Special son, I have told you on many occasions that it is extremely difficult to express in literary terms how pleased I am with you and your brother. I have told you that you have now fully and completely suffered for the good of this cause. What this means, My little son, is that you and your brother are uniquely aligned with the Will of God, and consummately united in the Sacred Heart of Jesus. You have just completed a week of difficult events and imaginings, and yet here you are still praying as you have for decades. It is in turning to Jesus through Me that the world will be forever blessed. You have heard two quotations at the beginning of My message today for no other reason than that you enjoy them. I know that you have already written about Cardinal Newman, and you have been receptive to the intercession of the Dominion Angels your entire lives. It is extremely important that you remember that the joy in our relationship as Mother and son is wholly Mine. What could a mother do here in the exiled realms if not for her children who love so faithfully? How quickly would Creation fall into shambles without your relationship with God? Therefore, it is to the purpose of embracing His sustaining grace that you and the Church have lived. It is clear to Me that this age of baptized Christians is fighting harder to sustain their dignity than most others before. The Church has warned against the evil forces of relativism and pluralism. Popes and Cardinals have told Roman Catholics worldwide that there would be an attempt to marginalize the grandness of your faith. However, My Special and Chosen sons, every attempt to sideline the mission of the Roman Catholic Church will fail. Why? Because My Son Jesus Christ has said so. And, this is the reason why the endearing longevity of the Church will last beyond the ages. You see, therefore, that the imperative nature of your prayers is not solely to uphold the Church, for the Church will always be upheld, but to bless, sustain and guide it through these perilous modern times. The Cross is the true stature of Christians, and you walk through life with your heads held high because you have believed. All truth, glory, love, faithfulness, and trust are imbedded in everything I tell you today. Therefore, when we beseech the Father through Jesus to heal the lame and brokenhearted, He sees the authenticity of our desire to unite the Faith Church and the Church Triumphant in Heaven. This not only permeates time and space, it defies the dimensions that humanity sees every day. With all the goodness inherent in those who subscribe to the Holy Gospel, all human love and divine truth will eventually become one. This is another blessing for which the world has prayed from centuries long ago. Never has it been more imperative than it is today.

I spoke to you recently about Jesus approaching and knocking on the door of the human heart. I have said that He calls in piety and peace for humanity on Earth. Jesus goes calling at someone's door for a transformation to take place. The relationship between God and humanity is this transformation. The eternal Sacred Scriptures that are reflected so profoundly in the Catechism must impress upon humanity that there is always forward movement to the Kingdom of Righteousness. Every day and each new hour brings promises and opportunity for people to refine who they are. This must be accomplished through a heart open to suffering, to miracles and wonders, to sudden flashes of enlightenment, and yes, to the commonness that the months and years can bring. Imagine, My Special son. Think about all the millions of people who live by faith, and yet, have never heard of the Mother of God. If you could possibly conceive of a life led this way, you can understand what it is like for true blessings to occur. I am the Queen of Heaven and Earth, and every person living in exile should have the opportunity to know Me in the way of you and your brother. This is the reason that I came calling to Medjugorje 35 years ago. And, it is to celebrate this call, to enhance and strengthen it, that I came to you and your brother ten years later. You said it profoundly in the video that you have published in 2010. I came to establish a relationship with My children that takes them into the vaults of awareness that are still begging to be known. It is for this reason that I have rightfully given My advice, not only to the Church, but also to those who believe in other things. I am like you in so many ways that it would startle you to hear. There are some things that I do not yet know. For example, the day and hour of the return of the Son of Man is known only to God. This, therefore, necessitates that I also live in joyful hope along with humanity. There can be no misunderstanding that God did not do this to enlist His secrecy. He did so to allow for the impact of the prayers of the Church in exile and in Heaven to shape the final events of human history. What a compassionate Creator! This speaks as well to the Mysteries of the Most Blessed Trinity in that the Father, the Son, and the Holy Spirit are One God in Three Persons. And yet, the Second Person is also unaware of the day and hour that God will send Him to complete the mission of the Church of Faith. Jesus reigns as its Head. Moreover, My Special son, you and your brother, and the whole society of Catholic Christians know what My being, presence, identity, and intercession mean to the sanctification, conversion, and fullness of life for those whom My Son died to save. This is the touch of the Mother of Jesus on the collective cheek of Her children in exile. It is My embrace of the love and faith that has been offered throughout the ages. I have asked you to imagine. These are the things that I have asked you to wonder how humanity could do without. The Providence of God is bound in the stateliness He instills in those who speak for Him. Let this be the message to those who are still struggling to believe.

Therefore, the freshness of your faith as you see it every day is given this new life because Jesus has asked Me to serve. I am still summoning from Him miracles not to prove that He exists, but that there are deficits in the lives of humanity that must be addressed. I called for more wine at the wedding feast not to prove that Jesus is the Son of God, but because the guests there needed something. This is true yet today. I have told you and your brother many times that you need not provide evidence to the world at large that I am speaking to you, but to tell them that I want something. And, thankfully and blessedly, and without surprise, you and your brother want the same thing. I also have said that human life on Earth sometimes seems uphill. However, I have tried to impress upon you that Jesus and the Holy Spirit permit you to live in peace. All the confidence you will ever need, all the perseverance that could possibly be required are found in Him. My Special son, I am trying to assure you of the rest you find in Jesus if you will simply relax your mind. I realize that this is no easy task in a secular world that requires such intellect. Whenever you pray, you can sense this peace. Your prayers and invocations open the door through which the Holy Spirit enters. You are consoled and comforted by the response that you know to be coming from God. Please allow Me to speak another example. It is a cultural phenomenon when you see certain cultures of people begin rocking and moaning as if in response to the overtures from Heaven. This is not the kind of elation about which I am speaking. The actions of these individuals can commonly be attributed to their personalities. Indeed, the peace about which I am speaking is of eloquence and dignified rest. It is as though humanity kneels before the Most Blessed Sacrament and listens for the Messiah to speak. Here again, My Special son, I ask you to just imagine. Never mind the swirls and flares; disregard everything that speaks about bombastic force. I seek from My children to embrace the Fruits of the Holy Spirit, to reach out for God's hand that has strongly yearned to be touched. This is the hand that Jesus has offered for all to be blessed. His is the Blood that has redeemed all who believe in Him and accept Him, and this is what My messages to you and your brother have been extolling since 1989 and 1991. When you think about those cultures that so wish to dance about what they believe, this is the music of the heart that faith in Jesus brings. How many times can this be said? What else could possibly be shared that could glorify the Kingdom to come? I have an adequate response to this question. My Special son, imagine how many words about truth and righteousness can be assembled from an alphabet of 26 letters. My point is that writers, poets, lyricists, authors and orators have only begun to tap the resource. It is not an inordinate prospect to believe that the world could not contain all the books of what Jesus might say. In these modern times, the smallest and yet most voluminous instruments of words could not contain them either. Why? Because the content of the heart is as infinite as Heaven itself. My great purpose here has been not just to love you, but to prove that I love you. And, in accomplishing this, I have solicited your participation in writing some of those books. I have beseeched you to pray along with Me for the conversion of the lost. I have asked My children, just as Cardinal Newman said, that you would invite the Holy Spirit to penetrate your very being to supplant and reorient the purpose of your lives to be that of the Father in Heaven. I have sought from My children a new vision that will induce them to react to the overtures from God, just as the Dominion Angels have advised. There is no such thing as too much truth. Never will you find the exhaustion of the love of God for His people. What this means to Me is that we will strive for the conversion of every lost sinner living in exile until there are no more to be found. There will surely be many who will hold out and never accept what Jesus has asked them to do. We can only pray that they will accept His Divine Mercy in their most fateful hour. This, My Special son, is both the text and context of what I have come to tell you today. It has been a message of prudence and discipline, of loveliness and light, of prayer and wholeheartedness. It would take breaching the bounds of certain dimensions to explain to you what your friendship with God really means. I have come to you week after week to give you His blessings, to counsel you about the holiness of the Church, and to encourage you through your life's work. What will come of My message here today, for example, depends on what must be relevant for others to know. Could you have possibly imagined being at the Fatima miracle and speaking to a world a hundred years later that does not even remember that it happened? This is the difficulty that Jesus has in broaching to humanity the magnitude of His love. It is the seriousness of the state of the world in matters of faith and morality. When I speak about deficits, this is an example of what I mean. My Special son, you have said on multiple occasions that I always lift you and your brother up. I am saying that I have reams and libraries that could not contain what a blessing you are to humanity in exile. What you have given to Me is reason to go on. Throughout My message today, I have asked you to just imagine. Yes, what would it have been like if Saint Bernadette would have turned another way? What if I had tried 15 or 20 times and she would not have responded to Me?

Would she have continued to hear My voice until I finally said, 'Oh, never mind?' My Special son, I have just told you something that would never occur in the history of ten billion worlds. I do not give up. I never concede defeat. I forever persist in the message of eternal love. My prayers continue to be with your family, and all who are suffering for the success of the Church. You have seen tremendous sacrifices by those who are willing to endure what the Father has laid at their feet. Like Saint Bernadette, they never turned their backs or walked away. Let us remember in our prayers those who are mourning the loss of loved ones. May Jesus give them strength and peace to live out their lives in Him."

Sunday, October 2, 2016
9:17 a.m.

"In atonement for the sins of the whole world."

"My dear little sons, let it never be said that the Lord has not given exiled humanity the opportunity to convert. Let all the nations hear what we have done since the Crucifixion of the Son of Man. It is for this reason that I have come sharing My words and sentiments with you, and as I have duly proclaimed, it is a fruit of your love for Me. I have also come to you this morning to remind you of the tremendous gratitude that the Father has for your loyalty to Him through Jesus on the Cross. It is not something that can be easily said here – not even a grace that can be described within the confines of time. Hence, you are inspired and called to remember that God loves you beyond all telling. I am His holy ambassador; Jesus is His most redeeming proof. So, what does it mean that Jesus' Crucifixion made atonement for the sins of the whole world? It means that the Man-God was born into the created realms to suffer and die to reconcile humanity with its Creator. Atonement through Christ Jesus is the spiritual and literal definition of human Salvation. And, the Holy Gospel is the instrument for the conversion of lost sinners to the Cross on which Jesus died. My Special son, I keep telling you and your brother that you already know these things, but I wish to reemphasize that Jesus not only wants to save lost sinners, but He also asks them to become like Him. It is rightly said around the globe that humanity needs to accept the Blood of Jesus on the Cross so that one's soul can be saved from eternal condemnation. This is being communicated in truth. However, what is not as emphasized is that the converted human person needs to adopt a new identity and new way of life. Imagine that. Think about what it means to walk up to somebody and say that God wants them to become someone else, and to take-on a completely different orientation toward the affairs of life. Most people would look at you as though you have just arrived from a distant planet. However, it is true that the identity of mankind must be the identity of Jesus, and the new mode of conduct must be that mandated by the New Covenant. My Special and Chosen sons, I have never drawn the distinction between adopting the identity of Jesus and the behavior of the Christ-self in the way that I have this morning. Clearly, it is not a new pathway that I am charting. I am restating the truth that has been known for 2,000 years. My Special son, imagine all the implications that would come if the world dwelled on the distinction that I have made today. Adopting the identity of Jesus means that Jesus supplants the identity of the Christian. Do you suppose that this means that everything in total becomes Jesus, even the human will itself? *"Yes."* You have given the correct answer, except that the converted Christian retains his own will – he humbly gives it to Jesus of his own accord. If it were true that Jesus somehow stole the will of the human person, then this would not be conversion as described by the Church. *"I understand."*

    I would like to contemplate with you the moment of this conversion, even though the moment is a process that can sometimes take months and years. I have said that Jesus comes calling in the same way that the Archangel Gabriel came calling. Each was dispatched by the Father in Heaven in order to bring the Good News into the exiled realms. Yes, Jesus is the Good News about which Saint Gabriel was speaking. The moment of the conversion of man is when he realizes that there is Providence in being born into the world, that life has a purpose far greater than self-sufficiency and maturity in matters of work and the intellect. I am thinking the same thing that you are thinking. Many people do not come to the conclusion about the transcending nature of life until theirs has nearly ended. But, they will have their moment. My purpose here with you and your brother – indeed the entire efficacy of My worldwide message for centuries, has been to instill in My children on Earth that you are yet living in the foyer of the fullness of human potential. Estates and legacies are fine for what they mean to the living, but mortality makes them obsolete in the aftermath of time. As I have said before, I am like you in many ways, and the most important is that you wish for men and women, even children, to live one day at a time in the beauty of this world. On the other hand, you task them with learning the possibility that they can subscribe to the most ethereal facets of their holier selves. This is another way of saying that Jesus is the Savior and the image to which all men must be conformed. Do you understand this? *"Yes."* Here again, I have said that this is a process that leads to a moment, but rarely is it an instantaneous moment. Living one day at a time is extremely important for Christians because this is what Jesus did for 33 years. It means that you are imbedded in the created world to grow your own faith and that of others so that the identity of Jesus' Mystical Body can become more like Him. Imagine Jesus looking at Himself in the mirror every morning and seeing His reflection being different each time. This is the evolution of His Mystical Body into the portrait that will ultimately adorn the Father's house in Heaven. This is not only the essence of what we are doing in the world, it is the stature of hope by which I have lived for as long as I have been known.

It is more than a touch; it is an absorption of the Sacred Divine into the spiritual composition of humanity on Earth. It is a resounding union of faith and truth that rings throughout Creation like a million-ton bell. And, My Special son, this is the reason why I have asked you and your brother to remember how sacred you are. It is the reason that I came to you in 1991 and addressed you in a message as 'My divine ones.' I have regularly referred to My messengers and seers, and therefore My children at large, as My little angels. You may remember that a person told you in 1991 that the Mother of God would never refer to Her children as divine or angelic, but this individual was doing the best he could to understand the magnitude of what you and your brother have received from Me, even to this day. Please do not assume that I am criticizing this holy man, I am telling you that the idea that humanity can be divine and angelic is not something widely known. However, did not the Son of Man implore you to be perfect as the Father is perfect? There is so much fear in believing this, My Special son, because it leads to the expectation that the souls of Earth must live up to the title. I wish to tell you that I nearly began My message this morning with the Psalm 46:10 passage seeking the quietude of My children to know that God is their God. I have spoken about it here because I wish for you to remember that to know that God is God is a fruit of giving the human will to His Son. Taking on the identity of Jesus does not mean that someone asks Him to hide their true self from the Father. It means that the human person is remade from the inside out. This is what the Holy Eucharist does, and it is the reason the Holy Spirit in the human heart feels so welcoming and warming. It is clear that the Holy Spirit in the human heart is like a seed planted that grows the spiritual awareness of the faithful into discernible thought. This is how the heart rules the mind in those who are given to the Gospel. The thoughts of the righteous are made by the Lord of Righteousness, while both asleep and awake. It is true, therefore, that the devil tries his worst to infiltrate the mind, and drive out the holiness that Jesus instills there. This is a story for another day. Let us remember that Satan cannot enter a mind that is dwelling on the prayers of the Church. A man can only have one thought at a time, and this is best reserved for Divine Love!

Jesus makes an offerance to humanity not by just being more attractive than the devil, but by proving that the devil has no place in you. My Special and Chosen sons, I wish for you to not dwell on the devil because this will only serve his name. Jesus did not communicate with the devil in the desert as though the two of them were equals, but as Jesus knowing Himself to be the Way, the Truth and the Life. Satan came peddling lies to Jesus, but Jesus was of no mind to be patronizing. This is why the battle between goodness and evil in the world is not one that should be regarded as an even match. By all means, consider the entire Kingdom of God when observed through the Three Branches of the Church. Think about the birth of Creation through the love of God; there was no evil to be found. God never created evil, and He never will. But, He did give sentient creatures large and small the capacity of self-will. This, therefore, is what we are trying to tender to Christ Jesus for all who have lived and died. This is for the atonement that I spoke about at the beginning of this message. Reconciling humanity with God does not mean that God did something wrong to cause a breach. Humanity became disobedient and created the fissure, and God loves His people so much that He sent His Son to pay the cost and mend the breach. This, My Special son, is love in the way that the Father desires it to be known. This is the message of the Holy Gospel – the entirety of it. And, it is founded on the Old Covenant principles that Jesus fulfilled. All the heroes who have been born since; all the daring, all the dynamics, all the revelations – these things have come from the fact that the Love of One Man has created anew what once fell into shambles. There is eminence in what you believe, and imminence in what the Earth will eventually know. So, I commend you and your brother for staying the course with all who accept and live out what Jesus has bequeathed to the Church. As I have said, Jesus is its Living Head. He is its power and vision. Yes, Jesus is the Master and darling of the forgiveness of God for those who have disobeyed Him, but who will now rest in Heaven. I have completed My message for today. I join with you in praying that My messages will be read, accepted and acted upon with early dispatch. *"Thank you for being so generous to us in the last 25 years."* You are welcome beyond My ability to describe. I ask that you and your brother remember to pray for the upcoming public elections here and around the globe. I have asked Jesus to assist in choosing people who will safeguard the sanctity of life!"

Friday, October 7, 2016
Our Lady of the Holy Rosary
9:35 a.m.

"Triumphant faith and the spiritual aureole."

"My sweet little sons, I ask you to imagine what it feels like for the Mother of God to speak to two of Her children who not only welcome Me to pray with you here, but who inspire Me to return. Everything that I ever thought about humanity – all the opportunities, challenges and potentials – are unwrapped before Me like gifts from the eternal realms of your Christian faith. I am saying that you must tell your brothers and sisters that My messages to them through you have been by your allegiance to God. I am like you in this sense as well. I am the messenger in the same way that the Holy Spirit is the Divine Messenger to us all. You live a triumphant faith because you believe in the redemption of sinners in Jesus' Blood on the Cross. And, this encircles your lives and souls in the spiritual aureole of victory. It is your faith by which you have triumphed over the trials, troubles and tribulations of the exiled world. I once told My Medjugorje messengers that I could not make them happy in this life – but they can. My Special and Chosen sons, you have decided for yourselves that darkness and evil cannot diminish the strength or integrity of your faith in God. This is not only the reason why your faith is triumphant, but that it also has the power of transformation. Everyone who is baptized is transformed into new creatures this way, but not all who receive the Sacrament of Baptism live out its meaning. I have said that people become holier by reminding themselves that they are truly holy. This is the self-fulfilling grace in which the human heart basks. There is a certain beatific corona that enlightens the human heart and spirit, emanating from the presence of the Holy Spirit working through them. My Special son, you have often said that My messages are saturated with the eloquence of God. While this may be a qualitative measure, what remains factual beyond compare is that eloquence is only effective if there are listening ears willing to hear. It is the same phenomenon as the most beautiful sights on Earth to see, but is anyone willing to look at them? In spiritual terms as well, having eyes and opening one's eyes are not the same thing. Hence, My children throughout the ages have been told that they have eyes to see their destiny in the Lord, but it is messengers like you and your brother who have encouraged them to use them. You are the holy vessels in which the Father has deposited His intentions for humanity. You are the mediums through which He has imparted His Wisdom through Me, His Mother, the Morning Star Over America.

What we have done in the Church – I am speaking about the Most Blessed Trinity working through the faithful around the world – is procure the attention of those who are prone to see. They have not yet seen, but they are lent to doing so. And, when many have read your books over the past several weeks, they are rendered speechless because they have never seen such prolific messages from the Mother of God. When they are asked by others to describe what they are seeing, many of them can only make the sound of the schwa. They can only say, 'uh…' in an attempt to relate what they are feeling. My Special and Chosen sons, this is one of the greatest early gifts of your faith and My intercession. I ask for you to remember that your lives have manifested this blessing because you have been in the Lord's vineyard working every day, defying the odds and elements, holding true to what you believe, and trebling your determination to remain tethered to My Immaculate Heart from the inside. This, therefore, is the origin of the vision of the world to see with their eyes the eloquence that I have pronounced from My lips. It is their way of being instituted into the miraculous in the same way that the miracle of Jesus' birth was brought into the Bethlehem night. The whole concept of revelation is that it stems from humanity not knowing what it does not know. You cannot expect something, then discover it later, and call it a new revelation. This is only confirmation. What I have been able to give the world through your triumphant faith is a means to know who they are on a level that lies outside their sphere of consciousness. In this sense, it is not like somebody knocking on their door because they have heard people knocking on their door before. It is instead like approaching someone from a position already in their home – someone whom they did not even know was there. This is the assumed presence of the Holy Spirit that touches the human heart from the ethereal realms. My Special son, I have spoken a great deal this morning to finally broach the subject that I just mentioned, that of the assumed presence. This means that there is limitless potential for earthly men and women to know God, and then coupling this potential with humanity's faith to make it so. There are many metaphors that we have mentioned through the years that reflect this assumed presence, including the sensation of a person's bare feet touching the floor. No one thinks about what it feels like for their feet to touch a walking surface unless there is something peculiar about the surface. Extremely high and low temperatures are readily noticed beneath a man's feet. And, it is clearly discernible whether a person is walking on beach sand or on nails. I am speaking about another facet of the assumed presence of humanity's environment and ambience to which they have become accustomed. It is only by breaking beyond this assumed presence that someone realizes that life is not as it seems.

Now, enter God the Father, God the Son, and God the Holy Spirit. Enter the Holy Sacrifice of the Mass. Enter the Morning Star Over America. Yes, indeed. There are miracles flowing from Heaven through all these blessings, but humanity on Earth must be attuned to them to appreciate what the Father is giving. My Special son, this is the promise; this is the potential. It is in opening the human heart that the triumphant faith about which I am speaking marches on. It leads to the aureole, the corona of divine life that comes upon those who believe. It is as though you are speaking to Jesus in the Manger, Jesus on the Cross, and Jesus on Easter Sunday at the same time. By all means, you are. This is the timelessness that has revealed the Christ Child to be the King of Creation; not because He has changed, but because humanity has changed. Whatever the world chooses to call it – victory, triumph, satisfaction, absolution, renewal or whatever terms might describe the fulfillment of their dreams, they are all found in Him. There is nothing corrupt about feeling the positive emotion of knowing that one's soul has been redeemed. It is like being released from a dark dungeon after fifty years of captivity. It is like finding a cool, clear running brook in the middle of a desert. To recognize that God has given the soul the right to feel perfect once again is the purpose of your faith. This is the basis of the trust in what you believe. It is the touch of the human spirit to the divinity of Heaven. It is the warming of the soul in the cold, barren wretchedness of the exiled world. It is your recognition that your faith is as much a living being as all the elements of Nature combined. My Special son, I am speaking today about the assumed presence that tells you that you have inalienable rights before the Father through Jesus that cannot be rescinded. These rights include being able to see where other faithless men cannot see. It means that you have the capacity for movement amid a world of statues. You are capable of predicting what changes the future will bring in a world where men without faith have already conceded what time has set in stone. These rights give you the ability to imagine what Creation should become, what God first intended from the strains of Genesis reflecting His eternal love.

My Special and Chosen sons, this is where you and I have been meeting since you were born. All the scents and feelings that you have ever acquired or touched have come from your awareness that God the Spirit is thriving within you. I whisper it into every ear that is born into this world. I never depart from My children's presence – it is they who often stray from Me. I never surrender a soul to the netherworld. I have said this to you time and again. So, when the innocence that I spoke so much about in 2015 and 2016 regrows in the hearts and consciences of those who wish to know God, I am still there, reminding them that they are like budding trees, reaching for the Kingdom that will come to them. I realize, My little sons, that there is a fair amount of high hope in what I have said today, but there is certainly no hyperbole. Give Me the opportunity to take one of My children to the summit of a mountain, and I will hand him to the soaring skies. Give Jesus the chance to take someone by the heart, and He will carry them on His shoulders. My Special son, these may seem like empty promises to many people because they have not considered the suffering that comes with sacrificing for the Cross. They have not yet come to the conclusion that self-denial is crucial to the refinement of the human heart and soul. They see contradictions, where God in Heaven sees beatific conclusions. This is what comprises the holy triumph of your faith in Jesus. It is the precursor to your participation in the blessing of eternal piety that humanity must reflect back to Heaven. There are no great mysteries in this, even as there are Sacred Mysteries from which all blessings flow. It is not about illogical happenstance or ironies that abound. It is about a transformation that occurs the moment someone says that they desire to become like Jesus. From all the agonies in this life grow the glories of the next. Christ Jesus has given His disciples the ability to withstand anything they might face on the pathways of the exiled Earth. The heart decides which ones the faithful will conquer. This is the connection between God and man, between Heaven and Earth, between the soul and one's Redeemer. My Special son, I have concluded My message for today. O' I hope you enjoyed it. *"Yes, I did so much, thank you."* I ask that you remember to pray for all who are in hospitals and nursing homes, for unborn children, and for those who are contemplating religious vocations. Thank you for praying the Holy Rosary on this special feast day. It means so much to the Church and to Jesus that you are praying for the peace and love of His flock."

Saturday, October 15, 2016
9:29 a.m.

"Sometimes you just want to crawl inside a human heart and stay there; wrap yourself deep within its care, and never come out. I promise that this kind of love can heal a nation."

- Cristo, El Salvador (Christ, the Savior)

"My little ones, it is on the wonders of human redemption that your works have been focused. My Special son, we must ensure that the world accepts the peace and truth that you and your brother have come to know. This is, as you have said, been a year so far filled with sorrow and loss, confusion and false engagement, terror and disappointment. This is why those close to you and the nation in which you live must allow Jesus to take comfort in their hearts. He will give them the peace for which they have yearned. Let there be no mistake, My Special son, the difficulties of this year have come because you and your brother are within months of releasing another book. There is no other reason than this. I assure you that the devil is trying to stop you, using any means he can to prevent you from issuing to humanity My 2010-2012 book of messages and beyond. I know that you are not surprised to learn this, and that you have self-prepared for anything else that Satan may attempt to heave upon you in the future. My request is that you stay the course, live peacefully on the inside, and carry on as though unfazed. Yes, I realize that this is easier said than done. But, this is what the Holy Spirit is about – you are given deep within you the reasons for maintaining your joy because you identify with Jesus' Sacrifice on the Cross. The elements of your faith are sustained by your trust that God will always be there with you.

Let Me speak for a moment about this new book that you are preparing to release. Think of its content in the way that I first brought you the messages in it. Recognize that this book is, as you know, not part of the founding period of My Morning Star messages that you delivered to the Church, but it contains what I believe to be more beautiful strains of love for you and your brother for your continuing faith. My goodness yes, I have spoken about My life as Mother while Jesus grew up. I have said that He was far more about spreading the Gospel of Salvation than developing it. My Special son, do you know the difference? *"Yes."* This is the point that humanity has yet to realize. The people whom we are trying to reach through My messages and your apostolate seem unaware that Jesus said 'It is finished' on the Cross. In other words, they believe that Christian evangelists and evangelicals are 'trying out' their religion on nonbelievers to see if it actually works. We know that this is not at all the issue. They are sharing a message of redemption that was completed on Good Friday. The secular void believes that Christians are comparable to doctors who are practicing medicine. The practice of medicine is like a democracy – it is refined and improved as the ages come and go. Christianity is not that way. Your generation has been handed a 2,000 year old Gospel that has not changed since the Annunciation of the Archangel Gabriel. This makes your lineage not about prescribing the faith to others, but sharing it with them. My

Special son, it is always humanity that must change to comply with the Will of God. His Will is amendable, but only in response to prayers that will assist in the cultivation and purification of lost sinners. This is what prayer is for. I am near the cusp of broaching in Medjugorje the issues that I first spoke about in June 1981. This is in response to prayers that have been lifted there since My children began traveling and tendering their hearts to Me in good faith. I have said to you a number of times that your work is an echo of Medjugorje, and yet the substance of your messages contains profoundly broader ideals. Your messages from AD 2009-2016 are yours for the ages, and you are free to share them as you wish, or keep them to yourselves. I have said that I dictated them to you because you have esteemed yourselves before Jesus through your faith and service. You are the joy that He seeks in this life. He has entered your hearts the way He has said, and He will never come out. Through your trust and honor, God is bringing healing to a nation.

Today, I also would like to tell you that the differences within the Catholic Church are not inherently counterproductive. It gives humanity an opportunity to see what conservative faith is about. I promise and assure you that as certain as I am speaking to you now, the Roman Catholic Church will not be liberalized by any progressive factions – it cannot be; Jesus is its Head. When He touches His faithful flock, it is not a consolation as though to say that He is comforting someone who has lost something. He is engaging His people in victory because the oldest institution in the history of the world is His Cross Church on Earth. I observe, along with you and your brother, the attempts to dilute the sacred principles and doctrines that the Catholic Church has taught for twenty centuries. However, all attempts to do so will fail. No one could commit a heist this large in a thousand lifetimes. What the liberals are doing in the Church right now amounts to no more than two mischievous thieves crawling through a window and making off with a few hundred dollars cash. I am speaking to you today about a Church that is so strong and resilient that the complete implosion of the Earth could not bring it down. My Special and Chosen ones, we belong to this eternal permanency because we are united with God the Father in Heaven. You have Jesus' Kingdom at your right and left guards because you have committed yourselves to His Being. Jesus is knowable in your hearts as a stabilizing, viable, preeminent, divine human force because He has instilled this vision within you. The whole idea of spiritual infusion is based on this force. When I speak to you with all the love in My Immaculate Heart, I am sharing with you the essence of the Father's Divine Glory in a way that your consciousness understands. Here, even though I am speaking to you in your English vernacular, your perception of what I am saying is a parable that comes from your wisdom of truth. And, this is where you know that the skies are blue and ocean tides are cleansing. You realize that forgiveness overcomes the past, and shared compassion heals old wounds. Everything that you will ever know about the human heart comes from this splendor of God that is handed to you in faith.

My little sons, I ask that you do not give-in to the pressures from Satan that would knock your progress off course. It is here with the Holy Spirit as your comfort that you are living in peace – you are living in unprecedented peace! My Special son, Jesus has also been comforted and consoled because you and your brother are willing to feel more of what He endured while in the flesh on the Earth. Whatever the Father deigns that you undergo to feel the emotions of Jesus comes to you because He loves and trusts you. Imagine the day to come when you walk into Jesus' presence and He sees the image of Himself. All these are good days! It is clear that what you do for Jesus in this life, as excruciating as it may seem, takes you closer to being the likeness of Jesus that God ushered forth from the beginning. If humanity's supplication to the Father is to touch the inside of Jesus' Most Sacred Heart in this life, then your prayers were further advanced on Thursday, October 13, 2016. It was not just that two thieves came calling on you that day that matters, but that the pair of you said to Jesus, '...We know how you feel.' How could the Will of the Father be more enlightening than this? How could a more evocative lesson be learned? My Special son, thank you for your blessed faith and trust in what the Lord wills to unfold. I am remembering to pray for the United States, just as you have asked during your recitation of the Holy Rosary. And, it is quite heartening to hear you repeat My commendation that America will be given a second chance. Your love for your country means this much to God."

Saturday, October 22, 2016
8:56 a.m.

"Lord, make me an instrument of your peace."

- Saint Francis of Assisi

"Good morning, My beloved children, and welcome to the compassion of My Most Immaculate Heart. Thank you for praying with Me for the conversion of lost sinners to the sacred bastion of the Cross where all good men and women turn for wisdom and redemption. It is right and just that you should exalt the Lord's holy name, and invoke the truth of the Holy Spirit to guide your ways. Today, I have come to celebrate the sentiments of the Saint Francis of Assisi prayer because it reminds Me so much of you. I assure you that the melodies of the Saints resound in your hearts as they are caroling through the corridors of the Father's House in Heaven. To be made an instrument for God means that you realize that you are only idle without Him. It implies that you have given your will to His Kingdom, and desire to help Him play out the final songs of the ages. It does not mean that you are finished with the world, for it is in His earthly vineyard that your labors for Jesus are ongoing. However, it definitely means that you are capable of judging the Earth in ways that those who are far from God cannot know. My Special son, imagine the issues that require our prayers. One might ask the question as to where to begin. It is true that giving your heart to God opens the doorway where you can see what He desires for His Creation. When so many people in exile ask why God is so silent, the Father is prone to inquire in return why humanity is so noisy. One of the oldest commands in the world is for someone to say, '...be quiet and listen to me.' This originated with God – it was His first mandate to Adam and Eve. It has been said many times from the pulpit that God said, '...whatever you do, stay away from that tree.' Hence, it was the disobedience of Adam and Eve that brought down the whole of humanity into this exile where I am speaking to you now. The Father began speaking to His people after that Fall, and His final word is Jesus, the Messiah. With consolation, instruction, example, love, Passion and Sacrifice, God is again saying to humanity to be quiet and listen. My Special son, God has never asked those in exile to replicate His power. This has never been the point of the Fall of Adam. He is instead asking His Church to replicate His holiness. There is a stark difference in the two. 'Thine is the power...' says that the Father retains all divine dominion over the Earth and its creatures. Indeed, it is to be so holy as Jesus that humanity retains the power of perfection that leads to the Salvation of the soul. Jesus asks the Church to be like Him, and He will greet all righteous souls at the center of the heart. With this heart, all time and spacial dimensions are superseded, and the future is guaranteed for the everlasting life of all who believe. Therefore, making instruments of all true believers opens the narrow gate for those who love God to enter His sacred domain.

My Special and Chosen sons, I must tell you that it is never too late for souls to convert to the Cross, but those who wait until their last breath can do an awful amount of damage. This is the kind of suffering that is heaped upon the world by those who do not pray, who do not even know what prayer is for. We pray as one for the success of the Church's mission, and it has thus far been successful because of those who have been so faithful down through the ages. Those who have done the Will of God, even as they have learned it day to day, are the Saints who have blessed the Earth with peace and prosperity. And, there are no lessons to teach someone the correct way to suffer. It is not taught in schoolrooms or shelved in history books. Anyone who suffers comes upon it by virtue of their identity in Jesus, as He has shown humanity what suffering means. It is more than a mere acceptance in the mind. It is recognizing with the heart that Jesus elevates and extols the spirit of those who live in His image and likeness. My Special son, the Agony in the Garden and the Carrying of the Cross are humanity's best examples of handing one's self to the Father. I have said this to you before. I also have told you and your brother that the Holy Rosary helps you identify with Jesus' suffering because you are capable of attaching your realtime difficulties to those that Jesus faced. The idea that your worries, pains and sufferings are separated by a value of centuries is not relevant. Jesus' love and Sacrifice transcend the ages; they defy the element of time for the millennia prior to the Crucifixion and after. I know that you never question the Wisdom of God, and you also never doubt His motivations. I have said that everything according to God must surely be for the conversion and cultivation of the souls and the world that will culminate in Him. And, My Special son, the Father has chosen to commit this into being through His instruments. This is what Saint Francis knew. I realize that you have known this for the whole of your years as well, and you have given your life to Christ Jesus for the same reason. This can be said of all who accept the Blood of the Cross as their eternal Salvation. This is who you are in the Church, and in the Kingdom to come.

Today, therefore, I ask you and your brother to allow Me to tell you yet again how dignified you are in the sight of God. No matter what happens in this life, you are asked to always remember that the silence of God does not imply that He is not speaking. Your voice and your writings are evidence that you are also His instrument. The way you pray for goodness and justice; the way you have stood up for peace and holiness; your testimonies about the sanctity of life – all of these are proof beyond any doubt that the Holy Spirit lives in your heart. I know that you sometimes ponder the many years that you have given to Me as your Mother, your work here with your brother as My messengers, the seemingly countless hours, days and decades that have found you still standing beside Jesus for the redemption of the world. This also means that Jesus was raised from the Tomb by the Father so He could remain living here with you. You not only personify what the Father sent Jesus to the Earth to accomplish, you resound and reconstruct what lost sinners must come to know every day. I have said that the work of the Saints complements what Jesus has done, but I do not mean that this complement is separate from what Jesus died for. You are building not just upon His legacy, you are deeply imbedded in the architecture of the original plan that He laid out. You are helping Jesus bear the burdens of the modern ages in the same way that He carried them during His lifetime on Earth. People like you and your brother have been so helpful to Jesus that you retroactively lightened the Cross that He carried to His Crucifixion. I have said that this has been true of the Popes and Martyrs as well. You have been the instruments that the Lord has assembled into an orchestra that stretches from one century to the next. You are playing a score that comes to you by the wisdom of the Holy Spirit, and you are capable of writing measures of the score as well, just as you helped Jesus endure the burden of the Cross. My Special son, God has always hoped that anyone who sees the veil of Veronica will see their own face there too. And, in the setting of these modern new times, the perspiration wiped from Jesus' brow sanctifies the labors of those who believe in Him. The Father desires Jesus' disciples to be of this true essence in Him. Thank you for your prayers, for your holiness and goodness, and for taking such good care of your brother."

Saturday, October 29, 2016
9:39 a.m.

"Fresh as the morning dew, innocent as the lamb –
strong of heart, and peaceful of mind."

"My Special and Chosen sons, I have come again to pray with you for the Church, that the Lord will uphold and guide you, and for all who are working toward the Kingdom that will soon inundate the Earth. I visit you joyfully with My prayers to place them into the Sacred Heart of Jesus, and I know that you will help Me design My prayers according to your needs. Today, I come to pray for the many who will be wedded in Holy Matrimony, asking Jesus to bless their marriages with fruitful lives and healthy children. My dear sons, the Sacrament of Marriage is the most important safeguard against the scourge of abortion. We pray, therefore, that children be conceived within this Sacrament. It is necessary, however, for all mothers to recognize the precious gift of unborn human life, and that every child must receive the benefit of being born. A woman becomes a mother upon the conception of her child. I also have said that the greatest protection against sin is holiness, and this is the reason I have spoken to you for so many years. My Special son, I hope that you and your brother do not tire of Me telling you how blessed your lives are in the sight of Jesus. I cannot over-express what your mission has meant here in this city, and that your faith and dedication affects the entire world. I see that you understand what this means because you share your joy and hope in earnest. Imagine, My little sons, what it is like for Me to have blanketed the Earth with such plenteous grace, to have appeared in dozens of locations around the globe, to have given humanity untold blessings, signs and wonders – and yet there are only few who follow Me. The Roman Catholic Church celebrates and venerates My role in the redemption of humanity, but there are scarce others that elevate Me to this stature. My Special son, when you imagine what it feels like for your twenty-five years of hard work to be taken for granted, think about what it is like for Me to be looked upon as just another historical figure. I have no disappointment because I realize that the people of Earth will finally come to know Me before the ages are through. And, they will recognize Me as the Morning Star Over America as much as they have known Me by other titles; it is a certainty. I realize that you and your brother do not require attention for what you have done for Jesus. You have been blessed to remain as anonymous as you are. It must be obvious to you that I have given most of My messages to those cloistered in convents and monasteries where the secular void cannot impede them. You know the exceptions; Lourdes, Fatima and Medjugorje among the most prominent.

My little sons, I once told you about righteousness being given venue. This is what you have accorded Jesus and Myself. It is clear that we have amassed a deposit of works that cannot be set aside or discarded, even though some may attempt to do so through their faithless interpretations of prudence. You know who they are because you have approached them in pious humility, asking for their assistance in propagating My work. And, what has been their response? Yes, there has been no response. It is also clear, My Special son, that the book on which you are working these days to celebrate My messages from AD 2010-2012 is replete with lessons and teaching that were meant solely for you and your brother. However, you have gone even further in accessing the faith of those who wish to believe through your own writings for the book. I know that it is difficult to read your own writing in an objective way, but you must trust My words when I say that it is comparable to the most noted Doctors of the Church. Yes, and if you look at your prologues and prefaces to your earlier books, you can see what I mean. Please look at 'Supernal Chambers.' You can discern the contemplations and meditations of the Holy Spirit in these manuscripts that came into Creation through your most lovely heart. Seeing the hand of God in your own work is a tremendous blessing, and it is evidence that you had earlier set aside your consciousness in favor of the intercession of the Lord. This is the medium through which you have recorded the wishes of the Holy Spirit and the substance of My messages to the world. You have heard of such a phenomenon as a flawless storm, but what we have been doing together has been the perfect peace. How much more grandness can be captured through the intersection of your lives and the eternity of the Father? What further blessings and wonders remain for the Earth to absorb? The answer is that even as tremendous as your works for Jesus have been, they are but a seed of what will eventually be known. This is the unexpected dawning of the sunrise in the middle of the night. It is the coming of a tidal wave in the flatlands of a desert. It is resurrecting the hope of those who have given up any possibility of being forgiven by God. I said in My opening 1991 messages that new beginnings are created by faith and prayer, and these two gifts are the result of repentance and confession. This is what we have told humanity through everything I have said, and all you have written. At every reading, you can observe what promises this harbors for summoning the repentance and confession of those who are far from God. What I am saying is that the miracle for humanity in exile is not so much My appearances and what I am sharing, but what you and your brother are doing with My messages that conveys the miracles to the peoples of the Earth. Jesus gave His life for the Salvation of sinners, and you and your brother are spending your lives enlisting their conversion. Many would not have come to the Cross unless you and your brother had done this. We hold in our hands the power of prayer that the Father has given us – He loves us this much. My Special son, please pray for everything that will mitigate the errors of humanity around the world, and for your brother who is again enduring horrific attacks. Your works are waiting so bountifully to be spread like wildfire around the globe."

Saturday, November 5, 2016
William on employment assignment in Clearwater, Florida.

Saturday, November 12, 2016
9:30 a.m.

"The Heart of the Kingdom is the Kingdom, itself. At last, when all is said and done, God will have His way with humanity."

- The Dominion Angels

"My dear little sons, My messages to you each week for the past decades have not been an experiment. They are the real, true, lasting and viable teachings of God through the Holy Spirit, and thereby through Me, His Mother. It is for this reason that I welcome you into My Most Immaculate Heart from where you have never strayed. I have come speaking to you here because our work, not our experiment, goes on. My Special son, you are laboring very hard on your next book because I know that you desire humanity to hear what you have written, and also to know what I have said personally to you and your brother. The latter of these is your graciousness to share our more private conversations as we pray together for the conversion of the lost. I have said on prior occasions that your writings are not too stern, but you can decide if you would rather soften your approach. What you have written is benign compared to the reproaches that Jesus will give those who deny Him. I have brought you a saying from the Dominion Angels in My message this morning about the Heart of the Father's Kingdom. It is that humanity considers the heart a function of an entire whole, and that the heart is where love and memories abound. In truth, the Heart of the Kingdom of God is His Kingdom itself. How could this be true, some might ask. Because the origin and sustenance of life in its essential form is the heart. And, it is through the heart that pious reality exists. The heart of faith is a storehouse of hope and promise. It is where the memories of life are archived. Yes, the Heart of God's Kingdom is His Kingdom in total because there are no deviations or depletions in Heaven. I ask that you remember the fullness of your faith when times seem difficult because faith is nurtured in the heart. And, if your heart is holy and filled with love, it will overflow with graces.

My dear little sons, of all things, Christianity is certainly not delicate. There are seemingly endless dimensions to the battles against evil and secularism – and these two things are in no way mutually exclusive. Christians are being strong-armed physically and emotionally by a world that is bent on rejecting God at every turn. But, sometimes there are miracles. My Special son, I wish you to know that one of these miracles was in response to the prayers of millions who wanted your nation to embark on a different political course. The change in the American government from a culture of death to one of new life has happened because of people like you and your brother. You have My permission to tell anyone you would like in writing or speech that I have told you this. I also told you that your country would be given another chance – and this month's election is evidence of it. Imagine the prospect that the liberal partisan faction would have been allowed to seat the individuals on the so-called Supreme Court who would have shaped this nation's social policy for the next fifty years. Yes, God is all seeing and all knowing, prescient and omnipotent. You may consider it true that God shed His grace on the United States on Tuesday of this week. My Special son, the Dominion Angels also told you that God will have His way with humanity at the last. What does this mean? You know that it does not imply that He will command the love of His people against their will. And, it does not mean that He will punish those who did not search for His Kingdom soon enough – paying the tardy laborer a full day's wage is evidence of this. But, what having His way with humanity does mean is that the Father will welcome their conversion, their repentance and penitence. It suggests that He cries out for interaction between the Church Militant and the Church Triumphant in Heaven. It means that the whole world will finally see where the Saints have tread, even as they are intercessors for humanity on the Earth from the peace of Heaven. Indeed, especially from there! Hence, you must also know that the intercession of your own late father hastened the defeat of the angry woman who wanted to be president as much as anything anyone on the Earth has done. This is the communication, the interaction that I am speaking about that God has sought since Adam and Eve were cast down from the Garden.

Now, inside your hearts where the Kingdom of Love lives, you can dwell on the most pleasing things. You know that the Father touches you and the lives of the faithful with ratified hope and fulfilled promises. He hears the pleas of the poor who only wish to be fed. Here, you shall see what those who have come to power do with their appointed venue. They are sinners like the rest, but they are sinners who have been handed the ability to do what is right and just. Dwelling on the most pleasant things means that it will happen. And, it certainly means that our prayers are as needed now as ever before. You and your brother have stated on many occasions that My messages during the past three years have been about the benefits of beauty, power and purpose. I agree that this has been the case. I have given you these messages because I wish for you to focus on the Heart of the Kingdom as the Kingdom itself. Beauty, power and purpose are functions of the heart because they are descriptive of the love of God and the Crucifixion of His Only Begotten Son. God is beautiful because He says so. He holds sovereign power over all seen and unseen things because there is no other god. He owns the purpose of the redemption of humanity by virtue of the Crucifixion about which I speak. The purpose of the Crucifixion is to redeem everyone who accepts Jesus' Blood on the Cross. I have even gone so far as to tell you that Jesus' Holy Sacrifice is also beautiful. The Most Blessed Trinity is the spiritual providence from which these Sacred Mysteries are manifested, and a providence with limitless dimensions. My

Special son, you are seeing that it is as difficult to place into words the truth and wisdom of God as to describe the Holy Trinity itself. Therefore, it is not that I am asking you to understand why the Father, the Son and the Holy Spirit are the Most Blessed Trinity, and I am not asking that you know how. It is believing 'that' the Father, the Son and the Holy Spirit are the Most Blessed Trinity that matters. Theologians for centuries have tied their minds into knots trying to put pen to page and explain how the Sacred Mysteries were formed. The human mind has tremendous capacity for capturing knowledge that comprehends and amends the exiled world, but the Salvation of humanity comes through a love and truth that surpasses all human understanding.

Moreover, having His way with humanity means that God reserves the right to forgive anyone for anything He pleases. He remains objectively opposed to anyone who commits blasphemy. And, this comes not only in speech and writing, but by the very thought of something that runs contrary to the Sacrifice of His Son. If a person speaks as though to mock the Lord's forgiveness, this is the language of condemnation. Imagine what it is like for you to tell someone that they are forgiven for something, and they tell you to drop dead. How would this make you feel? This is the same sorrow that God senses when He hears someone deny and reject the Crucifixion of Jesus on the Cross. The rejection of Jesus' Holy Sacrifice is a permanent sign that a sinner belongs in the flames of Gehenna, and this is as it should be. This is where sinners go who scoff at the most absolving event in the history of all histories. It is something that should never be debated in the realms of this world. And, My Special son, it is pleasing to think about this because it preserves the Glory of Heaven for those who pray to be there. You have said many times that actions have consequences, and that doing the wrong thing is not committed without dire consequences. You are echoing the words of Jesus on the Cross. Remember that Jesus said, '...forgive them Father, for they know not what they do.' But, even as the Father agreed to forgive them at Jesus' behest, they crucified Him anyway. The point of this is that lost sinners standing before Jesus at the end of time will hear the words of absolution from the Man-God who laid down His life to save them. They will then decide for themselves what must become of their souls – many will choose self-damnation. Do you see the analogy between Jesus' death and their fiery condemnation? *"The world has already heard Jesus forgiving them. It is up to us to respond."* Indeed, and what does this mean for those who refuse to listen? *"Consequences."* My Special son, there are so many implications to what we have shared today that anyone of lesser wisdom would ponder them for the remainder of their lives. But, you and your brother have the capacity to integrate into your knowledge what I have said. We shall see how the Father decides to act in light of all the unbelievers that I have told you about today. It may be true that He deigns to eradicate this darkness before He places the gift of Morning Star Over America on the streets of this nation."

Saturday, November 19, 2016
9:35 a.m.

"Jesus died to redeem lost sinners,
the Faith Church suffers to convert them."

- The Dominion Angels

"My holy and lovely little sons, I make promises that are certified by God because, like you, I am also His messenger. I have come into this home because it is your place of residence – I have said that this Shrine goes with you wherever you may travel or lodge. It is not upon the bricks, mortar or lumber of this building that My grace has been bestowed, but upon your souls through the love in your hearts. The Dominion Angels have said that the Church is within you; this is where the Holy Spirit comes to dwell. My dear sons, you have been given numberless signs and wonders to sustain your faith, but My presence here is the most transcending. Why? Because of your response. I ask that you do not look disdainfully on those who have not yet joined the Church, who often mock its mission, and who scoff at My role in the conversion of humanity. Their disbelief does not make the truth any less true. I have even said that you should take pity on those who do not yet know, but not on those who already know and continue to reject. It is clear that not all souls will be admitted into Heaven at the end of time – this prophecy is of old, and is too stubborn to ignore. In earlier times, livestock owners sharpened the end of wooden branches and sticks, and used them to prod their cattle to move. These devices were called 'goads.' Fighting against the goads means that the cattle would not comply, and would move in every direction to avoid being poked. This is the origin of the expression that someone is trying to goad another person into doing something. However, God does not use a punitive goad to persuade the people of Earth to join His Church. If there is any goad at all, it exists within the human heart where it can touch the spirit of man with blameless truth. I am saying this morning that Jesus' Gospel is more an inspiration than a prodding. He implores humanity to follow His Commandments by their own good volition. My Special son, I agree with your thoughts that human suffering is a form of goading lost sinners to change their ways, but we must remember that the Faith Church suffers for lost sinners, just as Jesus laid down His life in expiation for their sins.

You have found that I speak occasionally about theologians who often attempt to connect logical strains that help the pragmatic of mind to understand what God wants of them. It factually does work on many intellectuals and those who have never called on the Holy Spirit for divine assistance. But, humanity requires more than logic when applying one's life to the mandates of the Gospel. Those who have much will be given even more, and those who have little will lose what they have. What logic is there in this? Let he who is without sin cast the first stone. How is this reconciled against 'admonish your brother?' Even so, the teachings of God are not contradictory, and they cannot be backed into a corner where the pragmatics of lost humanity can lock them in time. They are inclusive of all avenues of behavior. Life always changes; the world evolves, and the persuasions of human thought and action are as variably unstable. Imagine what a labor it would be to write a Gospel that would last not just beyond the early centuries, but wholly until the end of time. This is indeed what the Holy Spirit did. Timelessness means that something is relevant yesterday, today, and tomorrow. One might pose an inquiry about how the Crucifixion of Jesus could be timeless in much this same way, and the answer is not just that He saved all souls in His day and in the future, but all ever given the breath of life who accept His Holy Sacrifice beyond the parameters of time. And without question, Jesus made His Crucifixion, beginning at the Last Supper and on the Cross, an eternal Sacrifice that supersedes the elements of human life, including time and space. Everything eternal about humanity must begin somewhere, and it was initiated through the slain Man-God – everything about Jesus that a heart and soul can understand. I recently told you that the Sacred Mysteries of the Church surpass human understanding, but their acceptance is within the grasp of all who believe. While this does not seem any more logical than anything else, it speaks to the fact that giving the Lord one's will opens the door to learning what His wisdom is about. You see the letters MIR during My Medjugorje apparitions, and I have said that they not only stand for peace, they are the first three letters of the word 'miracle.' This is the type of linear thinking that Jesus has applied since His birth in Bethlehem. The Father imagines that if He can give lost sinners a sign about where they must travel, they will embark on the journey toward Him in pursuit of life's true meaning. It becomes a hunger that can only be satisfied by seeking the origin and aroma of Salvation that Jesus shares with the Church. And, this movement, this momentum, is brought into being by the prayers from the heart that I have been summoning from humanity for 2,000 years.

My Special and Chosen ones, the Father presents Himself to you in the personage and honor of the Saints, in the signs of redemption that He offers through them, in the architecture of Nature and the innocence of lambs, in the inspiration made possible by the wisdom of the Holy Spirit, by the reflections of the Gospel that are always made fresh in the parables of the heart, and by your own consciousness that you accord Him when you focus on His love. I am saying that there is no single dimension by which you can capture everything that Heaven has to say because you are comprised of multiple dimensions yourselves. Even in your thoughts, speeches and songs, there are registers. A statement and a question are seemingly opposite things. With this kind of parity, something as simple as syllables from one's mouth, how many dimensions can there be in the infinity of thinking about God? This is what I have always meant that a single interlude from beyond these realms is a miracle itself, if that interlude opens the door to righteous truth. An interlude is believed to be something that interrupts a normal cycle of events, and this applies to what Christians do because it begins a period of reflection that changes who a person is. When Jesus comes knocking on the door of the heart, He wants something. I told you this quite recently. He seeks the image of Himself, as though when the person on the other side of the door opens it, Jesus is looking into a mirror. This is not out of the question. It is the same phenomenon as when you meet someone on the street who is so evocative that you wish the Father would have created you to look like them. Through Jesus knocking on the door of the human heart, if the respondent complies with His request, this re-identification comes true. Jesus says, '...I love you so much that I want you to be like Me.' Here again, how logical is this? If there is any cause and effect, it is that Jesus comes to the door to say that human beings do not have to be bitter anymore. They are not forced to wonder why life on Earth is so unsightly and lacking holy design. He is the beauty and holiness that the world has sought since the first exiled man took his first breath. Everything about a man that God loved when He breathed life into Adam is restored to perfection by Jesus on the Cross.

So, My Special and Chosen ones, it is not true that the fastest runner is not allowed to win. It may seem so because of the current state of world affairs, but the finish line is not in the confines of this world. And, whether or not someone chooses to mock who I am and what I have meant to the Catholic Church, this neither bothers Me nor has any effect on the outcome of the Earth. It is as though someone is walking through a neighborhood in which they have never been seen, and people sitting on the porch feeling as though their private space is being trespassed. They will change in due season. This is how Jesus answered the man who denied Him three times. Did He not say, '...You are the Rock on which I will build My Church?' For certain, My Special son, this seems devoid of logic as well. But, what exists is proof beyond all doubt that Jesus owns the prerogative to change or make new any design, factor, force, mandate or creature that He might deign to modify. This is the power that He wielded even before the Annunciation of the Archangel Gabriel. And, who wrote many Epistles in the Sacred Scriptures? *"Saint Paul."* And, did someone not ask this same servant why he was persecuting the Church? *"Yes."* This is the reason that I said that there are a billion Sauls still walking the Earth. There are even more who are denying Jesus three times a day. This does not make it any easier for the mission of the Church. Waiting for lost sinners to convert is like watching ice melt, but it is happening. The future of humanity is never etched in stone – it is a living, breathing, growing, maturing prospect that is trending toward this conversion. This is what Christ Jesus pondered during His Agony in the Garden and Holy Sacrifice on the Cross. If He had not known this, He would have pronounced His Mystical Body dead from the moment He spoke His first words in the temple. So, one of the vast bounties of spiritual conversion is hope. There is no hope if someone believes that the ideals of hope will never come. Hope implies a relationship between truth and action. Hope, along with faith, love and charity, make up the foundation on which the stature of humanity is standing."

Saturday, November 26, 2016
9:26 a.m.

"For every wind that blows, the soul hath a song."

- The Dominion Angels

"My dear little sons, everything that has to do with love and the refinement of the human heart is present within you. You remain with Me because of your dedication to Jesus, and for the succor you find in My Most Immaculate Heart. Today, the Dominion Angels have told you that there are limitless songs in the soul that are yearning to be free, and they are given voice by the Spirit of God in you. It might seem that Jesus would eventually cease speaking about human potential in favor of the newfound realities that have become apparent in this world – but not everyone alive is listening. Hence,

His mission through Me is to resound the message of repentance, conversion, and renewal. I have said that I would have spoken to you and your brother even if there were no urgencies here, and this remains true. My Special son, this does not mean that there is no reason to celebrate the condition of the Church. The faith of righteous men is already strong. The warmth of the Christian heart transforms the world into the beginnings of what the Father desires for His Creation. It was finished by Jesus on the Cross. Yes, for every wind that blows, the soul hath a song. You voice its lyrics every day. You sing its melody in what you pray for. We are united in this cause in that we have been found in the arms of the Father from where we began. My little sons, you are stationed with Me in the familial ties that unite us with God because you have invested your lives in Jesus. How many times and in what number of ways can I tell My children all over the world that this is the beginning of the new identity of man? I assure you that there are limitless means of expression, but there is only so much linear time. I always believed during My earthly years that it may not have mattered whether the entire human race was converted in My lifetime on Earth. Why? Because of the eternal redemption that all generations have found in Jesus on the Cross. This is the same in your day. You and your brother have given a converting blessing to humanity that will transcend your own lives. Even as much as Jesus has redeemed lost sinners, you and your brother are helping awaken them. I wish for you to remember that this dignifies you before the Angels, and gives you a standing before the Father reserved for the humblest warriors. I do not tell you these things to curry your favor, I am stating a well known fact. This is why I ask you to always walk with peace inside, with self-assurance that the Kingdom of God to which you belong has itself been shaped by your faith. One of the most often asked questions that I receive from hearers and visionaries is why I am always so happy. How can I not be elated when I know that the human race has been saved by the Fruit of My Womb? During those rare times when I appear not to be happy is when My children turn a deaf ear to My pleas, and when they scoff at the graces that God is bestowing upon them.

My little sons, I ask you to remember that everything good is always a seed of something better. This is the building-up of the Kingdom that you celebrate to this day. And, even many things that seem to be bad can lead to something good. My Special son, do you remember the crime committed by the man whom Jesus canonized on the Cross? Yes, he was a thief. And, just as this thief found himself dying on a cross next to Jesus, he was taken to Paradise before the day was done. It took the penitence of the thief to make this possible, but it also required his faith to know that His Savior was being crucified beside him. There are thieves everywhere around the globe – and not just stealers of money and materials, but of innocence and truth. What we know to be true in your day is that there is also redemption in repentance, and this is what we seek through My messages and your books. Every day of the world, there is movement in My messages to you and your brother that you do not see. It is the same as the phenomenon of allowing all the guns to fire at once. I ask that you and your brother remember that your lives are filled with grace that does not always reveal itself upon every hour. Your exile is not prone to allowing such blessings to be witnessed. Everything that trends toward darkness on Earth is eradicated by the Light of the Cross. The Gospel of Saint Matthew speaks about salt and light. And, I have spoken to you and your brother about focus and magnification. When these elements are combined, humanity in the world gains a transcending desire for the truth, and a vision for the beatific architecture of Heaven. When you pray for all your causes in this life, when you imagine what the world ought to look like in alignment with the wishes of Jesus, you are focusing His attention on the matters that you have magnified as worthy of prayer.

There can be no advancement of the Kingdom of Love without the Holy Spirit in the heart. While the Earth is rife in the depths of despair, the Kingdom of God is advanced through the heights of human love. This is what we are doing right now – we are stopping sinners from delving more deeply into sin. We are reversing the error that has held billions of souls in dungeons of guilt for centuries. We are painting a picture that will be recognizable to all who have accepted the Cross, but who have never thought about seeing it. We are approaching the innocent and warning them about the predators who would exploit them. We are bearing heavily on the consciences of mothers who might take the lives of the children in their wombs. This is what you do every time you pray. It is not something that you can see with your eyes, but it is a matter that cannot be stripped from your hopes. This is the divinity of the human person that time cannot steal. It is a purity of heart that the devil cannot soil. And, My Special and Chosen ones, I am telling you this morning that you are allowing the potential about which I have spoken to come of age during this period on Earth when everything holy seems to be pushed toward the margins. You are assisting the victory of the righteous over the world's unrighteous because you have never wavered in your faith in God. You have known all along that God is God, Jesus is God the Son, and the Holy Spirit is God and the Son in the Kingdom of the heart. This connects you, My Special and Chosen sons, with the origin of the universe and everything that precedes the dawn of man. This is from where I have come, where all the glories and beauties imaginable find their beginning in the love of God. You must remember that the Father not only created humanity out of love, He created humanity because of love. If anything that I would like My children to never forget, it is due to this love that our lives have been shared. My Special son, I pray atop My prayers that you and your brother will find happiness in what you know of Jesus' love for you. It is sacred, perpetual, and irrevocable. Jesus' love is timely and timeless. His Sacrifice on the Cross is your eternal joy, just as His Glorious Resurrection has sanctioned your life in Heaven. Yes, you could end your writing at dawn tomorrow, and never place pen to page again. This esteems the dimensions of your blessings already given to the world. However, My own soul is serenaded by your prayers, writings, and reflections. You magnify what the Lord has inspired within you. It is in accompanying the melodies of the Angels that you have composed your symphonies in Him.

My children, you should never assume that your faith and good works have a given measurable effect, for they are immeasurable in the sight of God. Why? Because of the magnification that I just mentioned. A small prayer becomes the estate of lofty speeches that can touch the hearts of millions. One does not have to be president or ruler of nations to be known Kingdom-wide in the House of the Father. Not everyone on Earth will have their portraits hung in stately halls. Anonymous names will continue to be unknown. But, in the Kingdom of God where everything righteous matters, the growth and magnification of the simple Christian life is hailed as mammoth among the nations. This is the reason such people as Popes, Bishops, and state leaders bear a tremendous responsibility for which they should truly fear failing. It has been the burden of many a man and woman who rued the day when they let their own pride seat them in such places. Indeed, I would rather be in your place – here where the greatest prayers ever said to God and His Hosts have parted your lips. It is here that you have told those who must know that they are more innocent than they believe, but more culpable than they presume. Clearly, this is the paradox that you have laid before them, the quest that they must unravel in the fathoms of their hearts and minds. And, this is what makes you messengers from God more than anything else you might imagine about this life. I ask you to remember everything I have said to you today when it would seem that your work is being disparaged. My Special son, I prepared you from a child to be a messenger with your brother. You can see the tenderness of the Mother of Jesus in the lives of those who are devoted to Me. It is through the Will of the Father that this has been done. I will ensure that great blessings come upon the faithful who pray for My intercession."

Saturday, December 3, 2016
9:34 a.m.

"Dignity and honor – pray tell, why not?"

"My dear little sons, it is My privilege to pray with you this morning because we change the future of humanity every time we do. I have within My Immaculate Heart and flowering from My fingertips all the graces that the world needs to be converted to Jesus on the Cross. This is the expiation of human sin that reconciles the world with the Father. The Lord requests that His people live with dignity and honor as the disciples of His Son, and there is no reason that this should not be done. It is coming because the Father says that it will happen. It has been brought into being because Jesus declared its veracity from the Cross. Yes, it is a fact because humanity has accepted Him through the Church. Why not be dignified in the Blood of the Lamb? Why not accept the sacred honor of being claimed by the Deity once again? This, My Special and Chosen sons, is the reason we have been working with such diligence to prepare the world for the earthshaking miracle of The Morning Star Over America. If it is true, as Saint John Paul II foretold, that the messages of Medjugorje will convert America, then surely it will be through the Morning Star who has brought such revelations upon its shores. I have introduced decency where there is unsightliness. I have brought purity to supplant the sordid. I offer integrity to replace the corruption that you are seeing at all levels of secular human life. My Special son, I wish to make amply clear today at the behest of Jesus that innocence does not imply naivete. The Father protects those who place their trust in Him, and infuses His wisdom into those who turn to Him for guidance. There is a keen intelligence within those with faith because they know that the devil is always assailing them. This is why the holy sword in Saint Michael's hand is a replica of the Cross. He demands of all evil spirits, '...die, devil, die!' It must be made known worldwide that those who are devoted to God through Jesus hold within them the sacred knowledge that the powerful bulwark of Heaven supports them in ways that are not readily seen. However, this must be sanctioned by the person with faith by living a pious life, a life with discretion and sound judgment. It is the same as one's guardian angel protecting the soul who calls on him. The angel provides this protection if the person lives prayerfully in accordance with the stateliness of God. My Special son, people everywhere are moved when they see a child fall four floors down and land on something that saves its life. (*This refers to a recent news story that I had seen whereby I thanked God for the deliverance of the child.*) This is the work of the guardian angel protecting the innocent who have not attained the age of reason. Those who are older and more mature must work in tandem with their guardian angel because they possess the will to make decisions about their own safety and welfare. In essence, they are aware of the dignity and honor that they have found in Jesus on Easter morning. Indeed, pray tell, why not? This is the providence of the miraculous Paschal Resurrection, and the reason for the joy of the Church. Yes, it is right and just.

My dear sons, those who desire unity with the Father in all His glory and beauty must reach out to Him without fear of falling. They must use their faith not as a safety net, but a reason to act with the knowledge that there is no need for a parachute. Jesus walked the Earth and cured the sick, healed the lame and performed other miracles, knowing that the faith of those who solicited Him was their healing. When someone comes to Him even to this day with petitions that comport with the Will of the Father, He will respond. Yes, it is true that Jesus induces the Father to answer prayers that sinners on Earth would never have thought to be granted. It is all about the balance between suffering for the sake of the wicked and forbearance for those who will convert no other way. It is true that sometimes suffering is the grace itself. The point I am making is that the Church must approach God with beseeching invocations that are about more than simple survival. These prayers must be transcending in ways that eradicate starvation and warfare everywhere on Earth. God would have the Faith Church perform every miracle that Jesus gifted on the Earth during His ministry if its faith were that strong. Sadly however, so much time is required during these modern years to battle the secular forces that incessantly bombard the mission of the Church. How can the Church pursue the graces of dignity and honor in a world that demands there to be neither one? It is a matter of the constant fight to end the scourge of sin that is chaining billions of lost sinners to the darkness. Approaching God with the expectation that these things will be eradicated is one of the most benevolent petitions that someone can raise. God will act when the Church beseeches Him to do so, in acclamation, with the due spiritual evidence to prove humanity's faith in Jesus on the Cross. My Special son, it is as though God places the fate of humanity into a vat, and adds the Crucifixion of Jesus on the Cross. He includes a generous dose of prayer from the Faith Church and the intercession of the Saints. He then says, '..now, what do I use to stir this?' And, the answer is the volition of the collective human spirit to combine the elements together. This is what it means when a slain president says that it will become all one thing.

Humanity must return to the benignity in which it was created through the Will of the Father that birthed them. Nothing can be constant without the Will of the Father. Nothing good will ever come of those who reject Him. All what must be accomplished toward the goal of purifying the Earth has to be brought through the Sacrifice of Jesus on the Cross. And, there would have been no resurrection of anything mortal without the raising of Jesus from the Tomb. Truly, this is where dignity, power and beauty walk right up to the human person and say that they welcome the spiritual touch of humanity in the ethereal realms. What I am trying to share this morning is that these realms already exist in the world of exiled men within the human heart. This is where the true dignity and honor of people exist. This is where the Holy Spirit presides over the events that will eventually shape the only human history that will ever matter. If there are any intentions and accidents that comprise this history in any reparative way, they too must be connected to Jesus on the Cross – they are even fruits of His Sacrifice forced into time. And to this end, I have said that Heaven is limitless in its expanse and perpetual in its being. There is no room in Heaven for tears, sadness or regret – save Our Lady of Sorrows. There are no hiding places that harbor corruption or darkness. It is not that they do not remain in the Abyss below because they do not vanish into thin air. Only joy and confidence exist in Heaven, and this is the center of the heart that Jesus is trying to instill in those who are walking on Earth. Done right, this results in the outpouring of miracles for which the world has long prayed, but it cannot be done if men and women of the Faith Church do not believe and serve its purpose more than any other time. My hope is that all human prayer will be directed toward this expectation of jubilation for those who believe what I am saying. My Special son, I told you not long ago that all that is eternal about humanity must begin somewhere. It begins in Jesus on the Cross, and it is initiated by those who not only accept His Sacrifice and reflect upon what it means, but who assume their identity in Him and force goodness and miracles into being. *"And, that's what our work is doing – forcing miracles into being."* Yes, this is precisely what I am saying.

My Special son, many of your friends and neighbors might claim that I am speaking about a near impossible degree of pious faith. They sometimes take a more practical approach living in the shadow of the Cross because they cannot detect the wiles of the devil through their everyday lives. Being present in the flesh on Earth does not have to be lent to this type of consciousness. A second component that acts against their faith is the fight for self-sufficiency in a world that would rather see them starve. These are not distractions as much as they are obstacles. You have written with eloquence about roadblocks and gatekeepers. These sinners could not care less whether Christians have lives of dignity and peace. It is all about their own standard of living, and how much they can hoard for themselves and their bloodline heirs. It is a miracle of sorts that Jesus has not already felled them from their thrones. My Special son, most all of them will fall of their own accord. So, I have brought My sentiments about the willpower of Christians to realize that the Holy Scriptures are playing out right before their eyes. This is sanctifying for humanity and legitimizing for those who remain true to their faith. There are few wonders on Earth these days, but one of them is for sure – how much more rope do the enemies of the Church require before they take the way of Judas Iscariot? It will happen, just as certainly as I am speaking to you now. I have asked you not to pity them. It is not that you should not care, but that you already know the Will of God toward those who reject the Sacrifice of His Son. If there is any blasphemy in this world, it is when those to whom God offers His forgiveness respond that they would rather decline."

Saturday, December 10, 2016
9:33 a.m.

Psalm 85:11-12
Kindness and truth shall meet;
Justice and peace shall kiss.
Truth shall spring out of the earth,
and justice shall look down from Heaven.

"My dear sons, there can be no monotony in your Christian faith because God is always re-creating within you the designs of His Kingdom. How on Earth or anywhere else could the infiniteness of His Sacred Love be captured in the collective lives of man? The Psalm 85 passage speaks of the unity between the virtuousness of Jesus' Most Sacred Heart and those who love Him. You are accorded the fullness of His Truth on the ground where you walk. And, you look skyward and see the Holy Face of Salvation looking back down at you. Today, I ask you to help Me pray for all who refuse to believe these things. I ask for your prayers that will touch them through the miracles that your Bishop mentioned on My Feast of the Immaculate Conception this week. You were there at the Holy Mass to hear him resound the praises of God and the Son whom I bore, that His Providence shall reign over all the nations and ages. Yes, there is eloquence in this man, and we have found it. So, the psalmists can put pen to page and celebrate the dignity of God who takes residence within the human heart because the psalmists themselves are touched by His grace. My Special son, this grace comes to you naturally because you were an apostle of the Lord upon your birth. Billions of other souls must internalize this grace as a gift they receive upon their acceptance of the Cross through the conversion that the Church teaches. And, it is not enough just to reflect this holy grace; it must be nurtured from within by the same dominion that sends it down from Heaven. The innocence of Jesus looks into your eyes when you stand before the Altar and pronounce your belief in the Most Blessed Sacrament. Forgiveness, power and new life are given to those who worthily approach Jesus on the Altar, the Mount Calvary of the Church of Faith. Imagine, My Special son, what I must feel when seeing the Holy Sacrifice of the Mass on such solemnities as the Feast of the Immaculate Conception, and hear within your heart the voice of Jesus, asking Me to see how much His faithful disciples love Me. There is no lacking in the miraculous in this as well. I have said to you and your brother that the perpetual sanctity of the Church Triumphant is humanity's blessing from Jesus and the Father. It is where human faith is redeemed; it is where all the Saints have gone, and it is the destiny of all the souls whom Jesus and I saw adoring Him at Holy Mass on Thursday. This is where the perfection of God kisses the brokenness of humanity.

My little sons, I keep repeating the word innocence – innocence, innocence. Why? Because the loss of innocence is the inception of sin, and the restoring of innocence is the forgiveness of sin. Surely, it was the Incarnation of Innocence Himself who was crucified to restore the lost innocence of those who crucified Him. There seems to be an ironic circle of life in this, but remember that it is indeed life. It is about living and breathing the excellence of humanity that was first given to Adam, and that is restored by the New Adam at the behest of God in Heaven. My Special son, there have been centuries of debates about why God changed His mind about the fate of His people. Adam and Eve were expelled from the Garden because of their wilful disobedience, and the Father seemingly changed His mind about it and sent His Son to die for their reclamation. I must say that the Father is single-minded in all things beatific and ordinary. It is not that God changed His mind, but that He completed His moral sentence. It is somewhat like the forbearance seen on Earth, but it is more all-forgiving and permanent. It is as though the people of Earth can now hear the echo of the Father's eternal voice from Heaven saying, '...You are to be banished into exile, but I absolve you through the Sacrifice of My Son, if you will believe in Him.' Hence, it is as much about the manifest love of the Son as it is about those who accept Him.

You and your brother know that God would be as glorious even if no man ever called on Him. He will always be as sovereign, perpetually and supremely kind, forever reigning, and at all times and places capable of anything conceivable in the heart of a lamb. When someone says, '...come to me,' this does not imply that there is always something that needs to be changed. In the case of Jesus, '...come to Me' means that all who are broken, lonely and afraid should enter His Most Sacred Heart with the expectation that He will comfort them there. Indeed, accepting Christ Jesus on the Cross is not always a struggle because millions of sinners accept Him upon first hearing. They never reject His Sacrifice on the Cross at the initial moment of knowing. Yes, there needs to be a conversion of lost sinners into saints; this is the reason they must turn to Him at His first summons. We look again at Psalm 85. Justice, peace, truth, kindness – all these things are pouring down from Heaven in the same way that My graces fall to Earth upon those who will accept them from My fingertips.

So, innocence is always the heart of the matter, but also is glory. This is the marriage of Heaven and Earth. Innocence-restored is the call of the Holy Spirit to those who will join Adam in Heaven with all his successors in the presence of the Father whose forgiveness is as powerful as His creative love. There are three other words that should be said by men on Earth to rival the number of times that they say, '...I love you.' These three words are, '...I am sorry.' These are the feet upon which all human transformation stands. It does not matter which phrase is voiced first, but they together represent a tandem upon which the entire universe can be carried. Those who do not accept Me as their Mother often cast aside My meaning in the Salvation of the world, but they are lacking in knowledge about the reason Saint Gabriel came to Me. It is for the very souls who reject My Holy Love that I have come speaking to them through you. I come hailing the Divine Mercy of My Son because it is needed, not just because He is offering it. What would be the benefit of businesses on the Earth building new cars if no one ever purchased one? There is a need that has been created through the corrupt functions of man. And, through the sins of these same men, they are in need of the pardon they find in Jesus on the Cross. Jesus is saying that He is offering the Mercy of God through His own Sacrifice in such a way that those who require it can base their repentance on it. Sinners cannot account for their own wickedness other than to believe that it is absolved through their acceptance of Jesus on the Cross. This is how they recognize that the devil had them all along. They were snared in the quagmire of not knowing where they were, and refused to take the steps that would help them learn. In other words, they needed an enlightenment that they did not know was available to them until they, like Adam, found themselves naked before the Father. Does it not make sense that God must tell lost sinners that they are lost? "*Yes.*" And, this is what the Holy Spirit is doing on Earth through the Church, through miracles such as My apparitions around the world; through the suffering of the heart, soul, mind and body, and through the natural and unnatural events that drive sinners to the Church in droves. Why should buildings and towers have to collapse in order to impress upon humanity that God is calling them to repentance? Because they will listen no other way.

My Special son, we have arrived at a point in time when all these elements of My conversation today will culminate in an enlightenment never before seen by humanity on Earth. I am not saying that the sky is going to open and begin raining down balls of fire. It is not going to cause the world to shudder in outer space. But, the invigoration of the faith of men will come quickly from inside their hearts when they begin seeing signs and wonders they cannot attribute to anyone but God. The Morning Star Over America is one such revelation. So is the miraculous reversal of the socialist movement in America. And, the step by step occurrence of the signs in Medjugorje will unfold precisely as foretold. These events will not only justify the faith of all good Christians, they will vindicate My messengers in the world. It is not that they require vindication; this is not the issue. My Special son, you and your brother will someday have the gift that Jesus gave to humanity on the day He was raised from the Tomb. They will see the verities and beckoning that you have elicited in the fullness of the years. It is not that you require it either. It is that God wants the whole of Creation to remember what blessings He gives to those who are obedient to Him. Do you remember the strains of the song, 'The ages will praise you for all you have done?' I have spoken worldwide in remote places about the 'glory' of men that lives inside the heart. It is the reflection of the Glory of God in those who bear out His Name. This, My Special son, is 'All for the love of one Man.' This is the reason I have come to you. It is the reason you have lived. It is the way the world ought to remain. Thank you for praying with such sincerity and meaning. Bless you for seeing the truth when so many others refuse to open their eyes. It is incumbent upon them to believe what I have said. The burden of proof is not on you. I join your prayers in all ways that the Lord prescribes."

Saturday, December 17, 2016
9:41 a.m.

"Every day, there seems to be more,
every moment, somewhat less."

"What a beautiful grace has come upon you, My dear little sons, that I am here speaking with you about the Lord. I have said that the Son of Man knocks on the hearts of men because He wants something. Jesus is not just a casual caller. His Kingdom is not just another place. Therefore, it is with all peace, providence, glory and opportunity that we have found ourselves praying together this morning. My little ones, if you look at the conversion of humanity on a larger scale, you will see that the world is becoming more holy every day. But, if men get lost in the briars– if they focus only on the minutia of everyday sins, they might believe that there is less progress toward the Cross by the moment. I have always asked My children to be patient during the evangelizing of the Earth, but imagine the patience required by Jesus on the Cross. No man at any hour has had to exhibit the patience that Jesus offers humanity in the Most Blessed Sacrament of the Altar. The Old Testament speaks about taking a stranglehold against the enemies of human righteousness, and the Good Messiah reflects on relenting so that eternal life is not withheld from those who repent. I have come today in tremendous joy that you are praying for your country and for peace around the world. I pray with you as well for the end of abortion – the worst global tragedy to ever stain the history of man. It would seem that there are incremental successes of the Faith Church through the years, while evil is overtaking the Earth in waves. This is just an illusion because evil has only the parameters of time in which to work. God the Father and Jesus the Savior have both time and eternity to prevail. It is all according to the response of men in the earthly domain. I find every conceivable reason to focus on the Cross and Resurrection of Jesus because this is the expiation of human sin, and the destiny of all who believe in Him. And, My little ones, it is not enough just to believe that Jesus is the Redeemer of sinners. There is no virtue in holding this lovely Man's Sacrifice at arm's length. There have been billions of people over the past 2,000 years who have acknowledged that Jesus the Prophet died on the Cross, but that His death did not affect them. The tip of one's cap will never deliver a sinner into the light of Paradise. It requires the complete unification with the Crucifixion so that the very identity of the believer becomes supplanted by the identity of Christ. It is an immersion in the righteousness that drives out every form of evil. It is the reversal of the tides of human helplessness in favor of the power within the Most Sacred Heart of Jesus. My Special and Chosen ones, God ordains that humanity should be found in His Son. This is the way the world was fashioned. What Jesus said during His three year ministry still echoes in the conscience of every soul who will eventually enter Heaven. It may not be something that is dwelled upon during every moment, but it grows stronger and brighter every day. My great joy is knowing that the encounter of Jesus and the sinner is inevitable. Clearly, it is a matter of time, the course of human events, the Will and Providence of God, and the life of the flesh taking its last gasps, wondering what will happen next. Accepting the Blood of Jesus is like a splash of brilliance impacting the consciousness of the penitent to the measure that one wishes to be immersed in His grace. How much Blood must touch the human soul? How many hours of confession are enough? To what extent does a sinner need to be contrite to be recognizable by Jesus on the Cross and risen from the Sepulcher? These are questions whose answers are as infinite as the imagination. The soul must be immersed not only in the Blood of Jesus on the Cross, but in His sorrow, agony, and torment as well. The lifetime of a man on Earth must be his confession and sanctification, but humbly telling Jesus that you love Him suffices for one's conversion. This is all He asks. The words, 'I love you Jesus' are comforting enough for Him that He would trek through the darkness of the world and rescue you again.

My Special son, I am speaking about the rhythm of the Christian faith in the temporal world that sounds like steps on a boardwalk. Prayers are strides in the direction of holiness. Reciting the Stations of the Cross in the sanctity of the heart soothes the Father in Heaven. Why? Because it is done in adoration of His Son by the Faith Church that defies the temptations of the devil. Do you remember – whatever is holy, whatever is pure, whatever is excellent or just; all these things are within the grasp of the sanctified heart. Our meditations are focused on the gentleness of the Holy Spirit that has not only infiltrated the confines of this world, but has taken control of the thoughts of the faithful and protected them from error. It is in these blessings that you have found your purpose because this is what the Father has commissioned. My children, if there is an image of human splendor here in America that so many have spoken about, it is found in the children of the Cross. If there is any stain to be expunged, it is washed away by the King who was crucified there. All the peace that could possibly console the collective human spirit is imbedded in this gift. All the generations before you have received this joy. Those who are living around the nations at this time will finally realize this truth. And, the generations to come, whether still bonded in exile or raised to the heavenly New Jerusalem – each and every soul has the gift of remaining within the Salvation that Jesus has accorded you because this is the love of the Father. It is His absolution and preservation that He has given those upon whom His favor rests and His Kingdom bestowed. Therefore, when you see that holiness is coming to the Earth in ways that are containable by the history books on the shelves, thank God in Heaven that He wrote it that way. And, if someone fails in the moment; if a man or woman slips and falls along the way, forgive their missteps and help them try again.

My little sons, I have given you a message this morning that is about the new beginnings that I spoke of in 1991. I wish for you to remember that all the words I have said during those eventful days and even to this very moment have their place in the Salvation story. It is not that they make a contribution to the sacred deposit of redemption, but they are the wings with which one's Salvation in the Lamb of God can take flight. This is the way of all the works of the great Saints throughout the centuries of the Church. You and your brother have made contributions to the conversion of the lost that can be seen written in the skies over Jesus on the Cross on Good Friday. It has been seen by many, and it will eventually be seen by everyone given the breath of life. Yes, your faith, prayers and hard work will descend onto the world like the 1917 Fatima Miracle of the Sun. It will appear as comprehensive relief to the billions who have kept their faith alive; and to those who have allowed their doubts to linger, it will drive them to their knees in joy that their hopes have come true. A great deal happens on one's knees. It is the point of surrender to the Will of God in Heaven. It is where one can see the Light of the World within the heart. It is the posture where contrition takes its most essential form. My Special son, you and your brother are so endearing, so hearty and loving in your desires to preserve the dignity of the Church and the fairness in which Jesus guides its mission around the globe. Your prayers are never in vain. I promise that you are whispering into Jesus' ear every time you say a prayer that upholds the centuries-honored Traditions of the Church. You take your case directly to His Most Sacred Heart when you pray for them."

Saturday, December 24, 2016
9:36 a.m.

"*The Battalion of Hymns —*
Holding on to the concept of life."

"My dear little sons, your lives are veritable encyclicals to humanity about the righteousness of God. You have become living institutions of the peace and justice that men pray for in your day. You are accompanied by legions of angels that give you strength and vision to withstand the difficulties of the world. The Dominion Angels sing the battalion of hymns that make you great leaders in the ways of the Church. Today, I come speaking to you on this Eve of Joy because we are united in the Christ Child in the same way that we are one with the Holy Spirit. My Special son, you have written through the decades that the innocence and power of the Son of My Womb is the example God set forth for humanity to emulate. If ever there were a reason for humanity to understand the concept of human life, it surely must be found in Jesus in the Manger. Such innocence, such kindness, such holiness, such love. The themes of Christmas must resound these simple traits of the Savior of the world from the moment of His Birth in Bethlehem to His Resurrection from the Tomb. A lifetime of righteousness is encapsulated between these two events. We have long prayed for the eradication of abortion from the face of the Earth. All humanity needs to do is look at the Child Jesus, and the reason will become clear. We pray not only for the end of abortion, but any mother's thoughts of committing one. Within each conceived child is the incarnation of the Father's Will to perpetuate life through the ages and His wondrous grace. Many are the months, and untold are the prayers that we have accumulated, seeking His intervention in preserving the lives of unborn children. What has happened, My little sons, is that humanity has lost its hold on the beatific meaning of human life — its very concept handed down from the Wisdom of God. It has often been said that human life is a product of God's Will. And, while this is true, this product must not be seen as separated from the Father, Himself. His Creation is sown from His Kingdom, for all its beauty and providence. The viable nature of humanity's life is something that must be put into action through the good will of God-fearing men. It is for us to share with humanity on Earth this eloquent truth so that the Father's Will can indeed be done. Jesus was begotten, not made, one in being with the Father. This unity is what He seeks of His exiled children. Christmas emboldens this faith because Jesus' Kingdom is worth believing.

When the nations see the dawn breaking on Christmas morning, it is a rehearsal for the Second Coming of the Son of Man. The great light that breaks is most prominent inside the heart. The world was not prepared for the Nativity of Christ Jesus in Bethlehem. It is our duty in prayer to ensure that the world becomes prepared when He returns in Glory. The Church has been given the remarkable miracle of Jesus' Crucifixion on the Cross, and God has saved His exiled apostles through this same Holy Sacrifice. The faith of men is the agent that connects these two gifts. And prayer, the prayers of the Church and little children in their bedrooms, make known to the heavens that the heart of lost humanity belongs to the celebration of the concept of life. While all those angels are singing the battalion of hymns, the world around them struggles to maintain its peace. We have seen the terrible aftermath of the violence and degradation of those who refuse to believe. The Church cannot state in good conscience that it is a purveyor of peace, if it just stands idly by. The very meaning of believing in Jesus is to feed the poor, set free the captives, and do all the other things that make the Earth look like Heaven. There are no needs in Heaven other than the awesome echoes of the Saints' intercessions heard by the ears of the Father on behalf of those who petition their prayers. This Light about which I speak is magnified by those on Earth who call on Heaven for help. My little sons, the most brilliant reflector of light in eternity is the Church Triumphant. And, this same bounty of Paradise finds its likeness in the hearts of the faithful on Earth. This is the sanctifying arena where Saints are created. This is where Jesus was born to instill in humanity the desire to manifest new life in the form of saintly goodness. It must be made clear that billions of souls before you have made this transition because of the Birth of One Innocent Child. My Special son, we contemplate every year about what homilies might be spoken on the Feast of Christmas. What can priests and deacons say that can capture the eloquence of a Messianic Birth that would change humanity and the world in a simple cry? What tumult would this Child face before He would grow into the fullness of maturity and handover His life to redeem a world that despises Him? Reaching with His palm into the air from His place in the Manger was as great a blessing as all the signs of the Cross given by the entire College of Popes in the history of the Church. I would look into the eyes of this Child, and see the destiny of humanity staring back at Me. I wish that all sinners unto the ends of the Earth could feel the warmth in My Immaculate Heart that night, knowing that the Son of Man, newborn in the flesh, lay so innocently before Me.

I knew what must come beyond this sweet Nativity because all the laws of divinity were imbedded in this Holy Child. Truth and virtue, peace and justice, and everything else that God would require of His people would be learned from this Child of Bethlehem. The entire New Covenant and everything it espouses until the end of the Earth was embodied by this Christ Child, raising and waving His hands beneath the skies of that Bethlehem night. He spoke in strains of the Will of God that would be translated into the first syllables of His Gospel Truth. And there I was, His Blessed Mother, alongside the great Saint Joseph who never committed a sin in his life. I prayed that humanity would celebrate his obedience on their journey of accepting the divinity of God. If ever there were a man who perfectly embodied the heartfelt love of God, it was My dearly beloved husband, Joseph. So, let us think about how what I have told you here applies to the faith of men. The Dominion Angels sing out their battalion of hymns to those who will never depart from the truth they have known. This new millennium reflects the beatific echoes of Jesus' first-century words. Faith, purity and chastity are required for those who desire to know Him. Meekness, fairness, and prudence are attributes of God-loving men. We have within our grasp the means to prove to them that time has not changed these things. We have more than they could possibly imagine that would take them to perfection, if only they would defer to hearing our words. My dear sons, it is with this hope that I wish you a blessed Christmas in the Church and in your holy lives, both of which are willed into being by the Child of My Womb. My Special son, it is with particular gratitude that I bring you the peace of the Christ Child for your determination to tell the world about the Glory of the Cross. From all the Saints in Heaven, I assure you of your great standing before the Throne of God. I will be with you through these happy days of Christmas. Hear the Angels in your Christmas songs! Let peace saturate your heart with the presence of the Little King. Give yourself to the kindness of the season, and be with Me in the grace of Almighty God.

Saturday, December 31, 2016
9:42 a.m.

"Affixed to the truth, and built upon love.
Be thankful for the manner of it all."

"My dear little children, please do not be among those who wring their hands over the passing of the years. Instead, hold in your hearts appreciation to the Father for having given them to you. It is fitting that you remember that your lives are affixed to the truth, and stationed upon His royal love. The entire unfolding of the history of man has been at His behest because you are helping build an earthly Kingdom of Glory through your faith, actions and prayers. The whole manner of human redemption is a product of this faith that finds its origin in the truth and love about which I speak. I wish for you to remember that Jesus is with you always and everywhere, and that My presence here on the Earth is His blessing upon your lives. It has been said that there is no such thing as a solitary man. It has also been said that only one Master can rule the universe. Therefore, all flesh and riches, fame and fortune, are meaningless in the larger sense of human life. I hold in My arms the Savior of the world in whose hands humanity has found its future. So, what can be said about this year 2016 that is expiring? Where are the legions of earthly servants who are addressing the needs of the poor? My proclamation to you here today is that they are everywhere. All across the globe, and in all the nations, are worthy Christians who are doing God's work on His behalf. The Church remains holy, strong and undaunted. The principles of your faith have never waned. Hearing stories about straying Church leaders who have wandered from the apostolic mission handed down by Jesus does nothing to diminish the heroism of those who remain faithful to His Word. It is easy to become disillusioned about the good being done when all you hear in national venues is that the world is crumbling to its knees. I assure you, My precious sons, that the stability of Christ's Church is stronger than ever before. It is in this that I find My joy and desire to proceed in the goals that we have laid out. Second, it must be made clear that every gift from God, every miracle, every healing, every revelation, and every new beginning rises from the hope that remains in the hearts of the faithful. There is holy light when people choose to see. There is gratitude that the nations have declined to reveal. And, My part in enlightening humanity that began at My Immaculate Conception is ongoing to this day. So I ask, My dear little sons, that you join Me in celebrating the new year that is about to begin.

    What we have done over the course of the decades cannot be reversed. By all means, our Father God would not allow it. The work of your hands that has been set into being will manifest the fruits of converted human souls, just as we planned. Of course, there are no throngs calling at your door. Without doubt, they are wandering elsewhere in many other ways. This is the fulfillment of the Sacred Scriptures in your day. We have remarkable evidence that you will in the future stand united with the millions who will come to believe. Verily, it is not about you and Me. It is the historical focus of our relationship and everything we have done to bring an unwary world to the realization that their only new life is in Jesus. This is the blessing that we seek for humanity. It is a good and just conclusion to the annals of the Earth. Getting there from here involves a deeply imbedded investment in the Sacred Mysteries of Christian Salvation. How many millions of faithful believers have found this to be true? They came to know that being mindful of the purpose of life is to pour out oneself for the glory of the Cross. My Special son, while I am speaking to you in a language that you understand, I lack the means to express the gratitude of God for your devotion to My Most Immaculate Heart. I know that you and your brother realize your stature before the Father in Heaven. Your lives have had meaning all over the place, long past the futility of your brothers' and sisters' years. When you review your own conscience, you find it overflowing with obedience and consecration. When you remember what your pilgrimages to Medjugorje might bring, who would have guessed that you would have achieved such distinction as mortals on Earth. I once said that having in your heart the peace of the Holy Spirit is reward enough, but you have given spiritual excellence to the existence of man that cannot be weighed. I ask that you and your brother do not overlook the gift you have been to the Church. You stand defiant against the errors of secularism. You examine the deficits of life before the backdrop of the truth. You pray for your brothers and sisters to come of their own accord to their Salvation in the Cross. What better lives could be handed to God than this? What the Father offers for your obedience is the preservation of life that I recently spoke about. And, He asks His apostles to be thankful for the manner of it all. Standing beside Jesus with the Holy Spirit within you is an auspicious way to live. When you look outside your windows and walk through your doors, and see the lives of others journeying toward their destiny in Jesus, it must give you tremendous satisfaction to know that you have already inherited His holiness yourself.

    My Special son, I would be remiss if I did not speak about the future of your country today. You have just experienced a tumultuous election of your new president. I wish to add that this gift to humanity was willed by the Father in Heaven to help eradicate the immorality that is happening in the States. I am not saying that this new leader has a history of righteousness. I am suggesting that he is a welcome departure from the vile immorality of the left. This man believes that human life must be preserved in the womb. He also believes that the historic esteem of the United States of America must stand for something. Yes, you and your brother are correct to assume that there has been tremendous damage done here in America by those who scoff at the teachings of the Church. All the components that you have spoken about that led to the destruction of the past eight years were manifested by the demonic works of the devil. And, good people everywhere wonder how such a thing could have been allowed. My dear holy sons, it is because there are only few who apply their faith and recite their prayers the way you do. There is an awkward definition of social justice here in your country that includes giving to those who refuse to work a measure of wealth just for remaining idle. The Lord knows that mere existence is no reason to yield the gifts of reward. There must be a standard of conscience applied by every living soul that helps them look at themselves and their place in the world. They must ask the difficult questions about their part in building up the Church. They must greet the morning with the intention of making the world a better place. They must look into the mirror and decide how they will judge the face looking back at them. All in all, they must inquire of themselves whether they have been faithful to the Commandments, worthy of the Sacraments, and in a state of preparation for their lives to be judged. My Special son, if for no other reason, it is good that each day and hour provides ample time for these answers to be revealed. We have helped them, you and I and your brother, and all My messengers and seers, to realize this standard by which they should live. The Holy Spirit that has endowed us with God's wisdom has given us the mission of leading them to the Cross.

Therefore, My Special son, you and your brother are wholly aware of how I feel about you as My children. I have summoned no requests that you have not fulfilled. I implore you to remember the peace that has become your lives. You will hear more about wars and insurrections. You will be bombarded with news about the globe melting down. You pray about these things, but they do not unnerve you. They do not force you off balance. They cannot make you believe that the Father has lost His compassion. I ask you to remember the most destructive century in the history of the world where two great wars were fought. Those were times when even the most faithful questioned their fate. Is it not providential that My Fatima miracle came near the beginning of it all? And yet, here you are, one hundred years hence, and the Church remains standing tall. No bombs or fiery crashes will ever bring it down. Why? Because it is built on the foundation of truth that lives inside the heart. This is where I am speaking to you now. It is where Jesus has fashioned His Kingdom. It is from where the Martyrs summoned their courage. It is the origin of the star-lines of belief. My Special son, what would it be like if the Church built a Cathedral in the shape of a heart? What if its halls were marked with plenteous absolution? This would be a metaphor for its mission. Yes, the shape of a heart to which Jesus has come to reign beyond all the vestiges of time. My Special son, I have concluded My message for today. It is not My most majestic; it will make no hearers cry. It will not be hailed from the summits of mountains. But, believe Me here today, every soul who has ever entered Heaven and who will come to God in future times will memorize every word. It is all the same – every syllable that I have uttered here in this place and around the world will be celebrated by the Saints of the Church. It is in this sense that I pray that you enjoyed My message today. I will speak to you again in AD 2017 and thereafter, as long as the Father allows. Please remember that I ask you to live the joy that I bring into your lives. Avail yourselves to the love, beauty and grace that are unfolding from the hands of the Father in Heaven. Let nothing dampen your spirit, or take away the gladness in your heart."

The Final Colossus
With the Valor of Archangels
AD 2017

Saturday, January 7, 2017
9:30 a.m.

"Handed down to the worthy."

"My holy little children, the veritable essence of the Lord's Divine Love is exemplified by your lives because you are mystically and sacramentally His creatures. I come to you today with the fullness of joy because we are praying in ways to which humanity is called. I tell My children that they are worthy of the blessings from Heaven that you receive through My intercession because I want you to remember that I am your Immaculate Mother. Much has been made about the ongoing disagreements between the teachings of the Church and the opinions of the secular void about what is right and what is wrong. The Church's teachings are handed down from the Will of the Father to sanctify the lives of exiled men. Secular opinions, on the other hand, are just that. Most of them have no purposeful reason to exist or basis in fact. Those who turn a blind eye and deaf ear to the teachings of the Church are not only ignorant of the truth of the Gospel, they are its enemies. Accepting the Cross as one's mission in life is in itself the most important decision a person can make. With all the struggle and suffering that accompanies one's Christian faith, there also comes down from Heaven the Sacred Wisdom to guide the believer in all things good. Lyricists wrote forty years ago that humanity should let his love bind him to all living things (*Bellamy Brothers*). While we know that this has been stated with noble intent, only those living things that direct the human heart to the Kingdom of God should be pursued. My mission here is the same as the Church in that I wish to clarify God's Will for His earthly domain and assist the Church in converting lost sinners. I have strived along with the Hierarchy of the Church to seek out those who must hear the Good News of Eternal Redemption. It is you, My children, who help identify them and direct them to Me. We have in our hands a most auspicious purpose that explains to the world the reason why the Child in the Manger is the Bearer of Eternal Life. My Son adores those who seek Him out while He can be found. Therefore, My Special and Chosen sons, I ask you to remember your part in the mission of the Church. Look at what we are doing here today. Perceive yourselves joined in prayer with Me, prayer that will reveal to the masses the visions of God that He is handing down. He seeks His creatures to come to Him, not just in droves, not just in flocks, but as one humanity embedded in the Most Sacred Heart of His Son. My Special one, it would seem that you and your brother will live out your lives for this purpose, and for this reason you have already been vested in the holy elect. How many more are already there with you? What bright imaginings they have fashioned for themselves. It is never a service to the self to share the Holy Word of God, but to the larger benevolence of His meaning in the material world. All glory, laud and honor belong to Him, and rightly so as well. Today, I have come on this Saturday morning when there are barely five degrees of warmth just outside your doors. This tremendous gift of prayer cannot be overstated. It cannot be diminished or expunged. Its effects cannot be extracted from the eternal annals. I wish to state more clearly than humanity has ever heard that God in Heaven hears your prayers. My Special and Chosen sons, when I speak about the Lord's gifts handed down to the worthy, I am not just speaking about those who appear to be more holy. Being worthy and becoming worthy imply the conversion of the heart to the majesty of the Gospel. Imagine the unsightly woman who professes to preside over the national Planned Parenthood organization stepping before a microphone and saying that she has been guilty of violating the Commandments of God. Yes, imagine her stating to a nation and world that she has been complicit in the murder of untold millions of little children in the womb. My Special son, while I do not wish to state the obvious, this would be an occasion where a converted human soul becomes worthy of the Absolution of the Messiah. I am not suggesting that she will be summarily pardoned without significant reparation. I am saying that this is the transformation that the Father is seeking. Second, many of My children have inquired through prayer why Jesus and Myself have not appeared to such people as the presider of Planned Parenthood. Here again, the responsibility of Christians is to apply their best faith in complying with the mandates of the Scriptures. There are many Christians who believe that 'thou shalt not kill' is an Old Testament requirement that does not apply to their New Covenant faith. This is as errant as the followers of Judaism who deny that Jesus is the Savior of the world. I am speaking about practical matters that reflect great dimensions about mystical gifts. Here, My Special son, let us be inquisitive of you in our conversation today. What would you say to the presider of the Planned Parenthood organization should you be allowed to put a question before her at a public forum where she confessed her error? *"What approach would you take to change the hearts of people who think as you did before?"* While this is an excellent question, how would you answer it if you were her? *"I would ask them to recognize that I was just like them, just as convinced, then divine grace changed my perception of why we even have life in this world. And, it is to do good and to preserve that life."* My Special son, you are correct in your assertions. Speaking directly about the delusion to which this person had surrendered her soul is precisely the means to touch other sinners in the wake of her confession.

I have said on many occasions that this truthful discourse in secular communities is the way to break past the obstacles to benevolent faith. It is resplendent to adorn one's words with the eloquence of God. Truth shines like diamonds in the temporal realms. The resonating echo of righteousness will ring out beyond the conclusion of the world. And, My Special son, these are the blessings we are seeking from God in Heaven. Especially your prayers from your place here in exile have an impact on changing men's hearts. It is a matter of God working through human petitions to mend a Creation that sinners have broken. The Church implores Jesus to come into the sanctuary and upon the Altar to feed and nourish the souls of those who believe. This Eucharistic Liturgy is the most powerful prayer on Earth. Combined with the Sacrament of Confession and the penitential rite, those who attend Holy Mass are made aware of their part in the sanctifying of the exiled world. What we do here is more than a mere complement to these grand gifts to God. We are facilitating the transformation of humanity's natural landscape in preparedness for the Return of Jesus in Glory. Therefore, I ask you and your brother to remember that your lives will never be lived in vain. Given everything you knew from when you were but babes in the womb, combined with the elements of wisdom embedded within you by the Holy Spirit, you have come of age in the enlightenment that Jesus seeks from those who believe in Him. You understand the nature of your own suffering and the agonies of your wounds in the context of those Jesus suffered for you. To become like Jesus is to open yourself to His identity supplanting yours. I have said this before, and it is particularly more relevant here. So, we shall proceed with our prayerful relationship no matter what the future brings, and beyond all the difficulties that you and your brother face in this life. Among the incalculable number of correct conclusions that you have drawn is the fact that I have spoken to you and your brother in such length, intensity, and depth because you have remained with Me to the exclusion of what might have been an endless stream of pilgrims to your home. I promise you that life is better for you this way. I wish not to speak in a shallow manner about what worldly people might say, but millions of them are not prepared to accept the miracles that I have presented to you. Even thirty-six years past My first appearance in Medjugorje, I am still struggling to convince the secular masses that I have come into their midst. Nearly everyone who pilgrimages to Medjugorje already believes in Jesus on the Cross. Can you imagine that I might therefore be caroling My song to the choir? None of what we have done will be wasted—not a minute, not a prayer, not an imagining, and nothing that was ever intended to touch a human heart still unaware. I ask you and your brother to remain in this hope because you have captured the intent of My apparitions through your loyalties to Me. Jesus not only loves you, He adores you for remaining at His side. Hence, I have concluded My message for today. Do you have anything to discuss with Me today? *"What is the purpose of Jesus allowing Satan to thrust such hellish visions on Timmy?"* Your brother will one day speak to the many who have lived these visions in reality rather than being superimposed on his consciousness. He will speak to the truth about the grotesqueness of the devil's satanic presence. He will give to the world and those who inherit it a sanction to avoid the temptations of the devil or be induced to participate in them. It is the same as all priests and visionaries who have experienced the suffering of Jesus in their hearts and minds. The Lord's eternal wisdom is borne out and transferred to the exiled world by those who have come face-to-face with His demonic enemy. My Special son, does this help you understand more clearly? *"Yes, thank you."* The agony and torment that your brother is sustaining are profound. I ask you and your brother to always remember the meaning of tenacity that you are providing in this world. Please do not fall to the temptation of becoming cynical about the fads of disgusting things. They are as passing as the night. You and your brother are in My prayers in the presence of My Sacred Son."

Saturday, January 14, 2017
9:30 a.m.

"More plentiful than swallows in the meadow."

"My dear, sweet loving children, it is the delight of My Most Immaculate Heart to embrace you on this day of prayer. I have wished for centuries that all My children would surround Me with their faith and devotion in the way you have been your entire lives. Today, I come again in prayerfulness to ask you to join Me in soliciting the intervention of Jesus on behalf of His Church. There is much suffering ongoing around the world by those who hold fast to their Christian faith because they are persecuted by nonbelievers. It is for this reason that I come to you with My warm embrace. I wrap My arms and holiness around the strength of your faith. All accolades are yours for not surrendering to the distractions of the secular void. My little sons, this does not mean that you are isolated from them. It also does not mean that the Church itself has been banished from the public domain. Those Christians whom you meet on the street, in businesses where you go and elsewhere, contain the spirit of the Church in their hearts the same way as you. The Church of the Father is a spiritual gift to humanity on Earth. Your strength and vision are products of your belief that this is true. And, your prayers reflect that you have joined all your faithful predecessors in continuing the mission to which you have been assigned. My Special son, I have said that the gifts from God and yours in return to Him are as plentiful as the swallows in the meadow. The exchange of energy that flows between Heaven and Earth is visible in your life's actions, and discernible in the content of your petitions. Ask and you shall receive; seek and you will find, means that your relationship with God is transformative for humanity in exile. Let us consider a concept. There is a difference in saying that someone is riding a horse as opposed to taking a ride on a horse. The first implies control, while the latter implies passive action. Do you understand the difference? *"Yes."* I have drawn here the contrast between your direct action of faith through your works and prayers as opposed to those who only stand and wait. As your brother is proofreading your writing for your next book, you are hearing on a daily basis his reading of your text. And here, you can sense this genius of wisdom flowing from your magnificent heart. You have taken the reins of human understanding about the Kingdom of God, and brought this Kingdom into reality for generations hereafter. Did the likes of Saint Alphonsus Ligouri or Saint Francis, or Saint Thomas Aquinas know in advance that their doctoral works would become the foundation of so many nations' faith? Surely, they did not. But, I am telling you this morning that yours will do the same. It is with the humility that I just saw in you as I made My last statement that Jesus wells up with tears in gratitude for your love for Him. He seeks worldwide throughout His earthly domain those who are given to His Crucifixion in the way of you and your brother. It is as though you came knocking on His door instead. Imagine the joy to know that Jesus had callers who sought Him out in the way of Isaiah while He can still be found. Yes, My Special one, this is the unified relationship that the Son of Man seeks from all. You prepare yourself because you have a tremendous need to exercise your faith in extraordinary ways. For you and your brother, it is not just about believing. It is about propagating your belief into the realms and quarters of the exiled world to fish out men from the depths of their doubts. You have been more productive in your prayers and works than the ages have been in creating history for the books on the shelves. I have said that your faith is about making the world more holy in your day. Once this is done in any generation, the future takes care of itself. We have been refining the landscapes of the Earth as prescribed by Christ Jesus in His time. The Holy Gospel is more than a prophecy by a Prophet. It is the delineation of the purification, sanctification, and redemption of the souls whom Jesus died to save. There are untold agonies in this process, but there are also countless comforts there too. You and your brother have participated in the revelation of the personal lives of Jesus and Myself in ways that are rare to mortal men. I say again that this has been done because your faith has pronounced it good. You and your brother are endearing visionaries who inhabit Jesus' Most Sacred Heart in ways that comfort Him from the inside. And, He embraces you there. He offers you His own comfort and consolation on behalf of the Father in whose Kingdom you belong. This is the orientation that all Christians seek, even those who are unaware that this is their course. And, so it is that we must pray for them, that they must become the likeness of My Son before their earthly journeys are through. When we pray and ask Jesus to make this come true, He will help them magnify their spiritual belief.

I know that the weather is cold, dark, dreary, and unsightly. I wish not that My children would observe these signs of Nature as a metaphor for their faith. You are children of light whose future is bright and hopes are well placed. I have reminded the Saints throughout the centuries that there would be both good times and bad. I have asked that My children focus their attention not just on repentance and reparation, but also on savoring the rewards that accompany your faithfulness to the Church. You have seen the blessings of prayer in a world that seems shorn of righteousness. Indeed, it is the Mother of God speaking to you now. It is not lost on anyone with a grasp on the truth that this is the gift that you have described throughout your decades of writing. I also realize that it is sometimes difficult to take an objective view at the manuscripts that you have prepared. Therefore, I ask that you accept My word that the Holy Spirit is running through your veins. Jesus is inspirited in you, and your heart is as fulfilled as His. There seem to be vast demarcations in the history of the ages that help highlight the changes that Christianity can bring. You are about to witness the initiation of a new government here in the United States. This is a time when historians imagine what has led to this event. There can be no denying that the western hemisphere has been developed from the beliefs of the Christian religion from far across the seas. You have written many times that the framework of goodness, hard work and self-sufficiency is a product of the New Covenant Gospel. Rightly so, you and other visionaries have explained that Jesus is the foundation beneath the structures of decency being upheld by the tenets of the Church. When you ponder what this new beginning implies for the United States of America, remember that your reflections and observations are accurate and substantiated by the facts of the matter. You have such unimpeded vision because you know the potential for humanity to replicate the righteousness of God. It is here in this nation that it must be done, beneath the Morning Star Over America, and through the authenticity of your work that cannot be dismissed. I speak today about a hope that will be realized. I speak about your concerns that the enemies of the Church will continue to attack, assail, impugn, and assault the good people who are trying to rescue your country from the jowls of the devil. There is no question that you have seen evidence of what I am saying. My Special son, your very existence is a blessing for humanity everywhere. When you raise your hand, the ages defer with grace. When you speak of God, you speak on His behalf. You stand tall in the power of your own light that is reflected from Jesus on the Cross. You are more tender than the swallows in the meadow because you are unified with His love. The years and decades have been more kind to you than many would believe. You still possess the innate assets of your youth through your drive and loyal energy. You walk gently on the ground that shudders in awe as you pass by. I wish to ensure that you and your brother realize the relevance that you have lived in your consecration to Me. Wherever you go, whatever you do, and whomever you meet—all these things will culminate in the world's realization of what you and your brother have accomplished for Jesus since 1991. I ask that you remember the facets of your experiences as blessings instead of burdens. All we have done, everything that could ever matter in the history of Creation, will stand as a triumph in the final moment of the Earth for every soul to adore. Jesus waits in joyful hope in the Tabernacles of the Church for this triumphant moment to come. And, it is in this sense that I ask you and your brother to live victoriously in advance of these events. It is true, as Saint Padre Pio implored, that humanity must pray, hope and not worry. The Will of God sustains you. His Kingdom bears your names. His love supersedes your sorrows. And, His beauty is befitting of your faith."

Saturday, January 21, 2017
9:26 a.m.
Feast Day of Saint Agnes

"Mysticism and mystique; such is the aroma of faith –
Validating, triumphant and vastly beatific."

"My dear holy children, we have come upon the occasion of another moment when I shall pray with you for the conversion of lost sinners. I have given you at the beginning of this message a stand alone passage that you may cite as you wish. We call upon the Saints to intercede for the Faith Church, especially the powerful intercession of Saint Agnes. It is incumbent upon the Church to remember that the Will of the Father integrates the prayers of the faithful with His eternal wishes of goodness and piety. We must remember that it is to the refinement of the Earth into the likeness of His Kingdom that the lives of humanity must be devoted. Therefore, as we pray today, let us remember everyone who has found their new beginning in Jesus on the Cross. I wish to reaffirm My commitment to intercede for those who are suffering. I also ask Jesus to embrace the many who are considering entering religious vocations. I have said that His shepherds must be treated with kind regard and the utmost dignity. Theirs is a difficult life in fostering the relationship between the Church and those who would join it. All the Sacraments are blessings from the Father in that they remake the soul into the pureness of His Son. We see a beautiful and lasting image of Jesus cast upon the legacy of the Church for all the ages to adore. My Special son, the thoughts that you have written for your next book are among your most eloquent. Your text celebrates the truth of righteousness and discipline for a world that divides itself from both. It is not an exercise in negativism to give counsel to those who would benefit from knowing their station before God. You have included sufficient examples of the holy life in your manuscript that can assist your brothers and sisters find their way to Jesus. We must remember that everything that you and your brother have dedicated to Me on behalf of the Church is a lesson in prudence. Your work has been to the advancement of the Gospel here in your time. It must be made clear as well that everything you have produced that seems to have laid unattended will be embraced, engulfed, and absorbed by the whole of humanity in due time. The words I am speaking to you at this moment will eventually pierce the ears of every soul given life. Yes, it is just a matter of time. You and your brother have made this difference because you are consecrated to My Immaculate Heart. You have made successful the desires of the Father because you are occupants of Jesus' Most Sacred Heart. When you say your prayers, especially the Most Holy Rosary, you wrap Creation in the warmth of the Lord's embracing arms. Now, My Special son, you must be aware of the internal dynamics ongoing in your nation surrounding its new government and president given the oath of office yesterday. As we continue our dialogue about the sanctification of the United States, you will find that the movement toward goodness and protecting the sanctity of human life will be opposed by those who have held a stranglehold of death on your country for the past eight years. I ask that you not be overly concerned at the libelous and slanderous diatribes about to be unleashed against your new leader. As you have said many times, imagine what would have happened if the other candidate would have won. If you would be so kind here during our message, you may speak your petitions about the future of your country. *"I ask that the people of our country never look back in flushing the enemies of Christianity completely out of our history. I pray for the Marxist delusion to be unveiled for what it is; for abortion to be eradicated, and for the Morning Star Over America to be elevated as a beacon of revelation from your Immaculate Heart."* My Special son, these are good and worthy intentions that have found their way into the beatific benevolence of the Father's love. I join your prayers through Jesus that God's Will shall be done. There is tremendous benefit in praying for these blessings because they are emblematic of your knowledge of the New Covenant message. You and your brother, and all who have learned through the years what righteousness must look like, have the capacity to know the difference between secular humanism and religious truth. By all means, you have made this adequately clear in your prologues and prefaces. We pray that you and your brother are able to release your new book this year, and that it will fulfill its destiny as the Father intends. I ask that you remember the high esteem in which you are held for your devotion to Me and your desire to complete your work. Whether or not it seems clear to you, there is tremendous joy blossoming here. Any time the evangelization of the Gospel is made possible by men of faith, life grows in the direction of Salvation. What we do in the future adds more blessings atop the colossal blessings that you and your brother have already gifted to the Church. Thank you again for helping your brother during this distressing time of trouble that he is enduring.

When I come into the world and deliver My messages from God, I realize the fragile nature of mortal men. However, I also know about the tenacity of those who have heralded the vision of the Cross. Jesus asks His apostles to join Him there on a spiritual basis because it is from this vantage point that the perfection of humanity is most clearly seen. There will be a time when every soul who enters Heaven will see from this perspective of life. It might be difficult to imagine that this is a joyful occasion for someone of simple faith. This is where humanity should remember that Jesus takes care of His disciples. He watches over them, and strengthens them. He raises up those who elevate Him before the masses. He welcomes into His Wounds all who are broken and despondent. He looks with eyes of pity on the millions who are lonely and afraid. He touches deep inside those who are filled with pain; and My Special son, He blesses all believers with the glory of eternal life. It would seem apparent that My messages around the globe speak about future times, ones that make way for a platform of existence that is being constructed right now. I do not wish to disregard each moment of these present days. Tomorrow cannot come without the hours at hand. It is remarkably the decisions that are being made at this time that will shape that tomorrow. This is as it should be; it reflects the place where the answers to your prayers are manifested. Calling humanity to the bounty of My Most Immaculate Heart is the goal that I espouse. Why? Because Jesus lives within My Heart, and He finds the petitions of His brothers and sisters deposited there. I have a vast and unending love for My children on Earth. It is through this love that I beseech the Faith Church to pray for the Poor Souls in Purgatory. This grand procession of life is based on the penitential truth that wicked men must disavow their ways and accept their new lives in Jesus. There is plenteous room in My Immaculate Heart for these converted sinners as well. My Special and Chosen sons, it is good to recognize that there is righteousness and virtue in any heart dedicated to Christianity. This is how your light shines brightly among men. I commend you for exercising your faith to make the world a better place. The grace and joy that you are accorded from the Heart of God are too immense to describe. I ask that you receive the gift of His Spirit within you in wholesome assurance."

Saturday, January 28, 2017
Saint Thomas Aquinas, 1225-1274
Doctor of the Church
9:37 a.m.

"The palatial aura of humanity redeemed."

"My dear little sons, how joyful and splendorous that you have permitted Me to come speak to you this morning. Thank you from the depths of My Immaculate Heart that you are so caring about advancing the Kingdom of God and the mission of the Church here in the exile of men. I speak of the palatial aura of humanity redeemed in the context of the Faith Church and the Church Triumphant. You must realize the beauty of converted souls living on Earth because humanity, in its holiest poise, is reflective of Jesus in all ways righteous. You also know about the writings of Saint Thomas Aquinas; and like you, his body of works were somewhat ignored for most of his life. I cannot overstate to you what a blessing this was for him, and the same for you. The palatial aura of humanity redeemed means that you are prepared to prevail in the mission to which all are called by Jesus on the Cross. Yes, His most prolific strains were given to the world by virtue of His public Sacrifice. This is from where the adage that an image is worth a thousand words takes its most essential form. My Special and Chosen ones, the revelations that have come down from Heaven are rightly humanity's to share, and this is from where faith factually originates. The palace of the human heart is where the Father has chosen to reside here in your world because His Love and Peace are received and protected there. They are shared like drops of rain quench the thirst of flowers and trees. You live within one another's hearts the same way. What must be remembered by everyone who professes their faith in Jesus is that this is not just something that lies in the distant offing. Your faith is proof of your capacity to love other men in the likeness of the Lord. Your speeches and writings are echoes of this capacity – and in this sense as well, you are not unlike Saint Thomas Aquinas himself. To be a Doctor of the Church means that your faith has ethereal dimensions, that it has the ability to bloom and change according to your growing enlightenment about the Gospel. However, being a Doctor of the Church does not imply that you are 'practicing' in the way that a physician practices his profession. Men become Doctors of the Church because their hearts are the perfect receptacles of the Wisdom of God, and this Wisdom is reflected in their voice and actions. Remember that Jesus spoke in parables to those around Him, but He explained everything He wanted humanity to know to the Apostles when in their private presence. The point I am making is that not just Roman Catholic Bishops are successors to the Apostles in this spiritual way. Anyone on Earth succeeds the Apostles according to their acceptance, understanding, and sharing of God's Holy Word. So this morning, I come in prayer as we see the unfurling of the Church's mission on a global basis from the foundation of the heart that I have mentioned here today. Apostolates everywhere augment this preaching to complement the vocations of the Church. As long as there is intent by the faithful for spreading the Word of God to the nations, there is successorship. There is a mechanism for the Kingdom of the Father to flourish around the globe in supernatural ways. Why? Because the spirit-world has no boundaries. And, this is the reason it is true that humanity redeemed has a palatial aura. You are pronounced good by God when you emulate His Son – it is a matter of recognizing your station as one humanity in Him, and protracting this identity throughout Creation. O' My goodness! My Special son, you see that I am echoing your own writing this morning. I am reflecting what you have said in your next book that serves to exhume the consciences of the lost from beneath the layers of years during which they have languished in the darkness. You are placing the exiled world beside itself as if to be looking into a mirror, and you are giving its inhabitants the opportunity to see what a wreck it has become. Your eloquent strains are speaking to the billions who yet do not realize that the decades and generations will always be their enemies if they do not step forward into the domain of Jesus' Gospel Truth. Here, I am not only offering My gratefulness for your service to Jesus in your time, but assuring you that you will reach those for whom your writings are intended. I shall deliver your words to My children with you. You and your brother are exemplars of the palatial aura that Jesus has fashioned within you. He blesses your deference, your determination and faith ethic, your piety and responsiveness. I know that you are aware that this has been the way of it since He chose His First Apostles in His day. You are living in this new time, and you and all who are oathed to Him are apostles for Him as well.

My Special son, the Kingdom of God is about more than promises. You have seen that promises imply the trust of those to whom these promises are made. Your relationship with Jesus is more authentic than that. You and your brother, and all who stand united with Jesus on the Cross, are living the 'realized revelation' that is only affected by the element of time. If Jesus does not return during your mortal lives, your bodies will break and you will see Him as you are set free to inherit the Kingdom in which you already believe. When you read the Book of the Saints, you recognize those who appropriated this same life and vision in their day. The same can be said of hope. You hope for the things to come for which you pray, and your confidence offsets any questions about the validity of your hopes. I would never ask you to stop hoping, but I would add that your hopes should reflect and consider the variables over which other people have control. In other words, when you hope for the conversion of the lost, you are petitioning that they will submit themselves to the Mercy of God of their own volition. When good men hope and pray, they are seeking from the Father not only the ratification of their best holy wishes, but that those wishes that might seem most elusive will come true as well. Prayer combines what you already know about the conditions of the world with the Will of God that might not be wholly revealed. And, humanity's prayers must always be lofty and poetic, even when addressing one's practical needs. It is not wrong for someone to pray for a hundred dollars, but this prayer must be connected with whatever means its intent assists in the advancement of Jesus' Will for the Church. After all, the Church consists of a collection of private lives. Yes, accepting the Mercy of God of their own volition – this is part of the palatial aura that humanity possesses as an offering of active obedience. Prayer has always been the mode for communicating this to the Father. Prayer is where one's hands touch the hem of Jesus' garment.

It is where one's lips kiss the hand of justice. Prayer is the spoken intentions of the heart. And, My Special son, prayer as you know it is living the life of Jesus to the best of your ability – so help you God. When your brother said that you are intelligent, kind and holy, he was only beginning to touch the surface of who you are. I implore all My children to make prayer the most important part of their lives. I cannot require it because each person has their own free will. I can reveal the blessings of the gift of prayer, but these gifts must be solicited from God in Heaven and Jesus at His right hand. My Special one, you have known Me to be not only the Mother of God and Mother of the Redeemed, I am also the most prolific advocate that any person could ever know. This is based in Jesus' love for Me and My knowledge of what My intercession means to Him. Do you remember the first miracle that I asked Jesus to perform? *"Yes."* And, what was it? *"The miracle of changing the water into wine."* Yes, you have spoken the truth. And, what did Jesus later do with this same ability? *"He gave us the Eucharist."* Yes, and did He not also give you the Cup? *"Yes."* Indeed, the first request of the Mother of God from Her Divine Son became the symbol by which the Chalice of the Blood of the Lamb was initiated. *"He enshrined your request as the source of human Salvation."* Thank you for understanding. And, since Jesus did this in His day, do you suppose that He will likewise enshrine the other requests that I make from His brothers and sisters on Earth in your time? *"Yes."* What has yet to be seen is not only that He responds to these prayers, but by what venues He chooses to do so. His response is always imbedded in the conversion and sanctification of His people in exile. To put it in another way that you will understand, this is His 'prime directive' from the Father's Throne in Heaven. Jesus' whole life on Earth was a prayer to God. His intentions and explications were to enlighten humanity about what the Father desired when He created Adam and Eve. The world must remember that God knew that these first two humans would eventually fall. It is not something that appeared to Him unawares. But, He created them anyway because He wished to share His love with creatures who had the capacity to return His love. And, this could only be done by giving them the free will to choose love or turn away in disobedience. When someone decides that they desire to marry another person, they cannot just approach them and say that this is going to happen. The other person must love them in return. In other words, God said that He desired someone to love Him because they wanted to. Do you understand? *"Yes, very clearly."* And not only that, God wished to be like the great heroes who defy the odds and the most prevalent dangers to rescue helpless people in peril. He desired from the vaults of eternity to bring back to life those who have died. My

Special son, this is the framework of the redemption story that the world has been playing out for 2,000 years – God presenting Himself in His Only Begotten Son, the great warrior whom you have described many times in your books, who took on the burden of other people's guilt, and saved them in their day. The true charity in Creation is for humanity to have a receptive heart, the same heart that I spoke about only moment ago. And, what this means is that the creatures toward whom God's love is directed must be willing to recognize the gift of Salvation that Jesus has wrought. One must receive graciously the peace and forgiveness of the Father in order to understand what I am saying. The entire Catechism that you often cite is based on the willingness of the Church to be led and taught by Jesus' miraculous wisdom. This is replicated from the pages of Heaven and published in the world for humanity's learning. This is the same as you and your brother's books – anything that is given to lost sinners to help them find their way to the Grace of God by which all men have been saved. This Grace is based on an absolution that is validated not only by men's faith, but their ability to practice it with genuine deference to the teachings of Jesus during His life on the Earth. My Special son, I will continue this message in the future, as I believe that I have spoken sufficiently today. *"Thank you, Mama."* Thank you for taking such good care of your brother during this time when he continues to not feel well. He is still trying to cope with the horrendous attacks from the devil. His battles are painful, as you have seen. Satan attacks him not only because of his work here with you, but because the devil recognizes you and your brother's inseparable bond. Your attentiveness to your prayers and writings is too profound to put in words. I ask you to remember that yours is a life that is precisely the model for the perfect Christian disciple, and we pray that everyone will imitate this life in their own way."

Saturday, February 4, 2017
9:34 a.m.

"There will be glorious days – long in coming, forever lasting."

"Heartfelt is My love for you, My little sons. Throughout all the ages and beyond every human endeavor in the history of the world, your faith and allegiance to Jesus has matched the most holy souls who ever lived. I promise that the days will come when you will see those glorious times for which you have prayed. There may be dark and sorrowful moments in the meanwhile, but you must realize that you are on the path to victory that you have described in your writings. My Special and Chosen sons, you have given Me through your holy love the gift of humanity to whom I have been calling for the past 2,000 years. You are making the difference about which millions before you could have only dreamed. Why? Because you have accepted the Cross as your Salvation, your identity and your being. You have marshaled the Angels to take up the cause of the Morning Star Over America. You have spoken and written the strains that will awaken the sleeping masses. The years that the Lord has given to you have been for the reshaping of the world in which they have unfolded. Your prayers have become the template by which the Father has accorded His Will. Yes, there will be glorious days yet to come, forever lasting, much more brilliant than you could have imagined, destined to be the rise and fall of many, and fulfilling to the pinnacle of your most hopeful prayers. Today, I have come to pray with you for all who do not know God, that they will be awakened in faith the way the Holy Spirit wishes to inspire them. We pray for the end of abortion, for the conversion of lost sinners, for world peace, for the preservation of human innocence, for the purity of the Church, and for the untold other intentions that humanity must claim. Holy and avowed are those who not only recognize the need for righteousness to consume the Earth, but who strive to make it happen in their time. My Special son, your approach to your work here in your exile has manifested great undertakings by the Church Triumphant in that the Saints are readily recognizing the need for remedial intercession. This reflects the question of what they do through the timelessness of eternity. It will please you to know that their most excellent exercise is to respond to the petitions of the Faith Church on Earth. They accept the prayers of the Church in exile in much the same way that I offer My messages here on Earth, but they receive them all at once – the whole of the centuries is encapsulated in one vast petition and invocation of intercession to the Church Triumphant in Heaven. This is why I have asked My children here on Earth to never stop praying to the Saints. It is imperative that this communication continue until Jesus comes again and lifts the veil that orders the Church into three distinct parts. This is the reason that prayer is so effective. It serves to dissolve within the human heart the sense of separation. Today, I also wish to remind you that your writing for your next book is awe inspiring. And, My Special son, the most important part of My saying this is that, in your wisdom from the Father in Heaven, you know that your writing is stunning. It is not an act of pride to state that your writings are 'super-substantial' in His eyes because it is His Holy Spirit that has inspired you. The many stories, parables, metaphors and memories have been placed inside your heart because you pray to be united with the Father. You are not just inclined to know what He would have you say, you are seamlessly connected to His Kingdom so fully that He is speaking directly through your thoughts. And in this, you and your brother are already partaking of the divine life that first inspired God to send His Only Begotten Son to live and die for the redemption of the world. You are transferring the meaning of this redemption through your life-generating acts and works. You are giving emphasis; you are shedding light, you are aiding in the manifestation of miracles here in your age and time. Again, I am telling you a fact that you and your brother already know. There is, however, one issue that I would like to address this morning that is quite important to Me. I ask that you and your brother do not believe that just because you are My two Morning Star messengers that you are living in this world alone. You must believe that you will always be connected to your Christian brothers and sisters as the Mystical Body of Jesus. I sometimes hear you and your brother speaking about being the only two who think like you do, or that you are the only two who have a certain vision of the way humanity ought to conduct the affairs of life. In fact, the truth remains that I have placed the two of you together so that you will recognize your connection to the people of the world with whom you will share the brilliance of Heaven. My Special son, do you realize how meaningful this matter is to Me? *"Yes. Thank you."* In other words, you and your brother have not been set aside for any specific purpose other than to receive My messages for humanity, and even in this, you are wholly connected to the millions of people exiled on the Earth who accept Jesus as their Savior. The bond that you and your brother share serves to connect you with them in ways that would never have occurred if I had not called you together.

    This should come as profoundly good news for you because it speaks to the Triumph of My Immaculate Heart that is unfolding as we speak. You shall, however, be called forth upon the Return of Jesus in Glory to be recognized as the mediums who have been responsible for the receipt and transference of My Morning Star messages to the Faith Church on Earth. And, this will not just be a moment to take a bow, but to stand with joy and pronounce to the Church Triumphant in audible terms every syllable that I have ever said to you, and every syllable that you have ever written on Jesus' behalf. This will not be a linear experience because it will be done outside of time. You will not need to pause for your listeners to hear your next word because you will pronounce them all at once. And yet, you will experience this gladness throughout the essence of eternity as your gift to God, and His to you. It would seem that I have spoken in Lourdes, Fatima, Medjugorje and many other places about what will unfold in the future. However, you have seen plenteous evidence that the future is now. Day after day, humanity is fulfilling the prophecies of My messages down through the ages. And, during these same days, the prayers of those who are consecrated to Me are amending what might have come. This is the realtime relationship between God and the Church. And, I cannot overstate the truth that He can rewrite history with the wave of His hand. This is as sure as you are alive – all the Father has to do is Will something into being, and it will happen beyond any shadow of doubt. So, why does He wait? Here, you have written accurately about this in your books and pamphlets, but humanity must know that God is deeply invested in watching His heroes conquer those who reject Him. He takes true joy in knowing that the Mystical Body of His Son has shared His Will with the masses and lifted up His sovereign reign. He knows what it means to claw back from suffering, agony, torment and torture that the sinners of the world heaped upon His Son. And, My Special one, God the Father is inspired by humanity's own inspiration to make things right that went wrong in the Garden of Eden. It is true that the only way that these things could happen at the hands of courageous men is that they had to unfold through time. It would require years, generations and centuries for the Salvation story to be globalized. The Army of Believers who have served Jesus on the Earth stretch not only through the regions of the world, but through the decades and epochs in which the service of good men occurs. It takes time for change to come, and it must be this way for the collective human spirit to process it. Winning means that there has been a heated battle. Vanquishing evil implies that there has been a fight. It is a process of purification and sanctification that began at the burning bush. And, why dinosaurs? Because there will always be creatures larger and more dominating than men. Yes, but not in spirit! This has been given to the creatures of life who beget human life within the realms of Jesus' domain. This is where reflection and magnification take hold. It is where lyrics are penned and dramas play out. Yours is the stage on which history has unfolded with tremendous melody – where human courage has been the music that has comforted the Martyrs in the presence of their God. Yes, where you live now, where the fight for righteousness is still playing out, this is where the entire vastness of Heaven is focused on the Revelations to come. My Special son, it is not irony at all. It is logical attribution. You and your brother, united in all ways with the Faith Church in exile, are poised at the doorway between Heaven and Earth where you can partake in the unspoken conversation between God and His Creation. You share the miraculous experience of knowing what has been, and what is yet to come. The whole matter comprises the constitution of your consciousness, your knowledge and your wisdom about the way God has framed His thoughts. So, I say to you that to question His motivations and what He either wills or allows is not the point. The point is that the Lord has scripted a finish to the exile of humanity that is being written by humanity, itself. This is not as though He has asked someone to take on a menial chore; no indeed. He has assigned the Faith Church the mission of bringing out love from everyone who accepts who Jesus is and what He does. This requires a length of days. It speaks for the necessity of applying the precepts of holiness to the practicality of the world. It mandates that men shall suffer and die in the likeness of His Son. It alludes to the premise that there will be bloodshed on the road to eradicating evil from this world. My Special son, I have said what I wished to tell you this morning. *"Thank you, Mama."* Bless you for your providential prayers. Please remember to pray for the poor and those contemplating taking their lives. And, also for the preservation of children in the womb."

Sunday, February 12, 2017
9:39 a.m.

"This is the faith through which God's Kingdom is radiantly observed."

"I have come to you, My little sons, not just to nurture and gather your lives, but to participate in them. I come to bless your faith by telling you that its offerance is more than simple belief. If this were not true, there would have been 70,351 people who would not have seen the Miracle of the Sun 100 years ago. I ask for your prayers for all the intentions that I have mentioned throughout the years – that all the things that are supposed to be synchronized are smartly aligned, and everything that is meant to be syncopated is rightly sequenced. It is in praying not just for change that humanity is made whole, but that righteous change will inundate the Earth. You radiantly observe the Kingdom of God through your faith, and you actively participate in His Kingdom through your prayers and holy lives. My Special son, you are familiar with the mechanisms of life because you have seen how societies are constructed. You and your brother are old enough, and you have learned enough, to know the habits of mortal men and their penchant for preferring and pursuing various goals. It is not so much about the collation of these things that matters, but knowing about and choosing which ones manifest more clearly the Will of God for Creation. You can focus a camera lens to clarify a photograph, and you can zoom in and out again to view a larger scene. However, zooming does not mean that the image you see is focused, just whether it is smaller or larger. And, focus is what creating clearer faith means. This is what enhances the vision and clarity of the Kingdom of God. And, focus precedes the dimensions of the image. If humanity will focus their hearts on the right things; if men would find in themselves the capacity to see life the way the Father sees it, then He will in His own way provide the larger image of life that He wishes the world to see. If He did not do this, the Faith Church would have conceded long ago that while humanity can discern what God wants them to see, they would have no idea what it means. This is the transformation of faith – through prayer, you can see the redemption of the world in the Faith of the Church, and you can know what this redemption means in the fullness of time. My Special one, you have seen items depicted in photographs placed alongside a coin so as to determine their size. The coin is a reference to indicate the dimensions of the object being observed. This is precisely the point when humanity must judge what is to be accomplished to achieve the holy life. God places the Cross in the image so that those who wish to be saved can know what is expected of them – not that they should replicate Jesus' Sacrifice on the Cross, but that they will know their relationship with God compared to the Sacrifice that Jesus gave to redeem their souls into Heaven. My Special son, does this description seem clear to you? *"Yes, very clear, thank you."* So, once someone becomes focused on the intentions that the Father has for each life, they will be able to train their eyes on every aspect of the human experience and recognize their place in every setting. Men might find themselves one day in the confines of the confessional, and then 24 hours later be circling the globe in outer space. The focus of their spiritual vision can be clear and concise in both cases. This is why the beauty of supernal love is so important in the eyes of the human heart. And, there must be at least one witness to the consecration of the soul to the Savior who has redeemed them. It is true that the Holy Spirit serves as the Divine Advocate for those wishing to be united with God, and I am the witness for everyone who joins Him through the Crucifixion of My Son. You have known for many years that the beauty and power of the Cross has given the world the ability to live beyond its failures and prevail over its weaknesses through the wisdom of the Gospel. The New Covenant is the explanation of the Cross in literary terms. It is further true that a person can request that any additional witnesses be present when that person finally says, '…Jesus, I love and accept you. I desire that your Blood on the Cross be my Salvation.' This can be a witness from the Communion of Saints or a person who lives yet in exile on the Earth. To be clear, I am present even in the event that another Saint or witness is summoned. And, what is the role of this witness? Another heart, another assurance, another colleague is saying that what is happening is pleasing to God and regenerative in configuring the gloriousness of eternal life. It is like welcoming another child into the family on Earth – every time another soul converts to Jesus on the Cross, the Communion of Saints reserves their place at the Banquet Table in Heaven. The Mystical Body of Christ becomes more profound. When you place your hand on top of someone's head in prayer, that person knows that something larger than life is happening. This is the feeling that occurs when the Holy Spirit blesses someone's heart.

Today, I also am praying that My children will realize that their faith is the foundation on which their lives in Divine Truth are constructed. Each person has the ability to be self-preserving and self-sufficient in aiding in the assembly of this life. Dedication to Jesus on the Cross does not just mean that someone recognizes their future in Him, but that they help shape that future by living as He lived on the Earth. It is not about performing miracles that proves one's allegiance to the Father, but in becoming miracles incarnate through faithful works and humble service. Wishing that it would rain someplace is a prayer to God to bring forth life-preserving waters. Living in the faith that it will come means that boats and ships should be built in advance. The Lord's answers to prayers are not just promises, they are dividends that come into the mortal realms for lives well lived. And, My Special son, what we are doing here with your brother is creating the conditions that will bring humanity's prayers to fruition. We have built an endowment through the decades that will enrich the Church and quench the thirst of Creation for an eternity to come. This is what is meant by facing down the opposition of doubt that keeps creeping into the consciousness of those who are trying to believe. Joyfully, God provides ample time for converted sinners to realize what I have said here this morning, but the burden of acceptance belongs to those in need of conversion. You will be pleased to know that everything I have told you through the years is reflected in your writings already. You have borne witness to your faith through your experiences that have been collected in your memories from your youth. There have been battles too numerous to recount, but you have veritably survived them all. There have been blessings aplenty as well, and these have been the groundwork through which you have sustained your trust. I have said that you are a premier Christian. I know that you never question the veracity of My words. It is that you also know your own identity as a man in exile. The forces that have been aligned against visionaries like you down through the ages would have toppled a lesser man. But, it is that you have trusted Me that matters, that you have stood steadfastly with Jesus through your life as He would have you stand tall. Everything I have asked of you and your brother, you have welcomed, received and performed with the stature of heroes.

It would seem that I come speaking to you and your brother every week with different ways to describe the same Truth. I assure you that there are more ways to accomplish this joy than there are years remaining in the created world. I love you more than any metric could measure. I admire you to the ends of the universe. I cherish what you have meant to the Church. And, I honor you for being the companion of Jesus for whom He has searched for the past 100 years. You are defending the Gospel in a way that is rare in the history of the Church. I desire that you remember that My speech to you is not just a means to curry favor or keep your faith alive for another week. It is not something that I have told many visionaries through the centuries. It is true – that you and your brother have brought into being a grail that will change the outcome of the world. You have been seemly and sightly, obedient and charitable; and above all things, you have been holy and beautiful – Yes, beautiful in the eyes of the Beholder of Creation, God in all His Glory who lives and reigns in Heaven. I have spoken to you about posture on several occasions since February 22, 1991. I have asked you to strike a confident posture as you live out your days in this world. I have sought in you the willingness to see that your posture must be reflective of your stature. You have been made Saints by Jesus on the Cross; this is your stature. You accept this dignity and live as His royal servants – this is your posture. You are prepared to deliver to His people the final message of redemption that will come upon the Earth when Jesus returns again. I am asking that the whole world see you and your brother as they envision the stature of Saints Peter and Paul, Cosmas and Damian, and all who have been sent out two by two to spread the Good News of the Gospel. My Special son, there will never be any hint of negativity in anything that you and your brother have done for the past 40 years. It is all about advancing the Glory of God and clarifying His Will for those who do not know Him. It is about sufficing what must still be known to bring about the great reconciliation that we have been praying for. My Special son, it makes Me emotional to ponder these things. It brings to My Immaculate Heart comfort and joy to know that you and your brother have never turned back. All throughout the times of your journey when you could have doffed your tunics of faith and turned another way – you did not. You have remained with Me for the good of humanity. William Mary Roth and Timothy Mary Heather. This is who you have been for Jesus in whom you believe. It is clear that you and Jesus are united in the Will of God on behalf of His Church. I am here with you, and long live the Resurrection to which you are given."

Saturday, February 18, 2017
9:37 a.m.

"A fresh course, a flowering spring, a new beginning."

"My dear little sons, every sympathy that would aptly describe the conversion of lost sinners is summarized in the words that begin My message today. It is like restoring the sacred virginity of the human soul that is yielded upon receiving the Sacrament of Baptism, echoed by the absolution found in the Sacrament of Reconciliation. My Immaculate Heart is overwhelmed by My children who receive the Sacraments because they come to Jesus knowing that He is their Eternal Redeemer. My Special one, I realize that you are undergoing a fair amount of indecision and an extra burden of work because of your daily labors, but I ask that you maintain your peace and concentricity through it all. You must be focused on the matters that bring you thoughts of accomplishment instead of those that divide humanity around the globe. I have said that your writing for your next book is wholly appropriate for upbraiding wicked sinners for the way they are behaving. You are to be commended for relating what God wishes them to know. Your prayers and writings are gifts to humanity from the lips of the Father. Your willingness to receive Me here with your brother is the mark of your sainthood, your Doctorship in the Catholic Church. I cannot overstate what this means to the Lamb of God for the conversion of lost sinners into the bastion of Salvation in Heaven. What I am asking all My messengers through these years of the third millennium is to seek this conversion that we are praying for from those who will live in the House of the Lord forever. It is indeed about a fresh springtime and a new beginning that is initiated here in the exiled world. You must remember that you are blessed to have advanced this cause, you and your brother. Yes, you are fruit-bearing advocates for the Holy Gospel representing the Will of God here in your age. My Special son, the promises of Christ are being fulfilled as well, and I am helping My children become worthy of them by reaching into the lives of lost men and women who are only now coming to realize their stations in life. It is a pious and righteous station to which they are called by the teachings of Christ Jesus and their consecration to Me. We do these things with tremendous joy because we are given to the Will of the Father as one Church. Imagine the bright and shining dawns that are in the offing because of our spiritual collaboration. This is one of those matters that is difficult to place into words. Your lives, your gifts, and your petitions have been the making of the Earth into the likeness of Heaven. If I were to say 'thank you,' it would not be enough. Therefore, I say bless you, and may our Father God keep you in His care in all ways and times. You and your brother have ratified your obedience to God. Your obedience has been fulfilled, and the fruits of your sacrifices will be delivered to yourselves and humanity for whom this movement was begun. It is Jesus who discerns the degree of wholesome devotion to the Will of the Father in the image of Himself. Good things will come because the world is in such need. By all means, this does not refer only to you and your brother. Humanity as one people is being called to promise its obedience to God. Reaching out means tending to Jesus' sheep, feeding the poor, protecting innocent life, growing the message of the Gospel in places where Jesus' Sacrifice is impugned, increasing the world's dedication to Me as its Mother, and fulfilling the promises made by those who claim to be authentic Christians.

So, what about this fresh springtime and new beginning? What do we make of what the future might bring? You may not be surprised to learn that it is about the celebration of the virginity of the human spirit that has been restored by Jesus on the Cross. It is about the power of innocence versus the forces of guilt. It is a message about the ability of humanity to choose wisely instead of being lured by the devil into the dungeons of error. It is about prodigies making the most of their talents. Yes, these new beginnings are the ones about which I spoke in 1991. I broach this issue to say that endings are not truly endings when they hail the majesty of God. When we pray together, this is always a new beginning, and it is the enlightenment of the human conscience that will come to fruition before the end of time arrives. A new way of thinking and a whole new awareness is being handed to humanity as we speak, and it is captured at the moment when men and women say to Jesus on the Cross, '...I believe every word you said from there.' This is the Holy Spirit in them that seems to be unable to wait for that eternal joy. And, it is good, it is just, and it is right. I have often spoken about sacred emotion, an emotion that is not based on carnal passions or whims that serve to satisfy the self. It is sacred emotion that brought Jesus to tears during various times during His ministry. It is sacred emotion that makes priests weep during the consecration of the Holy Eucharist. And, it is sacred emotion that brought the Father from the beginning to assert that His lost humanity must be saved. He realized that error consumed the dignity and innocence of Adam and Eve, and His response by incarnating Jesus on the Earth restored the dignity and faithfulness of all who would follow them. My Special son, this is why human life is not about punishment; it is about transformation. Out with the old, and in with the new. It is about invoking the life-sparing Gospel from which the Apostles themselves became known to the Father. We remember that Jesus chose the Apostles not from the social elite, but from a group of commoners who were imbedded in secular life. This is how condemned prisoners on death row can come to Heaven the moment they die. When they are penitent and call on Jesus, He does not ask who they are when their souls arrive in His Wounds. He gives them pardon and consolation from having just departed a world that taught them to hate. He espouses in them everything that is good, expunging all that has been cast down by virtue of His Crucifixion in an earlier realm. All the fullness of the Cross inundates their souls with absolution because they give themselves to the eternity that He brings. They become among the absolved because their guilt has been borne by Jesus into the depths of the lasting abyss. My Special son, I beseech from you the understanding that linear life may be difficult to bear at times, but it has no sovereignty over the forgiveness of God. Your brothers and sisters tend to forget this, if they ever really knew how permanent the pardoning of God truly is. Once the righteous nature of the Father receives the penitent heart, the matter is concluded on Earth. The pureness and innocence of the human soul is harvested into His Kingdom irrevocably with seamless unity. Sinners in the world seem unaware of this miracle. Hence, we pray not only for the conversion of lost sinners to the Cross on which Jesus died, but for them to understand the reasons they must convert. It is not just about making the world a better place, it is about amending the constituency of Heaven to include those who might have been condemned. So, does exiled humanity have the capacity to shape eternity for themselves? The answer is yes, they do. And, why? It is not just that God wants it that way because He is the omnipotence that manifested Creation from the beginning, but because He desires to see the pureness and wholesomeness of His people that emerges from within. In this way, Creation becomes a reflection of God's Kingdom, and His love is glorified by the obedience of the Church. My Special son, it is about yielding a framework where the Father will be pleased, and the world will be saved. This foundation was platformed by Jesus on the Cross, and humanity in exile is still building their response. Do you understand? *"Yes. Thank you."* And bless you for offering your lovely morning prayers, for altering the face of the Earth and the outcomes that will bring the Will of God to fruition."

Saturday, February 25, 2017
1:24 p.m.

*"Redeemed humanity is a wonder in the making –
an eternal apotheosis of beatific life."*

"My lovely little sons, let it always be known that you never wavered in your faith in Jesus, that you remained with Me through all the years of your lives. I take pity on those who do not know God, and I am saddened by those who reject My Motherhood. Together, we are still changing the world. We are proving to the Father that the sinners whom He sent Jesus to redeem are working toward the holiness that He requested they achieve. It is not impossible for this to happen because the power of the Holy Spirit is both absolving and restorative. Reaching for the highest pinnacle of holiness known to man, the apotheosis of piety that Jesus seeks from the Church, is the mission of our prayers and the reason why converted men live toward the eternal. I remind you that there are many mysteries in these things, but they are true because the Lord wills them to be. Thus, it is in striving for the beatific life that religious faith is about. We shall soon see the revelations that make this a fact in your time. I again tell you that Jesus died on the Cross for the forgiveness of human sin. Expiation has been made by the Crucifixion of Jesus, but humanity must accompany this expiation with penance of its own. My Special son, many are the years during which you and your brother have wondered how, and when, the miracles of Medjugorje will come to pass. It is of concern to the Church because the Church Hierarchy requires miracles before it will apply an ample amount of faith to testify to the authenticity of My messages. This seems ironic and contradictory. I know that men's faith is tested when they are asked to believe in miracles that are foretold by My visionaries and locutionists who are sinners themselves. However, were not the First Apostles sinners too? Have there not been parishes and cathedrals named after these Christians of such faith? This is the reason why you and your brother stand out among them. What must be accomplished without fail is for humanity to recognize why Jesus chose as His Apostles ordinary men doing ordinary things. Their lives and legacies became the apotheosis of their day, and this is what is being summoned from today's world in emulation of those First Bishops. All the prayers in Creation can make this happen, but it requires the dedication of the present day Church and those who are being summoned to congregate it. Jesus is pleased by the progress toward this end by those who are responding to Him.

Today, I have come to tell you that I am focused toward the renewal of your country, its reorientation and healing from the degradation that it has suffered in the past eight years. There is no question that there is a certain gruffness to your new president, but is this not what is required to foster the changes that must come? If a person's mission is about protecting the innocent, safeguarding the future of impressionable citizens, and making sure that unborn children are not killed in the womb, does this not mean that this person is doing the work of God? And, if purity and benevolence are being manifested on the social level, is this president not himself a righteous man? We know that the answers to these questions are clear. This is the reason we pray for those who make decisions about how laws and policies are wrought around the globe. There is no reason to believe, and rightly such, that the woman responsible for the 1973 Supreme Court decision strolled right into Heaven without being held accountable for the legalizing of infanticide. No amount of public reparation could reverse this error. It would require more than one traveling to every nation, city and hamlet to proclaim that all human life is sacred. My Special son, I am not saying that the Divine Mercy of Jesus is limited, but it is based on the genuineness of the contrition of those who seek it. If it is not there, if someone mocks Jesus' Mercy during times of doubt, then there are qualifications on the destiny of that soul. Do you see how this is true? *"I would hope that it would be true."* There is a hollowness in the confessions of those who seek forgiveness without a firm purpose of amendment in their heart. I am speaking about a life free from blasphemy and hypocrisy. I know that you understand the ways that humanity must be rebuked and admonished, based on the presence of this hypocrisy. Jesus' Mercy will not be mocked. And, I tell you this upon having said that redeemed humanity is a wonder in the making. Overcoming life's trials and tribulations means that the tenets of one's faith are sustained. These are the fruits upon which the exiled human soul feeds on its way to the Promised Land. And, this is the nourishment that My children find in the Holy Sacrament of the Altar. My Special son, you and your brother are sharing the same grace and goodness by which you have always lived. Your faith and charity will be repaid a thousandfold. This is the transformation of self-discipline that all Christians should adopt. It has been the spiritual mantra of the Saints since the first century Church. I am heartened that you know what must be done to ensure the conversion of lost sinners in this age of glamor and materialism. It is as great a gift that you have given Jesus by praying the way you do as many who walked at His side. *"I pray for people who believe their utter lukewarmness and lives of sin are the stature of the Christian life. They so abuse His Mercy.*" And, this means that they also abuse themselves, yes? "*Yes.*" It is a benefit to the human spirit that obedience becomes the sacred identity of those who proclaim their allegiance to the Cross. All who pray must believe that their petitions will be heard. I have hope with you in the created world, and I have knowledge of the unfolding of these things as the Queen of Heaven and Earth. Thank you for praying with Me. Always remember that you are precious and good. You are everything that Jesus has sought since His Bethlehem Birth that He would find in those who love Him. I realize that there are untold miracles that have yet to come into this world. I promise that one of the grandest of all, the Morning Star Over America, will not be eclipsed by any other. It is for the soliciting, conversion and sanctification of lost sinners that we have done this."

Saturday, March 4, 2017
1:27 p.m.

"Love is the absolute sum of life's eternal meaning –
humanity's sole purpose, the emerald of its feast."

- The Dominion Angels

"My dearly beloved sons, I am with you for the cause of the love to which you have dedicated your lives. We are celebrating this purpose of humanity in your day, given to you by the Lord, and handed down through the ages in the legacy of the Saints who have preceded you. It is with utmost admiration that I hold you in such esteem for making your years here on Earth the substance of divinity. My Special son, while I always enjoy speaking directly to your brother during My messages, it is to you that I have primarily come. You are the energizer of the mission of the Morning Star Over America by virtue of your Roman Catholic birth. We must ensure that all Creation reflects the origin of love that lives in your heart and Mine. Today, I have not only come speaking to you, but also to pray for all your intentions that you share every day with Me. It is clear that while humanity en masse does not know how to pray as they ought, you are perfectly aware of what needs to be said to the Father in order to reshape the Earth into the likeness of Heaven. It is in this wisdom that you know that humanity in the world will always be 'becoming' the reflection of His Will. When Jesus said that there will always be the poor among you, it is not that He believed that the Church would fail in feeding them. It is that those outside the Church are constantly exploiting and neglecting them that brought Jesus to issue His words. My Special and Chosen sons, I pray that you never loosen your grip on the youngness that is within you. It is not that you will be forever young or that you will not depart from things that would define you as spiritually immature. I am asking that you do not become bitter about the happenings in the world that tend to draw your attention away from the hopes you find in Jesus. My Special one, it would seem that there is little I can say to add to your priceless reflections about life and the Gospel because you have made clear your wisdom in your writings and prayers. But, I ask that you bear with Me while I celebrate what you have already proclaimed. I have used the word 'becoming' with reference to the maturity of your faith and the advancement of your knowledge about the Kingdom of God. Imagine if you were prompted to sit down back in 1991 and write the book that your brother is almost finished proofreading. It would have been a task to which you were equal, but the terms and phrases that you have written would have been difficult to conceive. Life and your own suffering have given you a vision that cannot be purchased anywhere in the world. You are connected to Jesus more through this than the timely length of your earthly years. With Jesus, it is not that you have just learned to understand His vision of humanity, you have been conditioned to recognize His part in the conversion of lost sinners by becoming uniquely one with Him on the Cross. Thus, it is a gift to humanity to watch the providence of Jesus' intentions for the world playing out. This is an awe-inspiring experience to perceive how something so grotesque as the Crucifixion could be so beautiful to the human soul. One would think that the awfulness of Good Friday would be a manifestation that would make people cringe. And, if good Christians cringe for the right reason, this is what the Father avows. It is a recognition that beauty and absolution are perceived from the unsightly execution of an innocent Man. I have told you on prior occasions about the beauty of Jesus' Sacrifice on the Cross, but not in the way it would have been seen here in your day. Yes, I am saying that Jesus' Crucifixion was set in the first century so that men's faith could be passed down. There were no cameras or news reels to film the Redeeming Act because this would not have been conducive to two millennia of faith. Also, there existed the common mode of execution of the condemned during the first century, but not today. Would it not have been the case that modern humanity would have instead tried to put Jesus to death by lethal injection or hanging Him on a gallows? I know that you understand the reasons for the Crucifixion being 2,000 years ago. And, My discussion about this issue has greater dimensions than the evolution of humanity's religious faith. What do you suppose some of them are? *"Humanity would have never grown to be what we see if Jesus had not come in the ancient days."* Yes, and there are almost limitless degrees to which this has affected the Church. Not only have twenty centuries gone by, but also the arrival and recording of multitudes of evidence that everything recorded in the Gospel is true. The world has played out the prophecies that Jesus pronounced during His ministry on the Earth. And too, the promised miracles and conversions that He predicted have happened in places as far from the Holy Land as geographically possible.

My Special son, the point I am making is that the Gospel Message, the New Covenant between God and man, has spread because of the power of the Holy Spirit, not as much by courier and letter. *"I understand."* And, it is this same spiritual holiness that is making Saints and Martyrs of those who have fought in defense of the Cross. Jesus died without dignity so that humankind on Earth could live with dignity. This means that every facet of humanity and the lives of men on Earth could be viewed as having innate worth in the eyes of God. We are still watching this play out, you and I. We are seeing along with your brother and everyone else who inhabits the world that God has handed His creatures the ability to walk to Him on spiritual legs that have been preserved for the journey. This is another reason why Jesus' legs were not broken on Good Friday. It is a metaphor that all men can stand tall in Jesus' death on the Cross. There should be dancing that the Son of Man took the sins of men upon Himself. I speak about God esteeming the valorous faith of reborn sinners because they have been remade into the pure, absolute sum of truth by which His love is defined. And, this is the love in which men have been created. You have in your midst not only the True Presence of Jesus' Crucifixion, but His divineness that lives by the power of the Holy Spirit in the hearts of all who believe. No amount of movement, commotion, destruction or upheaval can annul or extinguish this power from the face of the Earth. You have it within you right now in the same way that you had it when you were first placed in the womb of your mother. It must be unleashed and unfurled, and this was done upon your baptism in the waters of this holy Sacrament. The witness of your soul to the divinity of God that is inherent in you became focused that day in the same way that you said I help humanity see more clearly the images of daily life. My Special son, when you get to Heaven – when everyone who accepts Jesus as their Salvation gets to Heaven – you will hear an echoing of the words of consecration through the corridors of Paradise. And, you will hear your own innocent voice crying out through the ages that you will forever belong to the Man on the Cross. Even as an infant, your soul spoke this of you. This will remain in your ears and the gleeful chambers of your heart as your consonance with God. He will speak to you with the fullness of revelation, and you will know more than just why you lived and where you were stationed. You will learn the reasons why God is eternal, why He has never had a beginning or an end. You will find out where all other creatures, great and small, have come and gone in the expanse of their lifetimes. The summation of the entire meaning of love about which this message began will be clear to you. Why? Because you already have the mind and conscience of God, here in this world, now in this time. So, I remind you that everything that speaks to the Will of the Father is unfolding before humanity now. You are privy to all this by virtue of your life in Jesus, but it is being handed to you in daily increments because of the element of time. You are seeing the Time-Creation connection because time on Earth is measured by the movement of the globe in space. I have said that all time is one, and you must remember that this is true for you here. This is where your peace begins. It is the way good men discern what is truly worth seeking and fighting for. And, it is the way these same good men know to shun the irrelevance to which so many lost millions have given their lives and fortunes. We are focused on the glory and the glorious! There is nothing spatial about this momentum other than to say that the spirit of faith in your heart supersedes itself every day. You are on a timely journey to the timeless joy of redemption. This should remain the source of your sacred confidence in everything you are doing. Yes, God told humanity to be fruitful and multiply, and He also said that those who are married should live as though they are not. All human focus should be on His Kingdom through the Son who has shared it. We are poised, you in exile and Me in Heaven, to witness together the changing of the world along the lines of your beautiful writing because the Father has said that the time is nigh. My Special son, I cannot imagine a greater reason for you to live in joy than this."

Saturday, March 11, 2017
9:33 a.m.

"Jesus has delivered humanity to a stature of life –
that can be neither diminished nor surpassed."

- The Dominion Angels

"Now listen– this is the reason that My joy is complete. I have come to pray with you, and My Queenship thrives in the fullness that we share together. This is the way with all My children who hold sacred the relationship given to us by Jesus on the Cross. My little sons, the Eucharistic Prayers reflect the friendship that you have found in Jesus, and I have been telling the world for twenty centuries about the new bloodline that you have inherited with Him through His Sacrifice on the Cross. I remember all the ages, My little ones. As you will likewise see upon your entrance into Heaven, all the centuries and millennia that have preceded your mortal years have led to this – that God has loved His people, and He desires His people's love in return. If there is anything beatific about friendship on the Earth, it is to spread this wisdom around the globe to those whom you may not even know. I have the great satisfaction of realizing that the Church inside your hearts represents your 'intent' for these ages and beyond. All the aspects of the Church that you can see with your eyes are founded upon and fashioned by the Spirit of God, the Flame of Truth, who is living in your hearts. My Special son, the content of your new manuscript, what you are reading there, is a reflection of the content of your heart that is situated in your knowledge of God's Will for the Earth. You have done well; your writing will have its intended effects. And, what you have written is based on the 'intent' that I have mentioned here this morning. It is this intent that helps you convey the 'meaning' that must be transmitted to the world of lost sinners. You mentioned that the Lord may ask what is the meaning of certain human actions because He wants humanity to learn the meaning of His actions conversely and reciprocally. The meaning of His Kingdom, as you know, is Divine Love. The meaning of humanity's actions is still being observed. My Special and Chosen ones, the whole matter revolves around humanness being drawn into sanctity by the devotion of the heart. There need not be a division between being human and being divine. Jesus has proved this through Himself. There is no reason to believe that there should be a contrast between Heaven and Earth, but there still exists one because men and women in exile are still taken by their own pride. I have said at least a dozen times over the past 26 years that God is looking for the innocence in you. It is through this innocence that one's identity is enlisted by Jesus in Heaven. He expiated the sins of mortal men by His heroic Passion and Crucifixion, and He is now searching for the signs of this renewed beginning in the innocent life of those who believe in Him. It is the true nature of Christians to begin again. My children, there is a combination of innocence and the mature wisdom of holy love in the humble Christian. There is beauty in one's confessions and power in his innocence. This amalgam of prudence is yielded when the human being surrenders to the intellect of God rather than the machinations of the world. Therefore, the pure Christian realizes the working of the Holy Spirit in his heart at the same time that he defers his own will to that genius. The origin of the Kingdom of God in the heart is the realization that men on Earth cannot find the meaning of life on their own. Their guilt must be expunged, and Jesus has done this. Second, their feelings of guilt must be let go – this is what My messages have been about. My little sons, I have just described the reason why a twelve-year-old Messianic boy would enter the Temple and tender His teachings there. Those who saw Him in this role observed and conceded to His innocence because they were in the presence of God's Wisdom. And, My little ones, this is the same way that the great Doctors of the Church have come to be admired for upholding the tenets of the Father's Will in their time. It is not that the blast of the trumpeters breaks in, but an overwhelming sense of rightness, decency and honor. These are the three elements of righteousness. Rightness, decency and honor. When you consider that sacred love is the root of all goodness, it makes sense that righteousness is the plant that grows from this root. It is rather simple – but not so simple that those who are ingrained in their own perceptions of what God ought to look like can understand it. And, My Special son, what do you supposed is the seed of this root of sacred love? *"Our sacrifice, united with Jesus."* You have just stated one of the fruits of righteousness. The answer I am seeking is the Will of God. This is the Will that has adorned the Earth with mountains and seas. It is the Will that manifests and sustains life when all other forces of the world would destroy it. My own beauty and your goodness are products of this manifestation because God would rather dress His Creation in reflection of Himself than the remnants of fallen Adam and Eve.

I have also said that it would seem that your faith is about something that is always forthcoming, but this does not imply that the future is not worth the wait. It took Americans a long time to lay a network of railroad tracks before the first steam engine headed from east to west, but there had to be that first steam engine before the effort of laying the tracks came into being. What was coming was the mode of movement when those ingenious men decided that such transfer was possible. Let us ponder something further. If someone asked you what happens when you boil water, what would you say? *"The water turns into steam."* Yes, and the answer is also that when you boil water, the train moves down the track. This is the larger picture that you and I and your brother have been giving humanity for the past 26 years. It is so obvious that the men of Earth look right past it. And, this leads to the passage at the beginning of My message this morning. Jesus is delivering humanity to a forefront of life that cannot be diminished or surpassed. What this means is that eternal Salvation is the destiny of the resurrected Christian person. It also means that there will never need to be anything greater than Heaven in which the human soul would desire to rest. The redemption of the human soul is irreducible because it is the basis for the eternal existence of man, the way it was supposed to be in the Garden of Eden. Adam and Eve were meant to live there perpetually, and you know the reason why they fell. Nothing can surpass the Salvation of humanity because the redeemed human soul has been restored to its original perfection, intended by the Father from the beginning. And, My Special son, everything that has happened since the fall of man, which is the old dawn, has unfolded to the glorious blessing of restoring the stature of man by Jesus on the Cross. By His Cross and Resurrection, Jesus has created the New Dawn toward which humanity has been traveling ever since. Do you understand? *"Yes. Thank you."* I have simplified what I have said today because it has more dimensions than the world has languages and publishers. One of the most profound attributes about the conversion of lost sinners to the Kingdom of God is the question about how something so simple as children following their Father became so complicated. It has been rendered so complex because it requires a barrage of reasoning, awareness and permeation to break through the illogical egocentrism of exiled men. It is not possible, it may seem, to just present the mandates that Jesus laid out during His life on Earth and thereafter because we are still trying to persuade 80 percent of humanity to believe that He exists. You and your brother have become the twentieth and twenty-first century personification of the Saints Peter and Paul, and Cosmas and Damian, and representatives of the paired seventy-two in your time. This does not set you apart from all the other imminent saints who live in your day, but it makes you more consequential in the formation of the Mystical Body of Jesus that will inherit His Glorious Kingdom. You are making the most of your lifetime in exile to prosper the cause of your joy and the message that you are transferring to the Earth from Christ Jesus in Heaven. You are becoming spiritual martyrs and mystics who have carried-on the mission of all who have gone before you, marked with the sign of visionary and hearer. This is the way God sees your lives from His Kingdom in Heaven and within eyelashes of your vision where His Spirit reigns. My Special son, all of this is your 'commonness' with Jesus, your identity in Him, and your union with the Most Blessed Trinity. You are sealed with the imprint of perfection that Jesus accords to all who believe in Him. And, it is not enough that this beauty should exist, My Special son. It is that it must be seen. It has to be made visible to those who will almost envy you for your relationship with God. 'How did he get there?' some may be prone to ask. And, you have given the answer by writing the beginning chapters of your next book, and all the other writings that you have recorded for humanity – especially your memoir. In other words, together we have initiated the concept of the steam engine locomotive, and its tracks are the metaphor for linear time. It is always a good day when you remember that you have not only gained this stature in Jesus, but that men accept it with love. I am pleased that you have allowed Me to speak to you today. *"Thank you, Mama."*

Saturday, March 18, 2017
9:34 a.m.

"And then, O' Father, there are these two – the Morning Star Apostles, so chosen by your Spirit, so special to your Mother, so still in truth, visionaries of perennial faith, a gift to the Church, immune to darkness, a miracle for the ages, upright and strong, devoted to the Cross, gifting of the signs of new life; willing to break through barriers, challenge convention, transcend the obvious, shock the unrepentant, defy the reckless, and humble the vaunted."

- The Dominion Angels

"Yes, My sacred little children, the Angels love you dearly, all the Orders of them, every single little angel who has the awareness that you have meant to God what Creation itself has been unable to convey. I have come to pray with you because the work of the Holy Spirit is yet ongoing – even as Jesus pronounced the Salvation of the world finished on the Cross. There is a question whether the Angels in Heaven have their own will as humans do. Their will is the reflection of the Will of God, and in this, they know who belongs to Him. They are aware of the warriors and strugglers who are taking the message of the Cross to lost sinners on Earth. Today, as they have come to pray with us, it is an honor on their part to share your lives in spirit and truth. You are approaching the arrival of spring where you live, and the Earth will come to life again. It is reflective of the changing of the seasons of the human heart that you have spoken about in metaphoric tones in the past. It is a rejuvenation of the spirit of life and existence that Jesus seeks in the hearts of those who come to accept His Sacrifice on Mount Calvary. It is a rising from the dormancy of the soul that keeps the world in such darkness. And, when we pray for the recognition by humanity that this must be done, cultivation begins to take hold. It is a new cognition – a 're-cognition' that the circumstances surrounding the spiritual deadness of the world must be changed. And, My little sons, this is what you are doing, celebrated in the words spoken by the

Dominion Angels to the Father opening My message here today. Let Me be clear. They are not words that were spoken by the Angels in the past; they were spoken as soon as you heard them the first time yourselves. And, they will ring through the hills of Creation and the vaults of Heaven eminently and forever. It is true that you have made this remarkable gift the legacy of your lives and the estate you have bequeathed to the future of your brothers and sisters. I have seen a great many blessings in My life on Earth and in Heaven, but your dedication to Me, to Jesus, and to your Morning Star Over America work is unprecedented in human history and deific eternity. Thank you for the gift of your lives. I have spoken many times about the fact that the Faith Church is always in the process of 'becoming.' This means that it is growing in faith and perfection in light of the Gospel Covenant. It implies that My children who belong to the Church have become 'aware.' This is the awareness that sustains your faith and gives you strength for the battles that you face. There is contention everywhere you look – there always has been for those who are consecrated to Jesus' Most Sacred Heart. There is a constant struggle to maintain your dignity in a world that wants nothing to do with recognizing or complying with the teachings of the Church. There is a battle against the perception that the leaders of the Church never do enough to condemn the secular awkwardness that comes when Christians are forced to engage the secular void to feed, clothe and house themselves. With what hypocrisy do secular humanists criticize My children who want to be self-sufficient and do right by their families and friends! Which of them would lay down their lives for a stranger in the night? I speak about the maintenance of your dignity because you will always have it in Jesus. You will forever be, as the Dominion Angels have said, a gift to the Church and miracle for the ages. Where you find beauty, My Special son, is not where the social elites choose to search for it. Your definition of beauty is opposite their wealth and glamour. Your vision of beauty is in the sacrifices that you make for Heaven. It is embedded in your desire to make manifest the mandates of the Gospel for those who refuse to hear. Some of the saddest words that could impact someone's ears are these – 'I warned you!' This means that people who suffer loss by their own neglect have allowed their pride and disbelief to bring them into catastrophic darkness. Indeed, My entire deposit of Marian works created by your lovely hands has been a warning sign to those who reject the New Covenant between God and His people. I must make clear to you and your brother that they will do as written in the Scriptures. They will call out your names from their death chambers and beg you to wet their lips from the moisture on your hands. You will do as Jesus proclaimed to your predecessors; you will commend them to the Father's justice and the Divine Mercy of Himself.

My Special one, the world is aware that the New Covenant Gospel teaches the difference between vengeance and forgiveness. The Bible verses hail the contrast of striking back in defense and turning the other cheek. Jesus came to say that vengeance belongs to the Father, but He does not say that it will not be meted out to the unrepentant. The parable of the prodigal son recited by the Church is reflective of the resilience of the Father's desire to see His lost sheep return to the fold. Who else would abandon ninety-nine sheep to find the one that is missing? The striking back that is occurring is the movement against Satan who divides one man from another over the effects of sin. Satan is the enemy who lures lost sinners away from the path of righteousness. He even speaks from their lips the lies of error and exploitation. So, what I am saying this morning is that Jesus of the Gospel is asking humanity to see more clearly where Satan is lurking and what demonic influence he is having around the globe. Jesus did not say that the evil acts of men should be condoned, but to focus the collective conscience of humanity toward eradicating their real enemy by investing the human heart in His Sacrifice on the Cross. Yes, and this means that prayer must be the thesis of human interaction, even between brothers and strangers on the Earth. One must approach those with whom he interacts with Jesus on his mind. And this, My Special son, is why your words to your friend on Thursday were given to you by Jesus in Heaven. It is a matter of discipline, and those who belong to Jesus accept it as what you must do. What was his response? *"He was apologetic."* Yes, this is the signature of a saint in your midst whose vision had briefly become clouded by the secular void. His response was adequate; he addressed the situation accordingly, and the matter was concluded – for now. Why have I said, 'for now(?)' Because sinners are in a constant state of 'becoming,' just as I said moments ago. My Special son, there is nothing to forgive in people like this because they are not on wayward paths; they have just had a stumbling block laid before them. There is another discussion about dealing with those who fall and rise again, but you already know what it entails. My Special son, you need not see each new day as another mission. Life was never meant to be lived that way. You have but one mission in this world that you have made clear to Jesus on an everlasting basis. You seek Him in all ways. You are knowing of the reason you are living on the Earth – you understand the origin of human exile. Each new day is another installment, another footprint, another milestone on your journey to the eternal side of life. You can find your solace in these things by not testing yourself about what you can inordinately sustain. Please remember that your peace rests in your confidence in yourself. As the Angels have said, you and your brother have given humanity the signs of new life that flourish in the faith you have shared. You are strong, vibrant, brilliant and determined. These are the hallmarks not only of the Doctors of the Church, but the warriors who still fight to give them venue. God is aware – the Father is always aware! He subscribes to those things that you find important in committing the Earth and its creatures to the fulfillment of His Will. This is why I find it necessary to remind you of your goodness, to ask that you take a look at who you are and what you have accomplished. I beseech you to remember what this means to Jesus on the Cross, as well as Jesus 'of' the Cross. We shall go forward with your awareness of your victories worn on your lapel like battlefield medals. Let us pray that all who belong to Jesus give Him a worthy Lent this year, and that they understand the reasons for Jesus' strength in the desert. It is always about fulfilling the Will of God."

Saturday, March 25, 2017
The Annunciation of Our Lord
9:27 a.m.

"The difference between somebody and someone."

"My little sons, I come to bless your holy souls and fill your hearts with the Wisdom of God. There has never been a prior time when you have been held in higher esteem than during these present days. You must remember that it is eternity everywhere I am; and thus, the eternity of redemption to which you have consecrated your lives has begun in you. My children, 'forever' means perpetual, never ending, everlasting and unceasing. I wish for you to always remember that this is the 'measure' of the Father's love for you. It is that humanity became estranged from Him in the Garden, and Jesus has restored your union with Him through His Blood on the Cross. Yes, this is the reconciliation that has saved your lives. There is a difference between being somebody and being someone. One might say that someone brought you a warm meal. This is emblematic of affection and dearness. On the other hand, you might say that somebody stole your wallet. This holds the person at arm's length because you feel alienated from them because of their offense. Jesus' Sacrifice on the Cross has transformed humanity from being 'somebody' to 'someone' in the eyes of God. Instead of being people whom He does not know, you have gained His affection through your identity in Jesus. My

Special son, I am not being elementary in saying this, and I am not telling you anything that you do not already know. I am speaking about the whole of humanity. This is the difference in knowing who somebody is and actually having a relationship with someone. It comes down to the touch of unity found in the righteousness to which the Lord calls His people to be devoted. Knowing someone means that your own identity can be affected by them. It implies that you are open to their influence on your entire being. It makes possible that the measure of several parts is larger than their sum. This is the magnification that comes from being unified with Jesus in a way that embraces everyone He died to save. Yes, My Special son, this is difficult to do when there are so many sinners alienated from Him through their reluctance to convert. But, this is the reason we have been praying for so many years, you and your brother and all the Church, so that you might know all who have preceded you in life and 'everyone' with whom you will spend eternity in Paradise. Today is the Feast of the Annunciation of the Lord. You know with certainty what this means to the Faith Church. The Gospel states that I was 'greatly troubled' by the appearance of the Archangel Gabriel announcing the Good News. How could someone be troubled by the Good News of the Salvation of humanity? I inquired how the conception of Jesus could be done since I did not know a man. This is rightly translated because it would seem impossible without the Spirit of the Lord coming upon Me. Emmanuel, 'God with us,' could not have been propagated without the whole world knowing that it was the miraculous work of the Father. Just as I have told you in the past, I knew all along that I was born sinless to accomplish My Motherhood of the Messiah, the Church, and the whole world. I was greatly troubled for the same reason that I am today – that humanity would mock, ridicule and disregard the gift of Jesus' Life, Death and Resurrection. I knew that I would need to spend My earthly years reassuring Jesus that His mission would not be in vain. It is not that He did not know, it was that His Sacred Heart needed the support that only the Mother of the Most Blessed Trinity could provide. My Special son, I would like to share with you this morning the most emotional words that I ever spoke to Jesus in My lifetime on the Earth or in Heaven. Indeed, these words were not as He was maturing in Nazareth or during His days in Jerusalem. It was after His Good Friday Passion, Sacrifice and Easter Resurrection. Before His Ascension into Heaven, we were walking on a moonlit night down a quiet and peaceful path. Imagine this. My Son had just suffered the most excruciating agony known to man, the affliction of the Cross by an Innocent Lamb, the beating, bruising and lashing, and He was raised from the Tomb on the Third Day. What He endured to redeem lost humanity was a gruesome torture that one would believe to be reserved for the most detestable villain. It was an unsightly, and yet beautiful event that has taken the world of sinners to the heights of Paradise. Jesus was as pained, pierced, taunted, and agonized as any criminal might have been in their day. And yet, here are the words we exchanged – Jesus said to Me, '...I hope I did My Father proud.' And, this Mother turned to Him with My eyes filled with tears and replied, '...Yes, My Sacred Son, you did the Father proud; you did the whole world proud. Salvation has come.' We were consoled by our memories; we were heartened by the thought of Heaven being filled with Saints. We were elated that God and His people would be united once again.

So today, My Special son, it is My great honor to tell you that Jesus said on that moonlit night that there would be prophets, messengers and seers aplenty during the centuries to come. He asked Me to look up into the nighttime sky while He told Me that, someday, there would be a Morning Star shining over a place called America that would draw as many people to His Kingdom as the star over Bethlehem. It would be an illumination to replicate the Pentecost Spirit. And, here we are, twenty centuries later, and Jesus' words that night are still echoing around the globe. It is not only that His Crucifixion destroyed the death of humanity, but that His prophecies would be handed down to the Church and those who oath their allegiance to His Sacrifice. Jesus' Ascension came within the passing of days, and I realized when He had gone to the Father that I had participated in a years-long miracle that began when the Archangel Gabriel came to Me and announced the intentions of God. It was a miracle that shall live beyond the ages. It is so brilliant that its light still shines in far-flung universes not yet known to man. Why? Because God loves us. He has drawn humanity back to Himself as 'someone,' and discarded the 'somebody' whom He never knew. My Special son, the Age of Mary is the Age of the New Adam. This is the year in which you live, as your brother is prone to say. And, everything that was meant to be elevated by God's Dominion is being raised as we speak. All the great titans are still standing tall, and more and more are coming about. If you could imagine what it means to transcend the problems and issues that face you everyday, you will know what it means to have been walking with Jesus and Me that night beneath the glistening stars. This is the peace that He gives you in your prayers. It is the solace that makes you smile in the presence of every contention. This is the origin of the memories of your childhood that preserve your innocence every day. It is what I will say to you here now and forevermore – you and your brother have done your Father proud. *"Thank you Mama."* And, you will see upon the passing of the allotted time that all this 'living' you have done has stood for something. It has meaning that you cannot yet possibly imagine. It will change what must be changed, and preserve what must be etched in stone. Nothing you do for Jesus will ever be in vain. My Special and Chosen sons, I wish for you to remember that even though My Immaculate Heart was prepared for the Annunciation of the Lord, the Father wishes the enlightenment of His children to be as much a surprise as they understand the Annunciation of the Archangel Gabriel and My response as described in the Gospel. What sense would it make for The Immaculate Conception to not know from Her first awareness that there was a special purpose for My life? I have shared these thoughts with you because they are purposeful in helping you understand your own stature with the Lord as you live out the years ahead. *"Thank you so much for assisting my perspective."* It is the mission of the Church through the First Apostles that must be safeguarded and honored. The symbolism of the former presidents of the United States boarding the helicopter on the inauguration of their successors is a fitting metaphor for the Feast of the Ascension. And, the awakening of the human heart through the gift of the Holy Spirit is an appropriate reference to the Feast of the Annunciation. My Special son, can you not see the reason for My joy when I come speaking to you? *"Yes."* It is because you and your brother have allowed Me to do so for over 26 years, when I cannot persuade many others to even acknowledge who I am. My Special son, you have something they all want; it will be their big surprise. I commend you and your brother for being so holy, decent and caring. I pray that you will remember that My high praise of you and your brother is meant to tell you about the truth of the ages, not to pour accolades upon you for no good reason. Obedience is the reason. *"I truly appreciate your consoling my heart and uplifting us."* There is nothing in your path that can impede you unless you let it."

Saturday, April 1, 2017
9:33 a.m.

Live not worldly but ethereally superb,
right down to the last fiber of thought,
down to the tiniest glistening dewdrop,
as though someone's life depended on it.

- The Dominion Angels

"Wherever your meditations take you, My little children, the Holy Spirit will greet you there. This is the sublime nature of your faith, that Jesus within you makes you remarkable and traceable. It is all for your goodness and redemption that He blesses you, and this is the reciprocal meaning of your lives in Him. My Special and Chosen ones, there is beauty everywhere these days. There is wisdom in your petitions and purpose in your actions. We have agreed long ago that the world will brawl and bubble, blindly taking itself into the abysmal darkness. It is not to trouble yourselves with these things about which you are concerned, but to rescue the yearning souls at its center. Yes, the Earth is good, but the world of men is not as good. As I have told you more times than you might remember, the world is rife with error and riddled with miscalculations that bring suffering to the innocent. Today, therefore, we offer our prayers to Jesus so that He will increase the poverty of spirit of those who need to be humbled. The Angels have spoken this morning of the transformation from the worldly life to the beatific life. My Special son, you and your brother have done this long ago. It is essential to whom you have chosen to be. You are compliant with the mandates of the Gospel and in company with the Saints before you. All I have ever wanted from My children is that they get life right. And, this means getting on with the responsibilities of conversion, and tossing from their hands all the distractions that are holding them back. It is far better for them to seek the Kingdom of God than for them to proceed on the path they are taking. I have said this morning that there is beauty everywhere. This means that change has already come; its hues and echoes can be detected in the corridors of human life. I realize that there are obstacles yet to be overcome, but they are as measurable and predictable as the errors of men themselves. It all comes down to pleasing God in the way that He has shown through His Son. My little children, I wish to tell you this morning that the sacrificial life given to the Father by all faithful Christians is the way of eternity, already coming into this world. It is sacrificial not just because it often leads to suffering, but because it denies the adversaries of the Church and the enemies of the Cross the opportunity to distract those who are loyal to God. It is with parables, sermons and images that Jesus has taught His chosen flock what must be known about Himself. He told the world twenty centuries ago that when they had seen Him, they had seen the Father. Hence, when humanity embraces what Jesus believes and teaches about Heaven, they are encountering Heaven on the Earth. Preparing for Salvation is supplanted by one's presence in Heaven upon departing from the flesh. The Dominion Angels spoke at the beginning of this message about conceiving this fact, and making it manifest in the conscience and consciousness of each person, right down to the last thought, and down to the smallest fiber of thought. This is the same detail to which Jesus has gone to unite those who accept Him. Acceptance cannot come without belief, and belief cannot be present without repentance. My Special son, the whole idea about restoring one's innocence and breaking past the dawn of all new beginnings is encapsulated when someone says 'I love you' to Jesus. It is in recognizing how the human soul, allied with the heart and good faith, is consecrated to living in alignment with the Gospel. To accept Jesus' Crucifixion in atonement for the sins of the world is to recognize the destiny of the soul. And, the entire beginning of the redemption of the soul is vested in the reorientation of the heart to the culture of the divine. As I speak of the divine in light of the gift of Salvation in Heaven, I am also referring to the divine that thrives within the faithful exiled Christian. One of the most notable aspects of Jesus' life as He walked the Earth is that even His First Apostles were not able to understand what it meant that He was mortal. They had to deal with the contradiction, '...How could God die?' We know where they found their answer. It was on Mount Calvary, and it was because Jesus claimed identity with the divine that He was crucified. Nevertheless, He was raised to teach again that sinners the world over should aspire to reach the divine, even as they believed they might not know how. Being perfect as the Heavenly Father is perfect implies that everyone should strive to reach the divinity by which the Son of Man was born. There is no futility in this if you look from the standpoint of the whole of redeemed Creation being united at the end of time in God's sovereign presence.

Yes, it means living beyond the worldly into the ethereal sublime as though someone's life depended on it. This is the same as breaking past the bonds of convention. This is what the Cross represents. No greater break from convention will ever be made manifest in the existence of the world than the prospect that God's Son could die. But, He did. The Father in Heaven was the first to utter the words, '...A part of Me would die if I could just have My people back.' While God is seamless and timeless, He reckons things that might be otherwise immeasurable. How much love, He wondered, would it require to prove that He desires humanity to return into His presence? My Special son, the Salvation Covenant is His answer. He thought that if the people of the world could believe that storm winds can rip a door from its hinges without seeing the breeze, then surely Creation would believe in the Kingdom of His Son. Yes, through one visible Man, in the likeness of Himself. This is where the mending of everything broken first began. It is where humanity's dark drive toward eternal oblivion came to an end and reversed course. And, it is where the universe itself coughed up a corrupt world of men and began breathing on its own. My Special son, it began in Jesus, and it will conclude in Him. The Alpha and the Omega. In the meantime, the Faith Church is making His case. It is disciples like you and your brother, with the tools handed to you by the Carpenter Himself, who are righting the ship of life. It is in your hands and rebuilding at His behest that the world is being remade. Your acts and prayers, even your accidents and questions, are leading the lost from their dark dungeons to the hilltops beneath the sun. You are His teachers, writers, poets and musicians who are making the most of your lives in preparation for the end of the world. Is there pride in this? Probably a small speck of righteous pride, but also a fitting share of reward. We have already voided the myth that little people in remote places cannot change anything. This too began with the Christ Child in the Manger. My Special son, these sentiments come from My Immaculate Heart, but hardly anyone is willing to listen. "*I will always listen to you, Mama.*" I find tremendous consolation in your company. I am comforted by your prayers. And, this is what I ask of the whole world that is called to place its hope in Jesus. I urge humanity to reach deep down into their craws and find the humility to be united with Him. I wait to hear their own poetic strains that might lift Him up before the nations. It is all for the power of the Cross in an exiled domain that has no power of its own. I wait for the descriptive verses that will prove to Jesus that the world is listening to what He is saying. This is the sense of divine romance that I wish My children to embrace – to make right the wrongs that have stormed against the dignity of My children since their fall from Paradise. This is why we pray as we do. It is the reason men climb to vast mountaintops and freeze to death along the way. It is the purpose of shooting oneself into the void of outer-space and looking down with gasps of utter awe. Indeed, it is the reason you were asked to help Me reignite the spiritual flame of the world. Besides the Sacred Scriptures, what you have written is all anyone needs to know. What you and your brother have done is the work of God's genius and a gift from the Sacred Heart of His Son. Just as certain as you are praying with Me now, the days you are striving to achieve will be lived, and they will precisely reflect what you have written. The Angels will rejoice; the dancing will begin, and the arrival of the joy of humanity will be celebrated in the halls of the Afterlife. Just as the Dominion Angels have said – you will live that day right down to the last glistening dewdrop, and Jesus will be adored. It is more than courage that I am speaking about today, My little sons, it is the healing presence of God's Divine Providence descending to the created realms. It is about ushering the innocence of faith to its proper place of residence. It is about defying the devil at every turn when he tries to exploit the trust and holiness of God's living Church."

Saturday, April 8, 2017
9:37 a.m.

"Structure plus function yields outcome – truth matters."

"My dear little sons, you have not only become acclimated to the Will of God for humanity, you have been advancing His Will for five decades. You are aware that His Will is enwrapped in the righteousness through which He first gave humanity the breath of life. My children, God has also given His creatures the 'will' to live. It is a dutiful devotion to which men on Earth are called because human life in exile is not just mere existence – it is a mission. The Father has given you the structure of life, an essential 'being' in a temporal and spiritual sense. With this, He provides that you have this 'being' and breathing in Him. Your function is the mission of righteousness that I just spoke. And, what is the yielded outcome? The recognition of one's sinfulness, and handing to Jesus the human soul in all its dimensions and potentials. This, My little sons, is the essence of being human. The outcome of your lives, of every life, must be that you unite yourselves with Jesus both in your own sacred identity and with Jesus on the Cross. This is in succession of the Holy Resurrection by which He has restored your lives. My Special son, I have begun My message today with this framework of thought because it leads to the requirement that the 'Truth' be the most crucial factor in the lives of mortal men. Anything that strays from this Truth – everything that strays from this Truth – possesses an origin of error. All the debates about secular things are mostly distractions because they are not founded in the integrity of the Truth. For example, there have been long-winded debates in the secular void about which month of gestation of an unborn child is appropriate for abortion to be legal. You can see how this deplorable debate is irrelevant because abortion is a mortal sin. The debate itself is based on a false premise. Or, perhaps the national debate is about the most compassionate way to carry out capital punishment. Here again, the practice of capital punishment strays from the Will of God, and therefore the debate is in error. Truth matters. This means that the structure of every society, of every nation and family, the structure of the entire world, must be based on the intent of God for what His Creation must become. It is as though the Father handed humanity an Earth on which to establish a just world that is fashioned upon His teachings and Commandments. Debates like how to commit infanticide and purge criminals from society by execution are not within the structure of the Lord's eternal framework. This is the origin, the genesis of the wasting of human lives that are spent arguing which kinds of sins are better than others. Yes, I think the term you use is 'psychobabble.' The structure of all the entities that I just mentioned must reflect the infinite structure of God's righteousness in the way that He fixed it into being at the beginning of time. If the structure is to be just, it must be founded on His Will above all other things. Do you understand? *"Yes."* And, the second component of this eternal model is function. This is the means through which the structure is animated by the actions of humanity in the world; it proves that men are aware of their intended purpose. Writing your books, for example, proves that your intended purpose is tethered to all things eternal as they are prescribed by the Father in Heaven. If Jesus told you to travel across the city and bring back five chickens for a feast, you would not return with five barking dogs. However, with some other men, this is where the function becomes perverted. My example denotes the errant understanding by secular men about what God wants them to do. Think about all the debates that you and your brother see on the television every day. No one knows better than you that the truth remains buried beneath all the secular blathering, if it is even part of the discussion at all. This is the reason why most debates are irrelevant. The structure is not based on the Will of God for the shaping of the world, and the function is not based on the mandates of the Gospel that will prepare the Earth for the Return of Jesus in Glory. So, if the structure is errant, and the function is errant, what does this say about the outcome? It will be errant as well. My Special son, I am making what appears to you and your brother to be a point of material logic. This indicates how attuned you are to Me and the Will of the Father in Heaven. But, the idea of ensuring the proper structure and function seems like a foreign language to those who are far from God. I include in this group so-called Roman Catholics who have sold out themselves to the secular monstrosity that is trying to keep the Church from succeeding. All the debating is nonsensical because those doing the debating are talking about the wrong issues. And, by the time you include all the activists who would rather see the Earth drenched in sin, all you are able to see and hear is a group of clamoring voices blaring from unsightly sinners who would not know the facts if they ordered them for dinner. My Special son, this is the world that Jesus is looking at today. It was much the same during His earthly years, but by now, twenty centuries hence, the entire structure of secular error has grown exponentially. Therefore, its functional actions have fallen into even more egregious corruption. And, what is the outcome? The whole world is a boiling caldron of sin. I assure you that the most gruesome horrors of the early centuries are in common with what is happening today.

Lost is the beauty; cast aside is the piety, and utterly destroyed is any willingness on the part of secular humanity to abandon their current structure and reorient their actions to comport with the teachings of the New Covenant Church. However, I am not speaking hopelessly here. I am not saying that the problems that I have told you about this morning are not being addressed. I am describing to you a structure and process that have already been defied. The house in which these secular people are living is wholly engulfed in flames, but none of them know it. We can see it because we have the eternal vision of the Father in Heaven. This is the joy of the purview that we hold over the earthly exile of men. With His Spirit, it is as though you and your brother have communication devices in your ears through which Jesus has told you to leave the premises with haste. And, He is asking you to warn everyone else through your books and prayers, but they will not pay heed to what you have to say. I ask you not to pity them. They will find out anyway. Once the floor of Creation collapses beneath their feet, they will come to know what Jesus meant when He declared that their houses are built on shifting sand. This must surely give you consolation as you realize that My messages in your home will ultimately mean the difference between their conversion and their falling forever into the pit. "*Yes. Thank you.*" So, My message today is about reorienting humanity to recognize their helplessness without the wisdom of God in them, through Jesus and the Holy Spirit. Humanity must 'touch' the structure of the Father's Divine Kingdom by ceding their will to Him in all ways. Men on Earth must listen to the invitation of the Holy Spirit to receive the graces that God wishes to bestow. This not only pleases the Father when men do this, it assists in defining the mission of life for those who are still unaware what the role of humanity in exile is supposed to be. Then come the prayers and servitude as described in the Sacred Scriptures – this is the function of humanity from the structure of the holy identity of God within the human heart. If these things are done well, My Special son, the outcome will consist of the reunion of God and man in the way He always wanted it to be. It is the obedience that Jesus lived on Earth according to the Will of His Father. My Special son, I wished not to be too academic in My message this morning, but I wanted you and your brother to take ownership of the components of this design as a consolation for your work and service. In the complex world of men, you and your brother have led simple lives of righteousness that Jesus summons from everyone. This is difficult for you to maintain because you are constantly being bombarded with the complications of the secular void where you are forced to grapple with complex systems and people who believe they know everything about them. It is a source of frustration and stress for you to commit yourselves to this engagement, but you are coping admirably. I wish that you could sense how fairly you are living here in America, and with what esteem you are held by Jesus in Heaven. *"Thank you so much. It is sometimes so hard to deal with such secular commotion."* Neither you nor your brother is wasting time in your earthly lives – you are Christian visionaries in the themes of redemption who are being inundated with the prattle of the secular void. This has been the experience of most all My messengers for 2,000 years; it is not something particular to you. You are not being hindered by your exposure to this worldly motion, but you will be hindered if you do not remain adept at compartmentalizing your reaction to what you are hearing and seeing. So, please do not take seriously what you are learning about the rest of the world, even in your own country. Thank you for allowing Me to speak about the process of life on Earth, that its purpose is in seeking the product of existence that is yielded by finding oneself in the structure of God's Word and acting with worthiness on what every Christian knows. I pray that humanity comes to know everything that you and your brother have lived for decades in response to the centuries of grace and knowledge that your holy forbears possessed."

Holy Saturday, April 15, 2017
9:33 a.m.

Life must be a heavenly anthem of sight, sound and word,
Marked by the embroidery of joy, laid in the hands of truth,
Spared from the perils of error, free from the voice of harm,
Like summoning a deluge on order, let the inundation begin.

- The Dominion Angels

"My dear little sons, some people see life as an erosion of days, others see it as their accumulation. Today, you are seeing that the Angels believe it to be neither one – that it is a condition in a particular place from which the eternity of the ages begins. And, this beginning has an even more crucial effect, that of the conversion of the heart. My Special son, I am especially close to you this morning because of the peace that has come upon you during the past twenty-four hours. It is because of the intercession of the Saints in whom you have placed your hopes for the purification of the exiled world. You must know that you have a great namesake among the Popes. There is one who was particularly devoted to My Immaculate Heart, even being the first to articulate My role as

Mediatrix of Creation and the Salvation of man. This same Pope is also known as the Rosary Pope due to his devotion to Me. He also promoted the Catholic education of the young here in the United States more than his predecessors. Yes, this is Pope Leo XIII. You will find in his biography many parallels to yourself and the dignity you have found in Jesus through My heavenly intercession. You are carrying on the same charity of heart toward Me in your day. You will meet him in Heaven – you will see them all. I only ask that you remember how much you are loved by all your Papal Fathers from which the guardianship of God has flowed. I wish you peace and joy, a gladness that cannot be taken from you, in knowing that the Almighty Father has so vested you with the grace for which billions who have preceded you have prayed. This is Holy Saturday, and the Angels have spoken about summoning a deluge on demand – on order, they call it. There is no reason to believe that the peace, love, trust and faith that come with your dedication to God will not be given to all the world. It is a matter of preparation that has been ongoing since the Angels were first dispatched to you. It is a principle of the 'touch' that I have recently spoken about, that there is such thing as a spiritually tactile dimension to your belief in God that validates who you are in Jesus. The touch of the Holy Spirit is what you felt when you read the article about the dying 4-year-old boy. This is real impulse, not something based on the power of suggestion. In truth, suggestion has no power unless it refers the human heart to the Kingdom of God. I have also spoken to you recently about perpetuity, infinity and eternity. Even as these things coexist, today matters. This is your day. Through the Morning Star Over America, humanity is living the legacy of Pope Leo XIII as his successor in grace. You share coequally with him the peace and passion of the Lord that has come to rest in you. This is My message for this Holy Saturday, to tell you that your prayers with Jesus during the Sacred Triduum is like that of the olden days. You and your brother are one with Jesus' Death and Resurrection in the same way that all who believe in Him are one body in Him. It would seem that high feasts like Christmas and Easter come about every year as routine events to some people in the Church. And, for about two-thirds of those who claim to be Catholic, these feasts come and go without much mention. I assure you and all who are devoted to My Immaculate Heart that the Passion of Jesus is your sanctification in His suffering, and the love in your hearts is the imprint of His Resurrection. My Special son, a person cannot love God unless they accept His gift of faith. Yes, this is what I mean to say. It is the Father who instills in those who tender their will to Him the desire to love Him, the willingness to know Him, and the obedience to serve Him. It is the same gift from which holiness itself is manifested. All one has to do is sense within himself the void that only God can fill, and then ask Him to inhabit everything about the human person that can be occupied. Once the cold winds of indifference stop howling through the empty chambers of the heart, this is when the soul is inspirited by the Third Person of the Most Blessed Trinity. Once warmth is felt; once there seems to be a light that is not of this world within the confines of the soul, then that person is bound for Salvation. All the undertakings that happen in between, everything that must be suffered, borne and believed – all this is part of the life that the Dominion Angels speak about. It is given to humanity when good men choose to serve. And, this is what you and your brother's lives have been about for the past fifty years.

My dear little sons, what is building up is not so much the accumulation of days, but the desire of the world to be overtaken by the same love in which it was created. Everything that Jesus was trying to teach humanity during His earthly life was that this must be a surrender, not so much dismissing suffering as though it does not matter, but tendering one's soul to whatever suffices the judgment of God to make His Creation whole. I once, many years ago, spoke of Jesus kicking the world in outer space as though it were a soccer ball. While this is symbolic and figurative, there is tremendous truth in its meaning. Shaking the dust from the lost precincts of the globe means that many places must quake and burn. Other places must ascend, and still more plummet. This is all part of the culture of cultivation that Jesus to this day speaks about through the Holy Spirit from the tongues of priests and ministers. Routing and rerouting, clearing and shearing – all of these things imply the changes that must come to humanity in order to free them from their shackles of sin. And, there is so much vanity in the so-called 'appalling' feelings that some people have about what God should allow. The whole concept of Jesus being put to death on Good Friday was a product of this false indignation. 'Who in the world is He to claim that He is the Son of God in the flesh?' This was the great question that led to the Sacrifice of My Son on the Cross. 'Who would even think about appropriating one's identity with God?' This is the same complaint that has been lodged against those who affirm that the Spirit of the Lord has come upon them. It is the same assault that has been leveled against the Prophets and My Marian messengers. All over the world, it is here. And, it is good. Jesus said that His suffering, Passion and Crucifixion were good. For what reason? Because the Father says so. This was all the Son of Mary needed to know — SOM. Yes, this is the way Jesus signed His name. It was for God the Father on My behalf, that My Motherhood would be protracted into the Earth and enliven the spirits of men. This is what I am doing here in America. It is what you and your brother have set into motion by your lives, perpetuated by your trust in God and love for each other. My Special son, I have waited the whole year of 2017 thus far to give you this message on Holy Saturday because it is a fitting metaphor for the placement of My messages to you and your brother in this home and in this city. Awaiting the Resurrection. This is where your sacred deposit of works stands today. Its Easter will come as sure as the Easter of the Messiah was brought into being by the Father in Heaven to the jubilation of all the world. My Special son, your brother told you last evening that his heart would have been crushed to death by now if you had not nurtured and comforted him – rescued him from the ravages of the mortal world. He has never spoken a more principled truth. This is the way the Father sees your life here in this place, that you and your brother have given Jesus comfort and solace in a Creation that is still trying to cast Him aside. Your births from your mothers' wombs assured Him that His Gospel message and life's legacy would carry on into the third millennium. The entire purpose of your incarnation has been to propose His Truth before the nations at My behest. Make no mistake about it; this is no tale of hyperbole. Just think for a moment. Envision what I see through My eyes, what you have given Jesus during your tenure of years. And, you have done this without reward or approbation either from the Church or those who declare their autonomy from it. But, God in Heaven knows! Everyone who has ever mattered in the dedication of the world to the Sacred Heart of Jesus is aware of your station already reserved in the Kingdom of Redemption. Your lives are like the silent beating of the human heart that goes on without recognition in billions of souls around the globe. You are part of the essence of life that the Father has deigned into being, both anatomically and spiritually. All that makes up Nature, everything that solicits the heart from beauties yet untold, with the most centering element of human existence intact – all of these things are sustained by your identity in Jesus and His teachings that you have spread before the destinies of men. And, this is what Pope Leo XIII knew. It is what made him the Rosary Pope because I told him the same thing in his day. He could have only prayed to have had the kind of effect through his Pontificate that you will have in your lifetime. So, I bring you at the Eve of Easter the kind of joy that you could only have dreamed about having. It is the peaceful presence of the Holy Spirit in your heart that tells you that life matters, that today matters; the years matter and the centuries matter. It is about the depletion of hours and building up the Eternal Kingdom of God. My Special son, thank you for allowing Me to give you this message today. *"Thank you, Mama. You are very gracious. I'm thankful so much for all my gifts."* And, thank you for the gift that you are to your brother."

Saturday, April 22, 2017
2:08 p.m.

Jesus the Christ

His is the most beatific face ever set upon a man,
for whom marigolds dance and the winds accede,
In him all things eternal find their new beginnings.
For he makes rich the paupers' broth, low their ire,
true their fathers' joy, and sweet the trumpet's song.

- The Dominion Angels

"My little sons, these are the most beautiful words that I have ever heard the Angels share with humanity in exile. No, I was not exiled. The Archangel Gabriel was speaking to a Woman already filled with Glory. I come today to share in your prayers because the dutiful urgency of the conversion of the world requires it. So, when thinking about the way the Angels share their meditations with you, it is important to remember that it is really the Holy Paraclete sharing with you the Will of the Father in Heaven. It is their way of complying with His wishes that the Gospel Truth be shared both temporally and miraculously. Soon, your brother will complete his proofreading of your manuscript. It is no less than a wholesome miracle that the two of you have done this over the past two years when so much else has been ongoing. Your brother likes the passage at the beginning of our message this afternoon so much that he would like it placed singularly on a page somewhere near the beginning of your book – at least until the Angels share one that he likes even better! My Special son, it is you who always have the final word about these things. Your brother likes the passage today with more emphasis because it is reflective of your Resurrection Prayer. All around the globe, the Angels and Saints are making their presence known, but noplace more prolifically than in this home. I recently said that you are both inspired and inspirited, and this is what our Holy God has vested within you. Today, to accompany our prayers that you have returned home safely, we must remember to pray for all who are lost, everyone who has for some reason given way to the solicitations of the world and gone missing from the fold. When you think about it; and you once said something to this effect, everything that advances the Kingdom of God in the realms of men is a miracle. All this speaks to His sovereignty, anything that celebrates His dominion over His Creation – all this is the sacred remnant of the first miracle He ever performed. The miracle of Creation; this has thus far been His greatest miracle. And, the Life, Passion and Sacrifice of Jesus on the Cross is His greatest gift. Why? Because the Crucifixion is the seed of the Divine Mercy through which billions of sinners have already been absolved. My Special son, when we speak about this 'Kingdom' that I have many times exalted, it is most often the unspoken things that have the greatest power. It is when people who fall into temptation realize that they can commit to their repentance in Jesus because they know He will forgive them. Here, try pondering how many actual thoughts that a person can have in a lifetime. Surely it is a greater number than the beating of the heart. "*Yes.*" It almost seems to be an infinite amount of thoughts and impulses, but you must know that there is a finite measure to their count. Truly, the Divine Mercy of Jesus cannot even be conceived in this context. It is not so much how deeply Jesus loves humanity, but 'that' He loves humanity. The mere mention of Jesus' Divine Mercy implies the infinity of the Father's Love. It cannot be measured because it cannot be seen. Therefore, when someone says that they cannot wait to get to Heaven because they want to see how much God really loves them, they are missing the point. Accepting the Love of God means that someone is eager to travel the road of righteousness that has no end. But, it has a destination – each person should remember that the Love of the Father takes them back to their origin in Him. What God gave humanity in the beginning was soiled by Adam and Eve in the Garden. Jesus, therefore, has not only cleansed the souls of the soiled, He has rescued from the perils of death the very meaning of their existence. The New Adam has in another age and a different dimension collected everything redeemable about Creation in His Sacrifice on the Cross and handed it back to God.

My Special son, messengers like you and your brother have asked the reason why everything you know about human redemption is so opposed. The answer would be complicated if given in the setting of the diversions and distractions of lost sinners in the world. We choose to look beyond these distractions and get to the point, that men in exile are under the influence and under attack by Satan. Everything that causes the separation of humanity from God is a result of the sin incurred by those who do not reject Satan. Even as the Faith Church on Earth celebrates the Paschal Resurrection, there are millions of people around the globe damning their own souls by refusing to believe in the Father's greatest gift. In fact, countless numbers of them do not even believe in the Father, let alone accept His gifts. But, the poor almost always do. Jesus makes rich their broth because He identifies with them. He draws low their ire because God's anger will suffice their cries for justice. It can even be described as focusing on the weeds instead of the flowers to dwell on what revenge must be taken against those who reject the Will of Truth as it has been laid out in the Gospel. When Jesus rose from the Tomb, did He set out to find the ones who put Him to death and punish them? *"No, not yet."* And, the reason is because those who put Him to death are still being born to this day. As you imply, the operative word is 'yet.' The world will know when this process begins. I will illustrate an example of the sound of this justice. Imagine the muffled rumble of slow-rolling thunder echoing across the sky. You hear it growing louder and louder, more ominous, and at times seeming as though it is going to break into a deafening roar. That is the first sound. Next, imagine this rolling thunder being coupled with the sound of a billion glass jars being dropped from the summit of a rocky mountain to the foothills below – indeed billions of them, each one smashing against the craggy surface as they fall to their destruction at the bottom. I am speaking about a sound so deafening that the rolling thunder can barely be heard. This is a metaphoric way that the souls of sinners will be awakened at the appointed time when Jesus comes again. It will harken to the noise made when someone unexpectedly hears just one simple drinking glass being dropped onto a concrete floor, but multiplied by infinity. This is the kind of shock that will awaken the dead consciences of these souls with such emphasis that they will become new people in an instant. Shocked people. Terrified people. *"Is this only the people who are alive at the time? What about those who have already passed?"* They already know. They have already rued their lives in the case of unrepentant sinners, and the Saints have already rejoiced in their destiny of light. *"How soon before this comes?"* There will be no AD 2100. I have said that all perils can be alleviated by the conversion of the lost and by manifest abruption, but nothing of essence has been done to change the course of the things I have said. *"Mama, we need miracles – especially for our Bishop to believe you."* You have given your Bishop the great miracle of The Morning Star Over America, and I will give his successor, whomever he may be, another Tilma-like sign that will rock the Church and the world simultaneously. I will also affirm that you should not assume that your Morning Star Over America deposit of works is not a secret that is to be revealed in another location. I am asking that you live with confidence that your work here has not been in vain – your lives have resounded the courage of the Apostles and the wisdom that inspired them. This is the story of your time. It is the making of the sacredness of every tomorrow in the confines of each single day. Why? Because the Lord looks at you with affection and admiration. Do you remember the vision of seeing your brother standing here in the living room while you were traveling. *"Yes."* Your heart told you that you were looking at a good man. My Special son, this event represents a scripted version of how the Father sees you from Heaven. So much love, so much caring and compassion, so much identification with your suffering, so much desire to help you succeed. And too, is this not the reason I have come to you for so long? *"Yes."* Thank you for your holiness, loveliness and goodness. Bless you for your prayers and sacrifices. Gifts to you for so many years of life on behalf of the Church."

Saturday, April 29, 2017
9:32 a.m.

"Breaking bread, building bridges, healing wounds, and nurturing hope. Pious platitudes of an arcane panacea? I don't think so. It is the still-reigning Kingdom of a Man who fought to the death for human life, a sinless wonder whose charity glowed like the sun. His only crime was offering His love to the masses. He was rejected outright, killed and laid in a cave – His only flagstone was the mourning of His Mother. His only request was that humanity would remember Him when carving out the history of its heritage."

- William Roth Jr.

"Little children, it 'becomes' you to live in the shadow of the Great Champion Divine, the lovely Christ Jesus in whom humanity has placed its eternal hope. I have come to pray with you for the sinners who have yet to accept His Blood on the Cross as expiation for their sins. Thank you, My Special son, for writing such an endearing passage to begin our message today. Each time you write another one of these meditations, it spurs the world to remake itself in the likeness of Heaven. These writings are the eternal dividends of your decades-long sacrifice that you have shared with your brother. I have within Me this morning not only My everlasting gratitude for this, but My promise that all you have given to God during your earthly years will bear the sweet fruits that He desires to savor once the Church Triumphant is complete. I also wish to share with you today the gratefulness of Jesus that you have such keen wisdom in matters of faith and morals. I commend you for recognizing the weaknesses of humanity, that these shortcomings cannot be eradicated overnight. If this were true, you would have seen Creation in its state of perfection long ago. If you think about the attitudes of those who lived in the earthly age of the Messiah, and if you consider the tenor of the Gospels as they are written, you will see that the mere presence of Jesus on Earth was difficult for them to understand. Yes, the fact that God would inhabit visible flesh was not something easily internalized. There were no cell phones or satellite televisions to distract these people. There were no automobiles or flying machines. There was no race to the top of industry and entertainment. And yet, as you have made clear in your video, 'they had as many distractions in their day.' So, the idea of distractions is relative to one's age – it is that men will do most anything to avoid being called into question about who they are and what their motivations should be. Jesus could have come to one soul in a vacuum, and that person might have looked for a means to avoid Him. It is the intersection of the human soul and Divine Light that is the core of this engagement. This occurs one person at a time in a world of over seven billion people. My dear sons, I realize that you do not take for granted that you have become so advanced, that you have so vastly excelled in your understanding and acceptance of Jesus on the Cross. After all, this is a gift from the Father. But, the prospect that what you know, and what I know as well, having to be made manifest to billions of unbelievers is the task that seems more daunting than the idea of 'savior' itself. The question from many men who are presented with redemption is where they ask, '...redemption from what?' The answer to this question rests in man's self-examination and reflections about how meaningful his life and future should be. Hence, you understand the purpose of growing old. Imagine, My Special son, if everyone on Earth lived for 70 years without growing older, and then all of the sudden they die. They would not experience the visionary transition that comes with maturing in one's faith and temporal poise. The aging of the flesh is the Lord's metaphor for saying that His Kingdom is not of this world. I have told you that the human soul does not grow old – it cannot be affected by time, and it is immune to the impressions of the ages. You and all who have lived here have the same-age souls that were conceived and placed in the wombs of your mothers when the Father said that you should have life. The point I am making is that your soul is the permanent evidence of your having existed on the Earth, while everything else except your holy consciousness passes away. Contrary to what some theologians teach, you do retain your awareness upon the transfer of your soul into Heaven that you held in your mortal years in exile. How in the world can anyone call upon the intercession of the Saints if those Saints in Heaven have no recollection of who is imploring them for their prayers? What these theologians should be saying is that the Saints in the Church Triumphant have no memory of the matters they choose not to recall. They cannot even remember what they wanted to forget. Were it not for the veil that mortal men cannot see, this would be made clear – that beseeching the Saints in Heaven for their prayerful intercession is not a long distance effort. My Special son, look at the palm of your right hand. Heaven in its vast entirety can fit in the distance between your eyes and your palm. Yes, and it is as endless as the most remote universes that the Father imagined from the farthest places in His mind. Therefore, the distance between your eyes and your palm is infinite as well. So, Heaven is not so much about focusing on a physical place, but emphasizing the redeemed condition. The two, however, are not mutually exclusive. For the redeemed soul, Heaven is all realms outside human exile that could be imagined, except for the dungeons of Hell. Heaven is not measurable; it is spiritual infinity that is immune to the quantities of size and shape. It is neither cold nor hot. It has no top or bottom. It cannot be diminished or divided. And, at this time in the Earth's history, there are only two bodies in Heaven. Do you know who they are? *"You and Jesus." (Our Lady then shared with me privately a sacred perspective of all those awaiting the Resurrection, Lazarus' resurrection, and Enoch and Elijah being taken to Heaven.)* Thank you, My Special son, for being so holy. Please accept My gratitude for everything you mean to Jesus – every day, with every thought and deed."

Sunday, May 7, 2017
9:27 a.m.

"In my opinion, the whole idea of being a good Christian boils down to whether someone authenticates his faith with eternal veracity."

- William Roth Jr.

"The complete obliteration of the diabolical construct."

"My little children, what would humanity say if it collectively discovered that the good Lord was in no hurry to close out the ages? How could this be reconciled with the Gospel Truth in which the Will of God is consummated with the Return of Jesus in Glory? The fact is, the Father is waiting on the world to conform to His righteousness, but He will not wait forever. This pleads the contrast between what is meant by 'forever' and what is meant by 'eternity.' Forever implies that something is still being awaited. Eternity means that it has already come. Yes, the complete obliteration of the diabolical construct is based on the premise that humanity must participate. This is why Jesus founded the Church – His Arm and Body within the exiled realms, to finish the work that He set out to do. To say that there is something afoot does not suffice the description of what the mission of the Church is about. And, in order for someone to escape from captivity, they must first try the door to make sure it is locked. These are among the thoughts that Christians harbor. It is about what capacity rests in the hands of men to break past every barrier they could possibly conceive – the ultimate, of course, is being temporarily bound to the flesh. My Special son, you have been proofreading your own writing for your next book, and one might say that your writing there is one of the facets of the face of the key. You and your brother have gone many times to have a key made from another one bearing its likeness. Is this not what Jesus asks of all His disciples? It is the same principle as lighting one candle off another. This replication is what the imitation of Jesus is about. Spreading the Good News, sparing the innocent, and all the other things that exemplify the Spiritual and Corporal Works of Mercy are indicative of the replication of the key. Here, the idea of redesigning does not apply because there is only one Kingdom. Your acts in Jesus' name are replications because you are reenacting as a spiritual reflection His carrying of the Cross. Your gifts and sacrifices are examples of His beatific conformity, although you shall never die on the Cross to redeem the world. This is the origin of the passage where Jesus bids His flock to take up their crosses and follow Him. It is a replication of His Good Friday suffering. Hence, since it seems to humanity as though the old Earth will go on forever, it is instead being transformed into eternity with each passing day. What this means in absolute terms is that the obliteration of the diabolical construct is happening as we speak; at every moment, at each sunrise, and throughout the exhausting of the decades and ages. Jesus annihilated Satan's power on the Cross, and He has handed humanity the authority to execute it for Him. My Special and Chosen sons, I wish for you to think about what I have said thus far today regarding what impacts your consciousness every day. Is there enough evidence to prove that the complete obliteration of the diabolical construct is happening right now? No, not at all. And, this is because the mission of the Church is being obscured by everything that opposes it, and some members of the Church are damaging the Church itself at the same time. Jesus said that Hell and nothing derived from it would prevail against His Church, but He did not say how misguided its self-professed members would become. More simply, the lack of faith of humankind is the greatest stumbling block to the eradication of evil in the world today. Some people argue that God is waiting to destroy every evil act on Earth in the same way that I have said that you might wish to fire all your weapons at once. But, this is not true when it comes to the eradication of the diabolical legions around the globe. Shooting offensively is not the same as sustaining oneself defensively. When God says that He wishes humanity to destroy evil in one righteous swoop, He means that He wants every creature in the world to fall to his knees before the Cross and implore Jesus to come back. This is man's best defense against evil on the Earth. Since this has not yet occurred, there is a systematic attack against the diabolical construct that has been ongoing since Jesus' Ascension into Heaven. Hour by hour, day by day, and so forth. My little sons, this is why time keeps going on. Humanity refuses to participate. There is a term that is used to describe the power of persuasion that Jesus employed during His Passion and Death. It is 'writ large.' This means plain and obvious. Witnessing the Only Son of God being crucified is as plain and obvious as any man will ever see. There is no vagueness. It is black and white; it is about truth versus lies, light conquering the darkness, and life prevailing over death. My Special son, do you understand what I came to say today? *"Yes. Thank you."* It is a topic about which you can extrapolate many things in the world today. And, at the same time, it can be captured in a single phrase that you use on a common basis – 'do the right thing.' There is a building up of human righteousness in your time on Earth that echoes the mission of the early Church. It is like a volcano from the first century building ferocity over the centuries, that might erupt at the dawn of any new day. The Lord God is anticipating that His Church will see that the Gospel is fulfilled, just as Jesus said. It is not that new life will come from that eruption because Jesus' Sacrifice on the Cross and Easter Resurrection have already secured that gift. It is that this eruption of the ages will awaken humanity to the mandate given them by Jesus to participate in the obliteration of the diabolical construct. And, this is where your quotation from the beginning of our message this morning comes in. The authenticity of one's faith must be attuned to the eternal veracity that the Holy Spirit instills within the human heart. It is about truth and justice, and it hails from humility and servitude. These things stoke the fiery flames inside the volcano of the ages that I have mentioned here today. I am not saying, My Special son, that this is not already happening. I am saying that humanity is blocking its own view of the process by its propensity to sin. It is like placing a bushel basket over a light. It is closing one's eyes when he has perfect vision. And, this is how a world can grow stale in which everything that is right seems wrong, and everything wrong is believed to be right. As Jesus said, the world is upside down. God the Father has handed humanity the tools to remake the structure of the Earth, but sinful men are on their knees trying to wipe a broken egg off the floor with a maple leaf. It cannot be done. There is no unrealized potential within exiled humanity that cannot be reached through the faith handed down by God. And, this is what we pray for; it is the means to merit the complete obliteration of the diabolical construct in your day.

My Special son, I ask that you and your brother do not have hard feelings against sinners who do not yet know Jesus, or Me as their Mother. For most of the world, it is not so much a rejection of the Divine as that they have not yet been told. They do not know what they do not know. *"I don't expect them to know or understand what you've taught us, but I expect them to do right by what every person knows inherently to be honest and true, such as abortion is murder."* This is well explained, My Special son, but most all who are either receiving or performing abortions have already been informed. This is not the group that I mentioned before your comment. As for the individuals you just spoke about, you have every right to be resentful toward what they do and say. You are in accord with what Jesus has taught the Church throughout the ages. Your witness is with Him in everything you have done, said and written. I ask you to believe that your work here with your brother is among the greatest offensive weapons toward obliterating the diabolical construct since the Scriptures, themselves. *"I believe that, I believe it is your greatest revelation, and I thank you."* I am speaking about the messaging of the Crucifixion of Jesus on the Cross when I speak about the Scriptures and the Morning Star Over America body of work. The true and real annihilation of evil itself was accomplished by Jesus' suffering and death on the Cross. So, as human beings, we arrive at conclusions that are formed by personal and social circumstances – Me from My purview in Heaven, and you from your vantage point on Earth. This does not imply that you cannot reach the same conclusions that the Saints in Heaven have drawn. You have prepared yourself for this enlightenment because you have spent the past several decades at My side. The world back then was far different from the one you know now, but the obstructions and distractions are much the same. The obliteration of the diabolical construct remains on course because the fruits of your life with your brother have been placed into being. There is no reason why the two of you should not greet each new morning with peace and jubilation, knowing that this has been done. *"I have joy for our work, and what it means. It's the mechanical subscription to the treadmill of materialism and secularism to maintain ourselves that is the burden."* My Special son, you see the reason for cloistered societies around the globe – the convents and monasteries. I wish to reassure you that I am with you in every way you will ever require. Jesus is with you, and the Father is with you. The Holy Spirit thrives within you. I ask you to remember what a gift you are to humanity, and the effect that this new book will have on converting lost sinners."

Saturday, May 13, 2017
100th Anniversary of Fatima
9:40 a.m.

"To some men, human exile is an ill-defined affliction that has nothing to do with daily life, no place in the human psyche. But to Christians, it is the begetting of the march toward love, peace, tenacity, reflection and redemption – and always and everywhere, true goodness."

- The Dominion Angels

"Yes, My dear little sons, I speak here in the precincts of the Earth to a Church that is basking in Jesus' Divine Light. I speak to a world that has been lost, but has now been found. I speak to those who will not listen, even though they can hear. And, I still speak of the same Russia about which the United States is concerned ten decades later. My children, I come into this home because it is lovely here. I take comfort in your presence. I adore your devotion to the Church. I cherish your consecration to My Most Immaculate Heart. And most of all, I offer My gratitude for honoring the Sacrifice of My Son as expiation for human sin. There are ten billion messages that I could give you on this day – all the lessons and teachings fit for humanity that yields so stubbornly to change. I could tell you that evil legions are gobbling up your neighborhoods like vultures. And, all of it would be true. However, that will be My focus for another day. For this day, I wish to tell you that My reflections are as dimensioned as those who recall My appearances in Portugal 100 years ago. This was Jesus' gift to a world in peril. My messages of Fatima are not so much different from My warnings today. And, this is appropriate for the measures of the Earth that have yet to be taken. My messages in Fatima have been imperative and important in defining My role in the salvation of humanity. Unbelievers who do not belong to the Catholic Church fail to understand God's Will. I have spoken about being seated perpendicular to something, and as such, seeing with a perfect angle what the Father asks you to see. Those who do not belong to the Roman Catholic Church are outside this vision. They have a skewed perception of what the Cross really means. Yes, it means that there are Seven Sacraments beholding its Fruits. It means that there is misalignment in those who cannot bring themselves to join the Original Apostles in the propagation of the faith. Hence, when I speak about the Truth of Christianity, I am speaking about humanity acknowledging the exile of men in the world and on the Earth. This is the preparation of God's creatures as much as the gifts are prepared for the Holy Sacrifice of the Mass. My Special son, you and your brother are seeing the continued development of your most recent book that will be published this year. There is no reason to rush this event – you have many more weeks and months to work on it, if you choose. It is not a coincidence that The Final Colossus will be published during the 100-year anniversary of Fatima. You have seen these signs and wonders all throughout your life with Me, just as I promised the pilgrims in Medjugorje. Why? Because I mean what I say when speaking to humanity in exile. Indeed, this is the furtherance of the love, peace, tenacity, reflection, redemption, true goodness and everything else the Angels charge to be true about the people of the Lord. And, this is the reason My message today is not about the dangers that will come to those who disbelieve and disobey. These things will become self-evident to them in the years ahead. My Special son, you and your brother have arrived at an awakening that is unknown to many. You have come to Me with your hearts wide open and your hands folded in prayer, ready for My intercessory messages, willing to record them, and prepared for the backlash of the unwary world. You will be Saints someday, and this makes you spiritual martyrs as well. What is your pain? That the world is not tendering their hearts to Me. They ignore and scoff at My messages in the same way that they rejected Jesus, the Word. This is the fulfillment of the Scriptures without which no one can be saved. It is the denying of the Crucifixion as a common practice. But, it is not just with sadness that I mark the indifference of man as much as it is disappointment. If the conversion of lost sinners could ever be described as a framework, it is within this framework that the identity of man is meant to be found. There is righteousness abounding in defining this framework, and certainly a light so bright that it casts shadows into the deepest voids of outer-space. It is the making of the human heart into righteousness, and the summons of the conscience to a new way of life. None of this can happen in a world without sacrifice – the denial of the self, and the avoidance of the comforts and privileges that are only lent to euphemizing mortal life. My prayer is always that My children will see as I see.

My children, conversion is about communication. It is about tendering the spirit of the soul to the message of redemption that is found in the Gospel. Your whole lives have been rooted in this message. You are fruits of the Word of God. You are sons of His wisdom, like the Sons of Thunder. You sit and stand where His loveliness goes. You breathe-in His glorious love. These are among the meanings that I transferred to the world in 1917, the same Mother, the same person who is speaking to you now. Time has no effect on Me, and it has no effect on the eternity of your souls. This is why Jesus has asked through the ages that His disciples be sown to the Spirit and not the flesh. My Special son, I will tell you what I would say to those who refuse to believe Me. My attestation is that, someday, a Man will stand before them. He will be delightfully awesome and striking to behold. And, as I have said on prior occasions, He will speak about wanting something. He will solicit a confession from every penitent, and He will look for conversion from the lost. He will listen for repentance from the tongues of those who have rejected Him. He will demand remorse from those who persecuted His Church. He will look with pity on those who have been downtrodden. And yes, He will hand over those who espouse the evils of the devil to the death they deserve. This is the truth of the framework that I have spoken about today. This is not a message about warnings and prophecies that may not come to pass. I have spoken this morning about the undeniable facts that have been laid out in the Bible. Jesus is the Merciful Messiah for whom humankind should seek, but He is also the Divine Magistrate who will sentence His enemies to their fate in the flaming abyss. What must happen is that a tremendous flash of light must occur within the consciousness of the world. Every man, woman and child must sense the justice of the Lord descending upon their beings. Yes, something like the sun plummeting to the Earth to dry up the rains and make those who have seen it awaken from their slumber. Even after the passing of 100 years, I still believe that this is an appropriate sign. Millions of souls have been converted and redeemed as a gift of My appearances at Fatima, Portugal from May to October, 1917. And, the Medjugorje Queen of Peace and the Morning Star Over America will usher the remainder of God's children to the foot of the Cross. I am there waiting for them. I come with all the stately elegance about which any world could dream. I hold high the Cross of the Lord. There will be no other lady standing before them – for I am the Final Colossus! My Special son, the poem that you transcribed with the assistance of the Angels reflects the brilliance that enshrines before the world My role in their salvation. How can I thank you? It is nearly unimaginable that I could place into words the sufficiency of My gratitude. So, I will close this morning with a reminder that you and your brother are holding fast to that great destiny of glory that I have mentioned many times before. Thank you for remembering Me on this special anniversary of My Fatima appearances. It is revealing before humanity that you have devoted your lives to continuing My mission. You have been blessed in ways that you are unable to fathom."

Saturday, May 20, 2017
9:31 a.m.

"The superimposition of the ancient truth."

"Here, My dear little sons, you have found on this day another installment of your reason for living – to glorify God through the essence of your faith. You are completed in His grace and reasoned to be Saints because of your sacred love for Jesus. Today, I have come to tell you about the superimposition of the ancient truth into the created realms because you are truthfully part of that superimposition. Outside the parameters of time, you were born with Jesus. You were given to Me by the Holy Spirit, and your faith is a fruit of My Womb. Also, you will remember this day because the Angels completed their help of your brother in proofreading My messages from AD 2010 through AD 2012. Since this series of messages includes 2010, the Angels completed setting their hand on that year today, May 20, 2017. It is the seventh anniversary of the arrival of your friend Michael into Heaven. Yes, it is the intercession of the Church Triumphant that has been your strength and fortitude, given to them by Jesus on the Cross and raised from the dead. The first words spoken to Moses were representative of the superimposition of the ancient truth in the world because it is where God touched the exiled realms with His eternal knowledge. My Special son, millions of souls throughout the ages have asked why God would create two people – Adam and Eve – who would thereafter sin. The answer is that the Father had nothing to do with their sin. They did this on their own because He gave them free will. So, the Creation story and the whole of the Salvation story became one at the moment God said it shall be done. Creating and redeeming are the hallmarks of the Father's Triune Love. Unfortunately, sinning and lack of repentance are the nature of fallen humanity. You must remember that Adam and Eve fell from the Garden of Paradise under the weight of their own sin. God did not banish two innocent people into the darkness. And, is it not therefore fitting that the Father would provide a framework through which Adam and Eve, and all who would follow them, could embrace through their own repentance the gift of redemption? God is therefore the Creator, and Jesus the Son is the Redeemer. It would follow that something cannot be saved unless it has been created. To say that something is fashioned into being means that it has been created with distinguishing features. To create man in the likeness of his Creator is the ultimate gift of liberty. The apt reciprocity is that redeemed-humanity should wish to emulate the righteousness of the Creator who gave them life. If there is a circle of life that began in the Garden, this must surely be it. And, as you know, what has happened during the centuries is what your lives and My messages are all about. My Special son, what God accomplished through Moses laid the foundation for the Greatest Superimposition in the history of any world – the Birth of Jesus Christ. This means that an unseen God with a spiritual essence took upon Himself the Flesh of His own Son and came to live among His people. Why? Because He wished to reveal to the world what it is like to be sinless. There is no unknowable secret in this. I am not telling you anything new. But, what I am saying is that the superimposition of the Creator into the realms of the created introduces a New Liberation into the land of the condemned. With Jesus came all the absolution that humanity would ever need – not mathematical formulas or complex equations – but the simple veracity of forgiveness that fulfills the Will of the Father. God in all His genius wanted humanity to come back to Him. This was the origin of the maxim that says if you love someone, set them free. If they come back, their love is authentic. And, this can only be done if the object of love has its own will, its own volition to choose the beginning over all endless sequels. God in His awesome wonder decided to write a story about a prodigal Creation that found its way back to Him through the mysteries of His own suffering. This is where the circle began. And, My Special son, you know that the Father has the capacity to think in linear terms and timelessly universal. Imagine, and remember, that God in Heaven does not require any sleep. 'Give them all the gifts that I have at My dominion.' This is what He was thinking upon the retrieval of Adam and Eve. My dear little sons, God has given humanity the ability to dream with Him. It is imbedded in the existence of men. It is given to all who imagine how great in the lineage of the Saints exiled humanity can be. These are the dreams of the lovely, the humble, the pure, and the deserving. But, who is willing to sleep unless they become tired? This is the question that the Father asks. What would make His people believe that sleep should belong to them? The answer is found in the divine quest to find Him again. It is in this marvel that humanity claims its perfect labors, its reason to be spent during the years of life, of designing and building a world that welcomes His Kingdom as its eternal core. When someone sleeps after accomplishing this task, it is a wondrous sleep – and these are true and delightful dreams. And, they are followed by a kind awakening in the embrace of God whose holiness shall never die.

My Special son, this is the superimposition of the ancient truth into the human consciousness. And, it is the permeation of God's wisdom into the minds of men. You and your brother have already reached this sacred plateau.

When someone speaks of whatever is lovely, whatever is pure and excellent, they are speaking about the spiritual domain where you and your brother live. You are joined there by all who have achieved your same holiness, your knowledge about the purpose and future of life on Earth. You have filled your own voids with the loveliness of Heaven. In Jesus, you have gained your identities through which your volition has been given to God. Yes, this is the circle within the circle, your concentric presence in Creation and beyond its measurable bounds. If Saint Thomas Aquinas had within him the ability to connect cognitive reason and Divine Wisdom, then you and your brother have the capacity to live with transcendental awareness in this world and the next. You are connected to the Afterlife through your faith in Jesus and your devotion to Me. This is what makes your lives and works so miraculous to humanity. I have given you signs that cannot be explained on the floor of the United States Senate. They cannot be hidden in the bottom of a well. They cannot be cast aside by con artists or devil's advocates. No amount of wealth on this planet could purchase the power you have gained through the Holy Spirit to tear down the walls of humanity's pride. And, you are humble in all this. Your existence in this world is of the same superimposition that the Lord ordained when He was born in the Bethlehem night. God placed a star before men – you have known this your entire life. And, we shall see the impact that this Morning Star has on leading the world to the Holy Cross instead of the dark neighborhoods of sin and death. As you can tell from My message this morning, I have tremendous hope that it will succeed. I would not be speaking about it otherwise, but I would be here nonetheless. My Special son, I lack the words to tell you what you and your brother have meant to Me during your years in this world. I suppose I could ask you to take a look at the grand new book that you are about to publish. Who would have guessed that this miracle would become such a matter of routine for you? The entire world is waiting to receive from us something they all want, but getting them to realize it is the task at hand. I promise, My Special son, that humanity is unsuspecting when it comes to your work and its future. But, soon all humankind will be called to silence like a vast performance hall, waiting for the artists to appear on the stage. There will be building up an air of anticipation for what God will do next. The sounds of 'shhhh' will hover from all corners of the globe to silence the commotion in near and distant quarters. Your soul will tell you that this is happening. You will all know – the whole of humanity will be aware. *"Thank you, Mama."*

Saturday, May 27, 2017
9:41 a.m.

"Making the transition from benign voice to outward action. What can be done when someone fails to recognize, refuses to listen, will not understand, rejects reason, embraces duplicity, and impugns honor?"

"A Savior being the Second Person of the Eternal Trinity implies that the human will existed from that same eternity before the incarnation of men in the flesh."

"The Honor of God"

"My dear little sons, the answer to the question that opens this message is that you should approach lost sinners with dignity, with calmness and patience, with reflection and stateliness. When righteousness is presented to the unrighteous in a confident manner, the soul of the one you approach will wish to emulate your confidence. For those whose final destiny is Heaven, this is the way you should react to them. There is no question that nearly everything mentioned in the opening statement today is a product of pride. And, a reason for pride is found in the narcissistic disorder. You are living in a nation where the emphasis on the self is being magnified. This is the will of men over the Will of God. My Special son, of all the behaviors mentioned today, the most ghastly is that someone would stoop to impugning honor. Why? Because honor is the antidote for all the rest. The absence of honor kills children in the womb. Its absence is the basis for the corruption of humanity. It is honorable to love God, to pray for His intervention, to approach Him in repentance, to appeal to His Mercy, to liken your lives unto His grace, and to seek in Him everything that will make the human person perfect. Yes, this is sacred honor. It is what you have lived for, you and your brother. It is what you have called for from America's youth and their fathers. It is what you and your brother have designed into your lives from whence you were old enough to know. Embracing honor means listening, observing, understanding, and obeying. Hence, faith, hope and charity are centered in honor, and honor is endemic to them. You belong to an honorable Church that has been fashioned by the Honor of God. You have built an 'Honor of God Cathedral' here in your home, constant in your hearts, widely spread, and dutifully celebrated. It is not wrong to believe that a nation should be founded on this same honor because it predisposes its citizens to the dignity of the holy life. And, it brings to mind the reason for giving oneself to those who have nothing of their own. My dear sons, we pray that all nations inherit these ideals from our prayers, even as they may not yet know their origin. When you hear the ticking away of the hours, remember that the Father is ushering the world into the presence of His Honor, knowing that those who love Him will respond. (*Our Lady then began a conversation with me (so I would better understand) about our conception and incarnation in the flesh and the origin of the will. She spoke about the stature of Adam and Eve, the battle that broke out in Heaven between Saint Michael and the devil, and between the serpent and the first woman, and between the serpent and the New Eve.*)

So, what is My purpose in broaching the topic? So you can have a better insight as to the effects of honor. My Special son, honor is not something that is solely concealed within the mind. It is the taking back of goodness from where it has been stolen. It is shedding one's blood to advance the Lord's Kingdom. It is rebuking the doubters who refuse to believe. It is lighting a candle in the darkness. Yes, sacred honor. It is knowing why there is life, where it exists, what its fruits are, and where it is going. It is realizing before one's birth the difference between right and wrong. So now, I will tell you even more. (*Our Lady then continued Her first discussion by describing those who "will to live" compared to those who "will to die" through unrepentant sin.*) My Special son, we have now made the circle complete. Does it not make perfect sense thereafter that the Son of Man, a sinless Creature, would be placed in the Womb of the Mother of God, another sinless Creature? "*Yes.*" This is the balance of Creation-renewed. An Old Adam, a New Adam. An Old Eve, a New Eve. A Death and a Resurrection. After a while, the entire framework makes sense when seen by humanity from the perspective of God. These are tremendous Sacred Mysteries, and the whole design is based on Divine Providence. My little son, it is all about humanity deferring to the Will of God. After the salutation, what is the first thing petitioned in the Our Father prayer? 'Thy Kingdom come.' This is the summons of exiled men to God to inhabit the earthly domain. It is the recognition by believers that the world is an insubstantial place. And, it is also the confession by the Church that one key compliance must be accorded. By what action will this Kingdom come? It is found in the next line of the Our Father. 'Thy Will be done.' And where? On Earth and in Heaven. So My message this morning is in fact not so much about darkness and disobedience as it is about hope."

Sunday, June 4, 2017
9:44 a.m.

"These two visionaries have recorded a celebration of redemptive genius that is so humanely dynamic that it defies the capacity to understand, a sublime annotation and utter miracle from the vast empyreal domain."

- The Dominion Angels

"My sacred little sons, what could the Mother of Jesus Christ say to two Christian disciples that the Holy Spirit has not already made known? It means that you and the Father have nearly said it all, that there are some things that go without saying. You will someday see that your work for Jesus and your lives for God have been of the highest beatific order; and that all the rest, the societies you have known, the just-wars waged and peace accords signed, the excesses of the secular domain, and your relationships with other people and institutions have only been collateral things. I ask that you view your lives as if looking at a profile of yourselves. You are capable of envisioning the highest peaks and deepest valleys from the side, and you are able to see the summits of your dreams in the way the Father has known them. My little sons, I invite you to remember that the Holy Spirit of God forms and acts on His own behalf from within you. Everything that emerges from your essential being is a remnant of the ancient grace that was instilled in you upon your baptism. Your trust, faith and propensities are products of this grace. What you see of yourselves during your prayers and meditations is part of your recognition that God is greater than this world. All of your work, every fiber of your lives, has been devoted to the advancement of the message of the Cross. There is something for all men that is as triumphant as eternal sainthood; it is one's unity with Jesus. Even as you have yet to die and part from the confines of the flesh, you have been consumed by the Spirit of Jesus, and He has reciprocally taken you in. This is a unity that can come through nowhere else but His Crucifixion and Resurrection from the Tomb. This is the glorious canonization of your souls into the realms of Paradise. It is your deliverance from this world into the next, even before you shall surrender your bodies unto death. What the Dominion Angels have spoken about today barely touches the surface of what your lives mean to God. There are no words that are sufficient; none can capture the power; few can scarcely come close to identifying the imaginings to which your lives have been destined. So here, on this auspicious day and lovely hour; here where I have dictated to you so many holy messages,

I thank you for your love. *"Thank you, Mama."* It is more than a miracle you have given the world, it is a monumental blessing that is awakening mankind from their sleep. It is one of the history-makers for which Jesus has always wept. It is proof that His divine legacy is living within you now. My Special son, I would like to address your work with your brother. It has the power and elegance to fulfill every expectation that might not have come by any other means. When the Angels speak of a celebration of love, life and commitment, these are deeply imbedded in what you and your brother have done. In fact, you will see that it contains so much love and obedience that it yields even more graces for the Church, enough to suffice the gladness of God. You have known that there are many passions within His Kingdom, all based on His eternal wisdom. You and your brother's writings represent these fruits from His Kingdom, and you will find yourself rightly honored there. What I am saying this morning is that many other worlds could have come, but the most perfect is that which the Father has given you here, the one where you live, and where you have knelt to pray. It is the world where you have become invested in the human experience by donning mortality yourselves. It is the world in which God finds you poeting the sonnets of His own sacred glory. Yes, realms and dimensions where you have found Him the reason for life and the Earth itself. All of this is contained in what you and your brother have done. It is not water-treading flippancy or casual happenstance. It is not transient or a cause of strike and run. It is the perpetuity of God laid in the palms of your hands, what He expects and solicits from Creation, what it would look like if only He were worshiped in every precinct like you do in your hearts, and what joy He takes from the sacred dynamics of His disciples' good faith.

My Special son, the world will see in your writing that human life is more than a metaphor. It is greater than the sum of all acts and promises between every new day's rising sun. The symbolism of the way humanity conducts its affairs is relevant to the Father because all acts of faith are emblematic of the world's trust in Him. You reveal this kind of symbolism in your writing. In its own right, it is reflective of the charities of the Gospel in defining what it means to behold the Cross. This symbolism affirms what the human heart knows – that Heaven on Earth consists of remembering that providence lives in humanity's obedience to God. The world will behold in your writings My Fiat to the Archangel Gabriel. They will recognize the courage of Jesus as He faced His execution. And, not only that, they will discover the hopes for eternity that humanity has forgotten to seek. My Special son, what you and your brother have written gives Me so much confidence in the Church's prayers that there is no way that evil could possibly go on. Why? Because it is about the two of you. Yes, you and your beauty, innocence and kindness. You have handed a gift to Jesus who finds His Spirit living so comfortably in the safeguard of your hearts. You are whom the Son of Man has sought from the Church on Earth. Is it possible for two Christian companions to be as humble as you? Can it be true that your modesty will not permit you to envision the miracle that you have set onto the page? I ask you these questions only because I pray that Jesus helps you understand what you mean to Him. You feel My Son deep within your hearts because the Holy Spirit is communing with you there. This is reflective of My prayers for the whole of humanity. The gift of the faith of two visionaries can be the touch that heals the entire universe. My Special son, these seers are you. Whether your self-impressions might coax you to believe otherwise is not relevant here. We are much the same, you and I. There came a time when I found Myself old enough to realize who I was, why I was born, and why God had chosen Me. It did not take Me long to understand the reasons because His decisions are always based on those whom He believes love Him the most. This is the same reason you are sitting here today, reciting your deferential prayers, receiving My words, hoping for the conversion of the wicked, waiting as I waited with love in your heart that what we have done will succeed. It would seem that you do not have the capacity to elevate yourself before other men, but I beseech you to make an exception when you think of your work for Me. I have the gift of blessing the world every time we speak, each time I receive a prayer into My arms, whenever the Consecration of the Sacred Body and Blood of Jesus is lent to His Altar in Heaven, and as the Earth's passing ages take their toll. Being the Mother of God is about teaching prudence to those who must judge in God's favor. I inspire the rightness of the spirit when choosing between the right and the wrong. I offer chasteness of the heart to those who might turn another way. My Special son, I am living proof that humility, fairness and chastity are more appealing than anything to the contrary. I am the Lady of Light who has annihilated the prince of darkness. I have given humanity reason to hope in the sanctification of their souls. Yes, My Special son, it is all about lifting up the truth. It is about the grand procession toward the fulfillment of life's meaning according to Jesus' teachings on the Earth. It is not just His legacy that matters, but how His legacy flourishes in those who believe in Him. Here again, My Special son, this is who you are. It is about claiming for Jesus everything that He has summoned from those willing to suffer in communion with the Cross. We pray for these things because we have a stake in them. We are obedient to the Most Blessed Trinity because we belong to the Father's Church. Our mission here in this world, My Special son, has always been about feeding and nurturing the lost, and enlightening and leading, uplifting and delivering. Our lives are this important to Jesus, and it is about intention and outcome. This too, you will find in metaphoric strains imbedded in your writing. Sacred overtones can be found anywhere the Holy Spirit is invited to speak. This is what makes your love for Jesus so profound. It is the making of your heart into a Messianic shrine. It is where the loveliness of God takes its most essential form. And, it is where I choose to come not just to offer My messages here, but to gain comfort from you in return. This is My message for this morning, My dear sons. It is what I have always wanted to say about what you have meant to Me and the Eternal Kingdom that is clearly yours. In the meantime, I urge you to remember that the sun rises and rests on your lives of Christian love."

Saturday, June 10, 2017
9:27 a.m.

"Arise dear brothers and sisters, morning has broken! On this new day, Providence gives you truth excelling, love ascending, exuberance for the heart, vindication for the soul, hope for tomorrow, grace for the journey, Salvation abounding, and a Church Triumphant 80 billion strong. Humanity has been summoned by the Father to assemble into a new beatific beginning."

- The Dominion Angels

"My little sons, will the words that I share with you this morning be sufficient to express to you how I truly feel? Perhaps. Is your touch of dignity found in Jesus on the Cross sufficient to lend your spirits to His most sacred love? Most definitely. Why? Because redemption is much more than the touch of dignity that most Christians actually believe. It is the whole and everlasting transformation of your identity, and the transfer of your soul into the heights of Heaven. My Special son, please know that I will speak to you and your brother today anyway, despite the inability of My words to convey the magnitude of My love. The Dominion Angels have given you and your brother an eloquent preface for My message today that offers a glimpse into this transformation. While I realize that you are already aware of this transformation, I am pleased to defer to the Angels and allow them to offer you their passage because they love you so much. The word 'beginning' at the close of their passage could easily be changed to 'song' because all who accept Jesus on the Cross are complementing and continuing to write the melody that He composed on Good Friday. There is sacredness everywhere you look and walk because, through your obedience to Me, you have paved a new way of life for millions of sinners. If you think about the word 'obedience,' it implies that someone is doing something that they would not otherwise do, as if a concession is being made. When you and your brother comply with My wishes, however, it is not because you would rather do something else. In simpler terms, some people are obedient without having to suffer the consequences if they do not. Indeed, with rare exceptions, there is no such thing as forced compliance in the New Covenant Gospel. In former ages, a man being swallowed by a whale might have been one. And, it is more clear to you now than it was thirty years ago; the will of men is a matter that the Father never takes for granted. Rather than say to humanity, '...get into this Kingdom!' – He invites all who would find deliverance from eternal death to secure their Salvation in Jesus. This, as you know, is a blessing that has been written into the Gospel, but even those chapters are insufficient to stir some men to respond. It requires the miracle of faith, and belief in miracles themselves, to move the human heart to conversion. It is clear as well that you and your brother may not be able to recognize the giantness of your service to the Lord. Yes, you can see it in your new book about to be published. But even there, you are unable to appreciate on an eternal basis what this means to God. I have never seen anyone other than you and your brother who can paint so articulately the spiritual picture of human conversion with such detailed intricacy. And yet, you can obliterate the ignorance of centuries of human thought within the breadth of a single manuscript. It is the classic metaphor of focusing a telescope inward and outward until you find the clearest vision of humanity's potential. I ask that you hold in your hearts the grandest expectations for what you have accomplished together through Me. My Special son, you and your brother should understand that I invite My children deep into My Most Immaculate Heart. This is the reason Jesus wants His brothers and sisters to be free from sin. It is as though the Holy Spirit is at the doorway of My Heart, reminding the people of Earth to go to confession before seeking My intercession. Taking off one's shoes before entering the house means that no one should approach the Mother of God without some intention of changing his life and working toward the sanctification of the self. This is one of the greatest fruits of the conversion experience. It is the reorientation of the heart to the Kingdom that is eclipsing the world. I am not saying that the Will of God is trying to impede the free will of His people, but that the will of His people will find in Him their new reason for life. When someone finds himself living deep within the Sacred Heart of Jesus, the idea of

'I don't know' slips from their consciousness. An entire bay of answers becomes available to those who give themselves to Jesus on the Cross. At its core, those who profess their faith can no longer claim that they do not know about self-sacrifice, but they may not understand all the reasons why. This is another purpose of the service of faith, and it is also where faith is most commonly tested. Prayer is the origin of all sacred knowledge. This is the means through which eternal wisdom nourishes the awareness of those who believe in God. The task for those living with faith is not to reconcile what God wants from the Church in the same way they might approach the issues of the world, but sanctifying themselves in such a way that the dichotomy no longer exists. Complete unity with the Most Blessed Trinity implies that the human heart is thrice consecrated to the Will of the Father.

So today, My Special son, I remind you that you and your brother live a grand and wonderful life through the Glory of God. Your lives touch the Father in such a way that brings Him infinity joy. Your beauty, sacredness, kindness and ethereal piety bring jubilation to Jesus in Heaven. No place in the world have these things been better exemplified than by your lives. Let Me be clear. I once told you that you will in Heaven be able to live the sweetest moments of life again. I wish to add to this promise that you will also live those moments that you wished had come. Truly, you will in your redeemed loveliness be able to recreate the world, and as many other worlds as you desire. And, in these worlds, you can choose what transpires. You can decide their purposes and outcomes. So, I wish you to feel righteously justified. Most of all, it is a prayer to the Father's genius. It will bear the fruits of your petitions as you have raised them. If the world would extol and embrace holy love in the way you and your brother have personified it, broken humanity would be healed. Why? Because your lives are a celebration of God's beatific promise. You hail the presence of innocence and charity that gives glory to the Father in every conceivable way. My Special son, in your new book, the world will be able to see the eternal dimensions of what your life with your brother has been about for the past 28 years. This book is different from those that constitute your initial Morning Star deposit of works. I am not saying that it is better, but it takes on another dimension of the mission that you have accomplished for Me. This is a great gift to Me from Jesus through the Father in Heaven. And, it is also a great gift to you and your brother. "*Thank you.*" Recognize your holiness, and celebrate it! It is a universal prayer to the Father's creative passion to bless humanity once again. Your love for Me is a reflection of your love for Jesus. Your prayers, labors and contributions are more than any two humble boys should be capable of offering. The fruits of your lives are sweet to the palate of the Lord."

Sunday, June 18, 2017
Saint Delbert Dayton Whitehurst Jr. 1950-2016
9:36 a.m.

"The Lord did not approach Saul to destroy him, but to convert him to the faith. Jesus did not ask Saul why he was persecuting his disciples, but why he was persecuting Him. It was a sacred reproval that echoes to this day. Saul took no effort to defend himself. By the Light of God, he was blinded to the world he knew, and given sight for the Kingdom to come."

- The Dominion Angels

An excerpt from the Wisdom of the Ages –
The demonstrative substance of beatific inquiry.

"My dear little sons, I told you recently that there were no words to describe the intensity of My love for you, but this will not prohibit Me from trying. I come today in the fullness of Grace because the Father has sent Me. Yes, He does so because I ask Him, and your entire lives with Me have been His response. When He opened the door, you both walked through. This is His summons to the whole world – that humanity will reach for His hand in the Person of Jesus Christ. Everyone knows the story of Saint Paul. It is one of miracles, a life that was changed because God needed Him in the plan of human conversion. Could this have been a man who might have asked the executioners to make the Crucifixion even more grotesque? Most likely so. My Special son, eventually, it could be said that everyone on Earth who does not find themselves deep inside Jesus' Holy Sacrifice is on the road to Damascus. It is with such irony that the Jewish people and others tell the world that they are praying for the Father's sacred knowledge. If they acted upon the response they receive, they would be more Christian than Jewish. This is why we pray for all the Jewish people, and for all others who are not yet in communion with the Church. It is also fitting that they receive the intercession of Saint Delbert Dayton Whitehurst who had the blessing of the Lord when he surrendered his soul for eternal rest. My Special son, Delbert is still celebrating in Heaven with us, and I wish to tell you about part of his arrival testimony. He said upon being escorted by the Angels into the Father's presence that his greatest blessing in his earthly life was to know you. This is the way of all who are open to your friendship, who are receptive to the wisdom you have imparted during the years. Perhaps there will be a time when your friend will speak to you and tell you himself before you join the Communion of Saints in Heaven. Today, I wish to speak about the true conversion that must come to all who inherit the blessing of faith. There is no question that Saint Paul is one of humanity's greatest exemplars. The lessons and teachings that he handed the world, the fruits of His charismatic mission, and His letters in the Sacred Scriptures do not even pierce the surface of what he accomplished on behalf of Jesus on the Cross. There is an overarching sanctity that spreads from the very identity of people like Saint Paul, bathing the Earth in the same light that blinded him during his journey on the road. This is the Good Light of God. It is the origin of one's awakening; it is the igniting of enlightenment, it is the dispensing of the truth to those who live far from justice. I have told you that blessings and miracles do not come in gallons or tonnage, but if they did, the massive superstructure that you and your brother are getting ready to publish would be immovable by any man or other world. If you do not mind, your friend and mentor Saint Paul would like to scrawl his signature on your manuscript that will be visible to all who believe. "*Thank you. I would be honored.*" It is not that you were halted on any road to change your way of life because you did not have to be forced to give your soul to the Church and the Kingdom of the Lord in this world. Your faith came naturally. You were born; you discovered that you are a human being, and you thereafter began searching for the Father who gave you life. This is a journey in itself; you have been on the journey to your sainthood in the Father by walking with Jesus all the days since. My Special child, how can I express what this means for exiled humanity? It seems clear to you because of who you are. But, what about all those whom we have tried to reach for the past 28 years? We will reach them! Everything you have already accomplished is enough. Indeed, the book you are preparing to publish is beyond what is necessary to convert the souls I came to inspire. I have said that you and your brother are in alliance with the Medjugorje seers in multitudes of ways. Even they prayed and implored Me to continue speaking to them in the sacred hills where My messages were meant to last fewer years. Imagine how God feels about such inspiration from His faith-filled children on the Earth? 'Please don't go!' is a prayer that says, 'Please convert everyone to the Blood of the Cross!' The human heart is capable of this type of translation because the journey and the destiny are one and the same love. The center of the heart is not only the touchstone of the spiritual universe, it is the nucleus of all the cosmic universes combined. Everything good that finds itself a part of Creation is concentrically connected within the core of the human heart.

My Special son, this is My message for the world; it has always been My message to the many generations of people, and decades and centuries, wherein I have deigned to appear. You know that Heaven is always about heights. It is about towering vaults and spirits in flight. And, here on Earth, love is about depths as well. It is about the deepness of humanity's love for God. It is stationed on the bedrock of Truth that rests at the depths of loyalty, sacrifice and obedience. Yes, deepness. How deep will humanity fall in love with Jesus? This is the only way they will rise again. How deep is the Church's commitment to My intercession? It is the fullest way to the Divine Mercy of My Son. How deep does this love go when everything in the world mocks and ridicules you? Is there any defense of the blessings and Mysteries that have been handed down through the ages to humanity grappling with death? Is there any reason to believe that new life will come from the fatal errors that lost sinners in the world keep making to defy their own redemption? This, My Special son, is the reason that I keep reminding you that the Earth is in transition. You have heard that time is neutral, but this is not always the case. When sufficient time passes, some things wither away and die. If one pays no attention to the clock, he will be late for something. There needs to be a sense of awareness about where the souls of men are located. It is not so much a matter of on which mountaintop or what continent, but where they are located in the realms of mystical life. This is where the 'value' of the soul is important for sure, but more crucial, what is its 'quality' before God in the themes of compliance with the truth? I realize that I appear to be speaking in the abstract, but it would seem that the human soul is situated in limbo on Earth until such time its eternal destiny is determined. This is what one's conscience knows to be true, and the determination about which I speak is made while men still live in mortal flesh. It is about the action of God and the reaction of man. It is about giving oneself to a Kingdom that will reign long after everyone has died. Yes, it is about trusting in a Promise that has already been proven to be true. My Special son, this is the 'validity' of the Gospel that has been chanted in prayers for centuries now. God does not need to prove anything more to humanity because Jesus has already laid the foundation of the Church. This is why you and your brother understand what I am saying. You have stood firmly on this foundation since your spirits were elevated enough to walk.

Finally, My Special son, the deepness I have mentioned here today must be authentic. It is not about acting holy or demanding holiness from others. It is about being from the center of the heart true, real and genuine. Some people tell others that they love them so the others will not complain. Sharing the true love of Jesus in the way of the Apostles is something that must be thought about intensely – that it not become a mockery of what Jesus expects from His Church. This is the sewing of the two garments together. Deepness and authenticity. This is where new life will take hold. And, it needs to be nourished and wrapped in the charity of prayer. This has been My second most prolific summons to My children in the world. Humanity must make the commitment to live out the promise and tenure of life by seeking the Lord. It is as simple as this. This is the definition of the exile of man. It is a preparation and culmination from the moment of conception to the hour of death. And, it does not matter whether the wicked disbelieve or disagree with what the Bible says. It may as well be their death warrant – if they reject what the Holy Gospel teaches, they are already dead. But, if they convert and adhere to the New Covenant of Salvation, then they have inherited their life in Jesus. One cannot hear any better news than this. So, My Special one, I ask you and your brother to rest comfortably in knowing that you have manifested here on Earth a new understanding of what God expects from His people. You have done this through Me, and on Jesus' behalf. The Spirit of the Father was the first messenger to Moses the Ancient. The Angels and Prophets chimed in. Saint Gabriel announced the Divine New Life; his message resounds here still. And, I have brought the Word of Glory to humanity in such a way that none other could possibly bear. So, who now is messaging what God desires His lost creatures to learn? Yes, you and your brother. This is the sacred spiritual bloodline that has given hope to millions, and closure to the Church. I told all the Popes that I would do this, and I have done it through you. Untold blessings will come through your life with your brother. Millions of Sauls will be stopped in their tracks by blinding flashes of light. The Morning Star will yield the freedom of all who have for decades languished in the dungeons of sin. Our prayers have already taken hold. The intensity of the Lord's Passion is saturating the Church with wisdom. The sun rises and sets; the clouds stir and scatter, the rains bathe the earth with new virginity, and the Church marches on toward the final dawn of man. All of this is what we witness as the Father reigns supreme. Please remember that you are 'Special' because you are loved. You are singly divine in the Sacred Heart of Jesus in the way of no other soul. You are given to eternity in the presence of the Father through your trust and faith in His Son."

Sunday, June 25, 2017
9:32 a.m.

God's definition of redemption –
"The apex encrypted in the contrite vesture of man."

"My splendid little sons, My Immaculate Heart is filled with peace and joy because I have the opportunity to speak to you again. It is with every sense of happiness that I tell you that the Father in Heaven is pleased with you. It is about the conversion of lost sinners that we have spoken so long, that they will come to know the definition of their destiny in the way that I have shared. Today, My little ones, I would like to reemphasize that the building-up of the Church is a process, not an event. This process is sometimes plagued by sorrow, danger and doubt, but it is more often characterized by trust and enlightenment. For every word that I have spoken to you through the years, and there have been millions, I wish for you to remember that there must be pious 'meaning' in the actions of men. Accepting the Blood of the Cross without knowing its meaning serves no purpose. The contrition that is mentioned at the beginning of My message this morning is a fruit of repentance. This is the key that unlocks the door to the meaning of human life. It is a way for the Church to explain why there is so much suffering. This suffering extols the meaning of Jesus on the Cross as much as His endurance of the Crucifixion itself. 'See the Victim whose suffering has reconciled the Church with God...' means that there must be within human faith the veracity to be willing to suffer. My Special son, you and your brother have suffered the ravages of the years in that My messages have been widely ignored since I first came to you. This does not comport with the fact that I have told you many times that millions upon millions would be converted by the Morning Star Over America miracle. Why? Because if it were otherwise until now, you and your brother would not be publishing yet another book that you have further dedicated your lives to completing. There would have been too many distractions, too many supporters and detractors knocking on your door, too much commotion, and too little peace. It seems logical that you understand what I am saying. 'Let these two holy souls work in peace.' This is what Jesus has proclaimed to the unwitting masses. And, how could your brother have built his academic credentials if there were so many rumor peddlers and curiosity mongers descending on your door? The process has unfolded as it should. We are achieving the goals that were laid out from the beginning. The reason that you and your brother said 'yes' to Me in 1989 and 1991 is being validated by what you are experiencing. In all truth, there must be eternal meaning. I have told you this many times during 2017. When someone turns to prayer, there is eternal meaning. When you feed the poor, this too has eternal meaning. And, just as these things foretell even greater blessings, there is also such thing as eternal consequences. These consequences can be either auspicious or foreboding, depending on the nature of the act. Humanity generally believes that consequences are some form of punishment. The term is even defined that way. I will therefore speak about eternal consequences in the sense of what the human soul must undergo for declining to behave prudently. There is no proper facility for eternal consequences unless they, themselves, have eternal meaning. Sending someone into the fires of Gehenna is clearly the ultimate punishment, but as you know, it is the choice of the damned. What eternal meaning can be taken from this? That the face of God is so fair, that the Crucifixion of Christ Jesus is so bountiful, that the mansions of Heaven are so fine that anyone who rejects the Gospel is unworthy of the glory it proclaims. This is the reason we have placed into being the awesome messages that will take lost sinners to their awareness of what the Father deigns for them. It is all about the pardon, forgiveness and absolution that Jesus handed humanity on Good Friday. The comprehension of this gift by those who do not yet know seems as far away as some distance universe. Here is where they are – when an archangel approaches them and asks what they think about the New Kingdom into which they are being invited, they do not wonder what this Kingdom might be like. Instead, they turn toward the archangel and say, '...what? Who, me?' They have yet to recognize that an Eternal Kingdom is calling them because they have not accorded themselves the opportunity to seek it. All the other deafening noises and distractions preclude them from hearing the sounds of redemption. My Special son, as advanced as you and your brother have become in your spiritual acumen, many things that I say in My messages appear quite elementary to you. I am not the kind of Mother who would impede the Holy Spirit from bringing to perfection in you the wisdom with which you observe and discern the lines and passages that will help your brothers and sisters convert. However, I will never let go of you. You will never leave My side like a fledgling might take flight from its mother's nest. You have come in your own right upon the capacity not only to see Creation through the eyes of the Father, but to decide for Him in your prayers what He might prefer for its future.

So, My thoughtful children, I have come today to celebrate who you are in the Sacred Heart of Jesus. I am with you there, and you are deeply imbedded in the love of My Most Immaculate Heart. I see the unassuming children within you simultaneously beside the Doctors of the Church you have become. I am absent the words to convey what the meaning of your prayers does for the world. It is not that God lacks the wisdom to already know your prayers, but that He does not feel as separated from His children when you recite them to Him. Is it possible for the Father to yearn for the company of His children? Yes, absolutely. And, we are helping Him feel comforted in knowing that His wishes are coming true. My Special son, I would like, if you would consider, for you to return to your labors for the Church this morning, as I have shared everything I wish to say today. *"Yes, but I have a question. I have the Field of Eternity diagram that you presented to us years ago. Is the date that is missing the publishing of The Final Colossus?"* The answer is a definitive yes. The Final Colossus and the Immaculate Triumph of Mary are coupled at the core of this beatific moment. *"That makes me happy."* Does it not, therefore, seem more apparent that your prayers have brought this miracle into being? After all, your book that I just mentioned was not initially supposed to be published. It was the pleading of you and your brother that made this time-dividing manifestation possible. I ask that you remember that your concessions in this life have represented the begetting of untold blessings to the world from the Father in Heaven. This has been your mark not only on the history of the Earth, but on the eternity of the ages. This is the eternal 'meaning' that you have made clear to Jesus and all the Hosts of Heaven. You have preempted the need for many chastisements that would have otherwise come. I ask you to consider the central themes of My messages since AD 2012. I have spoken about beauty and power, truth and consequences, and process and meaning. These are the elements of self-examination that sinners worldwide should apply when comparing their lives to Jesus on the Cross. Have their sacrifices been reparative? Do they have identification with the Passion of Christ Jesus? The answer rests in whether these sacrifices were in defense of the truth, and whether their meaning aligned with the teachings of the Church. Do you have any other issues this morning? *"Just that I'm proud of our Bishop for standing up for the truth against same-sex sin."* Yes, he did the right thing issuing his decree. You should remember that it was difficult for him to stand up for the truth because everyone wishes to be liked. He has created even more adversaries by proclaiming the tenets of the Gospel. Thank you for your holy petitions. I shall remember all for whom you have asked Me to pray. It is truly heartening that so many young people are taking a stand against abortion."

Sunday, July 2, 2017
9:37 a.m.

The suspension of disbelief —

*The outcome of the circumstance of trust —
confidence, ambition, empowerment and stature.*

"My dear little sons, freedom will never truly ring until humanity tethers its future to the sovereignty of God. It is with a jubilant Heart that I have come to pray with you this morning. What we have done through the years has been all about faith. This is the reason you are listening to Me now. My Special son, you and your brother have given your lives to Jesus because of your faith, and your undying love for Me and the God of your fathers. It would scarcely seem possible after what I have given you over the past three decades, but your faith is the keystone to what we are doing at this moment. I would never enter a world and practice trickery to induce My children to listen. This is the reason I have been so forthcoming to you and your brother about the Lord's expectations for humanity. You heard at the beginning of today's message the concept of the suspension of disbelief. This is not the complete story of faith, but it is part of faith. It is possible for someone to have faith in God without overcoming an earlier state of disbelief. This is the way of most Christians. Belief in God is a matter of gifting the heart to Him, freshly due, from the curiosity for eternal wisdom that the Holy Spirit instills. This is the outcome of the application of trust. All the other gifts, the benefits and attributes that result from trust, make up the transformation that the acceptance and inheritance of the Eternal Kingdom imbues. One of the ways that humanity does this is to open the heart to believe because people 'wish' to believe. It is the satisfaction of the need for purpose in life and the knowledge about what happens when life nears death. For example, you watch television programs and motion pictures knowing that the actors are pretending to be someone they are not. You suspend your disbelief in order to understand the message being transmitted by the script. It would not be possible to watch motion pictures and weep over their drama if the human heart was not integrally involved. I have taken the opportunity to cite a second example in My message today. It is the phenomenon of the visual replication of objects that appear to take on human form. When you see faces in artwork, woodwork and other structures, your mind is suspending disbelief that these things are only casual architectures. *"Or when a ventriloquist dummy talks."* Yes, indeed.

You have the correct idea. So, you understand what I mean by saying that people must suspend their disbelief in order to comprehend the message that is being conferred. These sorts of things must be fashioned into a certain construct to produce the intended message and transfer meaning. I wish to show you an image of a group of similar objects that accomplish the same thing. (*An artist had created a very insightful depiction where empty beverage cans were collected together to compose a choir. The spouts on the tops of the cans were bent forward and open as if they were mouths singing.*) Why did you believe that the image of these containers was so humorous? "*Because it was a creative illusion with inanimate objects depicting a normal human experience. You could see the human experience in the objects.*" Yes, it is precisely as you say. My Special son, there are many implications to this image that are relatable to man's faith in God. Collecting articles such as the beverage cans and assembling them into a singing choir elicits an imaginative state of mind from those who see it. But, once it is done, the individual attributes of each container and the uniformity they assume creates in the mind of the viewer an image that is more transcendental than what they are seeing. Whoever sees the image that I just showed you knows that these are only beverage cans, but the cans themselves seem to no longer exist. They have become elements of a different message, just like the actors on a stage. They are components of a single voice articulating a particular meaning that cannot be yielded when the cans are seen separately. And, this implies not only that something living has been created from something inanimate, but that another dimension is manifested from the result. What do choirs do? They sing; and singing implies the production of sound. My Special son, all of this is done within the human mind because of the impulse to believe what is seen with the eyes. Imagine what would have happened if I had not shown you the assembled beverage containers until after I had provided you an audio soundtrack of collective voices singing. Would this not have made the image even more striking? "*Yes.*" So, here is the point that I am making. If humanity can imagine that a collection of beverage cans could be a voice-filled choir, why can this same humanity not believe that the language of Creation can be broadcast throughout the universe by a God that made everything out of nothing? – no beverage cans, no pliers, no cutters, no nothing. I will leave it to your good offices to ponder what I have presented to you this morning, and imagine what I have said about the gift of human faith. The other things – confidence, ambition, empowerment and stature are the fruits of the trust that you have placed in God, and they are sustained by the 'life' you see with your heart. It takes faith to believe that an actor on a stage is Moses the Ancient. But, that production is one of your favorite films. It takes faith to acknowledge that trees can walk and talk, but you were drawn to tears by what they had to say. And, it requires faith to accept that the Son of Man died to rescue all souls from the dungeons of death, but it is as true as anything human ears will ever hear.

When I speak about this empowerment and stature, it kindles in Me the desire to spread the Gospel message across the globe in ways that humanity cannot refute. Why? Because unlike you and your brother, there are billions of people who would have to suspend their current disbelief in order to accept it. This, however, has not been the way of God through the centuries. Faith requires that men must concede that they are lifeless and helpless without the Messianic Spirit of the Father through the Son. There can be no viable self-confidence without Him. There can be no empowerment without the Spirit Advocate being allowed entry into the human heart to construct a framework of righteousness at the center of the soul. There can be no stature in this life or the next without true faith in Jesus Christ. There can be no standing before Him unless all who require deliverance from sin, death and condemnation accept the Sacrifice that He suffered. My Special son, there are a billion ways to explain this to the world, and I have only just begun. The Truth is all there is. You are the warrior who has made possible the venue for Me to share this message to all who should hear. And, the lovely soul praying beside you now, your brother, has been with you all the way. It is true that he was too little to play sports when he was a child. He wanted to be a worthy batsman when he was a boy, but they all said that he was too small. He wanted to play basketball as well, but they all said that he was too short. And, he wanted to have the prettiest girl on the playground as his closest romance, but they all said that he lacked the stature. And, now? Thanks to your love, friendship and faith, he has become a giant among men. I only wish that I could put into words how grateful is the Father that you have taken such good care of him."

Saturday, July 8, 2017
9:29 a.m.

"Nonbelievers are people to whom words often come easily, but courage rarely does."

- The Dominion Angels

"The case against humanocentrism."

"My dear little sons, holding dominion over the Earth does not imply human supremacy. It never has. It is not that humanity is not in charge of the world's social affairs, but there is no such thing as humanity owning the power to alter the natural course of life. The term 'humanocentrism' means that human beings believe that they are more than stewards, but gods that have the right to reshape the world in the likeness of their sinful selves. This is the pretext for supporting abortion. This is not what the Genesis passage is about. My dear sons, I have spent the past 26 years telling you how blessed and special humanity is in the eyes of the Father. This will never change. Truly, it is due to this specialness that brought God to send His Only Begotten Son to redeem the world. What could possibly be unnatural about this? It is the natural and supernatural evolving of the human person from his exiled condition to a state of grace and redemption. My Special son, whether you know it or not, you are a theologian. But, you are not a theologian who has been schooled in the finest institutions known to man. You have been lettered by the Mother of God. The Holy Spirit has been your teacher here in this place and throughout your life. Yes, this means that you have wisdom not known to worldly men, and it also means that you have been graced in the way of few among you. You and your brother are worthy stewards of this grace in the same way that the Father deigned to hand dominion to humanity over the creatures of the Earth. As I have said, it is not that humanity lives supremely, but that those who belong to God are obedient servants as temporary stewards of His earthly domain. This poses the question as to why He would hand such responsibility to corrupt mortal men. After all, it is not about power; it is about adhering to the mandates of the Holy Gospel. The issue is that there is an argument to be made against the humanocentrism that the world has embraced, and the basis for the argument is the teaching of the Church. It is true that the Book of Genesis outlays the dominion of exiled men, but the framework is about righteousness and service. My little sons, if we can make this point more clearly to those who should hear, it would help in sounding the voice of the Angels about the courage that is required to live it. I am not asking you to take this into the streets, I am soliciting your prayers that it shall be done. This is the premise of My message today. However, I wish to remain with you and pray for the conditions in the world that lay in ruins in the aftermath of humanity's callous touch. I wish for you to remember, My Special son, that you are leaps and bounds, and generations and centuries, beyond what your lost brothers and sisters know about the Kingdom of God. I am not saying that this gives you the responsibility to mediate the world, but to focus your petitions on what you know My prayers to be. This, you have done like a master for the past thirty years. I hope that you realize that you and your brother are so close to your work that you cannot know what it means for the rest of humanity. Imagine someone handing you a copy of your AD 2010-2012 book forty years ago and telling you that it was from the future when you and your brother began receiving My messages. You might likely have fainted. And yet, here it is; you have done it. The years have accorded you the opportunity to decide for God, just as they have for everyone else. I pray that you find My messages in this most recent book to be inspiring, and that you feel that they will be enlightening for the world. *"I think they are beautiful."* Imagine seeing this new book beyond the element of time. Think about someone else being spontaneously handed the book. They would want to learn everything they could possibly know about the two messengers and seers. This is something that you and your brother should consider. The book stands apart from everything else you know about yourselves – they all do. Dealing with the dailiness of being mortal, the morning rising and evening retiring, your works and chores, your interaction with others, the financial considerations with which you deal, your thoughts and emotions, your movement through time and space – all these are incidents of what your lives are about. You are here in this world to serve the Father in the same way that Jesus was sent upon the Annunciation. You have perfected what it means to be human beings in the exile of men.

My Special son, I pray that you will not grow so accustomed to hearing My accolades that you will not believe them to be sincere. *"Thank you, Mama. I appreciate your encouraging words."* It is not that you require them as often as I offer, but I cannot help but tell you the truth moreover. One day, My Special son, you and your brother will look back upon these decades and your whole lives with the satisfaction of knowing that you have lived as honorable sons of the Mother of God. You will see Jesus face to face as though you are looking into a mirror – this is what He will see as well. This is the moment that He has prayed for, with every soul choosing the eternal life that He has won. I do not wish to speak to you in unrealistic tones, but Jesus does more than welcome a soul into His presence. He reaches back in time and comforts the wounds that His brothers and sisters endured for Him. He kisses them with the healing balm of soothing gratitude. My Special son, I wish to tell you something that the Church has never known. Upon the arrival of the human soul into Paradise, Jesus turns over the bodies of those who have given themselves to Him to Saint Thomas the Apostle. This is done at the behest of the Saint who wishes to feel the wounds of his Savior in every person who ever endured so much as a scratch in the preservation of their faith. Thomas asks to touch the wounds of all who believed in Jesus on the Cross without first seeing Him there. Each soul who comes to Heaven has this signature of eternal alliance – yours and your brother's have already been inscribed in the halls of the Afterlife. It is your commission to rejoin the Mother and Her children beneath the guiding hands of their Lord. You are like sacred ushers for those who lived out their years without knowing who I am. Yes, this has been done retroactively for every soul given the breath of life. And, it is not just you who have stood tall for this commission. It is a grace for the Church Triumphant that I have asked Jesus to ordain. My Special son, you are not only singing the psalms of praise to Jesus, you are writing them from your heart as well. It is important that we pray for those who are suffering in foreign lands because of their Christian faith. They will not all become blood martyrs, but they are being spiritually martyred for Jesus on the Cross nonetheless."

Sunday, July 16, 2017
9:08 a.m.

"Vested, sanctioned and summoned – It shall be done."

"My dear little sons, as you know, what is imminent is already here. The preparations for the return of the Son of Man are in place. The Earth that lay in wait for the Birth of Salvation is now poised to receive the Second Coming of its King. I cannot describe the joy that this brings the Father, that this world has been positioned in the path of the Son to win for Him the victory of His Church. The commendation at the fore of My message this morning says it well. Is there anything lacking in this? Are the Sacred Mysteries complete? There is nothing lacking, and the Sacred Mysteries have been finished. So, My dear sons, for what is Jesus waiting? It is the same as when you take for yourselves the moment of reflection before framing a miraculous picture. It is inhaling a breath of satisfaction before reaping the bountiful harvest. The sense of imminence is as overwhelming to God as it is for those who believe in Him. Vested, sanctioned and summoned. This describes the Church and each person within it. My Special son, there is plenteous speech and contemplative prayer that precedes the Second Coming of Jesus. There are homilies and reflections. There are hearts and minds readied for the miracle. If you reach out your hand and look at your palm – this is as near as the Kingdom of God in the offing. It is a matter of the expiration of time that will suffice the great revelation of the Glorious Kingdom to all men great and small. I have told you and your brother that time itself is only a complement to your life's work. It is your venue through which to effect your loyalty to your faith in Jesus on the Cross. And, it is man's sequential moment to assess and evaluate what it means to be human in exile. Every thought and action that has been caused in the history of the world that fosters the Kingdom of God has been the work of God. The Holy Spirit has done this so that everything not of His Kingdom will perish – not just pale, but fall into an abyss that is so far gone that redeemed men cannot see it. My little sons, the foundation of this great miracle is still invisible. Prayer cannot be seen with the eyes, but prayer has built the bedrock upon which the future of humanity has been laid. Yes, even the prayers of men on the Earth have been fashioned by this love for God. One cannot pray for the Kingdom of God to come without God Himself being the origin of this need. This is how close the Father is to you, My Special and Chosen ones, as close as your palm to your face. When you speak to Him, as when I speak to Him, it is the foreshadowing of your unity with Heaven that has already begun. My Special one, there is no greater grace or benignity than to pray for the redemption of the world. It is not only that conversion must take place, but that each person who desires to be claimed into the presence of the Father must willingly choose to enter His Kingdom. It is not that you can point your finger to the left or the right and say, '...that is the Kingdom, over there.' The Kingdom is a spiritual manifestation that originates at the center of the heart. Please do not be confused about what I am saying. Those who are not given to the Holy Spirit and the Church can indeed point to you or your brother, or any other Christian, and say, '...there is the Kingdom, over there.' Why? Because they are identifying you as holding the Kingdom of the Father within you. You are the sacred vessels of the Holy Spirit in a temporally identifiable place. Do you understand the contrast that I have drawn? *"Yes."* I am asking you to ponder this for a moment. You have a Spiritual Kingdom inside your heart in the same way that I held the Incarnate Kingdom of God within My Womb. They are one and the same Kingdom. Does this not make your heart the semblance of a womb as well? "*Yes.*" And, what shall be borne of this? "*Jesus.*"

Yes, Jesus the Holy Spirit has been implanted in the hearts of Christians, to be borne to the world in the way of His triumph and glory. This has already been done by those who go to Heaven, but the emission of Holy Love from your heart into the world does not mean that Jesus is not there anymore. It is a transfer of glorious energy from your own identity into the created realms, but the Holy Spirit within you is never depleted. You are, in effect, deploying the capacity to destroy hatred in the world through the infinite glory within you. The seed of goodness that Jesus places within you never dies – it continues to bear the fruits of love and forgiveness both now and long after you shall enter the eternal domain. This means that you will take your spiritual heart with you when you go. And, just like the seed of love therein, this does not mean that your spiritual heart will not remain with those still in exile when you take your place alongside Jesus in Paradise. Is this not what I have done? "*Yes.*" And, you will be capable of communicating the wisdom you have inherited to those who are still facing the challenges of life in the temporal realms. This is a question of dimension, for sure, but it is more emphatically a matter of power. It should always be known that there can be no true power without 'presence.' God is all-powerful, and He exercises His power by being eternally present. Hence, proof has been established that God is everywhere because His power is more prevalent than anything else knowable to man. Another point, My Special son, is that humanity must desire that God enter their midst. There is no such thing as the Holy Spirit entering a heart that despises everything about God and His Kingdom. Nothing is worse than a person having a heart as rigid as stone, and then wondering why life is so difficult. This leads to another question. Does the Holy Spirit enter a human heart to make it tender, or must the heart be open in tenderness first? This has been a debate that has not been decided since the fall of Adam from the Garden. Which do you believe that it is? "*I believe it goes back to Saint Thomas Aquinas's discussion between actual grace and sanctifying grace. God created us to know Him, so there has to be some receptive tenderness from when we were born, which is a grace.*" Yes, precisely correct. And, this means that the Holy Spirit will enter a heart that prepares Jesus room. As you have known all your years, Jesus will not kick down the door to enter. This speaks to the matter of preparedness on behalf of the people of the world. It refers to someone's capacity to know that there is something more glorious about life than succeeding in the marketplace or championing the most victories in battle. It is about responding to the overtures from Heaven that are always there. It means receiving because one's reception is an act of invitation. If one perceives the veil of human exile in the context of a closed door, it is precisely that Jesus desires that His people keep the door open at all times. This is the whole idea behind the opening of the jubilee doors at the Vatican in Rome. One of these years, and not in the distant future, a Pope will open one of the jubilee doors and see an image of Heaven for the entire world to share. It will be a reflection of God's Altar in Heaven, a glimpse of the Banquet Table where the Church Triumphant is seated. I am saying that if all Christians around the globe would envision in their hearts how this scene might unfold, the conversion of non-Christians would happen overnight. The joyful realization that one's faith is justified would be too jubilant to contain. So, your response is accurate. *"That's what your presence with us has done for me."* Yes, this is exactly what I knew would occur. I ask you to remember that this has been Jesus' intention for 2,000 years. *"It seems that the Bishops and Cardinals, the Hierarchy of the Church, do not have this joyful realization of the power of Catholicism."* This is the reason I have come to you and your brother, to direct their attention to the Morning Star Over America. They are not listening because they have never been exposed to a modern miracle with such implications. I have said more than their consciousness can absorb. This is the reason I have told you that the Morning Star Over America revelation is more a process than an event. My Special son, you can sense whom and 'where' these individuals exist who are vested, sanctioned and summoned to extol the Kingdom of God on His behalf. You can also see others who claim to know Him, but who are instead using the Gospel to advance their own interests. Two things will happen. First, those like you and your brother will ultimately win. Second, those who are not like you and your brother will fail. In both of these cases – It shall be done. My Special son, I wish to repeat that your prayers for the Church are never in vain. The Lord hears your petitions for holy priests and for women to embrace their stations in life. I will always share your prayers with Jesus, just as you lift them to Me."

Saturday, July 22, 2017
9:30 a.m.

"The Kingdom calls and the Scepter shines. The Lord knows that exiled men have battled for centuries with genetic propensities over which they have no control. This proves that, in humanity's fallen posture, divine instinct was always supposed to be greater than bloodlines and heritages. It took the death of Jesus Christ to make this known – that the Messianic

Crucifixion is a redemptional reconciliation between God and man and Heaven and Earth, not just some overwrought atrocity of another origin."

- The Dominion Angels

"My dear little sons, you are beloved and honored, adored and esteemed. Your gifts to God through all the years have been comforting to Him. I have come today to pray with you for the conversion of the wicked. My Immaculate Heart overflows with love for you that cannot be rescinded. Today, the Dominion Angels have spoken about the trials and tribulations that come from your genetic inheritance. I cannot overstate the influence this has on the behavior of exiled men. All the learned habits of the world cannot compete with the impact that one's bloodline has on his demeanor and approach to life. My Special son, one of the greatest blessings of the Crucifixion is that it reorients the faithful to the saintliness of Jesus. This is part of the reconciliation between God and man and Heaven and Earth. The attributes that are specific to someone's genes are overcome and superseded by the new spiritual identity that is inherited through their acceptance of Jesus on the Cross. My little ones, there is more. In the grand framework of the Father's Will to dispense Jesus' Divine Mercy into the world, there is a specific condition of absolution for various sins and wrongdoings that are wrought by someone's genetic disposition. The Church speaks about mitigating circumstances in the judgment of sinners. This accompanies the forgiveness that comes for other transgressions that are lessened because of someone's force of acquired habit. While abuse of substances like tobacco and alcohol are manifested by habitual use, personality traits and outward actions are connected to a person's genetic code. God does everything He can to absolve sinners of their transgressions. He understands that not everyone is capable of snapping their fingers and becoming new creatures through their fledgling faith. As the Angels say that the Crucifixion represents a reconciliation between Heaven and Earth, humanity in exile must do their part to accept the 'radical reorientation' the comes with Christian conversion. My Special son, this is not the same as giving someone a hundred dollars for a product at a store. The Sacrifice of Jesus on the Cross cannot be purchased. It is a reciprocity where God redeems the human soul in reflection of the soul's repentance. I mentioned before the concept of 'imminence.' Imminence denotes that something of manifestation is in the offing, a prospect or a promise. *"I understand."* It also connotes that there is an expectation on the part of the person doing the waiting. *"Yes."* This is part of the reconciliation that I am speaking about this morning, introduced by the Dominion Angels before we began. God is saying that if humanity will give Jesus their lives in exile, He will bestow upon them eternity in His presence. If the world will become like Heaven as has been taught, God will encircle humanity within His beatific embrace. In these same terms, if humankind will serve Creation in the likeness of its Savior, God will take humanity to the core of His creative genius. What did the Prince of Peace declare that He came into the world to do? 'I did not come to establish peace,' He said. Yes, and does humanity believe this to be a contradiction? It is not divided speech because God owns the authority and transformation of everything that reflects His Eternal Will. My Special son, what do you suppose could be said about the ironies of Jesus on the Cross? First, they crucified an innocent Man. Second, a Man should die so that all men can live. Third, a Man of honesty and integrity was crucified between two thieves. On and on, the ironies go. Jesus' Kingdom requires the reciprocation of truth between God and man. Humanity must lay aside their flesh to see the face of the Father, while the Crucifixion of the Son of Man spares all men from death. The purpose of My message today is to help you understand the very nature of the Kingdom of God – that no man on Earth can appropriate the power to choose how the Father configures His own divine providence. It is all about obedience and sacrifice. God did not just wake from His sleep one day and decide to ask Abraham to sacrifice his son. There was redemptive purpose in soliciting the sacrifice. This was the Father's way of identifying self-obedience from His Throne in Heaven, and it is the same obedience that brought Jesus to turn Himself over to the Roman soldiers to die. Complete and absolute unity with the Will of God. One might think that the only way for light to overcome the darkness is to conquer it outright. Does it not therefore seem contradictory that the 'Light of the World' was nailed to the Cross by humanity's darkest forces? "*Yes.*" Sometimes, men must see what they believe to be contradictory as instead part of the sacrificial aura of love to which the world is being drawn. If someone steals your shawl, give them your tunic as well. If a person strikes your right cheek, turn your left one too. My dear sons, there are no contradictions in the Kingdom of God. There is only oneness and wholesome unanimity. Whatsoever the Father requires must be the measure of men's response. This is why Jesus came to fulfill the law instead of supplanting it. There is no such thing as bartering between God and man in the Crucifixion of His Son, but a sinner cannot be redeemed until he accepts Jesus' Sacrifice of his own accord. "*The reciprocity must be there.*" Yes, it is the same as friction igniting a flame. No one can win a war for peace until the battle begins. There is no such thing as grayness when all truth is lily white.

And yet, there are multicolor rainbows everywhere. My Special son, what I am telling you is that God has removed any footholds that men can use to manipulate His Divine Kingdom."

Sunday, July 30, 2017
9:06 a.m.

Christianity in the heart –
resolve, integrity, energy, momentum and valor.

"It is impossible to support abortion and believe in God."

"A rare reality versus a common simulation."

"Good morning, My precious little sons. It is with great endearment that I come speaking to you because your prayers mean so much to God. I have incorporated several themes into My message this morning that you may cite as you wish. They are worthy of discussion in your writings and oratories. Christian faith must have integrity and resolve. It must involve the sacred energy that I have spoken about, and it must move forward with courage. This faith, this deeply-embedded trust that God supports and encourages love and life, is a rare reality among men on Earth because many see Christianity as a casual affair. There is a false belief in societies that humanity must only simulate the life of Jesus. We know better. It is about becoming the 'reality' of Jesus in this life – the uncommon new identity that He gives His disciples that cannot be compared to the commodity of everyday living. In doing this, My little ones, it is not as difficult to discern who among you holds true to the faith that God has given His people. It is easy to tell who believes in Him, who loves Him with every fiber of themselves. Hence, it is not possible to support abortion and believe in God. I know, My Special son, that you will in the future share these thoughts if you choose. Mainly, however, they are meant for you and your brother to know what the Father is thinking. I have come to pray with you this morning, as I have said, because I love you. There is no question that you understand why My Lourdes and Fatima apparitions are not spoken about on the street every day. It is the same reason that the Morning Star Over America has not appeared in the national news. We do not care; we consider it a compliment. It is a badge of honor. If there were ever a reason for you to know what can be done to change this world, you have found it in the way secular elitists have shunned you. You are in good company – they killed Jesus outright. Yes, this is the Messiah who raised the little girl from death, who brought Lazarus back to life, who healed more sufferers than the doubters dared to believe, who has granted forgiveness and Mercy to the exiled Earth for 2,000 years. I welcome you and your brother to the fold of Saints who have done your work for Jesus well, but have been relegated to the margins of secular society. Congratulations for a job well done! It is a blessing that you have given to God. My Special son, I have on many occasions asked you and your brother not to take pity on those who have blasphemed the Church and taken upon themselves the power to decide what God should do. I have done this because they have the facility of their own 'will' to do the right thing, but they outwardly refuse. This is not just declining what is right, it is an intentional refusal based on their prejudicial thinking. It is the same as putting off having dessert after dinner, but saying that you will have none at all. There is aforethought in what the enemies of the Catholic Church are doing because they have an overt agenda to impede its mission. Why? Because they are unwilling to make the sacrifices that will set them on their journey to the Holy Cross. We have mentioned those who practice 'prosperity' Christianity that have become wealthy from the donations of their flocks. This is one of the worst kinds of abuse of the Gospel of the Lord. My Special son, you can discern who among you is and is not representative of the rare reality, and who is only conducting for themselves a fraudulent simulation. It all comes down to the matter of exploitation. Everyone must answer the question, '...why am I a Christian?' My Special son, their response is key to their beliefs, their behavior, and the substance of their spiritual life. The whole priority of being alive is reflected by their answer to this question. I tell you and your brother this today because I wish for you to think about how you have responded. You can see the 'saint' in yourselves in this life. You will four weeks from now order a number of your AD 2010-2012 manuscripts, a book that billions of people around the globe could never have written or published. You have prayed with Me here in this place for decades, wishing and hoping that God would finish the world with Justice and Truth. Your prayers and Mine are never in vain! When men speak about the 'glory days' to which they look forward, they will find their beginning here. This is the reason I have asked you and your brother to consider yourselves worthy in the eyes of the Father and the annals of the world. You have seeded a rare reality on Earth that will awaken the masses to My intercession in these modern times. Why did I come to America, and why did I call upon you? Because the whole world strives to be as fruitful as the United States, and every child of God should aspire to emulate your goodness.

My little sons, these are not just complimentary sentiments, they are statements of fact. You will see! You will see!

It gives Me tremendous joy to know what will be revealed to you in the years ahead because you have formed the basis for this joy by the way you have lived. We speak of the integrity that is required to maintain the Christian life, and it is exemplified by your response to Me. It is illustrated by your love for Jesus. It is made clear through your obedience to God. When I speak about 'reason,' I am speaking about the ability of a man to know his standing before his Creator, and then to anticipate what this Creator expects from the life He has granted. This is the 'reason' that is untethered to any condition. It need not be logical in the sense that ordinary men might know, but it suffices the logic that the Father had in mind when He first created the world. The sky is not high enough to allow men to see where the Father of humankind is seated. But, holiness provides this vision. Faith and hope manifest it as well. Yes, faith in God and hope in His Kingdom are the only ways for a man's heart not to be broken into a thousand pieces by the evils of this world. There is daring in this design because it requires an understanding of the duties and sacrifices of the Messianic office – this is the life to which all men and women are called – not just a simulation, but the veracity of action and faith that Jesus brought forth from the shelter of My Womb. He once told the Apostles that the most important place for humankind to stand is before the Mother in honor of the Son. I have known these Apostles here on Earth and in Heaven, and I realize that their journey below the stars was difficult. This is the life that humanity is enduring; it is the journey that you are traveling today. And, it is a worthy one. It is an ordination fit for the brothers of Christ. It is a battle that finds you alongside the Man on the Cross as He walked the pathway to the Crucifixion. It is your unity with the Savior of the world who has seen fit to call you His disciples. My Special son, I ask you and your brother to remember what I have said about you this morning. It is one of the requests for which I bow in endless prayer – that Jesus will help you know how worthy you are. And, I love you beyond all imagining."

Sunday, August 6, 2017
8:32 a.m.

"Regal, palatial, grand and splendid."

"My dear little children, you have come to another August morning where I am praying with you for the transformation of the world. It is always a good day when we inspire the Lord to challenge humanity to do better. It would not be improper to suggest that lost sinners should be aware that there is within them the capacity to reveal their holier selves to the exiled realms in the same way that Jesus' Glory was revealed on Mount Tabor. I speak of humanity in Jesus that is regal, palatial, grand and splendid. My Special and Chosen sons, it is imperative that the Church realizes that these four terms describe its excellence. If all in the world would remember the identity they have found in Jesus, they would embrace the virtuousness of their own convictions. My Special son, people across the globe are searching for the cause and effect relationship between faith and the manifestations of life. It is prayer that fosters this connection. However, you have seen that it is not like bargaining. You cannot pray for ten minutes to receive ten minutes worth of responses. The Father does not work that way. It is not a matter of numbers, it is a fruit of intensity. If you love the Lord with your whole heart, mind and soul, He will respond by gracing your life with righteousness and wisdom. This is the means to being united with Him through this life and the next. Intensity implies the unbounded spiritual investment of the heart and soul in the Messianic Kingdom to which humanity is called. I wish to tell you today that there are awesome gifts for the world in the books that you have published to lead lost sinners to God's Kingdom – this is where the effects of prayer are most widely known. By all means, what have you and your brother been doing since I began speaking to you? What are you doing at this moment? Praying. If there is any cause and effect in man's relationship with the Father, it is that He summons His people to righteousness – this is the cause of your joy. And, acceptance of the Blood of Jesus on the Cross is the eternal effect. One of the more unique attributes about My messages to you and your brother is that, as your brother has said, I have not kept repeating the same themes in My messages through the years. There have been multiple dimensions to My lessons, and varied visions about the way humanity ought to live. This is reflected in your writings, prefaces and prologues. There is no end to the ways sinners can be warned about their fate in the future without their relationship with God. It is an awareness that grows from the enlightenment of the spirit about man's station on Earth before the backdrop of His Kingdom. Today, I wish for you to remember all the intentions that I have asked you to pray for, especially for little children who are learning from others. We know that they are impressionable in the ways of old, but there are many more malevolent forces that can harm them during these times. Who could have imagined that there would come a day when a child would coax another child to commit suicide by sending an electronic message? This is a manifestation of the malevolence about which I am speaking. And, so is the environment of violence and degradation that has come with these new mediums of communication. Whatever venues can be exploited by the devil to bring discord and destruction that are available to him, he will use. However, Satan is no match for the righteousness of God. He has only at his disposal the tools that lost sinners put within his reach. It is true that scandal can find its way into almost anything, but it cannot corrupt a heart that is wholly given to Jesus. Purity in these modern times is difficult to find because there is so much pressure to travel the darker paths. This is another of the intentions that I ask you and your brother to pray for. I know that you have the faculties of wisdom from the years of your youth, and I am not telling you anything new today. The remarkable content of your AD 2010-2012 book is a gift that will help stop corruption in this world from happening, and it will reverse the corruption that has already come. My Special son, this seems like an elementary idea to you and your brother, based on everything you have learned. It would seem that all the Popes in history would view this as a rather simple prospect as well. However, it is the basis of the regalness, fairness, beauty, splendor and grandeur of the Roman Catholic Church. How do we know? Because its Messianic King was born an Infant Child. This is the measure of simplicity that the Father has fashioned for the faith to which men must subscribe. By approaching this faith like children, the peoples of the Earth will better understand the Father's Will. Yes, God in Heaven desires to be approached with the innocence of children without the assumptions that plague manipulative men. There is no agendum in little children, there is eagerness to learn. The mission of the Church is to return humanity to this innocence that should be welcomed by the sinners who inherit it. This is the wisdom and innocence that it learned from the Gospel.

My little sons, this is why the Catholic Church is the Holder of the Gospel of Faith. *"As one of the Moral Majors."* Indeed, and you see that this springs from the unassuming nature that Jesus has sought from His disciples. It is not childish, but childlike. This is best shown in the prodigies of the Earth. A three-year-old boy playing the world's most complex symphonies?

This is a metaphor for humanity and the Church. It is illustrative of what God wants the world to know about the reciprocity of His Kingdom. My Special son, you have seen televised programs where children do extraordinary things – feats of talent, memory and accomplishment that are rarely known to man. Yes, these are among the children who are divinely connected to the God of Abraham. Their abilities do not come from advanced intellects or the counsel of the years, they are perceivable fruits of the presence of God. They are gifts to humanity so the world can know the great commission that comes to those who are receptive to Him. Imagine how your Mother feels when I see these little souls? How much more does the world need to witness before societies believe that this is how every person on Earth can be in the arms of God? This is not a giant leap of faith; it is simple commitment. There are untold ways that the Father makes Himself known through the artworks of Nature and the wonders that usher believers through their days. My little sons, you have received these signs long before I began speaking to you. They were deposited within you by the intensity of your faith, just as I said when I began this morning. Your acceptance of Jesus on the Cross through your own volition is one of the greatest signs of human redemption that humanity will ever know. You never stepped back, you never held out, and you never walked away. You are the modern incarnation of the Apostles who gave their lives for Jesus and His Church. You have not laid down your lives, but you have laid out your lives for Him in the way of the Saints and Doctors."

Saturday, August 12, 2017
3:02 p.m.

"Let us love one another, and let us pray together."

"With the infinity of God's Glory, I come to you again today to pray for the conversion of lost sinners. My Special and Chosen sons, it is the pinnacle of My joy to speak to you because your prayers invite Me here. It is your wish that all souls be redeemed in Jesus' Blood on the Cross that matters with such intensity to the Father. Therefore, I bid you peace and happiness as I make My presence known. It should be clear to you that I find joy in all the children whom I adopted on Good Friday, for this is a good mother's passion. My Special son, you restored the health of the injured little bird yesterday by putting Holy Water on its body. It was broken and lethally harmed, but your love and the Father's Will brought it back to health again. You saw how gleefully the little bird skipped away from the place where you laid it. It should not surprise you that this happened. So today, I ask you and your brother to beseech Jesus to bring the spiritual and physical healing to the many for whom you pray. I do this as well, and I ask that those who are healed understand the reason. I have said this to you many times. It is the same principle as whether someone loves others, and do the others know it. I realize that you are getting plentiful exercise as you exert energy assembling your new building components inside the garage. Yes, this is the type of physical motion that your body needs. You will find that your days will be happier when you allow your body to shed the toxins that build up inside it. A sedentary lifestyle is counterproductive to good health. I am pleased that you asked your friend to help you today because he enjoys your company. You are such a good example for him. All in all, I believe that you are making good progress on the construction of your new building. There too, we are aware of the constitution of the spiritual realms that we are helping shape through our daily prayers. The Angels told your brother that your new book has the capacity to convert millions of people to Jesus on the Cross. They declared that it would be ironic if this new book, published at the behest of your pleas, would be the one that would set the world back in its seat – this after an entire twelve-book prelude containing My Morning Star Over America messages idles in ecclesial discernment. It is My hope that 'The Final Colossus' will stir the heart of your nation to accept who I am as the Morning Star Over America. My little sons, I pray that you realize that it would have been impossible for your work to have been celebrated around the nation and the world while you have been assembling your books. You have seen the reason why the Medjugorje visionaries have been unable to finish their memoirs – they have been overwhelmed by the pilgrims there, and others who are surrounding them out of curiosity. I have said many times that irony abounds. Yes, the official deposit of My works here might be slow in being accepted, but the extraordinary private messages you have prayed to receive are devastating to the indifference of this world. Who would have guessed? Let us see what the Lord has planned. I am saying that your original deposit of works will have its intended effect, but what will spark the books to reach far into the lost precincts of the Earth? I find this prospect to be intriguing and providential. It is to the joy of the heavens that you and your brother have invested your lives in this remarkable journey that will take the created world to the Kingdom of the Father. I would like at great length to tell of Jesus' gratitude, but I know that you are aware of His thankfulness. My Special son, I do not wish for you and your brother to believe that your best days are behind you. Please refrain from focusing on how it feels to grow older. By many measures, you are still quite young. Think about the fact that your heart and soul never age; these are your supernal connections to God. It is all about how you think, and what you take into your hands. What do you dwell on that preserves the reach of eternity in each and every man? I am saying that you have the capacity to create new life in the hearts of your brothers and sisters because of your response to Me. If obedience is the answer that Jesus is seeking from His apostles, then you have given Him more than that for which He has called. If love has a measure, then you have more than sufficed its surplus. If sacred energy can be seen with the eyes, then the whole world is witnessing the essence of Heaven in your holy speeches and writings. You have harnessed it and put it on display for the entire globe to see. This is why I have said that you have the capacity to bring new life to the world. You have imagined what it would be like to live on an Earth that is free from sin and error, and from the sheer desire to commit it. You and your brother have answered the question through your obedience to Me that is posed by millions of Christians everywhere – when do the disciples of Jesus get their chance to win? You are handing them a victory that is deeply seated in the Triumph of My Immaculate Heart. Surely, you and your brother already know the outcome of the world. You should live with this sense of purpose, but the devil hurtles the barbs and burdens of secularism at you every day to deny your awareness of the victory at hand. Your minds, bodies and spirits are overwhelmed by the world's unfairness, injustice, heresies, and outright demonic lies. I wish to reassure you that none of these evils can change who you are. You still hold in your thoughts and prayers the motivations of Jesus that will destroy everything that runs contrary to the Will of God. And, as I have said, you cannot lose. You may be offended, battered and slandered, but you cannot be defeated. How do you know that your Morning Star Over America books will prevail? Because you are not in the news every day. You have not been invited by the Church to make your case for My messages in local parishes and at social functions. Do you remember what the world told Jesus? 'Go away.' They have not gone this far with you and your brother because God will not allow it to happen. The Father is waiting for you to fire all your weapons at once, just as I have said years ago.

In the meantime, My Special son, you and your brother are quietly increasing the ferocity of your arsenal. You are putting the devil and the wicked men of the Earth on notice to prepare for the onslaught of righteousness that we are about to launch against them. They are wasting their time – they do not stand a chance. Their obstinance is like a huge inflated balloon floating around a room with pine needles jutting from the walls. And, this is our joy; it is our anticipation. We do not begrudge a man his day in the sun, but by the time the Father finishes glorifying your work here in the exiled realms, these men, all of them, will run for the shade and hide wherever they can. These are not just hollow expectations. These are not hopes for something that will never come. This is the truth as authentic as it has ever been spoken. And, it comes to a world that is in no less turmoil than 25 or 50 or even 100 years ago. Indeed, what is the commentary for humanity these days? 'Which of the nations is going to scorch the lands of another with a thermonuclear holocaust.' Please know that My Son Jesus is the Prince of Peace, but He looks upon this inflammatory rhetoric as though it may not even matter. Truly, only His Kingdom matters. It is the refinement of the conscience of humanity upon which the Will of God is focused. My Special son, I am not trying to downplay the dangers that the world is facing in these times, I am citing the priorities that should be considered. I ask you and your brother to remember how well you have lived. You own the 'properties of prudence' that Jesus has instilled within your hearts. Your wisdom is Jesus' Wisdom. Your ability to alter the face of the Earth is as profound as His desire to cleanse it. Your perceptions of the Holy Gospel, still relevant in your day, are as accurate as the parables He addressed 2,000 years ago. This is why you and your brother are so esteemed and trusted in His sight. So, I wish you to ponder these things as you think about what you mean to Him. I look at you with the same overwhelming appreciation. I pray that the Lord will always safeguard you, honor your accomplishments, and fulfill your dreams. I will take your petitions to Jesus with great dispatch, asking Him to bring peace to your hearts and rest for your souls."

Sunday, August 20, 2017
3:15 p.m.

"Is there such thing as spiritual distortion? Perhaps. You will have your share of aches and pains, hard times and disappointments, but you will always be flush with blessings – and soon enough, you will inhale the sweet, luxurious fragrance of eternal redemption."

- The Dominion Angels

"Now, My little children, I come to you in the heights of joy because you belong to Me. I have never been more pleased with your lives, My Special and Chosen sons, because you are the perfect reflection of Jesus in this world. Yes, the luxurious fragrance of eternal redemption reminds you of the beatific origin of life. I wish for all My children to remember what it is like to be embraced by the Holy Spirit from within. Today, it is incumbent on us to pray for all the social unrest and upheaval that are happening around the globe. It is because humanity has yet to collectively adhere to the Gospel strains about nurturing peace in the heart, made manifest by the teachings of the King of the Gospel. My Special son, the Christian love shared between you and your brother for decades has yielded a lifetime of graces. Yes, it is in this nation that you and your brother are revealing the wishes of the Father through My messages to you. I know that you have seen your brother's written words to the university doctors, and they are a prayer to God for the enlightenment of all the world. And, what was their first response? 'We are not for abortion.' This is an outright falsehood. The two of them have given funds to Planned Parenthood, and they have been seen a dozen times marching in crowds carrying placards calling for so-called women's rights to choose abortion. As your brother said yesterday, '...if you are for the choice, you are for the act.' Thus, we are praying for the changing of the hearts of everyone involved in the evil and grotesque scourge of killing humanity's unborn children. I have said that the demonism of the devil is inside the leader of the Planned Parenthood organization, and it will require God's purifying wrath to wash her clean. You and your brother know that I wish no harm on anyone, but sinners like these bring themselves to the retribution they deserve. Please do not pity them when they cry out for relief. I would rather speak today about the bounty of your faith and the love it serves. I would like to refer to the dignity in your heart and the authenticity of your humanity. You have within you the ability to see through the smokescreens of the secular void. You recognize what it means when others reveal their distance from the beatific truth. There are eagles and streamers surrounding your thoughts and actions because you have maintained your trust in the Will of God. You have upheld your promise to remain loyal to Jesus. You have remained beneath the guidance and protection of My Holy Mantle for the whole of your life. This means that you are engaging Providence when pondering the effects of your decisions. Your life course is set by the authority of the Father within you; this is because Jesus lives in you, and Jesus is living for you. This is the deference about which Saint Paul and the Sacred Scriptures speak. It can be exemplified by many metaphors. How can a mustard seed become the magnification of one's faith? By realizing that simple faith can move mountains. It is how a butterfly landing on the side of an orbital launcher can have more power than the detonation itself. It is how something as diminutive as the Earth's moon can blot-out the light of the sun.

It is the way the wisdom of a child can conquer an entire army. These are the polar opposites that illustrate the contrast between a man without faith and one who believes in God with his whole heart. It is the salt and the light narrative that demonstrates what it means to be one in being with the Father through Jesus on the Cross. This is what must be known about history and the ages – all things flow toward the coming of the Kingdom about which Jesus spoke. There must be prayer for enlightenment and sacrifice to procure ethereal power. There must be the diminishment of the flesh in order for the spirit to prevail. My Special son, you and your brother are so far advanced in your knowledge of these things that I feel as though I am speaking to an angelic choir. But, I needed to tell somebody, and I thank you for your willingness to listen. It is in your hearing that the world itself is apprised. This is the transcendent fashioning of the Father's Kingdom on Earth. If the hummingbirds hear what I am saying to you, they will tell the trees. If the trees hear the words from My lips, they will tell the mountains. And, if the mountains are inspired by your reaction to what Heaven proclaims, then they will also be moved to speak. Yes, they will roar and rumble around the globe with delight that the Earth is finally being cleansed.

My Special son, there is height and texture to everything you believe. There is light and reflection in the things you practice. There is power and outcome in the intensity of your prayers. If anything about this is cyclical, it is only that the Father is taking you back to the days of Jesus' ministry, not just so that you can learn from it, but that you can project what He has taught you in the twenty centuries since He founded the Church. Everyone who goes to Heaven finds themselves present on Good Friday. Yes, it is another retroactive gift that is itself outside of time. This is the origin of the height and texture by which you measure the good and the bad. The most important point is that you ponder what lives in every man – is there virtue in his heart, or is there darkness and malevolence there? We have the benefit of knowing the criteria by which these judgments are made. You have the foresight and vision to know what type of conduct God is looking for. When you judge a man's actions, you do not weigh the worth of his soul, for this is Jesus' domain alone. But, you have the capacity to determine what kind of world he is building. You know the difference between an empire and a Kingdom. You have the ability to discern what is worth pursuing on an eternal basis because you have allowed this Kingdom to take residence in your heart. Make life holy! This is the mandate that Jesus has given the Church and all who follow Him. Cast out demons and admonish the unrighteous. Give food to the poor, and tell them in whose name they have been nourished. Walk upright with the confidence that your Christian faith instills in you. And most of all, allow your heart to be touched by the tenderness of Jesus' love. These are the qualities that summon the Spirit of God to come into the presence of those who pray. My Special son, when you read your books of My messages, you are 'encountering' God through His revelations that speak to the dire nature of the modern world. When you listen to Me speaking about the wisdom of truth and love, you are hearing the words of the Father, Himself. I say this to you because the same is true of you and your brother. You speak for Jesus in a world of sinners that has yet to fully acknowledge His Providence. Imagine how it makes Him feel when you speak for Him? It is the same as if your Bishop called a press conference to announce that the Mother of Jesus Christ has come into this diocese as the Morning Star Over America. The effect on the Lord in Heaven mirrors your speech about the virtues of the Gospel. This may be difficult to comprehend at this moment, but I am telling you the truth. It is your innocent faith that inspires Him. Hence, I have completed My message for today. Thank you for attending Holy Mass in Ashland this morning and remaining close to your family. You have a holy presence during these occasions because of your grace and stately poise. Thank you for sharing your lovely petitions, and your devotion to My Most Immaculate Heart. Bless you for allowing Me to speak to you and your brother today. I will pray for everything you have lifted to Me."

Saturday, August 26, 2017
9:31 a.m.

"Peace will reign victorious, even if over a cataclysm."

"My dear little sons, the pursuit of the Kingdom of God begins in the heart because the spiritualism that humanity acquires is imbedded there. I know that My children are capable of this, that the Church and the world have the capacity to reach out to this Kingdom through your prayers and meditations. In this sense, the Spirit of God is not only seeded in the heart, His Providence is seated there as well. My little sons, when you think about it properly, the peace of God cannot be destroyed. The Father is peace forever, and His peace comes to the world perpetually. It is a matter of acceptance by those upon whom the Spirit rests. My Special son, do you remember that the Peace of God is like a dove that will light wherever peace is welcomed? *"Yes."* This means that the hearts of humanity must be prepared; they must be cultivated to receive the blessings of life. And in doing this, peace will reign victorious in the hearts of all who believe in Jesus, who give themselves to His dignity and power, who reject the devil's works and all the distractions with which he impedes humanity's vision of love. If we give this message to them in the way of the Saints, we will allow their legacies to flourish around the nations – Me as their Mother, and you as their devoted brothers. It is a consecration that men make to other men, to their lives, souls and futures. It is the connecting of the life's mission of those who search for something greater than the passing from this world into the next. It is not so much leaving an indelible mark on history or the ages, but creating an atmosphere conducive to welcoming the Lord's Spirit, just as I have said. My little sons, when the final pronouncements are made about the faith in the hearts of humanity, it must be said that something redeeming came of it. The Church must not just be an institution without producing holy outcomes. There must be fruits from the planting that are harvested for purposes larger than human life. A recognizable change must be there; a sense of transformation must be apparent to those who have been watching both up close and from afar. And, if this transformation has the power intended by Jesus on the Cross, life as men on Earth now know it will become just a shadowy memory. This is how the corruption of human history will be erased and supplanted by a new righteousness. This is how the virtue of 'glory' becomes both a process of human refinement and the product of its refinement too. My Special son, if I were to send someone out to get some 'glory' and bring it back to Me, where would they go? *"They would go live life, and secure it by their imitation of Jesus."* Yes, you are precisely correct. And, if their vision is according to the teachings of the Gospel, it would not be a problem equating glory with human conduct. And, what if the person I sent forward asked Me before departing what I wanted them to carry it in. What should I tell them? *"In the heart."* Exactly, the correct answer again. My Special son, this is more than the impression of faith by which most people live. It is a transitional faith that speaks to the actual purpose of believing in God to achieve a righteous end – a new beginning and the shedding of one's former life. This means that the human heart is a vessel where the meditations that find themselves within it overflow into the vast earthly domain. Does this suggest that the heart has a given capacity? Not at all; endless love and righteousness flow from the heart, generated and reflected from the power of God into the created realms. We know that there is no true wealth without this spiritual richness. It is a fact that the human heart can beat for 100 years, but without the Spirit of God at its core, it has no eternal purpose. It is just a part of the human anatomy that binds the soul to the flesh. My Special one, this is the reason that peace will always prevail over the cataclysms of the secular void. It is the reason there is life in Jesus, and death without Him. The entire prospect revolves around one's ability to take flight with the Holy Spirit in the heart as opposed to being earthbound separated from Him. The cataclysm that I speak of finds its origin in the indifference of impious men. It is shorn of peace because peace is its nemesis. Your lives, poured out benignly and profoundly, are generating the capacity for humanity to overcome every catastrophe known to man. It is not just that you are praying for peace, but that you are in Jesus' Most Sacred Heart, making it manifestly true. Can you feel this happening? "*Yes.*" It is because you have willed this into being within the Will of God that is spread before humanity and the Earth in deluges and overages – all for the purpose of purging the world of evil.

My Special son, I have just given you the definition of prayer. It is not that someone is walking down the street with a music box on their shoulder, it is that they are placing the box on the ground, taking to their knees, and giving their fullest attention to their unity with Heaven. God will listen when they set their sights on Him – He does not even mind if a young man begins his prayers with, '...hey dude.' Coming to the Father with the Spirit of Love in the heart is a greater connection with eternity than the touch that first created it. It is a more impassioned plea than that which spared the world from nuclear holocaust in October 1962. By all means, taking to prayer by invoking the presence of God in the heart has more meaning than any other act that either begets life or threatens it. Prayer is a reconciliation between those who have been estranged. It is bringing light into the darkness. It is quenching dire thirsts and stanching lethal bleeding. My Special son, My messages to you and your brother have been of this critical nature. My actions in past centuries have led to this. The greatest question that humanity could ask in the history of all the worlds combined is this – 'What is the Will of God?' How can there be such depravation; such turmoil, sorrow and annihilation, such disease and brokenness? It all comes down to learning the role of man in acquiring the wisdom of the Father. It is about uniting with Jesus on the Cross as Christians aspiring to His perfection. It is reflecting what the Crucifixion means to those who refuse to learn. It is about embracing passion and sacrifice in ways that humanity can scarcely understand. And, as you have seen, it is about making hard choices and exhibiting scrupulous conduct that gives venue for the Cross to shine through – these are the acts of men polishing their souls skillfully. This is why the Guardian Angels beg their chance to intercede. They will do so if humanity will stop chasing the infernal pathways of sin instead of the righteous path of holiness in Jesus, raised from the Tomb on Easter Morning. My Special son, I am giving you only a brief description of a world prone to sin that must turn itself to the righteousness of the Son of Man. And, as usual, I have not told you anything that you did not already know. I am speaking to you and your brother to amplify My own prayers. All I ask is that you join Me in the hope that has given Me such joy. It would have little effect for God to bring up the lights on this world until the world itself gets completely dark. My dear sons, it is almost there. This is the source of wonderment that is about to engulf humanity. The New World to come is brightly shining and forever esteemed. It is within you now, My Special and Chosen ones. It is just beyond the grasp of your senses. It will soon overlay your lives with new glory to supersede the laborers who will not report for work, the long days that are much too hot, stubborn affairs both here and abroad, flames that will not ignite, and lights that keep burning out. My Special son, I will add to this message in the future when you and your brother are more rested. I am filled with joy that you have prayed with Me here this morning, and that you are strong and vibrant in matters of the Spirit."

Saturday, September 2, 2017
9:33 a.m.

Fear lurks inside the mind.
Courage lives in the blood.
Peace births new beginnings.
Love inspires a gentle heart.

- The Dominion Angels

"Brilliantly you live, My dear little sons. You have manifested for your brothers and sisters an example of holiness that will remain far beyond the ages. Imagine what it is like for Me to watch you engaging the years. With what imagining you have taken on the burdens of life, that you encounter them with care and confidence, with sureness and a drive to succeed. I have such admiration for you, My Special and Chosen sons, that it cannot be placed into words. Here today, I have come to pray with you for everything that instills in your hearts the movement of the world toward the Kingdom of Heaven. My Special son, I hope that you do not believe that I am over-expressing Myself, but I cannot keep from celebrating the gifts you have given to Jesus and the Church. *"Thank you, Mama. I just pray for the Bishop to be heroic in defending and propagating your work."* I know the origin and purpose of your prayers, and the Father hears your voice. It reflects His own. All Bishops have their own self-will, even after being elevated to episcopal stature. They are attuned to the Holy Spirit as much as their faith allows. Just as Jesus did not cease being human during His earthly mission, His Apostles and their successors have clung to their humanity as well. This is the main point about accepting Jesus on the Cross and serving as His earthly disciples. Human beings remain human, even in this discipleship. As I recently said, being human does not infer inevitability toward corruption. I have said that just because human beings are susceptible to sin, and that they are prone to temptation, it does not mean that they are predestined to commit it. I have told humanity in Medjugorje that it is possible to be so holy that Christians will not realize their passage from this life into the next. It has always been My desire that My children will know that they have this capacity because they would not otherwise strive to be holy. My Special son, your brother said yesterday that not many people will try to become saints in this life if they believe it will only take effect in Heaven. He was correct in his assertion, but it must be made clear that being 'chosen and elect' implies that sainthood is built here on Earth, and is conferred in Heaven. People pass into sainthood in the afterlife by not carrying the stain of sin because they have received the penitential Sacraments of the Church. It is the same as pouring liquid into a cast that, once the liquid becomes solid and the cast is removed, the finished product is revealed. Men on Earth are being filled with the Holy Spirit, full and complete, here in this life. And, this is the shape that their lives and souls take in preparation for their journey into eternity. My Special son, you and your brother have never felt it, but there are millions of people who can discern when the Holy Spirit enters their heart. The reason you have never felt it is because, as a sign of grace, you and your brother were united in faith with the Spirit of God on the day you were conceived. Sinners yes, but united nonetheless with the Providence of God that is shedding this same holy light upon you now. Others have for their own reasons either disregarded or rejected the presence of God in their lives, and their conversion is like setting their hearts afire. It is an emphatic moment to behold. I have told you on many occasions that the spiritual enlightenment of an unholy person is much more striking when their consciousness is far from God. They have a longer journey to travel. The unity of the heart with the Spirit of God is the same as someone close to Him, but the distance is more starkly defined. This can be seen through the metaphor of dropping an object from ten miles in the air compared to one mile. The speed of descent is the same, but the distance is farther in the earlier case. Do you understand? *"Yes. Thank you."* This has wide implications on a spiritual basis for people like those who sat next to you and your brother at dinner last night. You could sense their disconnection from divine grace. And, you and your brother had the appropriate thoughts – you knew that they were enemies of the Cross and adversaries of the Gospel that Jesus has imparted to the world. One might inquire where is the sacrifice in what they believe? And, to make matters worse, they uphold and venerate Me as an example of perfect womanhood. This is as contradictory as anything you might see.

I ask you and your brother to remember that you have dedicated your lives to propagating the Gospel of Salvation that the Father has given to exiled humanity. You have had your own Marian vocations that have filled the void in human history about the knowledge of Myself in imparting the Good News to the world. You have wondered why these revelations of My role in the sanctification and redemption of humanity have been withheld until the twentieth and twenty-first centuries beyond the Life, Death and Resurrection of Jesus. It is because I wished to make sure that all the faculties were in place – the effect of time, the exchange of information, the modes of communication, the conditions in the world that make for the globalization of My Messianic messages. And, the Lord needed to wait until you and your brother attained a sufficient age to embark on the work to which you have been assigned. The latter is the most important part. I wish for you to remember what I am going to tell you now. I have said that parish churches where Masses are offered are transported to Heaven as you attend the Holy Sacrifice. The churches we see in Heaven have stained-glass windows too – and these windows have iconic images of you and your brother imbedded in them. *"Thank you, Mama. It's only because of you."* My Special son, these stained-glass windows were fashioned into being by Saint William Leo Roth, Senior. (*My father, who died in 2016, crafted beautiful stained-glass windows and prayer shrines as a creative hobby during his life.*) It is all connected – everything you see, hear and know about the unity of God and humanity is created through the lives and actions of those who have believed in Him. There is always the 'image of the splendor of men' that begins in the exiled world, and completes itself in the Church Triumphant. It is as though the eyes of a Saint see the fullness of Heaven while the Saint's feet are grounded on the Earth below. When I speak about consistency, commitment and confidence, I am referring to these eternal designs. You cannot offer a gift for the conversion and redemption of lost sinners that the Father does not see, bless and ratify. My Special son, I hope you have enjoyed what I came to share today. *"Yes, thank you."* Do you have any issues to discuss with Me this morning? *"I offer My petitions for people who are being treated so horribly around the world. Please change it for them."* I will do as you ask, and we need to pray that sinners will stop being sinners. There is tremendous light that can be seen by those who are willing to open their eyes, but there is much darkness in which wicked sinners can hide that is created by their own hands. However, My Special son, the latter of these do so to their own demise. I hope you and your brother will rest when you are tired, and avoid situations and people who are vexing to your spirits. I have given you countless blessings through the years, but you have gifted Me many in return. I wish to close today with a special word of thanks. I heard you say that My messages to you and your brother have been the venue through which you have learned to write about Jesus and the Church, about humanity and eternal promise, about the wrongs that must be righted, and the ills that must be cured. I wish to say that I wept in thanksgiving upon hearing your kind sentiments. Thank you. *"Please help me know how to reach out with your messages."* I will do precisely that, and Jesus through the Holy Spirit will inspire your heart with the wisdom, words and timing. I am grateful to everyone who elevates Me as Mother of the Church, and the Mother of humanity. I will make My gratitude known!"

Saturday, September 9, 2017
9:28 a.m.

Our Lady, The Virgin of Bethlehem –
"Forgiveness is love's finest hour."

"Sincerely, I wish you the best of all your hopes and dreams, and I do My noblest to intercede before Jesus to make them come true. It is always a good day when I tell My children that My love for you is more tremendous than the fullness of eternity. Today, I come to help you spread your prayers and petitions over the landscapes of the Father's domain, and I wish for you to know that He listens as intently as anyone might imagine. I have also come today, My Special and Chosen sons, because you are touching Heaven with your lives. You are partaking of the cultivation of the hearts laid fallow by indifference; you are bringing into being the awakening of the consciences that have been asleep for decades. What does it mean to touch Heaven? First, you know that it implies that God wishes your souls to encounter His divinity through His copious sovereignty and gentleness. He desires humanity to experience His charity and kindness. As you have been told that the Father is slow to anger, He is also swift to forgive. The richness of His absolution is worth more than all the gold beneath a billion cosmic suns. It is to this forgiveness that My children are called. Yes, and you are called to practice holy love here on the Earth because forgiveness is love's finest hour. Please ponder, My Special son, whether you believe that God has ever apologized for anything. If so, what do you suppose it would be? *"I don't know of anything for which He would apologize. He is not guilty of any offense."* I wish you to think of this possibility. Could the Father find within Himself the Spirit to apologize to every good soul who enters into His heavenly presence? Might He say to the Saints that He is sorrowful that His Spirit could not reach the wicked wretches who made the Saints' journey back to Him so difficult? Yes, He offers apologetic sentiments on a daily basis to the holiness of good men and women who suffer in His name. It is an acknowledgment of the torments of exile, but not an admission of fault that humanity was cast there. His apology is defined as His reacquisition of human souls into His presence, the Supreme Deity who is pleased to welcome them home. My Special one, do you suppose that the father of the prodigal son might have offered an apology of any sort? If so, it is only that he could not make his love for his son so apparent that the son would not have wandered into the prodigal life. Here again, this is not an admission of fault or guilt, it is a concession that living the responsible life, the holy life, is much more difficult than many sinners are willing to bear. I am saying to you that not only does God redeem the penitent; not only does He open His arms and welcome those who have lived according to His Word, He makes clear that He understands the struggles and oppressions thrust upon those who have lived for Him. It is one of the affirmative dimensions of His boundless compassion. My Special son, the Father does this for another meaningful reason. What do you suppose could bring God to tears as He invokes compassion for those who have led the saintly life? The answer is in their response. It is when the Saints say, '*...it is all right, Father. I lived the holy life because I loved you. I gave everything to your Church because the Church lives in me. I handed my life to your Son because He lived out the meaning of righteousness. I have loved you because you have loved me.*' My Special son, I have asked all My messengers, seers, visionaries and locutionists throughout the ages to think about what they might say to God when He tells them that He has empathy for everything they endured for Him. I know your heart as well as the Sacred Heart of Jesus, and I can imagine what you will tell the Father on that day. It makes Me teary-eyed thinking about it. The Father confides in every redeemed sinner His own compassion and empathy for the struggles they faced in the fight between goodness and evil. There are multiple ways that this can be interpreted, but there is only one conclusion to be drawn – God did not just deposit human souls on the earthen floor to fend for themselves without divine assistance from Heaven. Yes, compassion for the long, hard road of human life in a world infested by the wicked and the wretched. There is nothing illogical about it. He places in your midst evidence of the compassion that He has for your painful lives. It is in your awareness of who you are in Jesus. The Father does not ask that 'you' be diminished as a dignified person living in the world, but that your identity becomes the identity of Jesus. I have said that love itself cannot be weighed or measured, and the same is true of the human soul. Jesus does not ask for your soul to become any smaller as you live His image during your mortal years. He asks that you flourish in His likeness with your soul intact. You once wrote that the human soul does not enter Heaven in phases. This means that it cannot be divided or parsed into pieces. The human soul that God sees is capable of miraculous gifts, the best of which is adopting the identity of Jesus as its reason for being. It is for Jesus to live in you – this is what the Father is saying. My Special son, there have been times when speaking to My messengers that I have said that they are not aware of the immensity of their contributions to the Church. I have shared this with you and your brother. This time, however, I veritably believe that you are both aware of the masterpiece that you will be delivering to your Bishop in a few short weeks. No matter who assembled the messages into one book, regardless of who authored the stunning opening chapters, you and your brother are wholly aware of the impact this work will have on the future of the world and the mission of the Church. Please imagine what someone who knows nothing about your lives might say if presented your new 'Final Colossus' book without knowing its background. It is almost too much to take in.

My Special son, do you have anything to discuss with Me today? *"I pray for all the people who are suffering because of the bad weather and fires."* Yes, you may wonder whether these events are chastisements from God for the way the United States is conducting it affairs. The answer is not that these events are of the vengeance of the Lord, but they are allowed to happen to convert the hearts and minds of Americans to Him, in whom many have lost faith. There are prayers aplenty being said by people who have never turned to God. And, what is the result? Millions are seeing the fruits of their petitions unfolding right before their eyes. The twisting hurricane is drifting more offshore. This is reasonable evidence that God is listening. Thank you and your brother for holding fast to your faith, for being not only co-identifiers with Jesus, but completely unified with Him to the essences of yourselves. I know that it is often difficult to discern where your identities leave off and Jesus' identity begins – and this was the plan from the beginning. I ask you to remember that Jesus has always been patient with humanity and long-suffering in His desire to redeem them. He has been loving and understanding with those who are far from the Church, and it is according to their decisions what they will do to enter the fold or be further lost in darkness. The Father is awaiting their response. Please receive My blessings for living in such piety with your brother, for taking such good care of him, and for lifting your prayers for peace and justice to inundate the lives and nations that are far and near. Love cannot be stopped; righteousness cannot be diluted, and the conversion of the lost will never be in vain."

Sunday, September 17, 2017
9:30 a.m.

"What does it take to raise up a Kingdom? An Immaculate Conception, an Angel of the Lord, a Fiat, a Messianic Birth, a Gospel, one Crucifixion, one Resurrection, and one indomitable Holy Spirit."

"Seeking the Kingdom of Heaven is like searching for a pair of glasses that are already on your face."

- The Dominion Angels

"With profound gratitude, I come today speaking to you, My dear little sons. Thank you for attending the healing Mass at the parish dedicated to Christ the King. The Lord does not disappoint you. I wish for you to know that the faith of humankind is valued over all other treasures, and what you experienced was a blessing for leading your lives in the fullness of your faith. My dear little sons, the 'providing' that you receive from God is your life's support. The love you cherish in your hearts is your sacred energy. The miracles and blessings that you see and receive are your guidance through the darkest days. And, My intercession to Jesus on your behalf is your most endearing gift. My Special son, you have been told that faith cannot be earned, and neither can redemption be earned. These are literary terms. You also know that faith and Salvation cannot be purchased. Purchasing something is a literary device as well. However, faith, enlightenment and Salvation are granted in exchange for repentance so the human heart can be opened and filled with the truth of the Holy Spirit. Even as you have read the evocative verses and passages of the Sacred Scriptures, you must not believe that the redemption of the soul is something that the Father offers just because He has nothing better to do. The idea of 'earning' it is incorrect, for the Grace of God is your Salvation. The issue is that the mere presence of man does not mean that unity with the Most Blessed Trinity is a foregone conclusion. The exile of humanity exists for a reason. This, therefore, is the purpose by which you have taken pen in hand for nearly thirty years and written volumes for the enlightenment of the human species. Yes, the literary term that befits what is happening is 'conversion.' It could be said that the Father in Heaven is receptive to the conversion of lost sinners because this is something that each soul should give Him. There is a conversation that must take place between God and His Church. In a sense, when humanity on the Earth converts to the Holy Cross, it is their way of saying to God that they are thankful for the gift of life. And, it is by the Crucifixion that the Father says, 'You are welcome.' My Special one, there are other concepts that could be applied to the transformation of the world into the righteousness of God. One such term would be 'development.' Others would include words like transformation and transition – whatever provides the impression that the human soul is not stagnant on the Earth, and that each soul has a vision for something greater than life. Many Saints have compared the earthly experience to resting in Jesus beyond the tenure of their lives. While I appreciate what this means, I would prefer saying that living souls, either exiled or in Heaven, are always at rest in Jesus when their hearts are consecrated to Him. 'I shall not rest until I rest in Thee' is a noble oath, and this resting can begin with any man or woman still in exile. This is what I meant when I said that the soul, heart and mind can go to Heaven and never realize the transfer from this life to the next. My dear child, it is a matter of the senses. When someone accepts the Christian life, it is like putting one's ear to an invisible wall where the Afterlife is located on the other side. You can hear the sensations of glory reverberating in the human heart by virtue of the Sacred Spirit living there. It is also the same as imagining a beautiful mountain range in your thoughts, and then later seeing a mountain range precisely like the one you imagined. This is part of the 'providing' that God instills in the human spiritual conscience. The Lord says, '...I will help you envision My Kingdom, providing you remain true to your faith.' He asks men on Earth to nurture the gift of faith that He hands down. It does not require any food or water, but feeds on the devotion of the heart filled with love. Nurturing and protecting one's faith means that it must be accorded the fruits of prayer. This is not only the life-sustaining energy that keeps Christians strong, it is the faith-sustaining momentum that provides the vision to keep going. Walking a path unencumbered means that there is already an existing passage, or the traveler has a vision that cannot be impeded by any obstruction, fear or danger. In the case of the Christian soul making his way to Heaven, it is often concurrently both.

Yes, the senses. There is an expectation that builds up in the mind of the Christian that manifests thoughts of vindication. It is not the soul that is vindicated because sinners are forgiven, not found to be free from guilt. Vindication means that everything that the Christian does to safeguard and keep alive his faith is vindicated by God. This is the template for binding in Heaven what is bound on Earth. It is the effect of humble prayer. My Special son, you and your brother have found yourselves within this framework of life. All that you pray for is imbedded in the Providential Will of the Father. Your speeches, writings and intentions are built into the architecture of the world's final moments. The history that you have created here in this home and in your lives is the substance of glory. What you might see as minuscule in the eyes of humanity is immeasurable in the mind of God. My purpose this morning is to declare that you have a vision that can capture the instincts of all pious men in one place – the cornerstone of miracles that you and your brother have laid. It is appropriate that you sense this gift so you will never forget what you have done. I know that you would never boast before humanity or the heavens that you have taken on this stature. But, if you do not mind, I will do your boasting for you. *"Thank you, Mama. I appreciate your kindness. The things you do are so meaningful."* I will tell the nations and the Mansions of Paradise that you have done the work that the Lord has asked you to do. I will soon have the Morning Star Over America not only ringing out over the mountains of Medjugorje, I will take My messages given to you and your brother to the summits and valleys of every continent on Earth. The lands will tell the seas that the Morning Star Over America has come. It will be a liberating annunciation that will rival the Great Archangel Gabriel. It will lead souls to the Grand Enlightenment that the peoples of the Earth always wanted. Why? Because God in Heaven loves them. Because faith means more to human life than believing what someone sees. It means establishing a relationship with the Father whose face they have sought in their dreams. Yes, it is about having a conversation with everything eternal that begins here and now. It is regaining one's consciousness, and discovering what knocked you out. It is a providing that comes only from the presence of God. Yes, My Special son, it is the senses. It is in anticipating the aroma of redemption wafting through the air, the same as you inhaled the fragrance of the roses in the Christ the King sanctuary. It is about forecasting not whether a miracle might come, but what your miracle will be. These are among the feelings that Christians should harbor for themselves. 'It is not whether God loves me, but *that* God loves me.' It is in the touching of the Holy Spirit at the center of the human heart that gives the Church reason to believe. There has never been a more gentle touch in the history of Creation. Insight, glory, absolution, enlightenment, sanctification, deliverance and perpetuity – all these things are inherited from the touch of the Holy Spirit to the seen and unseen surfaces of the repentant human life. My Special son, I could write a poem to describe what I am saying today, but you and your brother have already sufficed the rhymes, rhythms, cadences and symbolisms that any Kingdom might ever need. You have laid your lives alongside Jesus and the Saints, and there is no wanting to be found in you. I ask that you understand why all this has been done. It is because you have said 'yes' to Me in the same way that I pronounced My Fiat to the Archangel Gabriel. I beseech you to know how authentic My voice is this morning. I do not come seeking your approval as if to be a creature from the unknown. I am asking you and your brother to accept to the depths of your hearts the sincerity in which I offer My gratitude. *"Thank you. I accept."* My Special son, My great prayer, My everlasting prayer, My most heartfelt prayer is that you will someday tell humanity that above all things, the Blessed Virgin Mary, the Mother of Jesus Christ, is the most grateful Woman ever given the breath of life. Will you tell them this for Me? *"Yes, with every breath."* I have completed My message this morning. I truly hope that you have liked it. *"Yes, very much, thank you."* I assure you that everything for which you pray is heard by the Father in Heaven, especially the prayers that serve to change the hearts of the wicked and expunge evil from the face of the Earth."

Saturday, September 23, 2017
9:06 a.m.

The redemption accord –
A sovereign with a plan makes a presence for a purpose.

"Yes, My dear children, the Infant Narrative and the Messianic Sacrifice comprise this plan, and the deliverance of lost sinners to the bounty of Paradise is its purpose. I have come to pray with you this morning because the God of your fathers is listening. It is as though the world is parched and hungry, and your only satisfaction is the Lord's response from Heaven. My dear little sons, if you ponder for a moment, you will recognize that people often think in images. If you would like a strawberry pie, you think about what it looks like on a plate. This thought then enhances your desire for its sweetness, and the pie-seeking quest goes forward. Thinking in images is the reason people see scenes when they dream. The whole matter is wrapped up in yielding meaning from the envisionment that thought creates. This is another reason why Jesus spoke in parables – they are literary images that transferred the meaning He shared. I have told you these things to say that love in the way of life and absolution must create in the heart an image that is suitable for rendering the holiness that Jesus teaches. It is all about forgiveness, which comes only when the heart is tendered to the righteousness through which the conversion of humanity occurs. It is a domain that preserves all that is perfect, and expels everything imperfect. It comes down to the rebirth and redevelopment of the human person through the Kingdom of God on Earth. And with this, each soul undergoes its own infant narrative. Its rebirth into the Father is borne through one's new identity in Jesus. My Special son, these are the fundamentals that unknowing people need to learn. Look and see how far you and your brother have advanced. You hold in your hands the published work of My AD 2010-2012 messages that appear subsequent to the true wisdom in your book – the seven chapters of brilliant theology from your heart. It does not matter what the world does with your work at this time. All you need is to publish it in a format to be seen, and the Father will do the rest. Just as the soul of collective humanity cannot pass to the Father without Jesus, these same souls cannot comprehend Jesus' Divine Mercy without Me. You will not see this prescribed in the Church – but it is true nonetheless. I have been looking for all the Saint Johns on Earth who were represented by the Original Saint John the Apostle on Good Friday. I have found millions down through the ages. And, I have searched for the sanctification of women who have created a legacy of purity and kindness in the likeness of Myself, and I have found millions of them as well. This is the transfer of deific grace from the Father in Heaven to the exile of man, and back again. The circle becomes complete. Today, My Special son, I will not be speaking at length to you and your brother because your lives are busy, and there needs to be resting going on. I only wish to make Myself heard, and tell you that the blessings of God and the distinction of Jesus' providence remain with you. You have seen the signs of exhaustion on your brother's face, and it is because of all the intense work that he has been doing for so many years. The college courses to which he is tending have no effect on him – they are not that demanding in any way. He has mastered their academic secularism multiple times over. I am praying along with your brother that conditions at your workplace become more peaceful. This has been a constant theme for the past twenty years of My appearances here. American workers are pressed into stressful duties. Leaders are sometimes crass and uncaring about their workers' lives. This is the environment in which you have invested your time and laid open your heart, and I realize that it has been difficult for you. *"I'm thankful for the beautiful people that work with me. A couple of them need a little work, but they will get better."* One of the things that would help is if they would ask themselves what it would feel like to be on the receiving end of their brashness. My Special son, one of the worst causes of workplace disorder is the inability of people to confess and communicate their own weaknesses and ineptitude. Low self-esteem is one of the greatest causes of conflict over all other feelings. I know that many individuals do not have the spiritual foundation that I have given you and your brother, but this does not exempt them from being kind and respectful. My Immaculate Heart is with you and all who are fighting for the Kingdom of the Father to prevail in this earthly domain. We have said that the struggle seems uphill, but there are vast and beatific periods of solace along the way. Every time you hand the gift of your days and lives to Jesus anew, God has reason to hope in the faith of men. Human life is a process toward the culmination of Creation in the hands of the Father who deigned it into being. I will pray as you are praying. I will remember to Jesus all who are searching for the truth, all who are touching the Cross in excruciating ways, and all who held fast to the Crucifixion long before passing into the arms of God at the final moment of their lives.

    I would like to draw a connection this morning that I have never mentioned before. I once told you that the most important word that I have said to humanity is 'patience.' This is a prayer, meaning that patience and prayer are complements in the bastion of the human heart. Patience implies endurance, and prayer implies expectation. It is possible for humanity to sustain the burdens of life without losing sight of the victory. I wish for My children to build a lasting friendship with Jesus through the Holy Spirit so they feel comfortable with Him. People confide in those around whom they feel at ease, with those they know they can trust. This is the kind of friendship, brotherhood and dependency that Jesus wishes to have with those whom He died to save. Yes, the redemption accord is empowered by this deep reflective friendship. It is the spirit that overcomes the flesh. It is the joy that drives away the sorrow. It is the life that vanquishes the death. I wish My children to know that there are times when measurable, identifiable triumphs will come. Some are small in nature, but others are great in magnitude. Some events divide time into segments, others suspend it altogether. This is the emphasis that the release of your new book will have on the unfolding of the Earth. Everything that the Church will accomplish from now forward will be affected by the deliverance of My AD 2010-2012 book of messages to your diocesan chancery. It will not appear in the morning newspaper the next day, but nothing that has ever happened on the battlefield, in Times Square or Cape Canaveral in Florida will have the impact on the future of man the way of your new book. I am not speaking in exaggeration today, My Special son, I am stating the facts. *"Thank you, Mama. You are so beautiful."* I am beautiful because I was given life by God to preserve your joy and make manifest the true meaning of your faith in Jesus. I cannot overstate what this gift means to the Church and to the Most Blessed Trinity in Heaven. The substance of glory is present in this."

Sunday, October 1, 2017
9:29 a.m.

"Humanity can assemble panels of experts; men have the capacity to make choices and render decisions. But, they must always manifest wisdom. They must counsel one another beneath the arches of virtue, calculate on the basis of reason, and make judgments along the lines of truth."

"In its quest for survival, the human body adapts to various levels of pain – and so does the heart. At the last, imagine which one prevails."

- The Dominion Angels

"My dear little sons, you are the heralds for Jesus who have redefined what it means to be visionaries of truth. You have outlasted your enemies and transcended the exile in which humanity has been sentenced. I wish you could know through these simple words what this means to Creation and the eternity that engulfs it. Today, I have come to pray with you for the conversion of lost sinners, many of whom have no idea that their lives are in such commotion. It is their own stagnancy in sin that has caused this. It is their inability to connect with the benign spirit within themselves. It is their reluctance to acknowledge that they are powerless without God. I wish for you to receive the sentiments of the Dominion Angels this morning with particular welcome because they are closer to the world because of your prayers. The Dominion Angels are known for their leadership in holiness, directing and assisting humanity to move forward on the path of righteousness. And, I would like to speak today about a topic with overarching meaning. It is the concept of 'there.' What does this mean? On a casual basis, it is a place. It is somewhere that someone or something exists. You put something 'there.' You send someone 'there.' You go 'there' yourselves. However, in the mind of the God of your fathers and the existence of the self, it has an entirely new meaning. You have been told that Heaven is a place, and it is also a condition. Saint John Paul the Great was known for saying that Heaven is a spiritual condition, but he knew that Heaven is both. There are many mansions in the Father's House. It is 'there' that sinners should pray to go. But today, I wish for you to consider that 'there' means that humanity is undergoing a spiritual transfer. One cannot be relocated unless he leaves someplace and goes somewhere else. He goes from here to there, and all the energy is focused on the journey. In spiritual and eternal terms, 'there' can only mean that human beings are moved from their place on Earth to the ethereal infinity of Heaven. They go from 'there' to 'everywhere.' Life on Earth is a place of preparation, and eternal life in Heaven is a 'place' of perpetuity. The human soul moves from a temporal existence to endless spiritual life. It is the transformation from a fragile property to a flawless estate by the existence of the human soul. While this is not difficult to understand, it is an overwhelming transition for the soul being redeemed. This is when the person can confirm through the freedom of Jesus' Resurrection that there no longer exists a 'there' for him. He speaks about the presence of God being 'here.' And looking back, the expanse of Creation is likewise 'here.' I wish for My children on Earth to make this proclamation before surrendering their lives to death. My Special son, this is what you and your brother have already done. You know that Heaven lives within your hearts, and you have accepted that the Spirit of God's Kingdom is alive in you. The fact that you are still in the flesh and inside the bounds of the created realms does not obstruct your ability to know. I cannot overstate at what a loss earthly people are by not seeing what you see. They cannot imagine the transfer of the human identity into the 'person' of Jesus because they are slaves to their own sense of self. They do not know what it means to relocate their personalities and preferences from 'here' to 'there' in order for Jesus to live within them. In other words, they have a distorted focus about what being a Christian means because they do not know what to do with their original selves. They see a chasm between who they are and who Jesus is. Remember that Jesus said that every Christian is His other self. This is the reason that the Church lives-on, to assist not only their understanding, but their transfer into the identity of their Savior. My Special son, many of the most ardent Christians have yet to understand this transference, but it is true. It is the presence of the Mystical Body that Jesus has given Himself – His own identity, self-sufficiency, direction and eternal meaning. This is the entire purpose of Jesus living within the enlightened human heart.

So, My message this morning is about the spiritual confluence of 'being' someone and 'doing' something. Identity cannot be separate from action. My Special son, the reason I am telling you this today is to illustrate that exiled men do not understand what it means to be both physical and spiritual at the same time. They see themselves as physical first, and spiritual second. A person cannot hit a home run without first becoming a baseball player. A driver cannot win a championship race without becoming a competitor. It is a sequence or process. However, the self-profession of becoming a Christian means that the person and the process are united in the spiritual domain where there is no concept of time. And, this began when God first said in the ancient days, 'I AM.' And through Jesus, the Father desires His creatures to be a perfect reflection of who 'He is' as the Mystical Body of His Son. It goes back to the existence of 'there.' Do you know why? *"Because we are in a process."* Yes, and because God through the Son will make the 'there' of the Earth a beatific part of His heavenly 'here.' It is no more complicated than this. I wish to impress upon you that only about a hundred people would understand what I have just told you. Others would throw up their hands, say 'good grief' and return to their dinner tables and fine wines. This is the reason I have told you and your brother that you have advanced in your understanding of the Providence of God to the degree that you have already laid claim to your portion of His Kingdom in this life. And, when you enter Heaven, you will see that this portion has always been with every soul who is delivered into His presence. You have only a portion now because of the confines of the flesh. You are stationed here; you are one of billions who are suficing the reason you were given life. You are one of the warriors for the redemption of lost sinners in the same way as the Saints and Doctors of the Church. And, you must live out your life to the final day in dignity, knowing that God has validated your decades on Earth. You must know that every day you live for the remainder of your years means that the shape of Heaven will be more glorious than if you had entered it the day before. There was a time in your life when you were the youngest person in the world. Yes, think about this. Now, you must strive to live as long as possible to magnify the blessing that you are to the Church. You have received Me here because you love Jesus. So, this is the spirit of My message to you and your brother today. We must remember to pray for all who are suffering the ravages of poverty and neglect, those who have been affected by the turbulent weather, and the many who find themselves victims of crime. I will close this morning by saying that the Illinois governor will be held responsible to Jesus for signing the bill advancing abortion."

Saturday, October 7, 2017
Feast of the Most Holy Rosary
9:28 a.m.

"The mind, nerve and flesh of humanity are no match for the light, truth and majesty of the glorious divine. However, men on Earth are getting there. After all, the corona of the sanctified human soul is breathtaking to behold. Repentance gives way to clarity, promise, esteem and direction. Redemption celebrates the constancy of God within the heart, while the world is only now beginning to realize that there is no such thing as provisional love. Every person who accepts this fact reinvigorates the universe and instills in humanity so much new life, so much energy, so much beatific romance. You do not have to know a melody to break into a song."

- The Dominion Angels

"My sweet children, you are grace-filled darlings of the Church. You have esteemed yourselves in the Holy Spirit because you have given your lives to Jesus. I have come on this brilliant day to pray with you for the conversion of lost sinners who reject the truth that you extol. Our prayers mark the beginning of millions of lives in the grace of the Father. Our spiritual convention is a prayer to which Jesus responds for the reorientation of His worldly brothers and sisters. The redemption of humanity depends on the finding of the lost and the contrition of the wicked. I hope you enjoy the words of the Dominion Angels that they have shared to begin My message. *"Yes, thank you, I like them."* It is important for the Church to know that the sanctified human soul is capable of all the senses of divinity from beyond the purview of your exile. A soul that does not belong to Jesus casts a dark shadow on the backdrop of the world, but a soul given to Jesus has the capacity to reflect redemptive light itself. Unconverted souls are mired in the filthy mass of unconfessed sin. There is no life in an unconverted soul – no glory, no vision, no divine inheritance. This, My Special son, is why it is so crucial that you realize the impact of what you and your brother are doing. You are giving Jesus the gift of converted souls who are proceeding to the Father through the Cross. Your witness on His behalf is the life-giving prayer that satisfies their desire for Jesus' Mercy. I have spoken about imperatives to you and your brother, about moral truth that serves as the foundation of the righteous human life. And, these things must begin somewhere. There must be a seed planted in the world to grow one's alliance with the Will of God. This is the legacy of your life in this home. The Angels have spoken about a 'corona' of the soul. What does this mean? It implies that those who reject the Gospel of Jesus cannot shine either here or in the Afterlife. Unconverted souls are all about being inundated by the darkness, rather than responding to the light. Dead souls feed on other dead souls as though to be consuming themselves. There is no life in them; there is no joy or eternal consolation. There is only dust and lifelessness, only the stench of dead flesh that will never rise again. On the other hand, those who have given themselves to Jesus cannot be driven back. They exhibit a brightly shining sheen like a diamond in a crown. And, even should anything nefarious try to dim the glory of a soul belonging to Jesus, the corona of the soul still shines through. There is more to life than days and years, materials and promises, conveyance and conclusions. There is sanctioning truth that each person finds in the Sacred Heart of Jesus, and it is within this truth that every facet of human imagining takes flight. You and your brother have reached this plateau; you have seen that even as love is permanent, it is not fixed in time and space. It harkens to My message last week. You find yourselves alive in Jesus, and your identities cannot be constrained within a physical space. You cannot be confined by the world's opinions of who you are. Your souls will always be free to travel to new worlds, and capture the triumph that is yours. Your hearts can paint the images that your prayers envision. The dutiful faith that you have embraced will be exchanged for the Salvation that you have sought. Your unity in Jesus will forever be codified by the petitions you have raised. My little sons, these are the reasons you should rise from your slumber in the morning and thank God that you belong to Him. It is true that your praises do not add to His glory, but pleasing Him is the greatest gift you can offer. I have said that the Saints who arrive in Heaven are told of the Lord's gratitude for their sacred lives, and this is the point where not only man's final awakening comes, but the Father's joy that His Providence is honored and His Kingdom adored.

My Special son, you and your brother are living days of grace that are spectacularly rare in these modern times. You are situated at the center of one of the most converting miracles in the history of the Church. Your sacred energy, your response to My call, your devotion to the Saints, your friendship with the Angels, and your brotherhood with Jesus are yielding the fruits that the Father imagined as His Son was being transfixed to the Cross, taking His final breaths on Mount Calvary. You have been consistent in believing, serving and witnessing to His Holy Sacrifice as the gateway to the Kingdom Divine. You have set out in your response to Me to rescue humanity from the lethality of its own errors. You have joined the Angelic Choirs singing the Psalms of Wisdom that are overtaking the clamoring world. I realize that it is difficult for you to see these things from your vantage point on Earth. There is no question that the distractions and burdens of human life make it uneasy to know. However, you must surely be capable of seeing the remarkable impact that you and your brother have made on the extension of the First Apostles' mission from their age to yours. It is as though twenty centuries have had no bearing on what you have been called to do; you have been handed a charter from Saint Peter as though you are standing right beside him. And, while I have given due recognition to the Saints in My messages to you, I wish to further celebrate the implications of one Saint whose veneration is not as widely sung in the precincts of the Earth. When asked by the Father upon Jesus' Ascension what was the origin of His prolific confidence, Jesus said two words – Saint Joseph. This Saint is the source of tremendous aid and intercession for humanity in exile. His life seems such a utility in the history of the Church. It is as though this lowly carpenter was a custodian at the Vatican one day as he was preparing the Sistine Chapel for the election of a pope. And, what miracle came that day was that the electing Cardinals reached all the way into the infinite Heart of God and chose this humble custodian as the leader of the Catholic Church. This is the element of surprise that humanity will know upon learning about Jesus' affection for the man whom He so loved and admired. Now, My Special son, do you have any issues to discuss with Me today? *"What shall we tell the Bishop when we go to see him?"* Say that the Holy Spirit has sent you, and that His Immaculate Mother in Heaven pronounces good favor on his service to the Church. Assure him that holy resilience shines from the Chancery of the Diocese of Springfield like a beacon in the night. Say that all the Saints and Angels are drawn to his simple piety like light from a flame. Tell him that God, the Church and the eternity of holiness are embracing him as he wakes and falls asleep. Make sure that he knows that the Mother of Jesus Christ wraps Her arms around his soul like a blanket in the wintertime. His moment will arrive; his spirit will be held aloft, and he will be esteemed as the First Apostles are esteemed because of his footprint in the Church. It is all about what we have done here together. Say that Jesus and Myself, you and your brother, and his own trust will dispatch the Good News of the Gospel to the far-flung corners of the world. Let it be known through the history of man and across the ages of the Earth that the faith of you and your brother has wrought a miracle into being through the intercession of the Mother of Jesus Christ that will convert millions to the Cross of Salvation."

Saturday, October 14, 2017
9:21 a.m.

"The categorical ambiguity of the secular void."

"My dear little sons, if you parked a limousine in the middle of a chicken yard where three pigs and a cow were walking, the sleek automobile would capture everyone's attention first. It would take a moment to distinguish the car from everything around it because it would seem so out of place. And, if you played out this situation into milliseconds, it would seem a long time until the limousine received its due recognition. Even if this were drawn out into what seemed like decades and generations, the appeal of the car would remain imminent. This is what is happening with your Morning Star deposit of works. You have laid a diamond atop a pile of coal. You have added a priceless gem to a collection of buttons. This comes amid the seeming eternity between Jesus' Resurrection and His Return in Glory. It is as though these gifts are frozen in time until all in the world realize they are there. Let Me be clear. What I am saying is that humanity is only now coming to realize that there is a limousine, a diamond and a gem in their midst. My Special son, if you carried a billiard ball in an airplane to 40,000 feet and dropped it from the plane, what would happen to the ball? *"It would either embed itself in the ground or break into powder, depending on what it hit."* What would cause it to hit the ground or break into powder? *"Whether it hit something hard or something that would absorb it."* What would cause the ball to hit something hard? *"It depends on whether you released it over something hard as it fell due to gravity."* Thank you – after everything you told Me about the billiard ball, you finally said that the first thing that would happen if you dropped it from an airplane is that it would fall. You leapt ahead to tell Me the effects of the fall, but you did not mention the fall. This is the issue I am raising about the status of the Church, the Return of Jesus in Glory, and the impact of My Morning Star messages. If the billiard ball strikes something below, it cannot do so until after the time it takes to descend from the airplane. Hence, you and your brother are watching the world, the Church, and My messages as though you are waiting for a billiard ball to hit the ground. Do you understand? *"Yes."* I have told you that your Morning Star works are a priceless gem or diamond in the midst of Creation. And, what would be the purpose of the metaphor about the chicken yard? It represents the vagueness of the secular void in which all holy things are intermingled. My Special son, there are so many distractions and irrelevant interests that compete for the attention of humanity. God has placed the attention of the world in suspension, but the Earth's people are only now beginning to know it. The human will is causing this pause. If someone asked you a question, and you said that you would be with them in a moment, but you waited a thousand years, this does not mean that you never intended to return. This is the preoccupation of men waiting for the return on their righteous investments. I am not saying that you and your brother do this, I am telling you that it happens. I do not wish for the two of you to become ensnared in this framework of expectations. Please be proud of your new book; it is only now being launched into the public domain beside your other manuscripts. As has been said by many wise thinkers, patience implies that you will win at the last. It is as though there will be refreshments for everyone at the end of the journey, but the travel is still ongoing. I have described to you the Lord's designs for many years, and you can see His Will in the finishing of His works. Your Bishop knows that I would not leave you idle during these crucial times. He realizes that the Holy Spirit will manifest something even more divine than what you have given him.

    My Special son, I address the fact that the world should come to a halt and take your new book in hand. There is no question about it. However, there are chicken yards all around the world. There are vague and ambiguous agendas that have humanity focused only on the mechanisms of life – it is all about the maintenance of the person and the family. What we have done here with your brother is for changing the world's present state through the invocation of miracles. You are asking people who are looking at chickens and cows as a source of food to search instead for a spiritual Kingdom on which their souls will feed forever. They must make the connection between the worldly and the divine in such a way that helps them understand the true priorities by which they should lead their lives. I am asking you and your brother not to take for granted the state of grace in which you are living. You do not see life in the way of other souls. You have inherited by the power of the Holy Spirit a perception that has escaped the rest of the world. You have reaped the benefits of My messages in ways known only to such individuals as the Medjugorje seers. This causes within you a certain impression that the rest of the world cannot see the truth. Yes, there is a spiritual limousine positioned among them that will not only capture the gaze of everyone alive, but will lead them to see the institution that fashioned it into being. My Special son, My purpose this morning is to instill in you a sense of awareness that the momentum of humanity flows in the direction of what we have done. There is such thing as the future already being here; this is not just a journalistic slogan. You once wrote about an elephant in the room. No sound conclusions can be drawn until someone finally mentions the elephant. This is the nature of what I have done here; it is what the world must address before their lives are through. Now, I wish to include one more sense of perspective. Jesus is asking humanity where their attention is at this time regarding His Sacrifice on the Cross. His Crucifixion is the 'passionate investment' that has yielded the redemption of lost sinners. He placed His life in a world of men who are embroiled in the categorical ambiguity called the secular void. And, your books and His Holy Sacrifice are waiting for the brawling vagueness and ambiguity of the secular void to end. It will surely auger its own demise. My Special son, do you understand everything I have said this morning? *"Yes. Thank you."* You have much to celebrate upon the publication of your new book. One would think that Jesus' miracles of healing and the resurrection of the dead would have found Him hailed among the nations as the King of the world. But, what happened instead? Yes, they sentenced Him to die on the Cross. You need no other means than this to understand that your way of life with your brother has been marginalized in a world so ingrained in sin. It should make you feel welcomed by the Father that your lives in Him have been so validated. It is that you and your brother are carrying out the mission of Jesus in your time and place. I share My heartfelt congratulations that you have accomplished this esteem. I am pleased that your beloved friend, Mary Jane, wept in jubilation when you gave her one of your new books. She is reading and learning about the stature of life to which I have called My children. She is believing every word, and being blessed by Jesus for invoking her faith."

Saturday, October 21, 2017
9:28 a.m.

"The consequences of lukewarm faith – such devastation, such enigma, such ill-conceived designs, such diabolical commotion, such desecration of the spirit; such suffering, such torrents among the nations, such brokenness, and barely a fraction of human potential ever realized. The world of men needs to remember that Christian faith, even greater than childbirth, is the single most clarifying element of the mortal experience. Those who yearn for the blessing of the ages always hold firm to their life in the Cross."

- The Dominion Angels

"My lovely little children, I can scarcely summon the words to tell you how humbly you are loved and admired for all you do for Jesus, for all you accomplish and endure, for everything you mean to the Church and the Glory of God. I have come today to pray with you as you remember in your prayers all who are far from Him. It is true that we have changed the landscape of the exiled Earth by what we have done together for nearly thirty years. My Special son, I wish to speak to you today about your recent health issue. It must be clear to you at this point that your fatigue from your workplace is causing a decline in your health. You have given your life to your workplace that is somewhat disproportionate to what is prayerful. Everything you do is a product of two things – the demands of a job, and one's approach to meeting those demands. You are being asked by Me and Jesus at this time to realize that you are being 'used' in a way that we will not allow. I am certain that you can take a new look at the way you approach your work responsibilities without My having to ask you to resign your position. I have not come to you and your brother to make your employer wealthy. I came to help build up the Church and convert as many souls to the Cross as possible. You and your brother have given this gift to the Father in ways of few others. You deserve your dignity. You surely must see by now that you have acquired a propensity to 'charge the gates' in the accomplishment of everything you do. This is an admirable spirit to approach your assigned duties, but it is not an intelligent one. I do not want you and your brother to endure the evils of the devil. It is the devil who takes advantage of physical, mental and spiritual exhaustion to make My children suffer. There is nothing weak about telling someone who is demanding a job from you that you need your rest. There is nothing errant in expecting this response. My Special son, I am saying that you deserve your esteem as My child – I shall not permit a person or organization to bring you mental or physical harm. It is not a signature of concession to tell someone that you are My child, that your Mother in Heaven requires that this abuse must cease. It is not from a position of surrender that you should demand that the grinding commotion of the secular void not mar you with ill health. My Special son, it would seem that you take no time away from your office. A day or two every three or four weeks, given the dimensions of what you do, are not enough. You defer to people who make extravagant amounts of money, and you do their jobs because you believe it will make you look bad when they fail. This is no way to live. I am telling you that the way you desire to succeed at your workplace is no virtue. It is counterintuitive to everything I stand for, and it is contrary to the peace that Jesus teaches. Please know that I wish to lift you up, and remind you who you are. *"I understand, thank you. We're trying to find more people to help."* I am wondering when the new week arrives on Monday whether all the 'we plan to' initiatives will only result in the same exhaustion that you have been suffering. It is clear that you have within your power the capacity to make this better. I will leave it to your good offices to set out on this path. I am asking that you understand My love for you, My need of you, My desire that you live peacefully and happily. It would not be appropriate for this reason for you to take any long flights until you achieve a more stable workplace. "*I understand. Thank you.*" I believe that I have spoken sufficiency about this issue. Do you have any questions about it? "*No.*" Thank you for your prayerful compliance.

    The Dominion Angels have provided a profound passage this morning about the problem of lukewarm faith, about anemic faith. You might find it interesting that they did not speak of the consequences of lukewarm faith as though there exists no faith at all. One would think that all the consequences that they spoke about would have to do with a complete absence of faith altogether. Why do you suppose they did this? "*Because faith has to be lived, not just known.*" Yes, and because there is no true faith without authentic faith. Let Me say it this way. If Jesus did not ask for the highest, most genuine faith from every man, woman and child, then human beings could decide for themselves what degree of faith would be appropriate. One is better to have no faith at all than lukewarm faith because the hypocrisy is not there. "*I understand.*" And, it is in this setting that the avoidance of the ills and evils that the Dominion Angels mentioned finds its power. Perfect faith – this is the word used in the Sacred Scriptures – drives out fear and clarifies the meaning of the life of the exiled soul because it leaves no room for ambiguity. The Angels have said that perfect faith is the most crucial element of the human experience because it delineates the lines between right and wrong. Without the expectation of perfection in faith, all realities become blurred, and relativism seeps in. Pluralism comes crashing through the door. These are all the things you already know because you have written about them in your books. The point in My message about them today is so you and your brother will not forget. It is in seeking this perfect faith that suffering finds its meaning. It is in rebuking those who walk away from their faith that discipleship is vested in its most stately attire. Yes, you could name a half dozen priests in your own diocese who have walked away from their religious vocations after being seduced by promises of worry free lives. Where is the sacrifice in this? Where is the loyalty to one's faith? What about the validity of someone's vows? My Special son, the whole issue comes down to a priest's ability to know what ruses secularism is peddling. Refusing to given in to temptation is key to manifesting the higher order of spiritual trust. It is a function of the innate knowledge that the Kingdom of God reigns supreme over all other facets of the human domain. Where is the latitude for interpretation in this vision? Where is the bond between a sinner and his Savior if someone accepts the allure of the world over the divinity of Jesus' Most Sacred Heart? These are the questions you have asked in your books and manuscripts. The rhetorical nature of these inquiries solicits the obvious responses that men must provide. So, as you publish the Dominion Angels' succinct passage somewhere in future times, please remember that what we have spoken about today has been a prayer for the strengthening of the faith of the Church. We have prayed for the perfection of Christian faith everywhere, not just spiritual faith in all forms, but for the advancement of the accepting of the Cross as the redemption of all souls with the capacity to know. I pray that you do not feel as though My messages have become the same old song with another verse. The dimensions of your understanding are larger than that. "*I don't think that. I'm happy to learn more.*" I am taking advantage of you and your brother's welcoming ears to speak to Creation in a way that the world has never known. Everything I have said to you will be revealed – whatever is done in secret will be known from the rooftops. The Holy Bible says as much. Thank you again for staying the course."

Sunday, October 29, 2017
9:40 a.m.

"The Blessed Virgin Mary, Mother of Jesus Christ, implores each of Her children not just to pray the Rosary, but to pray 'your' Rosary."

- Blessed Alan de la Roche

"Spontaneity of the heart and wisdom in the retroactive sense – plenary redemption is not about counting the price of glory."

- The Dominion Angels

"My lovely little children, the devil is attacking you because of the profundity of your new book. I commend you for bearing with the pain that Satan has caused you because it is never an easy burden to carry. The environment of the United States has become one of divide-and-conquer from the family unit to the world stage. My Special son, while I have compassion for those like you and your brother who endure as victims this plague, you have the tools to make it right. No two children of the Mother of God have ever been so blessed. None have achieved the marvels that you have given to the world. No two-by-two disciples have given the exiled realms the miracles that you have recorded at My behest. None have been as compliant in suffering and servitude as the Morning Star Over America visionaries. My little sons, the torment thrust upon you is all the work of evil, and I ask you to rise above it like conquering knights. Today, I have the gladness to share with you that the Father sees what you have been enduring. He is aware of your struggles. He knows of the accompaniment of your lives in the Cross. If you wish the success of My messages to be manifested in ways that even I could not imagine, please peacefully bear your discomforts and sacrifices. I have said that you have the right to determine how this story will end. It finds its fullest meaning in the peace in your hearts. What does it mean that plenary redemption is not about counting the price of glory? It primarily implies that there is no one keeping score. It secondarily means not looking behind to see whom you are thus far outrunning. Just take heart, and love Me! Trust and know that Jesus is at your side! Bring the consolation of the Church Triumphant into your presence. Be joyful that you will be accosted for your work for God. Resist the temptation to say, '...how dare the devil come attacking me here.' For everything I have ever said about justice – be thankful that this is the case. Live with gratitude that you have not conceded your lives to impurity and materialism. Offer your deepest appreciation that Jesus has claimed you for Himself. Tell all the world anew everything that you have recorded in your books – that this turmoil, these times, and all the universes combined have no bearing on who you have become within the Most Sacred Heart of the Messiah. You have already conquered everything about these things that could pull you away from the Glory you have claimed. There will never be anything lesser about who you are. The waters of your baptism will never be shed of a single drop of grace. The light shining upon your souls will never dim. The satisfaction that you have come to know in being My children should be your singular source of joy. And, My Special and Chosen ones, if you thought that you were going to change the world and the fate of humanity from here in this humble place without being attacked by the same devil that caused the fall of Adam and Eve, you were more naive than any souls should have the capacity to be. I am not saying that you are naive, I am only broaching the prospect that you could not have possibly known the tragic history of Satan and what he has caused in these created realms if you thought you were exempt from his radical attacks. These attacks are your assurance that everything I have told you is true. My Special son, you speak truths that are implanted in your heart by the Holy Spirit of God. I pray that you realize that this is the same wisdom that Jesus spoke from the Cross, that was transmitted to humanity during His Sorrowful Passion, that was given to the Faith Church from the beginning. Just as I told Blessed Alan de la Roche that the Holy Rosary is 'your' Holy Rosary, it is something of which humanity must claim ownership; you can also claim ownership of the ages and events that comprise human life on Earth. You have the ability to choose which of these events will be the cultivating ones, the culminating ones, and the instances that affect you most. I bring out your confidence that you are taming the Earth by a means through which you can celebrate the strength of yourselves.

My Special son, I speak of marvels and miracles being within the reach of exiled men because your life here with your brother has manifested them. How? Because of your obedience. Because of your sacred love for Jesus, Myself, Saint Joseph and the entire contingent of the heavenly realms. You have the courage and determination to choose for God during circumstances when He seems far from the world. You look at the secular drivel in the news and from hard-hearted people on the streets, and you choose not to become invested in them. You hold dear to you the meaning of the olden days, the yore-soaked traditional days, when morality meant more than a mere mention in a history book. You have more tenacity in your little finger than the entire body of humanity that has been born since 1961. You claim your share of divine grace from the Father by invoking the Father's wisdom. Your eagerness to ensure the Victory of the Holy Cross is the dynamic that is wiping His vineyard clean – this is your catalytic prayer. What is not as clear, however, is that your friends and contemporaries are running scared or have turned callous ears to any miracles that might mitigate the things they do wrong. It is not clear because they are withholding their faith from God. My Special son, please allow Me to put a hypothetical question to you. Do you suppose life in the United States would be any different had the events of September 11, 2001 not happened? *"I still think we would have been witnessing and responding to terrorist attacks throughout the world."* There is no question about it, but knowing about evil as Christians do, what did the devil gain by staging the attacks? *"I'm not sure."* I am citing September 11, 2001 as a metaphor for a transcending purpose. God gave the people of the United States of America a reason to stand up for the Truth of His Kingdom against a so-called faith that is antithetical to the teachings of the Catholic Church. But, what happened instead? The leaders of the nations refused to stand up in defense of the truth, and compromised with the enemy. They did nothing. Why am I telling you this? Because God in Heaven has given humanity two great faiths – Judaism and Christianity — The Two Witnesses — and He has given them the miracles of My presence among them. And, lo' and behold, a full eighty percent of the world's population will not follow His Son to the Cross. So, in the absence of any reaction to these gifts, God gave humanity access to its own egregious error – two full-blown world wars and the atrocious tragedy of September 11, 2001. And once again, what was humanity's response? Still, four-fifths of the world's population will not follow His Son to the Cross. My Special son, do you see? Neither blessings nor curses can pierce the obstinate faithlessness of humanity in exile. Even as God has given them the impetus to stand for the Truth of His Kingdom, they will not respond to Him."

Saturday, November 4, 2017
9:33 a.m.

"Like diamonds glistening in the sun."

"Here, My precious children, is where you pray and listen to the strains of comfort that are echoing in your hearts. I give all the world the peace of Jesus through My intercession, with the conviction of His Kingdom reaching deeply into your lives. My little ones, it must be made clear to humanity that I am imbedded here with you where you live, and that I care intensely about every detail of your exile in which you approach the Father in prayer. I never wish any of My children to believe that I have not cared about their happiness. It is for the conversion of the lost that I have come, to teach you about the joy of righteousness, to convey to you the profoundness of God's love, and to ask for your petitions, that the sanctification of humanity will come in your day. Yes, I approach you and reach out to you because you are the ones with true power. The Lord listens to those who implore Him through the authenticity of their faith. He sends His presence to those who call out to Him in the dark. He dispatches plenteous Mercy and Salvation to the many who seek redemption in Jesus' Blood. My Special one, it is My specific purpose today to tell you how much you and your brother are loved. I invoke the Angels and Saints to assist Me. Why? Because you are still praying to receive Me here. If you lived a hundred more years, there is no question that you would welcome Me into your heart and home. You will do whatever it takes to ensure that My mission is made manifest through you. This makes you a 'princely king' in your own right in the likeness of Jesus. You have daring and eloquence in your speeches and writings. You stand upright in the power of the Cross. You have made yourself aware of everything that the Father wants the Church to know. Most importantly, your life has been modeled after Jesus in the Garden – your obedience, reflection, prayer and self-denial. I am only asking that you see yourself as a beacon in the night to the billions who are living around the globe. They see what we are doing here in America, some of them. They look deep within their hearts and ask the Holy Spirit for what they should pray, and God fills them with the wisdom to anticipate with gladness the rising of the Morning Star. It has already come! It shines and glows like a lighthouse on a seashore. But, many are only now seeing it in the distance. It is like a moonbeam cutting through the night or a diamond glistening in the sun. I ask for you and your brother to remain at peace with Me in Jesus. This is not the frenzied world that many people have made it out to be. Men who cannot find their bearings are what makes the world seem frenzied. Yes, just look around you. See in your heart what sinners have brought the global consciousness to be. Know that Jesus is here with you because you are dear to Him. It is real suffering that the corruptness of humanity has wrought. So today, I would like to take your heart and thoughts to the rising of the holiness within you that you have nurtured for so long. It is not that you are alone in this, you know, and neither is your brother. It is that you have difficulty seeing through the dense indignance of other men. The soft-spoken voice of the Holy Spirit can sometimes be difficult to hear amid the clamoring of the world. The mechanical aspects of human life are always louder than the spiritual peace to which the Scriptures call the Church. I only wish that My children would be like you and your brother in knowing these contrasts, these lines of demarcation that identify those who truly belong to God. Everything that the devil uses to take people away from the Cross is found in the absence of their own sacrifices. There are distractions and illusions from the rising of the sun to the darkness of night. Whatever it takes to lure My children away from the Kingdom of the Father, the devil will attempt. Here, I am saying that you and your brother have not fallen to his wiles. You envision what beckons you to your prayers. There is no question that your insights are with the Cross. It is written in every word, every sentence, every manuscript that you have ever published into a printed book. My Special son, can you not see that everything that has been happening around you and your brother has been to distract the entire universe from what we have done here together? *"Yes."* I am saying that you recognize this because you have been the agents for sharing the revelation to the unholy, impious, and unchurched that the Mother of God is in their midst. The commotions of the Earth are trying their worst to churn-up humanity in the tempests that will take them from the peace we already know. Jesus calls His disciples to heed what the Gospels have to say, but the lack of peace around the world keeps them having to ascend to this peace like swimming up a waterfall. *"That's a good analogy."* I only ask that you remember that you and your brother are not one of them because you have met the Father uniquely at the center of My Most Immaculate Heart. You have never surrendered or relinquished your statesmanship or air of dignity through the Most Blessed Trinity in Heaven and on Earth. I have tried to reveal to you how blessed you really are.

My Special son, do you suppose that people who live out in the countryside feel more peaceful than those who live in the city? *"Yes."* And, why do you suppose this to be true? *"Because cities are filled with the commerce and commotion of worldly affairs."* Yes, both on an economic and social level, the heart of the cities is the marketplace for the exchange of goods, services and ideas. However, do any of these things really change the world in the way of the Gospel? *"No."* The point I am making is that people who relocate from the city to the countryside can take these life-affecting motivations with them, but do they really have peace in their hearts when they arrive? *"I think they truly have to search for it, even then."* I have summoned you and your brother to the peace of Jesus not by relocating you geographically, but in the sense that you recognize the piety in you that you have borne all along. This is what I have been trying to do – reach out to those whose tendencies have been toward the righteousness of God. I am asking them through you to tend to their preferences only to the extent that His Kingdom is advanced through their lives. My Special son, it all comes down to one's spiritual standard of living. If one builds up the Kingdom of God through their life's work, does this not mean that there is a sovereign marketplace of divine love within the earthly domain? *"Yes."* This is precisely where you and your brother have lived, where you are living still, and to which you are calling your brothers and sisters in faith. You have within you the desire to exalt God as the reason for the existence of the world. You rise to the challenges that face you every day. You are aware of the omnipotence that permeates your souls. You have seen, at least in a spiritual sense, the conclusion of the Earth as it is poised at the center of Jesus' merciful judgment. You have witnessed the origin of absolution; you have ratified its intrusion into the hearts of angry men, and you have warned those who disbelieve that you have come to know what future is awaiting their souls. While you and your brother have grown in wisdom and discipline along the lines of righteous truth, you have seen the diminishment of those who are handing themselves over to death without a foundation of love. My Special son, you know that it is impossible for a creature to physically devour itself. It is against the laws of physics. However, such is not the case with the souls of wicked human beings. It is wholly possible for someone to devour his own soul and spate it out into the bowels of Hell. This is a great deal to think about when it comes to knowing the fate of humankind. It is not a figure of speech to say that humanity can damn itself. And, My Special and Chosen ones, while all this fateful destruction is going on in the secular void, you have been living with modesty here in this home, here on the Earth and at the edge of Heaven, glistening like a diamond in the sun. You are part of the noble society of gentlemen who have done what you have been called to accomplish. For this reason, not only are you blessed, but humanity-entire is blessed and sanctified. Imagine if I had come to the Earth only once in the history of man and tersely said, 'Go get redeemed!' What kind of Mother would I be? This is not the way of My Immaculate Heart, and it is surely not the way of God. We are like you and your brother who not only yearn for peace in the world, we teach and represent it. I seek from you today your acceptance of the apologies of God for the kind of world in which you are living. The Most Blessed Trinity is deeply sorrowful for the way humanity is treating you here. It is caused by the devil bent on his own destruction, and humanity that is unaware of theirs. All the peace that could possibly be known in this world or the conception of a trillion more worlds is awaiting those who will accept the love that God offers. The reluctance of men to open their hearts and receive the peace and power of the Holy Spirit can be blamed on multiple forces – obstinance, ignorance, pride, delusion and sloth. But, it all comes down to the unwillingness of humanity to admit their own sins. This is why we pray, My Special son. The devil would have no force or effect in this world if exiled men and women would just tell him that they reject his evil works. He is like a soul-devouring predator flying around a savory meal – he will get what he wants until he is shooed away by the righteous conviction of world-weary men. This is the essence of what I have come to share with you today. I am seeing you and your brother, and all My children, shining and praying here in this life. I have devoted thousands of hours reminding My messengers and seers that you will win at the last. My Special son, do you have any issues to share with Me this morning? *"Your message is very beautiful."* O' thank you, My Special son. You and your brother are among the few messengers who say that to Me. I hope that you will remember everything I have said today that lifts you up before Jesus, and see My words in your hearts as though they are written in golden letters across the skies."

Saturday, November 11, 2017
9:26 a.m.

"Passing through life absent Christian virtue is a vacuous exercise that serves no ameliorative or redemptive purpose whatsoever. It is dreadful that someone could lead such an aimless existence, so estranged from providence, so dead of conscience, so devoid of heart, so distant from truth, so lacking in eloquence, so wanting for direction."

- The Dominion Angels

"My dear holy sons, the Dominion Angels have given you another installment of their reflection that began our October 21, 2017 message. They feel strongly about the necessity of humanity on Earth to come to the fullness of life. I offer My blessings and compliments today as I have come to pray with you for the conversion of lost sinners. I have said that I came to you early in your lives for this reason – that you would join Me as My children to reach your lost brothers and sisters who are embroiled in the estrangement of the secular void. My little sons, there is no such thing as accidentally coming to the Cross. Accepting Jesus' Holy Sacrifice is never by happenstance. It is not a divine awakening that someone stumbles into. And yet, its acceptance is provided by the will of men in union with the Will of God. The entire process of the enlightenment of man has always been about the world's response to Him. In other words, the Father came to Moses in the ancient days and asked His people, 'Do you love Me?' This is the overture that began the spiritual romance between the creature and the Creator. The purpose of My Marian apparitions around the globe since the early centuries has been to assist My children to prepare their response to the Father's first greeting. I have always desired that the Church remember that its sole purpose is to manifest this answer within the parameters of time. My Special son, it would seem appropriate that the entire world remembers one specific word that I uttered to be most profound. And, what is it? *"Yes."* Indeed, the word is 'yes.' This is the answer that My children must tender to God. It is an elementary prospect for you and your brother, but imagine how this simplicity affects those who are far from the Church. It began with the Lord God seeking this response from those to whom He gave life. No mortal man ever thought in the early ages to rise in the morning and say, '...I think I will go out and try to find God today so I can tell Him that I love Him." It never happened. The entire framework, the whole concept of the Man-God was fashioned from the fact that the Father knew that it was to be Him to begin the reconciliation of His Creation with Himself. My Special son, I have told you these things so I can now tell you this. Embedded in the history and the nations of the world have been certain people who have defied the silence of their forbears and reached out to the Blessed Trinity in prayer and conviction. These are the great leaders of the Church who acted not in advance of Moses, but in advance of a world of tragedy that might have otherwise come; a world of ignorance. You and your brother are among these visionaries. What must begin in the heart of a Saint is to understand that 'today' affects what will become the legacy of 'tomorrow.' It is not enough for someone to say that they will get somewhere; they must know where they are going, and why and how. This is the spiritual synthesis of the life of man with the Providence of God. This is the greatest prayer that could ever be said. It is the way the Holy Mass is the synthesis of the faith of man and the Sacraments of the Church. It is the same way that love in the heart becomes united with the Kingdom of Divine Truth. There is a multi-dimensioned opening of the life of a Christian to the endless and boundless eternity to which their future is bequeathed. Faith. I know that you clearly realize this because you have already written about it in ways that I have never before been able to impart. The whole matter comes down to divine auras and graces. Even as simple as the Christian faith has always been, there are as many facets to its beauty as there are people who practice it. When the poet Ralph Waldo Emerson wrote that all things swim and glitter, he was sadly ignorant of the Church itself in which all things of Nature and the intellect find their true meaning. Yes, their purpose and identity are authenticated in the Gospel of the New Covenant Christ. My Special son, this is the reason there are seemingly infinite numbers of gifts and blessings not only from the Sacred Heart of Jesus, but from humanity itself by its affirmative response. The circle is complete as exiled men are drawn to the relief, beauty and freedom of the redeemed spiritual state. The human heart hungers for Salvation in the way a deer is drawn to a stream. The food for the soul is the Most Blessed Sacrament of the Altar, but the hunger to receive this gift was not initiated until God told the world that it needed to be fed. A person cannot crave something that the spirit has never imagined. So, My Special son, I have spoken today about achieving the goal of sanctity in this life, here in the realms between the netherworld and Heaven, where so many souls have tendered their best efforts to the mission of the Church. I always ask you and your brother to remember the dignity that you have found in Jesus, and in My Most Immaculate Heart. The Father's poise and honor suit you. You have always been a prince of theological faith, and a blessing to the Roman Catholic

Church. I ask that you live in this stateliness all the days of your life. You should never ask for or demand it because those from whom you must prompt it are not honest in the presence of the Holy Spirit. Residing within you and your brother is the wholeness of everlasting life, prepared to make its finest revelations to the Church in exile."

Saturday, November 18, 2017
9:25 a.m.

"Faith is about love and constancy – something preservable, something transcending, the long-standing truth beyond the ages; gallantry, gentleness, honor, worthiness, and serving the right-minded spirit with peace and eternal joy."

- The Dominion Angels

"Good morning, My dear little sons. It is My honor to speak to you here in your prayer room where I always remain. I pray for you in all ways, that you will be happy and healthy, that your work in Jesus' name and in His Kingdom will be accepted by the world to which it is being given. My message today revolves around the words of the Dominion Angels who have added to their passages of October 21 and last week. When speaking of gallantry and worthiness, it is a means of awakening the sleeping giant in all men who profess to be Christian, and those who are only now converting to the Cross. There is little that I can add to your knowledge of righteousness because of all you have learned through the years, and everything that you have contributed in thought and reflection about the Gospel of Jesus. I wish to instill in you the confidence of knowing that you and your brother have contributed to the spreading of Jesus' Wisdom in such a way that is pouring forth across the ages. You have a living and abundant faith that cannot be impugned. You live with the hope that all who will eventually enter the Divine Kingdom will encounter their Mother sooner rather than later. With the intercession of the Saints, especially Saint Padre Pio, the millions upon millions of lost sinners around the world are preparing for their rendevous with the Cross. As you know, and as the entire Church realizes, this is a soul-awakening experience that not only changes who they are, but changes who they perceive themselves to be. The latter is as important as the first. The self-realization that one's soul is the property of God here in this life and the next opens the door for a new view of destiny. It is in this destiny that life's changes come about. It solicits a new definition of what it means to be holy and perfect in the sight of one's Crucified Lord. Humanity has the making of greatness in their faith in Jesus, and our prayers help them bridge the distance between their fears and the final commitment that will take them to their place in Heaven. I also wish to share with you the joy that you have inherited with the completion of your recent book, and the impact that it is having on those who have received it. Hearts are being touched and inspired by your chapters in your book, as well as My messages. With great discretion, the Bishops do pay attention to the lay people in their midst because they are aware that they are often seen as hidden in their closeted towers. It is easy for them to be seen as isolationists by the very nature of the role of Bishop. On the other hand, when they do reach out, they are often bombarded by aggressive people who accompany the public face of the episcopal life. This is all wonderful, My Special son – all about the encompassing companionship that you share with these men in whose custody the Church has been placed in your age. I ask that you remain aware of the time it takes for others to read the massive content of your books. Please be assured that all souls bound for Heaven will pass through every syllable of your writing before they enter the Holy Gate. And, please pray for the sick and infirm, for those who are contemplating suicide, for the poor and neglected, and for those who are carrying their baby children in their wombs."

Saturday, November 25, 2017
9:28 a.m.

Revelation 22:16
"The Root and the Offspring of David."

"My dear little sons, I come to pray with you perpetually. There is never a time when I am not in your presence. And sometimes, such as this moment, I reach out to speak to you in words that you can hear. This is as it has been for many years, and it is as it should be. I come with compassion for your suffering, My little ones. I bear in My arms the Root and the Offspring of David. I bring you reassurance that the Holy Spirit is with you, and the Father holds you dear to His Heart. My children, you are seeing worldwide the suffering that is heaped upon the innocent by malevolent forces. You are witnessing the persecution of the Church. You are yourselves seeing what happens to those who love God, the ones who trust in His power, the people who practice the mandates of the Gospel. My Special son, I hope that you and your brother do not see these things as happening solely to you. They are specific to the fight between goodness and evil. They are in keeping with the teachings of the Church. I wish to speak today about the Bright and Morning Star who is also My Son, equally present in My Womb as your own lives. Jesus, the Bright and Morning Star of Revelation is the hero to whom you have turned not only in your hours of need, but during the ordinary times of your lives. My Special son, the greatest obstacle to the Christian conversion of the world is not that Jesus has not made Himself sufficiently knowable, but that those to whom He has turned have hardened their hearts. They have lesser plans for their lives, plans that have nothing to do with the refinement of the Earth or the redemption of souls. I do not need to recount here today what all these things entail – the culture of anti-faith that has come upon America is too repulsive to describe. I am not speaking about the decent people who live down the block or across town. I am not referring to those of good will who live around the nation who work hard, defend what is decent, provide for their families, and tithe to the Church. The point I am making is that those who put the image of the United States in print and over the airwaves have hearts filled with impurity, profiteering and materialism. Whatever can cause people to react with shock and surprise seems to be the way they live. My Special son, the reason I have told you these things today, that I have reminded you of them, is because it is difficult to fight off the impressions that they have on the psyche. It is not often easy to realize that the national consciousness has nothing to do with the consciousness of God. Sensationalism, culture shock, materialism and victimhood are accurate ways to describe the national consciousness of America today. It is all a ruse to take people away from the tenets of the Holy Gospel. My little sons, I am not speaking about you today. I know that you are not caught up in the hype and lies that are being peddled by those who control the media and entertainment business. It is no surprise that most people learn the truth about their own societies by turning to one another in unconventional ways. It is not unfair to say that these people are doing the right thing. Why? Because it is a way of ignoring the off-putting lies of the media executives who are acting precisely as you described in 'At the Water's Edge.' My dear sons, I do not wish for you to become combative when thinking about them. Pay no mind to what they are peddling. Watch for facts as you know them to be facts, and disregard the rest. I ask you to do this because this is the way of Christians; you have the capacity to judge and discern what must be said and done in your time to challenge the world's error and remain at peace in your hearts. The latter of these is most important to Me. It is the call of God who loves you beyond all telling. If you do these things, My little sons, the peace of God will rise within you. The calling of His voice will resound through your minds. The center of His Holy Peace will reign inside your hearts. My dear sons, one of the problems that occurs in the battle against secularism is that Christians sometimes over-think what must be done to combat the enemies of the Church. This over-thinking is exactly what the devil wants Christians to do. There is always an over-analysis of what the devil is doing. Do you remember that I once called for My children to stop asking questions and ask themselves why they are asking so many questions? What I meant back then, and what I mean still today, is that the only answers that matter are the ones given you by the Holy Spirit when you lend yourselves to heartfelt prayer. Too many questions means that a person is distracted from the answers that the Father has already provided.

My Special son, I am again not speaking about you and your brother when I am saying these things. I am only trying to help you see what is happening outside this home and beyond your lives where the distractions that lie there have nothing to do with one's life mission. It is somewhat like the pages of your worldwide web – there is a movement to place as many parts of a single story on as many pages as possible in order to publish more advertising. This is a metaphor for the way the devil tries to piecemeal the ill-conceived content of his blather to those who give him the time of day. It is all about falsehoods, distractions, lures, fears and temptations. My Special son, you might not realize it at this time, but I came to speak to you and your brother in happy tones today. I ask the both of you to remember what a gift you are to each other. Know that Jesus, Saint Joseph and Myself are always with you through the days and nights. We pray that you will realize your own strengths and beauties that capture the Lord's eyes. Please pay no mind to the wayward ways of the secular void or the false pressures they try to inflict upon you. Being My children means that you belong to the steadfastness of the ages granted you by the power and providence of the Father in Heaven. You are part of this indomitable reign. You have within you the wisdom and wherewithal to withstand the challenges that you face. You have the holy criteria in your wisdom to know when to strike and when to walk away. You and your brother do not need to worry about life every day. This is why I ask you to pray for those who are ill and paralyzed, for the impoverished and incarcerated, for the people around the world who have no homes or food. I know already that you pray for the poor souls where Father Ted is working, that he is more in need of your prayers than anything else. Be thankful to God that you and your brother are still together and alive, doing what you have been called to accomplish from decades past. All in all, you and your brother can attest that life is good. All the individuals who have received your books have taken to their knees in humble adoration of the Mother of God. 'How could this have been going on right under our noses?' This is what they are asking in their prayers. 'Why has not the news of this Morning Star been propagated in lands far and wide?' This is what they are prone to inquire. And then, in their prayers, the answers come. It is about timing, and time itself. No two messengers could have amassed such a magnanimous work with a thousand curiosity seekers knocking on their door. It is all in true providence that they see the Morning Star Over America being commissioned this way. My Special son, I used the phrase 'pouring forth across the ages' in our recent conversations about what true righteousness should be doing. This is what will happen to the righteous remnants of the lives of those with whom you have met and communicated."

Saturday, December 2, 2017
9:25 a.m.

"Undimmed joy, undying courage."

"My little sons, I wish for you to always remember that the sole purpose of human life is to make God happy. We do this through all we offer Him, in the way we foster peace among His peoples, by nurturing the good will that ensures mutual prosperity, and by advancing those measures that protect human life and give meaning and dignity to the title of 'the Lord's creature.' My dear sons, you have come upon through Me an undimmed joy, and you have achieved by the power of the Holy Spirit undying courage. We pray together this morning that the whole of humanity will come to understand what I have told you, not just in 'knowing' what I am saying, but in effecting its meaning in their own lives for the propagation of the Gospel by which they are redeemed. It is clear that some individuals and societies find it difficult to believe that God loves them because He supposedly threw them out of Paradise. It is not the casting out that matters, but the gathering up and being allowed back in. It must be made clear that if a man stubs his toe and suffers excruciating pain, in the eyes of the Father, that pain is felt down through the ages, all the way to the man's last great-grandson. This is the connection of the spiritual realms with the earthly domain. It is the way that pardon and exculpation are shared across generations. Yes, it is the same way that a Man who died 2,000 years ago can redeem a child born in the last fifteen seconds. My Special son, I am so pleased that you are finding ways to rethink your approach to your workplace in that you do not get caught up in believing that you must micro-manage everything. Your health will improve; your thoughts will be less stressful, and you will enjoy the undimmed gladness that I have told you about so many times. I refer to your workplace in this message because it is part of the eternal continuum about which I speak. And, I wish to make the issue clear that the continuum is not as impactful as the consequence, as the outcome. Just as the purpose of life is to make God happy, the consequence and outcome of life is to share His happiness. Imagine a world in which there were no personal needs or ambitions, no requirement to be self-sufficient, no deadlines or taxes to pay. This is not the kind of world that the Father has in mind – it is not about the absence of identity, but about having a sense of community yielded from coalescing separate identities. Your comments, suggestions and propositions at your recent seminar showed your peers that you are deeply personal and reflective, that you have a creative concern for the success of your organization, and that you are within yourself a truly thoughtful man. You should be pleased by your presentation and the type of individual you are perceived to be. Why? For the same reason that a man stubs his toe in 1754 and the pain is felt in 2017. It is not really about the pain – good things are felt generations and even centuries afterward as well. The point is that it is all about a transcending purpose throughout the ages. The laws of Moses are not dead; they have been fulfilled by Jesus on the Cross. The waters of someone's baptism do not evaporate, they live on in the soul with the thirst-quenching prevalence of purity and pardon.

My Special son, few people think about what happened to Jesus' Blood that was shed on the Cross, that spilled down the tree and made its way to the ground. What of Jesus' Blood that stained all the facts and artifacts with which it came into contact. Very few people have ever wondered who 'cleaned all that up.' Do you suppose that it is written in the scriptures somewhere? *"I don't know."* The answer is that it was absorbed by the same environment that caused it to be shed. Jesus' Blood is still everywhere on Earth right now, seeking out souls to bless, cleanse and redeem, in the same way that it was freshly shed on Good Friday. Here again, the ages and nations cannot change this fact. Human sin and even human righteousness cannot alter what this means. Here is the climax of what I am saying this morning. The Sacrifice of Jesus on the Cross is yet ongoing in the minds, hearts, spirits, flesh and souls of those who believe in Him. The amassing ages cannot expunge this fact; the repetitive days and nights have no effect, wars and insurrections are helpless to void it, and all the Sacraments combined reflect what it means. My Special son, living in you are these Sacraments. They are alive in everyone who believes in Jesus and who accepts the Crucifixion as expiation for the veritable concept of human sin. All this potential is present in every man, woman and child. It is the human will in alignment with the Will of the Father that deigns which of these Sacraments shall be present in any man – whether he chooses to marry or walks alone in the grace of the Church. Or, if a man is called to the priesthood, or a woman to a religious vocation. You have already fathered a million spiritual children by the work you have done for Me. All of this is the purposeful, holy and triumphant identity that you have gained in Jesus through your consecration to the Cross. I am trying to turn your perception, and that of your brother, to the prospect that the entire Mystical Body of Jesus is not so much generational as it is beatifically eternal. There are grandfathers and grandchildren, teachers and learners, beginners and experts all around the world. It is not necessarily who comes of age in which century, but that everyone comes to Jesus at the last. My purpose here is to tell you that I have come to people like Juan Diego in Guadalupe and told him that I was his Mother – he was in his mid-fifties, and I was sixteen. I have appeared in places like Lourdes and Fatima to present the King of the world who was but a babe in My arms. So, I speak of perspective and insight, of undimmed joy and undying courage because I wish for you to gain a sense for the peace within you that is of old – and yet new and renewed every day. I have tried to impress upon you that this pleases God greatly. Do you understand everything I have said? *"Yes."* I will not speak a long time today because I wish for you to rest. I will begin in January 2018 to give you an even more evocative series of messages that will comfort your heart and enlighten your soul. *"Thank you. That's exciting to look forward to."* I will pray for all the intentions that you lift to Jesus in your daily petitions, especially for the propagation of your Morning Star work. I ask that you join Me during the Advent Season in praying especially for the end of abortion and the conversion of lost sinners."

Saturday, December 9, 2017
9:30 a.m.

"Yield your hearts to the filial domain of the Father's sacred truth. Make the cadence of the years resound His indelible Spirit. Come to life in the Cross of His crucified Son – for this redemption is about untrained heroism, tragedy, compassion and posterity; and good men already know it."

- The Dominion Angels

"My wonder-filled little sons, I ask you to ponder where else I might have gone to find two perfect likenesses of Jesus waiting for Me to appear? How can it be true that you are so filled with grace, goodness, eagerness and joy? Because the Lord has made you, yourselves, part of the miracles of these modern times. Within you, the Holy Spirit has a lifeline to the exiled realms. In you, God has found consolation for whatever else might occur in the precincts of His world. In your lives, He has found the remnants of His Son's Blood pouring through your veins. And, here in this place, He has seeded the beginning of what shall come to be the leading of humanity to the Cross. Here in the nation of courage and freedom does the Morning Star produce the fruit of converted souls for the Son who has redeemed them! My little ones, it is not an overstatement to say that your Bishop has not only found truth in My messages to the world, but comfort for his own soul, encouragement for his weary heart, company for his lonely spirit, and the regeneration of his energy to continue the fight. This is the way, My little sons, of all who become immersed in My miracles. It is the following and the legacy of Christians who put their hope in God. How, then, can I not have within Me the peace and gladness that I have come to know in you? Today, the Dominion Angels have given you a remarkable recounting of this peace and joy found in the Cross, in the Easter Resurrection, and the descending Holy Spirit of the Child I bore at Bethlehem. These weeks leading to the celebration of the Nativity are part of the new awakening, the twenty-first century awakening that is calling all with a conscience to take hold of their prayers and raise them. The Gospel message never changes, but those who accept and follow that message forever evolve in wisdom and piety until they see their Savior face to face. I tell My children that this can be done; it must be done, and it shall be done. Everything beautiful finds its origin in the Birth of the Christ Child. All that becomes known of newness and reflection resounds with His innocence. No wonder the world was taken by such surprise! A King wrapped in swaddling clothes? A Savior whose innocence would preserve innocence itself? A Man-God who would destroy evil and rescue wayward sinners caught in its clutches? Could it be true that all this would come from the Womb of a Virgin on Earth? Yes, as true as the truth has ever been told; and eternal too. My Special son, you and your brother are receiving a message today about the conversion of lost sinners and the demise of death itself because the Father has asked Me to tell you. This is how it has been for all these many years when you wondered when your work would take hold in the parlors of such unprecedented darkness. Through you, God has channeled the Light of His Love to those hidden from anything that might bring them hope in life. You have never in your lives seen

Creation as dark as it has been in 2017. And yet, what are we doing about it? The groundwork for propagating My messages throughout your nation has begun through the books you have recently sent. And now, the power that must thrust these new beginnings into the outlandish landscapes of the United States and around the globe began being manifested on the Feast of the Immaculate Conception, December 8, 2017. Not only will the Morning Star Over America be seen by the Church as a 100-year miracle of the Fatima visions, but so has the generation of the power to laud them been brought into being here in this home. My Special son, this would not have occurred if you and your brother had not remained in your unity beneath My Mantle. And now, we must continue to fight until the world's obedience becomes as routine as the breath in their lungs. Indeed, this new book that you have produced and shared is unlike those of your original deposit of works. Why? Because it contains the ribbons for the manes on those horses that I spoke about years ago. You have asked Me if you could release My 2010-2012 messages to show to everyone alive that the Mother of God does not cease celebrating the glory of Her Son or human redemption just because of the passing of time. What we have done over the past decades is the begetting of the conversion of entire societies before the end of the world. I humbly ask that you have within you the realization that all of this is true – perhaps not patting you on the shoulder every day, maybe not making the national headlines and bylines, but slowly and inexorably building up to the grand conclusion by a lost world that God has come, that He is displeased, that He has the power to destroy heretics and rebuild nations, and He will act when the time to act becomes right to the benefit of the Church and the condemnation of the wicked.

    Therefore, My Special son and My Chosen son, My prayers with you this morning are about thanksgiving and the preservation of your hope that is well founded in everything I have said. Your faith is not only a gift from God, it is your gift to Him in return. Your years and lives have not only been an investment in what He would have the whole of His creatures to do, they are the manifestation of the miracles needed to build faith where there is now only sheer uncertainty. Nothing we have ever accomplished will be in vain. Not a moment in your lives will be seen as futile before the backdrop of the Eternal Kingdom. My little sons, these are My promises because I am the Mother of the Promise. My Special one, as I have indicated, I will begin in 2018 a new series of messages that will take on an even more evocative tone than those of 2013-2015, but you and your brother will need to rest before then as you fight against the devil to prepare those messages for presentation to the world. I ask you and your brother to take joy in what you have done. See our mission together as ongoing, but ever-complete in the Sacred Heart of My Son. Breathe easily, take time to relax; live peacefully and quietly, allow no one to knock you off course; give the best of your heart to love, and always remember that I am with you. And, please never take for granted that you are responsible for living safely in whatever you do and wherever you go. Give your Guardian Angel the opportunity to protect you under the guidance of your own wisdom. Wishing you well; asking for caution in your travels, promising you the prayers of the Church Triumphant, and giving you the elation of the Angels, I will speak to you again next week."

Saturday, December 16, 2017
9:31 a.m.

"Some people acquire faith by emulating the faith of those they admire. This is the genuflection of the Holy Spirit in the mirror of life. And, the years can sometimes be painful, but a Christian reserves the right to shift the winds of consequence and vindicate the worries of his heart."

- The Dominion Angels

"My dear sons, most people ask if the Mother of God will ever say anything to them during their mortal lives. Here, you ask what the Mother of God is going to say today. This makes you blessed, but it also requires from you the fulfillment of My request that you be happy in all you have been given. Realize that you have been chosen because you love the Lord endlessly; you give to Jesus not only your hearts and souls, but your thoughts, actions and intentions. I have said that no one earns the right to communicate with God in a way that He seems to be sitting next to you. However, once someone is selected for this celestial conversation, this does mean that esteem is accompanying you. This, My dear little children, is only part of the reason why I have been speaking to you for so many years. One of the other reasons is that I cannot help it – you are too awesome, too beautiful, and too eager to unify with Me and Jesus. And, in My eyes, this makes Me wish to speak to you, to listen to your prayers and concerns, and to assure you that no matter what happens here in this life, you will be together with all the Saints when your earthly years are through. It is true that mansions in the world are built by people, and the mansions in Heaven are built together by God and His faithful who have come eternally unto Him. These words – all the sentiments that I have given you over the decades – are part of this sublime construction.

By your prayers here in the world, you are indeed shifting the winds of consequence in your favor, just as the Dominion Angels have said. You are enlivening and building up the Church; you are mitigating the sins of nonbelievers, you are tending to the lost and forsaken, you are drawing God's attention to the worries of your hearts, and you are signaling to the Angels that they should be with you in this world and the next. My dear little sons, mighty are your deeds, strong is your conviction, durable is your armor, and tender are your hearts toward those who suffer. These, My holy sons, are among the reasons that I keep returning to speak to you – not just that a world of sinners needs converted, not that the Earth should become the likeness of Heaven, but because I love you, and I wish for you to know it. I beg that you always remember that whenever you think of Me, wherever you see a statue of My likeness, no matter what concerns you might believe to be too insignificant to draw to My attention, please approach Me, invoke My Maternal intercession, call out 'Mama' and I will be there. I will hold and bless you. I will comfort you and bind up your wounds, and I will ask the King of the world to hasten for you the victory that you have found in Him.

My dear little sons, there are no barriers strong enough to keep us apart. There are no heights or depths that we cannot travel. There is nothing in life so dark that we cannot enlighten it with the power of our prayers. There are no hearts so stony that we cannot soften them, no callouses that we cannot shallow, no opposition that we cannot subdue. There is nothing in Creation that we cannot refashion. It is all because we are united in the Father. I am the Mother of God and His Daughter. You are brothers of the Savior, and sons and siblings of the Holy Spirit. You are not just called to be the champions of the redemption of humanity, you are commissioned by the mark of righteousness on your souls. It is clear that these are sacred mysteries about which humankind may never find an origin here in the exiled realms. The question that should be posed, and one that even the great Doctors of the Church have asked, does it truly matter? I have said to you years ago that Saint Thomas Aquinas himself thought about what he might have otherwise done with this faith and ingenuity, and he has concluded on the heavenly side of the veil that he could have at times been more like a child. He forgot that even in his theological inquiry, he was meant to frolic and play in the spiritual endeavors of benign innocence in the way of children in the park. Whom did he touch with this holy genius? The leaders of the Church, and this has made all the difference in the world. My Special and Chosen sons, the works that you have produced through My intercession cover the entire expanse of the existence of the Faith Church, the Church Suffering, and the Church

Triumphant in ways that the writings of no other Saints have accomplished. One of the reasons that your Bishop was inspired to establish the Commission to examine your messages is because they have touched Roman Catholicism in the way of the Doctors of the Church. However, your works containing My messages also speak to the Mystical Body of Jesus entire – and this is every converted soul ever given the breath of life; the holy and unholy, the lost and found, the tall and diminutive, the redeemed and the wandering, and all the vast precincts in this world and the next who will ever lay eyes on the Face of God. My messages to you are the 'all and everything' in which the Holy Gospel finds its future. I am the Mother of the Gospel, and I am the Morning Star Over America. My Special son, I am telling you this morning that your life with your brother has already shifted the winds of consequence in the favor of love. You have inherited a new faith in Jesus because you have seen how much I love Him; you have learned how He lived and died from the Mother who bore Him in the flesh, and endured seeing Him suffer and die. You are called the 'Special one' because this is who you are – of all the billions of souls ever to live on Earth in exile, you are the Special one to whom the Lord has come to resolve the issues that must be faced in the twentieth and twenty-first centuries. What does this mean for the Church? Not that a new Church needs to come into being; it has nothing to do with that. It means that the Church of old and the Church of this century are one and the same faith. All the distractions, alter-impulses, revolutions and reorientations that could ever be imagined in the collective mind of humanity cannot change this. You will see at the last that you and your brother were there on the days that Jesus dictated His most eloquent homilies. You came to Him upon the conclusion of these sermons and promised that you would later re-tell the world what He said 2,000 years earlier. And, here you are, doing just that. These are the themes of immortal genius that are written into the Sacred Scriptures, but are invisible to the human eye. I ask that you believe Me, that just because you cannot always remember the things that I am telling you does not mean that they did not happen. You will see; even better than the Spirit of Truth can see the center of your soul, you will see that all of this is true. So, I summon your confidence that the sanctity of your life in this world means something greater than the mere existence of a mortal man on Earth. You and your brother have always had a transcending purpose together; you have given to each other and to the world the presence of God's Holy Light. In the sense that one can be proud without being self-centered, you should realize that this is the faith to which you were called, and your response could not have been more noble. If I may give you a parable, you will one day take every lethal intercontinental ballistic missile ever conceived in the minds of men and train them on the devil who has brought such hatred and darkness into this world. You will do this in Jesus' name, and He will answer you in the same way that you have responded to His call for sacred love to banish the night. My Special son, I plead for you and your brother to believe what I have said here today. I beseech you to remember that all the secular palaver that you are hearing is passing away. You are polishing the 'finish' that Jesus spoke about from the Cross on Good Friday. You are holding high the Kingdom that will annihilate the empires of human error. With your brother's help and your continued prayers, this line of offensive onslaught will proceed until Satan's grotesque work breathes its last. I wish for you to remember that the Season of Advent and the Feast of Christmas are auspicious times for humanity in the world and the Poor Souls in Purgatory. I know that you remember them in your prayers, and they implore you and the whole Church to remember them to the Child Jesus on the anniversary celebration of His Birth. Whenever offering your Christmas prayers this year, please join Me in asking Jesus to touch the lives of those who do not understand what the meaning of His Nativity is about. Pray for the destruction of evil, for the conversion of non-Christian faith communities, and for the preservation of everything sacred for which the Roman Catholic Church lives. It is imperative that you and your brother always remember what I have said about your goodness and holiness. Why? Because I have spoken the truth, and everything that is aligned with the truth of God shall never die."

Saturday, December 23, 2017
9:30 a.m.

"The Virgin Birth of Jesus Christ –
Resplendent, absolute, glorious, sovereignly supreme."

"With this new morning, My dear children, I bring My good wishes and blessings from Heaven for your holiness and love. I offer you the Lord's gratitude for your faith, for the means of your lives, and for the prayers you offer for My intentions on behalf of the lost and forsaken. My little sons, we are here doing this because we can make a difference not only in the outcome of the world, but in what part each soul plays in manifesting the outcome. This is a portion of humanity's dominion over the Earth – your spiritual fruit will be carried by those who believe in God to the Gate of Heaven where Jesus will greet them there. My Special one, in a matter of hours, you shall celebrate the anniversary of what you have described as the 'Eve of Joy.' This joy will always be replete in glory and absolution. It will forever reflect the sovereign supremeness of God who was born of My Womb. Imagine that the Holy Spirit who has taken flight throughout the ages was given flesh from My flesh, that the Father would identify with the mortality of humanity by subjecting His Only Begotten Son to death, and that the trials and tribulations of the Messiah would not only bring compassion to the ages, but closure and forgiveness as well. Yes, it is all about a timeless and dimensionless God becoming incarnate upon the Annunciation as an infant boy, and hence on Christmas night being born into a world that would not welcome Him. It is fitting that this be the way the Lord would come to His people – as innocent and benign as He has called them to be. My Special and Chosen sons, you have the capacity to know, along with all who are close to Me by virtue of the mighty Paraclete, that Jesus' innocence and benignity do not mean that He was helpless. Jesus is the Father born incarnate as His own Son from a Blessed Mother who never relinquished Her virginity. It is these Sacred Mysteries that come to the fullness of light for those who pray to believe. We have what some call the 'audacity' to proclaim a Kingdom that cannot be explained in this world. We speak of righteousness that first took root in the hearts of men, and was born unto them in the Second Person of the Holy Trinity. We speak of pureness and power in the life of the Prince of Peace who would divide father from son and mother from daughter, who would become the subject of wars and insurrections, who would provide humanity the definition of human existence in consequential terms. So, My darling little sons, it is through this awareness that you pray and search for answers to questions posed by humanity that need no response of our own.

The Virgin Birth of Jesus Christ – a baby. Imagine that. The entire relationship between God and man has had nothing to do with armaments or war machines. It has no binding in wealth or social influence. It is as far from pride and secular advancement as anyone can be. And yet, it results in the deliverance of the population of the world to the Kingdom of Love through which it was inspired. All the ages; all the manifestations conceivable in the kindhearted and good-willed, all the healings and blessings for which a world could pray – all these things found their beginning in one baby. And, it is to this Christ Child that all men must be drawn for their redemption to come. My Special son, what do you suppose were the first two words spoken by the Child Jesus? *"Mama and Papa?"* Yes, He did say this, as appropriately shared, but the first two syllables He spoke were 'I AM.' And, He completed His thought by saying ' the Son of God Most High.' Never once did He say that He did not know who He was, or ask the reason He was born. At no time did

He cause Saint Joseph or Myself to question why we had comported with the Will of the Father. Even when Jesus was lost and found in the temple, My Immaculate Heart suspected that He was there. *"Why do the Scriptures say that you were disturbed looking for Him?"* So I would be the example for humanity that, if they feel as though their connection with God is lost, turn to the Church and find Him. It reflects the reason that Jesus was baptized, to be an example for the world. Go to the Church, become inspired by the Holy Mass, and be one with the Father where the Son lives in the Spirit and the Sacraments. How could the world believe that the Son went missing unless His Mother was worried about His absence? My Special son, you will find the mention of worries in the Annunciation narrative as well, that I was 'greatly troubled' by what the Angel Gabriel said to Me. These lines of Scripture were written in such a way as to indicate how anyone might respond in My place at that time. Another point should be made here. It was not until centuries later that the Catholic Church proclaimed the dogma that I am the Immaculate Conception. How could it be true that a Woman born without sin could question such a request from the Father? *"I understand."* I am telling you these things not to make you believe that I was more than human, but that being born without sin placed Me in seamless oneness with God. It must be made clear that the Father was as sorrowful as Myself and Saint John on Good Friday, but we knew that Heaven and Earth would be reconciled through Jesus' Crucifixion. My Special son, you and your brother know the Salvation story. *"What are the impressions of the people who have received our books?"* Mostly surprise. They are taken aback by what I have said in your home. And, they are prone to allow the miracle to go on without interrupting you. All of them are saying, '...let us see where the Blessed Virgin is taking us.' They are doing these things because there seems no end to what I am relating. There are new blessings and reflections, prayers and imageries about what I am asking the world to conceive. It is all too much for them, too pure and overwhelming, too filled with wisdom, and too beatific to dismiss."

Saturday, December 30, 2017
9:34 a.m.

"Man in mortal time – the year AD 2017, another courtship gone by, another virtue-driven covenant sealed; sanctioned, lettered, prescribed, inspired and adroitly divulged. So now, welcome 2018. Come in singing!"

- The Dominion Angels

"My dear little sons, this is My final message of 2017, and I wish you to know that I have instilled in My words today as much trust, love and loyalty to you as I did in the beginning – when the Archangel Gabriel came to Me far from your shores. There are always two ways to look at the passing into a new year. Some people breathe a sigh of relief, others rub their palms together in eagerness that another installment of modern time has come. Yes, there are others who even do both. For us, it is a moment of thankfulness that the Lord has accorded the opportunity to fight for His Kingdom, not that our hands might be rubbed together, but folded in prayer for those whom we must still reach on His behalf. My dear little sons, you once heard an elderly woman speak about human suffering while saying, '...isn't that wonderful?' There is nothing wrong with submitting to the trials and tribulations that accompany the Christian faith this way. In fact, it is endearing. However, many have found that the pains and torments run far more deeply in their lives, that rhetorical quips lack the facility to offset the suffering that comes. Here again, neither of these approaches is wrong. There are multiple levels of tolerance and emotion that come when accepting the Cross, different degrees of conviction and adaptation. No person is strong all the time, and no one is permanently weak. The energy in this is action and reaction, and even more in forward momentum. This is what the Holy Spirit instills in your hearts. This is what Theodore Roosevelt was speaking about when referring to entering the arena. My little sons, victors and champions are not determined during the fight; they are chosen by virtue of the fight. How could it be true that God would handover His Son to the Crucifixion that He would never ask mortal men to endure? Yes, He requested of Abraham that he sacrifice Isaac, but what happened thereafter? God said that Abraham's faith was sacrifice enough. However, when this same sacrifice of the Son came to the Father Himself, the Sacrifice was made complete. He placed the life of His Only Begotten Son before the judgment of sinful men, the same men who had betrayed Him through Adam, and they refused to love Him. This is to say that God passes through these same years with you. He accompanies His world through these time passages. He reaches deep inside the hearts of His disciples and seals His Covenant there, for all times and ages, for the conversion of the lost, for the encouragement of the faithful, and for the redemption of the Church. My Special son, your friends, the Dominion Angels, see what is deep within you and your brother's hearts, and all who have proven themselves to be future Doctors of the Church still exiled on Earth. These Angels are leaders of men who have never undergone the 'mankind' experience. They are advocates and advisers to those who profess the faith to which God has consecrated the many who believe in Him. And, they bring you from My presence the brilliance and wherewithal to go about your lives in peace and joy. After all, you realize that nothing about the Church makes you unhappy; it is secularism that brings you sorrow. I have said that Satan is a secular devil. We do not worry about him, My Special son. We care not about his welfare or well-being because there is nothing 'well' in him. It is the effect of human love against Satan's evil works that we dwell upon. It is the way My children hold fast to their obedience to God through prayer and piety. You and your brother have handed God in your time the gift of obedient humanity. This is the reason that 2018 will come-in singing, and those who must listen to the voice of God will hear Him. I wish that you could permeate the spaces of the world and the epochs of time to understand what this means to Him. Imagine how the Father feels knowing that His disciples on Earth are still going about the business of softening stony hearts and teaching the mandates of the Gospel to a world so devoid of light. Entering the arena means doing these things; it means standing tall when no one knows from which direction the next arrows will fly.

My Special son, it is for all these reasons that I cling to My joy about My children. I cannot allow My identity as 'Our Lady of Sorrows' to overcome the joy that I have found in My children like you and your brother. It is an honor accorded Me by God that He has enlightened you about His Will in these times. And, it is a greater fulfillment that you are complying with His wishes. I have said that I will offer much deeper messages beginning in the new year. I will speak to you as long as Jesus' Most Sacred Heart desires. It is all because you and your brother have never left Me. You have never said that you wish to become absorbed in the material world, and will see Me later in Heaven. This is what millions have done when considering the blessings of My Motherhood. Untold numbers of them say 'that's nice' when hearing of My apparitions around the world. Others say, 'I will believe it when it happens to me.' I have some news for them. They dare not say about Jesus being crucified on the Cross, 'I will believe it when it happens to me.' Why? Because God will put them to the test. He has already invited those there who accept Him, those who offer obedience to Jesus; the apostles, disciples and spiritual martyrs whose hearts, lives and souls belong to the Kingdom at hand. My Special son, you and your brother take time to read through your books and stand in amazement at we have done. Heaven is as awed as you! Even for all you have said, written and published since we began, this year of 2017 has been a flourishing year for My messages, a great gift to humanity and the Church, even more than you have the capacity to know. I only ask that you and your brother hold to your belief that you have already done enough. Everything that you are accomplishing now, as I have said many times, is doubling and trebling the effect that your lives and works are having in the Church and in the world. You are living your valedictory years that will prove to the world that your presence among the nations has been a reflection of Jesus on the Cross. My Special son, what good does it do to hand a message to a courier who shuts himself inside his house for twenty years and then dies? This has been the way of many messengers throughout the centuries. The Father has given truth, inspiration and opportunity to thousands of messengers around the globe in the past 2,000 years who could not endure the fight. They could not face the enemy; they could not bear the cynicism, they could not undergo the suffering. You and your brother have each other; you have the weapons, and you have the venue. Your lives and works have caught the attention of the Roman Catholic Church to such a degree that an episcopal commission has been seated to examine My messages. I could say this a thousand times, but its impact would not express what it means to Jesus. So, My Special son, I have completed My final message of 2017, and you will record it in your records for humanity and the posterity of the Church. Whenever we do this, no matter how often we pray, regardless of whether anyone else knows – this is the essence of the miraculous love between God and His Creation. Your brother once said that if anyone asks for one word to describe Me, he would say that the word is 'grateful.' He would not begin by saying that I am beautiful, even though he knows that I am. He would not just declare Me 'holy' because that goes without saying. Yes, I am grateful. No other person, not here or in the afterlife, is as grateful as I am for your divine help, for your devotion and consecration, for your faith and allegiance. Thank you for giving Me your lives during 2017 and through all the years. I remain prayerful for the Lord's response to your holy intentions."

The Final Colossus
With the Valor of Archangels
AD 2018

Saturday, January 6, 2018
9:31 a.m.

"Nailed to the boughs of a tree –
The Sacred Rite of Human Redemption."

"My dear sons, you have come to another year of praise and love for God, another year of making your faith the reflection of His glory, and another time for praying for the conversion of lost sinners. I hold you deep within My Immaculate Heart because I love you, as the Father loves you. Today, I am introducing you to 'The Sacred Rite of Human Redemption.' Yes, you realize that this is the Crucifixion of Jesus on the Cross, and it is the Holy Mass containing the Eucharistic Liturgy. There will never be a movement within the Church, rightly so, to divide the two. Some have referred to the Holy Mass as the bloodless Sacrifice, but this would imply that the sacramental cup does not contain the Blood of Christ Jesus. So, I am speaking of the Crucifixion and Holy Mass as one 'Sacred Right of Human Redemption' as a prayer for spiritual conversion. A sacred rite implies a ceremony, which is the Holy Mass – a feast of thanksgiving. It is the Last Supper and the Sacrifice of Jesus on the Cross in one sacred prayer. And, when the Holy Spirit speaks of Jesus being nailed to the boughs of a tree, God is saying that it is the crux of the reconciliation of His Church and Himself. Hence, the physical transfixing of Jesus onto the Cross bears the spiritual fruit of absolving those who accept Him from their sins, and reuniting them with the Father in Heaven. My Special son, I have said these things because I wish to emphasize this crux. It is where God and man come together. It is where the boughs of the tree were connected. It is the intersection of one's soul and beatific absolution. It hails from the same providence as Jesus' birth of My Womb, the echo of His teachings through the nations and ages, the imprint of His feet upon the ground, and the impression of righteousness that He makes on the conscience of His disciples. All these things are replications of the crux that was formed to connect the boughs of the tree on which He died. It is an ethereal touching of Heaven and Earth in the same way that the Holy Spirit implants the 'divine' within the hearts of those who believe. It is the touch of God, and the world feeling it. This concept of 'crux' is the way that the Crucifixion and the Holy Mass are one and the same Sacrifice. I realize that this seems a simple concept, but it is often the simplest ones that are most difficult to see. My Special son, you will remember that the Scriptures say that Jesus did not come into the world to convert the righteous. While you know that this is the case, it is by reason that those who reject Jesus as their Savior that this distinction is made. Of course Jesus' Blood has redeemed all who are cast into exile – believers and nonbelievers. No one can come into Heaven unless through the Blood of Jesus on the Cross, including the righteous. The reason that the Scriptures say that Jesus was not born to convert the righteous is another aspect of the crux. The crux is that Jesus' Holy Sacrifice, as accepted by those who believe from the age of reason, is the bright and shining star for which all who wish to be redeemed have searched. For them, Jesus on the Cross is the response of God to their prayers. The Prince of Peace was born the King, and He died to prove His love for those who accept Him. Conversely, and this is where the crux emerges, it is those filled with hatred and disbelief who nailed Jesus to the Cross, who took Him to His death. These are the wicked ones mentioned in the Scriptures, and they are the ones who stand in contradiction to those who believe. Jesus came to rebuke those who not only refuse to believe in God, but who reject that God could appear on the Earth in the flesh of a Man. Jesus came to convert and redeem those who have no righteousness. The Sacred Scriptures are rightly written – the crux is exemplified again. Do you understand? *"Yes. Does this crux relate to the original battle in Heaven where you spoke about the difference between the souls of men who were thrown down to Earth compared to the ones who had already accepted Jesus who would battle for the souls of the fallen?"* Yes, and how did you know this? *"Because those are the righteous ones who didn't need Him to suffer to accept Him."* Yes, but the Father wills that no one can enter Heaven unless through the Blood of Jesus on the Cross. From where do you suppose these two boughs were derived? *"From the Earth."* Yes, the horizontal beam came from a tree on the Earth; and in all His genius, the Father implanted in this same tree the vertical beam that was taken from the Tree of the Garden. God said, 'Stay away from that tree, or My Son will die.' There are all sorts of implications for the reason this was done. The main one as you surmise is that it reinforces the fulcrum that we spoke about as the veil separating God and man. And, it reemphasizes the crux to which I have referred today.

My Special son, I have shared supernal knowledge with you and your brother this morning that has never been revealed. *"Thank you, Mama."* I further wish to reinforce that you and your brother's works are complete – there is nothing more that you need to accomplish for your Morning Star Over America deposit of works, and even the supplemental manuscripts that you are fashioning on your own. Anything more, everything more, is your generous gift to Jesus on the Cross, Risen from the Grave, Ascended into Heaven, and bestowed upon humanity through the Holy Advocate in your hearts. You and your brother are generous to the Father in that He sees your lives as miracles to His Kingdom in the same way that He dispenses miracles to the world. There is no mystery in this. Look at your lives; make an accounting of what you have given to humanity since August 1989. Imagine what it would be like if the whole of humanity gave to Jesus what you and your brother have accomplished in the past twenty-nine years. You are esteemed and distinguished. I have made Myself clear on a number of occasions – your poise and stateliness, your wisdom and kindness, your peace and goodwill. These things stand in stark contrast to what you see in your country and around the world. I beseech you to believe that, someday, when humanity asks what I would like them to do for Jesus, what preparations they should make to see Him face to face, I will show them your lives. I will say, 'be like them!' "*Thank you, Mama. We are not finished yet.*" It is with this most grand thankfulness that I understand what you are saying. But, you must make sure to get your rest. The schedule on which you are working at your office is profoundly inadvisable. You have not yet taken into account your age and susceptibilities. There is a possibility that you will again be hospitalized before the next month is out. It is unique that you seem unaware of what this is doing to you. And notably, the Father is responding to the healing for which we are praying for children here and afar. My Special son, you may reveal everything I have said about the Church, Creation and Heaven. I pray that you realize what joy is brought to My Immaculate Heart when you welcome Me here to speak to you and your brother. Please permit Me to say it this way – There has never been anyone else on Earth who has better complied with Jesus' commendation from the Cross – 'Behold your Mother.' Here, you have beheld Me. You have dared to stare down the world that despises your devotion to Me. You have said to Jesus 2,000 years beyond Mount Calvary, 'yes, I see our Mother, Lord. Thank you for Her Motherly love, guidance and care. Bless you, Brother, for allowing us to be the sons of Mary too!"

Saturday, January 13, 2018
9:32 a.m.

"*Laying out in speech the glory of a nation.*"

"Thank you, My dear little sons, for kneeling to pray with Me today on this bitterly cold winter day in your city. I wish to remind you that you are keeping your promise to be faithful to Jesus as profoundly as His Promise to deliver your souls into Heaven. There is a phenomenon that happens to My messengers through the years that finds them growing and maturing in faith as My messages come and go, as they supersede one another and become more intense. My Special and Chosen ones, neither of you required this kind of development over the past twenty-seven years. You were filled with sacred knowledge and wisdom from the start. Your hearts were as wide open as any could be. You have spoken prophetically and eloquently about what the Father expects from His Church. You have laid out in speech the glory of a nation. There have been geniuses of this same magnitude throughout the ages whose vision comes from the Holy Spirit, that can be derived only through one's openness to prayer and their conviction to religious faith. When history speaks of the likes of Winston Churchill and Ronald Reagan, it is only touching the surface of the brilliance that you have stated here in this country and to nations far and wide. Why? Because you have within you the friendship of the Spirit of Truth and your unity with the Son of Man. You hold in your hands the reins to other men's hearts. You speak of a Kingdom that eclipses the entirety of Creation. You have imbedded in this world a gift to Jesus that glows like a diamond in the night. You have accorded the Roman Catholic Church reasons aplenty to celebrate the Mother of God. You have opened the eyes of the spiritually blind, shocked the consciousness of incumbent prelates, brought light into the darkness by the power of your love, and driven out demons who will never be heard from again. These are the reflections that I see on this cold January morning. It is a way to celebrate your esteem before the Father because nothing outside the Father's sight even matters to Him – there is no such thing as being beyond the sight of God. My appearance today is to bring to fruition, on another level, your self-perception of your place in the lineage of Saints. O' how I wish you could see yourselves from the other side of time. This is the reason that the victory of your lives rests in the Triumph of My Most Immaculate Heart. What is a life, anyway? What does it mean to spend the years fighting off one's enemies and enduring the elements, if not for the Glory of God? What does it matter that someone lives a hundred years because they only eat vegetables and drink filtered water? These are just details of the times; they have nothing to do with the intricacies of human love that are wedded to the Divine Truth of the Father. My Special son, life is all about the propers and priorities. It is about taking to task everything that downplays the sacrifice of the self. In all that Jesus brought the world, the greatest is that humanity has been taken to its knees. This is from where the heart best finds its oneness with God. Jesus did not come to condemn, but to save. This is what the Scriptures declare. Indeed, He has left the condemning to the soul's judgment of itself. 'Come unto Me and I will give you rest' means that all sinners should find in

Him the cleansing of their conscience and strength for their days. At long last, this is what we have been praying for. It is not only that we are willing into being prayers for which the Father might forgive His people, but an installation of peaceful forbearance that will spare the dying from their pain. I am not speaking of physical pain in this sense, but the pain of the spiritual void that has made wicked men of millions throughout the years. The dark, cold, hollow, shafty, unwhole and unholy emptiness that makes them ache for God. This is the reason that I have always told you that prayer is curative. It is an analgesic that not only takes away the pain of daily life, but heals the spiritual maladies that manifest the agony from inside. My Special son, from where I come, and to where you and your brother are going, you will perceive your lives in this world as capable of knowing true love innately, just as the Father sees us all. You will be amazed by how accurate your spiritual vision has been. You will see that while humanity has been blinded by their own transgressions and prejudice against God, you and your brother have lived from within the essential element of divine wisdom that first brought the Father to position the Earth in the void of outer-space. This does not mean that you do not battle what all others face in their lives. Yes, you have seen and endured those bitter winters about which you often speak – those 1977 and 1978 blizzards and rooftop snowdrifts and driving winds. But, you look back fondly on them because you survived. You discovered their quaintness amidst their harshness. You learned about your own capacity to deal with adverse conditions, and place your sights on fairer days. This is a metaphor for the way you have always lived in a spiritual sense. It is a call, My call, for humanity to remember that the paths, even though not always rosy, eventually lead to the sunrise of victory that Jesus has promised in the end.

You are seeing these days come and go. It is about saying 'yes' to the sublime components of human life that bring you to feed, clothe and shelter the poor whom you do not even know. My Special son, as the Mother of God, I have lived alongside every soul ever given the breath of life as closely as everyone's guardian angel. I have listened with My face against the breasts of dying men to their last heartbeats on Earth and their entry into Heaven. And, I have wept both happily and sadly as conditions might depend to the joy of human conversion, and the depths of mortal sin. As you have so aptly written, I have been 'Mother' to the world who is looking for a relationship with My children, precisely as I have been Mother to you. It is all according to the volition of My children to have Me with them so I can hold them close to Me. There is no such thing as a stranger in Heaven, and there should be nothing strange about embracing humanity in your exile. This is what Jesus died to prove. I have said that absolution is not the same as exoneration. Jesus reaches out to Saints and sinners alike, and His purpose, as you have known for decades, is to exemplify the unity that the Father wishes His Creation to find in Heaven. What is so mystical about this unity? That oneness with Jesus on the Cross is so counterintuitive to living in the exiled world that most men can barely understand. This is another reason it is said that the world is upside down. All the Saints have known this before you. Saint Peter even perfected his own example when he chose how his martyrdom would unfold. Yes, he inverted the vision of man by the very way he died. All of these things make sense to those who comprehend the protocols of sacrificial love and the way the miraculous is intertwined with ordinary life. My dear Special son, I have used the word 'superseded' in My message this morning to describe another term, but it serves perfectly to indicate you and your brother's vision of what human life is about. What you have given to Jesus has superseded anything you could have imagined in your years of youth. Your prayers and manuscripts have superseded any of your peers. The intensity and volume of My messages here have superseded any in the history of the Church. And, these are the things that are so difficult for you and your brother to see because you are yet dealing with the overwhelming faculties of your lives. This is your continuing prayer to God for the conversion of the lost. It is your endurance of the brashness of society that is still giving Jesus such consolation during His suffering on the Cross. It is finally being revealed to anyone who will see that you and your brother were kneeling alongside Jesus during His Agony in the Garden, so He did not feel so alone in advance of His Great Absolving Commission. Here, My Special son, I have concluded My message for today. I hope you have enjoyed what I came to share. *"Thank you, Mama."* I know that you are continuing to work long hours at your office, and you can detect when your heart begins its dysfunction. I only ask that you get the rest you need. Do you have any issues to discuss with Me today? *"Did you talk to Jesus about His Kingship as He was growing up, or did He really already know it? I mean like you talk to us?"* My Special son, remember again when it was said that I reflected upon all these things in My Heart. It was that I was preparing not what to say, but how to say it. Jesus was uniquely aware from a young boy who He was and the capacity of His purpose. I knew it as well, but I was His supporter and advocate in the image of the Holy Spirit. I spoke as the Father would have His Son hear, here in this world. This sufficed His own wisdom that He gained from the Spirit of the Father who lived, and still lives, within Him. So yes, I did speak to Jesus about His Kingship, and He asked Me to. He wished His Mother to reassure Him that His worthy Sacrifice would find Me strong enough to endure His death for the harvest of souls that I knew would come. We were, are, and will always be two hearts united as one. I spoke to the only sinless Man who ever drew the breath of life as though I was reflecting to Myself. "*I understand.*" And, do you understand what it means when I say that I speak to you with the same admiration with which I spoke to the Savior of the world? "*Yes, thank you, Mama.*" Remember your peace; remember your rest, remember your dignity in Jesus, and remember the blessing you are to His Church."

Saturday, January 20, 2018
9:31 a.m.

"Faith and the vast ambiguities of the secular void."

"My dear little sons, most Christians believe that in order for them to be in Jesus' good graces, they must first earn His trust. It is proper to trust Jesus, but He must come to know you so well that He will always know your response in return. Trust implies that someone believes there might exist certain conditions where another person may not live up to their words, or may not perform or conduct themselves according to their promises. Of course, the literal sense is that one trusts his friends and companions, but the idea of trust still implies that a counter-relationship could develop if certain conditions are not met. This is not the same kind of trust that Jesus espouses. It is not a casual relationship that Jesus seeks from His disciples, but a 'realization' relationship instead. There is no conditional thought in accepting the Crucifixion of Jesus as expiation for the sins of men. It is binary at the outset in that someone either accepts or rejects the Cross, but once this acceptance happens, there is no need to be on guard. All eyes, all consciousness, all energy, devotion and direction are given to Jesus as He manifests the beatific identity of those who believe in Him. My Special son, I hope that you do not assume that I am parsing words, but I am trying to draw the parallel between commitment and faith. The secular world tries to persuade Christians to believe that this type of realization and relationship with Jesus is too ambiguous for someone to be so committed. They call for such things as moderation and balance. There was nothing moderate about the Sacrifice of Jesus on the Cross, and there was surely no balance in the trial during which He was condemned to die. My dear Special son, it is to these ambiguities that the Scriptures test the fullness of one's loyalty to Jesus, and it is to combat these ambiguities that My messages to you and your brother have been about. I came to you twenty-seven years ago not just to enlighten the world about the Kingdom of Salvation, but to clarify what elements of human conduct are in agreement with His Kingdom. Your union with Jesus through the Holy Spirit is by every means the Father's ability to touch the world through your faith. There is nothing ambiguous about this. When you walk into a church vestibule and hear people speaking ill of a priest or prelate who is upholding the teachings of the Church, you are listening to ambiguity. It is ambiguous when you see and hear of so-called Roman Catholic Christians who hold public office and vote for the desecration and destruction of human life. There is no question that none of these politicians would concede to what I am saying, but their mantra becomes as ridiculous as this – 'We've never heard a single unborn child complain about being aborted.' This is how utterly vacuous their perceptions are; their penchant for evil has become this clear. The problem that occurs is that good Christians, faithful Christians, are labeled as radicals when they attempt to rid the world of the ambiguity that causes so much evil. This is exactly the reason why your brother was figuratively expelled from city hall by the mayor who once called him one of his key advisers whom he had known for years. All it took was for your brother to affix his name to the newspaper letter* about the malevolence of selling the body parts of unborn human children. To be sure, there was nothing ambiguous about what your brother wrote. It was the truth as clear and cogent as it has ever been told. However, what was the result in the field of public opinion? Your brother was declared the radical. My dear Special one, I am telling you this because I would like for you to take another look at the profound accuracy of your beatific vision. What you wrote about the great thoroughbred Secretariat is a testament to what I am saying. You write as if speaking aloud, and this is the best way to drive your message deep into your readers' hearts. Truly, you learned this technique from receiving My messages, and it is one of your greatest gifts that you are sharing with the world. I am unsure where to begin in telling you what an impact your AD 2010-2012 book of messages is having on everyone to whom you sent them. To say that they have been rendered speechless would do this impact a disservice. Simply try looking at your work objectively, if possible, and you will understand what I am saying. My Special son, these are not unexpected reactions from these individuals because we have known all along that My messages would accomplish what we set out for them to do. They are part of the clarifying enlightenment that the Holy Spirit is attempting to share with humanity in the same way that a farmer might plant a seed in the soil. There is nothing ambiguous about digging a hole in the ground, placing a seed at the bottom, and covering it with dirt. While this is a parable, it is what Jesus attempted to do from the moment His ministry began. The world did not like its spiritual landscape being so painfully cultivated, so they crucified the Planter on the Cross. As I say, there is nothing ambiguous about this.

So, faith must be the catalyst that fights against this ambiguity, and a faith that includes outward action. This is part of the definition of Christian love that changes the ways of men. If there is any trust in this process, it surely must be the kind of trust that includes faith in other men, sinners in other sinners; so that faith becomes the vehicle through which this trust is shared. It is not that Jesus has faith or trust in His Church, but that He becomes aware of the authenticity of those who enter it. The ideas of faith and trust, in this sense, are attributes belonging to and displayed by those who accept the responsibilities of holding to the Kingdom of God. Yes, outward action – such things as transforming one's thinking into writing and committing feelings to the page. This is what you and your brother have done for Me. Why? Because you are disciples who hold no ambiguities about your life's mission. *"I understand, thank you."* And, thank you! The point I am making is that the clarifying element of truth drives out ambiguity, but humanity believes that there are multiple definitions of 'truth.' This, therefore, is the original source of human disobedience. Sin is the result of straying from the truth. And, as you know, all kinds of negative impacts can result. This is the source of errant thought that manifests social rules and public laws that stand in opposition to the Holy Gospel and the teachings of the Church. In fact, this is one of the greatest struggles that the Catholic Bishops are having to fight against – how to eliminate the ambiguity of what they are charged to defend so there are no questions about what the mandates of human conduct must be. This same ambiguity has led to the widespread practices of relativism and pluralism. My Special son, when it comes to areas where ambiguity has caused a departure from the teachings of Jesus, you know it when you see it. This is one of the topics about which someone like Saint Thomas Aquinas could write ten books in attempt to clarify what I am trying to describe in these moments. You have done well to comprehend My point, although what I have said adds little to what you already know. You captured the entire essence of what I have said today in your excellent discourse about humanity's frames of reference. The concept of ambiguity is a subset of what you have written. So, My Special son, I would like for you to speak to Me about anything you wish. *"I just want to tell you how much I love you. And, if I had only just a few words to say in life, they would be in honor of you and Jesus."* O' My goodness, thank you! I also wish for you to accept the initials that were so many times etched into the tides of time and history – you are S.O.M. – Sons of Mary. *"Thank you, Mama."* It is clearly your part to recognize that we have done our work in bringing the world to the brink of enlightenment that must be taken on if humanity is to change. It is not yet certain, however, whether your Bishop will make a formal public declaration about My messages before his episcopate expires. *"Please give us a great Marian Bishop to succeed him, if that is the case."* I will ensure that Jesus hears your prayers, and you must remember that the secrets of Medjugorje will take precedence over all the Bishops that this diocese will ever have. No one Bishop in any diocese can overrule My Medjugorje secrets – and this is good news for your life's work. *"Thank you, Mama. I am filled with joy by that."* Thank you for sharing the sentiments of your heart with Me this morning. I have concluded what I came to say to you and your brother – and if the impact of timing is here, I will speak to you again on his birthday this year. I keep thinking about what it means to have children such as you, so many holy priests, so many self-sacrificing souls who know what Jesus believes and takes it unto themselves. At no time in American history has the secular void been so damaging to the fabric of human life. At no time has liberalism been so poisonous. At no time has it been more important for My children to pray. Your brother was pondering yesterday about the number of elderly people you know who are still living in their exile – all of these people are not many sunsets from seeing their final reward. This is the effect of the march of the ages that has come upon you, but it need not be seen as a liability to the world. Thank you again for listening to what I came to say today. Bless you for being such spiritual support for so many good people."

* State Journal Register
Springfield, Illinois July 27, 2015

Now the United States is witnessing the merchandising of aborted children's body parts. Do we suppose the advocates of abortion are mortified yet? Has anything of their humanity been awakened that is worth salvaging from this nightmare?

We who have been pleading for more than 40 years to stop this macabre insanity of slaughtering children in the womb stand vindicated by the most recent news stories of the gruesome obstetrics of Planned Parenthood and their harvesting of infant body parts for sale. This is what abortion advocates have given their assent to. This is the darkness in which they have enshrouded America. This is what they are participating in by their approval. It is damning personally and socially, and especially immortally.

Any reasonable person would have imagined Dr. Kermit Gosnell's revelations would have been enough to make pro-abortion advocates question their deranged pathologies. Alas, this has not been the case. So I ask again: is this current revelation of outright demonic butchery going to be enough?

- Timothy Parsons-Heather

Saturday, January 27, 2018
9:31 a.m.

"After the Pentecost of the Holy Spirit, Pope Peter wore with sureness his seemly vestiture and humble heart, declaring that Heaven would suffice his commission of building the Lord a Church. When Peter said that the Church would become the image and likeness of its Savior, everyone began laughing at him. Look at the providence of the ages – no one is laughing now."

- The Dominion Angels

"With wonder and awe, My little sons, humanity is seeking the answers to the secrets of Creation that the Father is depositing in their hearts. They come from among you, dear ones, in the Person of the Holy Spirit, matched to your own faith and obedience. This is the true power of the Church from within; it is the reflection of God in your own being, and it is the harbinger of the destruction of the wicked. We pray here because you invite Me to. We offer the world the Divine Mercy of Jesus because I desire that it be done. My Special son, I have said that the first Pope saw the world as being upside down; and through his commission to build up the Church, he set out to upright it. One might imagine in your time if the day of Pentecost had not occurred until 2,000 years after the Ascension of Jesus into Heaven. The quickness of the Pentecost means that the world cannot survive without the intercession and intervention of the Holy Spirit to foster the sublime works of men. I have treasured My children's capacity to respond to this summons from the moment in the Upper Room. I have augmented, supplemented and replicated the prayers of the faithful since that day. I understand what it means to be human – to be perfectly human – not only in the sense that I was born without sin, but because I have seen the effects that the life of Jesus has on other men, and their capacity to be remade in Him; to be reshaped by His righteousness, and to begin anew to live on Earth in advance of their great reward. As Saint Peter said, the transition from nonbeliever to faithful Christian is made essential in the understanding that Jesus is the New Life of the human soul and its afterlife. The Cross of Mount Calvary constructed a spiritual scaffold around the world inside which the identity of humanity is being renewed. There is much tearing down and building up again. There is destruction and replacement, and there is New Light supplanting the old darkness. Yes, this is the spiritual renovation of the created world that began the moment Jesus was conceived in My womb – and it was a miracle for men and the ages. I hold in My arms and in My presence the reason for good men's lives and the demise of men who oppose Him. My Special son, of all the prevalent feelings that you have through the hours and years, it surely is your satisfaction to know that you and your brother have become part of this miracle in the way of few others. Hence, humanity has made the transition from being motionless in indifference to advancing in holiness. Even as the Earth appears to be still in space, you know that it is rotating around the sun and spinning on its axis. You cannot feel it because of its constant pace of movement. This is a good metaphor for the cultivation of the spiritual identity of humanity who inhabits it. Yes, it is an inexorable excruciation for those who deny the sovereignty of Jesus, and a source of infinite joy for the Christians who accept Him. You can see that the days and years are measured by the motion of the Earth as related to its proximity to the sun. This is yet another metaphor for the growth of the Church as it revolves around the Providence of God through the ages. All in all, one might wonder whether all the movement of the celestial skies will ever stand still. Is it possible that the Earth will never again be privy to the climates and seasons that are yielded from humanity's exile? The answer is that these things will continue in Heaven for those who enjoy them. I have said that the world became the Cross on Good Friday; and on that day, the day of the Crucifixion of the Son of Man, is the only day that, for one brief mortal moment, the Earth stood still. I am telling you this, My Special son, in an effort to express to you that while the lives of men are uniquely connected to the temporal environment in which they live, they are severed from that physicality when they receive the Body and Blood of Jesus during the Holy Sacrifice of the Mass. And, they are separated from it as well when they go to sleep – in the sense that all consciousness is yielded to another form of existence, of rest and surrender. This is the reason so many priests and theologians have referred to sleep as rehearsing for death. And, awakening in the morning refreshed and renewed is a metaphor for the resurrection of the human soul in the arms of their Savior. My dear Special and Chosen sons, it is not so much that you endure your lives that matters, but that you manifest them within the beatific realms of Sacred Truth. You relish the surrender that you make to My Son in Heaven. You celebrate your ability to become what God desires that you must be through His Son on the Cross. It is through this glory that you make yourselves miracle workers, holy believers who are making the charge against the night on behalf of the Messiah of Light.

My Special son, I have sometimes spoken to you about the concepts of expression and expectation. What this means is that a man can ask a question, which is an expression, with the hope of receiving a response, which is an expectation. It is like the movement of a saw blade through a piece of wood. Pushing it forward for cutting is the question, and pulling it back is the answer. I have with this parable described the framework of Messianic redemption. This can give you a great deal to think about – what has the Father expressed to humanity through the Angelic Annunciation from which He expects a definitive outcome? It is clearly that He wishes to reunite Himself with His earthly creatures by cutting through the thickness of the veil. Without going much further into detail, I would like for you and your brother to remember that you have already witnessed the cleanness of the severance between humanity and their sins. You have heard the echo of the two worlds being torn apart like a pair of boards impacting a concrete floor. How have you done this? By accepting your portion of the sacrifice needed to operate the saw. You have given your energy to the Father through Jesus the Carpenter on your journey of making yourselves Saints. And now, you are His sawteeth in the wind, cutting through secularism and indifference as though you were there with Me on the day of the Great Annunciation. You have wisdom that has yet to fall upon the ears of men. You have courage that can outlast the squalls over the seas. You have vision that can permeate any obstacle in the path of the truth of My Son. This is the reason that I keep telling you that you are different in a reverential way, in terms that both the righteous on Earth and the divine in Heaven can see and understand. And, unlike many others, you do your best not to get in your own way of prospering these things because you are deferential to Me. This is the same reason that we are trying to bring the whole of humanity around My feet, for the same enlightenment, and the same new beginning. My dear Special son, you have the capacity to perceive and judge what is said, and what must be said, about God, the truth and His Church. Your brother is more an academic than a contemplative thinker, and the two of you complement each other in these realms. This is the reason he keeps telling you that he cannot construct the strains of the Spirit in the way of your vision. Everyone has certain talents that they share toward the building up of the Kingdom of God on Earth. Yours is particularly spectacular because you were born to the Earth from within the Original Apostolic Church. You are adored and blessed because of your capacity for the mystical, for the miraculous and the ordained. One of My favorite quotations from the mouths of men is the one that your brother showed you this week from a 1984 convention. 'Born not to the blood of kings, but of pioneers...' This best describes you, My Special son. *"Thank you, Mama."* And, what it means is that you have been assembled with Jesus in the sovereign domain that I mentioned a few moments ago with the greatest wisdom and eloquence that the world has ever known. You have been reborn in the Blood of the King, and this makes you royalty in this world and the next. This is the way of all men who accept the Cross of Christ Jesus as their Salvation. I have told you these things not only because they are true, but because you have the ability to share what I have said in ways that only few before you have had. It is a miracle, when you think about it. The fact that God in Heaven wished to be reunited with His people is a miracle. The whole mysticism of the Salvation story is itself a miracle. Faith, the ages and the conversion of men are miracles as well. And, it is one tremendous miracle what you and your brother have given to those who must hear – that the Mother of Jesus Christ has willed through the Will of the Father to awaken the sleeping for that new resurrection that shall come to them in time. All mysticism and the miraculous are part of the expression and expectation to which God has devoted Himself since the days of the burning bush. My Special son, thank you, and bless you for being My child. You have the divinity of God within you. The Earth continues to live in anticipation of the miracles that will change it, and we are their answer."

Saturday, February 3, 2018
9:38 a.m.

"Remain in the Gospel, and keep a sharp eye.
The Cornerstone is also the whetstone."

"I am so deeply grateful, My dear little sons, for your tenacity in doing the right thing in all matters of grace. I pray for you in ways that would stagger your thoughts if you heard them. I told Jesus that I was going back this morning to My Morning Star boys, that I am gladdened beyond all telling that you have assembled here in this prayerful place to greet Me again. Yes, one's vision is kept sharp by focusing on the Cornerstone that the builders rejected, the whetstone that keeps keen your wisdom of the truth in a world so filled with lies. I come today to adore you with the same love and adulation that My children have during the Exposition of the Most Blessed Sacrament. I love you as if the world will yet see a billion tomorrows. I love you as deep as the vastness of cosmic space. My devotion to your lives on Earth is as intense as your desire to convert it. All in all indeed; you are more than just men! You are Saints in My arms, and you are precious to the good Father who has vested you in His Providence. My Special son, you and your brother are esteemed. I have told you this dozens of times, but I must ask whether you know what I mean. It is more than just that you are in good stead with Jesus' wishes. It is more than the certainty of your union in His Kingdom. It is about the luster with which your souls shine – the brilliance of your love for the Father is a massive glow of peace and confidence that you have inherited from Him, through your acceptance of your sacrifices by which human conversion is advanced. It is about what you have done to inspire the Holy Inspiration Himself! Yes, there is truth in knowing that the Father would have given up on many sinners who have rejected Him tenfold, a hundredfold and a thousand times more if you had not prayed for Him to remember them. My Special son, it is all about the centuries that you have collected at the Father's feet. Yes, centuries filled with sufferers and conquerors, of the giants of the ages who were looking for a home for their bravery, and the sweet maidens and gentlemen who were searching for the origin of their holiness. You and your brother, through your prayers, actions and writings, through your obedience to Me, have helped them find their home in the Sacred Heart of Jesus. You have transcended the meaning of life by helping Jesus on the Cross rewrite it. You have given the Son of Man, the Babe of My Womb, the joy to realize that whoever has lived, breathed and died have found themselves in Him.

My dear sons, the Holy Scriptures reveal that you should not wonder what you will say when your hour arrives; you will be given all that will glorify the suffering you have found, and the purpose of your lives. What will be given then was handed to humanity in the proclamation, '...It is finished.' My dear Special son, the entire manifestation was finished because Jesus saw on Good Friday, as I have said more than once, the disciples like you and your brother who would be born of the essence of providential love and handed back to the Kingdom that personifies it. There is glory in you! There are miracles yet untold because your journey is still ongoing. I am saying to you that '...It is finished' incorporates the real time in which you and your brother are living. All the roaring commotion and blaring sounds, every sight that could conceivably be beheld, every notion that could surface in the thoughts of mortal men – all this was finished by Jesus on the Cross through His Mystical Body during the twenty centuries since. This is the power of the Holy

Spirit to build a Church and strengthen a world for the fight against the devil. We have within us now this same vision that Jesus saw from the Cross on the day He died. And, the question is not what we do with this vision, but how we can induce the exiled world to listen. The answer is that the Cornerstone is indeed the whetstone, and the slow sharpening of the vision of humanity is being clarified now. We are generating the sacred energy that is refining it. Imagine, My Special son, how many words I have spoken to you and your brother since February 22, 1991. It is assuredly not infinite, but a person would be befuddled trying to number them. I would dare anyone to try, but in that effort, they would be missing the point. You and your brother and Me have been trying to sharpen the vision of humanity to 'see' their Salvation in Jesus the Savior, the Messiah on the Cross, the Victor over death, and the Man-God who belongs to Heaven and Earth. You have become conquerors in Him not as though you have been walking on crutches, but in flight alongside the Advocate who has been searching for the lost and forsaken, to rescue and invigorate them. You have had the Spirit of God within you, and the Second Person of the Trinity beside you. You have lifted high the Cross as a lighthouse for those lost in the seas of their own transgressions.

Yes, My dear children, one would think that there is a tint of timidity in those who claim to be Christian. The world should not see it this way! I have said that all the weapons will be fired at once, not just the weapons of war against the devil, but all the thoughts and actions that have saturated the Earth since the Crucifixion occurred. Imagine, My Special son, what your contributions have meant to the Saints looking on from Heaven. Consider what they thought when each of them arrived in the Father's House, knowing that the best of the clarification of human vision would happen here in this home, here in your nation, here where the Morning Star Over America shines. There is a cascade of wonder that is overcoming the nations by virtue of the prayers that you and your brother have shared since you were yet young men. You were priming Creation for a response from God, and My Morning Star Over America messages are His answer. Hence, when we speak about the manifestations of God, all the things that He chooses to do and reveal, whatever sightings and healings He ordains, what must become of the world once all souls have been redeemed, and those who reject Him have been damned – we are speaking about a world that has been framed and fashioned by your relationship with Him. You have learned that it is not enough to know God as a conceptual figure who has created the world and watches it from His heavenly throne. Human beings in exile must engage Him, search for Him while He can be found, implore His intervention, invoke His deific pardon, and handover to Him every particle of their being that they can possibly yield. This relationship is the center of the existence of humanity in the world because there can be no world without Him. Why did the sun rise this morning? Because the Father said so. Why will it set again tonight? Here is a fallacy for you – it is not because the sun is tired and wants to go to bed. This is what some people metaphorically believe. No indeed, it is because the Father says so. This is the same Father who has ordained that men should be saved, that the world should be set aright, that every good deed done in His name should be glorified, and much that I shall say to the Church will be spoken to My Morning Star Over America visionaries. This is how future-changing our messages have been. This has been the essential meaning behind your lives. And, the Church and the world around you is beginning to realize it now.

The whole matter of your consecration to Jesus and Me has meant the enlightenment of the twenty-first century world about what the conclusion of its exile implies. It is about working toward the eradication of evil, and the acquisition of righteousness by those who have yet to decide. Please do not worry; they will get there. I am speaking the strains of their transition now. As My words fall upon your ears at this moment, the Glory of God is overtaking the Earth like the slow eclipse of the Moon. My Special son, we celebrate this fact, even as you and your brother do not see it every day. When you are driving your truck down the road, there are thousands of explosions happening inside your engine that you cannot see – nearly countless detonations that are powering your vehicle on its way. This is the same thing that is happening now as you, I and your brother are speaking. If humanity were to place its collective ear against your Morning Star Over America published works, they would hear the humming of this cultivating power. This is a metaphor that only a Woman in Heaven could relate. I am saying that you and your brother should live the practicalities of your days with the knowledge that there is always a great force, a larger purpose that is unfolding beyond the realms of your sights. You have said many times that I am always kind to you when I come speaking every week. Thank you for this observation, but I have not even begun to voice the praises that you and your brother deserve for your lives devoted to Me. Jesus will give you more than redemption, something greater than distinction, a wealth more valuable than accolades, and a standing in Heaven so high that you will be able to see the architecture of Creation on the Father's drawing board from the first day of the world. Let there be light? Yes, the answer is yes. And, the first thing this light has revealed, exempt from the constraints of time and space, is the lovely faces of you and your brother, poised to receive the commission you have known. 'In the beginning...' This is what you will see, and you will know Jesus as you know each other now. You might refer to this as prophecy, if you wish. Refer to it as the planned 'might' to come in your future. Call it miraculous or beyond the reach of mortal men, but it is coming nonetheless. My Special son, I pray that you have enjoyed what I came to say today. *"Yes, thank you very much. I love you."* Do you have any issues to speak about today? *"How is our Bishop doing? I pray for his health and peace."* My little son, your Bishop knows what you have given him. But, the history of the Church and the protocols of the process find him having to ingest more and more of what I have said. It is his belief that it would seem imprudent, given the immensity of your works, for him to make a public proclamation now. *"I understand."* Your brother has helped your young friend with the baby's supplies. This young baby girl will become the next likeness of Mother Teresa. It is true that someone can be born into poverty and become the darling of the nations – Saint Joan of Arc, Mother Teresa, and all the gentlemen Saints and Martyrs. Let us remember this today as we bless all who suffer dearth and lacking."

Saturday, February 10, 2018
9:33 a.m.

"Human life on Earth is about faith, victory and commendation – the world should pray, hope and welcome its inheritance of Salvation bequeathed to them by Jesus on the Cross."

- The Dominion Angels

"Yes, My dear little sons, the constancy and apparency of your faith proves that you are within the exhaustive presence of goodness that has overwhelmed the world with love. It is My desire for you to remember that you have found yourselves in the caress of Heaven where you have strived to be, where your souls are destined, and from where your strength to be sustained in this life is derived. My little ones, Jesus comes to you here. He comes to you. What does this mean? It is that a distance is implied, that there is another dimension unknown to you that must be transcended so the Son of Man can live and reign here in your day. He comes to you as the Holy Spirit in your hearts and through the Sacraments of the Church – there is nothing new in hearing this. My description of Jesus' coming to you is that humanity accepts Him. He is the mandated course of life for those seeking redemption. 'He comes to you...' means that you invite Him into your hearts and lives as a permeating love, always and everywhere. Just as humanity moves through time, it is humanity who must come to Jesus. This is how Jesus comes to you. When you travel to another continent and breathe the air, it is not that you have never breathed air before, but you have never been in that location to inhale the air that is common to all the world. This is the way of the conversion of men. And, men who are converted are already 'breathing' the air of Heaven before they shall die. My Special son, the Dominion Angels have spoken this morning about humanity welcoming its inheritance of Salvation bequeathed to the world by Jesus on the Cross. Coming to Jesus on the Cross is assuredly the movement of sinners to the Savior who was crucified there. It does not mean that God takes the Cross in hand or carries Jesus on the Cross to every soul seeking eternal Salvation; it is lost sinners who must come to Him. And, My Special son, there is a proposition that the spiritual aspects of the Crucifixion come to humanity inside the heart; this is where the Holy Spirit deposits the faith, hope and enlightenment that Christians gain from Mount Calvary. I have no difficulty with this proposition, but it requires that each human soul must open itself to this reception; it is a movement of the heart and conscience in the direction of supernal truth. All the initiative for the conversion of lost sinners, in this respect, must be manifested by those seeking redemption. There has never been a stream, even those running downhill, that has moved itself to the lips of a thirsty traveler. The traveler must take a drink. There has never been a bird that grabbed the sky and placed it beneath its wings. The bird must take flight of its own accord. The point here again is about what initiates the contact between Heaven and Earth, and you know that it was the Father who first came into the world. From the burning bush to the Manger, from the Spirit to the Flesh, from the beginning to the end – it has been God who has summoned the peoples of the nations to respond to Him. The Salvation story is complete. The response of humanity has been heard – the Church stands in faith at this moment, waiting for its time to stand in glory. So, let those philosophers say all they wish about the contrast between the sinners in the Church and the Spirit that fills it with Truth. I have never dwelt on this differentiation, and I never will. While there can certainly be Truth without mortal men, there can be no resurrected man without the Spirit of Truth – the Living Spirit that has been handed to the ages by the Messiah on the Cross. What this means, My Special son, is that being 'transcending' is more than changing places in space and time. It means that there is a renewal of the course of humanity on Earth and the meaning of his existence. It is as glorious as the Transfiguration of Jesus on Mount Tabor, but for men, it is not about revealing their glory, but inheriting it. The Divine Living Spirit is about harvesting everything righteous about a man in the expanse of his time, and feeding the Apex of Salvation the fruits of his triumph. This is the origin of the nourishment of Adam and Eve, the holiness and obedience on which they should have fed at that moment in the Garden. I once told you that new beginnings come from things like these, and this is how eternity itself has been rewritten. It is about the forgiveness of God and the obedience of His people.

You and your brother are enduring the winter's weeks and months by safeguarding this glory within your hearts. You are practitioners of the faithful legacy of those who have preceded you. It is clear by the fruits of your lives. When you pick up one of your books in the future, pretend for a moment that it is the first time you have seen it, and you have yet to meet its authors. This will place you in the mind and thoughts of those who have seen your books from out of the blue. 'How can the Mother of God ever have said so much here in the exiled world?' This is the most common question that they ask. And, when they keep reading, they realize that no one who has ever been exiled could have written what is being absorbed by their eyes. Who could know so much about the unwritten history of the Church, about the Apostles and the personal lives of Jesus, Mary and Joseph? Who has gone into the private archives of the Father's Will, and discerned the genius that He has laid onto the page? Where did the Virgin Mary get all these lessons and parables about the human and the divine being intermingled so eloquently in the Three Persons of the Most Blessed Trinity? Who would have the time to record all these messages, to transcribe them from Mary's lips to the page, to digitize and format all this glorious speech? And still, the questions just keep coming. 'Why have I never heard about this before...' is the most common inquiry derived from the curiosity of the United States Catholic Bishops. 'This must be Providence...' This is the way they see that twenty-seven years, nigh at hand, can pass so quietly, and the Lady of Peace has laid Her hand so gracefully on the landscape of this great American nation. This, My Special son, is the reaction that is happening around the states and cities where you have lived the whole of your years. It must be so! – It must be made manifest that I have come to you and your brother so the most profound nation in the history of the created world can come in its own right to the Cross. A leader of men? Let that nation lead in this! Let it raise its face toward Heaven in the darkest of its hours, and proclaim that the Morning Star has come! Yes, this is the Morning Star that shall precede the Second Coming of the King in Her arms. My dear Special son, it is the noblest thing that any man could ever ponder – that Jesus will return with justice in His hands and the Salvation of the blessed in His

Sacred Heart. This will be the moment when Adam and Eve will hear what you and your brother have etched into time and eternity from your lives here in this world. It is the transcending inspiration about which I speak, the glory that I celebrate. And, to say 'thank you' is not sufficient to express what the Lord feels about your gifts to His Kingdom. My Special son, there are ordinary days, and extraordinary ones, mundane and rallying ones, and days that reveal the brightest light perceivable by humanity in the flesh. They come and go, all of them. They rotate and exchange one another for a newer pursuit of the future. But, what they all have in common is that they rest inside the Providence that I have mentioned. They are like the inner-workings of a clock. What time is it? Providence – every hour, every waking and sleeping moment, every tint of darkness, and every peak of light. It is Providence when it is time to pray, and it is Providence when it is time to die. But, the greatest Providence is when it is time to live again! – time to be resurrected into the New Jerusalem that is, as we speak, being re-inhabited the way God always hoped it would be. This is what makes for the Glory of His Kingdom; this is what prayer is for. This is the reason for the sacrifices of the Church and the culmination of the Sacraments that have saturated the Earth with love. My Special son, I have concluded the message that I came to give you today. I pray that you have liked it. *"It's fantastic, thank you for talking to us this way, with such words to share."* I also hope that you and your brother will take these days to rest and reflect, and to relax and remember the peace that thrives within you. Thank you for taking such good care of your brother. Thank you also for praying so faithfully for everyone you mention in your daily petitions, for praying for your nation and its leaders, and for praying for the leaders of the Church. It makes all the difference here in this world and beyond it that you remember these things to God. It is important that you remember the significance of your writing that you are presently composing for yet another book, AD 2013-2015. You have such vision and charitable awareness of what needs to be revealed to humanity and the Church. Your writing is blessed beyond all imagining."

Saturday, February 17, 2018
9:36 a.m.

Pardon yielded from the Blood of Truth.
Admonish the vengeful, shun the darkness.
Shame the wicked, honor the righteous.
Tame the wilderness, but not the heart!

- The Dominion Angels

"My little children, while your love must be as tender as silk and petals, your faith must be as strong as iron and oak. Here, we have again joined in prayer for the Faith Church, and for the Poor Souls in Purgatory who are suffering the legacies of their lives. I wish for you to remember that there are stark differences between regrets and the outright guilt of unconfessed sin. Hence, the Faith Church does its best to cleanse humanity of those wrongs that are not yet righted. Yes, we pray for everyone to convert to the Cross, to the life of Jesus, to the purifying Sacraments, and to the confession that will make them whole again. Today, I have come to pray with you, as I have said, for the end of war and the begetting of peace. My thoughts are with everyone for whom you are praying, and your thoughts are with those whose prayers have yet to be said. Jesus acknowledges not only the intent of human beings, but the potential of placing their intentions into action. The preferences of the world should always reflect the Will of God in transforming the essential existence of humanity into the perpetual life of the sanctified redeemed soul. My Special son, the nation in which you live reels from the sins about which we speak. All the destruction and loss of life is doubtlessly attributable to the lack of prayer in homes and public places. If I were to speak to you every day for the next fifty years, I would remind you that these conditions are changing because of our work. You have welcomed Me here in your home for almost twenty-seven years, an anniversary that you will mark this week; and you and your brother should remember that your blessing of the world is complemented by My blessing of the Church. The Holy Spirit comes naturally to those who welcome the presence of God. This is your rightful encounter with the Father who has given you life. This leaves open the question whether the Holy Spirit comes naturally to those who do not welcome the presence of God. The answer is yes, but it is only by the miracle of the conversion of these sinners. Conversion to the Cross is the greatest gift ever to be bestowed by exiled sinners upon the Messiah who was crucified there. Conversion of the heart is humanity's way of thanking Jesus for His Passion and Holy Sacrifice. And, the resurrection of the human soul upon one's mortal death is Jesus' way of saying '...you're welcome.' Imagine, My Special son, what this means in the aftermath of so many millions of lives spent wandering the Earth, contemplating what the essence of life means, taking care of those under one's charge, enduring the effects that the years have on the mind, body and spirit. Even if after 90 or 100 years passing, it is less than an instant that the raising of a soul is manifested into the eternal realms of God. It is a miracle beyond all telling. You remain imbedded in the days of winter that are still ongoing, and you are still hopeful in your heart that the coming of spring will be a metaphor for the awakening of the world to God. So many people around the globe want to know why the Father is always so quiet. Why does He not shake the nations with jubilant revelation that the Son of Man draws near to them in prayer, or that He touches them with true healing and new awakenings. These things are His voice of triumph for the waiting world, and the jubilance that He expresses lives in the strains of faith spoken by people like you and your brother. If it is true that My most-known attribute is gratitude, beyond My grace and beauty, it is because I am thankful that God does indeed speak through such brilliance of His children. He does not mandate that His disciples be beautiful like artworks and Nature, but beautiful in resemblance of He who has fashioned them both. If a person wishes to sing like a whippoorwill, his song should reflect the Maker of the songbird. If there are favorite sunrises and sunsets seen over the crests of coastal waters, their origin in Jesus should be celebrated like a feast. Many sinners speak about a heaven that is far off from them, and it is certainly true for those who keep their distance from God. But, Heaven in the way of Salvation, in the way of peace and justice, is already present in this world. It lives in the conscience, consciousness, thoughts, motivations and actions of those who accept Jesus as their Redeemer. My Special son, please hold your palm to your heart for Me. Can you feel Jesus touching you in return? *"Yes."* The point of this exercise is that you feel Jesus within you as though the flesh of your body is like the spiritual veil that separates Heaven and Earth. Does this make sense to you? *"Yes."* This is the simplest metaphor that can be applied to the principle that Heaven is this close to the exiled human soul. The body is like the veil, and the spirit is the sacred energy that permits the exiled soul to touch the unseen Heaven inside.

My Special son, I concede that telling you how lovely you are so often might bring the risk that you could assume that I am not being sincere. Many people believe that this is the case. My response is that, even as a person says tens of thousands of Hail Mary's in their lifetime, is any one of them less sincere than another? The answer is 'no.' I am simply reciprocating by telling My children 'thank you' in the same way that Jesus' thank you is the resurrection of the soul from the grave. When you adopt the attitude of prayer, you are saying to God that you will see Him soon. The peace and loveliness that you feel in your heart after that are His response of, '…I know.' I will tell you something. It is possible for humanity on the Earth to 'teach' God that you love Him, much like a toddler would 'teach' their parents a talent they have newly discovered as if they do not already know. Similarly, it is not as though God is unaware, or that He has no idea what is inside the hearts of His people. But, teaching God about your love for Him lends evidence to the intentions of your life. It is as though someone says that it will be cold out tomorrow before tomorrow ever comes. It is one's promise to love and worship God in spite of what might happen here in this world. And, this speaks to the prospect of whether God ever tests His disciples to discover whether this promise is true. The whole concept of tested faith comes from the earthly side of the veil. The Lord gives His gift of faith freely, and without encumbrance. It is conditions 'on the ground' in this life that determine the mettle of that faith. It is as though 'faith' in the human heart is the speech of God, telling the soul that its final destiny is at hand. The 'testing' of that faith is when mortal men and women find themselves in circumstances where the devil is trying to steal their faith away. And, there can be no mistaking this; the sinister forces in this world and in societies here in America are doing this. My Special and Chosen sons, you have the capacity of knowing precisely the reasons for all the destruction, mayhem and loss of life within the confines of your shores. You may call it leftism, collective agnosticism or outright evil works, but the ends are still the same. If people's faith is tested during these awful trials, they should think about the reasons they are remaining so quiet while the devil keeps whittling away at the righteousness in their hearts. If anyone complains that the voice of God is too silent, they should instead ask themselves why they are being so silent – given the evil works and indifference that are consuming what is left of the mutual goodness on which this country was founded. Therefore, My dear little sons, I ask that you take heart in knowing that you are fully apprised of the problem. It is the stunning silence of the faithful, refusing to make a difference in a nation that prides itself on free speech. I do not wish to claim that these changes will happen soon. The concept of 'soon' is a relative term that people without patience do not understand. It is the same as referring to the Poor Souls in Purgatory as being only in a place, not suffering the effects of a spiritual condition. When they leave Purgatory is not an accurate description of their entry into Heaven. It is not 'when' they leave

Purgatory, but 'because' they leave Purgatory. They leave Purgatory because of the intercessory prayers of the Church. This is the way 'soon' is applied as a matter of principle to the eradication of evil works from the Earth. It is according to the prayers of men, matched to the Will of the Father who shall proclaim that their response is enough. Do you understand what I have said? *"Yes, thank you."* I am only saying that the iron and oak of your faith is the structure behind the power of your prayers for the Lord's intervention. Yes, you have silk and petals in your heart, and Jesus resides comfortably there as His domain of hope on the Earth. I would be remiss if I did not mention the sweet poem that the Dominion Angels dictated to you at the opening of My message this morning. I know that you understand what it means, that a heart given to Jesus does not need to be tamed. It is as lively and spontaneous as Jesus ever was in His youth here in the world, and in the Father's heavenly realms."

Saturday, February 24, 2018
9:36 a.m.

"Yes, fishers of men – with dreams deeply fathomed."

"Greetings to My dear little children, and love and hope for your hearts and souls! Today, I have come to pray with you again, that all the world will realize what a gift love is to them. I bring with Me the fullness of gratitude from Jesus and the Father, and the blessings of the Holy Spirit abounding. You are moving more toward the spring of the year as the days pass by, and I wish for you to know that the spiritual conscience of humanity is awakening too. Spanning the many years that I have come has been an overarching presence of divinity that has lived in you, that has been broadly cast over the landscapes of the world, that has touched the lives of the suffering poor. My children, I heard you speak recently about what constitutes prayer. Yes, it is lauding the Son of Man in word and deed. It is imploring God to lend compassion to your lives. Prayer is about curing the ills of the temporal world. And, just as you have said, prayer is living in 'accourse' with the Will of the Father. It is as though you speak a phrase here in this life, and hear it when you enter Heaven. Just as Jesus is living within you now, and you in Him, you have already made the connection between this life and the next. Your presence in Heaven is already being felt. My dear sons, many people ask how the Earth can be the likeness of Heaven as long as there are sinners in the world. The answer is that Heaven comes down to Earth. Divine Love transforms the exiled realms of men by flourishing within the faithful. As you can readily see, this process is not yet complete. The Lord comes to change sinners into Saints by entering their hearts. And, it is clear to us, My children, that it is not so much the stubbornness of the veil of human exile that separates men from God, but men's reluctance to lead lives that transcend it. I have told My children, especially My seers and locutionists, that the grace to find God in this life is already made manifest through the faith you have been given. You are commissioned to welcome Jesus in Glory by tending to His Kingdom in the way that the Scriptures mandate. This commission begins with prayer as I have described it this morning, and includes granting God the most humble chambers of your hearts. My Special son, you are writing ingenious strains of enlightenment in your prayerful sessions. You can feel the Holy Spirit permeating the physical bonds that keep you from seeing Heaven right now. The wisdom that you are writing is not just a dictation of the grace of truth from the mouth of the Father, but your own wisdom about the way the Earth must be enlightened. In other words, the process of converting lost sinners is prayed into being by exercising your own awareness of what God desires. I have said that humanity tends to speak in trite phrases and vague rhetoric. I have said that acts of the conscience are routinely clouded by the call for expedience. These are two reasons that genuine prayer is not lifted from the hearts of everyone in the world. And, inexplicably, prayer usually follows some sort of catastrophe or undue challenge that must be overcome. Flowers are laid at sites where people have died, in foyers and entrances where well known souls have lost their lives. It must be made clear that if humanity would give Me those flowers in the beginning, these tragedies could be avoided. If it is darkness that prevails over the endeavors of men, then something must be done to preempt it. My Special son, humanity has yet to draw the connection between embracing the light to avoid disaster before these disasters come. It is like trying to give a man a drink of water who has already died from thirst. Yes, even in the way of Salvation, there is a sequence that must be followed in order to become one with the timelessness of God. If Heaven is going to be allowed to sanctify the domain of mortal men, then the sequence laid out by the Scriptures and the Sacraments of the Church must be observed. Conversion requires repentance. Confession precedes Communion. Marriage comes before the conception of children. You see that conversion, confession and such gifts must preempt the darkness. This is the preventative life that Christians must avow. To use the adage about crying over spilled milk, it is better to pet the cow than slip and fall on the milky floor. Yes, it goes back this far in time – to the origin of the goodness of men, to the thought of a world not yet set in space and time, to the desires of God to build a Creation that reflects the presence of His love. So, we speak about Fishers of Men who have dreams that are deeply fathomed in the commission to which they are appointed. Every person who accepts the Cross becomes one of these disciples – not just descendants of the Apostles like the Bishops of the Church, but apostles and disciples who are sent out to convert lost sinners who will someday live in Heaven with all the Saints. This is the commission that is handed to a Christian once he pronounces his Profession of Faith.

Also today, My Special son, I have come to remind you that the Great Commission of the Roman Catholic Church is more blessed than the world believes. Popes and Cardinals come and go, but the Church is the Constant Star in the constellation of the earthly domain. You and your brother once reflected about all the people you have known through the years since you have lived in this city. Most of the faces have changed; the families are smaller; the pews are sparsely occupied, the voices are fewer, and the singing of the anthems less heard. This does not mean, however, even in a nation that has grown to 330 million people, that the Church is being defeated by the wiles of the secular void. It means that the charge of being Roman Catholic has not been handed from one generation to the next. It means that surviving the distractions of the world has become more difficult because of the lures of the flesh. This is not the result of secularism overcoming the faith of men, it is about men choosing not to embrace their faith. Faith is called living for a reason. My Special son, whenever a Bishop is required to issue a public reprimand to a Catholic United States senator about something so basic as protecting unborn human life, it is not about the advancements of the secular void. It is about a Roman Catholic parishioner becoming the new Judas Iscariot of the 21st century. There is no such thing, as the Church now lives centuries beyond the fall of Adam, as someone claiming that, '...the serpent did it.' It is instead all about sloth, fame, profit, power and inconceivable pride. It is about facing down the very grace that has laid claim to the still-converting human soul. As much as I would like to blame the secular void for these things, it is more about people lying to God from the drivel on their tongues about how faithful they are to His Church. They even couple this evil with the strains of rhetoric that I mentioned earlier today, saying that there is no such thing as equality in a nation that refuses to permit private citizens to choose how to sin. My Special one, you can tell that this has the stench of evil from the beginning. It is about someone who had the 'light' inside him, but who chose the darkness instead. You know that there is a stark particular judgment reserved for these politicians, and I ask you again not to pity them when it arrives. My dear son, I have concluded what I came to share this morning. I pray that you and your brother remember how precious you are in the sight of God. Let us pray for the intercession of the Saints in the blessing and healing of the sick, for those being held against their will, and for the Poor Souls in Purgatory. Yes, let us ask the Father that there will be no more abortions in the aftermath of our prayers of love."

Saturday, March 3, 2018
9:28 a.m.

"Blue flames, alcoves, pontiffs and laces."

"Good morning, My darling little sons. I wish for you to remember that it has been you who have called Me here. You have invited Me to pray with you because you know of the advocacy that I hold before Jesus. You understand that Beauty Incarnate has the constitution of the Spirit of God, and nothing else considered beautiful matters. I pray that you are enjoying these days, My dear children. Many people say that human beings are forced to 'endure' life. This is not what the Father intends. Humanity should not view life as an undue burden. It is claimed that people live their lives, and then die from it. We know that your years in exile have the effect of purifying the soul, elevating your vision of Divine Love, and preparing you to meet Jesus in the Kingdom of God. I have said that Paradise can begin in this life and, if not for your responsibilities of maintaining your own self-sufficiency, you would recognize Heaven here with you now. If you were to compose a list of the five most difficult aspects of living in the world, you would likely list as number one the same thing that the Saints say when they reach the Father's side – engaging the secular void. And, being around a humanity that believes that there are numerous ways to Salvation that have nothing to do with Jesus on the Cross is another. Appropriating freedom and power that conflicts with the teachings of the Scriptures is yet one more. My Special son, as the world has grown older; and notice that I have not said 'matured,' it has come upon a disordered conclusion that progress in human affairs translates into being more like God. We know that the opposite is true. The Father wants humanity to be like the Son of Man, His own Son, whose tortured years on Earth were meant to teach lost sinners everything that the Father wishes them to know. 'When you have seen Me, you have seen the Father.' This, My Special son, seems to be the most controversial statement that keeps the Jewish people from accepting Jesus as their Savior. It is the Messianic Proclamation that sent Jesus to the Cross on Good Friday. However, its truth rings throughout all times and places; it lives before and beyond the existence of man, and it embraces eternity in clearer ways than anything else Jesus said. Humanity seems too imbedded in developing its own sense of 'self' than striving to become the likeness of Jesus, of God, through the power of the Holy Spirit. It is no wonder that some people say that there is no such triune as the Blessed Trinity because the sinners who say this are not receptive to the wisdom of the Holy Spirit, the Third Person of the Blessed Trinity that they deny. They believe that the entire concept of the Messiah is misplaced because they cannot accept that a God so powerful would come to Earth as a Man. They are secular blatherers. They do not take it upon themselves to realize that God can do anything He pleases. You have written that $2 + 2 = 4$ on Earth and in Heaven, which is true. But, God can make it equal 116 if He wishes. Those who refuse to believe in the Most Blessed Trinity are unaware of His power to do so.

Blue flames, alcoves, pontiffs and laces. This is what atheists have reduced religion to in their minds. What they refuse to acknowledge is that Jesus can reduce their entire existence down to two or three words as well – damned, irrelevant and cowardly. Add to this such things as obstinate and arrogant, and the entire sum describes the eventuality of their fate. There is nothing damned, irrelevant, cowardly, obstinate or arrogant in Heaven. In essence, people who refuse to believe in God, and those who claim to believe in Him that live in ways that displease Him, will find their lives and souls being trampled underfoot by the parade of Saints making their way through the Gate of Paradise. Unbelievers view the Faith Church as having one dimension that has no connection to the Church Triumphant. Hence, in their minds, it burns like a blue flame that will finally douse itself out. They see the whole institution of Messianic religion as an alcove off the main stage of human life in a world that offers them far more to engage. As for pontiffs, we know what they think about the infallibility of sinners claiming to speak and 'make policy' on behalf of God. They see chief priests and Bishops as dressing up in lacy vestments to get other people's money – this is the position held by vile despots throughout the world. My Special son, I am telling you these things because it reinforces My point that engaging the secular void is the most difficult part of living in the world. It is something that must be dealt with, not defeated by. It is the same point that life is something that must be lived, but not to die from. Why? Because life on Earth is the beginning of a journey to Salvation that yields the fruit of eternity for the exiled human soul – it starts where you have lived, and it never ends. Remember that it is the flesh that passes away, but not the perpetuity of the soul. So, we pray for the conversion of lost sinners who have not grasped what it means to be in alignment with the Will of God in all things human and divine. You have seen that there are geniuses all around the globe, people with multiple doctoral degrees, and at least some who understand the presence of God. The problem is that their own hubris gets in their way – this is the arrogance that I speak about – and they refuse to believe that something that Adam and Eve did thousands of years ago has anything to do with them. They do not understand that they are saying something as a figure of speech that literally applies to them. When they are surprised by a certain piece of knowledge, they are prone to say, '...well, I'll be damned.' And, they are absolutely right. Their speech is a parable for their standing before the Father; and at the end of time, Jesus will remind them that they have already spoken the answer to His question about their eternal destiny. He will ask which they prefer, Heaven or Hell, and they will have the same response. One might think that what I am saying is an attempt at humor, but I am stating the facts. I have said that this can be averted, and it can, but many deathbed conversions are more about fear than acceptance. In fact, most of them are. My Special son, one of the key issues that keeps unconverted souls from accepting the Blood of Jesus on the Cross upon their deaths is when they see the record of their lives. I have never told you this before, but the decades that you and your brother have given to Me and the Catholic Church have expunging power for sinners in this position. Why? Because their penance is to hear every word I have said to you, every book you have written on your own by the wisdom of the Holy Spirit, and to see every moment of sacrifice that you made in your life so Jesus could be known. My Special son, no one who has ever seen your manuscripts beyond this life has ever failed to understand what every word means. No soul has ever approached Jesus and asked how a particular passage applies to them. They also realize that the Holy Gospel is imbedded in everything that you and I have ever said in this world and the next. The point I am making is that they believed that the Gospel of Jesus was encrypted in the dimensions of the world while they lived here in exile, but they later recognize that it was before them as clear as day. The Holy Gospel lives in every person who exemplifies the life of Jesus on Earth and in Heaven – thus the Faith Church and the Church Triumphant are one by the benevolence of the same Spirit. You may notice that I have yet to mention the Church Suffering in Purgatory because no one who enters Heaven remembers the 'time' they spent there. It is the Divine Mercy of Jesus' Holy Sacrifice that brings people to enter Purgatory when they see the sacrifices of the Church and the legacy of the Saints when they stand before Jesus. These are not the souls who say, '...well, I'll be damned.' My Special son, do you have any questions or reactions to what I have told you today? "*I understand. It's part of the clarity of your Wisdom.*" Have I said anything that you did not know? "*No, it's something that I would have thought to say.*" Your lives of sacrifice emulate Jesus' life and death on the Cross; and to God, this reflects His absolving grace from which all reconciliation comes. His Mystical Body emanates His Light and radiates His Grace. Thank you for everything you are doing to keep Me encouraged about the conversion of humanity, especially not conceding your hopes about the success of our mission to the routine of the years. It is not just about blue flames, alcoves, pontiffs and laces, it is about inducing lost sinners to accept the Cross that will open their eyes to the truth. Please remember that you are loved beyond all telling, and that your life and soul are precious to God."

Saturday, March 10, 2018
9:30 a.m.

"The Son of God – Redeemer and Cultural Paragon."

"My dear little sons, this beautiful morning that has broken for you is the reason that your hopes shine as bright. It is more than men can imagine that I have given them the grace to change through My messages to you. Jesus is not quiet. He does not remain still in the presence of those who follow Him. His Spirit invigorates what you do, how you feel, where you travel, and what you say. The billions of years that the universes have existed are but a moment's pause to Him. The magnitude of the love in your hearts is even larger still than those same universes. I wish you peace on this pretty morning, and I urge you to remember that all days are blessed when you realize your standing before the Father. My Special son, the Redeemer of the World is also the Earth's Cultural Paragon. Jesus is the highest form of human life that will ever be revealed. I will not be telling you anything about Him this morning that you do not already know. My intent is to relate His message to you and your brother that you can find His Spirit within you, alongside and united with the spirit of your own souls. To reach the pinnacle of something in an active sense is to 'paragon' it. I have made use of a word that does not imply action, but a state of being. You have gained your own 'propriety of being' in unison with the Being of Christ Jesus because you have laid your lives in His hands. My Special one, I realize that Christians sometimes feel helpless on Earth to effect the changes that must come because of the sins and failures of those who do not believe in God. It is equally as difficult to believe that you have all the power that I have told you about so many times over the past twenty-seven years. Please do not misunderstand what I am saying to you, but if you did not have this power, you and your brother would have never amassed the miraculous body of works that you have placed into being for the glory of the Father and the enlightenment of the Church. It is not that you lack an appreciation for it, but that you are so well acquainted with your years-long contributions that you have become accustomed to its content. You have acquired within you a unification with the culture of the Paragon. This does not mean that you will not be surprised by the profound new miracles that have yet to come. When? It is the Will and pleasure of the Father to make these pronouncements at any moment, or tomorrow, next week or next year – so the element of time is not the issue. What percentage of ten billion years is the twenty centuries since Christ Jesus walked the Earth and brought forth the Salvation of the entire human race? It is important to you, your brother and humanity at large because, here again, what percentage of twenty centuries is the seventy or eighty years that most men live on the surface of the globe? I am saying that time is relative, that the linear nature of human existence is measurable but not consequential, and that the actions and reactions of the life, death and resurrection of human creatures is best viewed through Jesus' eyes. So many more questions follow these, My Special son. How old would Jesus have lived if He had not been crucified on the Cross, the same seventy or eighty years? Would He have lived 400 years like some of the ancients? The answer rests in the fact that Jesus never sinned – He was incapable of sin. In what way does this answer the question about how long He would have lived? *"He would have never had to die as a wage for sin."* Exactly and precisely. Jesus would have lived until God said that the old world should exist no more, and forever beyond.

My Special son, I am saying that humanity's sins brought death upon a Man who would not have died, in the same way that His death brought new life to exiled sinners who would have never lived again. You are able to see the parallel that I am drawing between the life of Old Adam and the death of the New Adam. And, to make My message clear, this is how the culture of redemption took its first form in the mind of God after the events in the Garden. It is all about this – the Father knows that He can draw a circle. He makes a sphere out of a straight line; this is the way God thinks. This is where the concept of time loops emerged. It is where He thought of making the motion of the planets determine when you get out of bed, when you eat and socialize, and when you take your rest for the night. And, it is not so much the motion of the planets that decides the longevity of the ages, but the effects of the motion on your physical body. Does this not mean, therefore, that your life on Earth is more a condition than a manifestation of time? *"Yes."* Now, I have just given you a practical view of how this is true for the Poor Souls in Purgatory – it is a condition rather than an effect of space or time. *"I understand."* What I have been doing by the examples I have given is refine your understanding of the culture of human life over the backdrop of the miraculous gift of the life of Christ Jesus as He has always been known. I have given you earlier messages saying that '...in the beginning' does not mean the beginning of God or Heaven, or Jesus. However, do you suppose that Hell existed before the beginning? *"No, because it's a condition generated by sin."* Exactly correct. What I am also saying is that you are so close to the Cultural Paragon that you already knew the answers before I asked them. Imagine if you put these same questions to people walking down the street. If you asked if Hell existed before Adam and Eve fell from the Garden, half the people would want to know who Adam and Eve are. But, they know what Hell is! Some of them celebrate and promote it. This is the counterculture with which your works often come into contact. *"Was there a time when Satan was happy and sinless with God?"* Yes, you must know that God never created evil. It was the point when Satan, through pride and disobedience, caused the corruption of his own volition that tempted Adam and Eve. The point you should remember is one that you often highlight – consequences. *"Was his act of disobedience the act of tempting Adam and Eve?"* Tempting Adam and Eve was the effect of his disobedience. His disobedience was violating the love of the Father. *"What did he do in that moment with his will?"* He chose to perpetuate evil, placing him in contradiction with the love of God. He set out to supplant the Glory of God with his own definition of what glory should be. This is the same as sinful men on Earth who have been doing things that are contrary to the Will of God. *"I understand."* This is a reflection of how one fallen angel created the crucible in which the sins of men would take place. And, God said to humanity, '...if you wish to sin, go somewhere else." Hence, Adam and Eve were cast down from the Garden. *"What did Satan see as glory compared to God?"* That he would be God, himself. *"I'll decide."* Yes, and what deadly sin produced this error? *"Pride."* My Special son, do you see how My message this morning speaks to the conflict and contrast that the world embraces that stands against the Cultural Paragon, the Redeemer of the World? *"Yes."* Can you see the circle that I have drawn? *"Yes."* Hence, there exists in the Heart of the Father the desire to return all lost things to where they can be found. This is a great prayer that we have offered today, My Special son, that we have spoken about this. God is glorified, Jesus is uplifted, humanity is enlightened, and your work is enhanced. *"Thank you, Mama. Does God have an even bigger universal plan to redeem all the angels that fell, including Satan?"* No, Satan and his demonic followers will always be condemned because they will never convert; they will never love, they will never accept God as the Sovereign Providence of Heaven and Earth. If anyone tells you otherwise, they are lying on behalf of the devil's works."

Saturday, March 17, 2018
9:39 a.m.

"It is only a beginning, always. The young must know it; the old must know it. It must always sustain us, because the greatness comes not when things go always good for you, but the greatness comes and you are really tested, when you take some knocks, some disappointments, when sadness comes, because only if you have been in the deepest valley can you ever know how magnificent it is to be on the highest mountain."

Richard M. Nixon 1913-1994
Farewell Speech
August 9, 1974

"If opportunity doesn't knock, build a door."

Milton Berle 1908-2002

"Good morning, My beautiful and cherished sons. I have brought you the quotations of two seculars today because their thoughts seem wise; their souls are in Heaven with Me now. There is a similar theme between them – that Salvation must be sought with truth and love in the heart, and one needs to build within himself the structure of holiness that opens the door to redemption. My Special son, I have with you and your brother today fulfilled a tremendous wish of Mary Jane Kerns, that I would continue speaking to you until the end of your lives. It is not for Me to say when this will come, but I shall offer My messages to you and your brother as long as the Lord allows. My dear Mary Jane, your friend and fellow Christian, is in her latter times in the mortal world. She will go to Heaven and be a tremendous intercessor for the cause of My messages to you. I also have the high honor of saying that I am your Mother, that you accept Me as I have adopted you, that you care deeply about the benefits of hope and reconciliation, and that you bear no animosity against those who have been unkind to you. The world and your generation are moving on; they are getting on, but we have much more praying to do for those who will populate this country and inherit the Church to which you have been so dutifully faithful. Please notice that I have not said that we have much more work to do, but more praying. Your work for Jesus as visionaries and messengers has been fulfilled. These are your days of victory and triumph in this sense – everything you are now doing is supplemental to what we set out to achieve in August 1989 and February 1991. I know, My Special son, that you realize how you and your brother have impacted the mission of the Church. I have spent many hours during My messages lifting you up for this, and rightly so, that you would never forget what you mean to the Father. You have helped open and heal the hearts of millions of Americans, and billions of other people around the globe, but you have not yet seen it. This will happen; your lives of prayer and piety here in this Springfield, Illinois home will yield everything providential for which Jesus sent Me. It is an amazing thought, after all. Some people spend their entire lives creating an imaginary world in their minds to push back the tragic real one at the center of their hearts. I refer to this as an 'amalgam illusion' that they have generated because the pain of accepting what reality has wrought is far too difficult to bear. The work that you and I and your brother have accomplished will heal these people in time. We take their thoughts to Jesus on the Cross, to the Sacraments, to the immeasurable love that God has for them, and to the light of joy to which they are being called in faith. The tragic world in their hearts will be eclipsed by the Kingdom of Love that has overcome every sorrow ever laid on a man who has been inclined to believe. This is a prospect that was accomplished the moment that the Archangel Gabriel said that I am blessed. Hence, as I speak to you today, there are mountaintops preparing to receive the climbers ascending them now. This is the great spirit of achievement that lives in Christians like you. I wish the world to never forget what you and your brother have given them; it is etched in the tides of history and deeper than any fathoms of the universe. I also wish to make clear that you and your brother and I have asked the Father for specific gifts. There are curious people around the world who want to know what the Blessed Virgin Mary asks them to pray for. If anyone asks you about this, it would be proper to tell them that My first request was to simply ask them to pray. Seeking the prayers of the faithful and those who have yet to believe is the purpose of My calling. The substance of these prayers, the needs of humanity and the Church, should include the expectations that the world desires in its relationship with God. My Special son, it may surprise you to know that there are men and women on Earth who have never formulated in their thoughts what it means to communicate with God whom they cannot see. If they were able to see Him, they would likely not pray at all because they would believe that He is already aware of everything they need. This is not the way man's relationship with the Father unfolds.

It is as though the life of Jesus on Earth, His ministry, Crucifixion, Resurrection and Ascension were components of a single statement by God. He says that He loves humanity, and He proves it through the Sacred Mysteries of Redemption. Now, exiled men on Earth are asked to respond to these gifts, but their reply to God is, '...what did you say?' After all the miracles, blessings, healings, revelations, absolutions and deliverances, broken humanity in the world has turned to Heaven and said, '...what did you say?' It is the sort of question that someone might ask if they were not listening at all, if they were not paying attention, if they were distracted by something else. This, My Special son, is the reason the Father secures the attention of sinners through suffering – it is loud, clear and unambiguous. Suffering cuts through the distractions of the world, and impacts the core of the human heart and mind. As I have said, this is not suffering for vengeance, but awakenings. God directs the attention of lost sinners to Jesus on the Cross, and allows them to see and feel firsthand what He felt on Good Friday. After that, as you might surmise, these sinners receive the answer to their inquiry of, '...what did you say?' My dear little sons, what God said on Mount Calvary is the same thing He is saying now. It is about coming together as one body of people for the cause of reconciliation. It is about making amends for humanity's wrongs against the sanctity of human life. It is about wealth-holders and fund-merchants recognizing that money is the root of all evil. How many millionaires do you know who receive taxpayer-funded abortions? It was all about the economy and convenience that the governor of Illinois signed a law that allows these abortions to happen. He is an example of a lost sinner who not only asked God what He said through Jesus on the Cross, but has willfully and wantonly ignored the reply he received. And, why? Because the old Eve to whom he is married wanted it that way. All this cries out for justice. I am aware of it, and the Father and Jesus know it as well. Justice in the form of change is not sufficient for these atrocities; the response from God is that there must be amendment and reparation. You and your brother will recognize them when God brings them. So, My Special one, I have completed what I came to tell you this morning. As you know, I do not have a practice of quoting secular voices to preface My messages to you and your brother, but you can see the reason they are applicable to the modern times. Going from the deepest valley to the highest mountain is a metaphor for sinners becoming great Saints.

Making one's heart open to an approaching Messiah is one way to ensure that the knock is forthcoming. I am pleased by any attention the Commission may give in examining My messages that you tendered to your Bishop. I am saying that your works must not lay somewhere collecting dust. I hope that you can sense the progress that you and your brother are making here in the middle of your 28th year of messages from Me. I wish for you to remember that you and your brother lead your lives and accomplish your work before the backdrop of this miracle. These are tremendous times of faith and progress for the Church in America that is so in need of the Morning Star Over America to invigorate its spirit. *"I'm realizing again as I reread 'Supernal Chambers' what a miracle it is."* Yes, it is one of the best fruits of you and your brother's years-long sacrifice of love. You wrote 'Supernal Chambers' with such beauty, eloquence, symbolism and power because you were obedient to the call of the Father to make sacrifices that you might have never made before February 22, 1991. I have said that this book is the sleeping giant among your published works. I will proceed with My prayers that will envelop humanity in My grace, that will urge good men to speak out in the face of unrighteousness, and that will aid the poor and end the scourge of abortion. Thank you for praying as I have prayed with you, and please remember that it is '...only a beginning, always.' Every moment of every day, all the hours and minutes comprise the miracle of your relationship with Jesus and Me. The toll of the Earth is growing against those who do not accept our love. My dear sons, the longer you live, the more you recognize the gifts of your lives to the Church. You will be heartened to know that everything you have done for Me has been to the enhancement of its mission. I love you."

Saturday, March 24, 2018
9:46 a.m.

"Not just more blood, but New Blood."

"My dear little sons, your heroic lives are augmented by the courage that you receive in the presence of the Holy Spirit. Your designs and actions are facilitated by your faith in Jesus. Your endearing prayers are a manifestation of your loyalty to God. I have come to pray with you today for all who have fallen victim to the enemies of the Church, to the unbelievers whose lives will have no effect on the outcome of the world. As long as humanity has lived on Earth, there has been blood-soaked soil. Fighting, in-fighting, wars and insurrections have saturated the ground with the blood of the fallen. Not until

Jesus came into their midst did the Blood of One Man have the power to stop these wars. It takes a different perspective to understand these things. My Special and Chosen sons, I showed you this kind of different perspective on this date in 1991. It was from My vantage point in Heaven. It was a way to look down upon the Earth through My eyes, in the wisdom of the love that I have for you. We speak about what supports the Church, what is the foundation upon which your faith is stationed? The love of Jesus for you is that ballast. If your lives were considered a length of rail tracks, His Holy Sacrifice is its bed beneath your feet. Yes, Jesus is this ballast, this cornerstone, this intersection of the walls of Truth and Justice. I have come to you for many years not to regale what we accomplished in the beginning, but where you are going, where you have come since then, and what you must know about the fruits of your faith. My testament today is that your faith has given you access to the miracles from God, but also access to the wisdom of the Crucifixion to all others who are enriched by My messages. I ask that you have peace in your hearts. It is this peace that fosters your patience, that gives you a sense of accomplishment in what we have done, and allows you to secure in your consciousness the ability to understand. My Special son, I know everything that the Father allows Me to know. Even though I have seen the end of the ages, I am unaware of when Jesus will return. It is this way because God knew that I would be coming to My children on Earth through the centuries to ask for your prayers. And, without doubt, My visionaries would ask when Jesus will come in Glory. The Father realized that I could not tell My seers that it was not for them to know. After all, preparing for the Second Coming is the purpose of human life. And, I could not tell My visionaries that I did not know, if in the case I had this knowledge, because it would be a divergence from the truth. So, the fact that I do not have the knowledge of this tremendous event makes sense. Do you understand? *"Yes."* It makes sense because I am given to have hope in the same way of the world. We spoke last week about new beginnings. We looked out into the great expanse of human affairs, and willed that we would never give up on the souls who are still straying. It is not just about the time required to foster the conversion of the lost because time can be seen as relative. You and your brother recently proofread a message from 2013 in which your brother mentioned that he could not remember the word he spelled correctly to win the county spelling bee, but he remembered the one he spelled incorrectly to remove him from the next contest. This is an interesting point to make, but an even more interesting point is that the county contest took place a half-century ago. It is stunning to think about in these terms, but this is what it means to look with transference on the passing of time and the eminent goals that must be accomplished in the

Christian's heart. I have said many times that the movement of the sun is only a molecular measure that cannot change the heart of a man. What changes the heart of a man is the revelation that life is a destiny. You and your brother, and all who belong to the Church, have received this revelation through My Son on the Cross. You have known all your days that men have fought and died for freedom, for what they believe in, to preserve life and posterity, and to prosper the future for those they love. These battles have been ongoing since the dawn of humanity on the Earth. Millions upon millions of fighters have died for such causes. But, there is a difference in dying an 'institutional' death and a death that seems arbitrary. All the Martyrs of the Church died institutional deaths. Casualties of war die institutional deaths. People who are shot by home invaders die arbitrary deaths. The difference is in the reason, the motivation behind their dying. The reason that I have raised this point is because only Jesus died both an institutional and arbitrary death. What do you suppose was the institution for which Jesus was handed over to death? *"For the redemption of humanity."* Yes, it was the institution of the condemned state of collective human souls. And, why was Jesus' death considered an arbitrary one? Because He was crucified between two thieves who were themselves victims of the world's unmitigated sins. In other words, Jesus' executioners did not perceive Him to be the Incarnation of God.

My Special son, there are several reasons in this context why Jesus shed His New Blood instead of just more blood. It was more than the fact that He was not a sinner, but that His Blood is the only Blood with Redeeming Grace. When men speak of more bloodshed in prosecuting wars, they are speaking in a single dimension. When Jesus died for the sins of humanity, His Blood took Creation to more dimensions than anyone could see. It is the same principle as God making a sphere out of a straight line. *"I understand."* It is to this point that the New Adam shed New Blood. And, not only that, the freedom that earthly warriors yield by bleeding on the battlefield is concentrated in the same world. The New Blood of Jesus has transformed the existence of men into the realms of the Father in Heaven. It is tied together with the example of the miracle that we shared on this date in 1991. The way you and your brother perceive human life has also made this transition – you are creatures of the Earth at the same time that your hearts and identities are in the presence of God in Heaven. When some people say that they would like to go to Heaven someday, what they should be saying is that they would like to become one with the Kingdom in their hearts. You can feel the presence of Jesus there through the Holy Spirit. You feel warmth in your heart and the presence of light because of what you believe. After that, it all comes down to manifesting benevolent fruit that grows from the dynamics of your faith. In the case of you and your brother, for example, you have issued a series of works that will always stand for the 'preexistence' of the Church. And, in this vein, I wish to add another dimension to My discussion about time. It is something your brother said yesterday that is absolutely true. Here in 2018, and in all the years since 1991, I have said that you and your brother have given humanity a handhold to the Cross. I have always told you that millions of souls have believed. I have promised you that everyone who enters Heaven does so upon hearing and knowing everything I have said as the Morning Star Over America. The point that your brother made, and that I am reinforcing now, is that all these things are true in the same way that Jesus says that sinners who accept the Cross will never die. I am not saying that humanity will not presently take your books in hand before Jesus returns in Glory, I am saying that many of the praises, speeches and sentiments to be spoken on the last day are being given to you now. So, it is both; you are receiving the best of this life and the afterlife, the best of both worlds – the old and the New. Before I close this morning, I would like to gain a sense of what you foresee being the content of your next book. You have said to your brother that it could be prepared for release in 2019, but I would like to know what you perceive to be your preface compared to the book you published in October 2017. *"I was going to have a preface of answered questions."* Yes, excellent. The only reason I raised this point today is to tell you that I am profoundly pleased by that choice. You will feel the Holy Spirit harvesting the sentiments of your heart, outlining and explaining your feelings about the subjects of those questions. My Special son, I would like to make the request of you today that you never believe that your work with your brother has been in vain. *"I don't believe that, even if it never flourishes in this world."* Thank you. The content of My 2013 messages should prove that they will. I am pleased by your progress on your next manuscript. It is clear that you are struggling with some difficult personalities in the secular world. It is all about the cynicism that exists in America today, the latitude of other people to say that they despise you, the doubts they have about the legitimacy of your claims, and the fact that they believe they will never have to defend the errors they are making. *"Mama, I want peace, goodness and cooperation to have a chance to be the order of our days. People such as these need to be moved aside."* It is all in the force of the Father's justice that this shall be done. I ask that you believe that nothing unjust, unfair or irreverent will ever be allowed to stand without this dismantling taking place. It will be a bright, moving and illustrative Holy Week that the Church will celebrate this year. The thanksgiving that My children will offer Jesus on the Cross will be worthy of their faith."

Holy Saturday, March 31, 2018
9:29 a.m.

"The True and Glorious Presence."

"My dear sons, the reign of the Father is upon you here; it has been with you since the inception of your days. And, all the glory that can fill a heart with providence is upon you as well. I am your Mother. I am the Blessed Virgin Mary, Mother of Jesus, Mother of God, Mother of the Holy Spirit, Mother of My children in Heaven and on Earth. You have given yourselves to Me because your faith demands it. I have given Myself to you because the Kingdom of God demands it. My Special sons, we are commended to one another through the extraordinary grace that lives in the Father, the same grace by which you have been saved. This grace has a beatific component and an earthly component. Grace itself is from Heaven; this is the first one. The second one is the grace of men to be obedient to the call of righteousness. In this call, and in this response, is found the Will of God. I have spoken about the True and Glorious Presence of Jesus in Heaven, seated at the Right Hand of the Father. I have spoken about Jesus the Holy Spirit in your hearts, and I have spoken about Jesus in the Most Blessed Sacrament. It is clear that His Truth, His Glorious Presence, is also living in all that you do for the Church. Hence, your hearts are the tabernacles of the Holy Spirit here in this life. When the Church observes the Paschal Triduum, especially the grand Feast of Easter, humanity is saying that the Earth is preparing for its own transition. This creates the distinction between the Faith Church and the world in exile – they are not the same thing. The Faith Church is situated in a world that has no grace of its own. The Catholic Church is the seed of righteousness planted by Jesus during His birth, life, ministry, Passion, Crucifixion, Resurrection, Ascension and Pentecostal Descent. These are the Fruits of the Messianic Age that have been shared by Christians throughout the ages. And now, all times are imbedded in this Eternal Messianic Age. When you observe the Paschal Triduum, you also celebrate it. You witness to the True and Glorious Presence of Jesus in all the forms that I just mentioned, but you also celebrate the response of humanity to this grace. God is saying that He wishes to call on lost sinners in the hope that they will answer. Jesus knocks on the door with the expectation that He will be allowed to come in. The Holy Spirit travels through the nations looking for open hearts to welcome Him. My Special son, when looked at in its essential form, this is what spiritual faith is all about. Everything else that builds upon this sacred principle is a fruit of this essence

– the teachings of the Gospel, the mission of the Church, the Church's eloquence, pageantry, piety and stateliness are all the offspring of the willingness of holy men and women to believe. My dear sons, I am speaking about an expectation and an entrance. People pray to receive blessings that will purify their lives and enhance their well-being. This is the expectation of the response through the same grace that redeems penitent souls. The entry is not only God's response, but the ability of enlightened Christians to realize that this response has been given. This is what the Sacraments are about as well. Does it require faith to believe that the Holy Eucharist is Jesus' Body, Blood, Soul and Divinity? Of course it does. This is the continuation of humanity's response. However, not having faith in Jesus' True and Glorious Sacramental Presence does not mean that He is not there. The pronunciation of the Eucharistic Prayers is the Church's invitation for Jesus to enter under the rooftops of all who believe. In this sense, Jesus does not have to knock on the door of human hearts. He is called there and received. The door is opened by the Eucharistic Prayer before Jesus knocks. My Special son, this is the distinction that keeps so many people outside the Catholic Church from believing in the Most Blessed Sacrament. After all, it is called 'Most' for a reason. The greatest faith required by a Christian is called upon in the belief of Jesus on the Altar and in the Tabernacle. Thus, when someone looks at the tabernacles of the Church, they are looking at replicas of the spiritual hearts of those who accept and practice their faith. So yes, this is Holy Saturday. It is a time of preparation for humanity to welcome the Resurrected Son of Man. Does this not make every day of the world Holy Saturday? It is not only a time of prayer, but a time of self-examination and reflection about what someone will say when he sees the Son of Man raised from the Tomb and Returned in Glory. I have told you and your brother that you are prepared to greet Jesus when He comes again. Your baptismal gowns are unstained. Your souls are illustrative of this commendation. Your hearts are filled with everything that Jesus asks you to deposit in them – holiness, goodness, purity, compassion for the poor, dedication to the preservation of human life, a conscience toward forgiving those who have trespassed against you, and so on. So, it is not about you that I speak about in My messages when calling for the restoration of these virtues.

My Special son, the point I am making is that humanity must make a transition during the hours of Holy Saturday that demonstrates the conversion experience about which the Church has spoken since the Miracle of Pentecost. It is not possible for someone to be converted without the presence of the Holy Spirit in their heart. The Holy Spirit preserves the spiritual heart in the same way that the physical heart preserves the body. The Holy Spirit does the same thing on this level, as well as assists the Christian to be transcended in his own self-identity by his new identity in Jesus. We pray that this happens to everyone who is not converted during all the days of the Earth, and more profoundly during the Easter Triduum. This is the reason the Church celebrates the seasons of the liturgical year, that new beginnings and awakenings will occur as a result of these observations. I am telling you that your prayers with your brother in communion with the whole Church foster this process. Through Jesus, who is the Head of the Church, humanity is being asked to accomplish on Earth everything that the Lord desires. It is not unlike a baton relay. It is true that generations hand the future of the Church to their descendants, but this does not mean that these first generations fade away. They become sainted for their service, for their faith and generosity. And, their greatest gift is that God continues to bestow power in their prayers. To become a Saint is to fulfill the purpose of human life. This is the sacred rite about which I have spoken since I responded 'yes' to the Archangel Gabriel. My Special son, I know that you will allow Me to speak about Myself, knowing that My words are not from self-aggrandizing pride. "*Yes.*" The first Saint was not the good thief whom Jesus took to Heaven with Him on the day He died – it was Me. "*Yes, I know that.*" And, the moment I was canonized was when the Father brought to mind that He would like to have a Mother. It was not when I was conceived in My mother's womb or when I was born. It was not when the Archangel Gabriel came to Me or when I was assumed into Heaven. It was not when the 'Crown of Queen' was placed on My head by the Father in Heaven. It was in the thought of the existence of man in the mind of God – from the moment that He chose to create spiritual souls with metaphysical identities. Yes, this means that I was created higher than the Angels, not a little lower than them. So, I am saying that My Most Immaculate Heart is of the Father's preeminent Will. I am not God, and I have never equated Myself with His Providence, but I am 'of God' to the extent that any primordial thing could be. This is not Church dogma or doctrine. It defies what every theologian, but the most sanctified, will say. I never died because I was not subject to the wage of sin. This, My Special son, is what all those dignified thinkers inside and outside the Church have never known. It is beyond them; they have not thought in such supernal terms. They cannot imagine a Mother so perfect that She could be in the grace of God by personifying grace itself. And, My Special son, to make My point complete – this is how I knew that Jesus, My Son, would walk out of the Tomb 2,000 years ago, just as He said. It was for Me to wait and see the faces of those who believed, once their faith was fulfilled. It was not enough for them to see the little girl brought back from death, or Lazarus given another opportunity to live. Why this is true remains a mystery. But, to await the Resurrection of the Man who performed these miracles was difficult for them. Not for Me. Yes, I prayed along with the others as a means of supporting their anticipation. I augmented their lives of faith. I prayed not just that they would believe, but what they would do with this new revelation once Jesus walked again in their midst. What would they do with this miracle? How would the world be changed? What did it mean that the temple was rebuilt in three days? I prayed that they would realize that it would never be razed again. The Savior of the world would live forever on, His Kingdom would not be destroyed, the future of converted souls would be encapsulated in their own miraculous resurrection. My Special son, the prayers that you are saying now are in union with Mine that day. Your heart is resounding the same hopes; your thoughts are in alignment with the Father's when He first created the world. And, this places you and your brother in the lineage of Jesus and Me; given life, holiness and love at the same moment that God thought of Me in His Presence. Now, I have completed My message for today. I pray that you have liked it. Thank you for your lovely prayers, for receiving Me here, and especially for taking such good care of your brother. I know that you see the great challenges facing the Church with the tremendous prayers that you have been lifting through the years. The Father cares what you believe about the Church, and I join you and your brother in asking Him to guide and protect it."

Saturday, April 7, 2018
9:30 a.m.

"Origins and intentions."

"My dear little sons, the interaction of humanity in the world comes to two questions. 'Where are you from? What do you want?' This is it. The matter of who somebody is seems secondary and even tertiary to these issues. The question of origins means that there has been a beginning to someone, to their thoughts, persuasions, desires and motivations. Your origins are based in your rural American culture and your Christian faith. The origins of other peoples and nations are oftentimes wholly different. What you want, on the other hand, is not necessarily separate from your origins because you utilize your origins to plot the future and accomplish your goals. The origins of the Messiah are quite clearly the Deity of God, and His intentions are profoundly spelled out by what you know of Him. One point that I am trying to make clear is that your identity in Jesus is Jesus, Himself. What remains to be articulated is that you have found your origins in Him. This is part of the transition of someone being a nonbeliever to becoming a devout Christian. So, identity springs from one's origins, and those origins beget one's intentions. My Special son, I have mentioned these things because this is the way theologians have examined the phenomenon of private religious revelations, and this is the stage that your works are in with the Bishop's pastoral commission. They are determining your origins without contacting you because they have already discovered them through My appearances here. In other words, there is no question that your origins are of God because of My prolific presence in your home. The commission is heading toward the inevitable conclusion that your intentions are those of God because of the many years, even decades, that you have given to My cause. There is no such thing as someone giving his life to, or for, something in which that person does not believe to be the primal essence of his soul. You and your brother have seen in the past twenty-four hours what the secular domain thinks about your work for Me. Your brother was rejected from the English Department at the university, and your Morning Star trademark request was denied. It should seem neither a surprise nor coincidence that this has happened. I assure you that they are badges of honor that you should wear with glory. And, whether either of you wishes to appeal these rejections is fully yours to decide. My Special son, you likely would not have realized or internalized how the Gospel is fulfilled in your day if these things had not happened to you. There is a history-filling record of everything you have learned about the error, indifference and apostasy of the secular void for you to ponder, but I wish that you not dwell on these things. I am only asking that you see them as signs that you are in complete alignment with the Will of God and the prophecies of the Sacred Scriptures. It is also interesting to realize that some people defer to the origins of their birth to determine their intentions. These things tend to hinge on heritage, pride, social rigidity and the calculated collusion that drives the social collectives of mobs and hordes. You would not be surprised to know how many people see a parade, and then fall-in behind it not knowing what it stands for or where it is going. This is how such laws are approved that allow the scourge of abortion and assisted suicide. Most people believe that if the majority accepts these things as worthy of practice, then who are they to argue? This is the origin of the Pope's statement about same-sex couples. He asks who he is to judge, as though he has no power to speak for the Church in this crucial matter of moral truth. So, the people who make decisions based on the origins of their birth have to make a transition if those origins are against the teachings of the Church. This is what conversion means. It is often difficult because of the reasons I shared a few moments ago. But, their intentions cannot be changed until their perception of their origins is changed. The repentance of sinners is based on this premise. All we have done since 1989 has been based on this premise. You may know that I have not identified individual people separately in My call for the conversion of humanity, with the exception of those you have mentioned during our messages. As I have said, the reason for this is because the concept of identity is not as important as one's intentions. Let us now take a moment to exemplify what I have discussed. If you were to speak before an audience who knows nothing about you, what would you say to introduce yourself? You do not need to record your comments because you will never forget them. Yes, you have just now mentioned your origins. Now, what about your intentions? Yes, you would relate that you have been placed on a mission to help them understand how special they are. However, can you see how the people to whom you would be speaking might believe that you are trying to regulate their perceptions of life through the sharing of your own identity? *"Yes. They want to believe what they want to believe."* Indeed, this is the experience of Jesus trying to convince the world who He is, and what He desires – His origins and intentions.

So, I gather that you would be speaking to this audience from a position of humility and confidence. *"Yes. That is what I would try to do."* Does this sound familiar? *"Yes."* And, you are aware of the exiled world's reaction to Jesus, in the Flesh, making the case for God's Kingdom in places filled with people who do not wish to be regulated. These circumstances are the reason that people like you and your brother are rejected. As your brother said this morning, '...the Gospel is fulfilled.' He is also prone to say that you do not win every game you play. No hero has ever emerged victorious without taking his share of falls. It is a human and divine thing – I know a Man who fell multiple times while carrying a Cross to the top of a Mount. To encapsulate what I have said this morning, your origins and intentions are your two figurative legs on which your embodiment of life stands. You are able to walk on them; your mission is mobilized by where you have come from and where you are going. And, it is this sacred internal passage that creates your daily consciousness, your moment-to-moment awareness of how you have chosen to live. Yes, it is to this same framework that the redemption of humanity speaks – the origin of man is the Holy Father in Heaven. The intention of the Father is to return His people in their redeemed state into His presence. The entire discussion is no more complicated than this, but hardly anyone in the world bothers to learn it. I was once described by a young Far East visionary as being 'simple.' I have been described as the 'simple Maiden' on many occasions. I feel that these descriptions are endearing and appropriate, but I have asked you to describe Me, as well, as someone who could have sent men to the Moon with no afterthought. It is not that I am two separate people, or that I have more than one personality. I am empowered by the Holy Spirit in the same way as you and your brother. And, I wish for both of you to accept that you have once existed in a sinful state, but that your origin in Jesus on the Cross has raised you from the condition of sin. You have allowed the Holy Spirit to regulate who you are, and what you desire to achieve. God knows this to be true. You have come to pray with Me for decades now, and you have listened to My voice and wishes without complaint. Even the great Saint Padre Pio did not suspend his wishes this much. So, I have come to speak to you without eloquence this morning to reassure you that your lives are in complete alignment with the life of Jesus in His earthly days, and also in His days on Earth in the Blessed Sacrament and through the Holy Spirit. You are in pious company – all the Saints who fought and became disappointed eventually recognized their life's events as being times that both inspired and exhilarated Jesus, Himself. Your brother is not prone to challenge or protest his rejection from the English Department, but he has not yet decided. He is likely to say that he has no problem not being permitted to study there, but he does not understand the crass, cold hatred that they plied against him since April 2017. You and your brother need not depend on that program for your brother to write his memoir. He has not yet begun this work because he has concentrated on proofreading your latest anthologies. What you and your brother are doing is not easy. The construction of your works is a long and arduous process. They are filled with beauty and wisdom, there is no question about that. And, I have artfully described what I would like from humanity. But, the mechanics of it all is painstaking and exhausting. I believe that you have been stellar and saintly in the composition of your works."

Saturday, April 14, 2018
9:28 a.m.

"Imagine capturing a bagful of daylight,
and setting it free into the midnight skies."

"This morning, My dear precious sons, we pray for all the victims of war and the destruction that results from humans battling one another for territories and jurisdictions. It is clear that this has been ongoing since the first two swords of earthly warfare clashed against each other. I have given you a thought to ponder at the opening of My message today because it was once said to Me by the Dominion Angel, Blessandarie. I also ask you to pray for the Roman Catholic priests who are fighting against the squalls of ridicule that are heaped against them for their faith, that they will remain strong through the Holy Spirit, and steadfast to the promises of their vocations. My Special son, you might inquire why your brother is again battling such evil visions that have transformed into physical torment. You have spoken it correctly – it is all about your progress on your next book. It is not that Jesus does not love him that these things happen. It is not because the Father does not want you to live in peace. It is because the devil is lurking, striking, clawing and scratching against the death that he faced by Jesus on the Cross. It is because holiness lives in this home in the persons of you and your brother. It is because My messages here have such power to change the condition of the world. Yes, it is because you are so connected to the mission of the Church in your companionship with Jesus. Thank you for being so compassionate with your brother. He does not wish to become a burden on you. When thinking about My 2013 messages that you are about to publish, you might understand why the devil is gasping in such fear. You and your brother have given to Me what no other mortals have given – the right to claim that you have changed the world in ways that invoke My Marian miracles. I have never said that I have undue influence on the redemption of sinners, but I have facilitated the conversion of the lost because visionaries like you and your brother have helped Me. So, your brother is tired and beaten down, but he has not been broken. You have likewise faced conditions of torment in your engagement with the secular void. All of these things are the designs of the devil in attempt to coerce you to abandon your work for Me, for Jesus, for the Father and the Holy Spirit, and for the Church Triumphant in Heaven. Imagine all those people who find themselves in powerful places that are making unholy decisions about life and government, and who seem to always be walking in sunshine. It seems as though the world is truly upside down. It will soon be inverted in favor of the righteous, as you have been told. Today, I also wish to commend you on your continued writing for your next book. It is clear that you can sense the presence of God's Spirit in your thoughts and passages. I ask that you and your brother remember that this unity cannot be broken, no matter what the future brings. It is that you have such holy and visionary impressions of what the Father desires of His Creation. You have the capacity for manifesting miracles through your writing, and you have recently had the ability to make a Roman

Catholic Bishop weep happily in the solace of his own room by your message to him. These are the things that no one ever sees. It is all about committing to the heart what plays out in the company of the Church and its parishioners. I beg you to believe that Jesus is present within your heart, and living vibrantly through your life, because the fruits are sweet to God. Yes, it is said that the Father comes calling with consolation to humanity, and it is those who believe without seeing Him that give Him such comfort in return. Out of My compassion, I recognize your sufferings as they occur even now. (*Our Holy Mother recognized the litany of torments that we endure that satisfy Her revelation that mystical gifts only come through the diminishment of the flesh.*) But, you are still here. You still welcome Me. You bear out your consecration to Me because you have learned to live in faith. It is not unusual for My messengers to undergo what you and your brother have suffered. Yes, I am holding the devil back from doing anything worse right now, but imagine what Jesus is thinking while seeing you carrying on. He weeps like the Bishop whom I mentioned because someone such as you and your brother have the courage to suffer in His likeness for the conversion of the lost. It is all about remembering the Passion of Jesus, and His Suffering on the Cross. All throughout the ages, this has been true. You and your brother have had the right response – carry on and glorify the Son of Man by your lives.

My Special son, there may even come a time when you and your brother will need to seek medical care as a response to the devil's attacks, but this will not inhibit your progress. The whole world may be in a secular panic these days, but you and your brother are stationed on the strength and wisdom of the Father through your faith and imitation of Jesus' life and glory. I look at you and your brother with the same love that I saw Jesus on Good Friday. It is a certainty that you are one with Him through everything you do. So today, I wish for you to remember all the little children who have been so injured by the poison gases being used on them by the despots in Syria. I ask for your prayers in defeating the devil in this conflagration. And, our prayers together are bringing opportunities all across the country for new conversions to take place, for the preservation of unborn human life by expectant mothers who are changing their hearts, and for the eradication of pestilence and disease in poverty-stricken nations in lands far from America. I realize that there are mountainous problems here in the United States that need to be overcome as well. It is true that capitalism does not guarantee everyone the right to eat. There is disparity in the marketplace, and corruption in the government. These are the issues that plague so many people who only ask for a place to lay their heads, and a meal to eat during the day. People are sleeping in parks and on street corners, in vans and automobiles, and in empty crevices in cities where no one ever goes. All these things are mitigated by the suffering of Jesus on the Cross, and Christians like you and your brother who ask Him to bless their lives. My Special son, I do not wish for you to believe that My message this morning is all about what is wrong with the world and your country instead of what good is happening around the globe. The Church is safeguarding its mission. We have seen the benevolent acts of pious men taking care of the less fortunate. We have seen feeding, clothing, housing and nurturing in massive measures, even as we speak today. This is what I ask you and your brother to dwell upon. God is good. He gives to those in need in His time. He unites His people with the suffering of His Son, and He will unite them in His Resurrection. It has only been two weeks since you celebrated the Feast of Easter, and this is the focus that I ask you and your brother to take into the summer. I beseech you to remember that you will hear every word I came to say from February 22, 1991 as long as the Father allows. I tell you that you must do everything in your power to travel safely, and return on time next week. I will be with you, but I ask that you make sure that whomever is driving your vehicle does so with extreme care. And, please do not wander off alone while you are away from home next week. Thank you for your warm embrace of love. I am with you and your brother with Jesus in My arms more than you know. Thank you for remembering in your prayers the Pope in Rome, that he will guide the Church with the distinction of his predecessors. I join you in these petitions."

Saturday, April 21, 2018
9:28 a.m.

"Let there be no mistake."

"So much are you loved, My dear little sons. So much cherished and admired, so many times-over blessed. Here in your company, I bring the Sacred Christ who delves into your lives and encourages your hearts. You have remained with Him during your entire days, and with Him in the fullness of eternity you shall remain. I have come speaking to you this morning in the aftermath of a week that had a few bumps in the road – nothing that rocked you, nothing that brought you down, and nary a thing that knocked you off course. I have told My children throughout the ages that you will know when you are perfectly united with the Cross; and here, you have realized it. My dear little sons, Jesus is with you, as I have said. And let there be no mistake, you will succeed in the work that He has given you to do. My Special son, I ask that you always remember the immense help that you have given your brother through the years, especially during the events of last week, because you are representative of the compassion of Jesus. Your prayers and petitions are remarkable of this truth. Your brother stands with you in everything you have always done and believed because he is aware of what he means to you. It is not something that he does not know. He will proceed with his work next week on proofreading My 2013 messages, and the progress that you are both making will not be impeded – make no mistake about it. So today, I come with My love and sentiments to ask you and your brother to send your holy prayers into the world where many people are enduring desperate lives and unimaginable torment. The starving and abandoned conditions in war-torn countries are too grotesque to ignore. The killing of innocents and the neglect of the elderly are two symptoms of unaddressed evil that is rampant around the globe. My Special son, I send the love of My Most Immaculate Heart to them; and most primarily, I ask Jesus to end their suffering. I call on Him to invoke the power of the Father against all that assaults and assails His Faith Church on Earth. It is not enough, it would seem, to say that the good people shall win at the last. This is little consolation for what they are enduring now. The invocation of Jesus' Crucifixion and the prayers of the Church have the power to alleviate these ills and wrongdoings. My point has always been that humanity is reluctant to do so, and this is the reason I have come to you with such fervor. We are constructing the new 'now' that will foster the changes that must come. I am not just speaking about our work together over the past three decades, or what you and your brother's lives have been about, but that the whole Church is establishing this new 'now' to preclude and supersede the catastrophes of time. My Special son, I realize that this may seem difficult to believe as you experience life, but the essence of what I am saying is clear to you by virtue of your monumental faith.

I have often spoken about the intersection of innocence and eminence. I have also said that, without sounding confusing, that eminence in humanity's life is imminent. The intersection of innocence and eminence is based on the assumption of power – the power of God, the power of change in those who believe in Him, and the power of possibility in knowing what God can do. This gives rise to the notion that God is about action and culmination, that the prayers you offer Him will lead to definitive outcomes. While it is always a blessing to pray, you might imagine that the prayers of the innocent reach His Throne with the swiftness of lightning. I have said these things because I wish to make a larger point. In Jesus, the Father allowed an Innocent Man to suffer for the sins of the guilty. This means that there is manifest Providence in uniting the guilty with Him through the suffering of the innocent. This is true for the conversion of the wicked, as much as it is true for the redemption of the world. So, Jesus is not only the Greatest Innocent, He is also the Only Innocent. Every other person on Earth is a sinner who becomes innocent in Him. They remain innocent in Him by virtue of His light, pardon, peace and grace. And, as this innocence remains, those who possess it become the targets of evil. Hence, Jesus lives in them, and they suffer in Him. Is this clear to you? "*Yes.*" So now, imagine a scenario where an innocent soul is approached by another innocent soul to procure a favor that will bring about much suffering. This would be exemplified by the Annunciation of the Archangel Gabriel. Here, an innocent being approached another Innocent being because the guilty needed to be redeemed. I have said that there is one mission that supersedes all others in Creation, summed by the premise that you recently heard, '...nothing else matters.' The Archangel Gabriel, therefore, came to speak the Good News of the Resurrection. This is the effect of the Annunciation. He might have said, '...Hail, full of grace, the Lord is with you. You shall conceive and bear a Son who will rise from the Tomb.' This is the thesis of what Gabriel said – his was an Easter prophecy before there was ever a Conception. My Special son, I am implying a sequence because this is what the hope of Christians is founded upon. It is simple for you to understand because this is what you have always believed.

The crux of this process, therefore, is based on the willingness of those with faith to accept what they have been asked to accomplish. It is a fruitful acceptance based on a promise that a joyful outcome will arrive. After all, this is the foundation of a trusting faith. I had faith to trust and accept not just because I am sinless, but because everything that God does is in accordance with His Will of Truth. It does not require an angel in the night for someone to oath their allegiance to the wishes of God. As I have said, look at the condition of the world. If for no other reason than to respond to what you see, this is enough motivation to assist your decision to call on the mission of the Church to succeed. This is the prayer of all good men. I am saying that the innocent and eminent converge in righteous sacrifice that pleases the Father in the same way as the Crucifixion of His Son. Here is the measure of what I have said this morning – every time someone suffers for the good of the Church in the name of the Cross, they should remember the 'Easter' Annunciation of the Archangel Gabriel. They should realize that suffering is not an end in itself, but the most powerful component of human conversion for populating the Church Triumphant in Heaven. This is the most stately, elegant and worthy elevation of humanity that could possibly be undertaken. When Jesus says the words, '...be like Me,' He is saying that He desires to share the Glory of the Cross with His Mystical Body. This is done through man's participation because Jesus and His Mystical Body cannot be divided. Now that I have said these things, Christians might ask, '...where is the joy in this?' My Special son, how would you respond to them? *"It's in the joy of knowing that Jesus loves you so for loving Him enough to suffer with Him."* Yes, and this is the sacred unity that makes humanity 'divine' through Him as well. You might suspect, My little son, that someone may approach you and say that they would rather have no part in this kind of love. *"Yes."* Would you describe this as part of the paradox of Christianity? *"Yes, because you have to believe the joy in faith."* Why has this been such a faithful practice of you and your brother, even more than other Saints? *"Because we do it together in our love for each other."* Exactly and precisely correct. What you just said is the message of the Christian Gospel. Please never forget that this is what Jesus has been saying from the beginning. It is the basis for His calling forth the fishers of men. It was imbedded in His parables and teachings. It is the call of the Holy Spirit from the olden days to the moment we are spending together right now. Well said, and well done. This is the joy and torment, the agony and ecstasy, of upholding your faith against a devil who is determined to destroy the Church. He will never prevail against the Kingdom that Jesus offers – make no mistake about it. I have heard your prayers for the Church, for the suffering, for the end of abortion, and for the justice that the world seeks to restore decency and purity everywhere. You and your brother have blessed lives because you have blessed the Lord in return. Thank you for your stately faith, for your compassion for the poor, and for your wisdom that you are sharing so prolifically through your writings and anthologies. Please remember that your brother loves you in greater dimensions than any human being has the capacity to understand."

Sunday, April 29, 2018
4:06 p.m.

"The eternal resolve of human love."

"My lovely little sons, I make My presence known to you today as a means of reassuring you that Jesus is veritably aware of your goodness. Every time you undergo suffering, in whatever form it may take, you must remember that it is because of your union with Jesus on the Cross, and the apostleship that you have inherited from the Father. It is not that He does not wish you to have peaceful lives that you fight against the devil, but because you have the ability to deal defeat to evil by your prayers and through your faith. You have within you the resolve of human love that brings dignity to those being tormented and persecuted for their faith. My Special son, I have told you on multiple occasions that suffering yields your unity in glory; it is your means of capitalizing on your discipleship that you have promised the Father in return. My little sons, you have become the 'knowing' among other men. You are capable of extrapolating what God would have you do in instances that have yet to unfold. In Jesus, you have been given a divine template with which you guide humanity and the exiled world through the vast undertakings of mortal life. Your lives have been provided; your future has been assured, and the power of your prayers lays the foundation upon which everyone else is living. When you speak to Jesus with the atonement that He seeks from lost sinners, He knows that you have not only been found, but that you are signaling to the nations the paths they must travel to reach their destiny in Him. It would appear, My little sons, that you have come under specific attack during the past few months that seems much more severe than before. This is because My messages are growing nearer their proficient announcement by the Church and across the nations. It has nothing to do with whether you feel deserving of these attacks – it is a badge of angelic valor that you have been subjected to these tests. I ask that you remember your strength in Jesus, and bring your troubles to Me so that I can support you in the love of My Motherly care. My Special son, since you and your brother are so tired, I have come briefly to bless you, and assure you of the confidence that you hold in Jesus raised from the Tomb. When it seems its darkest in the world, this is where the light of Easter shines most brightly from within. These are unprecedented times that require you to have extraordinary patience. There is nothing that will ever come upon you that you cannot sustain.

Also today, I offer you My additional prayers for your intentions, that everything you ask of the Father will come to pass. It is all about the resolve of your love for humanity, for fairness and justice, for the light of peace to come to warring lands, and for health and prosperity to follow the people of the Cross. I am asking that you and your brother look outwardly at the world when you pray, as you always do, and to specifically remember the injustices that are being heaped upon those who are closest to the Church. It is a profoundly difficult time to be a Roman Catholic priest not only in America, but in other nations where they are routinely subjected to persecution and martyrdom. These are the shepherds whom Jesus has chosen to administer the

Sacraments in places where the Holy Spirit is rarely welcome. We are invoking the presence of His Spirit to permeate the places where love is rejected, and to enter the hearts of those who refuse to pray. The light shines most brightly where humanity opens to the intercession of their God. Healing and manifest righteousness appear when wicked men convert. These are among the petitions that I have sought in locations like Fatima and Medjugorje, that all the world will know that humanity does not suffer alone. The Earth does not turn by its own axis, but by the Will of the Father. There are worldly empires that cannot stand alongside the Kingdom of God, and they will be put down and destroyed by the end of time. This is a painful prospect for those who control them, for the leaders who harbor the wealth, and for the armies that are sent out to defend injustice and hatred. If you ever wonder why there is yet wrath left in God, it is because He has prepared it for those who persecute His Church. This is part of the justice of His love, and it magnifies the faith of those who are closest to Him." (*Our Holy Mother continued speaking to us privately.*)

Saturday, May 5, 2018
9:29 a.m.

The overarching power of love –
Defining purpose.
Soothing pain.
Clarifying vision.
Creating peace.

"*The Earth was quiet before humanity corrupted it.*"

"My holy and precious little sons, the divinity that comprises the perfection of Creation surrounds you with love and protection. It is your faith that has brought you to believe this, but it is more in the power of the Holy Spirit that has sent wisdom to your lives. I have come again today to pray with you and bless you, to share the remarkable glory of the Father with you, to listen to your concerns, to console your pain, to bring lovely sentiments into your day, and to seek from you the prayers that you have so loftily offered Jesus for so many years. My Special son, the theme of My messages has always been about the power of love, the ability of love to retake the Earth from the jaws of hatred. I have said that God's love is overarching and omnipotent, that His presence is comprehensive of the spiritual and material realms, and that His purpose is to transform humanity from a collective body of sinners into Jesus'

Mystical Body whose place is in Heaven. You see various elements at the opening of today's message that describe this healing and comfort. It is the Will of God that you would assist Him in the undertakings that He has manifested through My messengers and seers. It is true that the Holy Spirit comes to humanity to share the Will of the Father about which I speak, but the substance of that Will has to be understood by the masses. I will liken it to you this way: Imagine if I appeared before someone and never said a word. Think about what it would be like if a Marian seer would set eyes on My presence every day of his life, but I never uttered a word. Even as awestruck as this seer might be, there would always be an empty place in his heart for wanting to know why I came. In other words, beauty is a remarkable gift, but it must convey a beatific message to be complete. It would be frustrating to know that the Mother of God has come to you, but that She never explained the reasons why. It is all in the process of the intent of the intercession of the Lord, and the purpose behind it. After all, there can be no intervention without intercession. In order for the grand and noble purposes of God to be complete, there must be a message imparted from His Son's Sacred Heart about the deliverance of humanity to His arms. The Earth was quiet before humanity corrupted it. What does this mean? What broke the silence? When did the first unholy act occur? This was initiated by the fall of Adam and Eve. It has therefore been the penchant of lost sinners to create corruption everywhere they turn, not that it is their nature, but because they refuse to accept the divine identity that will transform them into saints. One might imagine that the first silence was breached by a young chirping bird or an owl sitting on a limb. Or, it could have been the rolling of a stream against a passel of rocks. My Special son, I have said these things to you this morning because I want you to venture a guess as to what broke the noise of the exiled world with a new solemnity of peace? When did the corruption of men find itself in the midst of a new song? "*The moment you were conceived in your mother's womb.*" Yes, that was an awe-striking moment that changed the course of human existence, but the moment about which I am speaking is the Annunciation of the Archangel Gabriel. "*I understand. Did he appear to you at night, or when you were in prayer, or when?*" It was in the nighttime hours as I was sufficing My prayers, praying for the imminence in Me to be fulfilled by the Father who had fashioned My soul with such Immaculate Grace before humanity and the created world. The Archangel Gabriel's voice brought a new song into the world that would bring an end to humanity's commotion, the end which has yet to occur 2,000 years later. My Special son, the Archangel Gabriel said much more to Me that night than what is recorded in the Scriptures. He said, '*Mother of the divine, a*

Church needs to be born. The grace of your soul has been enlisted to personify the world in the ways of God's love. There is joy and sorrow in the offing for you, but there is glorious redemption for the people for whom you have prayed. Will you do this as the Lord has asked?' My Special son, you know the remainder of this sacred story that the Church has shared with you, that I have recounted for you, that the Holy Spirit has celebrated in your heart.

When I speak about Jesus being conceived in and born of My Womb, this was the fulfillment of the Immaculate Conception that you mentioned a few moments ago. I was born into the exiled realms only for the purpose of bearing the Son of Man and the Church. There would have been no Church without Him. This is why I have made the statement that love has an overarching presence that cannot be annulled. We have spoken about Jesus' Life, Death and Resurrection in the context of time and beyond it, and there is no pragmatic way to describe what it means between humanity's life and death. It is relevant in mortality for preparation for eternal life, and it is relevant to eternal life because of the deliverance of the soul. I ask that you always remember that the transfer of the soul into Heaven is not about time. It is the changing of life, not ending it, which means that it is not a distance traveled, but a different condition. Entering Heaven is not so much about going somewhere or leaving the Earth, but about arriving in Paradise outside the flesh. There is no such thing as someone saying that they got to Heaven before someone else who died at the same moment in time. And, outside the influence of time, there is no such thing as someone going to Heaven after someone else who died 100 years earlier. Do you understand? *"Yes."* My Special son, this is why I have been saying for so many years that the time you are spending on Earth is so important. Life seems briefer for those who spend their lives working for God. The efforts are more charitable, more prolific and meaningful, more creative in the fruits of faith. If you look anywhere in any of My messages from centuries' past, you will notice that I have spoken about the realities of the present before the backdrop of the eternal. This is something that a person knows from the moment they are aware that they are alive. They see the sun rising and setting every day. They read the passing days on the calendar. They feel the changing seasons and accumulating years. What this means to their mind and heart is that they are evolving; they are moving, they are on a journey toward a destiny that they have yet to see. Of all the genius in the world; of all the capacity of men to discern, dissect and design, the most elusive of everything they know or hope to know is the exact composition of that destiny and how they will get there. The medium for their understanding is Jesus on the Cross; and the wisdom for being united with

Him is the exercise of faith. I realize that I have not told you anything new about this, but being able to voice what I have said this morning echoes the meaning of My messages around the globe to lost sinners in the same way that the voice of the Archangel Gabriel still resounds through the epochs of time. My Special one, I ask that you remember in your prayers the instincts of your country to preserve the love and goodness from which it was founded. Remember that God has provided for the United States by interceding during the selection of your president in November 2016. As you know, it was nothing less than a modern miracle that happened that day. The Lord will someday let you and your brother hear the deafening magnitude of the dynamic explosion that occurred when your brother completed the proofreading of My 2013 messages. It was an amazing moment that changed the world in the same ways as your previous books. It is all about your prayer for the Will of God to be done. It is in your witness of His miracles, your part in the conversion of the wicked. *"Your messages are so beautiful. I am so thankful."* They are beautiful because you are beautiful. I am praying with you that peace will be restored around the world, that humanity will allow God to share His overarching faith with them, and that a culture of life will supplant the spreading of death in nations around the globe."

Saturday, May 12, 2018
9:27 a.m.

"Conditioning and acclimation."

"My dear little sons, we have tried to impress upon humanity that the journey to reconciliation with God begins with human repentance, and concludes in Jesus on the Cross. We have succeeded in transmitting this blessing because you have been willing to pray with Me, receive My messages, transfer them to the broken world, and wait patiently while humanity responds. You have been as dedicated to building up the Church as the Saints in Heaven. We know that it is clear that human redemption would be just as full without our work because the Father has sufficed it in His Only Begotten Son. So, Salvation in Jesus stands alone in itself. However, we are responding to the question of how many sinners are willing to partake of this Salvation. How many are in the flock? What will the final face of Jesus' Mystical Body look like? How many exiled human bloodlines will be absolved by the Blood of Jesus on the Cross? We have been conditioning humanity to become acclimated to repentance through the messages that you have recorded for Me.

My Special son, millions of people worldwide have asked what the Mother of God knows about redemption. I am remembered for bearing the Son of Man onto Earth at Christmas, and appealing for additional wine. The Holy Scriptures rightfully describe these things. Those same millions would like to know where it is written in the Bible that I was assumed body and soul into Heaven, and crowned with twelve stars. My little son, do you suppose the Book of Revelation is enough to make them believe? *"It should be, but they need more miracles."* They need more miracles in addition to all the Marian shrines that have come through the centuries? *"They are behind a veil of distractions that are diminishing their ability to understand."* Yes, what you have said is completely true. It is more than a matter of perception, it is a matter of acclimation, just as I said about accepting Jesus on the Cross. I am reinforcing the fact that your work with your brother has built a bridge in the world across which these detractors can walk to see more distinctly My role in the redemption of lost sinners. I wish to tell you today that you need not focus as much on My role as such, and focus instead on My role as Maternal Converter. The Morning Star Over America messages that I have given you are about imploring humanity to convert to the Messianic Sacrifice that has brought about the Salvation of the world. More wine implies that there are more people in need of conversion than are coming forward; and more miracles, more wine, is needed to serve them. Your statement a few minutes ago says precisely what I just stated. They need more miracles; they need more wine. They see the waters of their indifference in surplus. They require the intervention of Jesus to realize that their own repentance, their own conversion, is found within themselves by receiving the miracle of His Holy Spirit. My Special son, I do not wish for you and your brother to take lightly what I am saying about conditioning and acclimation. The reverse is also true in the exiled world. When you speak about distractions, you realize that the things that take sinners away from the Cross are also heaped upon humanity through conditioning and acclimation. People become used to sinning by these impulses. They become lulled to sleep by their wrongful doings. It is a matter of habit, and therefore not unusual for them to commit any number of unholy acts. So, conditioning and acclimation work both ways. It all comes down to exposure. Whatever occupies the consciousness finds its way into the center of the heart. If a person leads a life of darkness, there is no light in their heart. The inverse to this applies to spiritual conversion. If there is light in the heart, there will be light in the consciousness. It is an inverse of itself in that conversion is a product of spiritual light, but dark hearts are a product of dark consciousness. Do you understand? *"Yes."* It is like putting an object in front of a mirror and looking at its image. What did Jesus say about the righteous when He was declaring the reason for His Life, Death and Resurrection? He said that He did not come to convert the righteous, but the unrighteous. My Special son, I ask you to think about this because it will bring you great joy. Has there ever been a moment, even in your youngest years, when you did not believe that our sovereign God has been guiding you? *"No. I have always known that He is there."* The same is true of your brother who willed his compliance with the teachings of Jesus and allegiance to the Gospel of redemption from his first age of reason. You and your brother did not require conditioning or acclimation to the grace that you accepted the moment you were conceived."

Saturday, May 19, 2018
9:24 a.m.

"Please don't trip over the guard dog."

"My dear little sons, there are melodies playing in your hearts that only your souls can hear. There are rhythm and harmony to your lives that are apparent only in Heaven. There is peace and joy where you are bound, so much so that it overflows into your exile here beneath the City of Light. This is the fulfillment that you feel when you pray, when you live in accordance with the Father's wishes, when you realize that human life on Earth is not that bad after all. There are too many paradoxes, too much irony, and too much hypocrisy in the earthly realms, and this is what My introduction this morning means. Who is watching over the Earth? It is Jesus the Incarnate Father! It is the Holy Spirit who blesses you with wisdom, courage and tenacity. My Special son, God does not have His hands on you as if your soul is attached to strings. He has His hands on you from within your heart, caressing and comforting you. You are tethered to Jesus by your acceptance of the Cross, and it is His Paschal Resurrection that overflows from Heaven to inspire your thoughts and actions. This is the over-abundance of Providence by which you live in this world, profoundly in advance of your inhabitancy in Heaven. Today, I have come to pray with you for every intention that you raise to Heaven, asking My intercession, and beseeching Jesus' intervention. I have described humanity's journey to redemption as a process, one that requires conversion that occurs throughout the sequential life of men in exile. This implies that conversion must result in an outcome, that the destiny has spiritual and ethereal mass. And as such, this outcome has an eternal design. If you imagine a rope going through a hole in a door that you cannot see through, you have no way of knowing its length on the other side. You might know that you can pull on the rope, for sure, but you also know that you cannot push it and gain any headway toward knowing what is at its other end. This is the struggle of human life that seems to exist for men in exile. It is like being caught in a boat upside down in the water. When you hear someone knocking on the outside of the hull, your spirit is lifted because you know that you have been found. The discernment that wise men must make, however, is whether the knocking is some kind of serpent wanting to devour you. This is the decision that Christians must make when encountering the designs of the world. Who is knocking, and what do they want? From what origin has this being been sent? This is what is meant by the perils and hypocrisies of the human realms. I am pleased that you and your brother are keen discerners of the world, that you realize that there are certain traits that guide you in these matters. You know which facets of life will lead you to smiles instead of tears. My dear little sons, I ask you today to remember everyone in your prayers who has asked Me to pray for them. You know many of them by name, but not their identities. There is Marsha and Joe, John, Sarah and all the anonymous people who call on My Maternal help. The Kingdom to which you belong is a magnificent, universal entity that begins with the Faith Church to which you belong, and makes itself manifest in the Church Triumphant. My Special son, if there is a process to what I am saying, the conveyance for all things benevolent is prayer from the heart. I have said this for centuries, and you first heard My plea for prayer from the heart most prolifically in your early encounters with My Medjugorje shrine. I am not saying that someone should not meditate on the difficulties of life or one's personal requests during canticle prayers. I am saying that everything for which humanity prays must be directed to Jesus and the Father through the investment of the Holy Spirit, with the involvement of the Holy Spirit, at the behest of the Holy Spirit. This is benignity at its best. It is the straightest path between a lost sinner and his unity with God. So, I speak about not tripping over the guard dog in the sense that Heaven is awake, unlike the dog. Jesus is aware of His Messianic mission, as the Church is aware of its Apostolic mission. It is all a timely matter that is encapsulated by everything eternal. This is the transmission of one's prayers into the Heart of the Father. My Special son, there is no question that you and your brother have perfected what you are doing for Me. You receive My messages when they come; you work with eager merit on your daily chores; you are kind and generous to other people; you produce more spiritual works in a month than most people do in a lifetime, and you maintain your loyalty to the

Holy Spirit who has for decades been guiding you, ever since the Father deigned that you be conceived. These are gifts that you offer His Kingdom so appropriately that you have built them into your lives. I am telling you this today so that you will recognize the contrast between what you do and what the rest of humanity seems to be doing. Your lives are a reflection of the Cross and a gift to the Church. I plead with you to always remember that I have told you this.

My Special son, I would like to create an image in your mind before I become silent for the day. I wish for you to consider, to remember that human life for Christians is not always uphill. There is great satisfaction in knowing the purpose of your life on Earth, and you are completely aware of what it is. You are not distracted by materials or other lures that would pull you away from the Lord's dominion. You live modestly here with your brother compared to everyone else who has your means. You are not burdened by addictions or financial distress. You have the profits of purity and chastity. You understand the teachings of the Bible as well as any Pope. And, My Special son, the Father sees all this. God is aware of your faith-conscience that has become such comfort to Jesus on the Cross, and Resurrected from the Tomb. Your thoughts and meditations that you commit to the page are the workings of genius because they are founded in everything that He asks the Church to believe. Your published books have been the consolation of Bishops and clergy for years. And, with the spreading of My messages that will eventually come, and please know that it will, you have laid the groundwork for thousands in your company to establish a relationship with Me. Just as Heaven is not some far off place that nobody ever sees, I am here with you and your brother in the same sense that the Holy Spirit is unaffected by the element of time. Exiled sinners must realize that human flesh is not your captivity, human sin is one's captivity. It is not a sin to live in the flesh; Jesus proved this through His Incarnation on the Earth. This is the reason humanity will be given glorified bodies in Heaven, to celebrate their re-creation through Jesus' Resurrection. I am saying this morning that everything I have ever shared with you and your brother is based on your commonness with Jesus that manifests your reunion with God. When Adam and Eve had thoughts of wanting to be like gods, the Father said that if they wished to be like Him, then they should be like Jesus. This is the testament that lives to this day. As I have said many times, it is not at all complicated. You summarize so many beatific qualities when you assert to others, '...just do the right thing.' It is your worthy commendation of humanity to Jesus in Heaven. I urge you to remember that the dailiness of your life with your brother is a precursor to an infinity of joy that you will receive as your eternal reward.

Saturday, May 26, 2018
9:26 a.m.

Living vis-a-vis "face to face."

"My dear little children, if there were words and phrases to describe how you are loved, I would surely share them. We use symbols, My little sons, to communicate how we feel. Yes, visible and audible symbols that create thoughts and confer messages about how the world and humanity are surviving. Spiritual survival depends on the thriving of the soul in the Holy Spirit of the Lord. My Special son, you and your brother have learned through the years that facts and circumstances are always dependent on other facts and co-conditions. For example, My children are baptized to cleanse them of original sin; it is a fact. Another fact is that this must be done willingly; no one is baptized against their will, not even infants. Humanity establishes a relationship with the Father through the spiritual communication and connections about which I speak. Imagine standing on the earthly ground 2,000 years ago, and looking the Savior of the world straight in the eyes. This is the vis-a-vis, the face to face encounter with the Son of Man that fosters one's unity with God. The distinction that I wish to make is that through your faith and the Sacraments, through your prayers and sacrifices, through the love and virtue in your heart, you are looking Jesus in the eyes as though you walked with Him twenty centuries ago. And, this is the spiritual vision that I have been describing to you since February 22, 1991. There is no way of escaping this perception of Jesus; no person ever born can decline seeing Jesus' face, even if after they succumb to mortality. This is a gift from God to those who believe in Him here in the earthly domain, and it is a moment of torment for those who do not. I am saying that those who look Jesus in the eyes during their years in exile, and proclaim that they love Him, will not be ashamed in His divine presence. The righteous have already been saved before departing the flesh. Thus, '...coming to judge the living and the dead' means that those who are confident of their standing in Jesus find their affirmation. They come to have their faith redeemed. This was the way of Saint Paul, just as he foretold. On the other hand, those who reject Jesus on the Cross during their earthly lives have already jeopardized their judgment by the record of their error. In this sense, critical judgment is reserved for those who are far from God. All the rest, those who have remained loyal to Jesus, receive a confirmation of the redemption that they have inherited. My Special son, does this make sense? *"Yes, completely. How do infants choose to be baptized?"* Their souls are in alignment with the virtue of whomever takes them to receive this Sacrament, and the Father sees it as an extension of His Will. Even those who reject their baptism and are eventually condemned are baptized through this virtue because the Sacrament of Baptism can never be an evil act. A person cannot be 'un-baptized.' "*I understand.*" And, to connect this with My thesis, once someone is baptized, they are situated vis-a-vis, face to face with Jesus; the impression of Jesus' face is imprinted on their soul the same way that His face was imprinted on Veronica's veil. It is through this grace that the New Covenant is made manifest to souls in exile, that the gate is opened for Christians to exercise their will to accept the Cross in the same way that Jesus exercises His Will to come knocking on the door of the heart. The New Covenant is the living, breathing, redeeming Second Person whose life and Holy Spirit are written into the Gospel. So, when you are reading the Sacred Scriptures, you are seeing Jesus vis-a-vis. This is not metaphorical or symbolic, it is true and tangible. And, when the priest or deacon reads the Holy Gospel during the Holy Sacrifice of the Mass, he ends the reading by kissing the sacred text. This is the righteous kiss of the Church on the cheek of its Savior, multiple times a day, thousands of times, to rebuke the betrayal of Judas Iscariot. My Special son, do you understand? "*Yes.*" God rebukes the world's evil by sufficing whatever goodness might come through His people in their reflection of His Son's holy life. And, it is good to imitate Jesus once your heart and soul capture the impression of what Salvation looks like. When you kiss the Cross, you kiss Jesus' face and dress His Wounds. The moment the words, '...Our Father' part your lips when you begin the prayer, you are invoking the impassioned emotion of Jesus to speak to you through the Holy Spirit emanating from the Divine Soul whom your own soul sees. As I have said, how many times have human beings looked at pictures of other people and said, '...I wish I looked like that.' In Jesus, they are given the opportunity. Jesus says in the Scriptures to all who will believe, '...Come to Me, be like Me, look like Me, and love like Me.' My Special son, this is an elementary concept that I have described this morning, and I wish for you and your brother to remember that Jesus' identity and God's Kingdom are deeply imbedded within you.

    This is the reason that I keep telling you and your brother that you are so holy, that your lives are sacred and replete with grace and purity. Living in you now is not only an image of the Kingdom of God, but the essential, spiritual love of God with tethers to His celestial being. It is certain that you are living rightly in the flesh, and it is certain that your flesh is not a burden because you do not yield to the temptation to sin. Hence, you are not cut off from God just because you are living in exile on the Earth. Your soul is standing tall in truth and peace, and you are looking Jesus in the eyes with everything in your heart. You are living vis-a-vis with the same Messiah who looked upon His Apostles and disciples with such love 2,000 years ago. You can feel this in your heart. You are aware of it, right down to the footprints of your spirit. The co-dependent fact is that you know everything that I have told you today. It is another means of describing the eminence in your faith on which the framework of your trust in God is founded. The Father would not allow you to spend the past twenty-seven years of your life working for a Kingdom that has no meaning. He would not have sent Me here to speak to you if there were no fruitful harvest in what we are doing. I did not come just to extend My cordial greetings. I pray that you will see your patience as one of your greatest virtues. We are taking to task everyone who is trying to hide their face from Jesus; there is no way to avoid Him. And, why does Jesus not incinerate a nation that decides that its unborn children should die? Because the Church still lives here. It is a greater sacrifice for the Church to stand and fight than to die with the souls that are already dead. It would have been easy for Jesus to have taken the lives of His executioners on Good Friday at the moment that He died. However, what statement would this have made? There is Divine Mercy for every soul, for everyone who still has a spirit to keep their flesh alive. Nothing evil in the world will go unpunished. My Special son, do you have anything you would like to discuss with Me this morning? *"I pray that the Hierarchy of the Church will become filled with warriors in obedience to you."* My Special son, I have said this prayer many times in the past twenty-four hours alone. *"Give them the grace they need to make them warriors; show them how to fight for God's Kingdom."* O' My goodness, My Special son, this is what your books are for. This is what I have given you. It is their will that prevails at this time. *"We need miracles to help them get past their will."* Yes, all souls do. I only ask you to remember that anything you do will not steal Jesus' thunder; you *are* Jesus' thunder. My Special son, there will be street battles and insurrections to advance the preservation of human life that the people of America have been unwilling to wage for forty-five years. Your brother was remarking yesterday that he was viewing the postings of abortionists in the United States who are dancing in the streets that the children of Ireland will die. These abortionists will suffer agonizing deaths, and be condemned to the fires of Hell. This is an unarguable truth that no one can hide; this is the fate they have chosen for themselves. Thank you for the infinitude of your love for Jesus, for your devotion to His Kingdom, and for your consecration to My Immaculate Heart."

Sunday, June 3, 2018
9:33 a.m.

How much does God love humanity?
Never an age too long.

"Composite religion and lethal arrogance."

"My dear little sons, your Mother is with you through all your blessings and sufferings. I will always be with you. I will never leave your side. It is for the cause of this love that I have come speaking to you, to share the Lord's bounty, and pray for the conversion of lost souls. It is for the Church that we live. My Special son, I am mindful of your suffering and hospitalization because of your labors on your outdoor building. I have tremendous compassion for what you have undergone, and I pray for your recovery. You must remember that the human body has a self-survival mechanism to counteract the decisions made by the mind that might harm you. Your body became spent because of what you asked it to do last Monday and Tuesday, and it responded that it was unable to do so. I ask that you tend to this matter according to the direction of your physicians and family members who know what this issue is about. It requires a month for your body to adapt in the aftermath of the trauma that it has suffered, and it may subject you to the same injuries if you demand from it more than it can produce. As for your new building, I realize that this problem happened because there was an insufficient number of workers who would come to help you. Nothing that happened is your fault, and a great burden of responsibility rests on those who neglected to appear. My Special son, I ask that you remember that you are requested by the Lord to take care of yourself because of your friendship with Him in the Church as His disciple. Yes, His holy apostle. You must remember to take better care of yourself. These things are in your hands. Are there any questions about this matter? *"No, thank you."* You are welcome. I wish to speak to you this morning about composite religion, which is another means of describing pluralism, because it reveals the lethal arrogance exhibited by those who detest the Roman Catholic Church, and refuse to comply with its teachings. My Special son, can you describe your impressions of pluralism? *"It is a grand compromise that is willful."* How would you describe pluralism to someone who has never heard of it? *"Everyone gets to believe whatever they want?"* So, you are saying that it is not something confined to religion? *"Yes."* You have stated it correctly. The reason that I have asked you to define pluralism is because men on Earth believe that religious pluralism can coexist with all other forms of pluralism without consequence. And, this is the reason that I am saying that religious pluralism can be defined as composite religion. What this means is that any form of belief can be included in this composite. I have mentioned this topic this morning because, as you know, humanity needs to be drawn to the Sacraments of the Church, to the primordial truth of Christianity in the Original Catholic and Apostolic Church, for Salvation in the Blood of Jesus on the Cross. *"It is this compositism through which the devil is trying to create a new church absent Christ's Sacrifice."* My goodness, the Father Himself could not have said this any better than you just did. Thank you! My Special son, the only source of ethereal eloquence is the Roman Catholic Church. All uprightness, spiritual reason, divine revelation, penitential power, and beatific grace come through the Papacy of the Roman Catholic Church, through the power of the Cross and the prayers of the faithful. Humanity has never learned what uprightness in the Cross means because of this 'compositism' about which we speak. Satan has always believed that if he can dilute and distort the spiritual vision of humanity, then he can destroy the mission of the Catholic Church. I have told you that those who stand outside the Catholic Church are living a lethal arrogance that will lead to their eternal demise. I have also said that the devil has inadvertently diverted to Protestantism those who would attempt to destroy the Catholic Church from within. This remains true, but it does not mean that we should not try to convert them to the faith by which all authentic believers are saved. My conversation with you and your brother this morning is our prayer that it will come, that those who attack the Church will be stopped; not just impeded, but removed from relevance in these realms. Uprightness means being united with the Apostolic See, and unified with the Church that Jesus founded in the beginning."

Saturday, June 9, 2018
9:30 a.m.

"Faith and synchronization."

"My dear holy little sons, it is with tremendous joy that I come speaking to you again as you pray for the conversion of lost sinners. I wish to make clear today that all righteous gifts from the Father, no matter in what age or generation dispensed, are blessings upon the Earth from the timeless hands of love. And, everything you have contributed to the Church, to humanity in exile, to the world in which the love of God prevails is given simultaneously.

Faith tells you that this is true, and life convinces you that the Will of God could have been no other way. You have written about these things with profoundness because you have participated in them yourselves. You are living, viable, truth-loving Christians who are ahead of your time. You have afforded Jesus on the Cross your consecration to His Sacrifice through My Most Immaculate Heart. Never let it be said that you have not been one with Jesus. So, what of this synchronization? The mainstay of your relationship with God is the synchronization of your lives with the Crucifixion. You must begin to see that this synchronization is also deeply imbedded in Jesus' Resurrection from the Tomb. My dear sons, your realization and acceptance of this fact is the bedrock of your faith. This is the message that we have been attempting to spread into the world since we first began. My intention here today is to remind you that your work remains on course and intact. I have further come asking for your prayers for the broken and the dying, for those being held against their will, for those addicted to alcohol and drugs, and especially for the children in the womb who must be preserved into the fullness of birth. Each of us shares a part in asking God to deliver these individuals and societies to the perseverance granted to all humanity through the power of the Holy Spirit. This is in keeping with the promises of God to those who love Him. My Special son, your brother spoke yesterday to your dear friend Mary Jane Kerns. She expressed to your brother her sense of abandonment from God when she fell and broke her hip, and as she lay recovering in the hospital. She also said that Jesus, Saint Joseph and Myself felt far from her during these times. She further explained that she did not feel our presence during the early days of her arrival back home. My little son, is there any better way to describe Jesus' Agony in the Garden? Even so, Mary Jane will be a great saint in the likeness of Mother Teresa of Calcutta. How do you see this equation? *"It helped her see how close you have been throughout her life."* Yes, what you have said is correct. Her experience reflects Jesus' Passion and Crucifixion. She asked the Father why He had forsaken her. And, who else said this long ago? *"Jesus."* My Special son, it is not that Heaven abandoned Jesus or Mary Jane. It was a perfect time for them to hand their will to the Father in the most unselfish and beatific means. Having said this, you surely see that every suffering soul is given the venue during their lonely agony to magnify the Father's Kingdom and diminish their own will. It is not that God desires suffering humanity for its own sake, but for the deliverance of the Church into His presence.

    I wish not to diminish the excruciating pain and torment suffered by anyone who contributes this way to the conversion of lost sinners. Suffering cannot be relegated to syllables on a page. Holiness can be sustained by physical pain and spiritual torment. The whole matter must be viewed through the eyes of the Father as He claims His earthly domain as part of His Kingdom. My Special son, I wish not to understate the Sacred Mysteries of human salvation by confining them to a brief supernatural passage. It is to the benefit of the exiled world that we have shared our relationship for so long. It is for the advancement of the mission of the Church, the Church in which you live, and where you and your brother have found your friendship. I ask you both to remember that these gifts to the Church that you have so generously given are wrapped in the grace of My Most Immaculate Heart. When you look around the world, you read the reflections of the holy; you understand and recognize the heresies that are spoken, and you wonder how these things can coexist. Truthfully, they cannot. The illness of the world, its sullenness, its ugliness, and its anti-Christian movements cannot be synchronized with the gifts and blessings from God. Everything that stands in contradiction to His Will dies in its own age. Only the gifts that reflect His Providence are timeless and ageless. Only these things can be synchronized with the eternal faith living in your hearts. So now, My Special son, please remember that the Church Triumphant is interceding for you and your brother in ways that you cannot see. *"Thank John Paul the Great for his blessing yesterday."* Yes, the great Saint John Paul II did bless you for your holy lives in honor of Jesus' Most Sacred Heart."

Saturday, June 16, 2018
9:30 a.m.

"Leaders of empires will someday pay you homage."

"My dear beautiful sons, with meaning and purpose I appear in your presence to share the loveliness of God. How many more weeks and years will pass before the Son of Man returns in Glory? The Father has never prescribed the conditions upon which this tremendous event will happen. It is all in His divine plan for spreading righteousness far and wide, in this world and the next. Please be assured that you have been His sacred ambassadors throughout this process. It is true that leaders of empires will someday pay you homage. The days that you spend in seeming irrelevance are truly those during which you are structuring the framework on which your brothers and sisters will follow you to Heaven. Today, I bring My good wishes and requests that you pray with Me for them, and that they will listen to what I have said here in this home. My Special son, I have often spoken of the world's environment in which Christian holiness must grow. It is a pious culture that must be made manifest to those who are far from God. I say that it is a pious culture because everything that is not of God is counter-cultural to His love. I am speaking of the institution of the redemption of humanity contained in the Sacred Mysteries of the Church. You and I and your brother have aspired to share this institution with those who are unaware that their participation is required. It is often difficult to perceive a spiritual Kingdom as a measurable institution. However, Jesus instituted the Holy Eucharist as a Sacrament of His infinite love. To be in love with Jesus means to transcend everything in life that defines limits and sets conditions holding the souls of men in exile. If humanity on Earth believes that life is a containment of sorts, Jesus gives the freedom to expand the spirit beyond these boundaries. Yes, it is possible to be impeccably free in a world so saturated in corruption. This is what our relationship has been all about in reflection of the mission of the Church. Also today, I bring My promise that I will continue to intercede on your behalf, and on behalf of all My children who feel abandoned and alone in a world that is itself embroiled in anonymity. I share through My Immaculate Heart and intercessory prayers the perpetual divinity of God here in the world that is encased in the confines of time. My Special son, this is also what your books represent. There is wisdom and divine presence between the covers of all your divine works. There is a Kingdom extolled by the glorious strains of faith and sacrifice imbedded in your words and My messages. They are here, My Special son. No one can destroy them. No passages of time can render them irrelevant. No old or new world can supplant the truth that shines from their pages. Even absent new revelation, they are an effusion of the Sacred Scriptures themselves. They are a work of the Holy Spirit whom Jesus said He would send.

    So, My Special son, I wish for you and your brother to realize the honor and homage that are in your future. I tell you these things not to grow your pride, but to offset the suffering that you have predicted to come. As I shared on the Feast of Saint Patrick, great men have always said that one cannot appreciate the view from the summit of a mountain until he has seen the depths of the valley. It is natural for humanity to seek the highest form of peace, even in its brokenness. There is a buoyancy to the human spirit that seeks to carry humanity from the hard, heavy burdens of exiled life. It would seem that the days become heavy to those who do not seek a spiritual way. And not just any spirit, but the Spirit of the Father. We must ensure that we pray not only for this ascension here in your day and time, but that all generations present and future will be united with the timeless Salvation that men have found in the Cross. My Special son, do you suppose that a soul who has surrendered his flesh would be more prone to accept eternal redemption if the first vision he sees would be Jesus on the Cross or Jesus exiting the tomb on His Paschal Resurrection? *"Jesus on the Cross."* Yes, you are precisely correct. And why? *"Because compassion is summoned from the human heart for the innocent Lamb who was slain."* And, what about sacrifice? *"The human heart spontaneously asks how can I heal this."* Yes, and the answer to this question is through acceptance. Why do you suppose that this is also true? *"Because the soul knows that Jesus' suffering was caused by them."* Absolutely correct. Thank you. So, what of the vision of Jesus exiting the tomb? *"The soul realizes that Jesus does not need humanity's help for anything, just their worship."* Yes, indeed. I will relate to you now the vision of those who accept the Cross upon their passing from this life into the next. After first seeing Jesus on the Cross, and bowing in deference to their Salvation, they see what the world did not see on Easter Morning. It was by the design of the Father that they should see the Resurrected Christ before they witness all humanity exiting the tomb in the aftermath of Jesus' emergence from death back to life. Yes, the first passageway to Heaven is the opening to the Sepulcher of Jesus Christ. All redeemed souls see themselves the way they would have walked out of the tomb of the Messiah on the third day. Therefore, My Special son, we are not just celebrating a Kingdom here, we are prescribing the images that represent humanity's entrance into its presence. Divine and sublime, rendering and upholding, and feeling and everlasting. For a world always searching for the effect of every cause, this is the one that matters most. Truly, it is just as you recently heard; nothing else matters at all. The Father wishes to render His people blameless not because they are innocent, but because they are forgiven. I wish to tell you something now that may be surprising to many. If one were to approach a Saint in Heaven and ask what is the nature of sin, this same Saint would question in return, '...what is sin?' All souls redeemed into Heaven have no concept of corruption. This is not a new revelation, it is confirmation of what Jesus has been saying all along. It is a new world reflecting the pristine nature of Eden at its finest. It is the Promised Land, the New Jerusalem, the Land of Milk and Honey, and the home of all the redeemed. My Special son, I have reflected here today about a glory that is indescribable in the confines of the exiled realms. Not unlike Saint Padre Pio, I can read minds, hearts, and souls from My lofty station in Paradise. I know that you understand what I have shared with you for twenty-seven years. You have created a spiritual miracle through your faith and love for God. You have made your own designs of awareness and revelation, handed to you by the power of the Holy Spirit. This is the way of Christ Jesus and Christians, united in love and peace. So, I have completed what I came to share with you and your brother this morning. I pray that you have enjoyed My words. *"Yes, thank you very much."*

Saturday, June 23, 2018
9:40 a.m.

*"The Holy Gospel – scrupulous, prescriptive, tenacious.
Is the iceberg upside down?"*

"The lands still echo the voices of the Saints."

"Good morning, My dear little children, on this day that we praise the Lord and uplift the lowly. The key component of My message today is in the inquiry of whether the iceberg is upside down. My children, your brothers and sisters who are lost in the deep of the world and its ugliness cannot see the danger ahead. It is our intention to lead them to the Holy Gospel of Christian Salvation. We must raise them up from the darkness and the sinfulness in which their souls are floundering. We have celebrated the legacies of the Saints and their gifts to the Church through their writings, preaching, and sacrificial witness. Today, we pray that their message of conversion will be spread far and wide into lands that defy the faith they are given from God. My Special son, the implication of the iceberg being upside down means that the souls of lost sinners are not breathing the air of holiness. We must ensure that humanity comes to the Cross for life, freedom, redemption, conversion, and enlightenment. You see at the opening of the avenue on which you live a sentence on a sign that says, 'It all will become one thing.' I have mentioned this sign on a prior occasion, and today, I wish to refer to it again. I speak of humanity's oneness in the Cross as one such eternal moment. The bloodlines of humanity converge in Jesus' Sacrifice on Good Friday. Of all the moments, hours, years and decades that men live on Earth that contribute to the consciousness of the world, the Crucifixion of Jesus is its most sanctifying event. When one speaks of a moment of eternal certainty, this is the Cross. It is about spreading righteousness around the globe from one supernal font. We have in our hands and in our hearts the message of Salvation that is of old, that extols the future of the world at its finest. My Special son, Jesus loves a good review. He has asked those to whom He has appeared throughout the ages how they would describe the Gospel message. What in the New Covenant can be illustrated by suitable language to capture the miracle of the Sacred

Mysteries? What words, what terms, what phrases and metaphors could be used to describe this redemptive gift? Here, if you should think about it, how would you respond? Please consider your answer in light of the terms at the beginning of this message. *"Unyielding, uncompromising, definitive."* Yes, My Special son, all of these apply. It has been said of Christianity that compromise is another word for surrender, and it is scrupulous to be unyielding in defense of the Gospel. The argument is that there are so many seeming contradictions in the Sacred Scriptures. People from all walks of life are curious how Jesus, the New Covenant Messiah, can fulfill the Old Covenant. Indeed, Jesus said that He not only came to fulfill the Old Covenant, but to personify its Messianic prophecies. He said that it is not to hate your enemies, but to love and pray for them. This is not a contradiction. It is an extension of His Divine Mercy through His disciples who have espoused His Kingdom. My Special son, these are the days when those seeming contradictions culminate in the greatest contradiction where the Son of Man, a sinless Savior, died at the hands of the sinners whom He came to save. Participating in the cultivation and purification of the exiled world by humanity who is lost is part of the acceptance of His Kingdom. Surrendering one's life for his friends resonates the summons of the Gospel. It is true that Christianity comes down to one thing – handing one's life and soul to Jesus without counting the cost.

My Special and Chosen sons, you are seeing the framework of your lives in Jesus on display before the world, before Heaven and all the Saints, as your own gift to the Lord's Kingdom. You are in a way constructing your own spiritual mansion within your hearts that you will deliver to Jesus upon your passing from this world. You will say at the last, 'Lord, is this the way you wanted me to build it?' The response from the Lord of Peace will answer your question with the words, 'My dear brother, this is the way I built it in you. This is the Kingdom that you inherited from the moment you were baptized. It is the Kingdom that has supplanted all your labors with the blessing of sainthood. It is the Kingdom in which you will eternally rest forever beyond this day.' My Special and Chosen sons, everything we have done together from the beginning will culminate in this moment. Wholly, it will become all one thing. Imagine what this shall mean to your souls. Please give yourselves the opportunity to meditate in your prayers upon what this means to those who have already passed into the presence of the Father. It is true that you rarely hear from any of them once they have entered the realms of the beatific. However, in their eyes, to inhale a breath to tell you that they have arrived in Heaven could be seen as a thousand years on Earth. The Saints speak to you here through their intercession to the Father. His gift of life and Nature represents their response as a prayer not just of interceding, but of providing and grace. The Church Triumphant is the honor of your own faith in your desire to someday join them. You aspire to reach the pinnacle of Paradise by your memories of them in your hearts. My Special son, the Church Triumphant and the Faith Church on Earth are not separated by different definitions of love. They are not kept apart because of the effects of death. By all means, faith implies that death does not matter. You and your brother are representative of humanity's wisdom in knowing this fact. When the Church canonizes a Saint, it does not place the Saint into an historical archive without relevant life. The Church is recognizing the perpetuity of the soul of the Saint, the thriving and essential form of newness that was created in the beginning. And, this is more than mere hope or speculation. It is truth, reality, fact and practice. My Special son, I am asking humanity worldwide to place this perspective in their hearts when considering terms and phrases to describe the New Covenant Gospel. Thoughts of love, life everlasting, perpetual piety, unending light, ceaseless joy, and undimmed beauty can be used to describe the condition of the soul that has been washed in Jesus' Blood. We think about what this means to all the broken people who are suffering in the world. Even here in America, there are countless individuals without food and shelter. Millions of them would given life and limb to be allowed into the backdoor of their neighbors' home for food, water and shelter in the same way that you have so kindly done for the animals next door. This is a perspective that is lost to the millionaires who drive their fancy cars and prance down red carpets around the globe. We know it because we are people of God who have been given the wisdom of truth.

My Special son, I have been listening to your casual observations and self-critical assessments of your life here with your brother. I implore you not to look at yourself as though you are in any way to blame for the contentiousness that you engage in the secular void. I have spoken on prior occasions about the hubris and deceptiveness in those whom you often meet. It is true that you should disregard the error of these people in the same way that Jesus said that others know not what they do. Yet, this does not absolve them of their guilt. What we have done together, the way they will see themselves in the shadow of the Cross, will be sufficient to destroy their pride when all things become one. History and the annals of human existence have proved this to be true. My Special son, you and your brother have always been goal-oriented, responsible, honest, and good-willed human beings. When you see others who do not espouse these virtues, it is frustrating for you. I ask that you defer to the call of peace in your heart so that you will not be disturbed by the obstinance of others. Do you have any issues to discuss with Me today? *"Should the leaders of our country be worried about the overwhelming influx of immigrants, or simply throw the doors open? It seems the Bishops are on the side of everyone entering."* My Special son, the Gospel and the Catechism teach that it is not improper to recognize the sovereignty of a country's domain and protect its sovereignty from enemies who may attempt to enter it and destroy it from within. Indeed, would Jesus allow His Church to be infiltrated for this reason? And, therefore, I agree with the implications of your question. *"It is just sorrowful that what was so special about America is being diluted, and ultimately will be rendered extinct, maybe forever."* I assure you that your sorrow is unfounded because the paternal purity and essential identity of America that you have described will never be lost. *"That makes me happy."* My Special son, your recognition of the possibility of your concern is a prayer to preclude it from happening. I ask you and your brother to realize the gift you are to the world. Thank you for helping so many people, especially the poor and broken, to be uplifted in heart, mind and spirit. What you did for your friend this week has opened the floodgates of Mercy from Jesus' Most Sacred Heart for those suffering in Purgatory. You know of his tenderness, and you are aware of how special he is to Me. From a thief to a prince; this is the way Jesus sees the transformation of the human family. Please remember that you are blessed beyond all imagining, in every way holy and eternal."

Saturday, June 30, 2018
9:34 a.m.

"It is not so much that the human soul needs sanitized or disinfected like a porcelain bowl, but liberated from sin – cleansed and purified from the inside out through Jesus' Blood on the Cross."

- The Dominion Angels

"On this remarkable day of grace for you, My children, I have come speaking about the power of God and the efficacy of your prayers. It would seem that humanity throughout the ages has spoken of God and His Son, '...please send Our Savior back to either help us or condemn us – at least just do something.' For My part, My little sons, I stand with your position that 'something' has already been done through the Crucifixion, the Resurrection, and the Descent of the Holy Spirit. I am not saying that time is irrelevant or that the frustrations of human life do not matter, but that the maximizing of your faith rests in your capacity to bless and reshape the world in the image of Jesus. My Special son, today I would like to speak to you about whether God judges you every day, or if He reserves His judgment for the moment you enter His presence. This appears to be among the reasons why humanity is reluctant to accept the Cross and take their place in the lineage of Saints. They claim that they do not wish to live under a microscope every minute of the day. They are concerned that they have to erect a firewall in their mind to keep them from forming thoughts that would displease the Lord. They fear that they would be always on guard, that their conscience would never have a moment's rest. What do you suppose we should tell them? *"That they should more see it as the story of their lives, and how they want to write it. What do they believe would make them proud of themselves?"* Yes, My goodness, you have provided a profound answer to My question. And, what should be said to them in response to their contention that Christianity is all about sacrifice and suffering instead of triumph and fulfillment? *"That sacrifice and suffering are the heart of the victory and fulfillment. And, the reward will be eternal life forever."* Yes, you have again spoken profoundly. However, the stumbling block in their mind is the idea of reward. We know that reward implies the achievement of something, that it means the passing of time and the conclusion of an endeavor, mission or journey. This is the part that the Lord has difficulty conveying because it requires faith. I have said that faith can change a heart, and righteousness can heal a nation. Hence, it is not just that faith is its own reward, but it is a mode of transcendence for everything that human beings know about life – the good and the bad, and everything in between. My Special son, can there be true righteousness without faith? *"No, because one cannot have a vision for righteousness without faith."* Yes, you are correct again. So, we know that righteousness is a manifestation of believing in the eternity of God that cannot be completely grasped here in this life. It is the fruit of the alliance of the human heart and Heaven. Faith is the energy that connects mortal time with the sphere of perpetual being. I am not speaking of a measurable sphere that can be equated with the circumference of a globe, but a sphere of glory that has been ordained by the Father through the infinity of His Wisdom. My Special son, if you were to take in your hands a large spherical object, and then took a thin wire and touched the sphere as though drawing a line on a page, how many places on the sphere do you suppose this tangent can be made? *"Nearly endless points."* Yes, you are always correct in your responses. Now, imagine having an infinite number of sizes for the sphere, and an infinite number of diameters for the wire. Does this not increase this endlessness to an even greater degree? *"Yes."* Thank you. The point I am making is that those without faith have in their grasp only one sphere and one wire. They can touch their lives to the fact that they are alive and situated in space, moving through time. However, they do not have the capacity to be, or become, any larger than this on their earthly journey. I am comparing the finite with the infinite in a way that geometrists can understand. I am using material parameters to explain the infinity of the immaterial. And, it is only through the 'faith experience' that you understand what I am telling you because you have given everything that is eternal about you back to our eternal God from which it came. This is not only your claim of faith, it is your ability to apply beatific reason to your claim in the setting of the mortal domain. In other words, righteousness can only have its transcendental property through the exercise of faith. *"I understand."* So, when another man stands before you and says that he believes in God, you know that you are looking at all men of good faith in this single person. When the congregation offers its collective Profession of Faith to God during the Holy Mass, God sees the reverse – He sees from this assembly a single person, united and origined in His Only Begotten Son. It is the growth of Jesus' Mystical Body in the same way that an infant grows into an elder statesman. Does this make sense? *"Yes."* I am saying that the Holy Mass is the transition of the old earth into the New World that will supplant the broken landscapes that you see every day.

My Special son, it gives Me tremendous joy to tell you that you have within your heart the entirety of the spirit of the Church Triumphant because of the transcendent nature of your faith. The love of all the Saints lives in the heart of every faithful Christian. It is not a mystery that cannot be seen until the old earth passes away; it is living in Christians like you and your brother because of the meaning that you have attached to your faith. You and Jesus are one; and together, you are facing down the evils and perils of this world in the wisdom that the Father has dispensed. In other words, you have set aside what non-Christians believe to be 'meaning' in favor of the Messianic revelations of the New Covenant Gospel. This entails all the gifts of the Holy Spirit, the Commandments and Beatitudes, the morals imbedded in the Gospel teachings, and the vibrantly-living grace that comes to you from the Paraclete of the Lord during your every waking and sleeping moment. You are receptive because the Holy Spirit is generative within you. You are welcoming because Jesus is calling. You are willing to be claimed by Heaven because you seek His redemption. You stand for the truth because you have been so victimized by lies. Your spiritual heart bleeds because Jesus shed His Blood on the Cross. You preach the wisdom of the Church because you are one of its disciples. Your feet walk firmly on the bedrock of holiness because Jesus has stood you erect. All in all, and on and on, the messages of deliverance and arrival have made their way deep inside your consciousness because, as I have said, you were conceived and born with your 'fiat' on your tongue. My Special son, this is the message that I came to share with you this morning. It was forty years ago today, June 30, 1978 that you first asked your brother if he ever heard of the appearances of the Virgin Mary around the world. "*That is nice to know.*" Yes, look where we are now! I have accolades for you, My Special and Chosen sons. I beseech you to recognize your standing before the Father in Heaven."

Saturday, July 7, 2018
9:29 a.m.

"Honor is the ultimate test of holiness."

"Good morning, My wonderful little sons. It is an exceptional day when the Mother of Jesus Christ comes speaking to you about the Church and the piety that you hold within. I have long spoken about the honor that you possess because of your faith in God. It is a fruit of My own Maidenhead that you have embraced the holiness that the Father renders to you. You must remember that honor is the ultimate test of holiness. All other things – glory, faith, trust, truth, righteousness; all of these are products of honor. My Special son, I recently shared that you often say that honor is best described as 'doing the right thing.' You have perfectly told of the spiritual perfection that Jesus seeks in His disciples. It is in being honorable that humanity does good things. Hence, all goodness is a manifestation of honor. It was honorable for the Archangel Gabriel to come to Me at the Annunciation, and it was My honor to respond with My affirmative Fiat. The honor of Jesus being placed in My Womb is the greatest honor ever known to man. Yes, it is all about the communion of honor and holiness within the human heart. It is also My joy to say that I am beseeching miracles from Jesus on behalf of those who pray. I have said that the little child for whom you prayed would receive one of these miracles, and it began, My Special son, the moment that you asked Me to render it. "*Thank you.*" You must be clear that the miracle you seek is in accordance with the Will of God. The Father will respond to your prayers as much as Mine. It is clear that humanity is refined and cultivated according to its petitions on behalf of its own redemption. We shall see what Jesus deigns for all who are broken, what tremendous graces are dispensed to the world through those who live in His likeness, and how the Father configures the conclusion of the Earth according to their sacrifices. My Special son, you have said that some of My humble visionaries are suffering the effects of the coming secrets of Medjugorje. I ask that you and your brother realize that the Medjugorje manifestations will soon be revealed. And, it will logically follow that the events I have told here in this home will unfold briefly thereafter. It suffices what we all must know that this be true because of the investment of our prayers in the conversion of the lost. You must remember that the occurrence of some of the secrets was meant to be contingent on the prayers of the faithful. And, in the absence of these prayers, some of the secrets that could have been avoided will happen. This is the origin of the grief-stricken appearance on the faces of My visionaries. My Special son, you have also said that if this is what is required to make right everything that is wrong, then it should be done. Here again, you have reflected the sentiments of Jesus, Himself. You have further said that clemency should be reserved for the penitent. This is still true. My dear Special son, I am elated that you are resting and giving your spirit the peace it deserves. I ask that you remember that the preservation of your body and health are preeminent in the completion of your work. If it becomes true that you are unable to sustain undue levels of stress and exhaustion, I implore you to set aside your engagement with the secular void and trust that God will sustain you. It is clear that you see your earthly mission as an analogy of hammer swings. I am simply asking that you take more time to reflect and relax between impacts. I shall connect this topic with the subject of honor. It would seem that you have been taught during your entire life that working until exhaustion is honorable. I am telling you here this morning that this is not wholly true. You and your brother, and all My children beneath My Mantle, should realize that you harbor attributes that are expended, but not totally lost. Your mind, heart and spirit require rest so that you will not be fully spent. It is more honorable, and it is an honor for Jesus, that you should remember this as the future unfolds. It is more wise to walk slowly than to spend oneself into exhaustion and get nowhere at all. My Special son, I am telling you these things not only from the standpoint of being your Mother, but I am a human being as well. It is not necessary for you to fall on your life's journey. Jesus did this for you on the way to Golgotha.

    I wish that I could convey to you the manifest clarity that you hold about the vision of the Lord's Kingdom to come. It is more than supernatural that you have believed not only in what I have said, but that it is Me saying it. I promise that you and your brother will see to the jubilation of your hearts a mystical rendering of your lives here on Earth. Yes, it may be on the last day, but you will witness in America and around the world the story of your time written by your faith in God. I also promise that you will hold in your hands the wealth of the nations to which all men have aspired since the dawn of the ages. You will give this gift to the world's poor who for so many centuries have pleaded for help. You will hold to the designs of the Father for the purification of the Earth, and explain to your fellow brothers and sisters, fully assembled, the reasons for your perseverance in these crucial years of the world. This is the saturation of your honor into the places where it has never been known. It is not just a privilege to be a messenger for the Mother of God. It is a gift to honor Her Son that grows the faith of children, and rewards the lives of the Saints. So, on this beautiful day in July 2018, I make you these promises because I know that you believe Me. It is a strange mystery to many that the Father would not reveal to His Son or His Mother the hour of the Second Coming. Does this not mean however, that the Mother and the Son still enjoin the mysteries of faith? Yes, everything about knowing and experiencing the faith of God is made manifest to His Son and Mother. I have the particular benefit of knowing that My children on Earth aspire to be like us, even absent of sin, for the purpose of satisfying God's Will. Those who emulate Christ Jesus and Myself are of the bounty of the Lord's providential Heart. There could be libraries across the continents and seas filled with the revelations of these souls. In the final hour of human endeavors, honor will be their greatest gift. My Special son, I ask that you receive My gratitude for being one of these holy men whose life and legacy will be celebrated in the annals of time. Thank you for being patient while your brother tries to rest his mind and spirit in the same way that I have sought from you. Is there anything you wish to ask Me this morning? *"What are the things to come that had the Medjugorje visionary so burdened? Can you tell me?"* They involve suffering, deprivation, punishment, and recrimination from the divine domain upon those who have rejected the Cross. If it seems as though this is reflective of the Mosaic Covenant, please remember that Jesus came to fulfill it. He also came to share His Divine Mercy with those who accept and practice His New Covenant. There is still time for the chastisements to be avoided. Thank you for your prayers and remembering the miracles that God gives to those who trust Him."

Sunday, July 15, 2018
10:05 a.m.

"Handing the world the property of change."

"My dear little sons, it is not a time for worry or consternation because the Will of God is present within you. There is divinity and providence in everything you think, speak and accomplish. I have come to tell you this morning that the gift of prayer represents handing the world the property of change. There is no stagnancy in the life of a Christian. There is constancy, but there is also the process of adapting not yourselves to the world, but the constitution of the world to your faith. When we speak of handing the world the property of change, it begets the benefits of hope and inspiration. Nothing painful will ever be permanent. And, nothing joyful will ever expire. We seek the change of humanity because it is humanity itself that changes the world. The efficacy of prayer is that My children all around the globe shall become more holy, and therefore more pure. I come speaking to you on this midsummer's day because your prayers are especially fruitful. We seek from the nations the view of the world that the Holy Spirit has given to you. This is a view of peace and wisdom, one that cannot be expunged by the world's evil. My Special son, the angels said through your brother yesterday that the Holy Gospel scatters and disperses everything that has nothing to do with the Kingdom of God. Everything that distracts humanity from accomplishing the mission of the Church within the Gospel teachings is turned away by the righteousness of men. This gives all Christians the power to facilitate the changing of the Earth into the likeness of Heaven. Please speak aloud the heading of My message this morning. Yes, the most important word in My statement is not so much that change shall come, but that change is a property. It is an element more crucial to the future of men than any natural element that can be inscribed on a periodic table. The property of change is manifested through prayer from the heart. This has been the essence of the entire redemption story. If God did not believe that humanity has the property of change, the capacity for change, He would not have dispatched His Only Begotten Son onto the exiled Earth to sanctify the hearts of men. It is in this property that the future of the world rests, and the future of men's eternal souls resides. I have had the great joy of speaking about this manifest change for centuries. And, it must be known that change can come to the world at various velocities. Change comes slowly to those who pray only little. Change comes not at all to those who do not pray. It is clear that this represents the movement of the world not only in the direction of Salvation, but at the pace of human supplications. Hence, the relevance of velocity is appropriate here. We pray together that My children of the 21st century will understand what I have told you here today.

It is also clear that the change that the Lord seeks is not just for the sake of change. Eradicating evil and demonic works from the face of the Earth is not the only goal of the Gospel. The ultimate purpose of Jesus' teachings is the conversion and purification of those whom He calls into His Church. The entire matter revolves around one's willingness to repent. My Special son, those who are unaware of the teachings of the Gospel are also unknowing about what repentance means. A human heart cannot repent without the reception of the Holy Spirit to its depths. Nothing else can bring to humanity the wisdom and truth needed to foster this redemption. Conversion to the Cross and the enlightenment of the New Covenant consists of this. It must be realized that the Gospel message, written on the pages blessed to receive it, is good whether it is observed by humanity or not. It is the same principle that says God is glorious even without the worship of men. Praise from the lips of the faithful does nothing to intensify His perfection. On the other hand, however, praise from the lips of the faithful cultivates and perfects those who believe. It is along these lines that change is made clear to those whose vision has been refined. It is a property reserved for believers who have opened their hearts to receive. My Special son, this is how miracles are wrought, healings are given, evil is eradicated, and men around the globe seek to live in peace. You are living in the midst of these changes that are coming more rapidly than you have seen in previous decades. Why? Because you can see the radical extremism that has accosted the Church from both behind and beyond its doors. When we have spoken in times past about the influence of outside forces on the ordinances and decisions of the Church Magisterium, it is here in these times that you are seeing its awful effects. As I have stated many times, you need not worry that the foundation of Truth on which the Church is standing will ever waver. You can see, however, the effects that come when secularism, materialism, pluralism, and relativism take their toll on those assigned to ensure the sanctity of their Apostolic charge. The Church is comprised of sinners who are striving to become the likeness of its sinless Head. My dear Special son, this entire prospect reminds Me of little children trying to escape from a playpen with walls twenty feet high. They can only tinker around the edges, boast of the progress they have made, celebrate among themselves their attachment of the ancient Church with the modern day lives of unrealistic men, and then lie down and either fall asleep or die without so much as making the slightest impact on the constancy and integrity of the Church. My Special son, you and your brother are committing yourselves to the future to which you are called. You are in realtime changing what must come by the property of your own holiness. You are giving to modern men even without their awareness the foothold they require to be elevated in stature in the likeness of the Saints. I pray that you and your brother never tire of accomplishing this greatness during your lifetime on Earth. I also pray that you are aware, even through the darkness and commotion of worldly time, that you remain within My Immaculate Heart where you were placed before you were born. I wish that I could inspire within you a perfect understanding of what unending joy really means. I call you again to consider the metaphor of a basketball or football game where the clock is ticking down while you have achieved a score that cannot be surpassed. This is the sense of inevitability by which you must live. Indeed, when the stately Secretariat accomplished his goal forty-five years ago, he could have stumbled three times and gotten back up, and still won the race. It is to this inevitability that every priest should call his parishioners during his homilies, visits to religious institutions and social gatherings, and especially during the Feasts of the Liturgical Year. It is the imminence of the heart that keeps hope alive for all who believe in God. This, My Special son, is My message for today. Manifesting to humanity the property of change through prayer is the great high mission of the inspired heart. I ask you to remember the gratitude that the Most Blessed Trinity holds for you and your brother with unsurpassed intensity. Please give yourselves the opportunity to reside in the peaceful Heart of Jesus your whole life through. You must remain in the peace that the Father has given you through Jesus' Paschal Resurrection."

Saturday, July 21, 2018
No public message this week.

Saturday, July 28, 2018
9:28 a.m.

"The richest soil is the human heart."

One Truth in a world riddled with 'ologies' and 'isms.'

"Here now, My dear little sons, the Mother of Jesus spreads Her loving blessings upon you. I come praying with you to assure you that I am also praying for you. What we hold dear, My children, is the love that we cherish in the Father, the Son, and the Holy Spirit. We share a common humanity that was given to us the moment we were conceived in our mothers' wombs. My Special son, it is possible to be human and divine at the same time because this is the creative Will of the Father for His Church. I come today with God's blessings in everything you have given to Him, for the work of your hands and the meditations of your hearts. They are indeed acceptable in His sight. We hold to and speak of One Truth that thrives in a world that is riddled with -ologies and -isms that have been wrought by the misgivings of non-spiritual men. The readings about the sower who finds his richest crop in the good soil are speaking about the love in the heart, and this is where the entire foundation of our messages has been placed. I come to share with you the Good News not only of the Gospel message, but that everything we have done together here in this home has found its own peace in the Kingdom of God. Your work with your brother on My behalf is the energy that has allowed the New Covenant to eclipse the Earth in the way that Jesus intends. There are hardly words to describe the fruits of this energy because it is too panoramic for you and your brother to take-in with your senses. If there is a sixth sense, it is the super-ratification of your faith in everything you have believed, espoused, taught and propagated about the future of man and the destiny of the world. My Special son, it is unfair to relegate the definition of Christianity to pain. This seems the common way to understand what it means. Yes, pain is redeeming because it drives out sin. But, pain is only the underpinning of human redemption that captivates the annals of the mortal ages and brings out the glory of good and decent men. My messages have extolled this glory, as well as all the fruits that are borne when a world engages in magnifying the Cross. If you think in heavenly terms that are marked by sacrifice, by human self-denial, you have a means of reckoning the immeasurable aspects of faith, and complying with the Father's Will. There are strange and awkward circumstances that surround the development of human sacrifices because most of them are mental and spiritual, rather than corporeal and material. All in all, the faith that you practice and the Church in which you believe comprise the two pillars on which your association with your religion rests. You have donned the Holy Spirit, taken your place in the arena of life, and offered yourselves as sacrificial victims of those who refuse to believe because Jesus is alive and working through you. Yes, too many -ologies and -isms. I have mentioned this concept before. It is about human beings believing that everything that has a thesis or purpose needs to be categorized. This is their means of creating distractions that blind them from seeing the One Single Truth. It is a way for lost men to spend the hours and years looking at the painting of life without giving any attribution to the painter who so artfully laid it on the canvas. Wise men imagine through prayer not only who might be the artist of life, but what other renderings He might have created. It is all in the imagination of God, made manifest in the presence and consciousness of those who believe in Him. My Special son, I would ask you and your brother to promise Me something. I ask that you remember that you have the capacity to see beyond your own viable vision into the Sacred Heart of Jesus in ways that reflect not only the beginning of life on Earth, but its joyful and glorious outcome as well. It is a strange and beatific vision that you possess because you have not been given foresight to the makings of the world; you do not know what will come tomorrow, which nation might fall to another, who will come to the leadership fore, and what magnate might die and leave his fortune to those who will hoard it the same way he did. All these things are part of your life on Earth because God wishes for you to engage your capacity for trusting in Him. It has been this way for centuries. He wishes you to find your way through the smoke and fog of all those -ologies and -isms by walking in your awareness of His presence within you. Philosophy? Realism? Naturalism? Paganism? How many more can there be? Only about ten million atop a hundred million, but they do not matter here. They are not relevant in the mind of God because God is thematic in terms of human deference to the glorious divine. Even in the Blessed Trinity, God is single-minded in His own glory because there is no other sacred love. His Kingdom is seeded in the Sacred Heart of His Son because the Sacred Heart is the richest soil. And, this is the Heart that Jesus wishes to implant into everyone who will come to Him. The Sacred Heart of Jesus is the most powerful gift ever created by the Holy Love of God. It is a clear and present blessing.

There are hundreds of intellectuals poring over everything I have said in Medjugorje and elsewhere, wondering what the thoughts and motivations of the Mother of God might be. Reams have already been written and archived in private places about the Queen of Peace and the Morning Star Over America, but the world of humanity does not yet know it. And, this also does not matter. What matters is that the march toward victory continues on. What matters is that the transition of exiled men to resurrected Saints goes on. And, what matters most is that men, women and children are praying that what the Father wills for His Creation will come to pass in their day, during their knowing hours before their flesh fails and their bodies fall asleep in death. They shall all rise again at the same moment in time! We should remember to pray for them because they are in union with us. They are our company in the presence of righteousness that was given to the world before the sun ever began to shine. My Special son, the designs of men are not the same as the Providence of God for a reason. God does not want them. He does not recognize them any more than you might imagine what graffiti has been placed on the back of an abandoned drug store in a lonesome city. Everything that is of God is welcome in those who trust what He asks them to believe. And, all that is contrary to His love is appalling to the Church in which His Spirit reigns."

Saturday, August 4, 2018
9:27 a.m.

"The intersection of truth and expression – the Holy Gospel revealed and spoken; chanted, said and sung; verbalized, vocalized, pronounced and preached. The First Word irrevocably declared; forever and uniquely told; documented, disseminated, heralded and complete."

"Now comes Eternal Truth; boulder-strong, brightly shining, promising, vindicating, impassioned; copiously lettered, consummately enduring, wholly innocent; transcending, fearless, fervent, incorruptible, and peer to no one."

- The Dominion Angels

"My precious little children, there are plenteous reasons to be hopeful about what the future may bring to the Church and to the world of humanity, and the fact that I am speaking to you now is the most auspicious of all. I welcome you into the love of My Immaculate Heart where you have resided since before you were born. My Special and Chosen ones, I ask you to remember that there is no such thing as compromising with the devil. Evil legions must be destroyed, not just turned away or set aside. Everything that is of God is of Divine Light, and all that is of the devil is the darkness. It is possible for even little children to draw this distinction within their hearts and souls because they are capable of understanding love. Love and light versus hatred and darkness. It is said of such things as sports competitions that, over time, most competitors are equal because they are all human beings. At last, it becomes not so much a matter of whether or not you win, but when you win. Stringing together enough victories over a period of time can make you a temporary champion. However, what we do is more than championing what the world puts before you, but vanquishing your opposition so the battle need not be waged again. This is why we are praying for lost sinners, that they not only be found, but that they find themselves, that they gain their bearings in life to realize where they are standing in exile, the reasons why, and what they must do to be beatifically rescued from the throes of this world. My Special one, if a person says that he lives hopefully and happily, it does not mean that there are no dark or questionable times. It means that his hopes overcome his doubts. This is the setting in which Christianity is positioned in a world that is mostly about faithlessness, violence and fear. It is said that perfect faith drives out fear, and in doing so, it conquers even the fear of living in fear. The new month of August 2018 has come upon you with this grand vision of courage. You are delightfully in love with God because you know what He has done for you. Jesus has given you among all things the faith to believe in Him. This is the product of His love, your ability to understand what sublime love is in a world that has so misconstrued its meaning. Yes, it is about sacrifice and penance; you have known this all along. And, it is about the capacity of humanity to change in the ways that I have described in past weeks. Today, however, I would like for you to remember that faith is about humanity's capacity to remain constant. Constant, but not rigid. Holding true to your faith is the basis of this constancy, a willingness to weather the storms of life beneath the shelter of the Cross, and the ability to sustain whatever might test everything you believe. Relativism and materialism, as I have said, are more about the human will succumbing to its own pride than about perfectly choosing unerring paths. This is likewise the origin of pluralism. I also spoke in past weeks about One Single Truth, a facet of human excellence, and the Divine Domain that cannot be debated away. This One Single Truth is the foundation of the constancy about which I am speaking. And, it is from this sense of loyalty to the constancy of God that you battled back against the girl who demanded with such pride that she be called a woman. She was trying to make relative your perception of humanity, and she was making an attempt to liberate herself from the ages-old lexicon by which those of her identity are known. You were in the presence of the original Old Eve who was trying to tempt you into abandoning your oath to the constancy of the Original Church of Christianity. One of Satan's minions had wandered into your presence, and she set her sights on you. So, I ask that you feel confident of your reaction, your position, and the way you processed the situation because it was a metaphor for what women are doing around the globe, especially in the United States.

    Constancy. It is your capacity to view humanity through its own ability to change into the likeness of Jesus Christ. While this seems like a contradiction, it is an effect of the elements of time and condition, emotion, preference, circumstance, and the truth of God simultaneously staring everyone in the face. From My viewpoint in Heaven, it is a unique and promising coalition of events that proves that the Holy Spirit is succeeding. And, My Special son, if you at a later time describe to someone what I am telling you today, it is important for you to remember that the underpinning of constancy is the truth, and the energy for the truth is the pious conscience. The truth conscience. This is the way you and your brother have lived since you were conceived in your mothers' wombs in 1953 and 1960. It is from this origin that you have found your own ability to remain intact through everything in life that has tried to shatter you in both spirit and consciousness. The truth conscience is what kept you from conceding to the girl who was proclaiming her independence from the childlike identity that Jesus calls for in the Gospel. Jesus saw the woman at the well as a girl because all the children of God must reflect the innocence of Jesus at His birth. 'Unless you become like little children...' does not mean that a girl must demand that she be referred to as a woman. The girl who wore the Armor of Sainthood in France never demanded that the world call her a woman. I realize that the whole matter may come down to terminology, but the principle behind it has many implications. It was not just a Man who overturned the tables in the temple, but a boy who was also a Man. Any sinner who demands aggrandizement for their simple identity is far from God, holding themselves up before the world as being someone greater than they are. Your own reaction to her about being a 57-year-old man and knowing exactly how to speak was suitable because you were simultaneously the boy in the temple. You sustained the proposition that you are a child of God, living within the Most Sacred Heart of the Man-God whose wisdom has become your sight. Yes, this is the constancy and conscience by which you live, and through which you and your brother are amending the world, just as you summoned a change in the heart of the self-possessed girl who confronted you. I have told you this because it is the sacred impression that all Creation will eventually have of you; it is the means by which the Church of Faith and the Glory of Heaven will celebrate what you have given to Me, My Son and the Father. This is your life of faith and trust. These are two more pillars on which the Morning Star Over America has been built. The faith and trust of two men in exile on Earth – not the balance of reality and presumption that the world might demand, but the faith and trust of two deferential, holy, beatific and charitable children of Mary who have capitalized the gift of human existence with the codex of conversion that exemplifies and complements the Divine Gospel of Salvation. This morning, therefore, I assure you that we are winning when it matters; not just that we are winning, but that we have already won. This is the reason I have called on you and your brother to live your hopefulness and happiness in a world that is doing its worst to put you down. It is all about good will and lifting people up; you and your brother are experts at this. It is an honor beyond all imagining that you and your brother have remained so close to Me. It is a gift to God, to Jesus and to Heaven that your faith remains so strong."

Saturday, August 11, 2018
9:30 a.m.

"Prayer and the weaponization of sanctity –
Human life isn't rainproof."

"Good morning, My beloved little children. It is an intense honor to be here before you and with you in prayer to God that He might change the hearts of humanity and heal the world. I have said that prayer is the ultimate weapon against evil. We have come together in prayer tens of thousands of times toward this end. I give you My assurance that each prayer is like a fiber sewn into the sanctity of the world so that it might be blanketed in the Father's grace. Humanity is exposed to the buffets of evil that attempt to take your souls away from God. It is as though My children represent a mighty army, not only in defense of the Church, but of each individual as well. I have said that human life is not rainproof. What does this mean? It is clear that the world endures its share of sorrows and setbacks, but it is also true that the flourishing graces that God offers enlighten His Church about the consistency of His Will. We have within us the power to touch Him in a way that He will, through Jesus, take Mercy on those who repent. There is no greater compassion either on Earth or in the Glory of Heaven than that which lives in the Sacred Heart of God's Son. My Special and Chosen ones, you live gloriously within this aura of grace because you have accorded the Father your hearts that are devoted in Him. Yes, you endure the monsoons and rainfalls of suffering and sacrifice in the way of Jesus. This makes you the chosen elect, even as you find yourselves still living in anonymity on Earth. The latter of these is your blessing. The Father, the Son and the Holy Spirit sustain your hearts and prayers as you proceed through the days and years toward the accordance of the Earth's final ages. I ask you to remember that your petitions rise to listening ears, and the tone of your holiness is welcomed by the Father in Heaven. My little sons, you live beatifically in a world of mundane seculars.

You engage your friends, peers, acquaintances, and even strangers on a level of piety that helps everyone fight for righteousness. If you think in terms of the transformation of the world into the image of its Savior and the likeness of Paradise, you will recognize your place in making the Father's wishes come true. I once said that a day is a window too small to reveal all the glory that God possesses. However, we know that Good Friday and Easter Sunday are exceptions. The purpose of life is to accept the Sacrifice of Jesus on the Cross, and consecrate the human soul to His Paschal Resurrection. If it is true that sanctity can be weaponized, it is for battling the indifference and evil works of those who do not believe in God. Holiness is an offensive and defensive weapon against the onslaught of evil. The impression that Christians are timid and fearful of forces that attack them is an errant perception. This does not mean that you should take battering rams against the neighborhood demons next door. It does mean, however, that you should not defer to their devious schemes that would dilute the audacity of your mission. Of all the wisdom that Christians share in common, it is the knowledge that evil will ultimately die. This, My Special son, is the foundation of Christian hope. And, on this foundation is built the spiritual courage to which the faithful aspire.

Today, therefore, I offer you and your brother My guided efforts in sharing with you the hope that even the Lord possesses. It is in Jesus that the nexus of hope and love finds its origin. While it is said that hope is a timely thing, it is also a timeless blessing that the Father has dispensed to the Church. This is the hope of the ages on behalf of humanity in exile, and of those who know that living in peace is the precursor to everlasting life. Jesus wishes you, My Special son, so much happiness that you can scarcely take it in. The happiness about which I speak is seeded in this hope. It is not happiness in a worldly sense, but an internal joy that the perpetual sanctity of the Church will be celebrated in this life and the next. It is not happiness based on who finishes first, which team bests another, or whose trophy is taller than someone else's. The entire framework of happiness is based on the possibility that humanity can comply with the Father's Will. Time cannot change this, My Special son. The darkness and evil of the world cannot de-weaponize the power of prayer or the perfection of love. Looking at and reviewing the mighty writings that you have composed in recent weeks proves that you have a perfect understanding of what I am saying. The Holy Spirit lifts you into the hands of the Father as though you are a weapon for Him to wield. Wherever He points the faith in your heart, your wisdom looks there. You have residing in you not just the potential to turn back the enemies of the Cross, but the means through your words and actions to defend everything the Cross represents. In effect, My Special son, you and your brother, and we together, are attempting to disrupt the conniving of men who would see the Church put asunder. I am speaking about the Gospel Church that cannot be annulled. It cannot be outlived. It cannot be reversed, and it cannot be silenced. My Special son, I speak of blessings and charities from the heart of God that are not handed down based on someone's good works alone. The Father would rather sustain the faith of His Church than allow succeeding generations to go on. It is all about the essence of a man to reach for his salvation with his arms of compassion open wide, despite the criticism hurled against him by those who do not believe. Faith. My Special son, when I speak of the essential mind, heart and soul of an exiled man, I speak of faith. It satisfies a hunger for supernatural wisdom that cannot come from a plate to a palate. It comes instead in the form of Bread and Wine, the Eucharistic Host from the Sacred Altars of the Roman Catholic Church. Yes, My Special son, faith is the reason that you and your brother are before Me now. Faith is the reason that your trust in God has always been strong. Faith is the reason that your love is so prolific for broken humanity among whom you live. These are the designs of the gifts of faith that prescribe the handiwork of your actions on Jesus' behalf. My messages throughout the centuries have hailed these blessings before men. I have invited and pleaded with My children to hear and comply with what I have said. I have never made a demand or issued an ultimatum that a lack of response will result in certain death. I have simply said that death is forthcoming nonetheless. Preparation for this momentous event is what My messages are all about. I have sought out humble seers in remote places and intercontinental cultures with whom to share My wishes. I have seen the suffering that has come upon them. It is the greatest facet of My certainty, seated within My Most Immaculate Heart, that the faith of these servants shall never fail. You and your brother are among those about whom I speak. Your faith, founded on your love for the Father, the Son, the Holy Spirit and Myself, is becoming the origin of the conversion of the American people. God has called upon two stately gentlemen with boyish charm and open hearts to enlighten and convert the most advanced democracy in the history of the world. Our work here has not only highlighted the failures and weaknesses of those who are prone to dismiss My intercession, it has become the framework around which those pesky naysayers will soon shape their lives. I realize that this may be difficult to envision in your day, but My promises to you and your brother have always come true. My Special son, the Holy Spirit will provide these signs and wonders. You are a charitable Christian for asking that signs be given. Please remember that to live peacefully implies that you need not take on every battle. Not every adverse word needs to be refuted, and new mornings will always give you the opportunity to be refreshed again."

Saturday, August 18, 2018
9:30 a.m.

"I've seen countless men stagger – not from drunkenness, but from the battles of this world. They poured out their lives in rhymes and ballads, built empires, and even rocketed themselves to the moon. But none of them, even as they aspired to the blessings of the ages, possessed the wisdom to fend off the devil in the way of Jesus Christ."

- Archbishop Fulton J. Sheen
1895-1979, [unpublished quotation]

"My beautiful little children, it is a tremendous blessing for the Church and the world that we are sharing our prayers again this morning. Yes, we pray for humanity in the Church around the world, that all men might come to know the Father through the Son in the way that you have lived your faith. My Immaculate Heart is filled with pity for those who do not understand the mandates of the Gospel because they are unaware of the prescription for their future. My Special son, I have shared with you this morning an unpublished quotation by the great Saint Archbishop Fulton Sheen so that you will realize that his mission and accomplishments are much larger than many people realize. I have seen in your thoughts that Saint Sheen was fifty years ahead of his time. O' that he would be here on the Earth today to rebuke the enemies of the Church, and reassure the faithful that their love for God is not misplaced. None of the opposition to the Roman Catholic Church should surprise you, My Special son. If the Bishops of the American Church would have made My supernatural appearances around the world the most notable blessing to your nation, there would be no such thing as a Church touched by scandal. I have brought My purity and wisdom to the United States decades ago from other shores with messages of prayer and repentance. I have told of My willingness to intercede before Jesus and God the Father for the needs of the most democratic nation on Earth. It is the Bishops, My Special son, who have left Me behind because of their collective hubris. Regardless of the defense of the Church that you just shared with your brother from the noted Catholic advocate, it cannot be sustained to lighten the offenses of the Church by comparing them to something worse. It is appropriate, however, to defend the Church against untruths, distortions, and outright lies by those who detest what the Church teaches. My dear Special son, you have correctly assumed that much of the grief in the hearts and on the faces of My Medjugorje visionaries is the manifestation of the attacks against the Church. It must be said that the American Bishops are responsible for the unfolding of these circumstances that I foretold to the Medjugorje visionaries in the early days. I spoke of a world filled with sinfulness and tears, of death and destruction, and of humanity's separation from the grace of God. There needed to be a great light, I told My Medjugorje seers, to overcome the world in the way of the Fatima Miracle. The greatest light ever to shine above western civilization is the Morning Star Over America. So, we set out to call on humanity to pray. We invoke the intervention of the Holy Spirit to shine the light of the Father into the world's darkest places. We ask God to shed this light on those who call out to Him. We ask the faithful to reflect this light into its own generation. Now, we summon the Holy Spirit to give strength and courage to those who do not relent in their support of the truth. My Special son, the entire discussion about Church scandal is a terrible distraction from its eternal mission. Yes, the Hierarchy is comprised of sinners who lead the Lord's flock in the direction that He would have them follow. They consecrate the bread and wine into the Most Blessed Sacrament – the Manna from Heaven – the Eucharistic Body of the King. This is the great miracle that supersedes any degree of doubt, and this is the sacred gift that the Bishops should be celebrating before the world. We have in our presence the Son of the Most High whom I bore onto the Earth for the expungement of every form of scandal. You and your brother realize that it is all about Jesus and His Eucharistic Communion. I have said that the Holy Spirit will light where there is peace, to sustain peace. You and I realize that it is an appropriated cause of the secular void to criticize and ridicule the Roman Catholic Church. I have spoken about their lack of legitimacy in doing so, and that they will be judged before the backdrop of eternal truth. They are not sanctioned by God or any holy voice to assume this false practice. When will the time come, some ask, when Jesus and Myself stop calling for prayer in favor of defensive action? This is the question that millions of Roman Catholics ask around the world. While Jesus and Myself will never stop seeking prayer, we are in the making of creating a response to the enemies of the Church and those who persecute the innocent who hold it dear. Just as sure as there are dozens of shrines dedicated to My Queenship around the globe, there will be an equal number of repudiations against those who persecute the Catholic Church. I invoke your trust to know that this will be done. The Father owns the benefit of handing defeat to those who hate Him. Other people ask why the Mother of Jesus speaks about what might happen, as opposed to when it should happen. It is enough to remind humanity that the gates of Hell will never prevail against the

Church. The Spirit of God is too truthful to allow it. His holy will is too prevalent to condone it. And, the Sacrifice of Jesus on the Cross is too powerful to concede to it.

My Special son, millions of Roman Catholics around the world are wondering where the American Church will go from here. What about the Church in Europe with its lack of continuity and empty pews? What can be said of the Church in South America where the appearance of scandal is causing its mission to be ignored? I say again, My Special son, it is all a distraction created by the sins of a few and the hatred of the many. As you and your brother pray here together with Me, I ask that you do not become frustrated or agonized by what you are seeing and hearing. I have spoken about constancy and courtesy to which your living hearts are devoted. It shall never be known that there was ever any bitterness in you. My Special son, it is visionary that you might wonder why ordinary men from all walks of life do not step forward in defense of the Church as it should always be offered. They are afraid of the revelation of new sins that could be revealed from amongst a body of over a billion Catholics. But, we are not afraid. We speak about a Church that is a beatific family. When you touch your knuckles to someone's front door, and they answer it, it is because the facility of your actions has raised their attention. This is the same principle as the Holy Spirit allowing individuals inside and outside the Church to communicate in practical ways. We refer to a spiritual Kingdom that is found everywhere except the depths of Gehenna. Hence, there is hope for change that I spoke about before. The entire conflict created by sinners inside the Church must be seen in the light of this eternity. Jesus came to call humanity to turn away from sin. He did not pronounce them as not being sinners. The Holy Gospel written about Him, and at His behest, is about purifying humanity so that sin no longer exists. This is the potential for the highest form of piety that a man could ever know. Given that it rarely happens, sins within the Church, attacks against it, and the publicized criticisms will go on. My Special son, I have completed My message for this morning. Do you have any issues to discuss with Me today? *"As I attempted to research the Church's position on when the soul is created, I wanted to know if the soul is created before being incarnated in the womb; and does the soul converse with God before being placed there?"* My Special son, the human soul in its entirety is as timeless as God, Himself. The communication about which you speak is the soul's connection to Divine Love that has no timely beginning, just as it will have no end. I realize that this gives you another dimension upon which to ponder. For example, where is the soul before the Father places it into its mother's womb? The answer is that the soul is where it should always be, in the Eternal Heart of God. Adam and Eve created the chasm that casts souls into exile. However, they have been redeemed, along with the souls about whom you speak. Does My response clarify your understanding? *"Yes. The soul has always existed in God, but was placed here due to the sin of Adam and Eve to be redeemed to its original place."* Yes, My Special son, God does not reach to another place for a human soul, separate from His presence, to conceive into its mother's womb. This would imply that there is a division in the Father's Kingdom and, of course, you know that this is untrue. How do you perceive what I have shared this morning to be different from the conclusions of the theologians? *"They do not seem to believe in a soul's existence before the incarnation of the human person in the womb."* Please tell them that the Mother of God says that they are being inconsistent. How can a gift of the human soul be perpetual if it somewhere had a beginning? Do you have any other issues to speak about today? *"No, thank you."* My Special son, even as you and your brother shall celebrate the Feast of My Queenship this week, I ask that you remember the great miracle of yourselves to God and His Creation. Never allow a dark thought to enter your heart about your standing before Jesus. Remember your brilliance and piety, your honor and faith, your trust and good will. Stand tall in the light that is shining upon you. Rest peacefully with the knowledge that your lives have been for the good. And, never surrender your happiness to any wound, callous or negative word."

Saturday, August 25, 2018
No message this week.

Sunday, September 2, 2018
9:45 a.m.

"All Creation echoes His name –
This is the poetry of virtue in the Christian soul."

"My dear beautiful children, please always remember that Jesus on the Cross is the only source of redemptive mercy. And you, My beautiful sons, are truly suffering for the good of this cause. I come speaking with you today as your Lady of Grace because I wish for you to have peace in your hearts. I desire that you understand with the fullness of wisdom that you are perfectly united with God the Father through His Son, the Holy Spirit and Myself as your Mother. I ask that you remember the courage of your faith as the poetry of your virtue. You have encapsulated in your thoughts and hearts the meaning of sacrifice on humanity's behalf. My Special son, you have in your lifetime never seen such aggressive attacks against the Roman Catholic Church and its converting mission. The Church will be sustained by Jesus through these difficult days. You and your brother have also witnessed relentless attacks against My Marian messengers. The world must remember that the devil is not capable of redemptive mercy. Jesus is the origin of your strength and prayer. Yes, My seers and visionaries are agonizing like My Son in the Garden, and carrying their crosses that God has asked them to bear. While I wish not that you live in fear, you must realize that you and your brother are under equal assault. There is danger everywhere. My Special son, I have spoken about the poetry of virtue inside the human heart. This is the virtue that pushes back against the devilish attacks being launched against the Church. The Church is undergoing lies, misjudgments, mischaracterizations, and unappealing commentary about its stature and stamina. Christians like you and your brother are the living reasons why the Church will prevail. You must think, pray, and act in ways that seem inordinate to other Christians. This is what your lives have been about for the past twenty-seven years. These years have proved that you do not question the motivations of God. Your viability in grace is asking that Jesus might have mercy on those for whom you pray.

Here, My Special one, I would like for you to render your comments about the recent attacks against the Church. *"People are functioning in the realms of fanaticism and refusing to maintain perspective and equal analysis of the overall composition of society in our modern day. The Church is being scapegoated for the failures of a secular society."* Yes, My Special son, and it is not that some Church leaders have not failed, but the magnitude of these failures is being judged out of proportion. Imagine for yourself and relate to Me what you would say in November to the Conference of Catholic Bishops. *"I would present my words as you have taught me to speak. I would lift up their hearts and tell them that Divine Mercy will not be allowed to fail in the world. I would remind them that you have been trying to help them, but they have yet to collectively summon the courage or the vision to realize the times we are in, and who is their refuge."* These are profoundly relevant sentiments, My Special son. And, you just days ago read another response from your Bishop about the moral crisis within the Church. While his testimony is holy and admirable, those who are reading his response are wondering how fasting and running will produce practical solutions to this issue. I am not criticizing your Bishop for saying that prayer and fasting are appropriate for refining the hearts of humanity, I am telling you that parishioners of the Catholic Church across the United States are asking what actions will be taken by the Hierarchy to eradicate this problem. This is what American Catholics nationwide are wishing to know. My Special son, you have accurately cited same-sex attraction as being the core of the matter. You have also correctly said that the Church would seem filled with hatred to address the problem by ostracizing those who suffer from same-sex attraction. So, My request of all members of the Church is to ask what response is appropriate for this crisis. May I have your comments please?

"The perspective of the Church and society itself must be replaced by something larger and more consequential to our lives. We are hopelessly attached to a cudgel, no matter what the Church does, until it is superseded." It is here that I wish you to communicate an advisory to your local Bishop that he might share with his peers in November. You may speak about taking on the opponents of the Church with the weapons handed to the Church by Jesus on the Cross and upon His Paschal Resurrection. It must be about producing the graceful effects of human conversion, both now and in the times to come. My long-standing messages to you and your brother are extraordinary. It is why so many sacrifices have been made by those to whom I have come. It is not just a sign of wherewithal to continue this struggle, but the rhyming sanctity of the virtue in the human heart that lasts beyond the ages. Humanity and the Holy Spirit are unified through the Will of God. The juncture about which I speak is that men will comply with God's request to manifest on Earth the bounty of His Kingdom. My Special one, I hope that you and your brother realize that I do not speak about matters of the Church from a position of weakness. Just as Jesus had the power to decline to be crucified, the Church has the power to sustain with grace the attacks being leveled against it. Why? Because only the Church stands on the foundation of truth. Only the Church propagates this way of life that leads to peace, purity, and redemption. This is the message that I wished to share with you and your brother today. O' how I hope you have enjoyed it. *"How do I know what to put in the advisory that will matter?"* Your advisory must be clearly centered on your knowledge of what Jesus would do in these times. And, it surely must include the message that you believe I would relate if I appeared to all the American Bishops during their gathering in November. I will help you in its composition."

United States Conference of Catholic Bishops
Advisory Statement

Dear Prelates of the Roman Catholic Church in America,

We address you in humility, reverence and in the Name of the Most Immaculate Virgin Mary who is poised to intercede for you in these heart-wrenching times.

> *Who would believe what we have heard?*
> *To whom has the arm of the LORD been revealed?*
>
> *He grew up like a sapling before him,*
> *like a shoot from the parched earth;*
> *He had no majestic bearing to catch our eye,*
> *no beauty to draw us to him.*
>
> *He was spurned and avoided by men,*
> *a man of suffering, knowing pain,*
> *Like one from whom you turn your face,*
> *spurned, and we held him in no esteem.*
> *- Isaiah 53:1-3*

Yes, what we have heard amidst Her beauty, we declare to you. The Queen of the Church loves you. May we repeat—the Queen of the Church loves you. Her devotion to you is unwavering during the present troubles being inflicted upon you by both the wolves and the world. She has great empathy for your discomforts, yet She asks that you remember well that you have yet to truly suffer for the propagation of the Gospel of Jesus Christ. Our Immaculate Mother asks you to recall that Jesus was rejected by everyone, while some believe they should be rejected by no one. Posturing is not conviction. Compromise is not courage. Devotion sings of sacrifice and resolve. And, Truth still resounds from the housetops of old, from hovels to hamlets and villages to your great cities. Everywhere you look, the Truth reflects like a beacon off of corruption, impurity, division and human misery.

Do not be tempted to dismiss these words as merely pious platitudes. Your Heavenly Mother speaks to you thus.

The secular void demands much but contributes nothing. Be not tempted to concede to its demands of the flesh, remembering that your Lord simply asked whether the rest were going to leave Him too. You are to be reminded that Divine

Mercy will not fail in the face of calls for condemnation and retribution; and that purity and truth must be allowed to rightfully assume their reign to the exclusion of all opposed.

Our Lady recognizes that among you are the few, the unfortunate few, the misguided few, who have conceded the stature of your holiness and the integrity of the Church to the impurity where lost sinners revel. She would have you know that the Sacrament of Reconciliation stands waiting for your return to unity with the wisdom you are asked to defend in the image of your Savior.

The Church has been affixed to the Cross, no matter which administrative path you take, no matter how heroically you sacrifice, nor what you surrender to the secular realms. You are bound to their condemnation until their retribution is superseded by something larger, something more consequential and glorious, something that leaves them in awe and speechless in tears. Again, the Queen of Heaven stands poised to intercede for you.

She has extended Her miraculous intercession repeatedly to help you, but you have yet to collectively summon the courage or the vision to realize the times you are in and who is your Refuge. Orthodox rhetoric does not validate one's consecration to Her Immaculate Heart.

Jesus would tell you that His sinless Mother is not a stumbling block to any ecumenism that matters. Unity at the expense of morality and truth cannot withstand the test of virtue.

Your Heavenly Mother wishes to relate that when She looks upon your episcopal gatherings, when She looks into your eyes, She sees power, sacrifice, devotion and honor, perhaps dormant, but present nonetheless. She sees through the ages to Her beloved Peter, brilliant and bold, standing and addressing the crowds on Pentecost from whose words conversion was loosed. When She looks into your faces, She sees this Vicar whom Jesus knew would die for Him with conviction still alive in his final breath. In you, She sees that faithful group of original shepherds who loved Her so, who quieted themselves so as to hang on Her every word. In you, She sees the resolute heroism that will bring humanity to Her side where Jesus wishes to find His children. In you, She sees the True Faith vibrant and alive, ready to be wielded against anything that would obscure redemption in the Resurrected Christ.

In our efforts to engage the spirit of this age, might we together consider possible actions that may accompany our devotion to the Truth.

First and foremost, might you manifest and elevate the Sacrament of Reconciliation with a public reception of this Sacrament by every American prelate, openly and visibly to the world? Not a public penance service, but lines of prelates preparing to be the next to kneel and offer his confession, not to each other, but to the humblest of priests.

Secondly, might you request publicly the resignation of any cleric or religious who does not have the intention of honoring their vows of celibacy? Then, let the Holy Spirit help them to decide.

Third, might you never again allow any man or woman that condones, embraces or practices a sexuality that is in violation of the Language of Creation to be admitted to the reception of religious or Holy Orders?

Fourth, might you summon yourselves and all the faithful to respond to the gift of Our Lady's miraculous intercession as the superseding principle of these times?

Dear Prelates, Christian civilization is failing and the world is falling into the darkness of the ages. Our Heavenly Mother says that it is your faith that must meet the challenge of the night. Know true that She is the Morning Star over this land, appearing proudly and prominently as the sparkling jewel in the heavens who will enlighten, guide, comfort and convert. This Holy Matriarch is beautiful, stunning, magnificent and unafraid. She asks that you accompany Her into the world through the conduit of your faith. Let Her immaculate motherhood resound from your pulpits, one and all. Recognize and respect Her miraculous efforts. Let America see that you love Her and obey Her. Challenge your own faith to greater heights. Witness to your belief in Her. Call to the corners of the globe for everyone to look up and upon Her succoring Queenship manifested in these times. We repeat, the Queen of the Church loves you and is poised to intercede for you. Then, She will supersede this troubled age in Her Triumph, making intentional disciples of us all; and the Roman Catholic Church will be found standing proudly once again alongside the Savior in all His Glory.

All praise, honor and glory to Christ the King through the Mother who proclaimed,
"May it be done unto Me!"

Asking your episcopal blessing, we remain loyal —
William L. Roth Jr.
Timothy Parsons-Heather

Saturday, September 8, 2018
Nativity of the Blessed Virgin Mary
9:46 a.m.

"Pray for all things benign."

"My holy little children, it is My hope that you do not consider these days to be among the most corrupt and dark as those in times past. Imagine living through an age where the Vatican itself was in danger of being sieged and destroyed by enemy forces, as was the case in the 1940s. What would it be like to not know which Pope to declare one's allegiance at a particular point in time. Yes, these are perilous years for humanity and the Church, but they are not threats to the mission of the Gospel. There is no such thing as destroying the Gospel of My Son. Therefore, I have come to pray with you today for all things benign, and that you would join Me in asking the Father to bless all who are loyal to Him, that they might alleviate their fears and moderate their concerns that the world is under oppression. My purpose this morning is not to misrepresent the lack of holiness around the globe. Surely everything I have said and you have written about the chasm between the world and the perfect new world is true and real. Mortal sin is still engulfing the societies of the Earth. This, My little children, is why we pray with such devotion for the propagation of the Gospel in your time. My Special son, you have authored a good and worthy letter to your Bishop about the status of the Church that he might share with his fellow Prelates. It is clear that your heart is filled with spiritual vision because you have encapsulated the way the Father views them in their clerical roles. You have underlined the foundation of My honor given to them as they live out their episcopal lives. Notice that you did not write in your advisory anything that would suggest the undermining or destruction of the Roman Catholic Church. Hence, you inherently realize that while these times are agonizing, they do not carry the threat of the destruction of the Faith. Nothing can destroy the spiritual realms of the Church from which it has been given. Nothing on Earth can remove the Cross from the annals of history. The shedding of Jesus' Blood cannot be reversed, just as surely as a river cannot run uphill. The redemption of the penitent will never be in doubt as long as the Earth shall last. Hence, when I say that we pray for all things benign, we ask God through the Holy Spirit to proceed with the plan that He has coursed for humanity. The salvation of the human soul is on course. What prayers we might add to this great benediction will surely serve to annihilate the enemies of His disciples. My Special son, the Father implemented the redemption of the world while including in its framework the prayers of the faithful. God did not establish the salvation of humanity lacking humanity's knowledge and participation. Through Jesus, God will save any human soul, but the human soul must agree. There must be a communion and reconciliation between the Father and a man for this deliverance to take place. Here, My Special son, I am not telling you anything that you do not already know. Indeed, you have known for the whole of your years. I could celebrate the refrains of the Gospel in a thousand tongues published in repetitive reams, and My words would still resound anew with every syllable. I know that you and your brother have dedicated your lives to this rhythm in the way of the other great servants of Jesus' Holy Kingdom. You recognize the stark differences between the secular void and the new world as it will be known. This tends to create an inner-conflict in those who have handed their lives to Jesus. However, this conflict need not be one that destroys a Christian's peace or brings darkness where there is eternal light. It is not appropriate for a Christian to see the world the way it is, and believe that it will never change. It has taken untold lifetimes for the Church to have arrived in the century in which you live. Every word and every verse of the Holy Gospel is as true and relevant today as in the beginning. Believers have knelt to pray to the same God who deigned that there should be a Creation in which they have lived. All to which good men aspire, all that is holy and benign is still living in the hearts of humanity, as I say, just as it was in the beginning. My Special son, imagine what it would be like if all seven billion people on Earth could have their collective attention drawn in a contemplative way to the Cross on Mount Calvary. I have alluded before that if this were done, Jesus would drop the veil between Heaven and Earth and engulf humanity in Glory. The world is not too large for this to happen. It is not beyond the power of God. However, the spiritual posture of humanity must be aligned with the Will of its Maker. When we pray for all things benign, the image of all sinners simultaneously focusing on the Cross is the most unique of all. To say that everyone must be one in Jesus is to declare that the unity about which I speak must come. It is to the destruction of the devil's work; it is to the denial of temptation. Yes, it is to the glory of the Kingdom of the Messiah that human oneness be achieved in His name. My Special son, when men pray to God, they often write their intentions on a page or speak them in song, or etch them in sand, snowdrifts, or layers of soil on the ground. The medium for these things is all the same. It is about the transfer of meaning from the lives of humanity into the bountiful Heart of God. And, this same humanity often sees signs and wonders that their prayers have been answered. It is true that God does not reserve His best responses for those who seem most deserving. He answers the prayers of all who approach Him, even the dishonorable, if their prayers are from the heart and propagate the majesty of His Kingdom. This is a certainty, and a promise that cannot be annulled.

My Special and Chosen sons, I ask you again today to not become disheartened by what you see other people do because their reluctance to be holy cannot be permanent. When Jesus endured the Agony in the Garden, He thought of all the hopes and dreams of His Apostles and disciples that would be realized through what He was about to do. This great Sacrifice would be the source of graces for billions of souls who would believe in Him for ages to come. This is the consolation that He gathered on that dark night of wonder. We must remember that nothing that Christians suffer is lost in the turning of the tides. My Special son, I once told you and your brother that the days are like numbers, and that you do not know where you are in them. While this is still true, you have fortified your understanding of your own position in time so that all your days are blessed with the momentum of grace about which I speak. There may seem around you certain people both inside and outside the Church who have different definitions of what benignness is. There is an ongoing great debate about which human conduct is or is not acceptable to the Father in Heaven. Let the Gospel teach them. Let the purity of the Messianic King be their wisdom. Let them be the example that Jesus has provided by His ministry, Sacrifice, and Resurrection. And yes, I am just now being reminded by the Archangel Gabriel that they should see Me as their example too. Tell them, Gabriel just said. I wish for you and your brother to endure your sacrifices and sufferings with the knowledge that your lives are deposited in the Cup of the New Covenant during the Holy Sacrifice of the Mass. No omissions or mistakes by other broken people can reverse the unity you have found in Me. No tawdry riddles can dismiss the purity that you have inherited by your consecration to My Most Immaculate Heart. No amount of time can render obsolete the newness that you shall always have in Jesus' most favorable blessings. This, My Special son, is the heart of My message for you and your brother today. Thank you again for writing your advisory to your Bishop for transfer to his colleagues. You may reflect upon and revise it as you will, but it is timelessly perfect as you have written it. I will always pray for you and your brother as My distinguished children who live in a world that you, yourselves, are shaping into the image of the Cross. It is clear that you and your brother have more strength than you realize. Only as your faith has been tested that you have learned this. Let us pray among all benign things that your brothers and sisters will join you in this cause."

Sunday, September 16, 2018
9:40 a.m.

"Manifesting a pattern of peacefulness."

"My beautiful little children, I have come to you this morning to celebrate the heroic holiness by which you are living. As you examine the conditions of the world in these modern times, it has never been more clear that the battle between righteousness and secularism rages on. This is why we proceed in our prayers for the faithful and the expansion of the Gospel message around the globe. Humanity in the west is living at a dizzying pace, it would seem. With all the diversions and distractions obscuring men's faith, Americans everywhere are refusing to take time for God. My little sons, we are asking for Jesus' intercession and intervention to reestablish the connection between God and man. We are praying to manifest a pattern of peacefulness that will overcome the staggering impiety of secular men. There is no question that the fate of many rests in the hands of those who are far from the Father. I ask My children to vest themselves in holiness for the difficult times ahead. It is much better to wrap oneself in holiness now than to quickly strive for it when true suffering comes. Understanding God entails the complete awareness of the self in one's relationship with Him. While it is known that people are unaware of their own reactions to life's issues until they eventually come, such is the case as to how someone might respond to the inexorable call of God. Humanity in the world aggravates suffering, and God utilizes this suffering as a pathway back to Him. So, My dear sons, what does manifesting a pattern of peacefulness mean? It suggests that you should not internalize the actions of other men over which you have no control, especially the leaders of the Church. You have recently been exposed to news of priestly conduct that is not only unsightly in the annals of the world, but detestable in the eyes of God. Concealing corrupt behavior, prostitution on behalf of the clergy, priestly alcohol and drug abuse, exposure to pornography, and the rejection of the Sacraments that priests are assigned to administer – all these are among the acts over which those who commit them have control. All sin is an act of the human will. People can choose not to sin. Having said these things to you, it must be more obvious to you now where the devil focuses his attention in weakening the resolve and effective message of the Roman Catholic Church. There is always the question whether salvation in Christ Jesus is a single act of conversion, or if salvation involves additional manifestations of sanctification. My Special son, which of these do you believe that the Church teaches? "*I believe it involves the manifestation of sanctification after the acceptance of Jesus as the Savior of the world.*" And, it would seem that the sanctifying process is precisely the presence of conversion. There are volumes written about whether salvation can occur at the point of conversion because of those who accept the Blood of Jesus on their deathbed. Here, what would be the appropriate time for the sanctification about which I have spoken? "*I suppose through their final suffering.*" Yes, and the exposure to every Saint's life, every sanctifying gift, every message that I have given through the ages, and one's unification with Jesus' Passion and Crucifixion. It is throughout one's life for sure that sanctification occurs. However, this same sanctification can come at the moment of baptism. There will be debates about this subject for generations to come, should Jesus not return by then. I have simply broached the topic today so that you and your brother will remember that your lives are gifts to those who are not only now being sanctified, but to those who are at this moment preparing to see the Glorious Face of God. What you have rendered to humanity is a blessing far too majestic to describe. It is in the love that you and your brother have shared for Jesus and Me that this gift has come into being. Your faith has rung a bell of holiness that will ring long into eternity for the Saints to hear. Your gracious obedience to My call as your Mother has fashioned the response of millions to the summons of Mount Calvary. Now, it is your duty to join Me in praying for those who refuse to listen, who refuse to hear. My Special and Chosen sons, you are witnessing during the present months the terrible effects that the battles of the Earth are having on good people everywhere. Your personal health is being adversely affected by your struggles to keep up with the world. There comes a time, My Special son, when people like yourself must decide if the continuing decline of your health and well-being is the appropriate course. In other words, you must begin to recognize that there has been a planned process by the evil one of burdening and breaking your heart through those you encounter in the secular void. My Special son, do you understand what I am saying? "*Yes, thank you.*" You and I and your brother have the unified purpose of converting lost sinners to the Cross of Jesus for their redemption beyond the ages. I do not believe that this mission has caused the same type of intense suffering that the secular void has heaped upon you. It is as though Jesus is calling you and your brother anew, away from your fishing boats, and asking you through the First Apostles to become fishers of men. Time will not be divided by what I have told you today, but I pray that your perception of life will be assisted, that your hearts will be healed, and that the manifesting of a pattern of peacefulness will result from meditating upon what I have said. It is all because I love you more than any language can describe. It is that I see in you the glory that brought Jesus through the Crucifixion and outside the tomb. It is for all the sacrifices that Christians have made throughout the ages that I am calling you to remember this peace. My Special son, your brother asked you yesterday to take seriously his heartfelt commendation about the way you live, about your advancement of goodness and propriety, about your righteous work ethic, and your sense of honor, duty, and fairness. These attributes help you shine in a world of darkness and depression. They define you, and set you apart from billions of others. I am telling you that Jesus desires for you to acknowledge the beatific image of Himself that you are presenting to the world. Self-dignity and self-preservation are the two primary components of this image. Why? Because Jesus took upon Himself the indignity and brokenness that the world would otherwise have you bear.

It must be also clear that the letter that you are about to present to your Bishop is another gift from your beatific heart. It is excelling, visionary, and prolifically sound. Do you have any other issues to remark about your advisory to the Bishops? *"No, thank you. I simply hope it will encourage them to give you a chance."* There is no question that this is all the Holy Spirit is asking. My Special son, you and your brother are aware that the Bishops have wrapped their lack of response within the framework of prudent discretion. It is obvious that they cannot dismiss it this way. I have asked you to share the glory of God with the masses during your years of holy service. You and your brother have done so. You have come to your feet with the message of power. You have called the nations to recognize the Spirit of the Gospel in Me. You have wielded the wisdom of holiness in such a way that draws all men to the Cross. You have preached the Father's life-giving absolution to all who will hear. My Special son, there has never been a moment in your life when you did not know about these things in you. You have paused along the way to bless your brothers and sisters with the meaningfulness of your soul. Like Saint Paul, you have spoken with confidence and vision to proclaim your place in Jesus' Kingdom. While these great blessings have come naturally to you, they are exceedingly rare in the history of the world. Thank you for your willingness to share the seed of the Holy Spirit within you with the whole of Creation. Bless you for being responsive to the call of your Mother. I know that I speak in terms that you understand, so it is for My own joy and to the Father who is listening that I am saying these things. Thank you for praying together with Me, and sustaining what must be done to give Jesus the hearts of humanity."

Sunday, September 23, 2018
Feast of Saint Pio of Pietrelcina
9:41 a.m.

Christianity is the basis for acutely focused reason.
Divine Truth is the currency of all prophetic faith.
Repentance is the birthplace of sanctifying grace.
So, may the designs of God be your cause for living.
May the Holy Spirit inundate your hearts with peace.

"*Pray from the heart, and the Lord will carve a refreshment into your souls to soothe the Earth's aching, to surpass every other beatific masterpiece, to restore to humanity the dignity that died in the wreck of Adam's error.*"

- The Dominion Angels

How Jesus deals with brazen, flagrant impiety –
Do they really not know what they are doing?

"Good morning, My lovely and holy little sons. With overwhelming joy, I make it My purpose to enrich your lives with My presence once again. We pray today for the continuance of the Lord's grace to nourish the hearts and souls of those who love Him. There remains the question now after twenty centuries of wisdom and blessings being dispensed upon the Earth whether sinful men really do not know what they are doing. It must surely be true that those who are far from God cannot depend on this excuse any more. My Special and Chosen ones, your advisory statement to your Bishop has been received. Please be assured that your nation of Bishops would profit from your holiness. Today, I also make it My purpose to remind you that Jesus and the Hosts of Heaven stand with tremendous affection for your servitude here in His earthly Kingdom. You have many ways of knowing that you are blessed because you can look at your own lives, the fruits of your labors, the changing of the spiritual seasons in the climate of God, and the certitude in your hearts that everything you have done for the Father will be celebrated in eternity. Praying and devoting yourselves to My Most Immaculate Heart has been your most prosperous work. I once said that one of the greatest gifts given to humanity in exile is the capacity to change. You and your brother, My Special son, are not only fostering this change, you are forcing it into being by the proficiency of your prayers. To say that a wild bull might enter a china shop would be comparing it mildly to the enlightenment you have gifted to the unwary and indifferent world of men. There seems to be a position that the examination of the Church must become the nature of its relationship with the secular void. While we know that this is only a distraction, the world must remember that these days also count toward the coming in glory of the King of the Church. In other words, a self-examination of the redemption of humanity is not like pausing the movement of a vehicle and checking the engine. No time in the march toward the conclusion of the ages is being lost. The sanctification and conversion of exiled men has not been placed into stasis. All the criticism that is being launched against the Church is an utter waste of time. My Special and Chosen sons, you are not surprised to learn that the writings of the Saints about the perfection of Jesus' Church remains intact. It is not perfect because its members are perfect, but because its Messianic Head is the perfect image of God the Father. It is not what humanity wills, but what the Father deigns to be the future of the Church He has founded. Everyone who is aware that God is in Heaven knows the nature of that future. The Holy Spirit at Pentecost gave every man the ability to turn to his brothers and sisters and say, 'I am going to Heaven, are you coming with me?' This is the essential architecture of the Christian consciousness. To understand this process is to realize that the change about which I speak must come. It is not just about who feels inspired to enter the religious life, it is about those who do so faithfully, and uphold their vows until they breathe their last. My Special son, when you hear stories about priests leaving the vocation without apparent reason or provocation, it is because their priestly mission has reached its pinnacle here in this life. It is not unlike Jesus taking their photograph of their greatest moment in service to the Cross, and sending them on their way. All in all, there is a priest or nun in everyone. There is truth, greatness, and eloquence on every tongue. These things are sought out by God to manifest His Kingdom on Earth through the servants He has chosen. There is no such thing as the priestly mark on a human soul being removed. At the same time, all who claim to be Christian bear a replica of the sacred priesthood on their souls by virtue of their summons to evangelize the nations.

It is today that I ask you and your brother to underscore in your prayers and meditations the consolation that all who believe in God give to Him. I speak of the sacred nature of the Christian heart that comes through the invocation of the Holy Spirit. We have said that the fruits of this invocation are not always visible to the human eye. This is because the heart sees better than the visual gaze. One can sense mystical feelings with spiritual sight. The human consciousness can be measured by the depths of this faith. All nature and natural things defer to the power of this true belief. It is the origin of the desire for prayer, and the satisfaction of those needs that prayer suffices. If this is the essence of the circle of life, then those who pray must realize that they are meeting themselves in the Sacred Heart of Jesus every time they pronounce His name. Those who truly wish to go to Heaven awaken in the morning and ask the question, 'Jesus, have you found me yet?' The response from Heaven will always be yielded by the fruits of those days and the measure of suffering that Jesus asks His disciples to bear. If it be tears or laughter, if the darkness should come at midday, if the rains might fall where the floods are still ravishing, if voices shriek of fear and devastation, these things are the clear reminders that the labor pains of birthing His Kingdom are present in your time. However, it also means that the newborn world will rest in His Sacred Arms as a child in the bosom of its father. The Lord will neither forsake nor abandon His people. He will not cast away those who aspire to be the likeness of His Son. He will dry their tears. He will grant the fruits of Christian hope. He will brighten the skies at high noon. He will cause the sun to shine at the midnight hour. And, He will alleviate the fear and devastation that keep so many sinners wondering where He has gone. The confidence of the Christian spirit is found in the knowledge that God is preeminently everywhere. This, My Special son, whether you realize it or not, is one of the greatest gifts inherent in your advisory to the Catholic Bishops. It all comes down to perception. Bishops are prone to examine their episcopate through the eyes of their younger selves. They see their lives in the circle that I mentioned moments ago. They wonder from the standpoint of their youth what decisions they might make today because they were laymen back then. It is conversely this same faculty that causes them to stumble. The ideal process of determination and discernment must come from the coalescence of their youthful innocence and the wisdom and service they have inherited in their apostleships. None of them have succeeded without the holy counsel of people like you and your brother. And, nary a single Bishop has led a soul to the gate of Paradise without My intercession.

Bishops have rarely become martyrs. The foot-soldiers on whom they depend to defend the dignity of the Church have always been those who have been most devoted to Me. My purpose in coming to you and your brother more than twenty-seven years ago was not for you to change the attitude of any wayward or lukewarm leaders of the Church, but to convince them that this change must come of their own accord. It may not surprise you to know how envious many ecclesial leaders have been throughout the ages to learn that the Mother of their God would come to anonymous people and paupers before

She would grace their presence with messages to them instead. This is why they have such difficulty accepting My intercession as being integral to their mission of converting the world. I speak in general terms about My intercession to specific people around the globe. You and your brother have known that I guide My work through those whose lives are not dominated by the responsibilities of people like Bishops and other clergy. The great stigmatist Saint Padre Pio is an exception because the Father willed that he be an exemplar for those serving in the priesthood. Your connection with Saint Pio has been obvious, considering the date of your birth. Your sacred promise to God has been the same. The miracle of your life has been no lesser. The gifts of your labors have been as flourishing. The awareness of your heart of the intentions of Jesus have been as intense. So, where does God turn? This has been His question of humanity every morning as well. My Special son, I offer you and your brother My gratitude for receiving Me here. It is clear to you that those who commit themselves to error truly now know what they are doing. This is the basis for God's judgment. It forges the legitimacy of the Father's power to decide the fate of lost sinners into the gift of Jesus on the Cross. Once He laid down His life on Good Friday, everyone in the world that day and the centuries thereafter discovered deep within themselves what they were doing in the wake of His Sacrifice. Please remember that I am with you always, that My Immaculate Heart enfolds you, that the grace of My wisdom becomes you, and that the peace and guidance of the Holy Spirit is your comfort. Remember that I came to you so long ago because I love you, and I have remained with you through the distance of your life."

Sunday, September 30, 2018
9:48 a.m.

"The term 'enigmatic,' meaning vague or
obscure, does not apply to the Gospel of the Lord."

"They will find us here, My little sons, praying together for the eradication of evil and the transformation of the world into the likeness of Heaven. Anyone who comes seeking, all who wish to find the scent and presence of the Lord's Spirit will reach Him through us. Thank you for joining in the prayers that procure the purification of the nations and the speeding up of the arrival of the Lord's Kingdom in your land. I have said at the opening of My message this morning that there is nothing hidden about the Gospel, nothing enigmatic, nothing vague or obscure. This means that faith is a reasonable path for accessing everything a man should wish to know in this world about the next. Jesus came among you to reveal Himself as the Messianic Son, a Savior without end, to offer the world a Kingdom without stress or evil, perfectly free from error and transgression, and liberated from the temptations that drive faithless men to commit mortal sin. My Special son, we realize that the New Covenant is no more complicated than this. There is nothing enigmatic about it because the mandates laid out by the Father through the Son are clear. The fulfilment of the Ancient Scriptures are present in Jesus. It is through our prayers that we help those who do not understand that they own a part in this. God provides a seed of faith for everyone to sow in the richness of His love. What humanity does with this seed is according to their degree of faith. This is the seed of life that possesses texture and form, aroma and wisdom. What we believe to be happening in the world today is that the devil is exhuming this seed from the hearts of men before it has an opportunity to take root. My Special son, I wish for you and your brother to have the full understanding that everything you have drafted, published, and prayed into being will be seen by the eyes of all who can fathom the grace of the Lord's Kingdom here in this place. I would wish that you reread the statement I just made when poring over My message from today in the future. I have said that your innocence, your devotion and dedication, your piety and sacrifices have been the reason that I will succeed in this twenty-first century, touching who must be reached to advance the mission of the Church and the cultivation of the Lord's vineyard over time. I have always prayed that you and your brother would not believe that I am being effusive with My comments to you about your lives in Jesus. Think about what you have done. Place your hearts and consciousness into those of the people who in the future will read everything that you have committed to the page. I hear you on occasion speaking about the Mother of God being charitable in praise of your lives. Thank you for recognizing that My love for you is sincere, that My reflections about your goodness are true, and that My promises of your standing before My Son will last long beyond the ages. It is more than a prayer to live out the purpose of your petitions. It is actualizing what you believe the Earth should become in a world of wicked men. Seventeen years ago, you published a narrative about the evil ways of the American media. Nothing has been accomplished by them to mitigate what you wrote in that piece. In fact, their conduct has only gotten worse. This indicates your visionary focus about the status of the lines of communication in the United States, and who has the power to shape them. I wish for you and your brother to not become involved in the analysis of this phenomenon because the media are manipulated by blind individuals who have themselves orphaned their souls from the outstretched hand of God. They have cut themselves off by their hubris. They have laid their heads beneath the rolling boulders of hatred. They have denied the teachings of the Church for fame, wealth, influence and outright demonic pride. It would seem, My Special son, that I should come among you to celebrate the great light that shines throughout the world from the Father's Throne on High. It is without doubt the promise of the future world. It is the origin of the Messianic Covenant to which all men must aspire. And, it is offered, available, and attainable by anyone hoping to inherit the blessing of eternal life. It is the acts of sinful men who believe that the Gospel is enigmatic. The Father is revealing a mammoth waterfall of truth and enlightenment, but humanity would rather focus their attention on a puddle of water in the bottom of a well.

My Special son, imagine a child being carried onto a 20th floor balcony of a city skyscraper. He looks across the landscape and sees hundreds of skyscrapers all around. He cannot see the ground below. Would it not be reasonable for this child to assume that these sky-bound buildings are infinitely high, and none of them placed on foundations on the ground? *"Yes."* This is the illusion that sinful men have about the infinity of their influence in this world. They do not realize that their lives are stationed on a foundation placed there by God in the beginning. He will decide in time to remove this foundation upon the Return of Jesus in Glory. All the skyscrapers will fall from the bottom. They will collapse into the hands of the Father, and be submitted to His judgment about the way they have lived. Truly, the conclusion of the Earth need not be this way. The ground should be sufficient height for men to walk through their lives in the presence of Jesus. They have constructed a false premise to elevate themselves as though one might publish his autobiography and declare himself the best of all men. I have said that I will not pity those who will perish in this grand realization imposed upon the Earth by God at the end of time. It is not that I do not love them, but that they refuse My overtures en mass the same way many religious leaders decline to accept their responsibilities in advancing the faith of the Apostles. It is all elementary, My Special son, but it is complicated through the guise and manipulation of people who believe that their legacy must involve their elevation before the world. There will come a time when radical progressive clergy, even before they shall die, will wish that they had never walked into a seminary to be accorded the honor of a Roman collar. I say these things not that you will have disdainful thoughts about what they have become, but that you understand the true gift of the historical sanctity of the Church. You and your brother are filled with fairness and justice, and I know that you will pray these priests into Heaven. My Special son, I herald your goodness across the nations and ages because I wish the world to become the likeness of your love. "*Thank you, Mama.*"

Saturday, October 6, 2018
2:00 p.m.

"Saint Nikita Vangelis"

"My dear little sons, it is impossible for someone to claim to believe in God, and yet support the scourge of abortion. My Special son, your rebuke of the election canvassers moments ago shed tremendous light on their error. The Father will use your testimony as a prayer on behalf of unborn children. (*A couple of Democrat election representatives came to my door this morning, soliciting my vote for their candidate. I asked them whether the one they represented supported abortion, even though I knew the answer. The woman present proudly replied that the female candidate was 'pro-choice.' I asked them whether they were Christians, and then recognized to them that they were both rather advanced in age and that they were coming closer by the day to meeting our Lord Jesus Christ. The woman reared back at me, knowing the intent of my words. Ignoring her, I then asked the elderly gentleman how he had come to a point in his life where he would support a person who believed it was right to kill babies in the wombs of their mothers, and why he would come to the door of a Catholic who has a statue of the Most Blessed Virgin Mary standing in front of the house? He stood shell shocked by the questions I asked him, while the woman seemed perturbed that I refused to dignify her arrogance. The look on his face was almost as if he had seen a ghost, while the woman knew her support had just been divided from her.*) Today, I have come to pray with you for all the innocents who require the invocation of God's protection from those who would harm them. My Special son, if I were to assign another name to your love here in the United States, I would tell humanity what I am going to say to you now. The beauty and eloquence of the Saint listed at the beginning of My message today is a good surname for you. Yes, you represent a graceful emulation of Saint Nikita Vangelis. I wish to tell you about this Saint this afternoon because he personifies the gift of Christianity in an exiled man. Yes, Saint Nikita Vangelis is also an appropriate name for Jesus because they are one and the same reflection of the Holy Spirit here in the world. You and Nikita are cross-bearers for the sanctification of men. Jesus bore the Redemptive Cross that saved the entirety of human souls from condemnation into the Abyss. My Special son, if you assembled all the attributes of Saint Augustine, Saint John Vianney, Saint Pio and Saint John Paul II into one person, you would come close to identifying the virtues of Saint Nikita Vangelis. I wish for you and your brother not to presume, however, that the Lord seeks competition toward who can be the better Saint because, in the aftermath of Jesus' Crucifixion, all who accept His Holy Sacrifice are comparable in their faith. It is believed that certain people have favorite Saints. This is because of the characteristics of each individual that aligns with the legacies of these Saints. I know that one of your most powerful intercessors is Saint Monica. And, even in your identification with her motherhood, her son is the reflection of the Christ whom she accepted. This makes you a stepson of Saint Monica at the same time that you are My son in Jesus. (*I was a parishioner of Saint Augustine parish in Ashland from the time of my birth. Saint Augustine's paternity was a gift to all the families of our parish. And through her son's spiritual paternity, Saint Monica accepted all of us as her children as well.*) I wish for you and your brother to consider all the benefits of your devotion to the Communion of Saints. You are dedicated to their intercessory prayers. And, the Poor Souls in Purgatory can be advantaged by your summons of Jesus' Divine Mercy for their admittance into Heaven. The prayers of the faithful for the Poor Souls in Purgatory are powerful. It is the reason that I call upon the Faith Church to pray for them. This is the unity of prayer beneath the guiding hand of God.

My dear sons, where does your Mother begin to reflect upon My messages to you since December 28, 2008? It would be necessary to cite the logical aspects of spiritual communication. If you had not been here and willing to receive Me, to whom would I have said so many profound things on the Father's behalf? He required two souls overwhelmingly special and particularly chosen who were devoted to each other for the cause of the conversion of the lost. This is an integration that involves your unity inside the Cross from whence your likeness of Jesus is derived. Many generations ago, a great Saint was told by interior locution from the Archangel Gabriel that the Holy Spirit would descend upon her and give her tremendous gifts and miraculous visions. When this Saint inquired what needed to be done on her part, the Holy Spirit replied that she should pick up a stone and slam it against her fingers so she would know what spiritual pain was about to come. This is not just a true story, it is a metaphor for all who accept the holy burden of enlightenment, servitude, and sacrifice for the conversion of lost sinners. My Special and Chosen ones, as the years have progressed, you have also realized the early extent of your own pain and suffering in response to My messages.

And, rather than dwell on this in the future, should anyone ask, you might reply that the greater torment has been enduring the indifference of the secular void. This is what makes Saint William, Saint Timothy, Saint Nikita, and Christ the Lord one witness for the Father in Heaven. For those who follow Jesus, the pain is not just that their blood has been shed or bruises sustained, but that the lost sinners for whom these things have been borne turn themselves away. My Special son, I have said that history is replete with hypocrisy from those who pray for God's presence, and then turn their backs on Him when they do not like what He says. When the Father asks a person if they love Him, He is often saying, "Will you suffer for Me?" There are overpowering dimensions to this question about the degree of commitment that humanity makes in His honor. You have seen it presently. The election caller who came to your door said that she prays to God too. In the name of His Kingdom, what in the world was she talking about? It is only through this thinking that they can canvass neighborhoods with such hypocrisy dripping from their tongues. It has yet to be revealed how these lost sinners will find themselves surrounded by the light of the Cross because of their concealment of the darkness in their lives. We will pray that they are awakened soon.

Let us return to Saint Nikita Vangelis. He is not unlike many other Saints who were named in your final anthology. And, the aroma of his sainthood wafts through this home and out into the world every time you and your brother open the door. It is the fragrance of providential victory that has been seeded here where you live to record the wisdom that has not been seen in this world since the scripting of the New Covenant Gospel. Yes, the aroma is as sweet, and the truth as profound. I come to your home not only to visit upon you My beauty and grace, but to share the Lord's assurance that humanity will change. My Special son, if you and your brother were to live 500 more years, you could do no more than we will do in the span of your natural lives. This is how graceful and meaningful your work has been. It is not that life is so everlastingly daily, but that the accumulation of the days has meant a lifetime of beauty for a world so stained by the ugliness of sin. You have read the Sacred Scriptures time and again, and your vision of what Jesus expects from you is precise. So, it is not that you just understand what the New Covenant means, you have beatific knowledge of how it will change the world. This is not a contradiction; even though human salvation is entire in the New Covenant, it requires the participation of those to whom the Holy Spirit calls for miracles to happen. There can be no message without a messenger, and there can be no compliance without a response. This response is the fiat of this American nation to accept My intercession as the Morning

Star Over America, whom Jesus is asking His disciples to welcome. My Special son, if there is greatness in humanity during this new millennium, surely it will be found in the embracing by the Church and secular society of the messages I have shared. You often say that you and your brother are too close to see the miracles in which you are involved, but I believe that you are poised right where you belong. This is My message for this afternoon. Let us remember everyone who is responsible for defining the criteria by which the Church conducts its affairs for the propagation of the Gospel. Soon the Holy Spirit will deposit in your heart the reasons why the great Fatima miracle remains so relevant in your day."

Sunday, October 14, 2018
9:45 a.m.

"Empires rise and fall, mortal men live and die.
God reigns over all; the oceans, earth and sky."

- Saint Robbie Nicholls, Martyr 1835-1844*

"Good morning, My distinguished sons and precious children. It is My honor to be with you again on this brisk autumn day to share our prayers and invoke the power of the Holy Spirit in your presence. I have cited one of the Saints who has come with Me this morning, a boy who was martyred in England just because he dared to declare the Cross of Jesus as the ladder of ascension to the summits of Paradise. Today, I bring you the good wishes of the Communion of Saints whose prayers of intercessions have blessed the Earth for twenty centuries with wisdom and peace. There will never be a time when their intercession is interrupted or delayed. My Special son, Saint Robbie Nicholls died because he refused to decline My invitation to fight for the Church that was even in his day much in peril. It must be known worldwide that one need not be an adult to realize the urgency of holiness that must come into the world. You have known that young children recognize this urgency even before their adult counterparts are able to understand. What we pray for today on this great observation in the Church, and on the occasion of your earthly mother's birthday, is that everyone capable of understanding the faith of the Gospel wraps themselves within it, in an outward way. I am prone to tell you about how beautiful these people are in the sight of God, and today is no exception. What does the Father wish the spirit of a man to look like? Is it an appearance, a presence, a manifestation of canonical glory, or a humble smile to supplant a sorrowful heart? The spirit of a man has the capacity to nourish his own soul, if his spirit and his heart are united in the Cross. Yes, there are appearances that cannot be seen with the eyes. These are the elements of sanctity that Jesus sees from the House of the Father. You and your brother recently discussed what the neighborhoods of the world would look like in the absence of wood. This is not a small prospect to imagine. Every building that you see in your neighborhood has been constructed from wood yielded from trees. Most people take this for granted. You and your brother realize that trees represent the key component in sheltering humanity. It is not surprising, therefore, and neither a mystery, that the life-giving and eternity-preserving Cross on which Jesus died is made of wood. If not for wood, what would you and your helpers have constructed behind your garage? If not for wood, how would the poor keep warm outside in the winter? If not for wood, how would the millions of souls been laid to rest over the centuries?

My Special son, I am not saying that wood is a worship-worthy object. But, in the case of the tree on which Jesus was nailed, it is a glorious one. This broaches the discussion as to whether the Church should focus more on the Cross or the Savior who was crucified there. It speaks to the difference between the authentic faith of the Roman Catholic Church and those who protest against it, and who refuse to practice its tenets. Have you considered whether you would find yourself arguing whether the Cross or its Savior should be more focused? "*No.*" The answer to this question is clear. It is one of those false choices that we have discussed before. Yes, the Cross and Jesus are inseparable. This is symbolized by the Roman Catholic crucifix compared to the barren cross used by the Protestant community. It is all about a tree that began as a sapling in the Garden, and was transformed by Jesus on Good Friday. This summons the question of many theologians. When the Church speaks of redeemed souls entering the House of the Father; when they deliver themselves into His presence, they wonder whether this House has dimensions. They are interested in knowing of what materials this House is constructed. The answer is that the House of the Lord is built from the tree of suffering to which all Christians are called. However, we ensure that humanity does not see suffering as an enemy of redemptive grace. Entering the House of the Father is the goal of those seeking eternal life. This is foreign to intellectuals who believe that life is an end in itself; so what do they understand about the prospects of glory? We have prayed that they come to know that heavenly glory is the fruit of suffering. An additional element that the Church cites is that suffering must be met with acceptance, which is not the same as coping. The latter of these lacks commitment to its fruits. My Special son, the third question that arises is why suffering is the key component of redemption? The answer is that redemption cannot take place without conversion, and suffering fosters conversion. The issue of Adam's error now comes to the fore. Did Adam and Eve bring about the suffering that is seen around the globe? The response to this question is not about the manifestation of suffering, but the effects of disobedience. This does not mean that Christians who are obedient to God do not suffer, but they suffer in the likeness of Jesus who bore the burden of the world's sins. The common thread through this process is that sins are mitigated and reparation is made for disobedience to the Father; and His Heart is pleased by those who offer themselves for the sake of His glory. Saints like Augustine and Aquinas have entered dimensional discussions about this topic. What they have in common, along with everyone else who wonders about the spiritual dynamic of human suffering, is that they pondered and wrote about them as mortal men. They were afflicted by the same suffering about which they wrote. They fixed their writings through the lens of the same torment. This is in reflection of Jesus' Passion and Crucifixion, while Jesus Himself knew as the Son of the Father the benefits of the suffering He came to know. This same principle applies to everyone who sacrifices their comforts for the conversion of the lost. In the final hour, each man must look at his life before the backdrop of these gifts, and ask himself if his devotions and self-denial mirror the Son of Man. My Special son, it has been posited by men of the Church that I have been spared this pain, as spiritual as it may be, that has brought about the enlightenment of the world. What then would be the purpose of observing the Seven Sorrows of Mary? God is a gentle Lord, and His Will has been accorded to Me as well. This prompts the question whether the Father felt the pain of Jesus' Sacrifice on the Cross, given their unity in the Most Blessed Trinity. Did God suffer the agony of His Son on the Earth? Before I respond to this question, what do you suppose to be the answer? *"The Father came to Earth with His Son to accompany Him in His Redemptive act that He not really be alone in it."* What is your response about whether the Father endured the pain of Jesus on the Cross? *"I believe in His love that He wanted to and did."* You are correct; so hear Me now. The pain and agony that Jesus suffered on the Cross replicates the pain and agony that God endured when Adam and Eve betrayed Him. Jesus' Crucifixion is God's display of what happened to Him when His children turned away from His word. And, exiled humanity turned away from His Incarnate Word in precisely the same way. Hence, you are seeing the components of commandment, disobedience, suffering, punishment, reprieve, resurrection, and redemption in the same eternal construct that is written into the Scriptures. You will remember that there is little to be known in the Old Covenant about the suffering of God upon the disobedience of Adam and Eve. For the whole of eternity, Jesus inscribed those feelings in one Good Friday. He personified God's forgiveness and glory through His redemptive act. And, the Father rewarded Him with the harvest of souls with whom He will spend eternity with no memory of sorrow or grief.

There are metaphors aplenty in the created world that illustrate the reunion between God and man. One of the most powerful that you have seen in your lifetime is the playing out of the prodigal son in a scripted presentation where a man with a rifle shot and killed another man who was about to gun down his father. This legend of the fall portrays in illustrative terms how the father and the son embraced each other once again. All around the world, you see references to the prodigal son in other settings that exemplify the chapters and verses of the New Covenant Gospel. It might seem unimaginable that the phrase 'let it be done to me according to your word' can be embodied by a mighty, majestic, miraculous work called the Morning Star Over America. Decades of devotion, prayer, commitment, obedience, and humility shine through these words of 'Fiat' to the Father's Will in response to the visitation of the Archangel. This, My Special son, is what the human heart seeks out in the annals of mortal life. It is the reception of the visitation of God in the womb of His converted Creation. For My part, I have come to you and your brother to share My Fiat with you, to echo My response to the Archangel in your day, to pull you into the center of Divine Providence, and make of your lives this glory to which we are devoted. When a man or woman declares their consecration to Jesus' Most Sacred Heart and My Immaculate Heart, they are reaffirming their obedience to the Father by their imitation of our love. So, we have spoken today about a succinct prospect. There is another phrase that I find particularly important. 'Do whatever He tells you.' This is the essence of obedience that defies the disobedience of Adam in the Garden. The fruits of My Fiat are encompassed in the lives of Christians like you and your brother. Your fiat decades ago has been to say to Jesus Resurrected and Crowned as King, 'Give my soul the divinity that is living within You, and make me like your Mother.' My Special son, I ask you to ensure that you prepare for the winter months carefully, remaining close to your brother as in the past. I love you forever, and I will never leave your side."

Saturday, October 20, 2018
9:43 a.m.

Genesis 1-3
"And God said, let there be light."

"A certain kind of light."

"My blessed little children, it gives Me tremendous fulfillment to know that you have sustained your faith in God, given that there is such turmoil against the Church, and against decent people everywhere. I wish to tell you this morning that these manifestations are nothing new. I have told My visionaries since I first began speaking to them centuries ago the same thing I just said to you. I have mentioned the Genesis verse where God said that there should be light. My Special son, I wish to engage you in conversation about this matter this morning. The first book said that there was darkness, and this is the reason that God created light. At the risk of sounding rhetorical, if there was no light prior to God's command, how could there be darkness to compare it to? Who would be there to notice the difference? The reason I mention this is because humanity on the Earth should realize that it is God who determines what is darkness and what is light. And, it is not just light to which the Father was referring, but a certain kind of light. What was the darkness about in the beginning? In addition to the creation of the Earth, does it connote the same darkness that engulfs the world today? Has humanity rejected the light of the Father in its original form? You may remember that I borrowed the phrase 'a certain kind of light' from a musical lyric that you have heard. The lyricist wrote that this certain kind of light had never shined on him. This is another way to consider humanity seeking the spiritual light of Heaven. Men on Earth are prone to avoid the light of God because they decline to seek and find it. The contrast of the darkness in their souls and the light of God wishing to come in is comparable to the Genesis statement reflecting that God knew of the darkness, and He brought forth the light. This is what He wishes to do with the spiritual identity of man. Therefore, My Special son, it is not just light that God created in the beginning, but a certain kind of light. You might believe that you purchased a certain kind of light that you installed in your basement yesterday. Yes, this is another metaphor for what I am saying. The bulb that you placed in the ceiling emits light with certainty, but it is a different kind of light, a light that spreads itself far and wide in ways not generated by other sources. This is the way Jesus has impacted the world through His wisdom and truth. The Earth has not changed, but its environment is manifestly more filled with light because Jesus has brought the light of His eternal truth. This leads to the supposition that what one person may consider spiritual light may be different from someone else. Here, I have just laid out the basis for relativism and pluralism. What one person decides to be more spiritually enlightening can be vastly different from what other persons believe. The means of addressing this contradiction is whether a person's concept of light aligns with the teachings of the Church. My Special son, I just gave you the thesis of My message this morning. Do different individuals believe that truth and light are of the same origin? And, if they believe that they are, do they hold that they are in any way connected or mutually exclusive? The truth and light of Jesus cannot be separated because they are innate to His Kingdom. God chose upon the conception of Jesus in My Womb to bear before humanity a certain kind of light. His light would supplant all other forms of light that preceded His birth. We have in our mission with your brother been celebrating the light of God that brings not a garish glow to the Earth, but a flourishing of wisdom that teaches humanity about His love. Hence, you know that God's light, truth and wisdom are undividedly descriptive of His love. My Special one, these gifts of Creation and the attributes of God's Only Begotten Son are united because the Father wishes to return His people to His presence in Heaven. This led to His sorrowful Crucifixion on Mount Calvary. Jesus on the Cross proclaimed with Blood, suffering, and death what God said in the beginning, 'Let there be light.' And, the Church recognizes that the kind of light to which Jesus was referring was Himself in the exiled world. The light in Jesus proves that truth and wisdom are one in redemptive sacrifice. My Special son, are you following My description this morning? *"Yes, I understand."* It must be made clear that all the sacred components of man's creation, his conversion to the New Covenant Gospel, and his deliverance into Heaven are products of the light brought into the world by Jesus, compounded and reflected by His Holy Spirit still saturating the globe. The matter seems elementary to us, but society has spent its whole existence debating the definitions of truth, light, wisdom, sacrifice, conversion, and redemption. The statement that you often make to chasten unbelievers is when they say, 'Let me decide.' We know that humanity is incapable of making such decisions. No sinner can decide what the definition of light should be because he is a descendant of the original darkness. Adam placed a blindfold on everyone who would be born into this world. And, Jesus not only removes the blindfold, He clarifies the vision with which each sinner sees, once they open their eyes. It is the ultimate eternal birthday gift.

My Special son, nothing in the world can escape being judged against the light of God. Wherever there is darkness, it will be flushed out because of His light that permeates every corner of the globe. Light represents new life, and darkness is a remnant of the transgression of Adam. I feel as though I am speaking to you in terms that you have mastered because you have written books, prologues, forewords, and manuscripts containing everything I have said today. I am speaking about these things because they are prayers to the Father. He listens to our prayers in the same way that you might replay a particular song. He enjoys the renditions that we offer, the new verses and rhymes that celebrate His creative bounty. Our Father in Heaven is not only the original Truth, He is the Only Truth. Wise men have known this since that silent night in Bethlehem. The final point I will make is where God's light can be seen in the world, from where is it generated in the precincts where you live? Yes, it is in the human heart. Just like that new bulb that you placed in your basement, the brilliance of supernal love must shine its brightest in places where it has never been seen. We have brought to humanity the wisdom to know that this light originates in the flame of the Holy Spirit. It would be difficult to display a hierarchy of all that I have mentioned this morning, as if on a chart. It surely would include love and truth, and thereafter, light, wisdom, and sacrifice. It is uncertain whether such a chart would be appropriate, but love is central to the entire framework. One might portray love as the trunk of a tree from which all the other attributes are branched. However men choose to see it, it must be fashioned on the fact that there is no other divine love or eternal truth than that brought into the world by God in His Son, Jesus Christ. Jesus is the Way, the Truth and the Life. The Father asks the Faith Church to come to Him by way of His Truth to find eternal redemption. This, My Special son, concludes My message for today. I hope you have enjoyed it. *"Yes, very much, thank you."* I have tried not to seem ambiguous about these holy and righteous things. I just wished to state how far from love that some men have strayed. Please remember My recommendations for you and your brother to live safely during the coming months. There are perils that would have you stop making progress toward My intercessory works."

Saturday, October 27, 2018
9:46 a.m.

"Is it more difficult to choose either option one or option two than choosing between one option and nothing?" Why ask? Because there are people who believe that all life is a matter of containment, that men live mostly in fear of the unknown, and that open-ended questions leave room for equivocation. Faith, however, gives humanity the courage to live beyond these constraints, to seek out and conquer the things that might frighten them in the moment."

- The Dominion Angels

"Here come I, My dear little children, not to interrupt your lives, but to complement them. I bring with Me the gifts and graces of love from My Heart in Heaven as the Queen of Paradise. We have spoken with such tremendous vision about the purpose of My messages to you for so many years. It is proper to tell anyone who asks that the Mother of Jesus has been speaking with you for decades. This commitment cannot be overlooked by anyone, either here in your exile, or having been sainted in the presence of the Father. You have known that time gives you the opportunity to prepare the world for its presentation to Jesus upon His Return in Glory. It is not that He does not know the composition of the world, but He wishes for humanity to be prepared to judge itself upon that glorious time. It is clear, My Special son, that your desire to pursue the sanctification of humanity will live long beyond the elder ages of the Earth. And even before that, you will be devoted to the conversion of lost sinners until the moment you hand your soul to God. Today, I wish to remind you and your brother that you are living in the final age of enlightenment that has come to America and the world. You may have believed that your work for Me might be seen as too magnanimous for those who are indifferent about My manifestations. However, it is their indifference itself that will die before of the grandness of My presence. You and your brother have placed yourselves at My behest in a position to be known as advocates for those who are unaware that the Cross is the meaning of life. Billions of people around the world are far from accepting Christianity. One would believe that My miracles of Lourdes and Fatima would have annihilated humanity's doubt that God is present in this world. However, as you have seen, and as the Angels have described this morning, there is equivocation that erodes the ability of lost sinners to become invested in the miracles they see.

Let us further examine what the Angels spoke about this morning. What is your opinion about the question they have raised? Is it easier to choose between two options, or decide one option or nothing at all? *"I believe it harder to choose one option because you do not have to invoke any decision. You can remain indifferent."* You are precisely correct because you are addressing equivocation. The latter seems to be the reason why My twentieth century apparitions have been ignored. You and your brother might conclude, however, that choosing nothing is a choice. God does not allow a human soul to have no opinion about one's destiny. Think about the response you just gave about options. When speaking about converting to the Cross, one either accepts the Crucifixion of Jesus or declines Salvation. This is a choice between options one and two. Conversely, choosing Jesus' Sacrifice or having no opinion is not an alternative, and God believes that a sinner's silence is the same as their denial. It is a condemning equivocation. No one can stand before a judge and, when asked for a plea, reply that he has none because the judge will declare the person guilty based on the evidence against him. This is the same scene that plays out when a person stands before their Savior and is asked for a response about their life's record, and whether they believe they are in good stead before God. My Special son, this seems too much of a burden for many sinners to discern. They seem too busy raising their families, being preoccupied with the distractions imposed upon them by the secular void. And, they remain this way until the undue demands of living and surviving come upon them. This is when they are prone to ask why God is doing this to them – the same God whose presence they deny until they are forced to seek Him to bear their agonies, sacrifices, suffering and deficits. This is when the Father asks them why they did not seek Him during the good times. Why was He not worshiped for creating the landscape of life on which they lived with peace and prosperity? The answer, My Special son, is that humanity often believes that graces and blessings are procured from the environment of their exile. They seem to have no notion that they are in the lineage of Adam and Eve, that they have been stained with original sin, and that they must be cleansed and purified to gain the sinlessness that was known in Eden. Yes, when the difficult times come, they wonder why God places such suffering on them, when it is their reluctance to search for Him beforehand that prompts their question. We are making remarkable progress in laying a foundation upon which the great orators of the Earth can stand and tell them why they are wrong.

My Special son, I continue to connect your contributions to the Church and the Kingdom of the Father with the holy heart that you offer Jesus. People often refer to something as 'back in the day.' What this means is that there is a connection between those times and the modern years that can be linked to a theme. It is usually a comparison of progress based on intellectual development or advanced designs. What I am speaking about is the spiritual development of the human heart that was itself, back in the day, unaware of the sacrifices expected from Christians who are only now maturing in their faith. Let us consider a circumstance. My Special son, who is the oldest Marian visionary that you know of? *"Lucia from Fatima."* I am speaking about the age of a seer when I first visited them. *"Some have been in their teens, such as at Medjugorje. I do not know of any adults."* I have commonly appeared to children for a reason. Young people are more believable because they are incapable of conjuring the religious framework in which I have come to them. It is not that older people are not innocent. So, it is not about the visionary as much as the way the visionary is perceived. Those who are the recipients of My messages have the choice whether to receive them. And, children are more likely to choose either option one or option two than do nothing. Do you understand? *"Yes, I agree."* And, it is mainly because children see things in a twofold fashion. There is black and white, right and wrong, and love and hatred. This allows them to see life without equivocation. Jesus says that unless you become like a child, you will not inherit the Kingdom of God. In other words, if a person equivocates in his approach to the truth, his soul is not wholly pure. My Special son, I have this morning given you another reason why relativism and pluralism exist. It is because people refuse to be childlike according to Jesus' dictates here in the world. I have achieved the objectives that I wished to accomplish on the Earth because of visionaries like you and your brother. You have been receptive to My miracles because of your obedience to Jesus and your trust in the Providence of God. And, it is not just that you would ask where else to turn, it is your determination to participate in the purification of humanity. It is about your awareness that the world is not right. It is about your comparison of what you know about Jesus' lordly love and those who live around you. The contradictory way that humanity lives is in contrast to the simplicity that the Father desires. What would be an example of this complexity? Perhaps, the intersection that you cited around the nearby railroad track. You are prone to ask what those people were thinking when they erected such a confusing number of signs. It is not about common sense. It is about complying with measurements that are written into regulations. My question is that, if men are willing to invest such efforts to ensure compliance with secular laws, why will they not, like little children, accept Jesus on the Cross? Every time you and your brother witness something on this level, it gives you confidence to know that you are living in communion with the truth. There is divinity in you because your devotion is given to this truth. There is peace within you because you allow this devotion to train your focus on the blessings of God. My Special son, I hope you have enjoyed My message today. *"Yes, very much, thank you."* Do you have any issues to discuss? *"How does equivocation impact the Church in America which the Bishops are trying to lead to holiness?"* The response to your question is about the battle that the Church is waging against the culture of modern secularism. The Bishops are trying to keep as many people in the Church as possible, people who place more value in what they reap from their secular relationships than the graces that they receive from the Sacred Altar. The Bishops are often in confrontation with parishioners who wish to modernize what they believe to be wrong in the eyes of diversity and inclusion. Another facet is that the Church requires resources from parishioners who hold a different view of their faith. This causes friction between the functions and values that the Bishops face every day. Your question revolves around why some Bishops do not stand more courageously by the teachings of the Great High Priest and My intercession; this is where equivocation is applicable. We wish for them to rise in defense of the Cross, even in the face of becoming martyrs. You are witnessing a manifestation by the secular void that will reveal most of the Judases. The secular government has infiltrated the Church. And, it is the fault of those who have fallen asleep that this has happened. Pray and allow Jesus to propagate My messages, and the results you seek will come."

Saturday, November 3, 2018
9:42 a.m.

"Internal dynamics and external effects –
There is no such thing as a nemesis of the Cross."

"Now I have come to bring the brilliance of My sacred love into your hearts because you feast there on the wisdom of God. My prayers are with you, and My intercession is for you. Today, I speak to offer you the love of God because I am drawn to His Spirit in mortal men. My Special son, I have given you two issues to ponder at the beginning of My message today. The first is a description of faith with multiple internal dynamics and incalculable external effects. This is the miraculous nature of Christian spiritualism. The second is the verity that the Cross of Jesus has no nemesis. I have spoken to you and your brother about the serenity of autumn and the new life of springtime. Yes, the harvest and the rebirth. This is the metaphor for the Christian life. I realize that you and your brother have given your lives to the cause of human conversion. There can be no greater gift to God and nothing paralleled to the sacrifices you have offered. What we must do here forward is to pray that your sacrifices are replicated by those around you because they will magnify the eternal blessings that you have given humanity through the years. All the Saints in Heaven are near you for the fullness of time. They anticipate you joining them with Jesus when the Father declares your earthly lives complete. You must know, My Special son, that there are manifest abruptions that come when the Father determines that conditions are right. This is the reason I ask you and your brother to live with deep spiritual reflection. No one but the Father knows when the truest blessings of life will be dispensed to those unknowing on the Earth. You and all who will eventually benefit from My intercession will realize that it is the spirit of love in Me that has made possible the miracles you have known. I am not saying that you are unaware of it now, but it will become more obvious when the fruits of your labors are fully dispensed. Therefore, I ask that you remember the peace to which you are called in the face of the commotion at your workplace and the personalities with whom you interact. It is to your credit that you have chosen to not allow these circumstances to cause you further stress. It is also to your credit that you have embarked on a spiritual journey that has lasted for decades, trusting that I am leading you in the presence of Jesus to a triumph that will outlast the history of the world. You notice that I continuously offer praise to you and your brother for the work you have done. It is not that I wish to keep you motivated when I say these things because your motivations are self-generated in that you have given your hearts to God. I praise you because your life is a prayer for the conversion of humanity. My praise is My way of pronouncing to the Church Triumphant that their likeness is living within you on the Earth below. So, let us think about the things that men need to survive in light of the principles they hold dear. It is a function of strength; and strength is the origin of power. Power requires conviction of pious belief and clarity of sight. You prevail in the world because you are principled in your exercise of power. Then, there is virtue. It is from virtue that honesty is wrought. You preserve your reputation because of the virtue in your hearts. You survive because the Spirit of Jesus identifies who you are, and this is what we are seeking in humanity.

The framework of American democracy will again engage itself next Tuesday in determining the future of your nation. I have said that shared values have given way to the great decisions that benefit the freedom of the many. However, this view of American democracy is coming unraveled. You have never witnessed a liberal political party that is so aligned with the works of the devil than the one you are seeing now. It must be made clear that the Mother of Jesus is not a political figure, but I have stood beside those who have espoused the truth as it relates to the governance of men. The prospect that individuals who look like you and your brother being accused of the falsities that are being leveled against your race is an act of evil works. The matter is not just an affront against your dignity, it is an attack on the Catholic Church to which you belong. This is the reason, My Special son, that the Church crisis is so horribly timed. You can see how the devil is taking swings against the Catholic Church while its reputation is under siege. It will not be a lasting conflict. The liberal partisans about whom I speak will soon reach their demise. God will not have His Church impugned this way. I must add that this is not peculiar to the United States alone. You see the same leftism eroding the holiness of the nations in Europe and South America as well. Prayer halts these things. Jesus did not say that it would require a thousand prayers over endless centuries to convert the world. He put no numerical equations on the purification of wicked men. It is not that He saw the cultivation of the Earth as an open question, but with a conclusion that ends in Him. Therefore, the right prayer, the most effective prayer for humanity is not that a heartless petition be raised over the course of millennia, but a unified voice giving Jesus due praise to the point where the Father declares it enough. You have noticed during your life that there are ebbs and flows like waves against a shoreline. And, once the waters of human contrition reach their high mark, the history of the world will find its destined end. This, My Special son, is My message for today. Do you have any issues to discuss? *"No, none that are more than curiosity."* You are allowed to be curious. *"How close are we to the crescendo of this secular evil in our government and culture?"* You have posed a legitimate inquiry. My response is that the time about which you speak is contingent on whether wicked souls undergo their destruction at the hands of the righteous. The silence of the good people makes way for those who do evil to prosper. This is a premise that you have known all your life. On the other hand, in the absence of the intervention of holy people in the public domain, the United States of America, as you know it, will reach its culmination of culture and identity in twenty to thirty years. I have said that Jesus will not permit the country you have loved to be dissolved into a nation that its founders would no longer recognize. A great deal of praying can be done in three decades, and the 2,000 year old Cross will preserve everything about western democracy that you have grown to love."

Saturday, November 10, 2018
9:47 a.m.

"Consciousness and etherealism –
The human spirit has the capacity to rust."

"My dear little children, to sanctify the world, we join our prayers with Jesus' love in adoration of the Father. It is here that we have altered the course of human life, and amended the record of history. I welcome you to the comfort of My Immaculate Heart where you are assured your dignity from the sorrows of the Earth. My Special and Chosen sons, I have begun My message this morning with concepts upon which you may later ponder. It is clear that the unearthly has to do with the Kingdom of God that must become the centerpiece of human faith. This is the etherealism to which I have referred. And, I have alluded that the human spirit has the capacity to rust. It is because of the hardness of heart that some people have before living the Christian life. The softness and dearness of the love of Jesus is a sturdy means of grace, but it is flexible in patience toward others. If one's love is not sacred, it will be subject to the corrosion that brings cynicism into the heart and the rusting of the human spirit. My Special son, I know that you did everything in your power to maintain your safety while you traveled to California. However, you were given a prime example of what I said about how the recklessness of other people can spontaneously affect your life. When you speak of a taxi driver nearly bringing you into an automobile accident, this is a metaphor for what I have been saying. It is the reason I have always asked through your brother to maintain your safety at all times. There is no question that the dangers of the devil are lurking to harm you at any time. We have again joined this morning in our prayers because you rightfully responded in that incident for the preservation of your life. I pray that you will realize how special you are to the conversion of the world. Today, I have come to speak about the consciousness of piety that humanity must inherit in their faith in the Church. I have spoken about My Son's Crucifixion as having been an earthbound ethereal Sacrifice. What this means is that the death of one Man became the sorrow of the Heavenly Father. And, it means that the sorrow of the Heavenly Father became the Salvation of the entire world. Not just one man or any man, but all men who accept the Cross have inherited their new life, their eternal life, their beatific life in the Passion and Crucifixion of Jesus on Good Friday. My Special son, one might believe that the Gospel message would be too single-dimensioned to be acceptable in the multifaceted inquisitiveness of the human mind. It would feel like transforming an object into a thought. This is the way some sinners see themselves alongside the Kingdom of the Father. It is as though His Kingdom is an object that they cannot place into cognitive perspective or embed in their identities. What our works have shown them, however, is that the Kingdom of God is the real and true human consciousness in this world and the next. And, their exile is the object that they must overcome to be unified with this truth. You and your brother have heard untold excuses why men and women of the secular void decline to accept their salvation in Jesus and My intercessory miracles. There have been no good reasons given to you because there are none to be had. It is a matter of faith that is based on hope and trust. These are the feet upon which humanity must walk to a destiny they cannot yet see. My Special son, do you suppose that most people who refuse to accept Christianity do so out of fear or obstinance? *"I suppose it is more obstinance because they lack the awareness to be afraid."* And, you are again correct. This obstinance, this stubbornness is based on their reluctance to forego pride in their heritage, along with the fear of the unknown. It seems an oddity that humanity must hold on to God by letting go of life. What we have proven here with your brother is that this can be done without relinquishing one's engagement with secularism, but in a righteous way. Jesus came to build a Church that would challenge the effects of secularism on those who accept the Cross. Imagine, My Special son, sitting in a Vatican office on your first day as Pope. What would be your thinking as the sun rose that morning? *"I need to lead the world to their Mother."* There have been masses of men whose faith has benefitted from this gracious approach. The great Saint celebrated today is one example (*Pope Leo the Great*). And, why would you declare to humanity that they should be taken to their Mother instead of to Her Son? *"Because it unites Christianity with the Holy Spirit's economy of salvation which Protestantism has fractured. They must contemplate and accept your station in order to understand Jesus' Sacrifice most completely. The Bread of Life was given to the world through you."* So, you would on your first day declare that Protestantism is the reason I have been rejected by the world? *"By focusing the Catholic world on you in relation to your miraculous intercession, it would immediately make them realize they are not in the center of the Original Church. All facets of Heaven and Earth must be in communion. Humanity cannot reject your miraculous intercession and claim that this communion is perfected and complete."* Thank you for your wonderful description of what must be done. Now, what should be accomplished to touch the other two-thirds of the population who do not believe in God at all. *"They must be approached through a testament to the miraculous. They cannot be won through intellectual argument. The Church needs to witness to your miraculous intercession as if it is a centerpiece from the God of Creation. We must testify to the miraculous as a motive of credibility that supersedes all worldly argument. Miraculous intercession takes the world into the heart. Only there is it understood. They must know that you are the Mediatrix of all Divine Grace, the Mother of their Redeemer and the Queen of Heaven."* Thank you again for your gracious perception. One might consider that this would be your first act while addressing the fractured landscape of Christianity in the process. Nevertheless, the point on which Christians agree is that the Blood of Jesus on the Cross is the only soul-saving Sacrifice, and that persuading all lost sinners to reach out to Him is the call of this miracle. *"Yes."*

I mention the word 'cynicism' today. I connect this with the term 'indifference' as if to be synonymous. It is an act of cynicism to be indifferent about Jesus' Crucifixion. This may seem unreasonable to many who just wish to live their lives in peace. And, they may believe that they are living in peace, but it is an impractical peace, a symbolic peace, a temporary way of life. Why? Because the tides will turn against them; their bodies will break, their minds will grow numb, and they will wonder where their peace has gone. They will recognize that their perception of peace was no more than a thought on a page. You and your brother have learned, along with all who accept the Kingdom of God, that true life-sustaining peace is the fruit of a great battle. The fight for righteousness must always precede the capturing of the eternal peace that no pain or sorrow can destroy. Time cannot wash away this grand and marvelous way of life that remains in the heart through the last days of the world. In the newness of the Father's eternal peace, always giving and never taking, is found the fresh new heart that will keep the life of converted humanity forever going. This, My Special son, is what I mean when I speak about the unity of the human consciousness and the ethereal realms of God. Here, there is no such thing as the corrosion of grace, the denying of forgiveness, or the rusting of the human spirit. You have been writing paragraphs and pages into assembled reams that magnify what I have said here this morning. The celebration of the Glory of God is amply represented in your writings, and no man would ever outlive the years it would take to exhaust the languages by which this Glory can be described. My Special son, I have said that you and your brother have been set apart from your peers by your salient awareness of the miracles that you wish to describe. Being set apart from this world means that you are closely united with the next. All human destiny is bound for the fruit of this miracle. It is through the Holy Spirit that this must be known. The fulfilment of your life and the culmination of the years in Jesus' Sacred Heart are intersecting this way. I have asked you and your brother to be humbly proud of your service to the Church because Jesus will reward you through the light of His Paschal Resurrection. This, My Special son, is My message for today. I hope that you have enjoyed it. "*Yes, very much, thank you.*" Please accept Jesus' gratitude for you and your brother who have given yourselves and your tenure of years for the conversion of the lost."

Sunday, November 18, 2018
9:48 a.m.

"Colorless, odorless, tasteless, touchless and inaudible – the great eternal divide. What does it mean to create something out of nothing? Perhaps only its genesis can advise."

- The Dominion Angels

"Good morning, My beloved little sons. I speak to you during these remarkable times, not only about the essence of life, but its purification here in this world in the presence of God. We have shown humanity that its innocence can be the beginning of its redemption. I have for many centuries tried to convey the message that the transition from mortality to eternal life is a product of the transformation of the human heart into the hands of its Lord. The Dominion Angels have today posed a question about what it means to create something out of nothing. They have not asked what it means for something to be created by nothing, but making visible something that never was. I have said that there are deposits of knowledge that are transferred to humanity in ways that appear too logical to be true. Humanity has been told that life has been created out of nothing. This is one of those instances where the deposit of knowledge about Creationism is to affirm that the Father can do anything He pleases. Rarely has He revealed to the world how His intellect works. However, what you can glean from the creation of something out of nothing is that all form, shape, matter, and energy are products of His Will. It might seem inconceivable by the human mind to understand that anything to which men are drawn never had a beginning. This is one of the paradoxes of faith that is resolved once the soul reaches its homeland in the presence of the Father. Humanity is prone to believe that everything knowable in the heart and mind had a beginning because of the effects of linear time. Hence, the Angels have posed an inquiry about the creation of something visible from something that cannot be seen, smelled, heard, touched or tasted. This seems a large leap for logical men. My Special son, if men wish to be logical, they should consider the idea of condensation because the principle is similar. The larger question implied by the Angels is not how something can be created out of nothing, but why. Yes, when speaking about the Providence of God, why a Garden? Why Creation? Why a man and woman? Why such beauty? It is all a manifestation of love that was betrayed in the Garden through the disobedience of Adam and Eve. My Special son, this is the query posed by the Dominion Angels this morning. The first is why not love, and the second is why not obedience. This is the premise upon which the messages that I have given you are based. There can be no love without ones's obedience to God. Clearly, deferring to God's Will is the fruit of obedience, and obedience must be supported by responsible action. You can see a hierarchy that connects not only the creation of man, but man's response to his creation by living the Will of the Father. Divine love requires this kind of sacrifice.

Today, I also come to speak about the genesis of the question asked by the Angels. What would make the Father deign to beget His people when He alone is so sovereign? Is it possible for Him to feel lonely? Can it be true that He requires the company of His children to enrich His joy? The answer is yes. And, as men build homes and furniture out of earthly materials, God gives life to humanity through the architecture of His love. The resource He uses is the creative Spirit of Himself. It is true that the mighty dimensions of the world are like His levels of thought, and humanity is His deepest contemplation. The joy of the Earth becomes dependent on humanity's ability to understand what I just said. All sanctity, soundness, safety, and happiness are dependent on whether exiled men recognize the hierarchy about which I have spoken. Whenever a man enters a body of water, he has engaged an environment that is not natural to his life. It is not wrong to delve into the oceanic depths or the fathoms of the seas. What seems wrong, however, is when a man does not know what perils are there. Being run through by a stingray would indicate that a man is not aware of the dangers to his life. This is a metaphor about the effects of sin. Diving into the darkness of impurity and transgression places one's soul as much in doubt as delving the perilous deep. A distinction can be made that unforseen incidents occur because of the effects of humanity's exile. This is where exceptions are made in the judgment of God for determining humanity's compliance with the mandates of His Word. My Special son, I would like to draw another distinction that has not been made clear through the centuries. It is a tremendous burden on the human soul to commit sins against the Lord. But, it is even more egregious to lure others into violating the Commandments. Such is the exploitation that places the destiny of two souls at risk, instead of one. Many believe that Jesus should absolve the victim and heap the culpability on the perpetrator. In these cases, He does this not through objective justice, but because the perpetrator must know that he has done the work of the devil. Jesus never asks what excuses draw men to commit sins against other men, but what reasons are applied. On the other hand, My Special son, this may appear to conflict with the events that transpired in the Garden of Eden. Why was Adam expelled with Eve when the latter yielded to the temptation of the devil? Because no man should allow any creature living or dead to rob him of his conscience about complying with the Will of God. If he does so, then he is also corrupt. Adam's portion of the burden was commensurate with that of Eve. Hence, what you are seeing in the exiled world is the same, but Jesus on the Cross told Adam that He is the New Adam who would show Eve how to live. Let us turn to the passage posed by the Dominion Angels today. Creating something out of nothing means that Jesus loved Adam and Eve and all their descendants because He wanted to. The Father did not have to coerce Jesus to love the sinners whom He has redeemed. Jesus died willingly on the Cross. He could have lived in Paradise with all the Hosts without the presence of the sinners in exile, but just like the Father's love living in Him, there needed to be salvation for the damned. Why? Would Heaven be any greater when filled with billions of Saints? The answer is affirmative in the same way that the Father chose to manifest Creation out of His love. We have spoken in times past about the reasons why God would beget creatures who were prone to corruption. The answer is that He gave His children the power of free will, and the abuse of their will is the reason Jesus was called to take on human flesh in the exiled realms. My Special one, it would seem in Heaven that every father needs a son. It is a remarkable facet of the durability of eternity and the light that shines on the ecstasy of being. On your best days in this life, you have felt this creative presence in the peace you have lived. In the deep recesses of your heart, you have touched the Will of the Father with your instincts of love. The impulses that have moved you to act in Christian ways were manifested by your connection with God. Lastly, My Special son, there can be no faith in this framework unless men on Earth embrace beatific curiosity. Faith assembles in the human mind the capacity for asking questions, not just about the origins of life, but about its purpose, survival, and destiny. In truth, sinners who are bound for Heaven seek out the answers to these questions, and they find them in Jesus on the Cross. We turn to the blessings of love and sacrifice once again. The Father said in the beginning that He wished new life to surround Him in Heaven. Now, this life is asking Him to visit upon Himself the company of His redeemed Church as a prodigal son might return to his roots. It is a glorious foundation on which this miracle is stationed – and as I have said, as it was in the beginning.

My Special son, thank you for your wholesome embracement of everything I have said through the years. I expect for you and your brother to measure your thoughts against the substance of My messages. You have the right to be curious about the outcome of the world. You have the ability to determine what shall be. You have arrived at Thanksgiving week, and your nation is on its economic course toward the end of December. You and your brother, and all of My children, live one day at a time in the majesty of My presence. It is in this moment that you know you are blessed. It is not that you are distanced from Heaven, but just one dimension from God. You transcend this dimension every time you work and pray, every time the thought of Jesus enters your heart. Imagine how many keystrokes you and your brother have committed to the page in the past thirty years. It is sheerly incalculable, a fitting means of bringing into being the fruits of infinite grace. Jesus chooses to see it as though each of your keystrokes is on a grand piano where you have been playing the great symphonies of the Communion of Saints. The songs have been echoing through the chambers of the Father's House since the moment you were conceived. And, Jesus has been singing as if performing an aria along with your playing to replicate the great melody commending that no one should sleep. At the last, this orchestral redemption will pierce the hearts of all who believe. The echoes of this grand performance will conclude in the applause of those who are sainted by His Sacrifice. This, My Special son, is a fruit of God's romantic love and His penning of the finishing of the Earth with sublime meaning, a meaning that will prove to universes unknown that something can indeed be created out of nothing. Bless you and your brother for your continuance of love and obedience in a world that cries out for the answers of life. I urge you to afford yourselves the opportunity to recognize your contributions to the redemption of the Church."

Friday, November 23, 2018
1:17 p.m.

"HEAR – Have Enough Ammunition Ready."

"Today, My little children, it is again My honor to come speaking to you in celebration of your Christian faith and the lives that you have dedicated to the Cross. Through this faith, you have implemented the venue not only through which you have been saved, but by which you are converting your lost brothers and sisters. Yes, My Special son, it would seem that the year is older than it is because of the observations that come through the secular void. I congratulate you and your brother for embracing the peace that Jesus gives, and allowing His peace to comfort your spirit as time passes by. I have provided a term at the fore of My message this afternoon that applies to every battle. You and all Christians have warehoused the graces from Heaven that will ensure your victory in this life. I am pleased that you have the perspective to know that the Lord will win at the last. I recently spoke about the glory that constitutes the Father's Kingdom. I shared with you an emphasis on love and truth, grace and wisdom, and faith and hope. These are the underpinnings of humanity's relationship with God, and they are the branches on which you might perch to see His Kingdom from your exile. 'Have enough ammunition ready.' This is what we have been amassing all these years in fulfillment of Jesus' declaration from the Cross and the promises that I made in February 1991. A great many battles have been won since, based on you and your brother's willingness to forego another way of life in favor of magnifying the Providence by which your lives are sustained. We speak about what constitutes God's Kingdom with the utterance of the word 'Glory.' It means beyond any doubt that there is no sin in Glory. There is nothing in humanity's lives that would make anyone believe that something more beatific is required. We have shared during all these years the great manifestation of enlightenment that reveals to the world the Glory of one's new life in Jesus. I wish to convey today My dearest wishes for everyone who is praying for this Glory to come. Yes, it is seeded within you now, growing outward in a miraculous way; and it will soon eclipse the materialism of the world that is destined for the darkness. It is clear, My Special son, that you and your brother do not patronize this materialism because you know that true wealth is the love in your hearts. Who would have surmised that being exiled from the presence of the Father would stand in such stark contrast to the Light of His Kingdom? This is what your lost brothers and sisters have never asked, and are unaware of their ability to do so. This comports with the spiritual curiosity that I recently mentioned. Prayer is based on curiosity because it is the substance of hope. The human heart is curious to know if Jesus, the Savior of man, is willing to respond in an affirmative way. The faithful know that the answer is according to the Will of God. My Special son, you rightly provided the correct response to the question of whether love or truth preceded one or the other. Do you remember your response? *"Yes, love is first."* This is the reason that the whole of human sanctity and the afterlife are fruits of His Will. 'God is Love and Truth' is an expression of truth itself. God is the only Truth. And, this Truth is Incarnate in Christ Jesus. As I have said, this is the way life must be lived. So, we connect your prayers with the Church Triumphant through your understanding of the Love and Truth to which you are drawn. You heard Saint John Paul II speak about Heaven being more a condition than a place. Saint John Paul II has found his redemption in the Father's House beyond the exile where he prayed and served. However, Heaven is also the condition of perfect salvation. My Special son, as I said in October, the whole matter revolves around seeing God's love and human life as a tree. Why? Because trees bear fruit. This is the essence of compliance with the life commissioned by the Holy Gospel. 'By their fruits, you shall know them.' These fruits, therefore, can be temporal and spiritual. They blossom from the faith of men. Every other virtue of your Christian identity is a product of this growth. When you smile and shake the hand of a stranger, your Christian faith is bearing fruit through the witness of your life. This brings Me to something that you participated in a few weeks ago. After admonishing the election callers at your door, you later said that you should not have spoken so coarsely to them. My response is that you spoke the truth perfectly; the fruits of your wisdom fed the callers the nutrition their spirits need to reconsider their faith. You made believers of two individuals who would have heard it no other way. Hence, when I speak about fruit, it can taste bitter to those who are not receptive to the Will of God. This is the way the Holy Spirit celebrates the invocation of Divine Love that satisfies the hunger of men. When someone goes door to door to testify that a candidate is worthy of public office, they align themself with their opinions. In such cases that involve someone wanting to promote the culture of death against innocent unborn children, they should be chastised to the fullest measure. So, your response was sanctioned. When you read the Gospel about vengeance belonging to the Lord, you are propagating this message.

What we will do for the remainder of this year in terms of My messages, both here and around the world, is to think about the coming of the third decade of this new millennium. I know that you and your brother have remarked appropriately that time seems to expire quickly. And, it is doing so because of the depths of your joy. It is from giving your heart so delightfully to the Will of the Father who has granted untold graces to the world. There are no distractions in your Christian life. You focus on the coming of Jesus into His Kingdom in which He shall remember everyone who has been faithful to Him. Jesus is the Incarnation of the Love of God. I also wish to mention the actions of the United States Bishops in the aftermath of their recent conference. My Special son, I know that you have heard the proposition that some words left unspoken are more deafening than those that are shared. This seems to be the echo of the Bishops' conference. They broached the subjects to which they were drawn by passion and pressure. However, there was little ameliorative policy passed that would effect the resolution to the Church's present difficulties. The Bishops summoned My intercession in their prayers, and I implored Jesus to accord them the opportunity to take heed of what you wrote in your advisory. Longstanding centuries of thought and meditation could not match the wisdom that you provided the Bishops from the depths of your heart. I have said that this transformation is a process, not an event. Therefore, your letter will not have been submitted in vain. All your works are prayers not only for the Church, but for the nations and their peoples. What you and your brother have done has been inspiring for the Church, and an invitation for God to intercede. I have completed My message today. Thank you for sharing your glorious, glorious life with Me on Jesus' behalf, and spreading the Gospel of redemption. Bless you for requesting of Jesus that He bring resolution to the issues being faced by the Church. And, thank you for praying for the birth of the unborn, and for feeding the hungry. Humanity is sanctified by your petitions."

Saturday, December 1, 2018
9:47 a.m.

"Love is the Person, Truth is His voice, Glory is His message."

- The Dominion Angels

"Good morning, My glorious little sons, you are My inheritance from a lifelong love of humanity and the legacy of the Church that has now spanned the breadth of twenty centuries. Your lives have bridged the expanse of two of them. And, yes, this third millennium is blessed because of your faith. I speak to you again with joy in My Heart, but not the kind of joy that men seek in victory over others. Mine is a unifying joy that claims My children for Jesus on the Cross. The world is colder outside than it was last summer, but I can sense the warming of humanity toward the righteousness that is needed to bring peace to the nations. My Special and Chosen ones, I come with clarifying grace in My message this morning that renders your vision acutely true about love being the foundation of all being. My Special son, the writing that you are composing at this time ensures the proficiency of this acuteness for those who will read your works. One of the great problems facing the teaching of the Gospel around the globe is that lost sinners have decided that they have the authority to define love in a way not sustained by God. The true definition of love laid out in the Gospel and the Roman Catholic Catechism is reflective of the holiness of the Father. And, those who subscribe to any other form of 'love' are not aware of the truth to which they are called. All throughout Creation, men are prone to redefine the meaning of virtue and admonition to advantage their own sinful perceptions of the relationship between God and His people. They do this because there seems to be no examination of the legitimacy of their decisions. This is why the Roman Catholic Church must share its message of 'Jesus the Truth' with humanity everywhere. There are untold numbers of false allegiances that are consuming the years of those who have only limited time to convert. The account of these issues runs pervasively through your writing. I wish to reassure you as you celebrate the Gospel of the Lord here in this place that putting into writing the testimony of your heart will never be in vain. All great manifests of love that clarify the relationship between God and man are penned in places like your home. You have alluded to the fact that your relative anonymity at this time is a blessing, and you are certainly correct. If the early volumes of your Marian messages would have been propagated worldwide, there would have been no more anthologies published for another fifty years. Then, it would have been left to the interpretation of those to whom you bequeathed My messages upon your entrance into Heaven. I ask you to believe that I am not euphemizing the time that has passed since we began our mission. I am trying to reinforce the fact that the Lord's Divine Providence has protected His venue here to continue My messages. If you could imagine the commotion that would have been prevalent over the past twenty years during which you and your brother have been accomplishing your work, you would understand what I am saying.

  I wish to reinforce this matter by saying that waiting is not denying. Please place this in the setting of Jesus' Return in Glory. It is also likened to the Poor Souls in Purgatory. The element of time does not seem as consequential as the outcome. Surely a Prince of Peace who supports and loves His Church would have returned to conclude the Earth prior to the 20th century, the bloodiest of them all. Surely, He would have protected the land of His Birth from destruction and desecration. The answer to these things is that He will ultimately do so. Jesus' Mystical Body will soon witness the response that the Father has planned against the evils of the Earth, concurrent with the most infinite Glory that Creation will ever know. This, My Special son, is another great gift of the Second Coming. How could God display His power and Providence as a response to the evil of the world if the worst of evil did not have time to rear its ugly head? Through Jesus' Holy Sacrifice, the devil has placed his head in the guillotine of justice. This is a product of linear time that transcends the lives of heroes and the prosecution of wars. I wish for you and your brother to ponder the proposition that Jesus might perceive the desecration of His legacy and the holy relics of those who have fought for Him as a badge of honor. How do you suppose this could be true? *"They are then united with the glorious restoration in eternal victory."* How eloquently and accurately you have responded. Did you feel the Light of the Holy Spirit shining through your words? *"Yes, I know when transcending truth is present."* Thank you for giving yourself so wholly and graciously to the Spirit of God living vibrantly within you. Just as it is a badge of honor for love to be opposed, it is the bestowing of this honor on those who remain faithful to Jesus that the Church will celebrate the Grand Feast in Heaven. You may remember that if your work is not opposed, it will have no effect. I speak the word 'shining' this morning about a spiritual manifestation of the heart. It takes the shining reflection of love to put down the darkness of hatred. I hope that you and your brother do not view My sentiments as pious platitudes. The truth comes easy to Me. This is the way of you and your brother. I have shared with you several conclusions about ongoing difficulties that are being redressed by the prayers of the Church. You see again, therefore, the necessity of time. I wish for you to accept My commendation of peace and happiness this morning as the month of December has arrived. You and your brother are making excellent progress on the production of your next book. Benign life is a fruit of your being here, and the Glory of the Father is your consummate blessing. We look out into a world that is changing both for the better and the worse. What you and your brother have done during your lives here has ensured that the better will prevail."

Saturday, December 8, 2018
Feast of the Immaculate Conception
9:44 a.m.

"The Kingdom of God, eternal before all things,
cannot be confined to world history.
But shine on until morning – Salvation has happened here."

- The Dominion Angels

"Good morning, My lovely little children, on this grand Feast of the Roman Catholic Church. It is a tremendous gift for Me to speak to you again in recollection of your blessings here in this life. The Dominion Angels have provided a worthy paraphrase of God's redemption of humanity and the accordance of Mercy upon those who are consecrated to Jesus' Most Sacred Heart. My Special son, we have spoken about the designs of God's love, and we know that these designs are for the glorification of His Kingdom based on His Will of Truth. However, something that is designed implies that it is constructed of parts or pieces that are connected to make a whole. There are no such components in God's Heaven. We also know that He wishes humanity to share the fullness of His Kingdom. This means that men on Earth live within His design. What was lost of its own doing has been found by its Creator. So, the Angels have said that time and space cannot contain the Kingdom of God, but humanity can contain His Kingdom in their hearts. Shine on until morning. This means that the world is engulfed in darkness, but humanity can embrace the light. You are celebrating the Advent of the Nativity of the Light of the World. It is by His light that the darkness is consumed. You once wrote a remarkable testimony about the Eve of Joy. It is here that Jesus' Kingdom can be understood beyond the bounds of world history. Hence, Jesus the Messiah is on Earth and in Heaven. It stands true that the faith, love, and trust of humankind are capable of transcending the breach between life and death. My Special son, as the weeks and months pass by, you realize in the maturity of your heart that there are multitudes of impulses and actions that have nothing to do with God's love. It is the purpose of Christian faith to recognize which of these are worthy of the virtuous life. I am aware of these distractions to the extent that Jesus allows Me to see them. You and I have discussed many of the manifestations against which Jesus has preserved the dignity of My Most Immaculate Heart. He does this not only to spare Me from sorrow, but because He knows that My witness to His Crucifixion was the most grotesque of all. Even in the redemptive beauty of the Cross, My sorrow and mourning still remain as monuments to the Salvation of the Earth. This is what one might say to be the stark contrast between the Nativity of the Prince of Peace and the Sacrifice of the King of the world on the same earthly soil. It is an irony that fosters the reconciliation between God and man that lives in the hearts of those who believe. Yes, it is the hallmark of eternal vision because the spirit of truth comes from within.

You and your brother have done things in your lives that would have created tremendous empires if for any other cause. But, your mission is about transforming the world into the life of Christian faith. Here, there are no bottom lines or costs to be calculated. Your lives have been a full and beatific gift to the Father and humanity of prayer, interaction, and the true nature of handing oneself to Jesus on the Cross. Many in the world cannot bring themselves to do this because they cannot see the connection between sacrifice and success. How many men have become rich by giving everything they have to the poor? They believe the answer to be none; this is the logic that humanity uses to judge the successful life. The Holy Gospel is filled with these kinds of contrasts. One of the greatest commendations of all is to remind humanity about laying down one's life for his friends. This is what the Scriptures say, but did not Jesus prove that it is a redeeming act to lay down one's life for the sake of His enemies too? One of the greatest affirmations that a man could ever make is to speak of someone who had laid down their life for him. What fruits are borne of this? The whole matter comes down to wondering what it is about someone that makes them worthy of another person's death. Surely, it is a concentration on the traits of the self that are hidden from the self. Christians who practice their faith already realize that Jesus died for them, not because they are perfect, not because they are His enemies, but to induce them to see their own worthiness in Him. My Special son, your brother's letter to the college professor yesterday was not to confirm that she maintained all the properties about which she received his praise. It was to confirm to her that she has the potential to reach the pinnacle to which your brother raised her soul. This is the same motivation of Jesus lifting His people to the heights of His love. Imagine this. Jesus came to the world to bring propriety, peace, love, and justice. One would have thought that He would have summoned the kings of the world to help in this redemptive cause. On the contrary, He sought out the fishers of the seas and the handlers of nets who owned no fortunes, who did not aspire to reign over the regions of the continents, who were living their lives as laborers under the sun. Why, My Special one, do you suppose that this was His plan? *"To reveal that His Kingdom was not of this world."* Precisely correct. And, to prove that righteousness is not a measure of wealth. Holiness comes from the poverty that fills a man's hands and the richness of his heart, inspired by the love of God for his soul.

My Special son, the measures of the Holy Gospel and the parables from Jesus' lips speak about the marvels of reconstituted life. Jesus speaks not only about dying to the self, but about being raised again in Him. He proved it on Good Friday on the Cross. His Crucifixion is humanity's divine vision for the way good men should receive the gifts of Heaven. There is no other direction for humanity to look. There is no need to search elsewhere. This is it. It is finished. And, the finest of all conceptions known in a world of such wonder is the Feast that the Church celebrates today. I aspire to give humanity the greatest example of prayer and piety that any of the Lord's people could know. You and your brother can attest that Christian humility is built on spiritual confidence. I am the lowly handmaid who can, through the utterance of one prayer, slay a million fire-breathing dragons at once. I can lower My head to the Earth and dare the devil to stand at My feet. Satan is deathly afraid of Me. There are ten thousand swords of Saint Michael waiting at My command to enter the world and right the wrongs that the devil has wrought against the children I love. The imposition of all that must come here and now, the great battles that suffice the commitment of men to Jesus Resurrected, and the future for which the Church prays, all rest in My power to see through the ages and nations the finishing of the Triumph of Most Immaculate Heart. You and your brother must understand what Saint Paul said about eating and working. Do you remember his proclamation? *'If you do not work, you will not eat.'* Yes, and it must be made clear that his words were also a metaphor to the redemption of the lost human soul. If men on Earth desire to taste the fruits of the Banquet Table in Heaven, they must work to purify themselves in the image of Christ the Lord. Indeed, these spiritual works are more imperative in the Lord's vineyard than building skyways and temples to celebrate the facets of life. My Special son, the entire proposition of living on Earth is a parable about the intentions of God. When He says 'Come to Me,' He does not ask one's arms to be filled with goods and the yields of harvests. God does not declare that he who appears before Him with the grandest record of worldly achievement to be the worthiest of eternal sainthood. The Lord says go to Him with your heart overflowing with righteousness. Empty-handed does not mean empty-hearted. My Special son, you and your brother came to Me in the Church filled with your love for Jesus. I knew you before you were born in the same way that the Father knew Jesus before He was conceived in My Womb. I am your Mother not just because Jesus proclaimed it from the Cross, but because, in the divine chambers of our home through the years, I spoke of the worthiness of His brothers and sisters to be seated at the Banquet Table with Him. It was at My urging that He should respond to everyone who might bid Him through their faith to be held, nourished and healed. Yes, there was not enough wine at the wedding feast. So, as I conclude My message here this morning, I wish for you and your brother to realize that I spoke to Jesus at the beginning of His ministry about the two-by-two who would be sent to cultivate, convert and purify His Faith Church. I said to Him that just before He might come again, to choose two disciples who would stand above them all in a modern day so fraught with danger and rife with disbelief. My Special son, you and your brother are His answer. For this, you are praised and given wisdom and prescience beyond your age. You are blessed and uplifted. You are adored and esteemed, and you are justified and poised for victory. Thank you for allowing Me to share the glorious dynamics of your earthly lives. Do you have any issues to discuss with Me this morning? *"Thank you so much for touching our hearts this way. Thank you for loving us."* You are welcome beyond all measures that I might describe. Thank you for placing your hearts in My hands for the touch about which you speak. It bears repeating this morning. You and your brother share the most consequential friendship in the modern history of the Roman Catholic Church. This has been willed by God in response to Jesus' promise that Heaven will be glorified by your lives."

Saturday, December 15, 2018
9:55 a.m.

"The Crucifixion of Jesus Christ is not just imbedded in the history of the world; His Holy Sacrifice is the existential bedrock of history itself."

- The Dominion Angels

"Good morning, My dear beautiful children. Today, we carry on and bear forth in this distinguished journey of your faith lives toward the goal of touching humanity in the way of the Father's Will. We do this by means of prayer and your consecration to Jesus' Most Sacred Heart, and My Most Immaculate Heart. My little ones, you must realize that your lives are prayers themselves. When you give yourselves to the conversion of lost sinners, it is when you wake in the morning that the devil's plans are destroyed. It is something that all men can possess because the Holy Spirit has the power to permeate every heart given faith by God. My Special son, we are battling a secular void that proclaims that what we believe is only a matter of the imagination. If they are unable to detect anything with their senses, they tend to presume not only that it does not affect them, but that it does not even exist. Those who do not believe in God see themselves as separate from His Kingdom of their own accord. And, they are precisely correct. However, they have no means of escaping the mandates and judgments of the God whom they deny. It is said that most outcomes in life are unpredictable. However, the condemnation of those who disavow any relationship with God through Jesus on the Cross is an absolute certainty. What does this say about Jesus' Divine

Mercy? It says that those who deny Him also deny God who sent Him. They deny the Holy Spirit as well. And, to reject the Blessed Trinity is to commit blasphemy against God who has fashioned Himself in Three Divine Persons. All the warnings and admonitions in the world are often too little to reach those who are so opposed to the religious life. My Special son, today I would like to address the practice of those who declare belief in God, but who disagree that He would establish an Apostolic Church. Some recognize the divine existence of God, but decline to believe that He would place His message of redemption in the hands of sinners. They are thinking as the world thinks. After all, should not the Lord expect that exiled men find their Salvation in a message handed to them by Himself? My Special son, please allow Me to give you the opportunity to refute what they believe. *"It goes to the nature of the relationship that God wishes to have with them throughout eternity. He does not want slaves that He captured from His enemies."* You have seen in your own response the reason why you will be viewed as among America's most prominent Marian theologians. The matter of faith must be upheld at the same time the redemptive Gospel is shared. The doubters to whom I refer are concerned that the Holy Spirit would speak through corruptible souls to share an incorruptible New Covenant. Jesus Himself chose His own Apostles. Everything that these doubters need to know has been personified by the Second Person of the Trinity. Jesus' decisions, instructions, examples, and parables contain what the Father wishes His Church to know. One of the most remarkable concerns about many who question the Messianic Gospel is its brevity. They believe that something so manifestly tide-turning and soul-redeeming should require the likes of great epics and novels. How could the Creator of the world lay out the resurrection of the dead in such few chapters? This is their question. The matter, My Special son, comes down to this – Jesus has shared the mandates of the Gospel as they are dictated from the Father's Heart. God did not appear on the Earth and ask humanity how they would like to be saved. My Special son, the statement that I just made is one of the most profound that I have spoken in the history of world. The Will of God is sound and true, based on His wisdom and the purity of His love. What this means is that He knows what is best for humanity. It was not the Father who broke humanity, but as you know, the two in the Garden who violated His decree. It is as though a waterfall of wisdom has come falling onto the Earth in tongues of fire. This means that the Father has all along intended to inundate the world with His oceans of truth, while incinerating everything that is opposed to His teachings. What I have said is that the justice of the Lord for those who love Him is not of vengeance through His Son, Jesus Christ. When the human person, therefore, denies the love of Jesus through His own Divine Mercy, justice is meted out and condemnation assigned. God is no hypocrite. He approaches His relationship with His people on Earth with His Will intact. He also approaches His relationship with these people with their will intact. This is the story of humanity's time. It is that sinners have the volition to comply with God's Will, or suffer the consequence of perpetual death. This too, My Special son, is one issue that nonbelievers have with organized religion. How can God give humanity a self-will by which they will be punished for using it? They are again speaking of a false choice. Through Jesus, God is saying that choosing the life that He teaches; the Way, the Truth and the Life, is a decision that is in the hands of men. It is not that damnation is not a choice, but the path to redemption feeds the heart everything it requires to accept the Cross. My Special son, this is our prayer for humanity.

We speak on this mid-December morning when the world outside is still brawling with infighting and terror. We see exploitation and harm being forced upon the innocent. We pray for the mitigation of these things because they are replete with suffering, and are in direct contradiction to the love of the Lord's Kingdom. We also choose to focus on the righteousness that is spreading like wildfire across the nations from the faith of those who believe. Yes, there is caring and goodness. There is prayer and reparation. One would not know if coming from another world what there is to discover about the benevolence of human life by examining the messages of the media. Placing something in print to the masses seems to lend legitimacy to what is being published. In this, lies are spread more quickly than the truth. It is no surprise that businesses and industries who practice this profession do so for profit. They create baseless panic within societies who would otherwise know nothing of life. They feed on themselves in a self-sanctioning pride that has no basis in fact. My Special son, the media empire in the United States has taken on its own institutional form. It consists, however, of an illegitimate collection of liars and hypocrites who are incapable of judging what must be done. You and I have spoken about the detestable media since I began speaking to you and your brother in discernable terms. If these same media conglomerates were to have condemned the atrocity of infanticide from the moment it was legalized on January 22, 1973, those who have aspired to public office would have passed legislation to end it by now. The American people have been misled and abused by these illicit power-mongers who have placed their future in the hands of Satan. They have gotten out of their beds every morning, looked in the mirror, and denied that they were the devil's tools. My Special son, nothing has been done to lessen this egregious affront to the dignity of human life. It has been the exercise of the human will along the lines of demonic action. Too many demons, too few prayers. And, the result? Here we are, still citing these damning conditions, still praying, still working, and still hoping. The effects that the lives of you and your brother will have on changing these things are too massive to describe. My Special son, you and your brother are anonymous lay persons living thousands of miles from the Seat of Christianity. And yet, here you are, just as I said, changing world history and the record that humanity will see of the prayers and commendations of those who truthfully love the Church. I wish to reassure you that your anonymity with your brother has not meant that you have not been seated on the world stage. Your hidden lives here have been your blessing from God. Thank you for praying as you have been asked with such constant grace and spiritual charm."

Saturday, December 22, 2018
9:53 a.m.

"Is humanity excavating or building?"

"My dearly beloved children, your faith, your love, and your prayers are deeply imbedded in My Most Immaculate Heart. There have been vast awakenings made possible by everything you have dedicated to Jesus on the Cross and raised from the dead. It is the Will of the Father that you should be here where it all began with your hearts grateful for the blessings of your lives. My Special son, it is clear that Jesus is the greatest blessing known to man, and that I am here to share the Gospel with you in the expectation that God will magnify what we have done in His name. The inquiry beginning My message this morning may seem rhetorical. It is a spiritual contrast that puts the question to exiled men as to whether they are digging more deeply into their secular lives or building up the Lord's Kingdom. It is a question that summarizes the reason I have come to you and your brother for so long. Excavation implies that something will be built at a particular location. However, excavation can also mean that something is about to be buried. This metaphor speaks to the souls of lost sinners who are engaging themselves in the world without caring what good could be constructed through true holiness. Saint Pope John Paul II characterized the love of God as a glorious allegiance to humanity so overwhelming that souls on Earth can barely take it in. He said that humanity need not match this love, but accept it. I am adding to the Saint's meditation by saying that Jesus not only asks God's people to accept His love, but that it might be shared worldwide as best as can be known. You and your brother have magnified what this Saint has said and what I have shared with you through your faith. Now, Americans everywhere and the people of the nations are witnessing the passing of another year. Everyone should pause to consider what their contributions have been to the Kingdom about which I speak. My Special son, millions of sinners around the world claim that they have done God no harm. While this may be true, it is not enough in the eyes of the Father. The Crucifixion of Jesus did tremendous harm against the dignity of God, but He willed it, He allowed it as a manifestation of His redeeming love. It is in His image that lost sinners should retrace their steps, confess their transgressions, repent their way of life, and stand in the light of confession so that they will know that they can be made anew. There is no immortal record; there is no eternal ledger bearing the sins of anyone whose soul has entered Heaven. Such things are but the measure of earthly archives that are used by societies and authorities to plague those who have committed sins here in this life with guilt. I have said that Jesus' Crucifixion and human redemption itself are not exculpating graces, but redeeming and renewing gifts from the Heart of the Father. The Lord has not declared the sinners He saved to be innocent, but absolved. My Special son, I wish for you and your brother to bear no regret for the way you have lived because your prayerfulness is being spread around this land and across the seas. The Earth and all its commotion may likely be ongoing when you both enter Heaven. However, what we have done through the decades will stop exiled men in their tracks, and give them pause to realize at last why Christianity was taken into the western hemisphere. The Morning Star Over America is the greatest fruit of any that will be borne in the Americas until the end of the world. It is difficult for you to believe; perhaps even you are incapable of understanding it, but we have yielded for your country and its neighbors, its allies, and even its enemies, the seed of reckoning to which humanity must be drawn in spite of itself. I have been speaking to you and your brother about sacrifice. This is the key to the framework of the deliverance of the human soul to the Land of Paradise. Jesus gave the ultimate sacrifice, while those who accept Him must sacrifice their lives for the burdens of faith – all the decisions that must be made to deny the self of all things worldly and impious. It is a gift to humanity and to God to take up this faith for His Glory. I have said that the Father does not require the redeemed souls of men beside Him in Heaven to make Him more glorious. He does not need His Son's Mystical Body to make Himself complete. It is a matter of whether the Father would be jubilant or despondent, given His desire to bring His lost creatures into His presence. In the wake of the Life, Death and Resurrection of Jesus, the world has found that it pleases the Father that His Church might pray its way into Heaven. Jesus is the Head of the Church, His Spirit is its Voice, and His Sacrifice is its Salvation. In all the great wonders that humanity will ever know, this is the manifest miracle that eclipses them all. It is a gift that cannot be earned in any other way than to accede and acknowledge that God's love is an undeniable blessing for everyone who ever lived. The light of Heaven shines brightly where it is not blocked by the indifference of sinful men. Remember that this light emits from the inside, where the heart is thirsty for the waters of wisdom. It must be made clear by all who preach the Gospel that belief in God is a gift from His hands. When sinners pray to have faith that they cannot fully understand, it is a sign that they are destined to discover the origin of all truth and the answers to their doubts when they enter the Father's Kingdom. My gift to the world began when God deigned that His Son would be born of My Womb. And this, My Special one, happened even before I was conceived.

So, you and your brother are about to enter another new year, about to reach another milestone that billions of people around the globe could have never conceived. I wish for you to remember that I did not come to you and your brother to ask if you wanted something. I came to inquire if you would be messengers for God. It is your response and obedience that have changed the face of the globe in a way that only dreamers could imagine. You have said that My 2013-2015 messages seem more elevated than many of those prior. And, you have speculated that it must be because I was seeking a crowning achievement for your subsequent works. This is not the case at all. It is because I made you and your brother a promise in December 2008 to offer you laudatory messages that were more profound and uplifting than any before. I wished to show you how the Lord keeps His promises. Your prayers and sacrifices on behalf of Jesus have brought into being a diary of works that has now blossomed in the likes of the mustard seed, where the eagles of the skies perch to survey the lands below. Yes, they see you here; they see your lives, and they guard, just like the angels, where you live and walk to assure your dignity in this dark valley of tears. You have seen transitions that expire with the passing of the ages. People come and go; their careers begin and end. Their decisions affect the lives of others in ways that are good, and at others times inauspiciously. The whole thing comes down to whether humanity is fasted to the teachings of the Gospel through all these changes. Have men given their hearts to the constancy of the Lord's Truth? It is clear as I have said that this is you and your brother's beginning point. It is the way you greet the morning every day. It is the summit of your expectations of human life. There is grandness and majesty in your thoughts and speech. What you have written and said, even privately between yourselves, will someday be shared through the open skies of Jesus' Second Coming. What you must remember in the meantime is that you have done everything right. My Special son, you often say that children are like tape recorders, and so is God the Father. He knows everything accountable and irrelevant about the world below His Throne. There is no filter through which the musings and actions of men pass before He sees them. This is to the benefit of humanity and the Hosts of Heaven who have the power to complement the pious labors of the Faith Church on Earth. This is December 22, 2018. Imagine what this day means for an unsuspecting world that will change for the better and never turn back, just because you invited Me here. Yes, a single day on a calendar can make this much difference, and look what you and your brother have done. This, My Special son, is one of the most monumental miracles of which you and your brother seem almost unaware. Due to the calling of your lives and the burden of your cares, you are incapable of knowing the magnitude of what you are doing. This is a design to keep you focused on the new morning sun and the details of your days that will culminate in your knowledge that what I am saying is true. I hope you will accept My sentiments shared with you today, praying that you enjoy the peace of Christmas that I bring you every year. *"Yes, thank you."* It is imperative that you be on guard while traveling for the holidays. With all the Saints and Angels, with the Spirit of the Lord and the commendation of the Father, I wish you joy and good fortune until I speak to you again."

Saturday, December 29, 2018
9:47 a.m.

"Tell them where it all began."

"Sweet as confection, strong and resilient, filled with peace and good will. This, My dear little sons, is the essence of your hearts. Your prayers rhyme perfectly with the Will of God. You are in alliance with the mandates of His Son for the purification of the Earth. So today, I bring you My good wishes and blessings as the final hours of 2018 expire. We have together made the difference for which Jesus called during His ministry to a world that was lacking in divinity and truth. I cannot imagine having approached humanity with the message of the Gospel on My tongue without your help. You have personified the gift of enlightenment to the world with the same degree of conviction with which the Martyrs laid down their lives. My Special son, you will one day reflect to many, far and wide, about this grand experience of being

My messenger. This speaks to the words with which I opened My message this morning. Tell them where it all began. This is the acclamation that will bring truth-seeking Christians to the fullness of understanding about what Jesus desires of them. Messaging for the Lord through the Holy Spirit is a succession in itself. The Father sent a message through the Archangel Gabriel. I proceeded this message of human redemption to My visionaries on Earth. And now, it has been your turn to spread the Good News of the Gospel as disciples of My Son. You are invested in the same sympathy of God for His Church. I speak of your alliance because this is the identity of the Communion of Saints. You have in common with them the same Holy Spirit that guided them through the perils of the world. My Special son, I will posit another question to seek your response. I will preface My question by saying that the Holy Spirit lives in all hearts in the world who accept the Blood of Jesus as their Salvation. Here is the question. Do you suppose that souls in Heaven have the Holy Spirit within them the same way that the hearts of Christians have on Earth? *"Yes, but those in Heaven understand the unity with the Holy Spirit perfectly."* Very well stated. It must be added that the Holy Spirit swallows up the souls of the Saints the same way that death is conquered by Jesus' Crucifixion. *"Yes, and also the Saints in Heaven no longer have the tide go out."* You have understood that the Holy Spirit is not only the presence of God in the hearts of men, but humanity's ushering to His Heavenly Throne. This is another way of knowing that the Holy Spirit is dispatched unto the Earth in distinct unity within the Blessed Trinity. One might not think of the Blessed Trinity as having components, but Three Divine Persons are present in One God, wherever He chooses to go. What, therefore, do you believe was felt by the Father when He raised Jesus from the dead? In other words, what effect did Jesus' Paschal Resurrection have on His Father in Heaven? *"It stated to Creation and all the realms of evil that He could not be driven out, and that He reigns supreme in His Son."* Yes, excellent; absolutely profound. As I stated earlier this year, your brother once cited the example of the end of a football game where the clock is still running, but the ball is dead and the players are walking off the field. The outcome of the contest cannot be recorded until the clock fully expires. There is a sense of imminence in this that speaks metaphorically about Jesus' Body in the Tomb. All who knew and loved Him, everyone who believed who He was, were waiting for the dawn, knowing that His victory had been won.

I tell you this today, My Special son, because this same metaphor applies to the 21st century world. You and your brother, and all believers, are dedicated to your service beneath the Cross here in your time. Imagine what

Jesus sees through the eyes of the Father as He watches you walking confidently into His arms through a victory that will stretch beyond your death. Tremendous elation. Wholesome triumph. Heartfelt expectation. This is the world to which I came when I first appeared after My Assumption and Coronation. I have been trying to tell humanity that the victory has been won, but the world cannot seem to understand what I am saying. In Jesus, there is no need for warring. All the great battles that have been fought and won would have found their victors anyway. It takes great faith to believe what I have just said, but do you suppose that what we have done will magnify that faith enough to bring the doubters and naysayers to their home in the Church? All of My Marian shrines have been tremendous gifts for those who have believed; and as I said in another message, they have been stumbling blocks for those who decline. It is not just that many on Earth choose not to believe in My miracles, but that they work to avoid them so as not to make themselves vulnerable to accept a God whom they have never known. Yes, Lourdes and Fatima and all the rest, dozens of them in the 20th century alone. I wish that My children would avail themselves to the graces that are being given there. My Special son, I will make a particular point about the headstrong faith of those who claim such allegiance to Me, but that is not imbedded in their hearts. Would it not make sense for someone with a child or grandchild who is physically broken to take their loved one to the healing waters of Lourdes? *"Of course."* And, you know that we have been praying for two certain individuals whose faith-filled parents and grandparents continue to ignore My blessings there. So, it is with distinct gratitude that I embrace you and your brother for giving another year of your lives to your Mother in Heaven. Imagine in your own hearts what it must be like for Me to see the way you live. I have said on many occasions that words are not sufficient to describe how I feel. But, look at what you and your brother and I have done over the past twenty-eight years. Yes, it is the language of love that uplifts the Father through the Creation in which you live. And, uplifting the Father means raising high the Cross of Jesus before the billions of sinners who inhabit the Earth. At this very moment, My Special son, I could break through the veil of what you are seeing right now and show you visions of Heaven and the celebrated Saints. I could bring you to the divine culmination of every expectation in your heart. These would be tremendous gifts to reassure you that there has never been any question about anything you have believed. I have not walked through the veil with this limitlessness because your faith does not require it. And your faith, My Special son, along with your sacred love, is the greatest gift that any man could give their God. To say that you believe in the bastion of His Providence before seeing Him in His everlasting Glory is the essence of His Will for the Church. Through your faith, you are extending His Kingdom in the earthly domain where His light is still shining through you. Yes, it is your faith that feeds humanity the nourishment of wisdom that defies their ignorance about love. My dear Special son, you and your brother have given life to spiritual faith in ways that you, yourselves, cannot imagine. I often find Myself concerned that I speak effusively of your faith with such repetition that you might not recognize My true sincerity. I have nothing more than to say that the Glory of the Cross and the grace of the Church have found their home in you. The eternal record, although already written, has placed you and your brother in such esteem that trumpets, pearls and laces cannot capture your dignity. Yes, remember always the refrain that in Heaven, you and your brother will be told, 'My friends, you bow to no one.' So, let this be your joy as I complete this final message of the grand year 2018. Let us go forward at the behest of the Father into the future during which I will speak to you as long as He allows. I have broached the topic of when it might happen that My messages would discontinue. I have said that I do not know when you and your brother will be called to Heaven. And, I have given you the reason. Let it be sufficient to say that come these events, the Lord Jesus will still find you working like Saints in His earthly vineyard here. My Special son, thank you for remembering everything for which I have asked you to pray, especially for the priests, the shepherds of the Church. I offer you My holy blessing for today. ✞ It is with My Heart filled with love that I promise to speak to you again."

www.ingramcontent.com/pod-product-compliance
Lightning Source LLC
Chambersburg PA
CBHW071055230426
43666CB00009B/1719